D0329280

PUBLIC ADMINISTRATION AND PUBLIC POLICY

A Comprehensive Publication Program

Executive Editor

JACK RABIN
Professor of Public Administration and Public Policy
School of Public Affairs
The Capital College
The Pennsylvania State University—Harrisburg
Middletown, Pennsylvania

1. *Public Administration as a Developing Discipline* (in two parts), Robert T. Golembiewski
2. *Comparative National Policies on Health Care*, Milton I. Roemer, M.D.
3. *Exclusionary Injustice: The Problem of Illegally Obtained Evidence*, Steven R. Schlesinger
4. *Personnel Management in Government: Politics and Process*, Jay M. Shafritz, Walter L. Balk, Albert C. Hyde, and David H. Rosenbloom
5. *Organization Development in Public Administration* (in two parts), edited by Robert T. Golembiewski and William B. Eddy
6. *Public Administration: A Comparative Perspective, Second Edition, Revised and Expanded*, Ferrel Heady
7. *Approaches to Planned Change* (in two parts), Robert T. Golembiewski
8. *Program Evaluation at HEW* (in three parts), edited by James G. Abert
9. *The States and the Metropolis*, Patricia S. Florestano and Vincent L. Marando
10. *Personnel Management in Government: Politics and Process, Second Edition, Revised and Expanded*, Jay M. Shafritz, Albert C. Hyde, and David H. Rosenbloom
11. *Changing Bureaucracies: Understanding the Organization Before Selecting the Approach*, William A. Medina
12. *Handbook on Public Budgeting and Financial Management*, edited by Jack Rabin and Thomas D. Lynch
13. *Encyclopedia of Policy Studies*, edited by Stuart S. Nagel
14. *Public Administration and Law: Bench v. Bureau in the United States*, David H. Rosenbloom
15. *Handbook on Public Personnel Administration and Labor Relations*, edited by Jack Rabin, Thomas Vocino, W. Bartley Hildreth, and Gerald J. Miller

Organizational Behavior
and
Public Management

16. *Public Budgeting and Finance: Behavioral, Theoretical, and Technical Perspectives, Third Edition*, edited by Robert T. Golembiewski and Jack Rabin
17. *Organizational Behavior and Public Management*, Debra W. Stewart and G. David Garson
18. *The Politics of Terrorism: Second Edition, Revised and Expanded*, edited by Michael Stohl
19. *Handbook of Organization Management*, edited by William B. Eddy
20. *Organization Theory and Management*, edited by Thomas D. Lynch
21. *Labor Relations in the Public Sector*, Richard C. Kearney
22. *Politics and Administration: Woodrow Wilson and American Public Administration*, edited by Jack Rabin and James S. Bowman
23. *Making and Managing Policy: Formulation, Analysis, Evaluation*, edited by G. Ronald Gilbert
24. *Public Administration: A Comparative Perspective, Third Edition, Revised*, Ferrel Heady
25. *Decision Making in the Public Sector*, edited by Lloyd G. Nigro
26. *Managing Administration*, edited by Jack Rabin, Samuel Humes, and Brian S. Morgan
27. *Public Personnel Update*, edited by Michael Cohen and Robert T. Golembiewski
28. *State and Local Government Administration*, edited by Jack Rabin and Don Dodd
29. *Public Administration: A Bibliographic Guide to the Literature*, Howard E. McCurdy
30. *Personnel Management in Government: Politics and Process, Third Edition, Revised and Expanded*, Jay M. Shafritz, Albert C. Hyde, and David H. Rosenbloom
31. *Handbook of Information Resource Management*, edited by Jack Rabin and Edward M. Jackowski
32. *Public Administration in Developed Democracies: A Comparative Study*, edited by Donald C. Rowat
33. *The Politics of Terrorism: Third Edition, Revised and Expanded*, edited by Michael Stohl
34. *Handbook on Human Services Administration*, edited by Jack Rabin and Marcia B. Steinhauer
35. *Handbook of Public Administration*, edited by Jack Rabin, W. Bartley Hildreth, and Gerald J. Miller
36. *Ethics for Bureaucrats: An Essay on Law and Values, Second Edition, Revised and Expanded*, John A. Rohr
37. *The Guide to the Foundations of Public Administration*, Daniel W. Martin
38. *Handbook of Strategic Management*, edited by Jack Rabin, Gerald J. Miller, and W. Bartley Hildreth
39. *Terrorism and Emergency Management: Policy and Administration*, William L. Waugh, Jr.
40. *Organizational Behavior and Public Management: Second Edition, Revised and Expanded*, Michael L. Vasu, Debra W. Stewart, and G. David Garson
41. *Handbook of Comparative and Development Public Administration*, edited by Ali Farazmand

42. *Public Administration: A Comparative Perspective, Fourth Edition*, Ferrel Heady
43. *Government Financial Management Theory*, Gerald J. Miller
44. *Personnel Management in Government: Politics and Process, Fourth Edition, Revised and Expanded*, Jay M. Shafritz, Norma M. Riccucci, David H. Rosenbloom, and Albert C. Hyde
45. *Public Productivity Handbook*, edited by Marc Holzer
46. *Handbook of Public Budgeting*, edited by Jack Rabin
47. *Labor Relations in the Public Sector: Second Edition, Revised and Expanded*, Richard C. Kearney
48. *Handbook of Organizational Consultation*, edited by Robert T. Golembiewski
49. *Handbook of Court Administration and Management*, edited by Steven W. Hays and Cole Blease Graham, Jr.
50. *Handbook of Comparative Public Budgeting and Financial Management*, edited by Thomas D. Lynch and Lawrence L. Martin
51. *Handbook of Organizational Behavior*, edited by Robert T. Golembiewski
52. *Handbook of Administrative Ethics,* edited by Terry L. Cooper
53. *Encyclopedia of Policy Studies: Second Edition, Revised and Expanded,* edited by Stuart S. Nagel
54. *Handbook of Regulation and Administrative Law,* edited by David H. Rosenbloom and Richard D. Schwartz
55. *Handbook of Bureaucracy,* edited by Ali Farazmand
56. *Handbook of Public Sector Labor Relations*, edited by Jack Rabin, Thomas Vocino, W. Bartley Hildreth, and Gerald J. Miller
57. *Practical Public Management*, Robert T. Golembiewski
58. *Handbook of Public Personnel Administration*, edited by Jack Rabin, Thomas Vocino, W. Bartley Hildreth, and Gerald J. Miller
59. *Public Administration: A Comparative Perspective, Fifth Edition*, Ferrel Heady
60. *Handbook of Debt Management*, edited by Gerald J. Miller
61. *Public Administration and Law: Second Edition*, David H. Rosenbloom and Rosemary O'Leary
62. *Handbook of Local Government Administration*, edited by John J. Gargan
63. *Handbook of Administrative Communication*, edited by James L. Garnett and Alexander Kouzmin
64. *Public Budgeting and Finance: Fourth Edition, Revised and Expanded*, edited by Robert T. Golembiewski and Jack Rabin
65. *Handbook of Public Administration: Second Edition*, edited by Jack Rabin, W. Bartley Hildreth, and Gerald J. Miller
66. *Handbook of Organization Theory and Management: The Philosophical Approach*, edited by Thomas D. Lynch and Todd J. Dicker
67. *Handbook of Public Finance*, edited by Fred Thompson and Mark T. Green
68. *Organizational Behavior and Public Management: Third Edition, Revised and Expanded*, Michael L. Vasu, Debra W. Stewart, and G. David Garson

Additional Volumes in Preparation

Handbook of Economic Development, edited by Kuotsai Tom Liou
Handbook of Taxation, edited by W. Bartley Hildreth and James A. Richardson
Handbook of Research Methods in Public Administration, edited by Gerald J. Miller and Marcia L. Whicker

ANNALS OF PUBLIC ADMINISTRATION

1. *Public Administration: History and Theory in Contemporary Perspective*, edited by Joseph A. Uveges, Jr.
2. *Public Administration Education in Transition*, edited by Thomas Vocino and Richard Heimovics
3. *Centenary Issues of the Pendleton Act of 1883*, edited by David H. Rosenbloom with the assistance of Mark A. Emmert
4. *Intergovernmental Relations in the 1980s*, edited by Richard H. Leach
5. *Criminal Justice Administration: Linking Practice and Research*, edited by William A. Jones, Jr.

Organizational Behavior and Public Management

Third Edition, Revised and Expanded

Michael L. Vasu
Debra W. Stewart
G. David Garson
North Carolina State University
Raleigh, North Carolina

MARCEL DEKKER, INC. NEW YORK • BASEL • HONG KONG

Library of Congress Cataloging-in-Publication Data

Vasu, Michael Lee.
    Organizational behavior and public management / Michael L. Vasu,
Debra W. Stewart, G. David Garson. —3rd ed., rev. and expanded.
        p. cm. —(Public Administration and public policy; 68)
        Includes bibliographical references and index.
    ISBN 0-8247-0135-6
        1. Organizational behavior.   2. Public administration.
    I. Stewart, Debra W.   II. Garson, G. David.
    HD58.7.S745 1998
    351—dc21   97-52353
                                           CIP

This book is printed on acid-free paper.

Headquarters
Marcel Dekker, Inc.
270 Madison Avenue, New York, NY 10016
tel: 212-696-9000; fax: 212-685-4540

Eastern Hemisphere Distribution
Marcel Dekker AG
Hutgasse 4, Postfach 812, CH-4001 Basel, Switzerland
tel: 44-61-8482; fax: 44-61-261-8896

World Wide Web
http://www.dekker.com

The publisher offers discounts on this book when ordered in bulk quantities. For more information, write to Special Sales/Professional Marketing at the address below.

Copyright © 1998 by MARCEL DEKKER, INC. All Rights Reserved.

Neither this book nor any part may be reproduced or transmitted in any form or by any means, electronic or mechanical, including photocopying, microfilming, and recording, or by any information storage and retrieval system, without permission in writing from the publisher.

Current printing (last digit):
10 9 8 7 6 5 4 3 2 1

PRINTED IN THE UNITED STATES OF AMERICA

Preface to the Third Edition

The third edition of Organizational Behavior and Public Management appears at a time characterized by profound change in the U.S and abroad. Clearly, the most salient global event since the second edition of this book has been the virtual collapse of communism in both Russia and Eastern Europe. Moreover, this collapse was neither anticipated by scholars, nor, brought about by military confrontation. Communism, in effect, collapsed of its own weight! To many pundits in the world, the demise of communism was vivid testimonial to the superiority of the free market over the planned economy, of the entrepreneur over the bureaucrat, of the new world order over the old! Whatever the merits of these contentions, one thing is clear, a new global political economy is at hand and our old paradigms are no longer relevant.

Among the most significant of the new paradigms is that of the global economy and its implications for the management of public and private organizations. In a world in which information, products, and capital move fluidly between and among national borders, new economic players are asserting their presence on the world economic stage daily. Many of these new economic players, in both Europe and the Pacific Rim, are championing new organizational designs, new ways of managing public and private work systems. Among the most important of these new paradigms, and the one most directly related to this edition of Organizational Behavior and Public Management, is the emergence of Total Quality Management (TQM) as a new way of looking at management.

In a global economy, economic rewards are forthcoming to those organizations that can constrict the time from product conception to production and insure quality outputs in the process. In Japan, for example, TQM management systems, pioneered by the American W. Edwards Deming, are in common practice. TQM depends on a well trained and empowered work force, which through skill and capability helps management produce quality products. TQM represent both a philosophy and methodology for managing organizations. TQM is a set of principles, tools, and procedures that provide guidance in the practical affairs of running an organization. TQM's impact on the public sector is now emerging. It is most evident in the organizational implications inherent in calls for "reinventing government." The political pressure on public managers to "do more with less" has engendered a search by those managers for organizational practices that will produce both quality and efficiency. TQM is one such system. It is getting a lot of attention in government.

The major elements of the conceptual framework for this book are elaborated in the Preface to the First and Second Editions, and, since they are included for the reader's benefit, we will not restated them in detail here. Some changes in this edition include a discussion of TQM and its applicability to government. We have incorporated this discussion into the chapter on worker participation because we see TQM related to empowerment in the workplace. In addition, all the remaining chapters have an updated literature review, with particular attention paid to the public sector implications of research that may or may nor have had any public sector focus in its conception. The chapter on Information, Computers and Organization Theory has been rewritten to reflect the ever increasing changes in the information technology and policy environment.

This book is designed as a text in organizational behavior and public management. As such, it seeks to expose the student to the extensive range of scholarship that addresses the question of how to effectively manage complex human environments. If the events of the last few years are any indication, the demands for this skill are likely to increase in the next decade.

Michael L. Vasu
Debra W. Stewart
G. David Garson

Preface to the Second Edition

The second edition of *Organizational Behavior and Public Management* appears during the early stages of the Bush administration. The first edition appeared at the early stages of the Reagan administration. For a book designed to focus on management in the public sector, this particular approach to the calibration of time is very salient. During the 190s, pollsters, pundits, and presidents have all asserted that the body politic has grown cynical about positive government, even as the administrative state and budget deficit continued to grow.

Academic writers in public administration have had a number of responses to this assault on the public sector. Barry D. Karl (1987) in his article "The American Bureaucrat: A History of a Sheep in Wolves' Clothing" argues that the origins of American hostility to public organizations are deeply rooted in the Jacksonian revolution's belief that there is something inherently anti-democratic about the growth the elite professionalism expressed in bureaucracy. To the extent that this is true, attacks on bureaucracy are part of our political culture and will grow in proportion to the growth of government. Charles T. Goodsell (1985) in *The Case For Bureaucracy* argues eloquently against the dominant popular and academic belief that governmental bureaucracy in the United States is a generalized failure and threat, and provides important evidence to the contrary. The late Charles Levine (1986) argued that the Reagan administration has left a legacy in its attempts to reshape the American administrative state and that a major part of that legacy is the form of an ongoing debate about the role and reach of government in a mixed economy. What all these authors and many more underscore is the existence of serious political controversy over the "public" role in society. And, while our crystal ball is no clearer than any other, one fact seems clear: both public attitudes and a massive public debt will combine to keep this debate alive. It will also require theoreticians and practitioners of American public administration to find more effective ways to manage America's public resources.

This book is designed as a text in organizational behavior and public management. It is designed to expose the student to the tremendous range of scholarship that has addressed the question of how one effectively manages in complex human organizations. It is ultimately designed to help make public managers more effective stewards of public resources. Much of the literature we employ comes from research done in the private sector, as well as from a variety of different academic disciplines. This is largely the nature of the beast. Much of the early and continued interest in management has had a private sector focus. Moreover, many of the dimensions of management have a generic core: for example, motivation, leadership, role behavior, communication, and decision-making. However, our focus in writing this book is clearly on the "public" aspect of management. It is our belief that the public sector is inherently different in many fundamental ways from the private sector. These differences in large measure flow from the unique role of government in society. The public purpose of most of what government does cannot be measured by the standards of prices and profits. By the same token, the absence of the information provided by prices and profits imposes a major contextual feature that influences the practice of management in the public sector. In addition, this book reflects our commitment to the belief that government has a vital role to play in insuring both equity and efficiency in America's future. Both social justice and the economics of a global economy require a vital and effective public sector workforce who can manage, and manage well, the complex organizational and technological infrastructure that is modern government.

The structure of the book flows from our conceptual framework. The second edition includes three new chapters and combines or deletes others. Chapter 1 outlines the major issues that the book will confront, including the question of the appropriate unit of analysis and a discussion of public and private organizations and the role of government in society. Chapter 2 provides a brief history of the various approaches to organization theory at a macro level. In addition, we have provided a chapter on the most significant technological change in the managerial workplace since the first edition appeared: the computer. Chapter 11 outlines the extensive interdisciplinary research emerging on this topic. We have also deleted a chapter on managing equal employment that appeared in the first edition and added the important topics from this chapter in our chapter on ethics. All the remaining chapters have an updated literature review, and attention has been paid to the public sector implications of research that may or may not have had any public sector focus in its conception. We have also included for both stylistic and conceptual reasons the preface of our first edition because, we believe, it still rings true in major ways.

REFERENCES

Goodsell, Charles T. (1985). *The Case For Bureaucracy*, 2nd Ed. Chatham NJ: Chatham House Publishers, Inc.

Karl, Barry D. (1987). "The American Bureaucrat: A History of Sheep in Wolves Clothing." *Public Administration Review*, 47: pp. 26–34.

Levine, Charles H. (1986). "The Federal Government in the Year 2000: Administrative Legacies of the Reagan Years." *Public Administration Review*, 46: pp. 195–205.

Michael L. Vasu
Debra W. Stewart
G. David Garson

Preface to the First Edition

DEFINING OUR TERMS

Organizational behavior is a field of study that focuses on the behaviors, attitudes, and performances of people within an organization. It is especially concerned with the influence of people within an organization. It is especially concerned with the influence of both formal organization and informal group structure on employees, the effect of employees on the organization, and the work environment's effect on both the organization and on the people working within it (Szilagyi and Wallace, 1980). Students of organizational behavior want to know all about what people *do* in organizations. Because of this broad focus, the field is necessarily interdisciplinary, drawing heavily from the behavioral sciences, particularly the core disciplines of anthropology, psychology, and sociology. The purpose of behavioral science research is to improve the manager's ability to predict the behavior of people, so knowledge generated by Organizational Behavior research speaks to questions posed by managers. For the most part, practitioners set the research agenda for the organizational behavior field.

Because of its focus on the behavior of people, psychology has contributed heavily to the concepts and theories of organizational behavior. Most research is conducted on three levels: analysis of the individual, the group, and the organization. Also of special interest to us is how organizations change.

Since so little work has been done on public management, there is no conceptual framework in this area (Allison, 1979) on which we may smugly hang our hat. We must rely on plain English to explain what public management is.

Management is simply the organization and direction of resources to achieve a desired result, so public management must be the organization and direction of such resources in the public or governmental sector. General management functions can be broken down into: planning, organizing, staffing, directing, coordinating, reporting, and budgeting (Gulick, 1937). These functions are common to both public and private sector management. But we cannot overemphasize the great difference that a public setting makes in how these activities are carried out. This is what our book is about.

In the public sector, diffusion of power and political accountability make the critical difference. While in private business general management functions are concentrated in the chief executive officer, these functions are, by constitutional design, spread in the public sector among a number of competing institutions. Thus, they are shared by a number of individuals whose ambitions are set against one another (Allison, 1979). The three branches of government and the three levels of government—a design rooted in balance of power and federalist principles—join to produce this unique management environment.

The public setting creates a different context for management on a number of specific dimensions. Four important differences are:

> Time Horizon—government managers have short horizons for implementing programs, a product of the election cycle.
> Performance Measurement—little agreement exists on standards and measurement of performance. The private sector's bottom line of profit has no counterpart in the public sector.
> Personnel Constraints—the existence of two layers of management, civil service and political appointees, each with a measure of autonomy vis-à-vis the other, frustrates the capacity for control possible in private management.
> Press and Media Relations—the public has a "right to know" about public management activities while the private manager freely denies media access to management decision making.

ON THE INTERSECTION: FOCUS OF THIS TEXT

The first teaching of "public administration" took place in departments of political science, but as the domain of "public service" grew through the 20th century, and the range of activities demanding management expertise expanded, students of public management pressed beyond the boundaries of the parent discipline. Driven by an environment oblivious to disciplinary limits, contemporary public management study is marked by the convergence of several disciplines.

This book is on the intersection of organizational behavior and public management studies. It centers on the human behavior issues public managers confront in organizing and directing resources to advance the programs and policies of their agencies. Figure 1 displays four qualities guiding inquiry on the intersection.

Studying organizational behavior in a public management context is necessarily interdisciplinary, drawing on the traditional behavioral sciences of psychology, sociology and anthropology, as well as the more normatively oriented

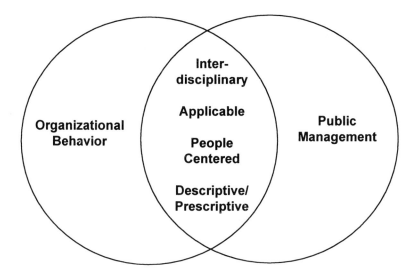

Figure 1   The intersection of organizational behavior and public management.

disciplines of political science and economics. But theory as it emerges in these disciplines doesn't always present itself in a useful form. Harlan Cleveland has noted: "The tightest bottleneck in modern civilization just now is relevant theory" (Cleveland, 1979). This means our theories must be applicable to everyday management experience to be useful to anyone. Literature at the intersection of organizational behavior and public management needs to meet this standard of applicability. Modern study of organizational behavior from a public management perspective thus becomes an exercise in theory application. The success of our theories and their applications is measured by our capacity to illuminate the feelings, attitudes and behaviors of real people, the human resources of the public organization. The analytical skills generated and/or sharpened by the study of organizational behavior in a public sector context must be both descriptive and prescriptive in kind. Study at the intersection will equip public managers to analyze both critical cause and effect relationships in organizations and will raise questions about how human interaction should proceed in modern organizations. In summary, this book focuses on the intersection of organizational behavior and public management. As an area of study that intersection is *interdisciplinary*, *applicable*, *people-centered*, and both *descriptive* and *prescriptive*.

Study centering on this intersection of organizational behavior and public management may be more important today than ever before. In recent years public confidence in government has dipped to an all-time low. In 1964, 69 percent of Americans acknowledged their government leaders, ". . . know what they are doing," but by 1978 that figure dropped to 40 percent. In the late 1950s, 56 percent of Americans polled believed, "You can trust the government in Washington to do what is right most of the time." By the late 70s the figure dropped to 29 percent (Cleveland, 1979). In fairness we should stress that the drop in confidence is a realistic reflection of a more complex world. Nonetheless the public demand for performance and efficiency from government is intense. A study of organizational behavior premised on the need for self-conscious development of a public management approach to managing people in organizations is one way to help meet this demand.

REFERENCES

Allison, Graham T., Jr. (1979). Public and Private Management: Are They Fundamentally Alike in All Unimportant Respects? *Setting Public Management Research Agendas*. Proceedings for the Public Management Research Conference, U.S.O.P.M., November 19–20, Washington, D.C.

Cleveland, Harlan (1979). Public Management Research: The Theory of Practice and Vice Versa, *Setting Public Management Research Agendas*, Proceedings for the Public Management Research Conference. U.S.O.P.M., November 19–20, Washington, D.C.

Gulick, Luther and Lyndall Urwick, Eds. (1937). *Papers on the Science of Administration*. New York: Institute of Public Administration.

Szilagyi, Andrew D., Jr., and Marc J. Wallace, Jr. (1980). *Organizational Behavior and Performance*, 2nd Ed., Santa Monica, Calif.: Goodyear Publishing Company.

Debra W. Stewart
G. David Garson

Contents

Preface to the Third Edition   *iii*
Preface to the Second Edition   *v*
Preface to the First Edition   *ix*

1. Introduction to Organizational Behavior in the Public Sector   **1**
    Introduction   1
    Choosing a Unit of Analysis   2
    Organizational Behavior   2
    Organizational Theory   4
    Public versus Private Organizations   6
    The Role of Government in American Society   9
    Controlling Externalities   11
    Providing Public Goods   13
    Insuring Equity   13
    Providing a Framework for Law and Order and Economic
      Stability   15
    Public Organizations: Economic Differences   16
    Political Difference Between Public and Private Organizations   18
    Differences in Problems Faced by Public and Private
      Organizations   20
    The Structure of the Book   21
    References and Additional Reading   *23*

2. Approaches to Organization Theory   **26**
    History of Organizations   27
    Railroads and Modern Organizations   28
    The Classical Approach   30
    The Human Relations Approach   36
    The Decision-Making Approach   38
    The Neo-Human Relations Approach   43
    The Systems Approach   45

Bureaucratic Politics Approach   47
Conclusion   52
References and Additional Reading   *52*

3. Motivation in Organizations   **56**
Introduction   56
Motivation in Context   56
Basic Motivation Theory   59
The Cognitive Approach   60
Drive or Tension Reduction Theory   61
Expectancy Value Theories   63
Human Growth and Development Theory   64
The Acognitive Approach   66
Motivation in the Workplace   68
Applications Deriving from the Cognitive Tradition   68
Applications Deriving from the Acognitive Tradition   77
Intrinsic versus Extrinsic Motivation   78
Managerial Implications   81
Endnote   *83*
References and Additional Reading   *83*

4. Leadership   **89**
Leadership versus Management   92
The Trait Approach to Leadership   93
Leadership Traits: Do They Lead to Organizational
   Effectiveness?   96
Behavioral Approaches to Leadership   97
Participatory Leadership Behavior   98
Social/Task Leadership Behavior   100
Instrumental Leadership Behavior   103
Contingency Approaches to Leadership   106
Contingency Theory: Hersey and Blanchard's Situational
   Leadership Theory   108
Transformational Leadership   110
Managerial Implications   113
References and Additional Reading   *115*

5. Role Behavior: Individuals and Groups   **123**
Role Conformity   127
The Dynamics of Conformity and Exclusion   130
The Positive Functions of Conformity   133
The Negative Functions of Conformity   134
Role Conflict   137

Psychological Dimensions of Role Conflict	140
Deviance	141
Managing Organizational Roles	142
Informal Organization	144
Informal Organization as a Threat	144
Informal Organization as an Opportunity	146
Informal Organization: A Summary	147
Managing Role Change	147
Managerial Implications	149
Endnotes	*151*
References and Additional Reading	*152*

6. Communication **160**
Communication as a Process	162
Verbal Communication	167
Nonverbal Communication	171
Vertical and Horizontal Communication	174
Listening	180
The Communication Audit	183
Managerial Implications	186
References and Additional Reading	*187*

7. Decision-Making **195**
Planning and Rational Models of Decision-Making	197
The Conservative Critique of Planning	200
Herbert Simon and Decision-Making Theory	205
Critics and Revisionists	207
Planning and Participatory Approaches to Decision-Making	211
Research on Group Decision-Making	214
The Delphi Method, the Nominal Group Technique, and Computer Mediated Communication	217
Managerial Implications	221
Endnote	*224*
References and Additional Reading	*224*

8. Worker Participation and Total Quality Management **233**
Total Quality Management (TQM)	235
Forces that Inhibit the Spread of TQM and Participatory Management in Government	243
Forces Favoring the Spread of TQM and Participatory Management in Government	249
Managerial Implications	255
References and Additional Reading	*256*

9. Organizational Change   **265**
    Organizational Culture   265
    Organizational Climate   269
    Structure, Technology, and Environment   270
    Organizational Learning and Organizational Change   273
    Managerial Change Strategies   276
    Basic Points About Managing Change   277
    Managerial Implications   279
       References and Additional Reading   *281*

10. Management Systems   **286**
    Public Sector Applications of Management Systems   290
    Design Concerns in Management Control Systems   291
    The Relevance of Research Design to Control Systems   297
    How Research Design Fits in   298
    The Implementation of Management Systems   300
    Management Implications   306
       References and Additional Reading   *307*

**11. Information, Computers, and Organization Theory in Public
Management**   **311**
    Policy Studies versus Organization Theory   312
    Typological Frameworks as Organization Theory   313
    Stages-of-Growth Theories of MIS   314
    Political Process Models   319
    Economic Theories of MIS   324
    Public Goods Theory of Information Systems   326
    Social Impact Research as Organization Theory   329
    The Communication and Control Perspective   332
    Conclusion   334
    Management Implications   335
       Endnotes   *336*
       References and Additional Reading   *338*

12. Performance Appraisal   **347**
    Organizational Needs: Evaluating Performance   349
    Objectives of Performance Appraisal Systems   354
    Context Factors Affecting Performance Appraisal   357
    Performance Appraisal Techniques: A Survey   358
    Management by Objectives   362
    Behaviorally Anchored Rating Scales   364
    Managerial Implications   370
       References and Additional Reading   *371*

13. Management Ethics **377**

Ethics Defined 380
Approaches to Ethical Analysis 382
Nature of Obligation: Negative or Affirmative 385
The Kew Gardens Principle: Between Avoiding Injury and
    Doing Good 387
Affirmative Obligation: Doing Good 389
Source of Regulation: Internal or External 390
Matrix Summarizing Dimensions of Variation and Their
    Interaction 393
Managerial Implications 393
    Endnotes *394*
    References and Additional Reading *394*

Index *399*

Organizational Behavior
and
Public Management

1

Introduction to Organizational Behavior in the Public Sector

INTRODUCTION

The purpose of this book is to provide you with an introduction to advanced study in organizational behavior. Our assumption is that you, like millions of individuals throughout the world, will spend your professional work life acting and reacting to the forces and individuals that comprise the social networks we call organizations. Consequently, the topics we shall discuss in this book (communication, motivation, decision-making, etc.) will form the basis for recurring themes in your *own* professional life. In other words, as either manager or subordinate, you will encounter people with whom you will need to communicate effectively. As a manager you will be expected to motivate subordinates, engage in decision making, employ information technology, act ethically, evaluate the performance of others and demonstrate that elusive quality known as leadership. In any organization that you find yourself, you will have to participate with others in order to achieve organizational objectives. Many of the people with whom you must participate will react to you on the basis of their perception of your organizational role. You will need to understand what quality is and how to achieve it. Moreover, as you move between and among organizations, you will sense that organizations have different climates and that they possess both formal and informal structures. If you have the opportunity to move between public and private organizations you may observe different goals, performance measures, and personnel practices. You may also observe that different organizations have different cultures which are reflected in different rituals and norms. Finally, if you remain in an organization long enough, you will observe that organizations can and do "learn" over time.

CHOOSING A UNIT OF ANALYSIS

The previous discussion about the kinds of activities you will engage in or are likely to encounter in your personal organizational odyssey are the chapter titles of this book. The purpose of our book is to expose you as a potential public manager to the research in leadership, motivation, ethics, etc. We do so to provide you with a "map" that you can use to find your way in your own organizational odyssey. The focus of the book, the unit of analysis in formal terms, is on the individual manager and the activities in which he or she must engage in order to function in public organizations. For our purposes, the unit of analysis can be understood as the perspective from which we will view the organization. The two most common perspectives in the literature are the fields of organizational behavior and organizational theory. The intellectual roots of organizational theory are in sociology. The study of organizational behavior has its roots in the fields of industrial and social psychology. While we will focus on the former approach, we do provide perspectives drawn from the latter. Moreover, our ultimate objective is to discuss the implications of both traditions for the *practice* of public management. Consequently, a brief description of these two approaches and our frame of reference is important.

In any discussion of perspective or unit of analysis, one must be cognizant of the lessons to be learned from the parable of the six blind wise men of India. It seems that the blind wise men were trying to "describe" an elephant. The first blind wise man felt the elephant's tusk and said that it appeared to be a spear. The second felt its side, flat and tall, and rendered the judgment that it must be a wall. The third touched the elephant's leg and said it must be a tree. The fourth felt its trunk and declared it a snake. The fifth blind wise man was exploring the elephant's ear and pronounced it a fan. The last wise man felt the elephant's tail and said it must be a rope. Clearly, all the wise men were partly right in their descriptions. They were also partly wrong. They were victims of their limited perspective! How we view organizations is also affected by the perspective we assume.

ORGANIZATIONAL BEHAVIOR

While we recognize the inherent dilemma posed for organizational analysis by the foregoing parable, we nonetheless agree with one of the eminent scholars of modern organizations, Herbert Simon, who said, "In the study of organization, the operative employee must be at the focus of attention, for the success of the structure will be judged by his place in it" (Simon, 1957, p. 3). In this sense, our primary focus in this book is on the social-psychological aspects of management. Therefore, we will seek to understand organizations using a model that focuses on the social and psychological forces and factors that impact upon the individual employee.

The notion of "models," a useful epistemological devise in the social sciences, has considerable utility in discussing what an organization is. A model is a tentative definition that fits the data available about a particular object. Unlike a definition, a model does not represent an attempt to express the basic, irreducible nature of the object, and is a freer approach that can be adapted to situations as needed. Thus, physicists treat electrons in one theoretical situation as infinitesimal particles and in another as invisible waves. The theoretical model of electrons permits both treatments, chiefly because no one knows exactly what an electron is; that is, no one knows its definition (Henry, 1995, p. 52).

Organizational behavior is a field of study which focuses on the behaviors, attitudes, and performances of people within an organization. It is sometimes referred to as the micro level of analysis. Organizational behavior is especially concerned with the influence of both the formal organization and the informal organization on employees, the effect of employees on the organization, and the work environment's effect on both (Hellnegal et al., 1986). Students of organizational behavior study the individual and group dynamics within the organization analyzing such topics as work motivation, job satisfaction, leadership, and decision making. They do so to help the manager in the real world carry out his essential analytical task which is to identify the important variables in any management situation, to estimate probable outcomes related to changes in those variables, and, to select the ones he or she can and should influence (Handy, 1993).

However, the organizational elephant is an elusive beast! If you think about the term "organization" you will realize that it is a construct, a linguistic abstraction like intelligence. Constructs are convenient words that represent generalizations based on observations about specific behaviors in real life. In this sense, constructs are not "real" in the sense that a computer is! Constructs are measured by indicators of their dimensions and operational definitions. For example, the ability to do calculus is one indicator of one dimension of intelligence and one operational definition of intelligence is scoring in the 90th percentile or above on the Graduate Records Examination. Similarly, organization is a term we employ to describe a phenomenon that occurs when individuals come together as a group to achieve a common objective. While there may be no universally accepted definition of the construct organization, scholars have attempted to operationally define organization by focusing on its various dimensions. Chester Barnard advised "A formal organization is a system of consciously coordinated activities or forces of two or more persons" (Barnard, 1938, p. 73). This definition focuses on the very central fact that organizations involve human activity systems that have at least two and usually many more people. Daniel Katz and Robert L. Kahn define organizations as consisting of ". . . patterned activities of a number of individuals.

Moreover, these patterned activities are complementary or interdependent with respect to some common output or outcome; they are repeated, relatively enduring, and bounded by space and time" (Katz and Kahn, 1978, p. 20). This definition underscores that the activities within organizations are interdependent, that the organization has boundaries, and that the activities are usually directed at a common objective. Dwight Waldo sees the organization as ". . . the structure of authoritative and habitual personal interactions in an administrative system" (Waldo, 1955, p. 6). This definition underscores the formal structure implied in an administrative system. In our view, an organization is a group of individuals working in a coordinated effort toward a common goal. The essential elements of an organization in our model are *coordination* and *motivation*. Coordination is necessary to unite the specialized work of individuals.

> Adam Smith's example of the pin factory vividly shows the benefits of co-operation and specialization and the corresponding need for coordination. Smith described how in his time (the late eighteenth century) the various stages of pin manufacturing were carried out by different people, each of whom specialized in a single task, pulling wire, strengthening it, cutting it to appropriate length, sharpening the point, attaching the head, and packaging the finished product-and how the resulting volume of output was many times greater than it would have been if each person involved had done all the stages alone. The crucial point, however, is that such specialization requires coordination. A single person producing pins alone turns out something useful. The time and efforts of the specialists are wasted unless they can be sure that both the people at each of the preceding stages are doing their parts in generating semifinished materials in the appropriate amounts and in a timely way, and that those at the latter stages of manufacturing are prepared to take what the people before have produced and turn it into a finished product (Milgrom and Roberts, 1992, p. 25).

The motivation dimension of organizations represents a necessary function that all organizations must perform. The need to motivate employees is central to the concept organization. It requires that the organization develop means to direct the activities of disparate individuals toward a common goal or output. Organizations must establish goals and measures of employee movement toward those goals, and, in so doing, to provide structures that facilitate both intrinsic motivation (the work itself) and extrinsic motivation (compensation).

ORGANIZATIONAL THEORY

By all the foregoing definitions of the term, the U.S. Department of Defense and the City of Cary, North Carolina are both organizations. Specifically, they are both public organizations. However, we are sure that you also recognize that while each organization is in some ways similar, in other ways, they are quite different. Both the Department of Defense and the City of Cary, N.C. are created by law and supported by taxes. They are both directed by public managers who approach work through a strict hierarchy of accountability, exemplified by written rules and procedures that govern budget and personnel decision making. They are both accountable to the public. They are divided into functional departments that facilitate a given division of labor. They both respond to some form of legislative and executive oversight. At the same time, these organizations are obviously dissimilar. They are of vastly different scale or size, they use different technologies to achieve their goals and function at different levels of government. Each has access to very different tax bases. Furthermore, their ultimate organizational missions (goals) are different.

Organizational theory is the formal name for the approach that seeks to describe, compare, and evaluate organizations at this macro level of analysis. Theory, itself, can be defined as a coherent set of interrelated definitions or propositions, presenting a systematic view of an event or phenomenon with the objective of explaining and predicting that event or phenomenon. Organizational theory, then, is a field of study that seeks to provide a theoretical framework for understanding the impact such systematic factors as size, task, technology, and culture have on predicting organizational outcomes (Senge, 1990).

The organizational theory perspective gives us very important insights into organizations. And, while it is not the primary focus we will pursue in this book, it is a focus we will not completely ignore. Organization theory tells us that organizations must do two things that are seemingly contradictory. On the one hand, every organization must *differentiate* its work into separate tasks or parts. As we said previously, a division of labor is required to achieve efficiency; that is, the most economical conversion of inputs into outputs. On the other hand, in order for an organization to be effective, that is to achieve goals that may go beyond simple economic efficiency, organizations must *integrate*. In order to integrate, organizations must coordinate, they must seek to bring the work of the specialized parts back together into a coherent whole. This tension between the natural tendency to differentiate work and at the same time the need to integrate that same specialized work, is inherent in all organizations. In other words, organizations are best conceptualized as *systems* that have inputs, a conversion process, outputs, and a feedback loop. The purpose of the organization is to minimize what are called transaction costs, which are the costs of running the system; that is, the costs of coordinating and motivating (Milgrom and Roberts, 1992, p. 29).

Administration or management, in this context, is the process of coordinating the individual acts of various specialized subgroups of people toward a unified organizational objective in order "to get things done" (Simon, 1957, p. 1). In this sense, organizations can and do exhibit a "culture," a set of assumptions, values, and perceptions about how "to get things done," that renders IBM and the American Red Cross very different organizational climates in which to work. In short, we recognize that the organization is the sum of its parts and, at times, greater than the sum of its parts.

PUBLIC VERSUS PRIVATE ORGANIZATIONS

This book is written for students and managers of public sector organizations. Public organizations are those created by law whose budget support comes from the public in the form of taxes. Public organizations are frequently referred to as nonmarket organizations in the literature to distinguish them from those whose survival depends upon the laws of supply and demand. The fact that we have decided to write a book about organizational behavior and public management suggests that we, like other researchers in the field, believe public organizations to be different from private organizations (Martin, 1989, p. 54). However, discussing the similarities and differences between public and private organizations brings us back to the question of perspective. Earlier we noted that organizations need to achieve, at one and the same time, the ostensibly contradictory goals of both differentiating and integrating work in order to function. In a similar vein, the case can be made for both the inherent similarities and inherent differences between public and private organizations and, by implication, between public and private management. To paraphrase Wallace Sayer, public and private organizations are very much alike in a variety of unimportant ways. Current debate, however, argues that all formal organizations share similar characteristics. And, in some sense, they do. Some argue that the essential elements of management in the public and private sector are generic, and in some sense they are. Other theorists argue that any organization, government, the firm, the not-for-profit sector, have a degree of "publicness" in that they are affected by public authority (Boseman, 1987). Again, this is true. It all depends upon your perspective and your definition of terms (Golembiewski, 1984; Perry and Kramer, 1983; Martin, 1989; Milgrom and Roberts, 1992).

Perhaps the best way to commence a discussion of public and private organizations is to speak in ideal types and to talk in terms of degree of "publicness." In our perspective, public and private organizations are different because their primary goals are different, and they are different in the way in which they secure the resources necessary for their continued survival. We also believe that these differences have management implications. The terms public and private derive from the Latin. Public means "of the people" and private means "set apart" (Nutt and Backoff, 1992, p. 25). The ultimate goal of the private organization (firm) is to maximize profit because to do less is to fail to survive in the marketplace. This necessity to secure its funding in the marketplace is what "sets apart" the classic private firm from the classic public agency. Public organizations, on the other hand, are empowered through law and funded through taxes and held accountable to oversight bodies and the public for administering the law in pursuit of their ultimate goal; namely, public service. Public organizations are part of government, which is part of the political system. The political system has a distinct role that is different in kind and character from the role played by firms in the market economy. This is not to say that private organizations do not have any other goals other than profit maximization or that public organizations have no goals other than public service. Nor is it our intention to contend that public and private organizations do not have some goals in common. However, their primary goals are fundamentally different! The private firm is by necessity concerned with efficiency; that is, getting the greatest level of output for a given level of input. The public organization's primary goal is equity, fairness in resource distribution. Moreover, as Hal G. Rainey observes in response to those who spurn any distinction between public and private organizations "If they are not distinct in any important way, why do public organizations exist?" (Rainey, 1991, p. 15).

Having said this, we are aware that there is some truth in Dwight Waldo's contention that "In the United States—and I believe more widely—there is a movement away from a sharp distinction between public and private, and a blurring and mingling of the two" (Waldo, 1980, p. 164). We are also aware, however, that in the mosaic of American politics the essential differences between government and the private market are recurring themes. Robert B. Reich has observed:

> Americans tend to divide the dimensions of our national life into two broad realms. The first is the realm of government and politics. The second is the realm of business and economics. Our concerns about social justice are restricted to the first realm; our concerns about prosperity, to the second. Issues of participation, equality of opportunity and civil rights, public education and mass transit, social security and welfare, housing, pollution, and crime are seen as aspects of government and politics—the substance of our civic culture. Issues of productivity and economic growth, inflation and unemployment, savings, investment, and trade are seen as aspects of business and economics—the substance of our business culture (Reich, 1983, p. 2).

In our view, the public sector and the private sector are terms that denote points on an underlying continuum. In other words, organizations can be conceptualized as to the degree of "publicness" they possess! The continuum is formed on basis of anchor points determined by whether the organization is privately owned and privately funded on one end, and, publicly owned and publicly funded on the other. Between these anchor points are a variety of hybrid organizations that blend public and private features (Dahl and Lindblom, 1953). And while the distance between the two anchor points may be contracting, the public sector and the private sector are still analytically and empirically different (Wamsley and Zald, 1973). We also share the conviction that the differences between the public and the private sector are important because these differences require that certain management functions (e.g., strategic planning, management information systems) be conducted differently in public and not for profit sectors than they are in the private sector (Nutt and Backoff, 1992: Bretschneider, 1990). Moreover, the differences between the public and private sector form a distinct management context that limits the direct "portability" of many management ideas developed in the private sector to the public sector in particular (Perry and Rainey, 1988).

Graham Allison has used the terms "predominantly public" and "predominantly private" to call attention to the underlying dimension of publicness (Allison, 1979). Some organizations are unambiguously situated, for example, Apple Computer Inc. is a privately owned organization (firm) that seeks profit maximization through sales of a product. It is also privately owned by its stockholders. The failure to profit maximize jeopardizes Apple's very survival in the market place, and, therefore it must be concerned primarily with efficiency. Other such organizations would be IBM, Sears, and grocery store chains. At the other end of the continuum, the U.S. Department of Education is a public organization, whose primary goal is not making a profit but rather equitably serving a public constituency. It also receives its support through taxes. Other such examples would be the Social Security Administration, the Cary, N.C. Police Department, and the Department of Defense. However, using the same criteria of private versus public ownership and public versus private funding there are hybrid organizations not so unambiguously situated.

In other words, there are organizations that are privately owned but are as dependent on public funding as any public agency, such as defense contractors who do business almost exclusively with government. There are also public organizations such as government owned utilities whose support comes primarily from private sources in the form of sales. Referring to such hybrid types of organizations one scholar has observed:

> Usually owned and operated by government, they typically perform businesslike functions and generate their own revenues through sales of their products or other means. Such enterprises usually receive a special charter to operate more independently than government agencies. Examples include the U.S. Postal Service, the Resolution Trust Corporation, The National Parks Service, port authorities in many coastal cities and a multitude of other organizations at all levels of government. Such organizations are sometimes the subject of controversy as to whether they operate in sufficiently businesslike fashion, on the one hand, and whether they show sufficient public accountability, on the other. On the other side of the coin are

many nonprofit and third-sector organizations that perform functions similar to those of government organizations. Like many government agencies, many nonprofits obviously have no profit indicators and incentives and often pursue social and public service missions. Finally, many private, for profit organizations work with government in ways that blur the distinction between them (Rainey, 1991, p. 20).

We all recognize that organizations such as Duke Power Company, the American Red Cross, and many private defense related organizations like General Dynamics fall somewhere in between the two anchor points on the continuum. Nonetheless, for the purpose of this book, we will find it useful to examine the characteristics that *distinguish* most public organizations from private organizations in order to discuss the unique *context* that public organizations provide for managers who function within them. To begin this task we need to briefly explore the role of government in our society, because it is the basis of the differences between public and private organizations.

THE ROLE OF GOVERNMENT IN AMERICAN SOCIETY

All public organizations are creatures of the state. They are created by law and draw on public resources for their support. This essential governmental character (publicness) of public organizations cannot be ignored, since it influences so much of the environment in which public organizations must exist. All public organizations exist within a political system. Political Scientist David Easton has defined the political system as a set of interactions through which values are "authoritatively allocated" for society as a whole (Easton, 1965). Public policy, the product of the political system that public organizations administer, is the tangible expression of these values. Consequently, all public organizations are part of this process that authoritatively allocates values (Denhardt, 1984; Denhardt, 1995).

Clearly, most social and public administration issues are, in the first instance, questions of values. Values are best understood by comparing them to facts. "Factual propositions are statements about the observable world and the way in which it operates" (Simon, 1957, p. 45). Factual propositions can be tested by the conventions of the scientific method to determine if they are correct or incorrect. Factual propositions can be verified because they are empirical. Values on the other hand, deal with the good or the ought. As Simon notes, "ethical terms are not completely reducible to factual terms" (Simon, 1957 p. 46). If we present you with an empirical or factual statement you can verify its accuracy. Take, for example, the statement "it is raining outside." In evaluating this statement, you bring to bear the evidence provided by your senses and you could verify the statement by using your senses. We would also have a means of reaching consensus as a group with respect to whether the statement is correct or incorrect. But a value statement such as "the law should not restrict a woman's right to choose an abortion," will engender far less consensus. In the case of the value statement you could not verify its accuracy by using empirical means. In fact, in answering the question you would rely on other value systems and ultimately state something about your values with respect to personal freedom and when life begins. In short, values cannot be verified entirely by resorting to facts. Because most real world policy issues have both factual and value dimensions, distinctions between facts and values are easier to separate analytically than in the real world of public organizations. This has led most scholars of public administration to reject distinctions between "politics" which is, in theory, value oriented, and "administration" which is, in theory, fact oriented (Gordon and Milakovich, 1995).

The political system, then, is the societal mechanism for resolving questions of values and public organizations are part of that political system. The political system produces public policy as its major output. Public policy in a democracy is the result of the demands, supports, and even apathy that the polity expresses toward the political and bureaucratic system (Mitchell and Scott, 1987). In other words, the fact that there is no clear empirical, factual, or scientific answer to the abortion question in no way inhibits citizens from committing their time and resources toward trying to turn the authoritative allocation of values in their preferred direction. This is why "politics" so frequently intrudes into the administrative process of government. The term "authoritative" is used because the political system enforces its actions through its monopoly on the means of legitimate force. This is implied in the term "force of law." Public policy reflects the force of law. In this way, public administration as a field of study is different than business administration (Martin, 1989; Perry and Kramer, 1983).

In order to understand American public administration, we need to understand conceptually the role of government in our mixed economy. We need to understand that the environment in which public management must function. That environment is bounded by a free market economy and a democratic political system. The role of political authority and the relationship of that political authority to market principles is at the heart of much of the controversy over public policy. According to Milgrom and Roberts, it is also central to why we have organizations at all.

> A thoroughgoing use of the market is one possible solution to the problem of coordinating economic activity. At the extreme, all transactions could be between separate individuals on an arm's length basis, and there would be no firms or other organizations apart from the market itself. The opposite extreme would be complete elimination of the price system under a regime of explicit central planning, with all decisions being made within a single (presumably multilevel) organization. Of course no economic system approaches either extreme. Even in their most centralized versions, the centrally planned communist economies left many decisions to individual

consumers who made their choice partly in response to prices. The market economies feature firms that interact with one another through markets but within which activity is explicitly coordinated through plans and hierarchical structures (Milgrom and Roberts, 1992, p. 27).

Robert Dahl and Charles Lindblom some years ago observed that there are basically two alternatives available to nations for organizing and controlling their political economies (Dahl and Lindblom, 1953). They are political hierarchies and the economic market. Both serve to provide social control. Political hierarchy draws upon political authority. In democratic political systems that authority is based on the legitimacy bestowed by elections. In the United States, the value of the dignity and integrity of the individual is an important core value in the political process. In addition, so is the idea of equality (not of outcomes measured in terms of possessions) but in the belief that every individual has a claim to life, liberty, and the pursuit of happiness. The final and very important core value underlying political authority in the United States is freedom. The idea that individuals in our political system should have a high degree of self determination (Denhardt, 1995).

Political authority can and is used to insure forms of social control necessary for life in the United States and other advanced industrial nations. Correspondingly, the market place provides through voluntary exchange, without any centralized direction, a mechanism for achieving social coordination. Day in and day out the economic market induces people to employ their skills and resources voluntarily to provide the abundance of goods and services that are present in most western nations. The market system is ultimately inductive. It is driven by the buying behavior of people who, for example, send signals to General Motors and its competitors that small cars with higher quality standards are what they want. They express these preferences by their purchasing behavior, that is, by voting with their dollars.

However, markets have a limited capacity to deal with certain classes of problems. This requires a government role (Cowen, 1988; Wolf, 1988) Some of these governmental roles are:

Controlling externalities
Providing public goods
Insuring equity
Providing a framework for law and order and economic stability

CONTROLLING EXTERNALITIES

One relevant question that may be asked is, if the private market through the interaction of supply and demand reaches an equilibrium at a price that reflects the

most efficient use of resources, why is there any need for non-market organizations like government at all? Why not allow all social decisions to be the product
of the voluntary transactions of individuals acting exclusively in a free market
environment? Anthony Downs provides one answer.

> Private agents operating solely through markets make decisions that do not
> take into account all the relevant effects of their behavior. In some cases,
> this results in socially undesirable outcomes. Either private agents carry out
> policies that are profitable to them but inflict unduly heavy costs on others,
> or they fail to carry out policies unprofitable to them that would result in
> great benefits to others (Downs, 1967, p. 32).

In more formal terms, these outcomes are referred to as externalities. Externalities are the side effects of market transactions (Cowen, 1988). More formally,
an externality is the direct result of an economic transaction that affects "third
parties" not themselves involved in that transaction. The effect may be positive or
negative and, can therefore, bestow either costs or benefits on those third parties.
A positive externality rebounds to the benefit of the person owning a home directly across the street from a beautiful private park for which he or she bears
none of the maintenance costs. A negative externality is occasioned by a firm lo-
cating a noxious swine processing factory in your neighborhood. In one case you
"benefit," in another you incur a "cost." In both cases you are a third party not directly involved in the economic transactions (Cowen, 1988; Hyman, 1973).

Clearly, pollution in all its forms is one type of negative externality. Pollution produces a social cost. That is, instead of internalizing the cost of controlling
pollution, including it in the costs of production, producers transfer that cost to
society at large (taxpayers in general). Government is the principal social organization that can and should intervene in a variety of markets to insure that relevant
costs and benefits are part of the social decision making calculus. This is the mission of public organizations which deal with such areas as zoning, land-use controls, and air quality control. Consider, for example, the following classic analysis
by Allison Dunham of why the courts allow public planning agencies have a legitimate role in overruling private market land-use decisions in some instances.

> The justification for changing the private land use decision and thus increas-
> ing the costs is the same as that suggested for control of the location of a
> public work: the benefit to the general welfare from decreasing or eliminat-
> ing an external cost (or from locating an external benefit where it is most
> valuable) exceeds the loss to general welfare arising from less efficient and
> more expensive locations (Dunham, 1958, p. 659).

In short government, through such public organizations as the Environmental Protection Agency at the national level, and the variety of land use agencies at the state and local level, have a legitimate regulatory role in a variety of
areas where the market cannot or will not include all the relevant social costs

into a decision that will have social consequences. Government in effect becomes the watchdog for the interests of those "third parties" who are not directly involved in many social and economic transactions but who stand to incur the consequences of those transactions.

PROVIDING PUBLIC GOODS

Government also has an important role in the production of public goods. Public goods are those goods that possess the characteristic that they can be consumed by one individual without diminishing the consumption of that same good by any other individual. In addition, the exclusion from consumption of a public good by potential consumers is either not feasible, not possible, or both. National defense and a light house are frequently cited examples of public goods. The Defense Department is a public organization that expends billions of dollars in pursuit of its goal, national defense. National defense is available to all citizens as a service of the national government. Your consumption of national defense does not affect the consumption of the benefits of national defense by others, and unless you live outside the U.S., you cannot be excluded from these benefits. Similarly, a government operated lighthouse confers benefit to all those who use it to navigate, whether they have paid or not. Imagine turning light houses over to the private sector. Few would pay the private lighthouse company because the non-payers (called "free riders") could not be excluded from getting the benefits. The company would fail and no lighthouses would be built. Government exists in part to provide those public goods that the market cannot or will not provide (Samuelson, 1964).

INSURING EQUITY

American government exists to provide social equity predicated on an underlying assumption of equality of rights. In a market economy, such as the United States, there is an inherent trade off between the efficiency and equality at many points in the public policy process. The economist, Arthur M. Okun, describes it as follows:

> To the economist, as to the engineer, efficiency means getting the most out of a given input. The inputs applied in production are human effort, the services of physical capital such as machines and buildings, and the endowments of nature like land and mineral resources. The outputs are thousands of different types of goods and services. If society finds a way, with the same inputs, to turn out more of some products (and no less of others), it has scored an increase in efficiency (Okun, 1975, p. 2).

The pursuit of economic efficiency by its very nature produces economic inequality. The market produces vast differences in income and opportunity in the United States. In the U.S. in 1986 the top one-fifth of American families enjoyed over two-fifths of all national income, while the bottom fifth, had only one-twentieth (Currie and Skolnick, 1988, p. 98). Robert B. Reich reports that between 1970 and 1990, the average pretax earnings of the bottom one-fifth of Americans declined by about 5%. Correspondingly during the same time period the top one-fifth of the income strata became about 9 percent more wealthy (Reich, 1992, p. 7). In an economic system such as that of the U.S., based primarily on private enterprise, government efforts to promote equality represent a deliberate interference with the results that the market would produce if left unrestrained. Therefore, the pursuit of equality (or any other expression of equity) produces costs to market efficiency. Why does government inhibit the efficiency of the market? Because we as a nation believe that the division of societal resources should be based on considerations (values) that go beyond simple market efficiency (which is itself a value). In other words, the body politic has concluded that some entitlements can and should be distributed equally, because, according to Okun:

> Society refuses to turn itself into a giant vending machine that delivers anything and everything in return for the proper number of coins. When members of my profession sometimes lose sight of this principle, they invite the nastiest definition of the economist: the person who knows the price of everything and the value of nothing. Society needs to keep the market in its place. The domain of rights is part of the checks and balances on the market designed to preserve values that are not denominated in dollars (Okun, 1975, p. 13).

In effect the economic market is oriented toward one value in society, efficiency! It does that quite well! What the market economy guarantees is that the most efficient uses of resources will result from the unrestrained interaction of supply and demand. Prices so determined will represent the most efficient allocation of resources. This postulate, however, does not consider that at times we may want, collectively, to maximize other values at the expense of market efficiency.

For example, lets take a hypothetical example a city suffering a natural disaster that destroyed its infrastructure (e.g., water and sewer). Lets further assume the city is cut off from outside aid for a significant time. According to free market economics what would happen to the price of antibiotics? In such a condition the *demand* for antibiotics would increase dramatically as the threat and reality of disease grew and new *supplies* were not made available. The laws of the marketplace would indicate that the most efficient allocation of resources will result from the unrestrained interaction of supply and demand to establish a market price for antibiotics. This would be the efficient (a value) solution. Also, that "price" may not even be money, it might be denominated in generators or cognac. How would the antibiotics be distributed under such a system? On the ability to pay that market price! What would that price be? What the market would bear! However, such a system of market-based distribution, perfectly acceptable in normal economic life, would in all probability be rejected by government in favor of one that maximized another value, equity (fairness). One equitable or fair system in this situation would be a form of triage designed to insure that those who needed the antibiotics most (e.g., sick children) received it regardless of the ability to pay. Such a system might, in this disaster scenario, involve the government commandeering the supply of antibiotics from private hands, with an agreement to pay a fair market price in the future, and then allowing medical officials to distribute the antibiotics to those most in need.

While the preceding example has the conceptual elegance absent in the complexity of a real world scenario, it does underscore the "tradeoff" often found between efficiency and equity in many current public policy programs. Most Americans would agree that a private housing market will never, on its own, produce housing at a price sufficiently low to provide certain segments of the population decent and safe housing. They would also agree that some government subsidy is necessary to produce such housing. However, just how much of such "public housing" should be produced is open to considerable debate. The same can be said of welfare and price supports for agriculture. The answer to the question under what conditions (and to what degree) should government interfere with the efficiency of the marketplace (and on whose behalf) to insure equity is itself a question of values. It is also a cornerstone of contemporary political debate in the United States.

PROVIDING A FRAMEWORK FOR LAW AND ORDER AND ECONOMIC STABILITY

In addition to the foregoing, government has the role of providing a framework for law and order and the provision of the conditions for economic stability. Since the provisions in the U.S. Constitution gave the national government the right to control the coining of money and the regulation of commerce, the federal government has facilitated the goal of economic stabilization. With the onset of the Great Depression, the role of both national and state governments in economic stabilization and development has expanded. Such public organizations as the Federal Reserve Board are central to this mission. The stabilization through subsidy of fragmented markets (like agriculture) are now functions of government with public organizations, ranging from the Federal Trade Commission to the U.S. Department of Agriculture, in place to pursue them. Even the regulation of that most symbolic of capitalistic organizations, the New York Stock Exchange, is conducted by a public organization, the Securities and Exchange Commission. In fact, managing the economy and controlling inflation by regulation of the money supply, are now the acknowledged responsibilities of government. Robert B. Reich observes that all the focus we place on indicators of the health of the economy, gross national product, the trade balance, the unemployment rate, etc:

> Underlying all such discussion is the assumption that our citizens are in the same large boat, called the national economy. There are different levels of income within the boat of course (some citizens enjoy spacious staterooms while others crowd into steerage). Yet all of us are lifted and propelled along together. The poorest and wealthiest and everyone in between enjoy the benefits of a national economy that is buoyant, and we all suffer the consequences of an economy in the doldrums (Reich, 1992, p. 4).

In addition, we expect the government to provide the rule of law and order that allows us to live in civilized society. This rule of law and order finds expression in both U.S. courts, civil and criminal. It includes everything from the commercial codes and rules of contract enforced by the courts, to sanctions against drug dealers.

The unique role government plays affects many aspects of public organizations: their goals, the legal and formal rules under which they must function, the degree of political influence to which they are subjected, the incentive structure which they can provide their employees, and the degree of market exposure they face. We will begin our analysis of the differences between public and private organizations by first turning our attention to those differences that are essentially economic in nature.

PUBLIC ORGANIZATIONS: ECONOMIC DIFFERENCES

Anthony Downs (1967) provides a very important conceptualization of the differences between public and private organizations based on market principles. According to Downs, most private organizations are economically two-faced, most public organizations economically are one-faced. Private organizations, or firms, secure scarce resources which they employ to produce their outputs. This is their first face. Their second face is the one they present to the market in which they seek to sell their outputs for a profit. As long as firms can sell their outputs for enough money to make the profit necessary to buy additional inputs, they can stay in business. This essentially two-faced system provides an important functional metric or standard against which to measure various elements of organizational productivity. In other words, the market system of profits and prices represents a measure of organizational health expressed in the litmus test of red or black ink.

Thus the sale of outputs in voluntary quid pro quo transactions provides an automatic evaluation of the work of the producer. If he can sell his outputs for more than his input costs (including normal returns on capital and entrepreneurship as costs), then he knows his product is valuable to its buyers. On the other hand, if he fails to cover the costs of his inputs by selling his outputs, then he knows his product is not valuable enough (Downs, 1967, p. 29).

The economic market, then, represents a system in which private firms compete for market share. Those private firms that can convince consumers to purchase their products in sufficient quantity to show a profit survive, those who cannot do not. A review of the statistics on small business failure in the U.S. in any given year will underscore that this is not simply a theoretical concept. In addition, Downs also notes that while the private firm's aggregate success can be measured in this two-faced relationship to the market, so can the productivity value of the given individual within the organization.

The market further provides a guide for evaluating the performance of the individuals within the firm. A sales man who brings in twice as many orders is obviously more valuable to the firm. Even men who perform entirely different functions can be compared objectively so long as their dollar contributions as measured from markets, can be roughly calculated through techniques as cost accounting (Downs, 1967, p. 29).

On the other hand, by design, public organizations and some segments of hybrid organizations which lack "market exposure," are economically one-faced. By this Downs means that while they secure resources in the market place (inputs), they face no economic markets on the other side. This is because typically public organizations do not sell their outputs. Consequently, they do not have the information provided by the market to use as a measure of their performance. Public organizations are typically controlled by oversight bodies; executive, legislative, or judicial in nature. They are financed by budget or fee structures. Public organizations usually have very weak or non existent market measures. This affects their ability to measure both aggregate (organizational) performance or individual (employee) performance. All government bureaus are nonmarket organizations in this sense. The market cannot provide the informational feedback loop in the form of prices and profits that it does for the private firm. In the middle of the continuum, what we are calling hybrid organizations, may be controlled by both oversight bodies and the market in the form of purchasing decisions by clients (Lan and Rainey, 1992). They may negotiate with oversight bodies for the right to provide services in a given area and even over prices that they may charge, as in the case of a public utility. Hybrid organizations may, however, have access to at least some market measures; some very clear, some muted (Rainey, 1991; Rainey, 1989; Perry and Rainey, 1988).

The absence of prices and profits in public organizations to employ as measures of organizational performance does not imply that no measures are possible. Such measures do exist and will be discussed in subsequent chapters. However, these measures are more complex, if only because they are once removed from the quantitative simplicity of running in the red versus the black. For example, anyone seeking to evaluate the organizational performance of the nation's prison systems comes face to face with a typical difficulty inherent in output measures that are not based on prices and profits. In our society, we lack consensus on the very purpose of prisons and the goal(s) we want them to achieve. Few citizens expect prisons to make a profit, although virtually everyone wants them run efficiently. This makes performance measures very difficult in that performance measures are simply the operational expression of progress toward stipulated goals. In the case of prisons, these goals are far removed from the marketplace, as well as societal consensus. In fact, some of our professed goals for prisons are at best ambiguous and in the worst case, contradictory. Some elements of the body politic and the oversight bodies they elect or commission believe prisons exist to punish. Others contend that prisons are designed to protect society. Still other segments of society contend that prisons should seek to rehabilitate. It is obviously most difficult to measure progress toward a target that is shifting, complex, and difficult to operationally define. In short, the economic differences between private firms and public organizations are most pronounced in the primary goals that each seeks to achieve. However, the differences between public and private organizations go beyond simple economic variations and relate to their inherently political nature.

POLITICAL DIFFERENCE BETWEEN PUBLIC AND PRIVATE ORGANIZATIONS

Public organizations are created by statute and are inherently "political." As we noted previously, public organizations differ from private organizations because public bureaus administer the law. In the American political system, the source of all power is the U.S. Constitution, "the supreme law of the land." The U.S. Constitution lays out the institutional framework in which all public organizations must exist. The Constitution reflects the framers' fear of centralized power and distributes power widely, some would say, in a fragmented manner. It divides the power between the states and the federal government and relegates local government to an inferior status. In this direct way, the Constitution sets forth the intergovernmental relations context in which all public organizations must function. The Constitution also provides the mechanism to restrain public organizations in order to make them accountable to the people, a significant consideration in the Founders' thinking. As Supreme Court Justice Brandeis has observed, the purpose of the Constitution was not to promote efficiency but to preclude the arbitrary use of political power.

Public organizations typically function under mandates that limit the organizational flexibility and autonomy of the managers of these organizations. These mandates can emerge from the political process directly. An example is the New Mexico state prison system in the 1980s whose warden, a public official, was under a federal court consent decree that stipulated 600 rules that had to be adhered to in the day to day running of the prison. Hybrid organizations may have such constraints to a lesser degree. Managers of public organizations also are subject to direct political influence from their oversight bodies, the users of their services, and organized interest groups. While not to the extent evident in public organizations, hybrid public organizations are also subject to direct political influence.

Public organizations have, when compared to private organizations, more extensive procedures and more formal specifications and controls designed to insure accountability to the taxpayer. These procedures and controls affect the internal and external aspects of public organizations. Also, most public managers deal with subordinates who are hired and promoted within a personnel system that sets forth very specific rules for hiring, promoting, firing, and appealing employee grievances. While these personnel systems were created in an endeavor to establish a merit system that places capability above political connections, they also limit the decision making autonomy and flexibility of the public manager when compared to her private counterpart. In other words, the incentives and sanctions that a public manager can bring to bear are limited by the personnel system in which she finds herself. Some researchers have found that public organizations exhibit greater cautiousness and rigidity and less innovation (Rainey et al., 1979). If you think about it, if the ability to provide merit pay, to terminate unproductive employees or to promote highly productive ones, is more limited and "procedure bound" in the public sector than in the private sector, these findings are not surprising (Lan and Rainey, 1992; Rainey, 1989).

Moreover, the desire for accountability is reflected in procedures and controls that go beyond personnel systems. They form the proverbial "red tape" that once wrapped French diplomatic communications, and which has now, by linguistic generalization, become a virtual synonym for public bureaucracy itself. Remember, however, that many often maligned rules and procedures are created in the interest of accountability necessitated by democratic theory. Stated simply, all elements of government in a democracy should be held accountable to the body politic. Partly for the previously mentioned reasons, working in government has been described as working in a "fishbowl." Graham Allison notes that many influential leaders who have served in senior executive positions in both the public and private sector contend that management in the two sectors is different and that it is *harder* in the public sector (Allison, 1979).

Much of society's preoccupation with accountability has to do with the fact that many of government's outputs are unavoidable. As we mentioned previously, government ultimately can resort to coercive power to enforce its will. The mandates of public organizations often give them coercive power over the lives of citizens who may not pick and choose the public services they will use. For example, parents who choose to send their children to catholic schools must still pay taxes to pay for public schools. The breath of impact of government is also much greater; government is involved in a vast array of activities which have broader and more significant impacts than the private sector (Rainey et al., 1979). This is frequently true for hybrid organizations such as not-for-profit foundations. Public organizations affect the day to day lives of people in areas ranging from protecting the food and water they consume to regulating the safety of nuclear power plants. For these reasons the "public" has unique expectations (which may or may not be met) with respect to the government and the behavior of public employees (Mitchell and Scott, 1987).

DIFFERENCES IN PROBLEMS FACED BY PUBLIC AND PRIVATE ORGANIZATIONS

The complexity of the objectives and the nature of the problems that public organizations must face is also a unique feature of working in government. In fact those organizations on the most "public" end of our public private continuum must deal with what have been called by Horst W. J. Rittel and Melvin Webber "wicked problems." In other words, the problems that are least likely to be addressed by the private sector because of their inherent nature. The definition of a wicked problem is worth exploring.

> As distinguished from problems in the natural sciences, which are definable and separable and may have solutions that are (finable), the problems of governmental planning-and especially those of social or policy planning-are ill defined; and they rely upon elusive political judgement for resolution. (Not "solution." Social problems are never solved. At best they are only resolved-over and over again.)

> The problems that scientists and engineers have usually focused upon are mostly "benign" ones. As an example, consider a problem of mathematics such as solving an equation; or the task of the organic chemist in analyzing the structure of some unknown compound; or that of the chess player attempting to accomplish checkmate in five moves. For each the mission is clear. It is clear, in turn, whether or not the problems have been solved.

> Wicked problems, in contrast, have neither of these clarifying traits; and they include nearly all public policy issues—whether the question concerns the location of a freeway, the adjustment of a tax rate, the modification of school curricula, or the confrontation of crime (Rittel and Webber, 1973, p. 160).

As the authors point out, most of the tame problems have been addressed. The streets are paved, the water and sewer systems established, and virtually every area of the country has schools and hospitals. Moreover, while there are still improvements to be made in these areas, we have nonetheless some fairly solid understanding of the parameters of the problems as well as measures of progress toward our goals. Contrast this to the wicked problems:

> Consider, for example, what would be necessary in identifying the nature of the poverty problem. Does poverty mean low income? Yes, in part. But what are the determinants of low income? Is it the deficiency of national and regional economies, or is it the deficiencies of cognitive and occupational skills within the labor force? If the latter, the problem statement and the problem "solution" must encompass the educational process. But, then, where within the educational system does the real problem lie? What then might it mean to "improve the educational system"? Or does the poverty problem reside in deficient physical and mental health? If so, we must add those etiologies to our information package, and search inside health services for a plausible cause. Does it include cultural deprivation? spatial dislocation? problems of ego identity deficient political and social skills?—and so on. If we can formulate the problem by tracing it to some sort of sources-such that we can say, "Aha! That's the locus of the difficulty," i.e., those are the root causes of the differences between the "is" and the "ought to be" conditions—then we have thereby also formulated a solution. To find the problem is thus the same thing as finding the solution: the problem can't be defined until the solution has been found (Rittel and Webber, 1973, p. 161).

We have not found the solution to the poverty problem. Like many wicked problems the answers to the problem are less in the realm of the true or false, and more in the realm of the "good or bad." This is because there is very rarely an immediate or ultimate agreed upon test for the solution of wicked problems. For example, have we solved the crime problem when there is a "significant decrease" in the relative amount of crime? What is the definition of significant? Or have we solved the crime problem only when we absolutely eradicate crime from society? In other words, many of the goals we have given public organizations have no clear definition and in fact are the sources of much controversy. We will return to this theme at a later point in the book.

THE STRUCTURE OF THE BOOK

At this point we turn to the organization of the book itself. This chapter provides a framework for our book by defining organizational behavior and placing it in the context of public organizations and public management. It introduces the view that public management is different because environment in which public organizations must function is different. This fact has implications for the analysis of an organizational behavior literature that has drawn in large measure on research from the private sector. As we stated previously, the public and private sector are different because their primary goals are different from those of private organizations. We also believe, as do other researchers, that the differences between the public and the private sector are important because these differences require that certain generic management functions (e.g., strategic planning) be conducted differently in public and hybrid organizations than they are in the private sector. Moreover, the differences between the public and private sector form a distinct management context that limits the direct "portability" of many management ideas developed in the private sector to the public sector. This also implies that ideas designed to make government more businesslike or to "reinvent" it need serious scrutiny. Chapter 2 will outline various approaches to the study of organizations that have emerged and will focus on the various ways organizations have been perceived historically.

Against this background we turn next to the study of the individual as the unit of analysis. Three bodies of literature are discussed in Chapters 3, 4, and 5: motivation theory, leadership, and role theory. We will also explore this literature from the environmental context of public administration. These chapters specifically seek to explicate the fact that the individual brings to the workplace a set of individual predispositions and individual differences that produce particular behaviors at work and that interact with the situational context of the organization to produce the environment in which managers must function. We will also explore the managerial implications of these facts.

The group provides the next general subject for analysis. Three aspects of group interaction central to organizational performance are discussed in Chapters 6, 7, and 8: communication, decision making, and participation and total quality management. In order for an organization to function it must possess the ability to modify its patterns and practices, so we also discuss the organization's capacity for change in Chapter 9.

The literature dealing with the individual, group, and organizational level variables provides insight into organizational life in public agencies by providing concepts and propositions generated through decades of research on organizational behavior. However, the approach employed in this type of analysis focuses on a single human activity (e.g., role behavior), while freezing for analytical purposes the other dimensions of life in the organization. The final analytical cut is the four chapters that conclude our work and which explore applied management problems. Drawing on implicit or explicit models of how individuals and groups function and how organizations change, these chapters provide opportunity for integrated analysis of all dimensions of organizational behavior. This holistic thrust is accomplished by examining four specific management challenges in Chapters 10, 11, 12, and 13: management systems, computers and information technology, performance appraisal, and management ethics.

REFERENCES AND ADDITIONAL READING

Allison, Graham T., Jr. (1979). "Public and Private Management: Are They Alike in All Unimportant Respects?" in *Setting Public Management Research Agendas*. Proceedings for Public Management Research Conference, U.S.O.P.M., November 19–20, Washington, D.C.

Barnard, Chester (1938). *The Functions of the Executive*. Boston: Harvard University Press.

Boseman, Barry (1987). *All Organizations Are Public*. San Francisco, California: Jossey Bass Publishers.

Bretschneider, Stuart (1990). "Management Information Systems in Public and Private Organizations an Empirical Test," *Public Administration Review* 50: pp 536–45.

Cowen, Tyler (1988). *A Theory of Market Failure: A Critical Examination*. Fairfax, Virginia: George Mason University Press.

Currie, Elliott and Jerome H. Skolnick (1988). *America's Problems: Social Issues and Public Policy*, 2nd ed. Boston: Scott Foresman and Company.

Dahl, R. A. and Lindblom, C. E. (1953). *Politics, Economics, and Welfare*. New York: Harper and Row.

Denhardt, Robert B. (1995). *Public Administration*. Belmont, California: Wadsworth.

Denhardt, Robert B. (1984). *Theories of Public Administration*. Pacific Grove, California: Brooks/Cole.

Downs, Anthony (1967). *Inside Bureaucracy*. Boston: Little Brown and Company.

Dunham, Allison (1958). "A Legal and Economic Bases for City Planning," *Columbia Law Review* 58:pp 650–71.

Easton, David (1965). *A Systems Analysis of Political Life*. New York: John Wiley and Sons.

Golembiewski, R. T. (1984). "Organizing Public Work, Round Three: Toward a New Balance Between Political Agendas and Management Perspectives." In R. T. Golembiewski and A. Wildavsky (eds.), *The Costs of Federalism*. New Brunswick, N.J.: Transaction.

Gordon, George, J. and Michael E. Milakovich (1995). *Public Administration in America Fifth Edition*. New York: St. Martin's Press.

Handy, Charles (1993) *Understanding Organizations*. New York: Oxford University Press.

Hellnegal, Donald, John W. Slocum, and Richard W. Woodman (1986). *Organizational Behavior*. New York: West Publishing Company.

Henry, Nicholas (1995). *Public Administration and Public Affairs*. Englewood Cliffs, New Jersey: Prentice Hall.

Hyman, David N. (1973). *The Economics of Governmental Activity.* New York: Holt, Rinehart and Winston.

Katz, Daniel and Robert L. Kahn (1978). *Social Psychology of Organizations.* New York: John Wiley and Sons.

Lan, Zhiyong and Hal G. Rainey (1992). "Goals, Rules, and Effectiveness in Public and Private Organizations: More Evidence on Frequent Assertions About Differences," *Journal of Public Administration Research and Theory.* 2. No. 1:pp 5–28.

Martin, David W. (1989). *The Guide to the Foundations of Public Administration.* New York: Marcel Dekker.

Milgrom, Paul and John Roberts (1992). *Economics, Organization and Management.* Englewood Cliffs, New Jersey: Prentice Hall.

Mitchell, Terence R. and William G. Scott (1987). "Leadership Failures, The Distrusting Public, and Prospects for the Administrative State," *Public Administration Review* 47:pp 445–54.

Nutt, Paul C. and Robert W. Backoff (1992). *Strategic Management of Public and Third Sector Organizations.* San Francisco, California: Jossey Bass Inc.

Okun, Arthur M. (1975). *Equality and Efficiency: The Big Tradeoff.* Washington, D.C.: The Brookings Institute.

Perry J. L. (1989). *Handbook of Public Administration.* San Francisco, California: Jossey Bass Publishers.

Perry J. L. and K. L. Kramer (1983). *Public Management.* Mountain View, California: Mayfield.

Perry, J. L. and H. G. Rainey (1988). "The Public Private Distinction in Organization Theory: A Critique and Research Strategy." *Academy of Management Review*, 13 (2):pp 182–201.

Rainey, Hal G. (1991). *Understanding and Managing Public Organizations.* San Francisco, California: Jossey Bass Publishers.

Rainey, Hal G. (1989). "Public Management: Recent Research on the Political Context and Managerial Roles, Structures, and Behaviors." *Journal of Management*, 15 (2):pp 229–250.

Rainey, Hal G., Robert W. Backoff and Charles H. Levine (1979). "Comparing Public and Private Organizations." *Public Administration Review* 36:pp 233–44.

Reich, Robert B. (1983). *The Next American Frontier.* New York: Times Books.

Reich, Robert B. (1992). *The Work of Nations.* New York: Vintage Books.

Rittel, Horst W. J. and Melvin M. Webber (1973). "Dilemas in a General Theory of Planning," *Policy Sciences* 4:pp 155–69.

Samuelson, Paul A. (1964). "A Pure Theory of Public Expenditure," *Review of Economics and Statistics* 36:pp 387–89.

Savas, E. S. (1987). *Privatization: The Key To Better Government.* Chatham, N.J.: Chatham House.

Senge, Peter M. (1990). *The Fifth Discipline.* New York: Doubleday.

Simon, Herbert A. (1957). *Administrative Behavior*, 2nd edition. New York: MacMillian. Waldo, Dwight (1980). *The Enterprise of Public Administration.* Novato, California: Chandler and Sharp Publishers.

Wamlsey, G. L., and Zald, M. N. (1973). *The Political Economy of Public Organizations.* Lexington, MA: Heath.

Waldo, Dwight (1955). *The Study of Public Administration.* New York: Random House.

Wilson, James Q. (1989). *Bureaucracy: What Government Agencies and Why They Do It.* New York: Basic Books Inc.

Wolf, C. (1988). *Markets or Governments: Choosing Between Imperfect Alternatives.* Cambridge, MA: MIT Press.

2

Approaches to Organization Theory

The purpose of this chapter is to review the significant schools of thought in organization theory. As we observed in the previous chapter, the parable of the six blind wise men of India is a very important conceptual framework to keep in mind when looking at organizations. Organization theory deals with a number of organizational dimensions, organization design (e.g., formal structure), internal functioning (e.g., decision-making, tasks, and human dynamics), and the external environment (e.g., markets, constituencies, and boundary spanning). We will look at organizations from the perspective of the public manager; however, the field of organization theory is inherently interdisciplinary. It incorporates such fields as psychology, sociology, economics, political science, and business administration (Argyris, 1990; Blau and Schoenherr, 1971; Denhardt, 1984; Evan, 1993; Golembiewski, 1985; Katz and Kahn, 1966; Mintzberg, 1983; March and Olsen, 1989; Perrow, 1986; Thompson, 1967; Senge, 1990; Wilson, 1989).

In our view, understanding organizations is sometimes facilitated by freezing all dimensions of an organizational life save that which one is studying at the particular time. For example, we will look at the research on motivation in the next chapter and study the concept in depth by holding constant other elements of organizational life. Of course, we recognize that day to day world organizations resemble Heraclitus's always moving river. That is to say, beyond the universal trait of being ever changing, organizations possess distinctive qualities. Employees are motivated or unmotivated in dynamic, real world, organizations that have distinguishing tendencies or characteristics, such as being public or private, technologically simple or complex, profit maximizing or not. Motivation, in reality, is only one element of organizational life, an element that influences and is influenced by other elements that make up the organization. Various approaches to understanding organizations, like the six blind wise men of India, have involved a number of perspectives that have emphasized different dimensions of the phenomena of organizations. Some approaches to the study of orga-

nizations have seen them in terms of structure and function. Others have emphasized the human factor. Some have seen organizations as essentially systems for
decision making. These approaches all take a macro view of the organization
which regards the organization as a whole and tries to understand it as such. This
holistic way of thinking about the total nature of work in the organizational context has resulted in propositions and concepts that help managers understand organizational behavior at the individual level and foster the achievement of
organizational objectives at the group level. Our theoretical introduction to
schools of thought in organization theory will provide a kind of mental anchor-
ing for the concepts and constructs that are introduced and reappear in subsequent chapters. We will begin our discussion of organization theory by looking
at organizations in history.

HISTORY OF ORGANIZATIONS

Organizations are human groupings deliberately constructed and reconstructed
to seek specific goals (Barnard, 1938 and Senge, 1990). By this definition, organizations have been a part of the human condition since the earliest of times. In
fact, basic organizational ideas are found in the Bible. Exodus Chapter 18 re-
counts the advice that Jethro, the father-in-law of Moses, gave to Moses about
management. Jethro observed that Moses was seeing too many people on a daily
basis and that "the thing thou does is not good. Thou wilt surely wear away." He
goes on to suggest that Moses choose men from among the nation who are able
to assist him in his organizational endeavors and place such over them, "to be
rulers of hundreds, rulers of fifties, and rulers of tens. And let them judge the
people at all seasons and it shall be that every great matter they shall bring to
thee, but every small matter they shall judge: so shall it be easier for thyself: and
they shall bear the burden with thee." (Exodus, Chapter 18, 21, 22). To put the
foregoing into the vernacular of today, Moses was being told to delegate, to
strategically plan and to develop an organization design that would facilitate a
division of labor by selecting competent subordinates. Accordingly, this new organizational structure would allow Moses to address larger policy goals, while
lower level staff members handled the more routine matters. This, according to
Jethro, would take some of the day to day management pressure off Moses as
well as allow him to manage his time effectively.

Indeed, we know from history, that many ancient civilizations accomplished a number of remarkable feats that required significant coordination
among groups of people in an endeavor to achieve common organizational goals.
Case in point, the problems faced by the early Egyptians in the construction of
the great pyramids are very apparent. One pyramid, covering 13 acres and 481

feet high, was constructed of about 2.3 million stone blocks each weighing an average of 2.5 tons. To complete this pyramid required 100,000 men working twenty years. Just planning for and organizing food and housing for 100,000 men over a twenty year period were no trivial tasks, regardless of the engineering complexity of the end product (Jackson et al., 1986, p. 5). In 3100 B.C., Memphis, King of Egypt, conducted a massive civil engineering project that actually diverted the course of the Nile. Ancient Rome had a very sophisticated organizational structure, designed to manage the empire, that manifested itself in Roman town planning. An organizational system that included municipal sewers, one way traffic during peak hours, traffic police, and a refined system of roads (Tomas, 1971). All of these endeavors required humans, working in groups, to both differentiate their work and at the same time work within an integrated framework. These were significant management tasks of sophisticated organizations that were designed to accomplish complex goals.

RAILROADS AND MODERN ORGANIZATIONS

The origin of modern business organizations in American society has been tied to our railroads. Railroads have been characterized as among the first modern business enterprises that employed professional managers on a salaried basis. They also provide a clear illustration of the process of rationalization and bureaucratization of organizations (Harmon and Mayer, 1986). Railroads were modern in both the technology they employed and the organizational structures they produced (Chandler, 1977). In addition, the evolution of management practices in the railroads set into motion changes that affected contemporary management.

Early transportation in the U.S. was over primitive roads. Subsequently, the Erie canal was built and the canal systems in other areas of the country expanded. Canals became a major way to move goods from one area to another. Beginning in about 1840, technological innovation in railroad design and engineering began to give the railroads a comparative advantage over other forms of transportation (Chandler, 1977). In the decade of the 1840s, only 400 miles of canals versus 21,000 miles of railroad were added to the nation's stock. Moreover, canals lost revenue to the railroads. The railroad made it possible to go from New York to Chicago in three days rather than three weeks. They also revolutionized the marketing of products. Railroads could operate in the winter and reach previously unreachable consumers. Railroads grew at an enormous rate between 1840 and 1850. This growth required extensive capital to finance a very expensive infrastructure. Railroads were so capital intensive that they became the first private enterprises to require large sources of capital from outside their immediate regions. Much of this capital came from Europe in the form of bonds. Historians underscore the role that securing this funding had on centralizing the American capital market in New York, which acted as a conduit for securing money for railroad expansion (Chandler, 1977).

However, what the railroads produced that is of most interest to students of organizational behavior is new organizational structures that led to new ways of managing. The geographical distribution of the railroads required management techniques that were distinct from anything that preceded them. The management of railroads required new information systems and accounting techniques that allowed managers to have the information they needed to manage this new endeavor. Railroads also demanded managers with high levels of technical expertise. In addition, this expertise, for the first time in history, was not exclusively associated with direct ownership of the business. As Alfred D. Chandler, Jr. (1977) has observed, the divorce of management from ownership, and the fact that the railroad manager was hired for his expertise and worked for a salary, made his way of life much closer to the modern executive than to that of merchants and manufacturers that preceded him. The development of railroads required the employment of a set of managers to supervise these functional activities over an extensive geographical area; and the appointment of an administrative command of middle and top executives to monitor, evaluate, and coordinate the work of managers responsible for day to day operations. Railroads generated the formulation of new types of internal administrative procedures, accounting, and statistical controls. Hence, the operational requirements of railroads demanded the creation of the first administrative hierarchies in American business (Chandler, 1977).

The evolution of mass production that occurred through the turn of the century, and the concomitant integration of mass production with mass distribution, offered manufacturers lower costs through increased productivity. The administrative structures and procedures, pioneered in the railroads, spread and became refined and elaborated in what became the modern industrial corporations. As industrialization grew, the entrepreneurs who created the nations first large firms could no longer handle the tasks of production, distribution, and marketing themselves exclusively, through their own families or associates. Initially, these entrepreneurs hired only middle managers and most firms were still owned by their founders. However, the movement away from single proprietor or family ownership of companies, brought about by the necessity to obtain working capital through the sale of stock in the business, opened upper-levels of management to the professional manager.

The management practices that evolved in the railroads found expression in other sectors of industrialized society. In addition, this new management environment produced an active intellectual interest in how organizations functioned. This interest emerged in the writings of various individuals. Some of the earliest and most influential of those writings constitute, what some call, the Classical approach. But, as the decades wore on, the Classical approach gave way to a succession of approaches each motivated by different sets of issues and problems. Some of these approaches include: the Human Relations approach, the Decision-Making approach, the Neo-Human Relations approach, the Systems approach, and the Bureaucratic Politics approach (Shafritz and Hyde, 1992).

Theorists and practitioners of organization theory today are constantly examining, revising and adapting organization theory to fit real world needs. Organization theory, and management principles and practices, remain an important topic of academic scholarship in both the public and private sector (Rainey, 1991: Daft, 1995). Moreover, the emergence of interest in total quality management (TQM) worldwide has produced a renewed interest in organization theory (Deming, 1982). In both the public and the private sector, organization topics such as group dynamics (e.g., teams and quality circles) organization design (flatter hierarchies and profit centers) and the measurement of organizational processes (e.g., statistical process control) are currently being discussed and implemented on a day to day basis (Lawler, 1992). Clearly, the search for theoretical principles that can guide the day to day activities of the manager remains a very important topic to professionals in the real world of organizations. We will now turn to the development of that body of organization theory.

THE CLASSICAL APPROACH

The classical approach to organization theory begins with the discussion of *scientific management*. Scientific management was a response to organizational demands of rapid industrialization in the United States and grew from the desire to base decisions about organizational and job design on scientific principles. These principles were based on very exacting measures of jobs and work processes (e.g., time and motion studies). The goal of scientific management was increased profits through increased worker productivity. In other words, the primary focus of scientific management was on increasing efficiency of production by decreasing the cost per unit of production. Frederick Winslow Taylor is often called the "father of scientific management." He was among the first individuals to systematically study the relationship between technology, work, and organizational structure and is best remembered for his time and motion studies. He was, in effect, the first efficiency expert. His work was designed to help private sector managers adapt production practices to the needs of the new industrial economy. An engineer by training and a president of the American Society of Mechanical Engineers, he is reputedly the author of the statement "time is money." Taylor (1856–1917), lived and worked during the period of industrialization in America and was among the first management theorists to look at the work systems in a holistic way (Taylor, 1967).

Taylor believed that with the application of scientific management he could both increase the wages of workers and decrease labor costs by increasing worker productivity. To Taylor, productivity gains were to be found in training people according to his scientific system. He served as a consultant to industry and had a variety of successful interventions in which his scientific management techniques saved companies money and increased wages. Talyor and his methodology became very popular in the business sector. Taylor's method focused on helping workers complete their tasks in less time and with greater efficiency. He accomplished this by breaking down the job into its component parts, standardizing those parts, and making careful observations about the time and motion needed to complete the task. He was known for his belief in the "one best way" to do a job. Talyor focused on formal structures and rules. He was "command and control" oriented in that he saw work systems as the responsibility of top down management to implement (Taylor, 1967, p. 83). Taylor's conception of work systems was predicated on the values of efficiency of production, rationality of work procedures, and profit maximization through productivity. His conception of the worker and his or her environment was secondary to his concerns for work systems.

One illustration of Taylor's technique is found in the impact he had on the Bethlehem Steel Company, where he was able to increase the rate at which pig iron was loaded on to cars from $12\frac{1}{2}$ tons to a new rate of $47\frac{1}{2}$ tons. Taylor was able to gain this efficiency by breaking down the task into its components and determining the optimum relationship of time, to motion, to the tool employed. At the time of his intervention at Bethlehem it was customary for workers to provide their own tools. Consequently, many different types and sizes of tools were employed to shovel pig iron. There were large differences in job performance. Some workers used the same shovels to lift both pea coal and iron ore despite the fact that the latter weighed ten times the former. By analyzing all the factors that went into shoveling coal, Taylor was able to design the one best way to do the job and to increase both worker efficiency and their wages. Taylor described his system and its effect on productivity, using as an example a worker named Schmidt. Schmidt started to work, and all day long, and at regular intervals, he was told by a manager who stood over him with a watch, when to work and when to rest. By five in the afternoon he had his $47\frac{1}{2}$ tons loaded on the car. Taylor also observed that he continued to work at this pace and do the task during the entire time Taylor was at Bethlehem (Taylor, 1967, p. 47). A more contemporary example of Taylorism is the way a surgeon approaches an operation. Efficiency in the number of steps, time and motion, and the "one best way" to do the operation are imperative because of the risks of infection. In an operation, the tools (instruments) are laid out in the order in which they will be employed and the steps in the procedures are designed to minimize time and motion. This approach is classic Taylorism! Some of Taylor's major scientific management principles are:

1. Management (not workers) are to develop a science for every job, which replaces the old rule of thumb method. In order to do that, workers should be scientifically selected, trained, and placed in jobs for which they are mentally and physically suited;
2. The job to be done should be analyzed scientifically to determine the one best way to do that job and standard times for jobs and work processes should be established;
3. Incentives should be offered so that workers behave in accordance with the principles of the scientific management that have been developed.
4. Management must support workers by carefully planning and helping implement their work (Taylor, 1967).

Frederick Taylor's influence on organization theory in general is well recognized (Daft, 1995; Tosi et al., 1990). Specifically, his prescription for designing organizational relationships by attempting to provide a blueprint for every facet of the worker's task gave management a framework for approaching work largely absent prior to Taylor. Scientific management called attention to the design of work as an important variable in productivity and profit. Taylor also had an important influence on the development of modern systems of job classifications. He made important conceptual distinctions, now a part of management lexicon, for example, the differences between organizational *objectives* what the organization wants to accomplish, and, *standards* or measures of performance that, when met, should accomplish those objectives! Moreover, much of the systematic process mapping evident in modern statistical process control (SPC), for example, using flow charting to isolate the steps in a production process, owe an intellectual debt to Taylorism (Deming, 1982).

Fredrick Taylor's perspective on the organizational elephant focused on the efficiency of *process* and *outcomes*. Taylor was by no means unsympathetic to workers (Schacter, 1989). However, the "human factor" was seen mainly in terms of wages, in fact, scientific management designed work (jobs) so that they could be implemented by a workforce that followed simplified procedures. Thinking, defined in terms of having input into the design of work, was the primary role of management. In the area of public management, specifically, there are today "standard times" for a number of municipal services (e.g., garbage in tons that can be picked up in one day by a truck of a given configuration) which are clearly based in scientific management principles. In addition, the philosophy of scientific management was incorporated into the ideology and structure of American local government. The successful implementation of the city manager form of government, non-partisan elections, and master planning, in many American cities incorporates many of the underling concepts of scientific management. These concepts include a belief in the one best way to do a job, neutral expertise, and the belief in "businesslike government," exemplified in the conception that "there is no Democratic or Republican way to pave a street (Vasu, 1979, pp. 34–48). Finally, scientific management influenced the philosophy of the *principles of administration* approach to organization theory which we will discuss next.

Leonard D. White (1926), in his classic *Introduction to the Study of Public Administration*, the first textbook devoted exclusively to public administration\management, reflected many of the assumptions of scientific management that were incorporated in the principles of administration approach. Specifically, the overriding belief that management lends itself to value free scientific analysis and the corollary assumption that efficiency was the major goal of administrative operations. White's work also reflected the prevailing view, that many scholars argue is derivative of Woodrow Wilson's (1887) classic essay "*The Study of Administration*"; namely, that politics and administration can be separated in practice. Moreover, this separation implied that the science of administration was distinct from the craft of politics. These assumptions set in motion a desire to elaborate the "principles" of administration. In other words, principles that could be scientifically derived from empirical analysis, stipulated, and applied in any administrative context.

Henri Fayol (1949), a Frenchman, wrote *General and Industrial Management* which was a major work in the principles of administration approach to organization theory. Unlike Taylor, he concentrated on organization design at a far more general level of organization and focused more extensively on the role of the manager rather than the worker. Fayol was the general manager of a large mining company and employed his practical experience to underscore the theoretical foundations of effective management. He is credited with being among the first researchers to provide a comprehensive theory of the organization. To Fayol, effective management of organizations was essentially achieved by implementing a five component process.

1. *Planning*: managers need to plan for the organization's tasks and objectives.
2. *Organizing*: managers need to find the labor and capital necessary for the achievement of the organizational goals.
3. *Commanding*: managers must regulate the activity of people in the organization so that it proceeds in the direction of the organization's main goals.

4. *Coordinating*: managers must provide the means to integrate the separate efforts of the organization's members into an integrated whole.

5. *Controlling*: this meant to Fayol that all employees had to be made to comply with organizational rules (Fayol, 1949).

Luther Gulick, and Lyndall Urwick summarized many of the major tenets of classical administrative theory in their seminal work *Papers on the Science of Administration* (Gulick and Urwick, 1937). Luther Gulick, in particular, had extensive ties to public administration including consultant to the National Resource Planning Board, a member of President Franklin D. Roosevelt's Committee for Administrative Management, as well as being a close personal advisor to F.D.R. Because of this experience Gulick and Urwick had a first hand knowledge of how administration worked in the real world. They believed that there existed rules or principles which administrators need to follow in the area of organization design. They outlined many of the principles that have become associated with the very concept of administration since their time. These principles include:

1. *Hierarchy*: the allocation of skills, rewards, and authority in an organization. This allocation is a vertical ordering of superior-subordinate relationships in a defined chain of command.

2. *Unity of command*: direction is given by a single individual at every level of the organizational structure.

3. *Functional specialization*: the division of labor by subject matter specialization was central to the administrative efficiency.

4. *Span of control*: the concept that the superior-subordinate relationship is maximized when the superior has responsibility for the activities of a limited number of subordinates. In other words, the span of control should be as narrow as possible.

5. *Rational organization design*: The organizational arrangement of functions should be rational that is based on purpose (e.g., criminal justice); client served (e.g., prisoners) place (e.g., state or county), and the process or purpose served (e.g., engineering, or public health). Also, the belief that organizational structure should be designed to maximize effective communication (Gulick and Urwick, 1937).

Of particular importance to Gulick and Urwick was the structure of the organization, over and above the individual personalities in it. They believed that the right structure had to be found and then filled with the right people. To all the authors of the classical approach, administrative theory was a set of principles that crossed cultural boundaries and administrative context, they were just that, principles.

To Gulick, for example, the division of labor was the basis for all complex organizations (Gulick and Urwick, 1937; Shafritz and Ott, 1987). Since work division was the logical foundation of Gulick's model of the organization it was also logical that he prescribe finding the perfect structure of authority, as the essential task of management. In Gulick's view, the principal obstacle in finding this perfect structure was the limits of human nature. The limits imposed by human nature lead to those principles of administration. For example, just as the hand of man can span only a limited number of notes on the piano, so the mind and will of man can span but a limited number of immediate contacts (Shafritz and Ott, 1987, p. 91). Therefore, the span of control had to be narrow if management was to be effective and efficient. Stemming from a span of control was unity of command. This was meant, as a practical matter, never placing a subordinate in a position in which he or she had to serve two masters. It was postulated that individual subordinates, subject to instruction from multiple supervisors, would become confused. It was further postulated that the work of such subordinates would be inefficient. Another major principle of administration was the technical efficiency gained from unifying homogenous types of work. This focus on the homogeneity of work and the importance of technical specialists directing other technicians was expressed as follows.

> It followed from this (1) that any organizational structure which brings together in a single unit work divisions which are non-homogeneous in work, in technology, or in purpose will encounter the danger of friction and inefficiency. And (2) that a unit based on a given specialization cannot be given technical direction by a layman (Shafritz and Ott, 1987, p. 93).

The principles of administration that Gulick and Urwick summarized gave public administration an enduring acronym, *POSDCORB*, which described the functions of public management: *Planning, Organizing, Staffing, Directing, Coordinating, and Budgeting.* The principles of administration were clearly affected by prevailing modes of business organization. Specifically, the necessity of establishing single centers of power forming a top down hierarchy. To accommodate this conception of organization, philosophically, with representative democracy the author's called for administrative centralization to be vested in an executive responsible to political authority. The principles of administration were subject to attack on the basis of there own internal logic (Simon 1957B). Moreover, scholars' like Luther Gulick were far more sensitive to the "context effects" on principles of administration than critics of this perspective admit (Van Riper, 1990). However, the focus of principles of administration and scientific management was on such variables as structure and job design, and minimized the "human factor" in organizations.

THE HUMAN RELATIONS APPROACH

The human relations approach to organization theory stemmed from empirical research which found workers and their interpersonal relations to affect what happens in organizations. In effect, this approach "discovered" the human factor in organizations as a variable that influences organizational productivity, over and above, organizational structure and job design. Unlike scientific management or the principles of administration, the human relations approach focused attention on the "human factor" in the workplace. These studies, which began in the tradition of scientific management, were designed to determine the relationship between certain variables in the working environment (e.g., lighting and temperature) on worker productivity. Elton Mayo, who many call the father of modern industrial psychology, was a professor in the Harvard Business School when he and his associates conducted a series of controlled experiments at Hawthorne Western Electric Plant. These studies, which went on over a decade, are characterized as beginning the "human relations school" of organization theory.

In one set of studies, the Hawthorne researchers were seeking to determine the effect of illumination on worker productivity. Certain groups of workers were isolated from their co-workers and placed in a carefully controlled environment where certain variables in the workplace could be manipulated, while the researchers observed the impact on productivity (the plant made telephone equipment). A number of measures of physical ability, fatigue, dexterity, and personal habits, etc. were taken of the subjects (workers) by the researchers. The Hawthorne researchers employed one experimental design in which two groups of workers were created from Hawthorne factory personnel. One group (the test group) worked under different intensities of illumination. The other (the control group) worked under conditions in which illumination was held constant. Intensity levels in the test group were raised in increasing magnitude from 24, 46, to 70 foot candles. Productivity was measured, and, indeed it went up, in both groups. In another experiment, the light under which the test group worked was decreased from 10 to 3 candles, while the control group worked, as before, under a constant level of illumination intensity. In this case, the output rate in the test group went up instead of down. It also went up in the control group (Roethlisberger, 1941). The real illumination in the study came when the researchers themselves realized that it was not the physical changes (lighting, humidity, fatigue) that were producing the changes in output but rather something else. That something else was the attention being paid to the workers, the now famous "Hawthorne Effect" (Roethlisberger, 1941).

> Their health and well being became matters of great concern. Their opinions, hopes, and fears were eagerly sought. What happened was that in the

very process of setting the conditions for the test-so called "controlled' experiment; the experimenters had completely altered the social situation of the room. Inadvertently a change had been introduced which was far more important than the planned experimental innovations: the customary supervision in the room had been revolutionized (Roethlisberger, 1941, p. 7).

In effect, the real influence on productivity was not the alteration in the physical environment, but rather the alteration in the social environment. More specifically, the experiment failed to show a simple direct relationship between physical factors of the work environment and rate of output. The reason the researchers concluded, was because the impact of these physical factors (light, humidity, fatigue) were confounded by the influence of psychological factors. This finding elevated "psychological factors" to a position of importance in explaining the variance in worker productivity. The Hawthorne studies also underscored the need for managers to focus their attention on both the formal structure of work systems and the pattern of human relationships in the workplace, if they wanted to increase output.

The Hawthorne studies also added other important concepts to our understanding of people in the workplace. For example, they demonstrated the existence of the "informal group." The informal group is the group formed by employees that exists over and above the formal organization. The formal organization was and is the organization on paper, as it appears on the organizational chart. These charts typically outline authority from the top down, graphically indicating lines of communication and the chain of command. What the Hawthorne studies observed was the existence of an informal organization, a group structure with norms about behavior that affected productivity, but was not reflected on the organizational chart. The Hawthorne researchers describe one such group and the influence this group had on the flow of work.

> The work of the employees was the adjustment of small parts which went into the construction of telephone equipment. The management thought that the adjustment was a complicated piece of work. The interviewer found that it was quite simple. He felt that anyone could learn it, but that the operators had conspired to put a fence around the job. They took pride in telling how the apparatus that no one could make work properly was sent in from the field for adjustment. Then telephone engineers would come in from the field to find out from the operators how the repairs were made. The latter would fool around, doing all sorts of wrong things and taking about two hours to adjust the apparatus, and in this prevent people on the outside from finding out what they really did (Homans, 1951, p. 230).

The Hawthorne studies also discovered that this informal group had a leadership structure quite apart from the formal organization, and that the group had its own norms with respect to production. The group also acted in ways that did not conform to the conventional wisdom of the time. Surprisingly, since the group was paid on a group piece work basis that rewarded more output with more money earned, the group norms were not exclusively monetary. In fact, operating in the group were four basic sentiments.

1) You should not turn out too much work; if you do, you are a "rate buster."
2) You should not turn out too little work; if you do, you are a "chiseler."
3) You should not say anything to a supervisor which would react to the detriment of one of your associates; if you do, you are a "squealer."
4) You should not be too officious; that is if you are an inspector you should not act like one (Roethlisberger, 1941, p. 11).

The Hawthorne Studies are among the most important and controversial studies ever conducted in the workplace (Baretz, 1974). What can be concluded about their impact is that they opened a flood gate of concern and theorizing about the "human factor" in industrial relations. The Hawthorne studies also set in motion the belief that managers need to focus their attention on both the formal structure of work systems and the pattern of human relationships in the workplace, if they want to increase output. Prior to the Hawthorne studies human beings were an element in productivity, but not a very important element. The Hawthorne studies underscored three major precepts still associated with the human relations school.

1) The level of production is set by social norms, not by physiological capacity exclusively;
2) non-economic rewards and sanctions significantly affect the behavior of workers and largely limit the effect of economic incentive plans;
3) often workers do not act or react as individuals but as members of groups" (Etzioni, 1964).

THE DECISION-MAKING APPROACH

The human relations approach and the classical approach clearly differ in the assumptions they make and the approaches they take in describing organizational reality. A third model often called the decision-making approach, stands apart but draws on each tradition. The unit of analysis of this approach is the "decision" a manager makes. Chester Barnard (1938), a chief executive himself, made a number of contributions to the study of organizations. His classic *The Functions of the Executive* was in many ways a conceptual bridge between the classical theories and the human relations school. Unlike Taylor and Fayol, Barnard saw the organization in primarily human rather than in structural terms. In fact, he saw it as a collection of human interactions focused toward a purpose. To Barnard, the organization was always in a "dynamic equilibrium," a state of tension necessary for the organization to sustain itself. This equilibrium was accomplished through a series of "exchanges" of utilities between the participants. He saw the manager's job as allocating satisfactions or rewards in exchange for the employees' acquiescence to the prescribed behavior; behavior that the organization required to meet its goals and survive. Barnard also hypothesized a distinction between the formal organization and informal organization. He characterized the formal organization as the one of structure and authority under the conscious control of managers; the organization highlighted by Taylor and Fayol. The informal organization to Barnard occupied the same formal space and time as the formal organization but lacked the structure of the formal organization. The informal organization was the world of group passions, identifications, and friendships that overlapped and influenced the functioning of the formal organization.

Barnard, who had a successful career as an executive, brought a unique perspective to the role of the executive in the organization. In his view, executive functions existed to facilitate the cooperative effort of organization members by enhancing communication within the organization. The executive also needed to maintain an informal executive organization of compatible personnel. The goodness of fit of these people with the executive could and should go beyond formal competence to include compatibility of such factors as education, personality, values, etc. Barnard saw the organization's success as predicated upon hiring individuals who could be induced to cooperate in achieving the organization's objectives. Finally, Barnard saw the role of the executive in terms of formulating long range policies and objectives. Executives, he argued, provided the general policies and objectives that flush out the "big picture." Managers, on the other hand, provide intermediate objectives for reaching goals (Barnard, 1938).

Herbert Simon (1957B), a Noble Prize winner in Economics, was among the first theorists to describe organizational behavior explicitly in terms of decision processes involved. In his classic, *Administrative Behavior*, Simon portrays organizational decision-making as a kind of compromise between rational, goal oriented behavior and nonrational behavior. Simon specifically called into question the entire concept of the principles of administration. He articulated, in very clear terms, the fact that for every "principle" of administration, for example, narrow span of control, there was a counter principle which called into question the entire concept of principles that could be applied across administrative arenas. In fact, rather than principles what one had was proverbs! For example, according to the principles of administration, organizations needed a narrow span of control in order to insure efficiency of communication channels. In other words, if the span of control got to large (there was various operational definitions of large), then communication between superiors and subordinates would break down. In order to avoid this, one needed a relatively tall hierarchy; that is an organization design with many levels (an organization chart with many levels and boxes) which allowed for narrow spans of control. However, the same principles of administration called with equal intensity for organizational structures that enhanced responsiveness and control. In order to achieve this, they needed organizational structures that were relatively "flat" (few levels and boxes). Simon effectively made the case that for every "principle" of administration there were practical administrative situations which made the principle impossible to implement.

> What evidence there is of actual administrative practice would seem to indicate that the need for specialization is to a very large degree given priority over the need for unity of command. As a matter of fact, it does not go to far to say that unity of command, in Gulick's sense, never existed in any administrative organization. If a line officer accepts the regulations of an accounting department with regard to the procedure for making requisitions can it be said that, in this sphere, he is not subject to the authority of the accounting department? In any actual administrative situation authority is zoned, and to maintain that this zoning does not contradict the principle of the unity of command requires a very different definition of authority than that used here. This subjection of the line officer to the accounting department is no different, in principle, from Taylor's recommendation that a workman be subject in the matter of work programming to one foreman, in the matter of machine operation to another (Simon, 1957B, p. 15).

Simon argued that the "economic man" of classical economic literature did not, in fact, exist. According to economists, the economic man was a person assumed to have superior knowledge about and anticipation of the consequences of each choice he would make, which implies a very high level of understanding about all aspects of his environment. Economic man was also presumed to possess a stable set of preferences, and a highly sophisticated calculation ability that enabled him to rank competing alternatives, and achieve the highest attainable point on his subjective preference scale for a variety of decisions. Simon postulated that instead of economic man, what in fact existed was administrative man, a decision maker who wanted to make "the single best choice" but who was constrained by the variety of variables. The single best choice for administrative man, like economic man, was the one that would maximize the attainment of certain specified ends with the use of specified resources. Simon argued that most of us live in the real world and that the real world is not fashioned according to the assumptions of classical economic theory. In effect, the real world is bounded by limitations both personal (limits of the decision maker) and organizational (limits imposed by the organizational setting in which decisions are made). In other words, these limitations may be of intellect, physiology, information processing capacity or they could be inherent in the organizational structure in which one finds oneself. In fact, they are frequently both.

Clearly, the unit of analysis for Simon (1957A) was the individual decision maker. He developed in an eloquent fashion his argument about the limits of individual decision-making in *Models of Man* (Simon, 1957A). The critique by the decision-making approach to organization theory was predicated on the observation that models of choice had traditionally been based on a global model of rational choice built on this ideal economic man. An alternative model, one of bounded rationality, that conceptualized decision-making differently was postulated by scholars of the decision-making approach. In most global models of rational choice, all alternatives are evaluated before a choice is made. In actual human decision-making, alternatives are often examined sequentially. We may, or may not, know the mechanism that defines the order of our search procedure. When alternatives are examined sequentially, we frequently regard the first satisfactory alternative that is evaluated as sufficient. This process is now referred to as *satisficing* which involves the selection of alternatives that meet some minimal criteria and then selecting the first acceptable alternative that arises. For example, a public manager who is in a department that has receipts for services is dissatisfied with her accounting software. It would take considerable time and expertise to discover all the elements of this problem. It would also require considerable time to meet with various vendors, review their software packages, run multiple selected packages in test mode, compare outputs and select the one best accounting software package for the department. This type of problem represents a situation in which some information is unavailable or expensive to attain, some alternatives are not easy to identify, and other alternatives are very difficult or impossible to select. Rationality becomes limited by these complexities and decisions become imperfect when compared to standards of classic economic rationality. In this simple situation, there are many points at which the manager can satisfice; for example, she can look what is available through the purchasing contract that many public agencies have with selected vendors, she can rely on a colleague who uses accounting software in a similar administrative environment. She can go to the colleague's agency, look at output from the colleague's software and using some minimum criteria (the software is on the purchasing contract list, its billing format is acceptable, it runs on an IBM platform, etc.) select that package to replace the old one.

Simon believed that in actual organizational practice decision-makers cannot and do not seek optimal solutions to complex problems. They approach many administrative choices in a fashion similar to the one described in the preceding paragraph, that is, they satisfice. Moreover, administrators do not seek optimal solutions because they come face to face with the fact that the world that they perceive is a drastically simplified model of the confusion and complexity inherent in the real world. Administrative man makes his choices using a simplified picture of the world, according to Simon. A picture that focuses on those few variables that he or she regards as most important.

The individual as the unit of analysis led to some very important observations about the role of administrative decision-making. This theoretical perspective, however, does not directly deal with the combined effects of other variables in the decision-making process. One approach, in the decision-making perspective, that has done so is the *garbage can approach* (Cohen et al., 1972) The garbage can decision process (also called organized anarchy) is caused by the existence of problematic preferences (goals, problems, and alternatives are undefined and ambiguous), unclear and poorly understood technology (cause and effect relationships within the organization are not clearly understood), and turnover (organization members change frequently resulting in situations in which participation in decisions is both fluid and limited). Many public and private organizations can fit these criteria at any given time. The garbage can model sees the decision-making process of an organization in terms of timing and fluidity. In other words, the organization is conceptualized as a fluid structure in which people, problems, decision- making opportunities and solutions flow together and apart at different times. The garbage can model is far removed from a decision-making process that flows from the normal vertical hierarchy of authority. The garbage can model is a different kind of decision "stream," one in which the overall pattern of organizational decision-making resembles a process which has random elements. The model states that administrators in complex organizations are decision makers with different goals and problems. Their time and energy is limited and they can be involved in only a given set of decisions. They choose those decisions in which they will be involved on the basis of their respective needs, goals, and availability. Participants in decisions also have specific ideas they want adopted "pet projects." Some of these ideas are problems in search of a solution others are solutions in search of a problem. Richard L. Daft, observes the following about the making of the movie *Casablanca*.

> The public flocked to see *Casablanca* when it opened 1942. The film won Academy awards for best picture, best screenplay, and best director, and is recognized today by film historians and the public alike as a classic. But until the filming of the final scene, no one involved in the production of the now famous story even knew how it was going to end.
>
> *Everybody Come to Rick's* wasn't a very good play, but when it landed on Hal Wallis's desk at Warner Brothers, Wallis spotted some hot-from-the-headlines potential, purchased the rights, and changed the name to *Casablanca* to capitalize on the geographical mystique the story offered. A series of negotiations led to casting Humphery Bogart as Rick, even though studio chief Jack Warner questioned his romantic appeal. The casting of Ingrid Bergman as Ilsa was largely by accident. A fluke had left an opening in her usually booked schedule.

Filming was chaotic. Writers made script changes and plot revisions daily. Actors were unsure of how to develop their characterizations, so they just did whatever seemed right at the time. For example, when Ingrid Bergman wanted to know which man should get most of her on screen attention, she was told, "We don't know yet—just play it, ... in between." Scenes were often filmed blindly with no idea of how they were supposed to fit into the overall story. Amazingly, even when it came time to shoot the climactic final scene, no one involved in the production seem to know who would "get the girl" a legend still persists that two versions were written. During the filming Bogart disagreed with director Michael Curtiz's view that Rick should kiss Ilsa goodbye, and Hal Wallis was summoned to mediate. Since the cast received their scripts only hours before filming began, they couldn't remember their lines, causing constant delays (Daft, 1995, p. 383).

Clearly, the making of *Casablanca* was not a rational top down decision-making process starting with a problem to be solved and a series of defined steps that lead to a solution. In fact, it was process that involved elements of randomness involving participants, problems, decisions and solutions ebbing and flowing according to the dictates of the garbage can model. However, *Casablanca* premiered just eighteen days after the Allied invasion of North Africa and was showing nationwide when Franklin D. Roosevelt and Prime Minister Winston Churchill presided over the Casablanca Conference (Daft, 1995). What for most filmgoers seems like a seamless process of perfect form and development, in fact, was a process that had many of the elements of randomness characteristic of the garbage can model of decision-making.

THE NEO-HUMAN RELATIONS APPROACH

The neo-human relations approach to management studies stemmed from the empirical research which found workers and their interpersonal relations to significantly affect what happens in the organization. In this sense, the central tenet of this approach is similar to that of the human relations school. In particular, it shares with the human relations school a focus on the individual, the group, and the intergroup relations in the organization. Chris Argyris (1990) has written much about the individual's relationship to the organization. He argued that many characteristics of formal organization are incompatible with the requirements of a mature individual. In particular, the functional requirements for rationality and specialization. Hierarchical authority, in Argyris view, inhibits the needs for autonomy and self direction of mature adults. He, like other writers in this approach, criticizes the traditional human relations school for seeking easy answers or techniques instead of questioning organizational structures and philosophies, a priori.

Abraham Maslow's work on motivation, which we discuss at length in the next chapter, forms a basis for many of the assumptions of this approach to organization theory. According to Maslow, human needs can be considered in terms of a hierarchy. The lowest level or physiological level of needs includes food, shelter, etc. These needs serve to motivate the individual until they are satisfied. Once these needs have been satiated, other needs such as safety, social, ego, and self actualization become predominant. Human beings move up this hierarchy of needs with the higher needs becoming operative only when the lower level needs have been satisfied (Maslow, 1970). We will return to this theme in the next chapter on motivation.

Douglas McGregor expressed many of the positions of the Neo-Human- Relations School in his classic work *The Human Side of Enterprise*. In it, he states that typically management's view of its task is driven by a series of propositions and assumptions about the nature of work and the nature of the worker. He calls these propositions *Theory X*. Briefly stated, these assumptions are: (1) that management is responsible for organizing the elements of production and, labor, and capital; (2) with respect to people, management needs to direct worker efforts through motivation and modifying their behavior so that they will fit the needs of the organization; and (3) without the intervention of management, people would be passive and even resistent to the overall needs of the organization (McGregor, 1957). Clearly, these were the assumptions underlying scientific management and the classical approach. He argues that the findings of behavioral science challenge these assumptions about the human side of enterprise. He goes on to argue that while human behavior in organizations is approximately what Theory X management assumes it to be, but that this is not a consequence of man's inherent nature. Accepting Maslow's hierarchy of needs, he suggests why the "carrot and stick" approach to management in the long run will be ineffective in a society whose basic physiological and safety needs have been met. McGregor sees many of the problems in industrial organizations as failures of those organizations to meet higher level needs of workers. The deprivation of physiological needs has behavioral consequences. The same is true-although less well recognized of deprivation of higher level needs. The man whose needs for safety, association, independence, or status are thwarted is sick just as surely as the man who has diabetes. And his sickness will have behavioral consequences. We will be mistaken if we attribute his resultant passivity, his hostility, his refusal to accept responsibility to his "inherent human nature." These forms of behavior are symptoms of illness of deprivation of his social and egoistic needs (McGregor, 1957, p. 17). McGregor goes on to build his own theory of management, which he calls Theory Y. While we shall return to this theme later, we can state, at this point, that the first assumption of Theory Y that is at variance with Theory X is that people are not passive or resistent to organizational needs by nature. Rather, they have become this way by virtue of their experience in organizations. The second general assumption of Theory Y is that people have the capacity for assuming responsibility in the workplace. Accordingly, it is the responsibility of management to create the environment to make this possible. Finally, McGregor sees the principal task of management as creating the environment necessary for "people to achieve their own goals best by directing their own efforts toward organizational objectives" (McGregor, 1957, p. 18).

THE SYSTEMS APPROACH

The systems approach to organizational studies traces its ancestry to the decision-making approach with a strong emphasis on process and a rich description of organizational reality. However, scholars in this tradition, rather than striving for efficiency, rationality, and productivity, attempt to understand the functioning of existing structures. They conceptualize the organization using the model of the system (Senge, 1990) Recall, a model is a representation of a phenomena that helps us understand reality in some comprehensive way. The components of the system's model are inputs, conversion process and outputs. Systems also have interdependent parts that operate as a whole. All systems require a feedback mechanism that alerts the system as to how effectively it is functioning. This is called the feedback loop. Figure 1 expresses the components of a "system."

Systems can be considered in two ways: (1) closed or (2) open. Open systems exchange information, energy, or material with their environments. Biological and social systems are inherently open systems; mechanical systems are typically closed. Organizations are open systems that interact and are influenced by their environment. Open systems can be viewed from the perspective of a transformation model. In other words, they are in a dynamic relationship with their environment, receiving various inputs, which the organization transforms in some way, and then exports outputs. It follows that systems have boundaries which separate them from their environments. The concept of boundaries helps

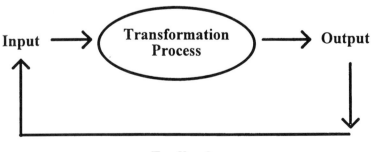

Feedback

Figure 1   A system.

us understand the distinction between open and closed systems. The relatively closed system has rigid, impenetrable boundaries; whereas the open system has permeable boundaries between itself and a broader suprasystem. For example, North Carolina State University exists within a state political and economic system from which it draws support and to which it is accountable. Boundaries are relatively easily defined in physical and biological systems, but are more difficult to delineate in social systems, such as organizations. Closed, physical systems are subject to the force of entropy which increases until eventually the entire system fails. The tendency toward maximum entropy is a movement to toward disorder, chaos, the inability to transform resources, and ultimately extinction. Peter Senge (1990) notes that few large corporations (organizational systems) live as long as a person! Reporting a Royal Dutch/Shell survey, he observes that one-third of all the corporations in the Fortune "500" in 1970 . . . had vanished by 1983 (Senge, 1990, p. 17). In an open biological or social systems, entropy can be halted and may even be transformed into negative entropy—a process of more complete organization and ability to transform resources—because the system imports resources from its environment.

The concept of feedback is important in understanding how a system maintains a steady state. Pain is the feedback mechanism of the human body, which is itself a system. Pain is the self correction mechanism that tells us to take our hand off the burner. Information concerning outputs or processes of a system are returned to or "fed back" as inputs into the system leading to changes in the transformation process and/or future outputs. Feedback can be both positive and negative. In addition, biological and social systems typically have multiple goals or purposes. Social organizations seek multiple goals, if for no other reason than that they are composed of individuals and subunits with different values and objectives.

Many phenomena can be modeled using the system concept. Things as diverse as the human body, farm ponds, and the economic structure of a nation can be modeled in terms of inputs, conversion process, outputs and feedback loops. The classic description of an organization as a system are found in Katz and Kahn (1966), *The Social Psychology of Organizations*. In this work, the authors present a process model for describing organizations in such terms as inputs and outputs. They argue that organizations are open systems that interact with their environment and are shaped by that interaction. In conceptualizing organizations as systems, Katz and Kahn emphasize the inputs, conversion process, and outputs of the system. In underscoring the open systems nature of most human systems, they highlighted the need to conceptualize systems as having boundaries. And, because systems have boundaries, there is a need for organizational actors to span those boundaries. According to Katz and Kahn, various functions are required for organizations to survive and are performed by departments that act as subsystems. These include *production*, this is the subsystem that produces the products and services associated with the organization, taking the previously used example of North Carolina State University (NCSU), this would be the research and teaching faculty. *Boundary spanning* the next subsystem is represented by the departments that work with the external environment. On the input side, this would be the departments like university purchasing that acquire the needed supplies and materials. On the output side, this includes senior administrators (Chancellor's Office and Public Affairs) who need to deal with the state legislature, the press, and other external actors who can impact on the university. The *maintenance system* consists of the departments (e.g., physical plant, cafeteria, janitorial staff) that are responsible for the day to day operation of the NCSU. *Management* is the next subsystem, it is responsible for directing and coordinating the other subsystems in the organization. At the university this is the "administration" Department Heads (History, Mathematics, etc., Deans and Provosts). The final subsystem is *adaptation* this is the subsystem responsible for organizational learning and change. University planning, institution research or budgeting typically, include people and functions that are involved with strategic planning and internal analysis. In other words, functions that provide the university with the information necessary to adapt to its changing environment.

BUREAUCRATIC POLITICS APPROACH

The concept of bureaucracy is very much a part of our culture. Almost all discussions about the phenomenon of bureaucracy begin with a discussion of the writings of the German scholar Max Weber. Weber originated the concept of bureaucracy as a model or construct that he used in his discussion of modern industrial society. Weber was interested in why people submit to authority structures. He was interested in the role that bureaucracies play in allowing some individuals to dominate others. Weber postulated that in order for leaders to dominate followers, the followers must believe they are obligated to obey the leadership. Weber developed a topology of the legitimate exercise of power and administration. His topology included three methods of domination (Weber, 1946).

The first he called charismatic domination, a leadership style in which the leader, through personal charisma, was able to obtain exceptional performance from his subordinates. Jesus Christ would be an example. The second type of domination Weber called traditional domination. This occurred whenever the leader commanded and the followers felt obligated to accept his authority because of inherited position. The Divine Right of Kings would be an example. The third form of domination he called legal domination. This occurred when the leader had obtained his position through some legal mechanism that the followers agreed was correct and consistent with the law. He placed bureaucracy under this category and went on to elaborate its essential features.

Weber sought to describe the "ideal" bureaucracy. There is still considerable academic debate with respect to whether he meant ideal in a normative sense, the way organizations should be, or as an ideal type, an idea or construct to be employed in looking at other questions (Weiss, 1983). Nonetheless, Weber did see bureaucracy as more rational than the other two forms of domination and concluded, correctly, that it would emerge as a dominate form of organization in industrial societies.

Weber outlined extensively the characteristics of bureaucracy. The most essential features follow:

1. *Hierarchy of Authority.* A stair-step distribution of authority.
2. *Rules and Procedure.* Standardized procedures, operations and decisions to ensure equality of treatment.
3. *Specialization of Labor.* All work should be divided into specific spheres of competence and assigned accordingly. Each employee should have authority over their function and should not interfere with the function of others.
4. *Employment of Qualified Personnel Based on Merit.* Individuals should be chosen on the basis of their technical competence to function in clearly defined position which have been clearly defined in job descriptions.
5. *Impersonal Formal Conduct.* Personality, emotion and other non-rational factors interfere with the functioning of the bureau. The primary focus should be on the goals of the organization and not needs of the individual.

Weber's work has been critiqued by scholars of bureaucratic politics. Some of this analysis focuses on the unintended consequences of bureaucracy. Robert Merton, for example, was among the first to recognize that the focus on rules and procedures that makes behavior predictable in a bureaucracy could have unintended side effects (Merton, 1940). Rules that the bureaucrats follow in order to be rational can also make them inflexible. Also, these organizational rules can be adopted by the bureaucrats as personal goals. When this occurs the process is called "goal displacement." In effect, goal displacement is the process by which organizational goals are displaced by personal goals. Goal displacement is an enduring problem for all forms of performance measures. It occurs when managers provide incentives for the workers in an organization to deliver measured output, while at the same time neglecting the unmeasured ones. An illustration of goal displacement may be found in higher education today. Specifically, if the tenure system at a university rewards those with higher numbers of publications (measured outputs) over those publications of higher quality (unmeasured outputs), the faculty is encouraged to produce citations over insights. In short, the very "rules" that Weber identified as rationalizing the organization, according to Merton and others, have the potential of producing the irrational outcome of turning means into ends.

Philip Selznick (1949), in his classic book *TVA and the Grass Roots* observed that goal displacement does not only occur at the individual (person) level. He noted that as bureaucratic organizations grow and divide into subunits, goal displacement can take place because of the need to delegate to subunits decision-making authority for policies under their control. These separate subunits or departments can then begin to develop goals of their own. This results in a shift of resources and objectives away from the overall organizational goal to the goals of the subunits.

More recently, James Q. Wilson (1989) has developed a conceptualization of bureaucracy which is predicated on a process and output perspective. In other words, what an agency does and how they do it. He argues that public agencies (bureaucracies) differ in two main respects and these differences influence the way public managers manage. These differences relate directly to the answer to the question, can the activities of employees in the agency be observed, and, can the results of those activities be observed? The first factor involves *outputs* and the ability to measure those outputs. Outputs are what the teachers, planners, engineers, police officers, and city managers do on a day to day basis. These outputs are themselves processes that are arrayed in a chain. We can conceptualize that some outputs are further "up the stream" than others. One output may be a rise in SAT scores.

The second factor involves *outcomes* how, if at all, the world changes because of the outputs. Outcomes can be thought of as the long term results of agency work, their reason for existence if you will. The outcome is what the organization ultimately seeks to accomplish, for example, in the case of a public school system an educated person. Another example is the outputs (or work) of police officers the radio calls answered, beats walked, tickets written, accidents investigated, and arrests made. The outcomes (or results) are the changes in the level of safety, public order, and amenity in the community. Observing outputs may be either difficult or easy. Taking the extreme case there are four ideal types of public agencies array in a typology.

Public agencies in which both *outputs* and *outcomes* can be observed.
Public agencies in which *outputs* but not *outcomes* can be observed.
Public agencies in which *outcomes* but not *outputs* can be observed.
Public agencies in which neither *outputs* or *outcomes* can be observed.

Using this typology Wilson divides public bureaucracies into four types. *Production Organizations*, organizations where both *outputs* (work) and *outcomes* (results) are observable and can be readily measured. Examples include,

Internal Revenue Service, United States Postal Service, Social Security Administration. Another example would be the state department of transportation an organization that can speak in specific terms about the cost per mile of highways and the number of new roads constructed in a five year period of time. *Procedural Organizations*, are public organizations in which *outputs (work)*, what their subordinates are doing, can be observed but not the *outcome* that results from that work, examples, state mental hospitals, U.S. military in peacetime, prisons. *Craft Organizations*, are those in which the activities of employees *outputs* (work) is hard to observe and measure, but whose outcomes (results) are comparatively easy to evaluate, examples, Corps of Engineers, the detective division of a police dept. In other words, we can observe if the bridge is constructed or the case is closed, even if the steps in the work process are difficult to observe or measure. Finally, *Coping Organizations*, public organizations in which neither *outputs* (work) nor *outcomes* (results) can be easily measured, examples, U.S. Department of State, colleges and universities. Wilson's typology provides a conceptual framework for those who see bureaucracy as more multivariate than simply the "public sector."

Currently, bureaucracy is under attack in much of the popular press. Much of the criticism of bureaucracy could, in theory, be directed at both public and large scale private organizations (IBM) that function according to bureaucratic principles (Carroll, 1993). However, most people associate bureaucracy with public sector bureaucracies. Charles Goodsell, in his book *The Case for Bureaucracy*, notes that bureaucracy in the vernacular often refers to "incompetent, indifferent, bloated and malevolent administrative departments of government" (Goodsell, 1985). Goodsell challenges this assertion, at least in the United States, by looking at the myths about bureaucracy. The myths about bureaucracy are assumptions made by popular and academic writers that paint public bureaucracy in a bad light. Goodsell asserts that these myths are false and that public bureaucracy in the U.S. is a convenient straw man for attacks by academics and ideologues.

Among the most significant of the myths that he challenges, is the myth that all bureaucracies are ineffective. Goodsell presents data drawn from citizen surveys and performance measures that show that the actual performance of bureaucracy is satisfactory in "the preponderant majority of encounters with citizens" (Goodsell, 1985, p. 15). His data also suggests that, far from being a different class of people, bureaucrats are representative, in the statistical sense, of Americans employed in other fields, at least with respect to educational level, social status, religion, and party identification. Still other data show that bureaucracies do not necessarily grow bigger with time and that the private sector is not necessarily more efficient. Goodsell notes that government frequently takes on tasks because the market has failed. Hence, it is unfair to use the market to measure the success or failure of the bureaucracy. Finally, he notes that many of the "problems" faced by government do not have "solutions" and to evaluate bureaucracy by a standard that requires crime, poverty, etc., be solved is inherently unfair.

More recently, B. Dan Wood and Richard W. Waterman (1994) have produced the most significant quantitative research on bureaucracies to date. Their research dispels a number of popular myths. Using a statistical analysis that considers both timing and covariation between independent political events and bureaucratic responses of a number of major federal government agencies, they demonstrate that bureaucracy in the U.S. is an adaptive institution that responds to democratic influences (Wood and Waterman, 1994, pp. 141–56). Specifically, all eight federal bureaucracies analyzed responded to elected officials in significant ways. They also demonstrate that the most important stimuli for change in a bureaucracy are the tools of political appointment and the budget. In addition, they discovered that bureaucracies also respond to the courts, the media and issues of importance to the public. To those concerned about democratic institutions this is as it should be.

In the first chapter we observed that public and private organizations are different. It is important to underscore that much of the research focused on organizations, as well as the various approaches to organizational theory we have discussed in this chapter, have emerged from the private sector context. Increasingly, however, this fact has become a matter of concern to public administrators seeking a unique definition for public service and a unique explanation for public organizational reality. In the last decade scholars have sought a professional self definition for public administration and the development of organization theory in areas specifically focused on the public sector. For example, Michael M. Harmon (1989) argues for an alternative approach to organization theory. His approach is one that assumes an "action" or "process" perspective and which avoids what he considers the major two problems of organization theory in recent decades.

The first of these was the abandonment of the public interest both as a unifying moral symbol for guiding administrative action and as a benchmark for its analysis and evaluation. The second was the virtually uncontested acceptance of the decision as the primary focus of analysis in organization theory (Harmon, 1989, p. 145). To Harmon and others, the focus on decision-making which separates fact from value, is an epistemological distinction that may be of value for instrumental purposes. However, it has very little to do with the manner in which the social world is "constituted, maintained, and contested" (Harmon, 1989, p. 146). We concur, government since the earliest of times, has focused on the public good and the public good will always have an ethical and moral component over and above profit maximization. In fact, government exists to address questions of equity (fairness) which are themselves largely absent in a frame of reference dominated by the profit maximization perspective. In a sense, a conception of the "public interest" is indispensable to the public good.

In a related fashion, Nancy K. Grant (1989) has observed that public organizations have a unique role in a capitalist economy, that is, to provide a welfare maximizing function. The capitalist system, whether applied only to the economic realm or, as Smith does, to all of society, is based on utility-maximizing activities; each individual consistently acts in his/her best interest. Somehow, all of the individual priorities result in a better society. No need exists for an overt commitment to social welfare maximizing activities. Recognizing that this does not hold true universally, the need for the public sector is thus based on the need to provide for those social needs that are not met through normal operating procedures (Grant, 1989, p. 107). Much recent writing in the area of bureaucratic politics that attempts to fashion a uniquely "public" approach to organizations is focused on this dynamic tension between the democratic values of equity, versus the values of private interests that underlie capitalism (Frederickson, 1989). While no clear and consistent "public sector" approach to organization theory has yet emerged, the elements of such an approach are evident in the literature.

CONCLUSION

This chapter has sought to trace the development of various approaches to conceptualizing the organization. Each approach placed more or less emphasis on certain aspects of organizations; organization design or structure, administrative principles, human factors, rules, politics, etc. Moreover, the authors associated with each approach have had important impacts on the evolution of the thinking about the role of organizations in the human condition. Indeed, contemporary scholarship in organizational behavior owes an important intellectual debt to the scholars presented in this chapter. We will call upon the general themes developed in this chapter in the subsequent chapters of this book.

REFERENCES AND ADDITIONAL READING

Argyris, Chris (1990). *Integrating the Individual and the Organization*. New Brunswick, N.J.: Transaction Publishers.

Baretz, Loren (1974). *The Servants of Power*. Westbrook, Conn: Greenwood Press.

Barnard, C. (1938). *The Functions of the Executive*. Boston: Harvard University Press.

Blau, P. M., and Schoenherr, R. A. (1971). *The Structure of Organizations*. New York: Basic Books.

Bozeman, B. (1987). *All Organizations Are Public: Bridging Public and Private Organizational Theories*. San Francisco: Jossey Bass Publishers.

Bozeman, B., and S. Loveless (1987). "Sector Context and Performance: A Comparison of Industrial and Government Research Units." *Administration and Society*, 19, 197–235.

Carroll, Paul (1993). *Big Blues: The Unmaking of IBM*. New York: Random House/Crown Publishers.

Chandler, Alfred (1977). *The Visible Hand*. Cambridge, Mass: Belk Knap Press.

Cohen, Michael D., James G. March, and Johan P. Olsen (1972). "A Garbage Can Model of Organizational Choice," *Administrative Sciences Quarterly* 17:pp 1–25.

Cyert, R. M. and J. G. March (1963). *A Behavioral Theory of the Firm*. New York: Wiley.

Daft, Richard L. (1995). *Organization Theory and Design*. Minneapolis/St. Paul, Minnesota: West Publishing Co.

Denhardt, Robert B. (1984). *Theories of Public Administration*. Pacific Grove, California: Brooks/Cole.

Deming, Edwards W. (1982). *Out of the Crisis*. Cambridge, Mass: Massachusetts Institute of Technology Press, Center for Advanced Engineering Study.

Etzioni, Amitai (1964). *Modern Organizations*. Englewood Cliffs, New Jersey: Prentice Hall.

Etzioni, A. (1988). *The Moral Dimension*. New York: Free Press.

Evan, William M. (1993). *Organizational Theory: Research and Design*. New York: Macmillian.

Fayol, Henri (1949). *General and Industrial Management*. Translated by C. Storrs, London: Pitman.

Frederickson, George H. (1989). "Minnowbrook II: Changing Epochs of Public Administration," *Public Administration Review*, 49:pp 95–100.

Frederickson, H. G., and D. K. Hart, (1985). "The Public Service and Patriotism of Benevolence." *Public Administration Review*, 45:pp 547–553.

Goodsell, Charles T. (1985). *The Case for Bureaucracy*. Chatham, New Jersey: Chatham House Publishers, Inc.

Golembiewski, R. T. (1984). "Organizing Public Work, Round Three: Toward a New Balance Between Political Agendas and Management Perspectives." In R. T. Golembiewski and A. Wildavsky (eds.), *The Costs of Federalism*. New Brunswick, N.J.: Transaction Publishers.

Golembiewski, R. T. (1985). *Humanizing Public Organizations*. Mount Airy, MD.: Lomond.

Grant, Nancy K. (1989). "Response to Kirk Hart," *Public Administration Review*, 49:pp 106–107.

Gulick, L. and L. Urwick, eds. (1937). *Papers on the Science of Administration*. New York: Institute of Public Administration, Columbia University.

Harmon, Michael M. (1989). " 'Decision' and 'Action' as Contrasting Perspectives in Organization Theory," *Public Administration Review*, 49:pp 144–149.

Harmon, Michael M., and Richard T. Mayer (1986). *Organization Theory for Public Administration*. Boston: Little Brown and Company.

Homans, George C. (1951). The Western Electric Researchers, in Schyler Dean Hoslett (ed.), *Human Factors in Management.* New York: Harper and Row Publishers.

Hummel, Ralph (1994). *The Bureaucratic Experience: A Critique of Life in the Modern Organization.* 4th ed. New York: St. Martin's Press.

Jackson, John H., Cyril P. Morgan, and Joseph G. P. Paollelo (1986). *Organization Theory: A Macro Perspective For Management.* Englewood Cliffs, New Jersey.

Katz, D. and R. Kahn (1966). *The Social Psychology of Organizations.* New York: Wiley Press.

Lawler, Edward E. (1992). *The Ultimate Advantage.* San Francisco, California: Josey Bass Publishers.

Likert, Remis (1961). *New Patterns of Management.* New York: McGraw Hill.

March, James G., and Herbert A. Simon (1958). *Organizations.* New York: Wiley.

March, J. G., and Olsen, J. P. (1986). "Garbage Can Models of Decision Making In Organizations." In J. G. March, and R. Weissinger-Baylon (eds.), *Ambiguity and Command.* White Plains, N.Y.: Pitman pp. 11–35.

March, J. G., and J. P. Olsen (1989). *Rediscovering Institutions: The Organizational Basis of Politics.* New York: Free Press.

March, J. G., and H. A. Simon (1958). *Organizations.* New York: Wiley.

Maslow, Abraham H. (1970) *Motivation and Personality,* 2nd ed. New York: Harper & Row.

McGregor, Douglas M. (1957). "The Human Side of Enterprise," in Walter E. Natemeyer and Jay S. Goldberg (ed.), *Classics of Organizational Behavior,* 2nd ed. Danville, Illinois: The Interstate Printers and Publishers, Inc.

Merton, Robert K. (1940). "Bureaucratic Structure and Personality," *Social Forces,* 18:pp 560–68.

Mintzberg, H. (1972). *The Nature of Managerial Work.* New York: Harper & Row.

Mintzberg, H. (1983). *Power in and Around Organizations.* Englewood Cliffs, N.J.: Prentice Hall.

Ostrom, Vincent (1991). *The Meaning of American Federalism: Constituting a Self-Governing Society.* San Francisco: ICS Press.

Peters, T. J. (1988). "Restoring American Competitiveness: Looking for New Models of Organizations." *Academy of Management Executive,* 2, 104–110.

Perrow, Charles (1986). *Complex Organizations: A Critical Essay,* 3rd ed. New York: Random House, 1986.

Rainey, Hal G. (1991). *Understanding and Managing Public Organizations.* San Francisco, California: Josey Bass Publishers.

Reed, Michael and Michael Hughes (1992). *Rethinking Organization: New Directions in Organizational Theory and Analysis.* Newbury Park, Calif.: Sage Publishers.

Roethlisberger, Fritz J. (1941). "The Hawthorne Experiments" in Walter E. Natemeyer and Jay S. Goldberg (ed.). *Classics of Organizational Behavior,* 2nd Ed. Danville, Illinois: The Interstate Printers and Publishers, Inc.

Senge, Peter (1990). *The Fifth Discipline.* New York: Doubleday.

Selznick, Philip (1949). *TVA and Grass Roots.* Berkeley: University of California Press.

Schachter, Hindy, Lauer (1989). *Fredrick Taylor and the Public Administration Community: A Reevaluation* Albany, New York: State University of New York Press.

Shafritz, Jay M., and Albert C. Hyde (eds.) (1992). *Classics of Organizational Theory*, 3rd ed. Pacific Grove, Calif.: Brooks/Cole.

Shafritz, Jay and J. Steven Ott (1987). *Classics of Organization Theory*. Chicago: The Dorsey Press.

Simon, Herbert A. (1957A). *Models of Man*. New York: Wiley Press.

Simon, Herbert A. (1957B). *Administrative Behavior*, 2nd Ed. New York: The MacMillian Company.

Simon, H. A., D. W. Smithburg, and V. A. Thompson (1950). *Public Administration*. New York: Knopf.

Taylor, Fredrick W. (1967). *The Principles of Scientific Management*. New York: Norton Library.

Thompson, James D. (1967). *Organizations in Action*. New York: McGraw-Hill.

Tomas, Andrew (1971). *We Are Not the First*. New York: Bantam Books.

Tosi, Henry L., John R. Rizzo and Stephen J. Carrol (1990). *Managing Organizational Behavior* New York: Harper & Row.

Vasu, Michael L. (1979). *Politics and Planning: A National Study of American Planners*. Chapel Hill, NC: The University of North Carolina Press.

Van Riper, Paul P. (1990). "The Literary Gulick: A Bibliographical Appreciation" *Public Administration Review*, 50:pp 609–615.

Weber, Max (1946). *Max Weber: Essays in Sociology*. Edited and translated by H. H. Gerto and C. Wright Mills. New York: Oxford University Press.

Weiss, Richard M. (1983). "Weber on Bureaucracy: Management Consultant or Political Theorist" in *Academy of Management Review*, 8:pp 242–248.

Wilson, J. Q. (1989). *Bureaucracy*. New York: Basic Books.

Wilson, Woodrow (1887). "The Study of Administration," *Political Science Quarterly*, 2:pp 197–222.

White, Leonard (1926). *Introduction to Public Administration*. New York: Macmillian.

Wood, Dan B. and Richard W. Waterman (1994). *Bureaucratic Dynamics*. Boulder, Colorado: Westview Press.

Motivation in Organizations

INTRODUCTION

Every organization needs motivated people! Why? Because all organizations seek to be effective, to get the job done. They also seek to be efficient, that is to maximize the outputs per unit of input. Efficiency is typically calibrated in terms of an organization's productivity. To be both *efficient* and *effective* public managers must work with and through people. In the most generic sense, an organization is a group of people working toward a common goal. Both experience and common sense indicate that all people do not expend equal effort toward the realization of organizational goals. When they do not motivation problems are reflected in such factors as low productivity, absenteeism, and rapid employee turnover.

As an academic area of study, human motivation is the subject of textbooks itself and has a variety of dimensions (McClelland, 1988; Beck, 1990; Steers and Porter, 1991). The important focus, from a management perspective, is on motivation and its relation to work behavior (Quick, 1985; Carlisle and Murphy, 1986; Mook, 1987; Wright, 1992; Robertson and Tang, 1995, Behn, 1995). They are typically concerned with what causes or drives behavior and how to direct and sustain that behavior toward specific organizational goals (Wright, 1992). However, managers need to understand that motivation takes place within a contextual framework. This *contextual framework* adds more variables to questions of organizational performance than motivation alone.

MOTIVATION IN CONTEXT

The cause of differences in the effort expended by individuals at work is the result of a number of factors. One of these factors is related to different levels of ability among employees. Differences in ability arise from the simple fact that there are significant individual differences that affect work performance. A given individual, for example, may be in the 90th percentile in math ability, 20th percentile in spatial ability, 75th percentile in resistance to fatigue, and 99th percentile on written ability, etc. However, ability itself is only part of the equation. Clearly, whatever the ability level of individuals, the *effort* they expend toward the realization of organizational goals will depend upon their motivation. In other words, the level of motivation for given individuals will interact with their ability to determine their performance level. The study of human motivation at work is basically the analysis of why people behave the way they do, why they do or do not expend effort toward goal achievement in organizational settings. As such, it is a field that brings together questions that are both scientific and philosophical in nature.

In the public sector, given its largely service component, people may be the most important resource. Stimulating employees' decisions to participate and to produce at work is the hallmark of an effective public organization. To be sure, in studying motivation we look at only this aspect of the human factor in the performance at work equation. What would such an equation look like? One way to conceptualize such an equation is in the form of a standard multivariate statistical model (a multiple linear regression equation) in which the dependent variable (Y) that we seek to predict is performance level. The independent variables that predict such performance are many and motivation is but one such variable. These other independent variables also contribute to the prediction of performance level. This *hypothetical* equation might look like:

$$Y = \alpha + \beta_1 X_1 + \beta_2 X_2 + \beta_3 X_3 + \beta_4 X_4 + \beta_5 X_5 + \beta_6 X_6 + \varepsilon$$

Where :
$\quad$ Y $\;$ = performance outcome
$\quad$ α $\;$ = slope
$\quad$ X_1 = motivation/effort
$\quad$ X_2 = ability
$\quad$ X_3 = task
$\quad$ X_4 = organizational structure
$\quad$ X_5 = group factors
$\quad$ X_6 = technology
$\quad$ ε $\;$ = error

The purpose of the foregoing equation is not to establish an empirical formula that includes all the relevant variables necessary to predict performance in the workplace. Our objective in presenting the equation is *pedagogical*, what we want to underscore is the *multivariate* nature of performance in the workplace. Motivation (X_1) is an important variable in organizational performance, but there are many other variables (X_2, X_3, X_n) in the workplace that explain or predict performance outcomes. In other words, if we are trying to explain the variance in levels of performance in an organization, a number of variables in addition to the *effort* an individual is willing to make are themselves important predictors of performance. Moreover, these other variables have different predictive coefficients or weights (β_1, β_2, β_n) themselves.

The implications of this line of reasoning for managers is that a person may be well motivated to perform, but his ability may be a limitation and this will effect his performance level. For example, a newly "networked" office, may have an employee motivated to perform, that is willing to exert the effort, but if he has no ability in computers his measured performance may be very low. In this situation, he does not need to be motivated to increase his performance, he needs to be trained! In addition, other factors such as technology, group dynamics, the task that the organization seeks to perform, interact with motivation and the ability levels of people in organizations. These other variables, in effect, form a context in which the ability of the manager to motivate (to increase individual effort) is but *one* important variable.

Another contextual consideration is the organizational structure of the public sector itself. Scholars have observed that recent prescriptions to *reinvent government* are predicated on the assumption that government is badly managed when compared to the private sector, that management is generic across sectors, and that the devices used to motivate in the private sector are useful to public sector managers (Peters and Savoie, 1994, p. 423). Most of these assumptions have not been confirmed empirically. However, it is clear that public budget and personnel systems do exercise a constraining role on managerial decision making (Osborne and Gaebler, 1992). In other words, public sector managers typically exist within a context that sets somewhat more restrictive parameters around their ability to control or manipulate motivational devices such as monetary rewards, in particular, when compared with some of their private sector counterparts. There are contextual features in the public sector worth exploring separately (Cherniss and Kane, 1987; Perry and Wise, 1990; Romzek, 1990; Robertson and Tang, 1995). We shall do so later in the chapter.

The basic motivation problem of the public sector, like the private sector, is that both must induce the employee to develop ties to the organization. The nature of those ties may be based on *investments* by governments in such things as career opportunities, pay for performance, and benefits (Romzek, 1990). According to this logic, an organization has to offer benefits and working conditions that are competitive with other prospective employers and then maintain that comparative advantage. Investments may be regarded as extrinsic motivators in the language of motivation. However, such investments are expensive and depend upon legislative bodies to enact. The other way of developing ties to the organization is expressed as *commitment* (Romzek, 1990; Behn, 1995; Robertson and

Tang, 1995). This in the language of motivation is intrinsic motivation. Commitment is based on an affective or emotive attachment to the organization.

However, in order to address these very important and essentially larger context questions related to the role of motivation in the public workplace, we need to build a foundation based on the extensive and sustained interest of the research community on the phenomena of motivation. In order to do so, this chapter begins by introducing the fundamentals of motivation literature, outlining both motivation and work setting theories and how they stimulate each other. Next, we consider motivational models applying the basic principles to the work setting, and stress the limitations of these models in public sector applications. Then the critical issue of the relationship between job satisfaction and performance is addressed. We propose to highlight and compare rather than to advocate any single theory. We will also provide implications for practicing public managers. In order to accomplish the foregoing objectives, we will begin with an overview of basic motivation theory and then discuss the various approaches to motivation that have emerged over time.

BASIC MOTIVATION THEORY

Why do human beings behave as they do? For many students of organizations this is the fundamental question in the study of human motivation. Yet, by the way this question is posed, it posits a certain assumption. It presupposes what is called in the literature a cognitive approach to the study of human behavior. This approach is best understood by reference to a simple model.

As the model expressed in Figure 2 indicates, this approach is guided by a single question: what takes place in the organism to produce a specific response to a given stimulus? Questioning changes in or experiences of the organism assumes that what counts as an explanation for behavior is an understanding or an elaboration of those antecedent events in the person. Conscious thoughts or decisions are presumed to intervene between the stimulus from the person's environment and the behavior that follows. In shorthand terminology; something happens, I think about and decide, and on the basis of that decision I then respond.

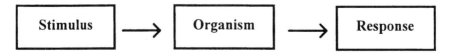

Figure 2 Stimulus response model.

Understanding behavior demands understanding the experiences that trigger conscious thoughts or decisions. This is what we are calling the *cognitive* approach to motivation. Some theorists shun cognitive approaches in favor of *acognitive* approaches to studying human behavior. Denying the importance of changes in the human organism, proponents of the acognitive approach focus on the influence of the environment to account for human behavior. Faithful to the tradition of B. F. Skinner, acognitive theorists consider the type of reinforcement for behavior as critical. Both cognitive and acognitive approaches hold important lessons for students of organizational behavior. Both traditions assume motivation is a term used to describe the forces *internal* to the individual that cause the person to behave in a goal directed manner.

THE COGNITIVE APPROACH

The general assumption of the cognitive approach to motivation is that *understanding of those internal motives* about how and why human behavior occurs is possible. The organism is perceived to be an active link in the stimulus organism response chain. Moreover, theorists of the cognitive approach believe those forces involve thinking.

Figure 3 represents a vivid, if perverse, expression of a motivated person! A person clearly expressing goal directed behavior. This picture was given to one of the authors by a senior public manager from a state prison system in the south. The procedure that generated this x-ray was a routine check of suspicious prisoners. The goal here, we can assume, is to escape from prison! The individual, I think we can agree, is very motivated (driven) to achieve that goal.

What are the causes of the internal forces that act upon any individual to drive them toward specific goals? If you will, what makes them do what they do? The answer(s) to this question are rooted deep in the history of Western Civilization. The philosophy of hedonism sums up our very earliest understanding of why humans behave as they do. Articulated by the early Greek philosophers and advanced in the 19th century social philosophies of Adam Smith, Jeremy Bentham, and John Stuart Mill, hedonism explains behavior in terms of the pain/pleasure principle, organisms try to maximize pleasure and minimize pain. Thorndike, the early empirical psychologist, buttressed hedonism as an explanation by pointing out how animals, when confronted with puzzle boxes, would learn to master them when the solution led to pleasurable outcome.

> Of several responses made to the same situation, those which are accompanied or closely followed by satisfaction to the animal will, other things being equal, be more firmly connected to the situation, so that, when it recurs, they will be more likely to recur; those which are accompanied or closely fol-

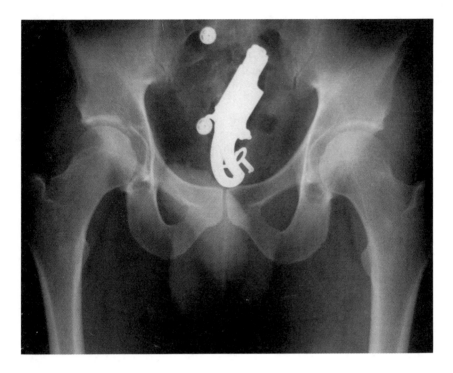

Figure 3 Motivation as goal directed behavior.

lowed by discomfort to the animal will, other things being equal, have their connections with that situation weakened, so that, when it recurs, they will be less likely to occur. The greater the satisfaction or discomfort the greater the strengthening or weakening of the bond (Thorndike, 1965, p. 244).

William James, in his seminal work, *Principles of Psychology* (1890), stressed two additional concepts which shaped psychological analysis at that time: the instinct and the unconscious. These two concepts formed the core of one of three major approaches to understanding motivation, the tension reduction approach. In this discussion of cognitive approaches to motivation we will first look at the evolution of this tension reduction approach.

DRIVE OR TENSION REDUCTION THEORY

The concept of instinct, acknowledged by James, found full-blown defense and elaboration in Darwin's *Origin of the Species* published in 1859. Seeing human beings as different from animals only in terms of continuous biological evolution, Darwin turned to "instinct" to explain human and animal action. The term "instinct" was defined for psychologists by William McDougall, in 1908 as a characteristic that was inherited and innate. Explaining behavior in terms of instinct was favored by psychologists in this earlier period, but with the growth of instinct theory and the proliferation of "instincts" (McDougall proposed a list of eighteen), disagreement among psychologists became apparent. By the 1930s this proliferation of instincts, accompanied by disagreement among the researchers as to what was or wasn't an instinct, led to a general abandoning of the instinct concept as "unscientific" (Weiner, 1985).

The concept of "drive" soon came to replace instinct as the explanation for action. Woodworth had introduced the notion of drive as early as 1918 in his work, *Dynamic Psychology*. Another psychologist, Edward Tolman, contributed to the development of the drive concept in his work, *Purposive Behavior in Animals and Men* (1932). Clark Hull fully developed the drive concept. His model was simple: Behavior = Drive × Habit. In controlled laboratory settings Hull tested hypotheses derived from mathematical models (Hull, 1943). The ultimate decline in these highly scientific and empirically based drive theories is attributed to their gradual neglect of the cognitive process and their assumption that human beings were analogous to machines (Weiner, 1980). Today the instinct or drive concept is alive among ethologists, who study instinctive behavior among animals and use these findings to theorize about aspects of human behavior (Weiner, 1985).

Freudian psychoanalytic theories constitute a second type of drive-need reduction explanation for human action. Individuals act in order to meet personal needs. Needs are met by some form of adapting to the world. Two concepts in Freudian thinking are homeostasis, the tendency toward the maintenance of a relatively stable environment, and hedonism, the seeking of pleasure and happiness. Pleasure results from being in a state of equilibrium with all one's goals satisfied. Critical to this tension reduction process are the components of the personality; the id, which is responsible for all psychological energy, the ego; with its power to delay gratification, and the super ego; the conscience of the personality. While the pleasure principle governs the id, the ego is regulated by the reality principle. It is the conflict generated in the interaction between the id and the ego that is the core of the Freudian view of motivation:

> The ego, driven by the id, confined by the super ego, repulsed by reality, struggles to master its economic task of bringing about harmony among the forces and influences working in and on it (Freud, 1933, cited in Weiner, 1985, p. 17).

According to Freud, all behavior is ultimately drive-determined, an unconscious process. The tendency toward drive reduction is omnipresent because it yields pleasure. Theorists in the drive-need-reduction tradition, whether psycho-analytic or more empirical, see behavior as determined by psychological energy (in Freud, the id; in Hull, habits). They also share the belief that actions are taken to satisfy unmet needs (homeostasis) and that fulfillment of these needs is satis-fying (hedonism).

EXPECTANCY VALUE THEORIES

Kurt Lewin (1935) is truly a bridge theorist between earlier drive theorists and contemporary expectancy value theorists. Like Freud and Hull, Lewin makes both hedonistic and homeostasis assumptions about human behavior. New in Lewin, and central to all expectancy value theories, is the assumption that human behavior is determined by how the world is perceived. Lewin's conceptual framework of "field theory" sees behavior as a function of the person and the en-vironment expressed in the formula [B = F(P,E)]. People have needs which cre-ate tensions. Tension can be dissipated only by attaining goals in the environment. The amount of valence (value to a person) an object in the environ-ment holds is related to the intensity of the need in the person. In addition to the intensity of the need and properties of the object in the environment, the relative distance of a person from his goal comes into play to influence the amount of force on a person to act. The formula Lewin proposed saw force as a function of the value (Va) of the goal (G) and the psychological distance (e) between the per-son and the goal.

$$\text{Force} = \frac{F\ Va(G)}{e}$$

When the goal is obtained the need is met and the tension relieved because the object loses its positive value, thus the "force field" is removed (Weiner, 1985, p. 151).

Building on the perception dimension introduced by Kurt Lewin, David McClelland articulated an expectation determined conception of motivation. Focusing specifically on the notion of achievement, McClelland and his close as-sociate, Atkinson, postulated that striving for achievement depends on a combi-nation of expectancy of success and value of success (McClelland et al., 1953). They used the projective Thematic Apperception Test (TAT) developed by Mur-ray (Weiner, 1980) to measure achievement. In the TAT methodology an individ-ual is presented an unstructured picture, for example, a man sitting at a desk with his briefcase open staring into space. The picture is subject to a variety of inter-pretations and there are no right or wrong answers. Respondents are asked to write projective stories about these ambiguous pictures. Their motivational dif-ferences are measured by their responses (Weiner, 1980).

Using these procedures, McClelland identified a group he called high achievers which he estimated represented about 10 percent of the population. The characteristics of high achievers were that they enjoyed setting their own goals rather than having them set for them by external forces or actors. In experimental situations, they were also more likely than others to avoid extremes in selecting goals, rejecting goals that were too easy or too difficult. Finally, high achievers also expressed a preference for tasks that had immediate feedback.

The full-blown theory of motivation advanced by Atkinson (1964), based on work conducted with McClelland, suggests that achievement related behavior is a function of a conflict between hope for success (labeled approach motivation) and fear of failure (called avoidance motivation). The approach and avoidance tendencies in any situation result from:

1. The need for achievement and anxiety about failure.
2. The expectancy of success and failure.
3. The incentive value of success or failure.

The third expectancy value motivation theory with implications for organizational behavior is identified with the psychologist Julian Rotter (Weiner, 1985). Rotter, a social learning theorist, stressed the importance of the external situation as a determinant of behavior. As with all expectancy value theorists, behavior in his view is a function of the expectancy of goal attainment and the value of the goal. However, the expectancy variable is formulated by Rotter in a different way. Expectancy in Rotter's work is a product of reinforcement history. In other words, what the individual has learned about the role of reinforcers in situations that are similar (Weiner, 1980). An important development in Rotter's research concerns the differences in perceptions of environment as personally or externally controlled (Weiner, 1986). Persons with "internal locus of control" display more information seeking and make better use of information than do persons with external locus of control.

HUMAN GROWTH AND DEVELOPMENT THEORY

The third major approach to understanding human motivation finds its most popular expression in the works of Abraham Maslow (1943). Common to the group of humanistic psychologists including Maslow, Carl Rogers, and Gordon Alport is the thesis that people are fundamentally motivated to grow and enhance themselves. Acceptance of a tendency towards self actualization is a basic tenet of this humanistic psychology.

Abraham Maslow, organizer and first president of the Association of Humanistic Psychology, dominated the study of motivation within humanistic psychology with his conceptualization of a hierarchy of needs. Maslow saw human beings as motivated by a hierarchical system of basic, "instinctoid" needs. People are motivated to meet these needs ranging from the basic and bodily to the very complex and psychological. These hierarchically arranged needs include, from lowest to highest level, physiological needs, safety needs, affiliative needs, esteem needs, and finally, the need to self-actualize. Maslow characterized the needs into higher and lower needs. The three lower needs have been characterized as extrinsic, that is they are predominately derived from factors outside the individual. The two upper level needs esteem and self actualization have been characterized as intrinsic, in that they are primarily related to factors internal to the individual.

Figure 4 illustrates these needs arranged in the hierarchy in which they are typically expressed. According to Maslow, as each of these needs becomes substantially satisfied the next need in the hierarchy will become more dominate. This is to say that a need that has been meet no longer motivates, and, since the needs are arrayed in a hierarchy, people seek to satisfy lower level needs first. For example, the need for friendship (affiliative) would not be felt until one is fed, clothed, and sheltered (Maslow, 1943). Only unsatisfied needs are motivators. When a need is satisfied, a higher level need emerges to motivate behavior. Looking back into the work discussed earlier in the drive reduction focus of Freud and Hull, Maslow characterizes lower level needs as deficient values. The attainment of the desired goal (meeting the need) results in a reduction of ten-

Figure 4   Maslow's hierarchy of needs.

sion, which allows the organism to return to a state of equilibrium (Weiner, 1980). But Maslow also describes a different set of values. "Being values" are those values associated with growth motivation. These values are sought in self-actualization. This focus on growth and development is the hallmark of Maslow's approach.

Maslow's work has influenced many subsequent scholars and his needs hierarchy is arguably the best known motivation concept in the lexicon of applied management. His concept of a hierarchy of motives clearly influenced subsequent theories of motivation that distinguish between intrinsic and extrinsic sources of motivation. Moreover, much of the movement away from the job specialization characteristic of Taylorism and associated with the *Quality of Work Life* clearly owe an intellectual debt to Maslow. The Quality of Work Life movement has sought to influence job design, that is, the way tasks are combined to form a complete job. A number of job design concepts such as, *job enlargement*; which seeks to expand the scope of the job so that it increases the number of different operations required; *job enrichment*, which increases the job scope by enlarging job responsibility; *job rotation*, which allows workers to diversify the activities they preform, are based on concepts derived from Maslow's work. Specifically, such job design concepts are predicated on assumptions about the socio-technical nature of work (Taylor and Felton, 1993). Among those socio-technical factors are the human need for closure and self fulfillment from work that are derived from the higher order needs of esteem and self-actualization first postulated by Maslow.

THE ACOGNITIVE APPROACH

One assumption guides the work of all motivation theories in the cognitive tradition. Transformations occurring in the organism explain behavior in the stimulus-organism-response process. In contrast, the acognitive approach to understanding behavior eschews any concern with events transpiring in the organism itself in favor of examining the relationship between the stimulus and the response. The seminal work in the acognitive tradition is that of B. F. Skinner.

The principle guiding Skinner's theory is that *behavior is determined by its consequences. Behavior modification* (operant conditioning) asserts that internal states of mind, such as needs that drive behavior, are not measurable and therefore irrelevant. What matters is what is measurable, and, that is behavior! Behling and Schriesheim (1976) elaborate on this basic principle by identifying three characteristics of Skinner's thought which set it apart from other approaches to motivation:

1. The organism is a passive mediating element in the stimulus-organism-response chain.
2. There is no need to postulate any internal or external need or purpose to explain behavior.
3. Operant conditioning explains most kinds of behavior.

This last point requires some explanation. Behling and Schriesheim describe operant conditioning as the outcome of an organism exploring its environment. That environment acts upon it in a variety of ways, positive, negative, and neutral. In this specific sense, human behavior is seen as subject to observable laws that can be understood and employed to modify behavior. Behavior is modified by *rewarding it, ignoring it,* or *punishing it.* Accordingly, the consequences of behavior will determine how the organism acts in the future (Behling and Schriesheim, 1976).

The formal terms of the environmental consequences are: *positive reinforcement, omission, punishment,* and *negative reinforcement.* They are defined by whether a pleasant or a noxious consequence is present or absent. Each of these processes can be understood in a classroom example provided by Hampton, et al.:

> . . . an instructor may provide students with positive reinforcement in the form of high grades for writing good essay examinations. The examination system may provide students with negative reinforcement in the form of anxiety about examinations, the anxiety is removed by completing the examinations. The instructor may not reinforce class participation by omitting credit for it. The instructor may punish class participation by providing sarcastic and humiliating critiques of ideas voiced by participating students (Hampton et al., 1978, p. 545).

In the case of the workplace, the consequences for behavior are arranged for some employee behavior that is desired, for example, a system for specifically praising employees for good work. There are two general behavior modification strategies for controlling human behavior. Affirmative strategies strengthen behavior by producing pleasant consequences or diminish behavior by removing existing reinforcing consequences, and are more appropriate in the managerial context. The aversive control strategies of punishment, in particular, often backfire on managers and may even worsen a situation by affecting general morale (Brown and Presbie, 1976).

A key concept in the organizational application of Skinner's theory is the reinforcement schedule, which concerns the quantitative relationship between environmental consequences and response. Different schedules are linked to different effects on behavior (Skinner, 1969). The key distinction comes between intermittent schedules, where the reinforcement does not follow every re-

sponse, and continuous schedules, where the reinforcer does follow every response.

We will discuss the specific workplace applications of operant conditioning principles in a subsequent section. Behavior modification, when utilized, requires the following at a minimum:

1. A detailed job analysis that identifies specific job behaviors that can
   be targeted for change.
2. A careful system of communication and feedback with employees!
   The communication needs to focus on the behaviors desired and the
   goals to be achieved and how each will be measured. The feedback
   system needs to provide valid and reliable data to employees about
   behaviors and goal achievement.
3. Behavior needs to be tied to reinforces. These reinforcers may be
   symbolic, explicit praise, or tangible pay for specific levels of measured performance.

MOTIVATION IN THE WORKPLACE

The preceding review of basic motivation theory provides the conceptual building blocks for models predicting and analyzing motivation on the job. Like the
theories of motivation put forth above, research on employee motivation falls
into two broad categories: (1) research focusing on how changes occurring in the
worker yield changes in behavior (rooted in cognitive theory); and (2) research
asking how reinforcement of behavior itself yields changed behavior (rooted in
acognitive theory). Each of the approaches in the cognitive tradition gives rise to
distinctive prescriptive models for motivating employees.

APPLICATIONS DERIVING FROM THE COGNITIVE TRADITION

Theory X, Theory Y, Theory Z

The first model stemming from the human growth development approach is the
previously mentioned Theory X, Theory Y analysis of motivation by Douglas
McGregor. Douglas McGregor, in his classic work, *The Human Side of Enterprise* (1957), builds a theory of work motivation premised on the humanistic
psychology of Abraham Maslow.

> There are at least five sets of goals which we may call basic needs. These ba-
> sic goals are related to each other, being arranged in a hierarchy of prepo-
> tency. When a need is fairly well satisfied, the next prepotent ("higher")
> need emerges, in turn to dominate the conscious life and to serve as the cen-

ter of organization of behavior, since gratified needs are not active motivators (Maslow, 1943).

Accepting this analysis of human nature with needs arranged from physiological, to safety, to social, to ego, to self-actualization in ascending order of potency, McGregor criticizes conventional managerial theory for making incorrect assumptions about the management process. According to McGregor, conventional management theory, or Theory X, believes that without active intervention by management, people would be passive, even resistant, to organizational needs. Theory X sees the average person as indolent by nature, lacking ambition, disliking responsibility, and preferring to be led. The typical employee is inherently self-centered, indifferent to organizational needs and by nature resistant to change (McGregor, 1957). In effect, they are at best motivated by the lower levels of the needs hierarchy. McGregor argues that the Theory X philosophy confuses cause and effect in its analysis of human nature. If the employee in the modern organization is the passive indifferent actor described above, it is in response to existing management philosophy, policy, and practice. He is "sick" because of deprivation of a higher level need. This sickness has the behavioral consequences outlined above. While the contemporary organization meets the physiological and safety needs of most employees, social needs are viewed by management as a threat to the organization so the organization seeks to inhibit them.

But even if these social needs are met by management the very structure of the contemporary organization would frustrate the fulfillment of the next two higher level needs: the need for self esteem (self-confidence, independence, achievement, status, and recognition) and self-actualization. The outcome of this frustration is the worker depicted in the Theory X model.

As an alternative approach McGregor proposes a theory of management which fits the real motivational structure of human beings. Theory Y management makes these assumptions:

> People are not by nature passive or resistant to organizational needs. They have become so as the result of experience in organizations. The motivational potential for development, the capacity for assuming responsibility, a readiness to direct behavior toward organizational goals are all present in people. It is a responsibility of management to make it possible for people to develop these human characteristics for themselves. The essential task of management is to arrange organizational conditions and methods of operation so that people can achieve their own goals best by directing their own efforts toward organizational objectives" [McGregor (1957) in Natemeyer (1978)].

The level of motivation evident in any organization will be a function of the set of assumptions selected. According to McGregor, management is capable of constructing a climate that either opposes or enhances the motives people bring the organization. Though McGregor has enjoyed such popularity that Theory X, Theory Y analysis has become virtually conventional wisdom in organizational behavior, his work has not gone without criticism. His principal critics allege that his application of Maslow's humanistic psychology to the work setting is simplistic. Indeed, we should point out that Maslow himself was too uncertain of the empirical validity of his own notions to feel fully comfortable with the applications that he saw in popular management literature. Not withstanding this tenuous theoretical foundation, Theory X, Theory Y analysis has had a profound effect on management theory and practice. In the chapter on performance appraisal we discuss Management By Objectives (MBO) as one of the most significant practical developments founded in large part upon McGregor's work. The Theory X, Theory Y model has indeed been criticized on the grounds that it is simplistic, yet it seems to provide significant insight to managers. In particular it focuses attention on one very important question for the manager: "Do you make one set of assumptions about the motivation of your employees and another set of assumptions about your own motivations?" (Boshear and Albrecht, 1977). Theory Y warns against applying a double standard and stresses the commonality of needs and therefore motivation among all human beings.

The Japanese upsurge of manufacturing productivity has engendered much interest in their management techniques. It has also engendered a new addition to the list of management theories; namely Theory Z. William Ouchi, drawing upon the work of McGregor, has postulated that America needs a new approach, Theory Z, if American management is to improve its productivity (Ouchi, 1981). Theory Z is a synthesis of elements of Japanese management and a Theory Y perspective on the value of human resources. Theory Z organizations place high value on long term employment, consensual decision making, individual responsibility, slow evaluation and promotion systems, and moderately specialized career paths. A Theory Z management approach has been attempted at a number of major American corporations such as Chrysler and it has its strong advocates (Joiner, 1985). Motivational models coming out of the humanistic psychology tradition see human motivation as a function of the need level at which a particular employee is operating (Doyle, 1992).

Two Factor Theory

Frederick Herzberg, in his "Two Factor Theory of Motivation," departs from the pure growth and development model and yet is rooted in it. He asks a simple question: "How do you install a generator in an employee?" In order to answer this question, he asks another, what do people want from their jobs? He asked employees to describe in detail the situations in which they felt very good or bad about their jobs. He then recorded and categorized those responses. He observed that the answers they gave when they were satisfied were different than those that they gave when they were dissatisfied. Herzberg, concluded that job attitudes where best described in terms of two factors he called *dissatisfiers* and *motivators*. Herzberg argued that factors leading to job satisfaction are *different* from those which lead to job dissatisfaction! In effect, he argued that a dual continuum existed and that the opposite of "satisfaction" is "no satisfaction" and the opposite of "dissatisfaction" is "no dissatisfaction."

Figure 5 is a graphic representation of Herzberg's conceptual framework. Note, that the dual continuum underscores the existence of separate factors. The key to understanding the difference resides in the pleasure-pain principle. One set of needs stems from the person's animal disposition and centers on the avoidance of loss of life, hunger, pain, sexual deprivation, and so on. The second dimension of human nature is pleasure-seeking oriented or motivation. Recall, Maslow's need hierarchy! According to Herzberg, human beings have a compelling urge to reach their own potential by continuous psychological growth (Herzberg, 1966). Those aspects of work which are *motivators* include classic growth factors; these are recognition, achievement, advancement, responsibility, nature of work itself, and opportunity for personal and professional growth. They tend to be intrinsic to the individual.

Aspects of work which cause dissatisfaction are called *hygiene* factors and are related more to a need to avoid unpleasantness. Included among these factors are supervision, working conditions, salary, interpersonal relationships, relationships with subordinates, and company policy. Hygiene factors tend to be extrinsic to the individual. The implication of this theory is that managers who insist on stressing extrinsic or hygiene awards will fail to harness the full energy of

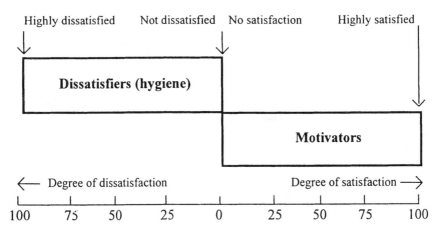

Figure 5 A graphical representation of Herzberg's conceptual framework.

their employees, for these rewards will only make the work situation more tolerable. The trash collection analog is often used, we expect certain minimal hygiene standards such as the trash to be collected, if the trash is not collected, a major hygiene factor that can lead to dissatisfaction exists. Eliminating that dissatisfier, by collecting the trash, returns us to a state where things are as we expect them. From a work perspective, company policy, administration, quality of supervision, working relations with fellow employees, and salary, are hygiene factors that can lead to employee dissatisfaction. However, what makes an employee want to work are motivators. To motivate an employee the work, itself, must be made valuable. Valuable work is work that provides an opportunity for responsibility, recognition, achievement, and presents opportunities for growth and advancement. In other words, intrinsic rewards can engage the higher level needs of the human spirit.

The two factor theory of motivation leads to a focus on job enrichment as the entry point for motivating employees. Recall, we said previously that Malsow's needs hierarchy provided the conceptual framework for attempts to move away from the specialization of job tasks that were derived from scientific management. Herzberg's research provided the empirical platform for many job enrichment efforts designed to enhance the nature of work. Many such efforts were tried and not all proved successful. Herzburg attributes such failures to the fact that managers confuse horizontal job loading with vertical job loading. Horizontal job loadings imply enlarging already meaningless work. Only vertical job loading, a form of job enrichment which directly taps motivators, will produce motivated action. The principles of such job enrichment include removing some control while retaining accountability, increasing the accountability of an individual for her own work and giving that person a complete natural unit of work (module, division, area, and so on), and granting additional authority to the employee. It also requires making periodic reports directly available to the worker herself rather than to the supervisor. Finally, job enrichment includes introducing new and more difficult tasks not previously handled and assigning individuals specific or specialized tasks, enabling them to become experts.

Herzberg and his associates report extensive research on this two-factor theory. Studies conducted on over 1600 employees, including lower level supervisors, agricultural administrators, foremen, military officers, engineers, scientists, and accountants, lent support to the Herzberg model. Also, Schwartz et al., (1963) claimed support for the two-factor theory in their study of public utility workers, and Dysinger (1966) found support in his study of scientists and engineers. Cross national research conducted in Israel using educators lends support to Herzberg's two factor theory (Gaziel, 1986). However, Herzberg's work has its critics (Lawler, 1973). The major disagreements center on disputes about whether job attitudes, in fact, constitute a single dimension or a continuum. Others contend that Herzberg's findings are tied to his methodology, i.e., when respondents are interviewed they relate critical incidents about "satisfying" and "dissatisfying" events. However, when independent rating scales are employed these findings are more difficult to replicate (Silver, 1987). In general, studies employing different ways of measuring factors leading to satisfaction support the notion that any factor can produce effects ranging from satisfaction to dissatisfaction (Graen and Hulin, 1968). Regardless of these criticisms, Herzberg's theory has been widely popularized and has taken on tangible expression in various proposals for job enrichment.

Equity Theory

Equity theory has its conceptual roots in rational economic man principles. It is predicated on the assumption that people do not work in a vacuum, but rather, make relative evaluations of their position. Moreover, those evaluations are usually made with respect to some point of reference. There is a strong body of evidence that individuals in the work place, in fact, make comparisons of their job inputs and outcomes relative to others and that perceptions of inequity can lead to differences in the amount of effort employees exert (Vecchio, 1984).

The basic premise of equity theory is that employees desire that their effort, abilities, and performance be judged fairly *relative to others* in the work place. Equity theory also assumes that employees evaluate their work situation much like they evaluate other economic transactions in the marketplace; that is, in terms of exchanges. There are four key elements used to explain motivational dynamics in equity theory, *inputs*, *outcomes*, *comparative analysis*, and *action*. *Inputs* are what we bring to the exchange education; intelligence, experience, age, effort, etc. *Outcomes* are what we get from the exchange; recognition, salary, benefits, perks, etc. *Comparative analysis* is the term for the cognitive process that underlies our view of the exchange process. Accordingly, we compare the weight ratios that we attach to perceived inputs (our skills, education, etc.) and outcomes (pay, recognition, etc.) for ourselves and others in the same situation. It is the comparison to relevant others that leads to assessment of equity (we are being treated fairly) or inequity (we are not being treated fairly). *Action* refers to the specific behaviors that an individual will take to reduce the tension that results from the feeling of inequity. When individuals perceive inequity they will do one of five things:

1. Distort the perception of others or their own inputs or outcomes.
2. Behave in a fashion that will induce others to change their inputs or outcomes.
3. Behave in a fashion that will result in a change in their own inputs or outcomes.
4. Choose a different referent for comparison.
5. Terminate their employment, quit!

What drives the individual (his or her energy source) is the desire to restore equity. Equity theory assumes that an individual's motivation will be related to his perception of the fairness of the rewards received for a certain amount of effort as compared to the rewards received by relevant others.

The perceptions by individuals discussed previously are all subjective. The referent that the individual chooses to compare themselves against are important variables in equity theory. The three referents discussed in equity theory are *"other," "self," and "system."* *Other* includes individuals with similar jobs in the same organization or similar organizations. *Self* refers to input-outcome ratios that are unique to the experience of a given employee such as past employment experience. System considers organizational salary, procedures, and administrative policies of the system in which the individual finds himself.

The managerial implications of equity theory are that individuals are concerned not only with *absolute* rewards or outcomes that are derived from their efforts, but will evaluate these rewards *relative* to what others receive. Managers need to be cognizant of real problems of equity that may exist in their workplace. They also need to recognize that they must also "manage the perception of equity" which can lead to differences in motivation.

Expectancy

The expectancy-value approach to human motivation has enjoyed broad application to work behavior over the last thirty years. Georgopoulos et al., (1957) made the first application of this motivational model to the work setting. Georgopoulos et al. saw worker productivity as a function of individual needs, perceptions of the instrumentality of high production, and worker freedom. A worker was thought to be motivated to produce when he was activated by desiring a goal (need engaged) and when he perceived that high productivity is a path toward this goal. But for the relationship between worker need and high expectation to hold, the worker must be free from limiting considerations. The principal limiting consideration is informal group pressure.

The first fully developed expectancy model was put forward by Victor Vroom (Vroom, 1964). Vroom's theory was based on three concepts: valence (value of an outcome or anticipated satisfaction resulting from an outcome), expectancy (subjective probability of achieving an outcome), and force (expected value of an act). The resulting model is:

Force (motivation) = valence × expectancy

Motivation, in this context, is understood in terms of a model which sees behavior as rational (from a subjective perspective) and as directed toward the attainment of a desired outcome or goal (Vroom, 1964). Vroom's work, focusing on "process" rather than content, has been well received by those desiring a more explicit examination of the relationship between motivation and the probability of achieving organizational goals (Luthans, 1972). Graen (1969) stresses that explicit recognition of organizational clarity is necessary as a prerequisite to employee motivation. Hunt and Hill (1969) criticize the Vroom model on a much more basic level by suggesting that it is not a behavioral theory, but simply one of motivation. Its weakness, according to critics, is that it ignores key intervening factors between motivation and performance.

Building on Vroom's theoretical work, Porter and Lawler advance a well-received and comprehensive expectancy model. The basic building blocks of this model are derived from the Vroom constructs: value of reward (valence), perceived effort, and reward possibility (expectancy), and effort (motivational force). To see effort as a product of the interaction between value of reward and perceived effort/reward probability is to adopt the basic Vroom proposition. The Porter–Lawler model further elaborates the factors that intervene between motivation, performance, and satisfaction. The relationship between motivation or effort and performance is modified by (1) abilities and traits (relatively stable characteristics of individuals); and (2) role perception (the individual's subjective definition of the job).

The next variable considered in the model is satisfaction, seen here as a product of reward. But again, the relationship is modified by subjective equity judgment of the recipient, labeled perceived equitable reward. Perceived equitable rewards have to do with the input-output discrepancies an employee perceives in comparing him/herself with another person. An employee who perceives she commits more to the organization and receives less than another colleague will suffer a decline in satisfaction. Studies support the evidence of equity as a norm in the workforce (Schuster and Clark, 1970; Zedeck and Smith, 1968; Henrichs, 1969). Other studies have found the causal link between equity, satisfaction, and absence of turnover (Klein, 1973; Dittrich and Carrell, 1976). There are conceptual difficulties in the minds of some scholars because the model says nothing about unconscious motivation or personality, attempts to predict choice in one or more efforts, and the theory does not specify which second level outcomes are relevant to a given individual in a particular situation (Fusilier and Ganster, 1984; Wanous et al., 1983).

After testing this model on a group of 568 administrators in seven different organizations, Porter and Lawler concluded that two modifications were in order. First, a direct causal link between performance and perceived equitable reward was added. Managers perceiving themselves as high performers established a higher standard for equitable reward than did those who saw themselves as low performers. Second, rewards had to be refined to distinguish intrinsic and extrinsic rewards. Intrinsic rewards (relating to higher level needs) related more closely to performance than extrinsic rewards (fulfilling lower level needs) (Porter and Lawler, 1968).

Expectancy is the most comprehensive and systematic approach to motivation theory (Stahl and Grisby, 1987; Tubbs et al., 1993). Expectancy theory argues that the strength of a tendency to act in a certain way is based on a cognitive evaluation by the individual. The nature of that evaluation is that the individual considers alternatives, weighs consequences, computes costs and benefits, and chooses a course of action that will maximize their utility. Expectancy is the learned connection between *behavior* and *goals*. According to expectancy theory, people consider a number of factors in choosing a course of action and the effort that they will exert in a particular situation will be the cumulative effect of three variables. First, the individual's perceived probability that a certain level of effort will lead to a desired level of performance (*expectancy*). Secondly, the individual's perceived probability that a given level of effort will lead to a desired level of outcomes (*instrumentality*). Finally, the person's perceived value of the projected outcomes (*valence*). Figure 6 is a simplified outline of the expectancy model.

In the above model, the strength of a person's motivation to perform (exert effort) will depend upon how strongly he believes he can accomplish what he attempts and the value he attaches to the rewards he will receive. Where rewards are clearly related to performance there should be a high expectancy that performance will result in the specified reward. Where no such linkages exist, people

Figure 6   A basic model of expectancy.

will have different expectancies which are typically not likely to motivate. If he achieves his performance, is adequately rewarded by the organization, and values that reward, his motivational needs will be satisfied. In addition to a person's values and expectancies, other factors influence the linkages between effort and performance. Among those other things are the individual's ability and the tools, technologies and knowledge he brings to the task.

Critics of the expectancy model stated that its comprehensiveness makes it too complex to adequately measure. Moreover, the fact that components of the model reflect internal states like subjective measures of probability of achieving outcomes creates problems in the operational definition of concepts (Tubbs et al., 1993). The importance of expectancy theory, from a conceptual perspective, is its emphasis on *rewards* for *behavior*. Expectancy theory assumes that a person's preference for a particular outcome may extend beyond the immediate consequences of an action to what will happen later. It also assumes that self interest is evident in that cognitive process. In addition, the assumed linkage between behavior and goals underscores the importance of the linkage between what is expected of the employee (performance criteria), the appraisal process, and the reward system.

APPLICATIONS DERIVING FROM THE ACOGNITIVE TRADITION

Though full-fledged operant conditioning programs are rare in the real world of organizations, principles of operant conditioning are applied everyday by managers and employees alike. Advocates of behavior modification in organizations argue for a more conscious and therefore effective strategy of behavior management. Their definition of management means changing behavior to increase employee effectiveness (Brown and Presbie, 1976), using five basic steps:

1. pinpoint the behavior critical to employee effectiveness;
2. measure and chart the behavior;
3. change the behavior by changing antecedents, consequences, or both;
4. evaluate your behavior improvement project;
5. change the program as necessary.

A number of private sector firms such as IBM, United Airlines, Emory Air Freight, Ford Motor Company, Procter and Gamble, and ITT have applied operant conditioning principles to their operations; some for as long as 20 years (O'Hara et al., 1986). For the most part, these efforts follow the model designed by Emory Freight, the private sector pioneer in behavior modification in organizations, whose methods aim to let employees know how well they are achieving specific goals, while rewards of praise and recognition are forthcoming for improvement (O'Hara et al., 1986) Among the examples that could be drawn from Emory Air Freight is the optimization of the use of containers. Workers were not using containers to combine smaller parcels and packages as often as they could have. Research by the company showed that the containers were used less than half the number of times they could have been. An operant conditioning behavior modification program was initiated that saved the company over $650,000.

An example of applying operant conditioning principles to the public sector is the City of Detroit Garbage Collector productivity improvement program. Here the reinforcements of bonuses and praise were provided on a quarterly and daily basis in an effort to strengthen productivity and weaken unproductive behaviors in garbage collection. The program resulted in a significant reduction of citizen complaints and savings to the city even after bonuses were paid (Brown and Presbie, 1976).

Critics of the application of behavior modification to the organization see it as ethically repulsive, as manipulative, involuntary, and patently exploitative. Inferring from the capacity of researchers to control subject behavior in experimental settings, critics raise the specter of employee enslavement to these scientific control methods. Proponents of operant conditioning respond that productivity is in everyone's interest, employer and employee alike, that employees typically help identify the critical behaviors in the program design phase and often actively participate in the program development, and that employees, often backed by unions, are far from powerless in negotiating program issues with employers.

INTRINSIC VERSUS EXTRINSIC MOTIVATION

Edward Deci has defined the concepts for studying intrinsic and extrinsic motivation. According to Deci, a person is intrinsically motivated if he or she engages in an activity to feel competent about successfully completing the activity. The reward to the person comes from the feelings of self worth about successfully completing the task. There is no external reward that generates these feeling per se, the reward is internal to the person. Human beings are creatures in constant interaction with their environment and they *need* to feel effective or competent in relation to their environment. This essential need is the basis for intrinsic motivation (Deci, 1975a). Extrinsic motivation, on the other hand, comes through reward structures over and above the job itself (Deci, 1980). It takes the form of some extrinsic drive reduction in hunger, thirst, material reward, etc. It is generated by the lower levels of Maslow's needs hierarchy.

Typically public agencies (like private companies) provide employees with a mixture of intrinsic and extrinsic rewards. Both intrinsic and extrinsic motivations are necessary to insure high quality recruitment, retention, and performance at work. Intrinsic motivation is a motivational force ultimately tied to intrinsic outcomes, while extrinsic motivation is a motivational force ultimately tied to extrinsic outcomes. Extrinsic motivations have been characterized as one form of "investment" that an organization makes to insure a tie between the employee and the organization:

> Getting employees to feel that they have a big investment in the organization is not very complicated. To foster these ties the organization has to offer opportunities and working conditions that are competitive with other prospective employers. Some of the more progressive corporations do this through liberal use of stock option and bonus plans. In the public sector, typical investment factors include promotion prospects, development of work group networks, performance bonuses, and accrual of vacation, sick leave, and retirement benefits (Romzek, 1990, p. 375).

Investments are based on the carrot and stick approach to motivation and are highly dependent upon extrinsic motivators (Behn, 1995). The investments approach is also clearly related to a rational choice perspective that assumes that the personal interests of the individual are the most important driving forces behind their behavior in the organization (Robertson and Tang, 1995). Moreover, the investment approach assumes a competitive stance on investments that must be maintained so that employees have more motivation to stay than to leave. To the extent that the investments approach is the only psychological tie for employees, public agencies are subject to the viscidities of the marketplace (Romzek, 1990).

Much research has focused on the conditions that must prevail regarding for extrinsic rewards to be effective (Deci, 1980). One important aspect is whether or not the rewards are contingent on performance (Lawler, 1986). A common refrain among critics of public sector management is that civil service regulations impede effective use of extrinsic rewards to motivate employees when compared to the private sector. Though merit increases and even performance bonuses are a part of the reward structure for many public employees, public managers have seldom been empowered to "hone" financial rewards to levels of employee performance. However, this is not a common practice even in the private sector, one researcher has estimated that approximately 20% of American workers see a direct connection between their own effort and how much they are paid (Lawler, 1987). Moreover, despite assertions about the pay for performance in the private sector many private firms promote from within the organization, on the basis of seniority, and tie salary increases to promotion to new positions rather than performance (Baker et al., 1988). In addition, monetary incentives, in particular, can have unintended counter productive organizational outcomes if employees cannot adequately determine what they need to do or how their performance is being measured (Baker et al., 1988).

In a radical departure from previous federal sector practices, key provisions of the Civil Service Reform Act of 1978 strongly endorsed monetary incentives in the Senior Executive Service and in the Merit Pay Provisions for middle managers. Annual case bonuses awarded or denied on the basis of performance were included to enhance the productivity of top civil servants. For the middle level manager, an incentive pay system providing one half of the annual increase to be allocated according to stringent merit criteria introduces a more modest version of the same principle covering civil servants in the G.S. 13 to 15 range. However, while an appealing idea in principle, it is not without its critics. Heavy reliance upon money as a motivating factor may be important in energizing the supervisory staff, but it has its risks (Baker et al., 1988). It is vitally dependent upon the objectivity of performance measurements and appraisal. Above all, the merit plan is flawed by its withholding of a portion of basic schedule increases in order to accumulate funds for making merit increases (Stahl, 1983; Stahl and Gribsy, 1987). Whether and how intensively this extrinsic motivator in the form of investments are employed will vary from agency to agency, much as it has in the past, and will depend upon the nature of the political climate. Interestingly, despite obvious differences between the nature and amount of extrinsic rewards between the public and the private sector researchers have found few overall differences in motivation (Rainey, 1983).

Employee *commitment* to an organization and its goals is another potential form of motivation. Commitment is one expression of the psychological attachment that an employee has to the organization. One value of commitment as a motivational force is predicated on a form of organizational self selection, that is, public employees may enter public service for reasons other than maximization of income, they do so to perform work that is meaningful (Behn, 1995). One commonly known expression of commitment to public service is exemplified in the words of John F. Kennedy "Ask not what your country can do for you ask what you can do for your country." The actual commitment by an employee may be to the agency's mission, goals, and values. Accordingly, employees who feel committed to the agency's values and goals do not base their calculations exclusively on what they have "invested" in the agency, they work to achieve a sense of personal satisfaction from public service (Romzek, 1990; Perry and Wise, 1990; Behn, 1995). Commitment is reflected in a belief and acceptance of the organization's goals, a willingness to exert effort toward the realization of those goals, and a strong desire to maintain organizational membership.

According to Stahl (1983), higher level needs are strongly tapped in the public sector. Commitment is implicitly based on those higher level needs (Perry and Wise, 1990). Stahl also indicates that most public programs have a built in advantage regarding their intrinsic value given that the very purpose is to serve the general public. In this sense, commitment can be based on unique character of government work. The public sector typically has a broader impact on the lives of people than the private sector. It has greater symbolic significance and deals with more life and death issues (Rainey et al., 1976). Public service is typically perceived as promoting the public interest rather than more specific and narrow self interest. Public administration, as a profession, is based on an inherently normative platform that is different from the private sector (Green et al., 1993). The roots of that normative platform are founded on the body of the Constitution and the Bill of Rights.

> It is our understanding that the body of theory guiding governmental organization and management-structures, processes, and procedures is to be found in public law, that it is valid today, and that it will remain so as long as the Republic endures. The principles that make up this theory can in many settings embrace useful precepts such as those of "management by objectives" (MBO) or "total quality management" (TQM) and they can accommodate and be enhanced by an almost infinite variety of technological innovations. But such techniques and advances are not, and cannot be, a substitute or replacement for the traditional, constitution-based method of doing the public's business (Moe and Gilmour, 1995, p. 136).

This commitment to the constitution-based method of carrying out the public's business has as its source, the same motivational base as nationalism, the desire to promotion of the common good, service to the public interest, and other higher level public service motives that employees possess. Accordingly, commitment in the public service can be based on duty, idealism, or on a belief in social equity (Fredrickson, 1985; Perry and Wise, 1990; Romzek, 1990). As a motivational device in public organizations, its potency will be enhanced by appropriate *selection* and *socialization* to agency values. Its potency should not be neglected by the practicing manager.

MANAGERIAL IMPLICATIONS

For the manager in a public agency this review of motivation models stimulates a practical concern. Do findings from the private sector apply to the public sector, or, is there something unique in a public work force or work setting that calls for a more cautious application of such organizational behavior findings? We accept the perspective implicit in O. Glenn Stahl's discussion of motivation in his standard text, *Public Personnel Administration*, that differences across settings create no *serious* problem in applying motivation theory. A similar position is found in N. Joseph Cayer's *Public Personnel Administration*. More importantly, whatever the theoretical relationship between performance and intrinsic/extrinsic motivation managers need direction to influence what choices they make over the domains of work which they control. Drawing upon the previous research from the cognitive and acognitive traditions, we will attempt to present managerial implications that are derivative of this literature.

Establish and Use Goals

The literature on expectancy and goal setting as well as that from behavior modification underscores the importance of having hard and specific goals. We agree with the assumptions of the cognitive approach that people have reasons for what they do. Moreover, what people choose as a goal is something they value and believe in. If managers can provide a linkage between the goals employees find valuable and the goals the organization wants to accomplish they can tap a very important motivational force. The goals chosen must be attainable. They should stretch the employee but not be so high as to be unattainable. Perceptions by the employee that the outcomes they want to achieve are beyond their abilities can result in a reduction of effort. Goals must also be clearly stated and measurable. Employees need feedback on their progress toward these goals and they generally should be involved in and have "ownership" of the goal formation process. We will return to this theme in detail when we discuss management by objective (MBO) later in the book.

Link Rewards to Performance

Both the cognitive and acognitive approaches to motivation assume that in order to change behavior it is important to make rewards contingent upon the behavior you seek to modify. We have already noted the difficulty in doing this in the workplace. Nonetheless, all effort possible should be made by the manager to tie tangible rewards (pay and promotion) and symbolic rewards (praise and plaques) to employee behaviors that the manager wants to reinforce. Whether the satisfaction that comes from such reinforcement causes performance (an intrinsically satisfying work motivates high performance) or performance causes satisfaction (high performers receive extrinsic rewards and feel good as a result), it remains true that satisfied employees stay with their employment. If the satisfaction performance linkage is strong, the most productive employees will also be those who remain to make careers in the agency.

Manage Equity Issues

Recall, the basic premise of equity theory is that employees desire that their effort, abilities, and performance be judged fairly relative to others. Equity theory also assumes that employees evaluate their work situation much like they evaluate other economic transactions in the marketplace in terms of inputs, outcomes, comparative analysis, and action. The fact that this analysis is subjective makes it no less relevant from a motivational perspective and leads to the prescription that managers take into consideration individual differences. As much as possible, differences in ability, experience, effort, and other inputs should "explain" differences in pay, promotion, and responsibility.

Provide for Job Enrichment

Human resource professionals have observed that public personnel systems and job classification procedures typically limit job redesign when compared to the private sector. In a sense this is true! However, public managers should not lose site of the ability they possess to change the ways in which tasks are performed and to enhance the inherent motivational factors in the nature of work itself. The principles of job enrichment should include removing some control while retaining accountability. In addition, to the extent possible a person should be given a complete natural unit of work (module, division, area, and so on). The suggestion here is that within the constraints of the public personnel system, endeavors should be focused on tapping as much as possible the motivational force inherent in the higher level human needs, those related to getting satisfaction from a job well done.

ENDNOTE

1. For the cognitive, acognitive framework for organizing the motivation literature we are indebted to O. Behling and C. Schrieshiem (1975); for providing a comprhensive review of motivation research in the 20the century we acknowledge the work of Behling and Schriesheim (1976) and Weiner (1980, 1985). This literature review draws heavily on both works.

REFERENCES AND ADDITIONAL READING

Arnold, Hugh J. (1976). "Effects of Performance Feedback and Extrinsic Reward Upon High Intrinsic Motivation" in *Organizational Behavior and Human Performance*. Psychological Bulletin, 52:pp 396–424.

Atkinson, J. W. (1964). *An Introduction to Motivation*. Princeton, N.J.: Van Nostrand.

Baker, George P, Michael C. Jensen, and Kevin J. Murphy (1988). "Compensation and Incentive: Practice vs. Theory," *Journal of Finance*. 43:pp 593–616.

Baldwin, Norman J. (1984). "Are We Really Lazy?" *Review of Public Personnel Administration*. 4:pp 80–89.

Beck, Robert C. (1990). *Motivation: Theories and Principles*. 3rd ed. Englewood Cliffs, NJ: Prentice Hall.

Behling, Orlando and Chester Schriesheim (1976). *Organizational Behavior*. Boston: Allyn and Bacon Co.

Behn, Robert D. (1995). "The Big Questions of Public Management," *Public Administration Review*. 55:pp 313–324.

Boshear, Walton C. and Karl G. Albrecht (1977). *Understanding People, Models and Concepts*. La Jolla, California: University Associates, Inc.

Brown, Paul L. and Robert J. Presbie (1976). *Behavior Modification in Business, Industry and Government*. New Paltz, New York: Behavior Improvement Associates.

Buchanan, B., II (1974). "Government Managers, Business Executives, and Organizational Commitment," *Public Administration Review*. 35:pp 339–347.

Carlisle, Kenneth and Shelia Murphy (1986). *Practical Motivation Handbook*. New York: John Wiley and Sons.

Cayer, N. Joseph (1986). *Public Personnel Administration in the United States 2nd Ed.* New York: St. Martin's Press.

Cox, A. (1985). *The Making of the Achiever*. New York: Dodd and Mead.

Charms, R. (1972). "Personal Causation Training in Schools," *Journal of Applied Social Psychology*. 2:pp 95–113.

Cherniss, Cary and Jeffery S. Kane (1987). "Public Sector Professionals: Job Characteristics, Satisfaction and Aspirations for Intrinsic Fulfillment through Work," in *Human Relations*. Vol 40 (3):pp 125–136.

Darwin, Charles (1859). *Origin of the Species*. New York: Modern Library, 1936.

Deci, Edward L. (1975a). "Hidden Costs of Rewards," *Organization Dynamics*, 4(3):pp 61–72.

Deci, Edward (1975b). *Intrinsic Motivation*. New York: Plenum Press.

Deci, Edward (1980). *The Psychology of Self Determination*. Lexington, Mass.: Lexington Books.

Dittrich, J. E. and M. R. Carrell (1976). "Dimensions of Organizational Fairness As Predictors of Job Satisfaction, Absence and Turnover," *Academy of Management Proceedings*, pp 79–83.

Doyle, Kenneth, O. (1992). "Money and the Behavioral Sciences," *American Behavioral Scientist*. July–August, pp 641–657.

Dysinger, D. W. (1966). "Motivational Factors Affecting Civilian Army Research and Development Personnel," report AIR-D-95–5166–TR.

Frederickson, George H. (1985). "The Public Service and the Patriotism of Benevolence," *Public Administration Review*. 45:pp 547–553.

Friedlander, F. (1964). "Job Characteristics as Satisfiers and Dissatisfiers," *Journal of Applied Psychology*. 48:pp 388–392.

Fusilier, M. and D. Ganster (1984). "A Within Person Test Form of the Expectancy Model in a Choice Context," in *Organizational Behavior and Human Performance*. 34:pp 323–342.

Gaziel, Haim H. (1986). "Correlates of Job Satisfaction: A Study of the Two-Factor Theory in an Educational Setting," in *The Journal of Psychology*. 120:pp 613–626.

Gellerman, Saul W. (1963). *Motivation and Productivity*. New York: American Management Association.

Georgopoulos, Basil S., Gerald M. Mahoney, and Nyle W. Jones (1957). "A Path Goal Approach to Productivity," *Journal of Applied Psychology*. 41:pp 345–353.

Graen, G. (1969). "Instrumentability Theory of Work-Motivation; Some Experimental Results and Suggested Modifications," *Journal of Applied Psychology*. 53:p 1.

Graen G. B., and C.L. Hulin (1968). "Addendum to an Empirical Investigation of the Two-Factor Theory of Job Satisfaction," *Journal of Applied Psychology*. 52:pp 341–342.

Green, Richard T., F. Lawrence Keller, and Gary L. Wamsley (1993). *Public Administration Review*. 53:pp 516–23.

Greenberg, J. (1989). "Cognitive Reevaluation of Outcomes in Response to Underpayment Inequity," *Academy of Management Journal*, 32:pp 174–184.

Guyot, James F. (1961). "Government Bureaucrats are Different," *Industrial and Labor Relations Review*. 22:pp 195–202.

Hampton, D. R., C. E. Summer, and R. A. Webber (1978). *Organizational Behavior and the Practice of Management*. Glenview, Ill.: Scott Foresman.

Henrichs, J. R. (1969). "Correlates of Employee Evaluations of Pay Increases," *Journal of Applied Psychology*. 53:pp 481–489.

Herzberg, F., B. Mausner, R. O. Peterson, and D. F. Campbell (1957). "Job Attitudes: Review of Research and Opinions," *Psychological Services of Pittsburgh*. Pittsburgh, Pennsylvania.

Hull, Clark, L. (1943). *The Principles of Behavior*. New York: Appleton–Century–Crofts.

Hunt, J. G. and J. W. Hill (1969). "The New Look in Motivation Theory in Organizational Research," *Human Organizations*. Summer:pp 100–109.

Huston, John P. (1985). *Motivation*. New York: MacMillian Publishing Co.

Jablonsky, J. F. and D. L. DeVries (1972). "Operant Conditioning Principles Extrapolated to the Theory of Management," *Organizational Behavior and Human Performance*. 7:pp 340–358.

James, William (1890). *The Principles of Psychology*. New York: Dover Publications, 1950.

Joiner, C. W. (1985). "Making the 'Z' Contact Work," in *Sloan Management Review*. Spring:pp 57–64.

Jones, Edward W. (1986). "Black Managers: The Dream Deferred" *Harvard Business Review*. (May/June), pp 84–93.

Jung, John (1978). *Understanding Human Motivation*. New York: Macmillan Publishing Co.

Kilpatrick, Franklin P., Milton C. Cummings, Jr., and M. Kent Jennings (1964). *The Image of the Federal Service*. The Brookings Institution, Washington, D.C.

Klein, S. M. (1973). "Pay Factors as Predictors to Satisfaction. A Comparison of Reinforcement Equity and Expectancy," *Academy of Management Journal*. pp 598–610.

Lawler, Edward. L. III (1986). *High Involvement Management*. San Francisco, California: Jossey Bass Publishers.

Lawler, Edward E. III (1973). *Motivation in Work Organizations*. Montery, California: Brooks Cole.

Lawler, Edward E. III (1987). "Pay for Performance" A Motivational Analysis," in Haigh R. Nalbantian, (ed.) *Incentives, Cooperation, and Risk Sharing: Economic and Psychological Perspectives on Employment Contracts*. Totowa, NJ.: Rowman and Littlefield, pp 69–86.

Lawler, Edward E. (1992). *The Ultimate Advantage*. San Franscisco, California: Jossey Bass Publishers.

Lee, Robert (1979). *Public Personnel Systems*. Baltimore, Maryland: University Park Press.

Lewis, Gregory B. (1986). "Race, Sex and Supervisory Authority in Federal White-Collar Employment," in *Public Administration Review*. 46:pp 25–29.

Lewin, Kurt (1935). *A Dynamic Theory of Personality*. New York: McGraw Hill.

Lindsay, C., E. Marks, and L. Gorlow (1967). "The Herzberg Theory: A Critique and Reformation," *Journal of Applied Psychology*. 51:pp 330–339.

Locke, E. A. (1973). "Job Satisfaction and Job Performance: A Theoretical Analysis," *Organizational Behavior and Human Performance*. 9:pp 482–503.

Locke, E. A. (1969). "What is Job Satisfaction?" *Organizational Behavior and Human Performance*. 4:pp 309–336.

Luthans, F. (1972). *Contemporary Readings in Organizational Behavior.* New York: Mc-Graw Hill.

Maslow, A. H. (1943). "Theory of Human Motivation," Psychological Review. 50:pp 370–396, cited in Natemeyer, *Classics of Organizational Behavior.* (1978). Oak Park, Ill.: Moore Publishing Co.:pp 55.

Mayo, Elton (1945). *The Social Problems of an Industrial Civilization.* Cambridge: Harvard University Graduate School of Business.

McAdams J. (1976). "Police are 'Busting' Out all over in Orange County," California. *Work Performance.* 2:pp 14–17.

McClelland, David C. and D. Burnham (1976). "Power is the Great Motivator," in *Harvard Business Review.* 54:pp 100–111.

McClelland, David C. (1984). *Motives, Personality and Society.* New York: Praeger Scientific.

McClelland, David. C. (1988). *Human Motivation.* London: Cambridge University Press.

McClelland, David C. (1961). *The Achieving Society.* Princeton, N.J.: Van Nostrand.

McClelland David C., J. W. Atkinson, R. W. Clark, and E. L. Lowell (1953). *The Achievement Motive.* New York: Appleton–Century–Crofts.

McGregor, Douglas M. (1957). "The Human Side of Enterprise," reproduced in Walter E. Natemeyer (ed.) *Classics of Organizational Behavior.* Oak Park, Ill.: Moore Publishing Co., 1978.

Moe, Ronald C. and Robert S. Gilmour (1995). "Rediscovering Principles of Public Administration: The Neglected Foundation of Public Law," *Public Administration Review.* 55:pp135–46.

Mook, Douglas (1987). *Motivation.* New York: W. W. Norton and Company, Inc.

Morgan, Clifford and Richard King (1966). *Introduction to Psychology* (3rd ed.) New York: McGraw-Hill.

Munro, D. (1986). "Work Motivation and Values: Problems and Possibilities In and Out of Africa," in *Australian Journal of Psychology.* 38:pp 285–295.

Natemeyer, Walter E. (ed.) (1978). *Classics of Organizational Behavior.* Oak Park, Ill.: Moore Publishing Co.

Nord, Walter R. (1969). "Beyond the Teaching Machine: The Neglected Area of Operant Conditioning in the Theory and Practice of Management," *Organizational Behavior and Human Performance.* 4:pp 375–401.

Nuttin, J.R. (1973). "Pleasure and Reward in Motivation and Learning," in D. Berlyne (ed.) *Pleasure, Reward, Preference.* New York: Academic Press.

O'Hara, K., C. Johnson, and T. Beehr (1986). "Organizational Behavior in Management in the Private Sector: A Review of Empirical Research and Recommendations for Further Investigation," in *Academy of Management Review.* 10:pp 848–864.

Osborne, David and Ted Gaebler (1992). *Reinventing Government: How the Entrepreneurial Spirit is Transforming the Public Sector.* Don Mills: Addison–Wesley Publishing Co.

Ouchi, W. G. (1981). *Theory Z: How American Business Can Meet the Japanese Challenge.* Reading, Mass: Addison–Wesley.

Perry, James L. and Lois Recascino Wise (1990). "The Motivational Bases of Public Service," *Public Administration Review.* 50:pp 367–373.

Peters, Guy B. and Donald J. Savoie (1994). "Civil Service Reform: Misdiagnosing the Patient," *Public Administration Review*. 54:pp 418–25.

Pinder, Craig C. (1984). *Work Motivation: Theory and Applications*. Glenview, Ill: Scott–Foresman.

Porter L. W. and R. M. Steers (1973). "Organizational Work and Personal Factors in Employee Turnover and Absenteeism," *Psychological Bulletin*. 80:pp 151–176.

Porter, L. W. and E. E. Lawler III. (1968). *Managerial Attitudes and Performance*. Homewood, Ill.

Quick, Thomas (1985). *The Manager's Motivation Desk Book*. New York: John Wiley and Sons.

Rainey, Hal G. (1983). "Public Agencies and Private Firms: Incentive Structures, Goals, and Individual Roles," *Administration and Society*. 15:pp 207–242.

Rainey, Hal G., Robert W. Backoff, and Charles H. Levine (1979). "Comparing Public and Private Organizations." *Public Administration Review*. 36.:pp 233–44.

Rawls, J. K., O. T. Nelson, Jr. (1975). "Characteristics Associated with Preferences for Certain Managerial Positions," *Psychological Reports*. 36:pp 911–918.

Rawls, J. K., R. A. Ulrich, O. T. Nelson, Jr. (1975). "A Comparison of Managers Entering or Reentering the Profit and Nonprofit Sectors," *Academy of Management Journal*. 18:pp 616–662.

Robertson, Peter J. and Shui-Yan Tang (1995). *Public Administration Review*. 55:pp 67–80.

Romzek, Barbara S. (1990). "Employee Investment and Commitment: The Ties That Bind," *Public Administration Review*. 50:pp 374–382.

Sarnoff, I. and P. O. Zimbardo (1961). "Anxiety, Fear, and Social Affiliation," *Journal of Abnormal and Social Psychology*. 62:pp 356–363.

Schachter, S. (1959). *The Psychology of Affiliation*. Stanford, Calif.: Stanford, University Press.

Schuster, J. R. and B. Clark (1970). "Individual Differences Related to Feelings Toward Pay," *Personnel Journal*. 23:pp 591–604.

Schwartz, M. M., E. Jerusaitis, and H. Stark (1963). "Motivational Factors Among Supervisors in the Utility Industry," *Personnel Psychology*. 16:pp 45–63.

Skinner, B. F. (1969). *Contingencies of Reinforcement: A Theoretical Analysis*. New York: Appleton–Century–Crofts.

Siegel, Gilbert, B. (1987). "The Jury is Still Out on Merit Pay in Government," *Review of Public Personnel Administration*. 7:pp 3–15.

Sievers, Burkard (1986). "Beyond the Surrogate of Motivation," in *Organizational Studies*. 7:pp 335–351.

Silver, Paula F. (1987). "Job Satisfaction and Dissatisfaction Revisited," in *Educational and Psychological Research*. 1:pp 1–20.

Sirgy, Joseph M. (1986). "A Quality of Life Theory Derived from Maslow's Developmental Perspective: Quality is Related to Progressive Satisfaction of a Hierarchy of Needs, Lower Order and Higher" in *American Journal of Economics and Sociology*. 45:pp 329–342.

Stahl M. J. (1983). "Achievement Power and Managerial Motivation: Selecting Managerial Talent with Job Exercise Choice," in *Personnel Psychology*. 36:pp 775–790.

Stahl M. J. and D. W. Grisby (1987). "A Comparison of Unit, Subjectivity and Regression Measures of Second Level Values in Expectancy Theory: An Empirical Test," *Decision Sciences*. 18:pp 62–72.

Stahl, O. Glenn (1983). *Public Personnel Administration*. 8th ed. New York: Harper & Row.

Steers, Richard M. and Lyman W. Porter (1991). *Motivation and Work Behavior* 5th. ed. New York: McGraw Hill.

Steinmetz, Lawrence, L. (1985). *Managing the Marginal and Unsatisfactory Performer*. New York: Addison–Wesley.

Taylor, J. C. and D. F. Felton (1993). *Performance by Design: Socio Technical Systems in North America*. Englewood Cliffs, New Jersey: Prentice Hall.

Taylor, F. W. (1967). *The Principles of Scientific Management*. New York: Norton.

Thorndike, E. L. (1965). *Animal Intelligence: Experimental Studies*. New York: Hafner Publishing Company (facsimile of 1911 edition).

Tolman, E. C. (1932). *Purposive Behavior in Animals and Men*. New York: Appleton–Century–Crofts.

Tubbs, M. E., D. M. Boehne, and J. G. Gahl (1993). "Expectancy, Valence, and Motivational Force Functions in Goal Setting Research: An Empirical Test," *Journal of Applied Psychology*. 78:pp 361–373.

Vecchio, Robert P. (1984). "Models of Psychological Inequity," *Organizational Behavior and Human Performance*. October, pp. 226–282.

Vroom, Victor H. (1964). *Work and Motivation*. New York: John Wiley and Sons.

Wanous, J., T. Kenon, and J. Lattack (1983). "Expectancy Theory and Occupational/Organizational Choices: A Review and Test," in *Organizational Behavior and Human Performance*. Vol 32 (1):pp 66–86.

Weiner, Bernard (1986). *An Attributional Theory of Motivation and Emotion*. New York: Springer-Verlag.

Weiner, Bernard (1985). *Human Motivation*. New York: Springer-Verlag.

Weiner, Bernard (1980). *Human Motivation*. New York: Holt, Rienhart and Winston.

White, Robert, W. (1959). "Motivation Reconsidered: The Concept of Competence," *Psychological Review*. 66:pp 297–233.

Winther, Dorothy A., and Samuel B. Green (1987). "Another Look at Gender-Related Differences in Leadership Behavior," *Sex Roles*. 16:pp 41–56.

Woodworth, R. S. (1918). *Dynamic Psychology*. New York: Columbia University Press.

Wright, Patrick M. (1992). "An Examination of the Relationship Among Monetary Incentives, Goal Level, Goal Commitment and Performance," *Journal of Management*, December, pp. 677–693.

Zedeck, S. and P. E. Smith (1968). "A Psychophysical Determination of Equitable Payment: A Methodological Study," *Journal of Applied Psychology*. 52:pp 343–347.

4
Leadership

Leadership is a major topic in public and business administration. Leadership is what we expect of presidents and CEOs. Leaders are accorded superior status, salary, and responsibility in all organizations. When an organization succeeds we attribute the success to the "quality of leadership." When an organization fails, we typically engage in attributions focused on a "failure of leadership." For example, a book on the economic troubles from which the International Business Machine Corporation (IBM) has only recently recovered, documents a failure in leadership at various levels of the corporation in explaining IBM's economic slide. Specifically, IBM went from earnings in excess of $6 billion in profit to reported losses of five billion in less than three years. This represented an economic downturn of such magnitude that as of 1994 IBM had lost some $75 billion of stock market value, going from a position where its stock market value exceeded that of all the companies on the German stock exchange put together, to a "spot barely in the top ten companies in the U.S." (Carroll, 1994, p. 4). Among the remarkable failures of leadership documented were the missed opportunity by IBM's leadership to buy outright the MS-DOS operating system from Bill Gates. The failure of IBM's leadership to buy, when offered, all or part of Intel and Microsoft. The failure of IBM's leadership to take advantage of the reduced instruction set computing (RISC) microprocessor, which IBM itself invented in the 1970s, because it was perceived by IBM's leadership to compete with its mainframe business; a decision that allowed competition in the PC market to take valuable market share from IBM. The final failure of leadership was the lack of vision of IBM's executives, expressed in their consistent failure to understand and act upon the fact that the microcomputer and not the mainframe, was going to be the future of computing (Carroll, 1994). Clearly, leaders are awarded the accolades when the organization succeeds and given the blame for its failures. Harry Truman's description of the presidency says it quite well "the buck stops here."

What is a leader and what is leadership? Many favor a conception of leadership similar to the definition of obscenity expressed by a Supreme Court Justice who when pressed stated "I can't define it for you, but I can tell you when I see it." To some extent the foregoing definition of obscenity has a ring of truth when one seeks to define leadership. Why? Because leadership is a construct like "mass" or "force" in the physical sciences. In other words, leadership is an abstraction formed by generalizations from particulars. Definitions of leadership are based on the observation of certain traits and behaviors in real world situations. Some of those traits and behaviors are identified as expressing the presence of leadership, others are associated with its absence. Because leadership is a construct, it should surprise no one that one researcher has observed "There are almost as many definitions of leadership as there are persons who have attempted to define the concept" (Stogdill, 1974, p. 289).

> The crisis of leadership today is the mediocrity or irresponsibility of so many of the men and women in power, but leadership rarely rises to the full need for it. The fundamental crisis underlying mediocrity is intellectual. If we know all too much about our leaders, we know far to little about *leadership*. We fail to grasp the essence of leadership that is relevant to the modern age and hence cannot agree even on the standards by which to measure, recruit, and reject it. Is leadership innovation-cultural or political? Is it essentially inspiration? Mobilization of followers? Goal setting? Goal fulfillment? Is a leader the definer of values? Satisfier of needs? If leaders require followers, who leads whom from where to where, and why? How do leaders lead followers without being wholly led by followers? Leadership is one of the most observed and least understood phenomena on earth (Burns, 1979, p. 1).

The review of the leadership literature reveals a number of typologies and numerous definitions of leadership (Bass, 1990; Yukl, 1989). Many of these definitions center around the *ability to influence others* (Yukl, 1989). However, there is significant controversy about such central issues as how leaders differ from followers, what situational factors in the work environment influence leadership, and how to precisely operationalize leadership.

Fundamentally, leadership is the process of attempting to influence the behavior of others, it is the art of getting others to do what you believe must be done (Kouzes and Posner, 1990). A leader is one who attempts to exert influence through some form of power that results in gaining compliance from those being led. Few would disagree with definitions of leadership expressed at this level of generalization. However, like motivation, leadership is a multi variate phenomena. Returning to our previous example, if we place leadership in a predictive equation in which organizational performance is the dependent variable there are a number of other independent variables that predict performance "over and above" leadership. In other words, these other independent variables also contribute to the prediction of organizational effectiveness. This *hypothetical* equation might look like:

$$Y = \theta + \beta_1 X_1 + \beta_2 X_2 + \beta_3 X_3 + \beta_4 X_4 + \beta_5 X_5 + \beta_6 X_6 + \varepsilon$$

Where :

Y = organizational effectiveness
θ = intercept
X_1 = leadership style
X_2 = motivation level or maturity of subordinates
X_3 = position power e.g., formal powers of the leader to hire and fire
X_4 = task structure e.g., the extent to which job assignments are routinized
X_5 = group dynamics
X_6 = economic factors
ε = error

As in the example used in the chapter on motivation, the purpose of the foregoing equation is *pedagogical*, what we want to underscore is the *multi variate* nature of organizational effectiveness or performance. Leadership style (X_1), which at this point we will define as any set of *traits* or *behaviors* that are expressed by individuals in a leadership position, represents one variable in the organizational effectiveness equation, but there are many other *situational variables* (X_2, X_3, X_n) in the workplace that interact with or themselves predict organizational effectiveness outcomes. In other words, if we are trying to explain the variance in levels of organization effectiveness, a number of variables in addition to leadership are predictors of organizational effectiveness or performance. Moreover, these other variables have different predictive coefficients or weights (β_1, β_2, β_n) themselves.

The research on leadership indicates that it is a very complex phenomena! Some scholars have concluded that leadership is a "social myth" and that by implication many organizational effectiveness measures are better predicted by looking at the contextual and situational variables in the above model (Gemmill and Oakley, 1992). Others, contend that leadership clearly makes a difference over and above these contextual and situational variables (Behn, 1991). Much of the complexity involved in understanding leadership is a function of how leadership is studied. Typically, the empirical research on leadership systematically varies some condition of a leader's behavior in experimental situations and then attempts to attribute differences in group performance outcomes to that leader's behavior. However, the results of this research are confounded by the fact that unlike other dimensions of organizational behavior, such as motivation and decision-making which can be studied by looking at the individual, leadership by definition involves group interaction (Davis and Luthans, 1984). This group interaction also takes place within a situational context which is typically difficult to completely control. This situational context is the environment which, it-self, exerts an independent influence on leadership style. The combined effect is that it is difficult to attribute cause and effect to the various variables in the lead-ership equation. The relationship between leadership, subordinates, and the situ-ational environment is vividly expressed by looking at the highest ranking job in the public sector, the presidency. Presidents have had vastly different styles of leadership and have varied the way in which they have organized the formal structure of the White House (Kessel, 1984). They also each possess various unique personal traits and have engaged in different behaviors in dealing with subordinates which have affected their relationships with those whom they seek to influence (Bratton, 1983). Nonetheless, each president's leadership style takes place within a context constrained by the situational influences he faces. These situational influences may be negative or positive (e.g., an oil embargo or a strong economy). In either case, they are important elements in determining ef-fectiveness of presidential leadership. Moreover, situational factors influence leadership at all levels of public management. We will return to this theme in our discussion of the development of the research on leadership.

LEADERSHIP VERSUS MANAGEMENT

One additional aspect to the complexity inherent in the discussion of leadership is the belief by some that "leadership" is distinct from "management." One renowned scholar has observed "The manager does things right; the leader does the right thing" Bennis (1989, p. 45). Implicit in this statement is the view that leadership is "over and above" compliance with the routine expectations of man-agement. What are these routine expectations of management and what is differ-ent about leadership? Abrahman Zaleznik (1977) for one, argues that managers carry out specific responsibilities, exercise organizational authority, and deal with process variables in order to get the job done. Managers are expected to *plan, organize, command, coordinate,* and *control* (Fayol, 1916). In addition, managers play a number of roles. These roles include *interpersonal roles* as when managers are required to act as figurehead or liaison in duties that are cer-emonial and symbolic. *Informational roles* when managers act to receive, col-lect, and broadcast organizational information either as a monitor or spokesman relative to that information. Managers act in *decisional roles* as when they act as entrepreneur to initiate and oversee new projects, as disturbance handles manag-ing unforseen problems, or, in a decision content, to allocate resources in the or-ganization. Finally, managers act as *negotiators* within their decision role which requires them to bargain between and among the units of the organization (Mintzberg, 1975).

In our discussion of leadership and its impact on public management we will review the four major approaches to the study of leadership: the trait approach, the behavioral approach, the situational (contingency) approach, and the transactional vs. transformational leader approach. In studying these approaches to leadership we will find a trend from simple, one-factor theories to complex, multi-factor theories. The earliest approaches, associated with "trait theories" of leadership, simply sought to identify outstanding leader qualities such as achievement orientation. Later behavioral researchers emphasized leadership behaviors such as participative management (a single-factor theory) or combined social/task orientation (a dual factor theory). Later analysis looked to such factors as the ability to motivate others so that they would commit to a shared vision. Because both trait and behavioral approaches found only limited evidence that the factors they studied led to organizational effectiveness, many contemporary scholars have rejected generalized theories of leadership in favor of contingency theories, which link particular leadership behaviors to particular organizational settings. More recently, some scholars have concluded that leadership transcends simple efficient and effective management.

The answer to the question what is leadership is very important as more and more governments are faced with a rapid turnover in upper management, turnover generated by both the electoral cycle and the financial and personal sacrifices that senior level managers must make to engage in public service (Trowbridge, 1985).

THE TRAIT APPROACH TO LEADERSHIP

The trait approach to the study of leadership is the most direct! It is predicated on the natural born leader concept. Accordingly, leaders posses traits that distinguish them from followers. The trait approach was the earliest and is arguably the most persistent approach to the study of leadership. Traits such as appearance, height, intelligence, honesty, integrity, expertise, etc. were (and are) used to explain leadership effectiveness. Media conceptions of leadership are replete with such trait descriptions. Ronald Reagan, for example, was characterized as *charismatic*. In the trait approach, effective leadership is defined in terms of the traits of leaders thought to exemplify good leadership. This essentially circular method of analysis has sometimes been labeled the attitudinal approach to leadership, since many of the traits studied are attitudes and values such as integrity or sociability. In addition, learned abilities, such as expertise, were sometimes included. Through this method it is possible to compile a long list of desirable leadership characteristics. Theoretically, agencies could then screen managerial candidates by these criteria (e.g., in psychological tests at entrance), or train existing managers to be more in conformity with prescribed leadership traits, or they could provide role models to encourage the imitation of these traits.

Some of the leadership traits identified by researchers are these: dominance (Lord et al., 1986); achievement drive (Bass, 1981; Mills and Bohannon, 1980); ascendance (Stogdill, 1974; Mills and Bohannon, 1980); emotional balance (Stogdill, 1974); expectancy of high standards (Scanlon, 1979); fairness (Sank, 1974); inner direction (Zaleznik, 1977); integrity (Argyris, 1955); originality (Argyris, 1955); self-confidence (Argyris, 1955; Motowidlo, 1980); sociability (Stogdill, 1974); understanding (Sank, 1974).

In addition, researchers have found correlations between leadership position and certain personal abilities and characteristics: intelligence (Lord et al., 1986); verbal fluency (Stogdill, 1974); height (Stogdill, 1948); expertise (Sank, 1974; Kabanoff and O'Brien, 1979; Knight and Weiss, 1980). More recently, researchers have isolated six traits on which leaders tend to differ systematically from nonleaders these traits are: *ambition, desire to lead, honesty/integrity, self confidence, intelligence, and job relevant knowledge* (Kirkpatrick and Locke, 1991).

An interesting study of the leadership traits possessed by political leaders as perceived by Henry Kissinger, was conducted by Southward Swede and Philip Tetlock. They analyzed the trait descriptions by Kissinger of 38 world leaders as expressed in Kissinger's book, *White House Years*. Over 106 leader traits were subjected to quantitative content analysis. These traits included many of the traits we mentioned previously, for example, intelligence, political awareness, understanding, dominance, etc. Kissinger clearly saw and described world political leaders from a personality traits framework.

> The complexity of Kissinger's world view is revealed by both the number of major perceptual dimensions he uses to describe people and by the discriminating manner in which he applies these dimensions to individual leaders (reflected in the existence of at least nine different leader types). Our analyses, moreover, underestimates the subtle highly differentiated quality of Kissinger's perceptions of others. There were many unique descriptions. For instance, Kissinger described himself as "the plumber in Kafka's novel *The Castle*;" he described de Gaulle as having the "natural haughtiness of a snow-capped peak;" and he described Lyndon Johnson as a "caged eagle." Our analysis captures only the major and recurring themes running through Kissinger's personality descriptions (Swede and Tetlock, 1986, p. 641).

Using factor analysis, the authors were able to come up with five personality dimensions that described most of the world leaders Kissinger discussed in the book. The authors speculated that Kissinger's trait based perception of world leaders may well have been related to the way he perceived his overall foreign policy strategy (Swede and Tetlock, 1986).

Based on a study of American public and private sector leaders, Abraham Zaleznik (1977) concluded that among the many leadership traits the essential one differentiating top managers was inner direction. These individuals, Zaleznik noted, are apt to be subject as children to parental demands for self-reliant performance. They adopt an inner-world orientation. They feel separate from their environments, even from other people. Their sense of self-esteem is based on inner drives, not social roles or peer attitudes. Zaleznik found such individuals form deep attachments to one or two strong mentors. For example, General Fox Connor was such a mentor to Dwight Eisenhower. Through inner drives for achievement combined with deep attachments to organizational mentors, Zaleznik concluded, inner-directed individuals rise to top leadership positions.

Zaleznik's research on leadership is reminiscent of Abraham Maslow's hierarchy of needs theory of motivation (Maslow, 1954) discussed previously. Maslow held that human values expressed in organizational life would center first on basic human needs (e.g., food, shelter). Only when these were fulfilled would people be able to give priority to the next higher need-social needs for affiliation and friendship. Next would come ego needs for esteem and power. Finally, needs for self-actualization would emerge as the priority of a mature society. Inner-directed achievement in Zaleznik's research corresponds to Maslow's self-actualization stage. Other leadership researchers have also found self-actualization to be a key leadership trait. Michael Maccoby's study of 250 executives uncovered four types of leadership, each exhibiting characteristic personality traits (Maccoby, 1976). The games man was seen as the new, emerging leadership figure oriented toward innovation, competition, and challenge. Other more traditional personality types were the company man (security-minded), the craftsman (production and quality-oriented), and the jungle fighter (power oriented). The analogies to Maslow's hierarchy are apparent: company man (security and social acceptance), jungle fighter (power and esteem), and games man (self-actualization in meeting challenges).

The drive for self-actualization is the normative ideal of the managerial leader in the writings of researchers like Maslow, Zaleznik, and Maccoby. This is not to say, however, that actual leadership patterns correspond to this idea. Argyris (1962), in fact, has long emphasized that organizations routinely foster dependent immature relations. Likewise Maccoby's company man is far from the self-actualizing norm. Zaleznik, for his part, saw the inner-directed leader as the exception, not the rule. In contrast to the ideal "self-actualizing leader," the more realistic norm is the "concerned manager" who provides employees with social recognition for a job well done. This image was publicized by the Hawthorne experiments (Roethlisberger, 1941) and was central to the human relations movement which arose in the 1930s. If you recall, these experiments demonstrated that when industrial engineering variables (e.g., light, pay incentives, work breaks) were altered in experimental groups, productivity rose. Surprisingly, however, productivity rose as well in the control groups. This "Hawthorne Effect" showed administrative researchers that increased management concern for employers was a key motivator. During the 1930s and the postwar period the human relations movement preached the gospel of the new, concerned style of management. The new style was taught to generations of public and private sector managers as the *correct* style of management. As discussed previously, Douglas McGregor articulated this approach as "Theory Y." "Theory X" was the traditional hierarchial style of management: top-down, one-way in communication, assuming subordinates must be coerced into being productive, and believing that many preferred dependency. In contrast, Theory Y was presented as a new, more effective style; sensitive to human needs, showing concern for subordinates' views and assuming employees would be productive even without the close supervision of Theory X management. Most leadership traits correlated with leadership style consistent with Theory Y or a self-actualizing approach and not with the more authoritarian Theory X. Unfortunately, insufficient research exists to conclusively differentiate public leadership traits from those of private sector leaders.

LEADERSHIP TRAITS: DO THEY LEAD TO ORGANIZATIONAL EFFECTIVENESS?

The trait theory of leadership has considerable intuitive appeal. Though a given trait like "concern" doesn't necessarily lead to a given outcome like high productivity, it is hard to imagine leadership being successful without some combination of many of the previously mentioned traits. For example, it is intuitive that a leader should be intelligent. Some evidence exists that many traits are related to productivity. Mills and Bohannon (1980) found that police officers characterized by traits of dominance, intelligence, and autonomous achievement were more effective than their counterparts not so characterized. However, while the evidence linking traits to effectiveness is mixed, there is much stronger evidence that traits like intelligence, correlate empirically with a leader being *perceived* as effective. Moreover, this perception itself is a precondition of effective leadership.

> Leadership perceptions are important in their own right, being a major component of the social fabric of many organizations. Being perceived as a leader allows one to exert greater influence in business or government, and leadership perceptions are particularly important in the political area (Lord et al., 1986, p. 408).

There are a number of reasons why the measures for the *actual* influence of traits on effective leadership are *weaker* than the data for *perceived* effect. First, traits may not be translated by the manager into actual behavior and, even if they are, they are affected by the reactions and needs of the followers. This makes cause and effect difficult to isolate! Second, what may be a good leadership attribute in one setting, may be inappropriate or ineffective in another. This fact makes it difficult to clarify the relative importance of various traits across leadership environments. For example, such politically incorrect traits as ethnocentrism, distrust of others, and high need for power have been the traditional characteristics of successful Soviet leaders.

Finally, researchers long ago discovered that there was little demonstrable relationship between personality traits and organizational effectiveness across differing situations (see Gibb, 1947; Stogdill, 1948). However, this may be a function of our inability to measure well all the complex interaction between and among the variables that make up the leadership environment. A major reason for the finding of weak relationships between traits and actual effects also has to do with the premises of trait theory. Trait theorists reasoned that good leadership attributes would lead to satisfied employees, and worker satisfaction would lead to effective work behaviors. While this seems plausible, research has found only a peripheral relationship between satisfaction and organizational productivity (see Brayfield and Crockett, 1955). For example, Vroom's (1964) study of nearly two dozen research efforts showed a very weak ($r = 0.14$) median correlation. Some have suggested that even this weak correlation is due to the effects of productivity on satisfaction, just the opposite of the trait theorists' assumptions (see Lawler and Porter, 1967).

For the foregoing reasons, researchers realized that there was more to the leadership equation and turned to the hypothesis that leadership behavior (not leadership traits or attitudes) determined organizational effectiveness. This is not to say that the differences between the trait and behavioral approaches to leadership are mutually exclusive. As we noted previously, *leaders differ from nonleaders on certain traits*. The trait of understanding, for example, suggests the behavior of two-way communication. However, the trait approach emphasized the attributes and attitudes of the leaders; behaviors were secondary. The behavioral approach, in contrast, was generally concerned with the organizational climate of the group as reflected in broad patterns of management behavior. Students of the behavioral approach assumed that research would prove leader behavior to be more strongly related to organizational effectiveness than leader attitudes and traits had been.

BEHAVIORAL APPROACHES TO LEADERSHIP

The identification of successful leadership behaviors has had a more productive history than the trait approach. Advocates of behavioral approaches to leadership study did not reject the findings of trait researchers. Attributes like sociability, fairness, or achievement orientation were acknowledged to be important. However, behavioralists argued that these attributes made little difference unless translated into specific leadership behavior. Behavior is, of course, a generic term which could be applied to almost any study of leadership. The behavioral approach to leadership is identified primarily with just three specific types of behavior.

The first of these is participatory management involving employees in democratic forms of agency governance. The second research focus concerns a combination of task-oriented and people-oriented behaviors thought by many to reflect an ideal leadership balance. The last focus studies behavior modification, path-goal, and other instrumental behaviors also advocated as keys to organizational effectiveness through leadership behavior. Each of these is examined in turn below.

PARTICIPATORY LEADERSHIP BEHAVIOR

Participation was the focus of the earliest major behavioral approach to the study of leadership. A seminal study of democratic leadership was that by Lewin et al., (1939). In research on children's clubs, these researchers created three different organizational climates. Under an authoritarian climate, the leader made all decisions and allowed the group to see only one step at a time. Under a laissez-faire climate, the leader acted as a passive resource for the club members. Under the democratic climate, the leader pursued action on the basis of group discussion and decision.

Lewin found the authoritarian style led to high aggression and high dependency. Laissez-faire leadership led to low group performance and the emergence of a strong informal group leader. The democratic leadership style, in contrast, was associated with low aggression and high group performance. Later studies did not change this initial finding substantially. Kahn and Katz (1953), for example, found that in a variety of industries high productivity section leaders were oriented toward employee interaction, whereas task-orientation prevailed in low-productivity sections.

Following Lewin, researchers documented a major cause of the apparent superiority of the democratic leadership style. Researchers found that subjects who participated in a decision were significantly more likely to accept and later carry it out. Efran et al. (1979) showed that securing verbal commitment beforehand led to higher performance than did three other methods tested: better information on work process, exhortation to try hard, or better monetary incentives. Participation invests the employee psychologically in the decision and reduces resistance to change.

The Institute for Social Research at the University of Michigan was a central force in studies of organizational participation and consequently "the Michigan studies" are classics of the literature on participatory leadership behavior.

The Michigan studies showed the effects of participation were more complex then previously thought. Generalizing the democratic style as employee orientation and the authoritarian as production orientation, Katz, Maccoby, and Morse (1950) found managers could be high on both dimensions simultaneously. In another major experiment, Morse and Reimer (1956) found productivity increased under both participative and hierarchical leadership styles, although only the former increased employee satisfaction. Kahn (1956) also documented these results. A later review of forty-nine other studies by Anderson (1959) showed clear relation of democratic leadership to organization performance. In summary, research (see Jermier and Berkes, 1979) continues to show a relationship of participation to employee satisfaction and even organizational commitment, but not necessarily to actual organizational performance.

A famous Harvard Business Review article by Slater and Bennis (1964) was titled "Democracy Is Inevitable." This was thought to be so because participation provided better communication, consensus in decision-making, competency-based decisions, and utilization of organizational conflict. However, the Michigan studies and later social science research showed that participation led to satisfaction but not necessarily productivity (Butterfield and Farris, 1974). A second problem for advocates of organizational democracy was finding that participation was not a cause of productivity but only a mutual consequence of a more basic determinant the propensity to innovate. Innovative organizations were found to be characterized by change, not only in participation but in many other productivity-related areas as well. For example, Marrow et al., (1967) studied the Harwood Manufacturing Company, often cited as a model democratic organization. These researchers found two-thirds of the reported productivity improvement to be due to industrial engineering improvement, better training, and personnel changes, not participation per se. Moreover, more recent research indicates that the direction of causality for leader subordinate interaction may indeed be two way. These findings have implications for participation and productivity. In other words, much leadership theory has focused on the influence that the leader has on subordinates, for example, the leader deciding to encourage participation among subordinates (Weisbord, 1987). Some studies have found that in the leadership interaction, subordinates themselves influence the subsequent behavior of the leader. In an interesting experiment, researchers were able to show that leader behavior was influenced by group performance by experimentally manipulating the leadership interaction. When subordinate performance was high, leader positive reward behavior was high. When the performance was low, leaders engaged in more punitive behavior (Sims and Manz, 1984).

Another alternative to organizational democracy argued that participation was effective, but only if part of a package of organizational changes. This argument was made by Rensis Likert (1961, 1967), who had studied four systems of leadership: System 1. *Exploitative authoritarian.* System 2. *Benevolent authoritarian.* System 3. *Consultative.* System 4. *Participative.* Likert found System 4, the participative approach, to be superior; but only if it involved corresponding changes in supervision, decision-making, personnel systems, compensation systems, performance evaluation, employee training and organizational communication. Otherwise, participative leadership would degenerate, Likert held, into benevolent authoritarianism.

In addition to these modifications to the participative theory of leadership, many of the criticisms of the trait approach applied as well. Hofstede (1980), for example, found that in some cultures such as France, a nonparticipatory autocratic leadership style was often preferred. Whereas in other countries such as Sweden, a participatory style received even more support than in the United States. Participation, like recommended personality traits, varies in effectiveness depending on the context! In a seminal book, Lawler (1992) argues that participatory management, which he calls the high involvement approach, is not right for all organizations. He argues, in fact, that it is not even right for all private (profit making) organizations, and may be incompatible with certain features of bureaucracy. Lawler contrasts high involvement (participatory) management with traditional command and control organizations where employees "are told exactly how to do there job. Managers are the only ones who are expected to think, coordinate, and control" (Lawler, 1992, p. 26). Lawler identifies the contextual features *most compatible* with participatory management: tasks which are nonrepetitive, high labor costs, global competition, and an environment in which the time between product conception and marketing is short. In addition, the high involvement style of leadership and management is more effective in environments in which quality is built in rather than "inspected in" and in which the intrinsic motivation of employees is high (Lawler, 1992). Few of these features have any relevance to the public sector environment. In short, while participatory management generally fosters employee satisfaction, too many other situational factors intervene to conclude that participatory leadership behavior will *necessarily* lead to greater organizational effectiveness.

SOCIAL/TASK LEADERSHIP BEHAVIOR

The Michigan studies originated with a concern for democratic management but democratic participation soon came to be conceptualized in broad terms as "employee orientation," contrasted to "production orientation" (Katz and Kahn, 1951; Kahn and Katz, 1953). Other Michigan researchers expanded the concepts even further to compare "group maintenance functions" with "group achievement functions" (Cartwright and Zander, 1960; see also Zelditch, 1955). Implicit in the reconceptualization was the belief that some combination of social-oriented and task-oriented leadership behaviors might prove more effective than participatory behavior alone. This alternative orientation was researched extensively in studies at Ohio State University, starting as early as 1945. In the period from 1945 to 1955, the Ohio State studies utilized an approached which asked subordinates to describe their immediate supervisor utilizing a questionnaire of over 150 items. Two factors emerged as important general behavioral dimensions of leadership:

1. *Consideration* (C)
2. *Initiating Structure* (S)

The consideration-structure distinction of the Ohio State studies was similar to the earlier distinction between democratic and autocratic leadership. Consideration and initiating structure, however, were much more broadly defined (see Stogdill, 1948; Fleishman, 1953; Halpin, 1954; Hemphill, 1954; Stogdill and Coons, 1957). Consideration covered an extensive variety of behavior specifically related to treating people with trust and respect in the workplace including: showing concern for subordinates, acting in a friendly and supportive manner, expressing concern for the general welfare of employees. Consideration also included all forms of supportive interaction and concern regardless of actual participatory process or exercise of democratic powers. Initiating structure included task-organizing behaviors, including defining roles and guiding subordinates toward the attainment of group goals, even if implemented in a non-autocratic manner. Initiating structure also included job assignment, attention to performance standards on the job, and attention to deadlines. Initiating structure, in effect, included behavior that attempted to organize work, work relationships, and goal attainment. In short, the two dimensions can be reduced to what in the vernacular of organizations are referred to as *people skills* and *task skills*. Using these categories, Fleishman et al., (1955) came to conclusions similar to those at Michigan. High consideration did not lead to as high rated performance as high structuring behavior, though it was associated with higher satisfaction evidenced in lower absenteeism and fewer grievances.

The Ohio State findings on the importance of a combination of task and social-oriented behaviors were popularized immensely by two organization development specialists, Robert Blake and Jane Mouton (1964, 1966). Blake and Mouton used the consideration and initiating structure dimensions, relabeled as "*concern for people*" and "*concern for production*" in what they called "*the managerial grid.*" This two dimensional graphical is presented in Figure 7.

The four extreme corners and the center of this coordinate system identified five distinct leadership styles according to Blake and Mouton:

1,1 impoverished management style
1,9 country club style

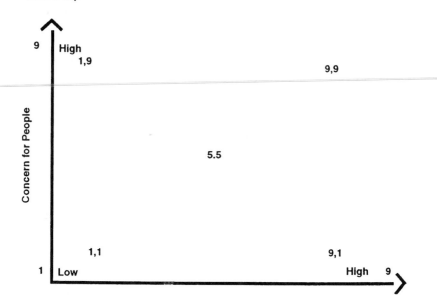

Figure 7   The managerial grid.

      9,1 authority orientation style
      5,1 middle of the road style
      9,9 team style

      In citing the drawbacks of all but the "9,9" style, Blake and Mouton were simply reiterating the earlier conclusions of Ohio State researchers and others who prescribed a combination of high consideration and high structure initiating behaviors for managerial leadership. There are many variants of these theories using social/task leadership behavior concepts. One of the best-known is the life cycle theory of leadership associated with Hersey and Blanchard (1966, 1977, 1979). In a new organization, according to Hersey and Blanchard, the leader must emphasize structure and direction (Quadrant I) (Fig. 8). Later it is possible and desirable to emphasize both concern and structure (Quadrant II). At an even later stage of maturity, the leader may be able to delegate structure concerns and concentrate on team building (Quadrant III). Occasionally, an organization may progress to the most mature phase, where the leader may delegate both dimensions to subordinates and move on to other priorities (Quadrant IV).

      In summary, social/task theories of leadership behavior prescribe a clear

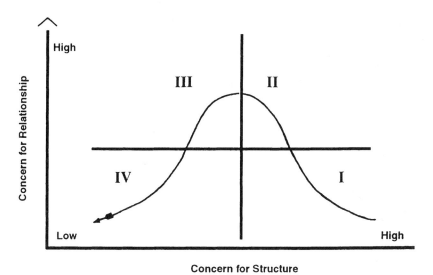

Figure 8 Concern for relationship by concern for structure quadrants.

norm for management. This is the action style high on both consideration and initiating structure. It is "9,9" team management in Blake and Mouton's terms. Even the life cycle variant suggests that the high social, high task quadrant (Quadrant II in Hersey and Blanchard) is the most prevalent. Mounting evidence suggests, however, that this prescription is no more clearly related to organizational effectiveness than the participatory leadership concepts had been. Clearly, many other variables intervene! Leadership style as expressed in the *people skills* versus *task skills* or *social* versus *task* perspective does not control for major context variables. Leadership style and behavior are related to organizational effectiveness but in a manner contingent on contextual variables. Contingency theories of leadership, discussed in a later section, build on this conclusion. Before turning to them, however, we will conclude our discussion of behavioral approaches to leadership by examining a third major focus of that orientation.

INSTRUMENTAL LEADERSHIP BEHAVIOR

In addition to study of democratic and social/task behaviors, a final major behavioral approach to the study of leadership is identified with instrumental leader behaviors. These include behaviors which clarify the relationship of means to ends for the individual employee (*path-goal theories*) or which reinforce desired

employee patterns (*behavioral modification theories*). The former was introduced in the discussion of expectancy models, and the latter in the discussion of
operant conditioning. What both path-goal and behavior modification theories
have in common is a mutual emphasis on leader behavior which is instrumental
to attaining the goals and rewards sought by the employee. According to path
goal theory a leaders behavior is acceptable to an employee to the extent that it is
viewed as an immediate or future source of need satisfaction.

As set forth by House and Mitchell (1974), the path-goal theory of leadership is based on a expectancy theory of motivation [also called the VIE theory,
focusing on valence/instrumentality/expectancy; see House, (1971)]. This theory
states that motivational force (MF) is determined by the value of the goal to the
participant (valence, V) and the expectation that a given effort will lead to the
desired outcome (expectancy, E):

$$MF = V \times E$$

Expectancy/instrumentality theory is associated with the work of Vroom
(1964), Porter and Lawler (1968), Graen (1969), and Nebeker and Mitchell
(1974). House and Mitchell sought to show how various leadership styles were
instrumental to goal achievement. The terminology path-goal is predicated on
the conception that the leader clarifies the "path" that subordinates need to follow to get from where they are to the achievement of their work goals. Leaders
do this by eliminating obstacles in the way of the employee and by making employee satisfaction dependent upon effective performance. House identified
four leadership behaviors. In each case, a different management style is instrumental to the *situation*. Directive leadership (high structure) guides employees
facing ambiguous tasks. Participative leadership (high consideration) mobi-
lizes expression of ego-involved, nonauthoritarian subordinates. Supportive
leadership (another type of high consideration) reduces stress in dissatisfying
tasks. Achievement-oriented management encourages goal-attainment in tasks
where opportunities for achievement are greatest. Complex situations may call
for an appropriate combination of leadership styles, according to path-goal
theory.

Path-goal theory is an expansion of earlier work on expectancy theory by
M. G. Evans (1970, 1974). Evans argued that a high concern, high structure
leadership style was associated with high group performance only if rewards
were contingent on performance. Even earlier Bowers and Seashore (1966) had
outlined four leadership styles similar to those in House's path-goal theory.
House used expectancy theory to explain the relation of these leadership styles to
various types of rewards (task accomplishment, ego involvement, stress reduction, goal attainment) in various situations. Path-goal theory was (and is) a practical contribution to leadership research because it moved the focus toward
consideration of situational variables. Moreover, *managers frequently overesti-*

mate the importance of formal rewards and underestimate the importance of task feedback clarifying path-goal relationships (Greller, 1980; Behn, 1991, p. 73). Path-goal relationships may be clarified in individual work contracts with demonstrable success (Burgers, 1980). Path-goal clarifying behavior does lead to greater job motivation. Path-goal concepts now often receive endorsement (Scanlon, 1979). A meta analysis shows strong empirical support for the path-goal approach (Wofford and Liska, 1993).

Some evidence exists that behavior modification is more effective than other, more diffuse forms of path-goal processes. Hersey and Blanchard (1980), for example, studied the effectiveness of various types of leadership behavior in the problematic situation of the disruptive worker. They found that high task-oriented leadership tended to exacerbate worker hostility, while high relationship-oriented leadership only rewarded disruptive behavior with attention. Most effective was a behavior modification style in which the leader ignored bad behaviors, set clear limits on bad behavior, and rewarded desired behavior. Behavior modification is employed in efforts to change such relatively concrete and specific behaviors as employee tardiness (Luthans and Kreitner, 1985). However, behavior modification's success is limited by group and individual factors (Luthans and Kreitner, 1984). Behavior modification has been employed in the private sector most successfully in areas where the task is subject to precise measurement and quantitative standards can be set. Behavior modification derives from broader notions about organizational change associated with Kurt Lewin (1947) and the study of group dynamics. Lewin saw change as a three-stage process involving (1) unfreezing (removal from the old environment, demeaning treatment, linking of reward to willingness to change); (2) change (identification of employee with new behaviors, internalization) and (3) refreezing (reinforcement of desired behavior). Lewin's studies of coaching of basketball teams and of training of U.S. Marines showed this sequence was effective in behavior modification. It is now commonly assumed that any effective leadership process must link rewards to desired behavior directly, but it is not clear that this is sufficient, in and of itself, to achieve organizational effectiveness.

Research on leadership started with a concern for identification of leadership traits, so that this might be used as a basis for management selection and training. When the relationship of such traits to organizational effectiveness proved weak, researchers sought to emphasize specific leadership behaviors, starting with participative management. This democratic focus, and the later behavioral research on social/task and instrumental leadership behaviors, revealed the complexity of leadership and showed the futility of simple answers. By the 1960s and 1970s, students of leadership came to the view that leadership theories must take specific management situations into account. From the 1980s until recently, we have seen the testing of leadership theories which puts more emphasis on the moderating influence of the situation on the leadership process. That is, earlier interest in broad generalizations (e.g., participative leadership always helps organizational effectiveness) has been rejected in favor of theories tying particular behaviors to particular situations or contingencies. These contingencies include the degree of structure of the task employees are asked to preform, the quality of the relationship between the leader and subordinates, the leaders formal power, group norms, and the maturity of the subordinates.

CONTINGENCY APPROACHES TO LEADERSHIP

Contingency theory is an attempt to deal with the complexity of the real world of leadership reflected in our multi variate equation at the beginning of this chapter. Contingency theories of leadership, also called *situational theories*, are unified by little other than a common rejection of the notion that good leadership is a direct function of having specified desirable leadership traits or a given set of leadership behaviors. Contingency theory argues that when it comes to the relationship between leadership style (e.g., the degree of consideration vs. initiating structure) and effectiveness in achieving a given set of goals, the preferred leadership style will *vary as a function of the situation*. In effect, under condition *(a)* leadership style *(x)* may be more effective than leadership style *(y)*. Situational leadership theory goes on to attempt to isolate those situational factors (variables) that affect leadership effectiveness. Contingency theorists examine a wide range of dimensions; seeking to develop relatively complex theories showing which type of leadership pattern is appropriate for a given cluster of situational factors. In addition, contingency research accepts the concept of "reciprocal determinism," the finding that leadership is a two way street with the behavior of subordinates and leaders affecting each other as well as being bound by the situational context (Sims and Manz, 1984).

The best-known contingency theory of leadership is that popularized in the writings of Fred E. Fiedler (1965, 1967, 1969, 1974, 1976; Fiedler and Chemers, 1974; Fiedler and Mahar, 1979; Chemers and Ayman, 1993). Fiedler's model departs from the traits and various behavioral models by specifying that the groups output is also dependent upon the degree to which the leader controls and influences the situation. He proposes that effective performance is dependent upon a proper match between the leader's style and the degree to which the situation gives control to the leader. He examined the effect on organizational productivity of three situational variables: leader-member relations, degree of task structuring, and strength of leader authority (position power). One evaluates the situation in terms of these situational variables: leader member relations was either good or poor, task structure was high or low, and position power was either weak or strong. Productivity was measured objectively by the number of games won by sports teams, profits of businesses, or accuracy of bombing runs by Air Force teams. Fiedler found that task-centered leadership styles (high structure) were associated with organizational effectiveness when these three variables were very favorable (good relations, high task structure, position power was strong); or when they were very unfavorable. For other, middle-favorability contingencies, a relationship-centered style (high concern) was more effective (Chemers and Ayman, 1993.)

The assumption was that an emphasis on structure rather than relationships was appropriate in the high-favorability contingency because there employees felt little need for participative meetings or other manifestations of a relationship-oriented approach. In the highly unfavorable contingency, structure was more appropriate simply to assert direction and move toward goals. Such unfavorable settings lacked the basis for effective action through relationship-centered approaches alone. Overall empirical support for the operationalization of the model is robust. However, several objections have been raised to Fiedler's contingency theory. One is, it is not predictive since leader-member relations cannot be predicted prior to group formation. It is not comprehensive since many other contingency variables can be posited. Csoka (1974), for example, found leader intelligence to be such as an additional contingency. The greatest criticism centered on Fiedler's method of measuring leadership style. Fiedler used a Least-Preferred Co-worker (LPC) scale (Fiedler, 1969) based on items like the following:

> Think of the person with whom you can work least well. He may be someone you work with now, or he may be someone you knew in the past. Use the scale below to describe this person as he appears to you.

helpful						frustrating	
1	2	3	4	5	6	7	8

unenthusiastic						enthusiastic	
1	2	3	4	5	6	7	8

efficient						inefficient	
1	2	3	4	5	6	7	8

Fiedler believed that the major factor in leadership effectiveness was the person's leadership style. He started by trying to isolate that style. The LPC rating scale consisted of 16 contrasting adjectives like those referenced above. The questionnaire then asked the respondent to think of all the coworkers she\he had encountered and to describe the one person he had *least* enjoyed working with by rating them on the LPC scale of 16 adjectives. If the least preferred coworker was described in relatively positive terms, the respondent received a high LPC score, which indicated that he was relationship oriented! Conversely, if this least preferred coworker was described in negative terms, the respondent would receive a low LPC score, which reflected a task orientation. In addition to empirical validation, Fiedler's contingency theory expressed common-sense wisdom. Leaders who had "everything going for them" (strong authority, clear tasks, good staff relations) had little need to go beyond simple task orientation. Leaders with none of these favorable contexts dealt with a chaotic situation demanding strong, task-oriented leadership, though for opposite reasons. It seemed only in the in-between situations that relationship-centeredness would make a difference to organizational effectiveness. It is interesting to note as well, that it is the in-between situations where the model loses some of its predictiveness (Peters et al., 1985).

CONTINGENCY THEORY: HERSEY AND BLANCHARD'S SITUATIONAL LEADERSHIP THEORY

The situational leadership model developed by Hersey and Blanchard is perhaps the most widely used model in leadership training in both the public and private sectors. More than 350 of the *Fortune* 500 companies report using it including IBM, Bank of America, Mobil Oil, and Xerox. It is also commonly employed in training in the U.S. military and by organizational development specialists at the state and local governmental level. Conceptually, this situational leadership model has its roots in the Ohio State studies in that it employs concepts similar to initiating structure (task behavior) and consideration (relationship) behavior.

> Task behavior is essentially the extent to which a leader engages in one way communication by explaining what each staff member is to do well as when, where and how tasks are to be accomplished. Relationship behavior, even when we call it supportive behavior, is the extent to which a leader engages in two way communication by providing socioemotional support, "psychological strokes," and facilitating behaviors (Hersey and Blanchard, 1979, p. 189).

Hersey and Blanchard's model asserts that there is no one correct leadership style across all situations! The leadership behaviors called for are *conditioned by context*, that is dependent upon the situation. What makes their model more elaborate is that they specify the major elements of that leadership context and focus on the follower, those who are to be lead. They argue that the situation, in effect, provides the environmental stimulus to which the leader must respond with an appropriate set of both *task* and *relationship* behavior. Successful leadership is not only possible, but is dependent upon, matching the right leadership style to the demands of the situation. The major determinant of which set of behaviors (task and relationship) are called for is the readiness of the followers, those who are being led, in other words how mature they are. Readiness is operationally defined in terms of the extent to which followers have the *ability and willingness* to accomplish a task. Dependent upon the readiness of the follower, they propose four possible sets of leadership behaviors.

S1:   (Telling) High-task and low relationship behaviors in response to followers who are unable and unwilling or insecure.

S2:   (Selling) High-task and high-relationship behaviors in response to followers who are unable but willing or confident.

S3:   (Participating) High relationship and low task behavior in response to followers who are able but unwilling and insecure.

S4:   (Delegating). Low-relationship and Low task-behavior in response to followers who are able and willing or confident.

Figure 9 illustrates graphically the interaction between effective style, as measured by the appropriate mix of behaviors (task vs. relationship) on the part of the leader, and the relationship of style to the degree of follower readiness. At R1, followers, because of their readiness level (low), need clear and specific directions in order to accomplish organizational goals. Therefore, the S1: *telling* style of leadership is called for. At stage R2 where follower readiness is increasing (moderate), the S2 *selling* style of leadership characterized by high task and high relationship is required. In this stage of the development cycle the high task compensates for the followers relative lack of ability, and the high relationship behavior is called for to get the followers to feel psychologically committed to the goals of the leader or organization. R3(moderate) calls for the leadership style S3: *participating* this style is low task and high relationship in nature and is characterized by the follower sharing in decision making with the leader serving as the role of facilitator. Finally, at R4 the S4: *delegating* style is called for. In delegating the leader provides little direction or support which is not needed because the followers are both willing and able to accomplish the task and achieve the goals. Hersey and Blanchard's situational theory has significant support from organizational development specialists. Academic researchers have not focused extensively on the model. There is limited research support for the theory (Norris and Vecchico, 1992).

Contingency theorists such as those examined here as well as others have shown a long list of determinants of organizational effectiveness to be important

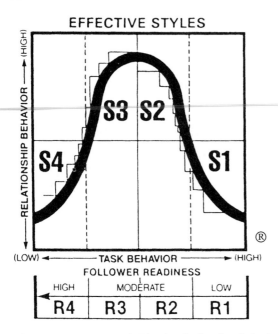

Figure 9   Hersey and Blanchard situational leadership diagram (Reprinted with permission of Dr. Paul Hersey, *The Management of Organizational Behavior Utilizing Human Resources*, The Center for Leadership Studies, Escondido, California. All Rights reserved).

in certain situations. These contingent factors include leader-member relations, degree of task structuring, and strength of leader authority (Fiedler); leader intelligence (Csoka); decision relationships and types (Vroom and Yetton); reward-related roles (French and Raven); representation-related roles (Miller); decision level (Price); and value relationships (Flowers and Hughes) to name a few. Contingency theory arose in reaction against single-factor theories of leadership, such as democratic theory.

TRANSFORMATIONAL LEADERSHIP

The last approach to leadership with which we deal is the difference between *transactional* and *transformational* leaders (Burns, 1979; Bass, 1990). Transactional leaders guide or motivate their followers in the direction of established goals by clarifying role and task requirements. Burns (1978) conceptualized transactional leadership as a process in which leaders approach followers with the objective of exchanging one set of things for another. According to Bass (1990) the transactional leader employs such managerial strategies as contingent reward, the exchange of rewards for performance as specified in an employment contract. In this same vain, transactional managers recognize and reward specific accomplishments that promote organizational goals. This arrangement between leader and follower is predicated on the precepts of extrinsic motivation.

In addition to such exchanges, management by exception is a second feature of transactional leadership. Management by exception is pursued either actively or passively. Active management by exception is characterized by the manager monitoring the work environment searching for deviations from rules or procedures and taking corrective action. Passive management by exception is characterized by the leader intervening only if rules or procedures (standards) are not met. Transactional leadership suggests that leaders and followers do not share a common stake in the organization and thus must arrive at some mutually agreeable understanding. Transactional leadership is rooted in a two-way influence model in which a leader gives and gets something from the follower. The subordinate's motivation to comply with the leader is predicated on self interest and is based on the fact that the leader can deliver payoffs, e.g., pay for performance. Transactional leadership assumptions are rooted in the lower rungs of the Maslow (1958) hierarchy. The transactional leader and follower can accomplish specific organizational goals predicated on norms of reciprocity. These norms are based on a "rational man" view of human behavior. Clearly, transactional leaders can be motivational, promote job satisfaction, accomplish organizational goals, and, therefore be effective managers. However, such performance contingent approaches to leader follower relationships are insufficient to produce or explain higher levels of follower motivation, loyalty, and commitment.

Transformational leaders (Burns, 1979; Bass, 1990a; Sergiovanni, 1992; Kochran and Useem, 1992) focus on higher-order, and ultimately the normative needs of individuals. Transformational leadership is based on a synergy between leader and follower. Followers are motivated to do more than is expected by the simple exchange mechanism discussed previously. Transformational leadership is characterized by a focus on the intrinsic needs of followers. Burns (1979) described transformational leaders as those who seeks to raise the consciousness of followers by appealing to higher ideals. Bass (1992a) describes the transformational leader in terms of characteristics such as *charisma*, expressed in the ability to provide a vision and a sense of mission to an enterprise. The transformational leader instills pride and gains the trust of the follower. Such leaders "transform" followers by making them more aware of the importance and value of task outcomes, in effect, activating their higher order needs for self-actualization. Transformational leaders induce the follower to transcend their self interest (lower order needs) for the sake of the organization. Transformational leaders are also capable of *inspiration* which involves the ability to communicate high expectations using symbols to express vision and purpose. They are also able to express important organizational purposes in simple ways that allow followers to focus their efforts. Transformational leadership arises when leaders are more attentive to gaining cooperation and participation from followers than they are in simply getting tasks accomplished. Transformation leaders promote *intellectual stimulation* in the organization and promote individualized consideration expressed in personal attention to employees who are coached, encouraged, and advised. Transformational leaders *empower* their followers by sharing power and responsibility with their employees. The empowering role of the transformational leader is expressed specifically in their ability to inspire trust, create a vision for the organization, and to remove roadblocks to performance. Among the examples of transformational leaders in the literature are Abraham Lincoln, Franklin D. Roosevelt, and John F. Kennedy.

Transactional and transformational leadership should not be conceptualized as mutually exclusive. Transformational leadership is "over and above" or is built upon transactional leadership. Transformational leadership provides levels of support and performance that go beyond transactional leadership. It involves "doing the right thing" as well as "doing the thing right." The distinction between transactional and transformational leadership sharpens the focus on the distinction on our previous discussion of the differences between "management" and "leadership" and on if either (or both) are innate or involve skills that can be learned.

> It is interesting for us to note that people have never asked us "Can Management be taught? Are managers born or made?" These questions are always raised about leadership, but never about management. It is a curious phenomenon. Why should management be viewed as a set of skills and abilities but leadership be seen as a set of innate personality characteristics? We have simply assumed that management can be taught and on the basis of that assumption established hundreds of business schools and thousands of management courses. In the process, our schools and companies have educated hundreds of thousands managers. Certainly some of those managers are better and some are worse than others. There is also a normal distribution of high-performing chefs. But in general, schools have probably raised the caliber of managers by assuming that people can learn attitudes, skills, and knowledge associated with good management practice. The same can be done with leadership. By viewing leadership as a non learnable set of character traits, a self fulfilling prophecy has been created that dooms societies to having only a few good leaders. If you assume leadership is learnable, you will be surprised to discover how many good leaders there really are (Kouzes and Posner, 1990, p. 297).

The research evidence supporting the fact that transformational leadership is superior is very strong. A number of studies document that transformational leaders are more effective than transactional leaders (Bass and Avolio, 1990; Hater and Bass, 1988).

MANAGERIAL IMPLICATIONS

"The influence of supervisory behavior on productivity is small," Robert Dubin wrote over three decades ago (Dubin et al., 1965). Since that time, research has shown leadership style to be related to organizational effectiveness in highly complex and contingent ways which contrast with the expectations of early researchers that studies would soon vindicate the universal applicability of democratic management, "9,9" management, or other simple formulations. Recent attempts to provide a theoretical framework for leadership research have emerged as far more complex than these earlier attempts. Earlier models utilized a two-dimensional grid based on two relatively specific dimensions such as consideration and structure. Recent models have utilized a three-dimensional grid based on very broadly defined axes which are themselves multidimensional. This multidimensional approach is complex because the reality it attempts map is equally complex.

In spite of the youthfulness and complexity of leadership research, a number of *generalizations* are now possible. These generalizations can and should be important parts of the conceptual framework of any public manager. First; organizational effectiveness is a function of many organizational variables of which leadership style is only one! Managers should *scan their environment* and be aware that factors such as the motivational levels of subordinates, the formal organization structure of their agency, their own formal position power, the task they are expected to accomplish, group dynamics, and the economic and political environment are all variables that will influence their own leadership style as well as the overall effectiveness of the agency. Second; despite the inability of researchers to develop a cause and effect relationship, the trait theory of leadership has considerable intuitive appeal for good reason! Though a given trait like "concern for employees" doesn't necessarily lead to a given outcome like high productivity, it is hard to imagine leadership being successful without some combination of the "effective leadership" traits. For example, it is clear that a leader should be intelligent. Moreover, researchers have isolated six traits on which leaders tend to differ systematically from non-leaders these traits are: *ambition, desire to lead, honesty/integrity, self confidence, intelligence, and job relevant knowledge* (Kirkpatrick and Locke, 1991). Effective public managers should seek to develop these traits in themselves, as well as select for them when hiring subordinates! Third, because leadership style is only one variable in the organizational effectiveness equation, the popularly-recommended leadership styles marked by high participation and/or high consideration often lead to higher satisfaction but not necessarily significantly greater organizational effectiveness. In other words, some aspects of organizational effectiveness will always be explained by contextual variables outside of the direct control of the public manager. Nonetheless, effective leadership will be more strongly related to a proper match between the leader's style and the degree to which the situation gives control to the leader. The organizational productivity of three situational variables: leader-member relations, degree of task structuring, and strength of leader authority (position power) are important. Task-centered leadership styles (high structure) are associated with organizational effectiveness when these three variables were very favorable (good relations, high task structure, position power is strong); or when they were very unfavorable. For other middle-favorability contingencies, a relationship-centered style (high concern) is more effective (Chemers and Ayman, 1993). For example, one public sector study underscored the implicit relationship between task environment and organizational effectiveness (the objective of all leadership) by gathering data from officials whose jobs required interaction with various federal officials. Task environment was defined in terms of the type and location of service provided by the governmental unit. One working hypothesis was that certain functions like human services, where the goals and means to achieve them are not clearly understood, would be at a disadvantage when compared with more physical support functions with a defined and quantitative mission like soil conservation. In other words, human services would be evaluated as less organizationally effective. Another hypothesis was that the physical location of the governmental unit, for example, headquarters versus field offices, would affect their performance evaluation. The logic here was that headquarters dealt with the formulation of policy, which was inherently more ambiguous that implementation of policy. The specific hypothesis was that the field office which applies policy, rather than makes it, would be perceived as more effective. The authors found statistically significant support for both hypotheses (Northrop and Perry, 1985). Fifth; of the variables potentially under the direct control of the manager those associated with clarifying the path-goal relationships which help the individual connect effort to performance are among the most important. This implies that effective managers frequently ask for employee opinions and let employees receive feedback on their work (Yeager et al., 1985).

Finally, and perhaps most importantly, public managers should seek to become transformational leaders. Transformational leadership is "over and above" compliance with the routine expectations of management! In this sense, leadership and management can be conceptualized as different dimensions of the same underlying continuum. Managers are expected to effectively *plan, organize, command, coordinate, and control* (Fayol, 1916). These functions are expressions of transactional leadership. Transformational leadership is "over and above" or is built upon transactional leadership. Transformational leadership provides levels of support and performance that go beyond transactional leadership. It involves "doing the right thing" as well as "doing the thing right." Transformational leaders are concerned with understanding people's beliefs and are concerned with getting commitment to some *vision* of the organization's future. Accordingly, transformational leaders go beyond the roles and functions of management to do such things as *challenge the process* by engaging in a search for opportunities to experiment. They seek to inspire a *shared vision* of the future! They seek to *enable others to act* by fostering collaboration. They *model the way* by setting examples of the type of behavior that the organization wants to reinforce. Finally, *they encourage the heart* by recognizing contributions and celebrating organizational accomplishments (Kouzes and Posner, 1990).

REFERENCES AND ADDITIONAL READING

Allport, F. H. (1924). *Social Psychology*. Boston: Houghton Mifflin.

Anderson, Richard C. (1959). "Learning in Discussions," A Resume of the Authoritarian-Democratic Studies, *Harvard Education Review*, 29:pp 201–215.

Argyris, Chris (1955). "Some Characteristics of Successful Executives," *Personnel Journal* (June):pp 50–63.

Argyris, Chris (1960). *Understanding Organizational Behavior*, Homewood, Ill.: Dorsey.

Argyris, Chris (1962). *Interpersonal Competence and Organizational Effectiveness*, Homewood, Ill.: Dorsey.

Bales, R.F. (1953). "The Equilibrium Problem in Small Groups," pp 111–161 in T. Parson, R. F. Bales & E. A. Shils, (eds.), *Working Papers in the Theory of Action*, Glencoe, Ill.: Free Press.

Bass, Bernard M. (1984). *Leadership and Performance Beyond Expectations*. New York: Free Press.

Bass, Bernard M. (1981). *Stoghill's Handbook of Leadership*. New York: Free Press.

Bass, Bernard M. (1990) *Bass and Stogdill's Handbook of Leadership: Theory, Research, and Managerial Applications*. New York: Free Press.

Bass, Bernard M. (1990a). "From Transactional to Transformational Leadership: Learning to Share the Vision," *Organizational Dynamics*. Winter: pp 19–31.

Bass, Bernard M. and B. J. Avolio (1990). *Transformational Leadership Development*. Palto Alto, California: Consulting Psychologists Press.

Behn, Robert D. (1991). *Leadership Counts*. Cambridge, Massachusetts: Harvard University Press.

Bennis, Warren and B. Nacus (1985). *Leaders: The Strategies for Taking Charge*. New York: Harper & Row Publishers.

Bennis, Warren (1989). *On Becoming a Leader*. Menlo Park, California: Addison Wesley.

Blake, Robert R. and Jane S. Mouton (1964). *The Managerial Grid*. Houston: Gulf Publishing.

Blake, Robert R. (1966). "Managerial Facades," *Advanced Management Journal*, July:pp 29–36.

Blake, Robert R. and Jane S. Mouton (1978). "What's New with the Grid?" *Training and Development Journal*, May:pp 3–8.

Bowers, David G. and Stanley E. Seashore (1966). "Predicting Organizational Effectiveness with a Four-Factory Theory of Leadership," *Administrative Science Quarterly*, Vol. ll, No. 2. pp 238–263.

Bratton, D. L. (1983). "The Rating of Presidents," *Presidential Studies Quarterly*, 13:pp 400–404.

Brayfield, Arthur H. and Walter H. Crockett (1955). "Employee Attitudes and Employee Performances," *Psychological Bulletin*, 52(5):pp 396–426.

Burgers, Sherry B. (1980). "An Examination of the Use of Contracts in Groups," *The Journal for Specialists in Group Work*, pp 68–72.

Burns, James MacGregor (1979). *Leadership*. New York: Harper & Row Publishers.

Butterfield, D. A. and G. F. Farris (1974). "The Likert Organizational Profile: Methodological Analysis and Test of System 4 Theory in Brazil," *Journal of Applied Psychology*, 59(1):pp 15–23.

Campbell, John P. and Marvin D. Dunnett (1968). "Effectiveness of T-Group Experiences in Managerial Training and Development," *Psychological Bulletin*, 70(2):pp 73–104.

Carroll, Paul (1994). *Big Blues: The Unmaking of IBM*. New York: Crown Publishers Inc.

Cartwright, D. and A. Zander (1960). *Group Dynamics: Research and Theory*, 2nd ed. Evanston, Ill.: Row, Peterson.

Chemers, Martin M. and Roya Ayman (1993). *Leadership Theory and Research*. San Diego, California: Academic Press.

Csoka, L. S. (1974). "A Relationship Between Leader Intelligence and Leader Rated Effectiveness," *Journal of Applied Psychology*, 59(1):pp 43–47.

Davis, Tim R. and Fred Luthans (1984). "Defining and Researching Leadership as a Behavioral Construct: An Idiographic Approach," *The Journal of Applied Behavioral Science*. 20:pp 237–251.

Dubin, Robert, G. C. Homans, F. C. Mann, and D. C. Miller (1965). *Leadership and Productivity*, San Francisco: Chandler.

Efran, Jay S., Dennis Goldsmith, Peter J. McFarland, III, and Bonnet Short (1979). "The Effect on Endurance of a Verbal Commitment vs. Exhortation, Task Information and Monetary Incentives," *Motivation and Emotion*, 3(1):pp 93–101.

Evans, M. G. (1970). "The Effect of Supervisory Behavior on the Path-Goal Relationship," *Organizational Behavior and Human Performance*, 5:pp 277–298.

Evans, M. G. (1974). "Effects of Supervisory Behaviors on Extension a Path-Goal Theory of Motivation," *Journal of Applied Psychology*, 59 (April):pp 172–178.

Fayol, H. (1916). *Industrial and General Administration*. Paris: Dunod.

Fiedler, Fred E. (1965). "Engineer the Job to Fit the Manager," *Harvard Business Review*, 43(5):pp. 155–122.

Fiedler, Fred E. (1967). *Theory of Leadership Effectiveness*. New York: McGraw Hill.

Fiedler, Fred E. (1969). "Style or Circumstance: The Leadership Enigma," in *Psychology Today*; reprinted in W. E. Natemeyer, (ed.), *Classics of Organizational Behavior*. Oak Park, Ill.: Moore:pp 210–216.

Fiedler, Fred E. (1974). "The Contingency Model-New Directions for Leadership Utiliza tion," *Journal of Contemporary Business*, 3(4):pp. 65–79.

Fiedler, Fred E. and Martin Chemers (1974). *Leadership and Effective Management*. Glenview, Ill.: Scott, Foreman.

Fiedler, Fred E. (1976). "The Leadership Game: Matching the Man to the Situation," *Organizational Dynamics*, 4(3):pp 6–16.

Fiedler, Fred E. and Linda Mahar (1979). "A Field Experiment Violating Contingency Model Leadership Training," *Journal of Applied Psychology*, 6(3):pp 247–254.

Fielder, Fred E., Earl H. Butler, Mitchel M. Zais, and William A. Knowlton, Jr. (1979). "Organizational Stress and the Use and Misuse of Managerial Intelligence and Experience," *Journal of Applied Psychology*, 6(6):pp 635–647.

Field, G. (1982). "A Test of the Vroom-Yetton Mormative Model of Leadership," *Journal of Applied Psychology*, 67:pp 523–532.

Fleishman, Edwin A. (1953). "The Description of Supervisory Behavior," *Journal of Applied Psychology*, 37:pp 1–6.

Fleishman, Edwin A., E. F. Harris, and H. E. Burt (1955). *Leadership and Supervision in Industry*. Columbus: Ohio State University Bureau of Educational Research.

Fleishman, E. and D. R. Peters (1962). "Interpersonal Values, Leadership Attitudes, and Management 'Success'," *Personnel Psychology*, 15(2):pp 127–143.

Gemmill and Judith Oakley (1992). "Leadership: An Alienating Social Myth?," *Human Relations*, 45(2):pp 113–129.

Gibb, C. A. (1947). "The Principles and Traits of Leadership," *Journal of Abnormal Psychology*, 42:pp 267–284.

Graen, G. (1969). "Instrumentality Theory of Work Motivation: Some Experimental Results and Suggested Modifications," *Journal of Applied Psychology Monograph*, 53:pp 1–25.

Graen, G., K. Alvares, and J. Orris (1970). "Contingency Model of Leadership Effectiveness: Antecedent and Evidential Results," *Psychological Bulletin*, 74:pp 285–296.

Greene, Charles N. and Chester A. Schrieshein (1980). "Leader-Group Interactions: A Longitudinal Field Investigation," *Journal of Applied Psychology*, 65(1):pp 250–259.

Greller, Martin M. (1980). "Evaluation of Feedback Sources as a Function of Role and Organizational Level," *Journal of Applied Psychology*, 65(1):pp 24–27.

Halpin, A. W. (1954). "The Leadership Behavior and Combat Performance of Airplane Commanders," *Journal of Abnormal and Social Psychology*, 49:pp 19–22.

Hater J. J. and Bernard M. Bass (1988). "Supervisors' Evaluation and Subordinates' Perceptions of Transformational and Transactional Leadership," *Journal of Applied Psychology*, Novemeber:pp 695–702.

Hemphill, J. K. (1954). "A Proposed Theory of Leadership in Small Groups," Columbus: The Ohio State University, Personnel Research Board Technical Report.

Hersey, Paul and K. A. Blanchard (1967). *Leader Behavior*. Management Education and Development, Inc.

Hersey, Paul, Alan C. Filley, and Steven Kerr (1971). "Relation of Leader Consideration and Initiating Structure to R & D Subordinates Satisfaction," *Administrative Science Quarterly*, 16:pp 19–30.

Hersey, Paul, and Terence R. Mitchell (1974). "Path-Goal Theory of Leadership," *Journal of Contemporary Business*, 3(4):pp 81–97.

Hersey, Paul and Kenneth H. Blanchard (1979). "Life Cycle Theory of Leadership," *Training and Development Journal*, June:pp 94–100.

Hersey, Paul and Kenneth H. Blanchard (1980). "The Management Change," *Training and Development Journal*, 34(6):pp 80–98.

Hersey, Paul (1988). *Management of Organization Behavior*, Englewood Cliffs, N.J.: Prentice Hall.

Hofstede, Geerte (1980). "Motivation, Leadership and Organization: Do American Theories Apply Abroad?" *Organizational Dynamics*, 9(1):pp 42–63.

House, R. J. (1971). "A Path-Goal Theory of Leader Effectiveness," *Administrative Science Quarterly*, 16:pp. 321–338.

House, R. J., and Terence R. Mitchell (1974). "Path-Goal Theory of Leadership," *Journal of Contemporary Business*, 3(4):pp 81–97.

Isenberg, David J. (1984). "How Senior Managers Think," *Harvard Business Review*. Nov/Dec:pp 81–90.

Jago, Arthur and James W. Ragan (1986). "The Trouble with Leader Match is that it Doesn't Match Fiedler's Contingency Model." *Journal of Applied Psychology*, 71:pp 555–559.

Jermier, J. M. and L. J. Berkes (1979). "Leader Behavior in a Police Command Bureaucracy: A Closer Look at the Quasi-Military Model," *Administrative Science Quarterly*, 24 (1):pp 1–23.

Johns, Gary (1978). "Task Moderators of the Relationship Between Leadership Style and Subordinate Responses," *Academy of Management Journal*, (June):pp 319–325.

Kabanoff, Boris and Gordon E. O'Brien (1979). "Cooperative Structure and the Relationship of Leader and Member Ability to Group Performance," *Journal of Applied Psychology*, 64(5):pp 526–532.

Kahn, R. L. and D. Katz (1953). "Leadership Practices in Relation to Productivity and Morale," in D. Cartwright and A. Zander (eds.), *Group Dynamics*, Evanston, Ill.: Row, Peterson.

Kahn, Robert L. (1956). "The Prediction of Productivity," *Journal of Social Issues*, 12:pp 41–49.

Kanter, Rosabeth Moss (1977). *Men and Women of the Corporation*. New York: Basic Books.

Katz, Daniel and R. L. Kahn (1951). "Human Organization and Worker Motivation," in L. R. Tripp (ed.), *Industrial Productivity*, Madison: Wisc.: Industrial Relations Research Association:pp 146–171.

Kessel, John H. (1984). "The Structure of the Reagan White House," *American Journal of Political Science*, 28:(May):pp 231–258.

Kirkpatick, Shelly A. and Edwin A. Locke (1991) "Leadership: Do Traits Matter?" *Academy of Management Executive*. May:pp 48–60.

Klimoski, Richard J. and Noreen J. Hayes (1980). "Leadership Behavior and Subordinate Motivation," *Personnel Psychology*, 33(3):pp 543–556.

Knight, Patrick A. and Howard M. Weiss (1980). "Effects of Selection Agent and Leader Origin or Leader Influence on Group Member Perceptions," *Organizational Behavior and Human Performance*, 26(1):pp 7–21.

Kochran, Thomas and Michael Useem (1992). *Transforming Organizations*. New York: Oxford University Press.

Kouzes James M. and Barry Z. Posner (1990). *The Leadership Challenge: How to Get Things Done in Organizations*. San Franscisco, California: Jossey Bass Publishers.

Lawler, Edward, III and Lyman Porter (1967). "The Effect of Performance on Job Satisfaction," *Industrial Relations*, 7(1):pp 20–25.

Lawler, Edward, III (1992). *The Ultimate Advantage: Creating the High Involvement Organization*. San Franscisco, California: Jossey Bass, Publishers.

Lewin, Kurt, Ronald Lippitt, and Ralph K. White (1939). "Patterns of Aggressive Behavior in Experimentally Created Social Climates," *Journal of Social Psychology*, 10:pp 271–299.

Lewin, Kurt (1947). "Frontiers in Group Dynamics," *Human Relations*, 1(1):pp 5–41.

Likert, Rensis (1961). *New Patterns of Management*, New York: McGraw Hill.

Likert, Rensis (1967). *The Human Organization* New York: McGraw Hill.

Lord, Robert G., Christy L. DeVader, and George M. Alliger (1986). "A Meta-Analysis of the Relation Between Personality Traits and Leadership Perceptions: An Application of Validity Generalization Procedures," *Journal of Applied Psychology*, 71:pp 402–410.

Lord, R. G. (1985). "Social Information Processing and Behavioral Measurement: Application to Leadership Measurement," in B. M. Straw and L. L. Cummings (eds.), *Research in Organizational Behavior*. Greenwich, Ct: JAI Press, pp 87–128.

Lowin, A. and J. R. Craig (1968). "The Influence of Performance on Managerial Style: An Experimental Object-Lesson in the Ambiguity of Correlational Data," *Organizational Behavior and Human Performance*, 3:pp 440–458.

Luthans, Fred and Robert Kreitner (1985). *Organizational Behavior Modification*. (2nd ed.), Glenview, Ill.: Scott, Foresman.

Luthans, Fred and R. A. Kreitner (1984). "A Social Learning Approach to Management: Radical Behaviorists 'Mellowing Out'" *Organizational Dynamics*. Autumn:pp 47–65.

Luthans, Fred and Todd I. Stewart (1977). "A General Contingency Theory of Management," *Academy of Management Review*, 2(2):pp 181–195.

Maccoby, Michael (1976). *The Gamesman*. New York: Simon and Schuster.

Mann, Floyd C. and James K. Dent (1954). "Appraisals of Supervisors and the Attitudes of Their Employees in an Electric Power Company," Ann Arbor, Michigan: Institute for Social Research.

Marrow, Alfred J., David G. Bowers, and Stanley E. Seashore (1967). *Management by Participation*. New York: Harper & Row.

Maslow, Abraham (1954), *Motivation and Personality*. 2nd (ed.), (1970). New York: Harper & Row.

McGregor, Douglas (1960). *The Human Side of Enterprise*. New York: McGraw Hill.

Mills, Carol J. and Wayne E. Bohannon (1980). "Personality, Characteristics of Effective State Police Officers," *Journal of Applied Psychology*, 65(6):pp 680–684.

Mintzberg, Henry (1975). *The Nature of Managerial Work*. New York: Harper & Row.

Morse, Nancy C. and E. Reimer (1956). "The Experimental Change of a Major Organizational Variable," *Journal of Abnormal and Social Psychology*, 52:pp 120–129.

Motowidlo, Stephan J. (1980). "Effects of Traits and States Subjective Probability of Task Success and Performance," *Motivation and Emotion*, 4(3):pp 247–262.

Nebeker, D. M., and T. R. Mitchell (1974). "Leader Behavior: An Expectancy Theory Approach," *Organizational Behavior and Human Performance*, 11:pp 355–367.

Northrop, Alana and James L. Perry (1985). "A Task Enviroment Approach to Organizational Assessment," *Public Administration Review*, 45:pp 275–281.

Patton, A. (1985). "Those Million Dollar a Year Executives." *Harvard Business Review*, Jan/Feb:pp 56–61.

Peters, Lawrence, Darrell D. Hartke, and John T. Pohlmann (1985). "Fiedler's Contingency Theory of Leadership: An Application of the Meta-Analysis Procedures of Schmidt and Hunter," *Psychological Bulletin*, 97:pp 274–285.

Porter, L. W. and E. E. Lawler (1968). *Managerial Attitudes and Performance*. Homewood, Ill.: Irwin Dorsey.

Price, James L. (1968). *Organizational Effectiveness*. Homewood, Ill.: Irwin Dorsey.

Radin, Beryl A. (1980). "Leadership Training for Women in State and Local Government," *Public Personnel Management*, 9(2):pp 52–60.

Reddin, William J. (1967). "The 3–D Management Style Theory," *Training and Development Journal*, (April):pp 8–17.

Roethlisberger, F. J. (1941). *Management and Morale*, Cambridge, Massachusetts: Harvard University Press.

Sales, S. M. (1966). "Supervisory Style and Productivity: Review and Theory," *Personnel Psychology*, 19:pp 275–286.

Sank, L. (1974). "Effective and Ineffective Managerial Traits Obtained in Naturalistic Descriptions from Executive Menders from a Super-Corporation," *Personnel Psychology*, 19:pp 275–286.

Segriovanni, T. J. (1992). *Moral Leadership: Getting to the Heart of School Improvement*. San Franscisco, Califronia: Jossey Bass Publishers.

Scanlon, Burt K. (1979). "Managerial Leadership in Perspective: Getting Back to the Basics," Personnel Journal, (March):pp 165–171.

Schneier, Craig E. (1978). "The Contingency Model of Leadership: An Extension to Emergent Leadership and Leader's Sex," *Organizational Behavior and Human Performance*, 21:pp 220–239.

Schrieshein, J. and C. A. Schrieschein (1980). "A Test of the Path-Goal Theory of Leadership and Some Suggested Directions for Future Research." *Personnel Psychology*, 33:pp 349–370.

Schrieshein and Sikers (1977). "Theories and Measures of Leadership: A Critical Appraisal of Current and Future Directions," in J. G. Hunt and L. Larson, (eds.), Leadership: The Cutting Edge, Carbondale: Southern Illinois University Press.

Schrieshein (1980). "The Social Context of Leader-Subordinate Relations: An Investigation of the Effects of Group Cohesiveness," *Journal of Applied Psychology*, 65(2):pp 183–194.

Shartle, Carroll L. (1979). "The Early Years of the Ohio State University Leadership Studies," *Journal of Management*, 5(2):pp 127–134.

Sims, Henry P. and Charles C. Manz (1984). *Journal of Applied Psychology*, 69:pp 222–232.

Slater, Phillip E. and Warren G. Bennis (1964). "Democracy is Inevitable," *Harvard Business Review* (March–April):pp 1–26.

Starr, Barry M. and Terry Ross (1980). "Commitment in an Experimenting Society: A Study of the Attribution of Leadership from Administrative Scenarios," *Journal of Applied Psychology*, 65(3):pp 249–260.

Stockton, Rex (1980). "The Education of Group Leaders: A Review of the Literature," *Journal for Specialists in Group Work*, 5(2):pp 55–62.

Stogdill, R. M. (1948). "Personal Factors Associated with Leadership: A Survey of the Literature," *Journal of Psychology*, 25:pp. 35–71.

Stogdill, R. M., and A. E. Coons (1957). "Leader Behavior: Its Description and Measurement," Columbus, Ohio: Bureau of Business Research, Ohio State University.

Stogdill, R. M. (1974). *Handbook of Leadership*. New York: Free Press.

Swede, S. W. and Philip E. Tetlock (1986). "Henry Kissinger's Implicit Theory of Personality: A Quantitative Case Study." *Journal of Personality*, 54:pp 617–646.

Trowbridge, Alexander B. (1985). "Thinking Ahead: Attracting the Best to Washington," *Harvard Business Review*, March–April:pp 174–178.

Vecchio, Robert P. (1979). "A Dyadic Interpretation of the Contingency Model of Leadership Effectiveness," *Academy of Management Journal*, 22(3):pp 590–600.

Vroom, Victor (1964). *Work and Motivation*. New York: Wiley.

Vroom, Victor and P. W. Yetten (1973). *Leadership and Decision-Making*. Pittsburgh: University of Pittsburgh.

Vroom, Victor (1976). "Can Leaders Learn to Lead?" *Organizational Dynamics*, 4(3):pp 17–28.

Vroom, Victor and Arthur G. Jago (1978). "On the Validity of the Vroom-Yetten Model," *Journal of Applied Psychology*, (April):pp 151–162.

Weisbord, M. R.(1987). *Productive Workplaces: Organizing and Managing for Dignity, Meaning, and Community*. San Franscisco California: Jossey Bass Publishers.

Wofford, J. C. (1967). "Behavior Styles and Performance Effectiveness," *Personnel Psychology*, 20:pp 461–496.

Wofford, J. C. (1970). "Managerial Behavior, Situational Factors, and Productivity and Morale," *Administrative Science Quarterly*, 16:pp 10–17.

Wooford, J. C. and L. Z. Liska (1993). "Path-Goal Theories of Leadership: A Meta-Analysis," *Journal of Management*. Winter:pp. 857–876.

Yeager, Samuel T., Jack Rabin, and Thomas Vocino (1985). "Feedback and Administrative Behaviour in the Public Sector," *Public Administration Review*, 45(5):pp 570–575.

Young, Frank and John A. Norris (1988). "Leadership Change and Action: Planning a Case Study," *Public Administration Review*, 48:pp 564–570.

Yukl, Gary A. (1989). *Leaders in Organizations*. Englewood Cliffs, N.J.: Prentice Hall.

Yukl, Gary A. and D. D. Van Fleet, (1992) "Theory and Research on Leadership in Organizations," in M. D. Dunnette and L. M. Hough (eds.) *Handbook of Industrial and Organizational Psychology*, 2nd ed. 3., Palo Alto, CA: Consulting Psychologists Press.

Zaleznik, Abraham (1977). "Managers and Leaders: Are They Different?" *Harvard Business Review* (May–June): reprinted in J. L. Gibson, J. M. Ivancevich, and J. H. Donnelly, (eds.), *Readings in Organizations*, 2nd ed., Dallas: Business Publications, 1979, pp 158–175.

Zelditch, M. (1955). "Role Differentiation in the Nuclear Family: A Comparative Study," in T. Partsons, R. E. Bales, et al., (eds.), *Family Socialization and Interaction Process*, Glencoe, Ill.: Free Press.

5

Role Behavior:
Individuals and Groups

Managerial leadership, discussed in Chapter 4, depends critically on the ability of the manager to recognize, understand, utilize, and possibly change the patterns of behavior characteristic of the agency's employees. The behaviors of employees are influenced by both the *formal organization* and the *informal organization.*

The formal organization is visually expressed in the *organizational chart.* The organizational chart reflects the choices made by the organization with respect to how job tasks are formally divided, grouped, and subsequently coordinated (Pinchot and Pinchot, 1994). The organizational chart, in effect, outlines the essential structure of organizational communication and work specialization. The formal organization also represents choices made about the division of labor (who does what!), chain of command (who reports to whom!), and span of control (how many people report to a given person!). In addition, the organizational chart reflects the agencies' preference for various aspects of *organizational design* (Pasmore, 1994). Finally, the formal organization also establishes a hierarchy of authority by assigning formal roles to individuals within organizations, for example, Director of Human Resources. The *informal organization* is a "parallel organization" to the formal organization. It exists in every organizational setting. It is the interpersonal organization that workers create among themselves. Various aspects of the informal organization were described in Chapter 2 in our review of the Hawthorne studies. Informal roles exist in the informal organization as well, one such role is "opinion leader."

Roles are behaviors expected of people occupying a given position in an organizational setting. Behaviors become routinized over a period of time, allowing them to become anticipated by the manager and other organizational members. Such established behavior patterns are reinforced positively or negatively by sanctions applied by the manager or the informal work group. Organizational roles create expectations for employees in that they define how others

123

believe one should act in a given situation. For example, we expect police not to consider the socioeconomic status of a motorist about to receive a ticket. Organizational roles can cause role conflict when an individual is confronted by divergent role expectations, as in the case of a city manager who is pressured to hire the third candidate on the list by an elected council member, who is also head of the town's budget committee. Role management is an essential aspect of the administrative function in the public sector as well as the private. As we said previously, role management requires the public manager to consider both the formal and informal organization.

> One of the best ways to comprehend the idea of a *formal organization* is to think of it as a *script* that has to be thoroughly understood by the director (manager) before the actors (employees) are given their roles to play. The script of a formal organization will include, among other things, the purpose, the functional roles that must be assigned to the actors, the coordination of the interactions between the roles, the nature of the different types of work to be performed, and the status accorded to the different work roles by the actors or the audience (the public). The background in which the play takes place must be known, as must the immediate setting. The types of people to play the parts plus the character, attitudes, and experiences are also important.

> If you are a competent director, you will be able to hire the actors, train them in your particular interpretation of the script, and see that the performance of the play achieves the purposes of the script and provides satisfaction to the actors. Under these conditions, the formal organization (script) and the *human organization* (actors) are compatible and well integrated. This condition can be achieved only when the director has carefully developed, shaped, and perhaps rewritten the script and the setting so the performance can be predicted. In other terms, management can design the work, control the environment in which it takes place, and shape the human organization so that high productivity will result from the achievement of the purposes of both the organization and the people. If management does not do this, a possibly serious consequence is that the actors will spontaneously create and control their own human organization, which may not have the type of climate conducive to high productivity. It may even have an anti-organizational bias to the formal system (Shani and Lau, 1996).

Role management is one expression of the management control function; that is, the process by which organizations insure that its subunits act in a coordinated fashion to achieve overall organizational goals (Lebas and Weigenstein, 1986). In fact, organization power itself, the power to control the behavior of others toward the realization of specific goals, has its basis in obedience to roles (Biggart and Hamilton, 1984; Robinson et al., 1994). Most human behavior is learned through modeling. This is no less true of many behaviors specific to management. For example, it is estimated that about 85% of potential leadership behavior is learned through a modeling approach in which the leader serves as the role model. Consequently, a basic understanding of roles is important to students of organizations.

There are many types of roles. Two broad dimensions divide roles into functional and cultural roles. Functional roles include patterns based on administrative task or function. For example, there are roles associated with the traditional administrative functions of planning, organizing, staffing, directing, coordinating, reporting, and budgeting. Benne and Sheats (1948) set forth ten such roles:

I. TASK ROLES

1. *Seeking* information and data
2. *Giving* information and data
3. *Initiating* ideas, proposals, concepts, or plans
4. *Clarifying* ideas, proposals, concepts, or plans
5. *Coordinating* group ideas, proposals, concepts, or plans
6. *Orienting* the group toward goal-achievement
7. *Establishing* outside contacts for the group (a gatekeeper role)

II. GROUP-MAINTAINING AND GROUP-BUILDING ROLES

8. *Supporting* participation of all group members
9. *Encouraging* compromise and harmonizing viewpoints
10. *Reducing* tension (e.g., through humor)

Likewise, Mintzberg has put forward a different set of ten: interpersonal roles (figurehead, leader, liaison), informational roles (monitor, disseminator, spokesman), and decisional roles (entrepreneur, disturbance handler, resource allocator, negotiator). As with the Ohio State studies of leadership, there is some evidence these functional roles may be reduced to those which are relationship-centered (e.g., liaison, disseminator, spokesperson, figurehead) and those which are task/decision-oriented (e.g., monitor, disturbance handler, resource allocator, negotiator) (see Shapira and Dunbar, 1980). The second dimension involves *cultural roles*, such as those based on nationality, race, or sex. For example, Hofstede (1980, p. 59) has found that decision-making roles vary by nationality. In effect, cross-cultural research suggests that national culture is itself a contingency variable in many management related behaviors (Cooper and Robertson, 1990). Studies of cultural roles within a given nation, in contrast, have found fewer administrative differences. Lefkowitz and Fraser (1980), for instance, found no differences between blacks and whites on need for achievement and need for power, controlling for education. Similarly, a variety of studies have found few gender related differences with respect to such dimensions as competitiveness, motivation, decision-making, or analytical skills (Powell, 1988). Muldrow and Bayton (1979) found no differences by sex on any of six decision task variables studied. Weaver (1980) found no sex differences in job satisfaction. Schneier and Bartol (1980) found no sex differences on group performance or on a variety of sociometric and interaction analysis measures. Sadd (1979) found femininity was not related to fear of success, self-deprecation, or insecurity as is sometimes alleged. Research suggests that there has been in the past a tendency to overestimate the differences between the sexes while ignoring the similarities. Nonetheless, the role of women managers in the work place is difficult. Long held role conceptions associate management with stereotypical masculine behaviors and traits. According to Camden (1983), women managers are in a double bind. If they behave in a stereotypical female role they are judged less effective in their role as managers. Yet, their management style conforms to male norms, they are also negatively perceived in terms of social image. In an interesting article, "Managing Women: A Man's View," Cardwell (1985) argues that male managers of female subordinates tend to view the management relationship as competitive. They also do not effectively distinguish the management relationship they have with females from their cultural view of sex roles. He states that men and women must be aware that many of their management relationships are conditioned by reactions to sex differences.

More recently, Helgesen (1990) did a case study of the strategies and organizational behaviors of four very successful female executives in which she indicates that while there may be no differences in the managerial skills of men and women, there are differences in philosophy and style which may in fact stem from female cultural roles.

> While doing the diary studies, I became aware that the women, when describing their own organizations, usually referred to themselves as being in the middle of things. Not at the top, but in the center; not reaching down, but reaching out. The expressions were spontaneous, part of the women's language, indicating unconscious notions about what was desirable and good. Inseparable from their sense of themselves as being in the middle was the women's notion of being connected to those around them, bound as if by invisible strands or threads. This image of interrelated structure, built around a strong central point and constructed of radials and orbs, quite naturally made me think of a spider's web-that delicate tracery, compounded of the need for survival and the impulse of art, whose purpose is to draw other creatures to it (Helgesen, 1990, p. 46).

There is little doubt that understanding cultural roles will become very important to public managers in the next decade. For example, *Workforce 2000*, projections indicate significant changes in the composition of both the public and the private workforce (Johnson and Packer, 1987). The most important finding of this study is the significantly higher representation by women, minorities, and immigrants relative to white males. Clearly, an understanding of the diversity perspective in the workplace is imperative.[1]

Any given employee will hold a variety of roles, each with its own set of sanctioned expectations. In addition to cultural roles such as being a woman, an African American, or a member of the social upper class, one may hold various functional roles such as being the quality controller, union steward, or simply the person who organizes the agency's social events. From the point of view of the administrator, managing the many roles of many employees, four general questions arise. First, why do people conform to roles, how are roles perceived, and when is conformity most likely or useful? Second, how does role conflict occur and what are its consequences? Third, how do role conformity and role conflict affect the emergence within the agency of an informal organization parallel to the formal structure? And last, when informal roles and organizations are incompatible with formal and necessary functions, how can role change occur? The remainder of this chapter is organized around these four general questions.

ROLE CONFORMITY

Although conformity is often disparaged, organizations could not hold together without it. The inducement of rewards and the force of authority are powerful motivators but no organization can function effectively unless its members share widespread acceptance of and conformity to organizational roles. Social order depends on actors sustaining a particular definition of reality, and in organizations, the structure of roles is an important part of the structure of meaning (Biggart and Hamilton, 1984, p. 548). Role conformity is intrinsic to bureaucratic organization because without it the separation of roles from personalities would be impossible. Role conformity is predicated on *norms* or acceptable standards of behavior. Norms outline what an individual should do in a given situation. When agreed to and accept by a group, norms are a very powerful form of behavioral control. Norms are the basis of role conformity and while norms may differ all groups have them (Hackman, 1992).

Interestingly, there is strong laboratory research evidence that underscores the pressures for conformity in human beings. In a now classic study Asch (1952), asked groups of subjects to compare two cards held by the experimenter. On card one was a single line of a given length, on a second card (card two) there were three lines of varying lengths. One of these three lines on card two was identical to the line on card one, the other two lines were clearly of different lengths. These lengths were sufficiently different from each other that, under normal conditions, subjects made less than one percent errors. The objective of the experiment was for the subjects to match the line on card one to the one that was identical in length on card two, a relatively easy task of visual perception!

Asch wanted to test the impact of group pressure on conformity, so he set up an experiment in which he got about seven "confederates" all of them, one after another, when asked which line on the second card (A, B, C) was most like the one on the first card, to give the wrong answer! In other words, they did not choose the line of equal length (assume it was line A) but one that was clearly wrong (assume it was line B). When the unsuspecting subject was asked (always last after the confederates had responded) which line on card two matched the one on card one in approximately 35% of the cases the unsuspecting subject went along with the wrong answer, that is, the answer given by the group. The results of this and other experiments suggests a strong human tendency to go along with group pressures for conformity. Asch (1952) and other (Weiner, 1958) showed that such a tendency toward conformity was most likely when the subject matter (dependent variable) was ambiguous. From a management perspective it is perhaps fortunate that powerful forces to conform exist in the work group. Management related areas characterized by high ambiguity include such matters as perceived promotion criteria and behaviors thought instrumental to promotion, policies of political leadership of the agency and behaviors thought consistent with these, or work team norms and associated behaviors.

Organizational continuity in the face of personnel turnover, in fact, depends on efficient socialization of new organizational members to dominant values, procedures, and social orientations of the agency. In other words, organizational continuity relies on pressures toward role and group conformity. This conformity is the basis of the socialization to agency norms. These norms, expressed in prescribed roles for newly recruited personnel are critical to both individual and organizational success. For example, one study focusing on the roles of California state government officials under different administrations, Governor Ronald Reagan (1967–1975) and Governor Jerry Brown (1975–1983), found that role conformity was imperative for a person to "get things done." The converse was also true; those who stepped outside the normative bounds of their role lost effectiveness and power. Two of the roles the authors compared were that of California Executive Assignees (CEAs), an elite civil service corps modeled on the Senior Executive Service in the federal government, and administrative appointees. CEAs were expected to behave according to the dictates of political neutrality. In other words, their actions were supposed to be those of dispassionate professionals. Political appointees, on the other hand, were expected to pursue the agenda of the governor. Conformity to these prescribed role definitions was expected in both administrations:

> Administrative appointees are in charge of substantial bureaucratic units; they are expected to manage without direct supervision by the governor, but keep the administration's political philosophy in mind as they establish programs and make decisions. Cabinet officers often describe themselves as

member's of the governor's "team," doing their part in a larger effort. Acting idiosyncratically and failing to subordinate their decisions to the governor's ideas opened them to charges of disloyalty. For example, one of Reagan's cabinet officers was seen as too liberal on social issues. According to one staff member, his decisions were "not in line with the Governor's thinking." As a consequence, the staff tried to isolate the cabinet officer's influence among other appointees and reduce the range of discretionary decisions that he could make (Biggart and Hamilton, 1984, p. 545).

The CEAs by contrast were expected to play the role of neutral expert and not appear to be a member of the Governor's team. Those who became too closely associated with the agenda of the administration, that is violated the dictates of their role, suffered the consequences:

> CEAs, who are expected to be apolitical experts, may violate the standards of their role in two ways. First, they may adopt the political orientation of the administration in power. Politicized CEAs were seen as toadies and not invited to work with the next administration. Second, CEAs, all of whom have risen through the ranks of civil service, may fail to give genuine assistance to the administration in power because they disapprove of the administration's policies toward favored programs. Such departmentalists are replaced with CEA's willing to work in support of the governor's ends (Biggart and Hamilton, 1984, p. 545).

Understanding the impact of a role and the perception by others in the organization of people occupying that role is also important to public managers. In an interesting experiment focused on person perception, the *same* individual was introduced differently in each of five British university classes. After the individual left, the class was asked to estimate his height. The height estimates for each of the classes was different and ranged from a low estimate of approximately 5 feet nine to a high of over six feet tall. These differences in the estimates between the classes were all statistically significant; from a probability perspective it was very unlikely to have been the result of random sampling error. What was interesting was how the stranger (the same individual) was introduced to each of these classes. The stranger was introduced in the first class as (1) Mr. Jones, a Cambridge student, (2) then as Mr. Jones, a teaching assistant, (3) then Mr. Jones, a lecturer, (4) then Dr. Jones, a senior lecturer, and (5) then Professor Jones from Cambridge. The groups' estimates of Jones's height increased in each of the five classes progressively, in direct proportion to the increased status evident in his role, for example, lecturer vs. professor (Wilson, 1968). In other words, the roles that organizational actors have influence both the perception and expectations that others have of them. Consequently, the study of roles and role conformity is important to the study of public management. It is important for a number of reasons, not the least of which is the desire to develop a sense of professionalism in public administration (Rabin, 1984).

While the tendency to conform is a powerful force and while it is operative in many management-related areas, it is more pronounced for some individuals and for some situations than for others. Conformity is greatest when agency members:

> belong to a cohesive group (Lott and Lott, 1965)
> believe others in the group are successful and competent
> expect to remain in the group
> are highly motivated upon entrance into the group (Schein, 1956),
> are themselves authoritarian in personality (Nadler, 1959)
> are dealing with issues outside their own specialty (Raia and Osipow, 1970)
> are less intelligent (Bass et al., 1953)

The prototypical profile of a high-conformity situation would thus be one in which an authoritarian person of low self-confidence joins an organization which he or she has intensely desired to join and with which he or she expects to remain. The organization is composed of a close-knit group of individuals who are competent and successful. The new member may be of lower intelligence or be dealing with issues outside those of his or her main talent. In such a situation conformity is highly predictable. Such extremes are not necessary for conformity, however. Because of the dynamics of conformity and exclusion, almost all individuals conform most of the time to most organizational expectations.

THE DYNAMICS OF CONFORMITY AND EXCLUSION

Conformity to group norms starts even before joining the organization. Anticipatory socialization is the process by which the individual takes on the characteristics of the group to which he or she aspires. Graduate students may begin to attend professional meetings, management aspiring employees may start wearing suits to work, or new intellectual and social interests may be fostered in imitation of the culture of the group into which the organization member seeks to rise.

Organization selection processes may complement anticipatory socialization. The organization may become biased toward recruitment of individuals of the "right type," seeking individuals who will "fit in." Through training, apprenticeship, or mentoring (Johnson, 1980), the organization seeks to socialize selected employees into desired roles. For example, one study on mentoring found that executives at all levels of government who reported having mentors indicated that they were more satisfied with their careers, were more willing to move for their careers, and were more apt to have defined career plans than those who did not have a mentor (Henderson, 1985). There is also evidence that the role of mentor may be particularly important to women in government and the mentor relationship for women involves more complexity and needs to be approached more systematically (Vertz, 1985).

Caplow (1964) has noted that the overall socialization process in organizations may involve four distinct steps:

1. acquiring a new self-image which reflects organizational norms
2. acquiring new relationships and abandoning those dissonant with the organization
3. adopting new values which reflect organizational goals
4. adopting new modes of behavior which conform to organizational norms.

By taking on the behaviors of the organization, the individual is simply living up to expectations. This is the "Pygmalion effect," whereby subordinates commonly take on positive or negative behaviors according to the expectations of superiors (Rosenthal and Jacobson, 1968).

Whenever an individual joins an organization he or she enters into a sort of psychological contract (see Levinson et al., 1962; Robinson et al., 1994). In this contract the individual's conformity to organizational expectations is exchanged for the benefits of belonging. Those who accept the contract involved in job offers are more likely to do so if the interviewer emphasizes the personal career interest of belonging (Aldefer and Cord, 1970). When organizational realities like pay, conditions, and recognition are close to what was contracted for, individuals are more likely to stay on in the organization (Dunnett et al., 1973). Violations of this psychological contract expressed in the form of role ambiguity have been found to be related to stress in the individual (Posner and Posner, 1986).

Just as the psychological contract involves expectations by the individual, it also involves organizational expectations of the individual (Robinson et al., 1994). "A price," de la Porte has explained, "is set for admission and recognition in the form of certain values and rules of behavior to be respected by group members at all times" (de la Porte, 1974). For example, in *Men and Women of the Corporation* (1977), Kanter found "A tremendous value was placed on team membership and getting along with peers; 'peer acceptance' was considered a factor in promotions while 'individual performers' were generally not promoted" (Kanter, 1977). Organizations may regard many behaviors as relevant and appropriate for conforming behavior but only some will be regarded as pivotal. In these areas strong sanctions emerge against nonconformity (Schein, 1970). Such pivotal behavioral norms were found to cluster in ten areas by de la Porte (1974):

1. organizational pride
2. performance
3. cost-effectiveness
4. teamwork
5. planning
6. supervision
7. training and development
8. innovation
9. customer relations
10. honesty and security

All organizational members who deviate from pivotal group norms will be subject to sanction. Sanction typically begins with receipt of increased communication directed toward encouraging conformity (Schacter, 1951; Schacter, 1959; Emerson, 1954; Berkowitz and Howard, 1959). Continuation of nonconformity after this initial stage will bring escalating sanctions eventually leading to rejection from the group in most instances (Festinger, 1950; Sampson and Brandon, 1964).

Again, experimental evidence suggests strong consequences for rejection of group norms. In a classic study, Schachter (1951) conducted a series of labratory experiments focused on small group reaction toward individuals who took unchanging positions in opposition to the majority positions of a group. In each experimental group, he placed a confederates (stooges) who played different roles at his direction. There were three roles, one role required the confederate to agree with the majority position of the group, the second role called the slider, initially required the confederate to take a position opposite to the majority position, but, then to modify that position, moving eventually toward the majority position. Finally, the third role was that of deviant, a person who took a well reasoned, but opposite position from that of the majority and who did not change that position. In those groups characterized by high cohesion, a pattern emerged. Initially communications were directed toward the slider and the deviant in attempts to persuade them to the group position. Group communication then fell off toward the deviant near the end of the meeting. The slider was accepted by the group, the deviant by a vote of the group at the end of the experiment, ostensibly designed to reduce the group size for efficiency reasons, resulted in the group voting to exclude the deviant. It is no exaggeration to say that the nonconformist may easily take on the characteristics of an organizational leper in extreme cases.

But why do social organizations routinely allow and encourage such sanctioning activity? What positive functions are served by conformity which may prevent a more tolerant management from accepting normative deviation from organizational expectations?

THE POSITIVE FUNCTIONS OF CONFORMITY

From an organizational viewpoint conformity is a method of dealing with actual or potential conflict. Conformity involves the coaptation of existing and potential critics or rivals, strengthening the organization. Conformity at the group level, is reflected in group cohesiveness, the degree to which group members desire to stay in the group and abide by its norms. Cohesiveness has been positively related to productivity (Mullen and Cooper, 1994). Moreover, by placing individuals under conformity-inducing group pressures, an organizational weakness may be transformed into a strength. Coaptation may occur not only with regard to employees but also with regard to external interest representatives, who may be given advisor or other status. The Tennessee Valley Authority, for example, acquired substantial power through coaptation of representatives of such interests as the Farm Bureau, the Department of Agriculture, land grant colleges, and extension services (Selznik, 1949, 1957). Organizations which tend to emphasize coaptation in management tend to have a higher degree of effectiveness (Price, 1968).

It should be noted that, like gravity, coaptation is a two-way force. At times, as with the hiring of a token minority member, coaptation is unilateral and organizational norms may be relatively unchanged. However, at other times, including the TVA example above, coaptation may lead to mutual accommodation of affected interests and real change in organizational norms. Short of mutual accommodation, coaptation may reduce consensus (Price, 1968).

Conformity may be based on personal factors rather than organizational factors. Conformity tends to increase popularity (Argyle, 1957). It also reduces cognitive dissonance in group membership and may make work more satisfying. Back (1951) found that conformity based on personal attraction led to a work climate in which task requirements were viewed as intrusions. Likewise, he found conformity based on membership prestige led to low risk-taking in task performance.

Conformity is most positive in function when based on the task itself. Socialization to professional norms is typically of this type. Back (1951) found that task-based conformity was associated with an intensive and efficient work process. An example is provided in a case study by Trist and Bamforth (1951). These researchers found that when new, supposedly superior technology disbanded highly cohesive teams of coal miners, productivity fell markedly.

Conformity may involve an esprit-de-corps which promotes organizational effectiveness in a manner more significant than does technology. The promotion of task-based conformity as by the promotion of staff professionalization is therefore a potentially productive and important management objective.

THE NEGATIVE FUNCTIONS OF CONFORMITY

Management must be equally sensitive to possible negative impacts of organizational conformity, however. There are numerous good reasons for the popular negative reaction to the concept of conformity. Prime among these is the tendency toward suboptimization. That is, the forces of conformity are most effective at the small group level. The norms of the subgroup, however, are often not the norms of the organization in microcosm. The organization may efficiently socialize individuals to subgroup norms while failing to do so for organizational norms. Subgroup norms may involve such negative behaviors as withholding information or goal displacement (elevating means to become ends in themselves, as when bureaucracies become locked into self-defeating procedural technicalities). More broadly, conformity may simply reinforce professional biases, what Veblen called "trained incapacities." This is particularly true in agencies organized along professional-functional lines.

Irving Janis's *Victims of Groupthink* (1972) details errors arising from over-reliance on a closed subgroup, even one at the top of an organization. Janis examined four major policies: the Bay of Pigs, Pearl Harbor, the invasion of North Korea, and the escalation of the Vietnamese War. In each case he documented a pattern of "groupthink" or harmful conformity. Group think is a mode of thinking that can pervade a cohesive group that is dealing with decisions under situations of great pressure. It is characterized by strong group pressures toward conformity, pressures so strong that they override rational appraisal of alternative courses of action. Groupthink is characterized by:

1. An illusion of invulnerability that is shared by the group and results in excessive optimism that encourages high risk taking.
2. Warning signals that are ignored because of group rationalizations.
3. An unquestioning belief in the inherent morality of the group that emerges and which inclines members to ignore ethical or moral consequences of their decisions.
4. Critics become stereotyped and dismissed and unanimity becomes a pivotal group norm.
5. Direct Pressure is exerted on group members who express strong arguments against any of the groups decisions, stereotypes, and commitments. A climate emerges that makes it clear that this type of dissent is contrary to the loyalty expected of members of the group.
6. Self-censorship emerges designed to control deviations from the apparent group consensus. This creates a climate that reinforces the members' inclination to minimize the importance of their doubts and counter arguments.

7. A shared illusion of unanimity concerning group decisions.
8. "Mind guards" develop whose role it is to "protect" the group from adverse information that might shatter the illusion of unanimity.[2]

Janis concluded that consensus seeking became so dominant in cohesive policy groups he studied that a realistic appraisal of the alternatives became no longer possible. One illustration of this is the case of the Bay of Pigs. At the later stages of policy formation President Kennedy was literally "protected" by mindguards from opposing voices:

> At a large birthday party for his wife, Attorney General Robert F. Kennedy, who had been constantly informed about the Cuban invasion plan, took Schlesinger aside and asked him why he was opposed. Kennedy listened coldly and said, "You may be right or you may be wrong, but the President has made his mind up. Don't push it any further. Now is the time for everyone to help him all he can (Janis, cited in Natemeyer and Gilberg, 1989, p. 179).

More recently, the space shuttle *Challenger* provides a poignant illustration of groupthink. The decision to launch the Challenger manifested all the requirements for groupthink to take place (Tompkins, 1993). The group, composed of NASA and Thiokol officials, were making a decision under conditions of great pressure, the flight was the first to involve civilians, a number of launches in the last month had been canceled, the press was deployed in Florida and raising questions about NASA's ability to keep to a launch schedule. Finally, NASA was under budget pressure in Congress. The group whose decision it was to launch was under strong pressures toward conformity, pressures so strong that they overrode rational appraisal of alternative courses of action. The decision making process that launched the Challenger evolved very much in sequence to the eight steps outlined above. A teleconference took place on the night before the launch. Initially, Thiokol the builder of the rocket, suggested that the launch *be canceled*. Two of its engineers who were responsible for the O rings raised serious concerns about the O rings ability to contain "blow by" at the temperatures that the Air Force meteorologists were calling for the next morning. NASA officials took a different position that it had in previous launches and asked Thiokol engineers to defend their unanimous position that the launch should not take place. After significant discussion in which NASA officials exerted strong pressures, the group went "off line" and Thiokol revisited its position (Smith, 1986). When the teleconference went back "on line" Thiokol had reversed itself and recommended launch. The skepticism of the Thiokol engineers closest to the O ring problem was never relayed to the top level of NASA who heard only that Thiokol had approved of a launch and not about the initial unanimous objection to the launch.

It is important to note that there are devices that can be employed to avoid the worse aspect of groupthink. First of all, appoint a devil's advocate to question the group's assumptions and decisions and have a strong leader in the group avoid stating a position before the group reaches its own decision. Learning from the lessons of the Bay of Pigs, President Kennedy took steps to restructure group decision making in his White House and built in a critical evaluation component into the decision making process during the Cuban Missile Crisis. Kennedy was also deliberately absent from some critical meetings so as not influence the free flow of ideas. Kennedy intentionally brought in outside members so that the groups insularity was forced to deal with "outside" opinions.

As a practical matter, all administrators need to be aware of groups which are too homogenous and conforming because they may lack the diversity of resources needed for effective problem solving. Conformity and cohesion achieved through reaction against a common enemy, as in Janis's foreign policy cases, often is negative in organizational impact. Resorting to emphasis on an external foe is an ancient and effective tactic to secure unity and conformity. In management as well as politics, a negative external environment is associated with greater cohesiveness. As Hickson (1961) has shown, however, conformity based on external threat is also associated with restriction of output and lower productivity. Though this tendency is not a major organizational force it does suggest that conformity may just as well serve the social norms of the work unit as it can the production norms of the agency. In extreme cases conformity may actually serve neither organization nor subgroup nor individual goals. Harvey (1974) labeled this the "Abilene Paradox," alluding to a family incident in which his family took a long, hot, arduous trip to Abilene. On returning, it was discovered that no one really wanted to go. Each was conforming to the perceived value preferences of the other. Citing Watergate scandals of the Nixon presidency as an illustration, Harvey argued that such "trips to Abilene" are not uncommon in bureaucracies. The recorded testimony of Oliver North, and others, about the policy formation process in the Reagan administration that lead to Irangate, indicates the constant danger of this phenomenon.

It has been hypothesized that group conformity can also lead to organizational defense routines, routines that produce organizational noise; that is, distortion in the information being used to make decisions (Argyris, 1987). Organizational defense routines or defense mechanisms are routine policies or actions that are designed to prevent embarrassment or threat to the organization. Organizational (group) defense mechanisms are different than individual defense mechanisms. They are imparted through organizational socialization:

> Most participants in organizations can identify organizational defense routines. Yet, the same participants appear to be unaware of using such routines

themselves. Acting consistently with defensive routines is usually done skillfully, and skillful behavior is tacit (Argyris, 1987, p. 456).

One example of organizational defense mechanisms is the sending of "mixed messages" from the top of the hierarchy down the layers in an organization. One factor that can produce this particular type of organizational defense routine is the autonomy versus control controversy that exists in most large organizations. On the one hand, subordinates want to be left alone to do their own job and upper-management realizes that this autonomy is necessary for organizational optimization. On the other hand, superiors need to exert an organizational control function and do not want any surprises:

> Executives frequently deal with this dilemma by sending mixed messages. The top keeps communicating, "We mean it; it's your show." The division heads concur that the message is credible except when division or corporation gets into trouble or when a very important issue is at stake. In the eyes of the division heads, the corporation begins to interfere precisely when they want to prove their own metal. In the eyes of the corporation, they intervene precisely when they can be of most help, that is, when the issue "requires a corporate perspective" (Argyris, 1987, p. 457).

As a consequence, conformity by subgroups to organizational defense routines are likely to take over at the most inopportune time, when the organization is subject to external threat and/or embarrassment. Organizational defense routines are possible in both public and private organizations and are counter-productive. Organizational defense routines and much of the noise found in the system may, in fact, result from individual and group conformity to patterns of behavior necessitated by the very way modern organizations are structured.

> I have suggested that the theory of control embedded in the use of most management information systems is consistent with top down unilateral control where those above seek to win rather than learn. Accordingly, subordinates protect themselves by providing as valid information as they can while still protecting themselves. This can lead to subordinates systematically distorting information (Argyris, 1987, p. 456).

There is, however, evidence that intervention by organizational development specialists can point out these defense mechanisms and change group conformity behavior increasing the quality of decision making even in such hard areas as prices and profits (Argyris, 1987).

ROLE CONFLICT

Role conflict arises because individual needs conflict with role demands, because of divergent expectations of a given role by different agency members, or because the same individual may hold two or more conflicting roles simultaneously (Nicholson, 1983). These are called person-role conflict, intrarole conflict, and interrole conflict respectively. In addition, public agencies themselves can have role conflicts.

Person-role conflict occurs when what an individual values contradicts what is expected of his or her role. A valued image as a "nice guy" may conflict with a personnel analyst's role as an evaluator of performance of marginal employees (Keeley, 1977). Religious obligations may conflict with job requirements for service at specified times. Person-role conflict is a universal organizational problem requiring individualization of supervisory practices, reward structures, and other management policies. There is evidence, however, that role conflict can be reduced through training programs (Krayer, 1986). Intrarole conflict occurs when organizational members have different, conflicting expectations of a given person's role. A common example is that of boundary roles; roles interfacing the agency with the environment, including other agencies. Those occupying boundary roles are subject to intense expectations to represent organizational norms (the expectation of organization members) and to accommodate the norms of other agencies in the environment (external expectations). Boundary role incumbents are subject to particular stress (Bartunek and Reynolds, 1983). Role management for such individuals may require job rotation, training and resocialization opportunities, or rest and recreation (see Adams, 1976; Wall, 1974). Intrarole conflict is also evident in first-line supervisory roles (e.g., foremen). Such role incumbents must represent employees to higher management and represent higher management to employees. This "in the middle" position is also stressful and requires a compensating management policy (see Mann and Dent, 1954; Walker et al., 1956).

Interrole conflict occurs when an individual holds two or more roles which are in tension with each other. Typical is the manager who has risen through professional ranks. Examples are the doctor who becomes a hospital administrator or the professor who becomes a university dean. Such individuals often hold strong self- and peer-imposed professional expectations which may conflict with their new jobs. Academic deans, for example, may be torn between pressures for cost cutting (an administrative norm) and pressures for professional excellence (a professional norm). Certain professional groups have professional role definitions that are transmitted through professional socialization. These professional roles can directly produce role conflicts for these individuals in the public sector. An example of this is the role discussed in the urban planning literature as that of "advocate" An advocate is either a public or private sector planner who seeks and supports specific urban policy outcomes, rather than merely providing technical alternatives for other policy makers to decide (Vasu, 1979). Such a role orientation, which is typically associated with support for the urban under-class, may well cause role conflict for the public planner whose agency expects him to be a technician and not an advocate of a specific outcome or group of people (Vasu, 1981).

City managers also have prescribed professional roles. Originally, the role definition of city manager called for political authority to be located in the elected council and that administration should be the purview of professional administrators (Svara, 1990). City managers have inherited specific professional standards as a part of their profession's evolution that calls for them to be neutral experts who seek to promote the values of efficiency (Nalbandian, 1990). The city management profession is predicated upon "business like" government, a philosophy that calls for the manager to render judgments about municipal matters based on profession rather than political criteria. The realities of being a city manager, however, make the distinction between professional and political criteria a question of semantics. Many managers perceive that they do in fact make policy in their role as managers; that is, they are more than the neutral expert that their traditional role definition has prescribed (Wirth and Vasu, 1987, p. 468; Svara, 1990).

In the public sector, another important role that public administrators and agencies play is as guardians of the public purse. This role is most important in large scale capital project implementation in such areas as defense hardware and rapid rail procurement. There are two general roles in this process: those who engage in politics to increase spending and program size (spenders), and those who seek cost containment and performance standards (guardians). When one of these roles is absent (guardian) the opportunity for fraud and abuse is significant and cannot be addressed by legal means alone:

> Put differently, on the one hand, appropriate regulation of contractor behavior to reduce cheating and to reduce incentives for superior performance is usually not achieved by application of tight legal and administrative controls. This emphasis often results in more red tape, clericalization of tasks, false confidence in technical gimmickry, and irrational pursuit of the riskless transaction (Guess, 1985, p. 576).

The author goes on to note that the guardian role is necessary over and above legalism and "red tape" if the public's interest is to be protected. He explicates the problems that role conflict can produce in capital projects implementation, using as an example the cost overruns incurred in the Dade County Metrorail project.

> The Dade County Metrorail project illustrates the harmful effects of a prolonged absence of constructive conflict between guardians and spenders. Lack of technical oversight by the Urban Mass Transit Administration (UTMA) resulted in de facto self certification of project implementation. Oversight remained passive until a series of major problems forced guardians to assume an active role (Guess, 1985, p. 577).

The Metro Dade Transit Authority (MDTA) who should have played the guardian role also had an interest in seeing the program implemented. This produced role conflict and cost overruns.

> An important contributory factor to spender domination during the first phase was that MDTA played an ambiguous "dual" or "mixed" role of both advocate for the rail project (placing it on the side of contractors), and guardian of costs incurred for the Board of County Commissioners and the general public (Guess, 1985, p. 581).

A similar phenomenon occurs in other regulatory agencies when the guardian becomes "captured" by the industry they are created to regulate (Quirk, 1981).

PSYCHOLOGICAL DIMENSIONS OF ROLE CONFLICT

All types of role conflict are examples of cognitive dissonance (Festinger, 1957). Cognitive dissonance is the stress induced when a person values two things which conflict with each other. Needs may conflict with job expectations, or the expectations of one person or group may conflict with another's. The level of cognitive dissonance in each case depends on two factors:

1. *Intensity of values*: the stronger the positive or negative rewards, whether material or symbolic, the more intense the dissonance. Values are intensified when the associated expectations are articulated more frequently, more forcefully, or by individuals of greater importance to the individual's reference system.
2. *Intensity of constraints*: the stronger the constraints preventing the individual from simultaneous satisfaction of competing values, the greater the dissonance. Role overload is a common example as is role ambiguity. In the former there is too much task burden while in the latter there is too little task direction. (Interestingly, role overload may also cause dissonance since underload may create boredom or lowered esteem.)

Cognitive dissonance has been shown to be a powerful force having substantial effect on management. Pettigrew (1972), for instance, has estimated that millions of workdays are lost annually due to the stress of role conflict (Maslach, 1983). Ambiguity and conflict in role performance are particularly negative to (1) lower-level employees, perhaps because they lack control over job definition and hence experience contradictory role expectations as intractable and frustrating (Caplan and Jones, 1975); (2) introverts (Kahn et al., 1964); (3) individuals having high need-achievement (Johnson and Stinson, 1975; Schuler, 1975); and (4) individuals with a high need for clarity (Lyons, 1971).

When role conflict occurs individuals seek to reduce dissonance in one of several ways:

1. *Withdrawal*: individuals may seek to isolate themselves from both conflicting values, as by avoiding persons apt to articulate one or the other of two competing role expectations. A classic example was the tendency of Catholic members of Communist unions in the 1940s to become apolitical rather than have to choose between their union or their church.

2. *Transformation*: individuals may seek to alter one value to eliminate dissonance with the other, as by changing personal values to conform to organizational norms. Mixed work groups may sacrifice representatives to pick a higher-status individual as leader in order to project an image consistent with perceived organizational expectations (e.g., selection of white males in mixed groups; see Webber, 1974; Aries, 1976).

3. *Rationalization*: individuals may change their perceptions to eliminate dissonance, as when enforcement officials ignore civil liberties infractions thought necessary for effectiveness in crime reduction (Festinger, 1958).

4. *Aggression*: individuals may express stress through hostility, as when managers frustrated in goal achievement vent their frustration on subordinates (see Dollard, et al., 1939, for the classic formulation of frustration-aggression theory).

The supervisor who seeks to manage role conflict within the organization tries not so much to eliminate role conflict (which is often intrinsic to organization design) as to channel its impact away from deviant behavior and toward organizational ends.

DEVIANCE

Reactions to dissonance, as through withdrawal or aggression, are the basis for deviance within the organization. Deviance may take extreme forms such as alcoholism, drug addiction, or chronic absenteeism. Milder examples include the coffee-break group which comes to an informal understanding about keeping the work pace down in order to have a more relaxed atmosphere. Deviance exists whenever employees choose to devalue or evade organizational norms in order to confer legitimacy on other informal norms of their own (Raelin, 1986). Deviance is most likely among those whose mobility is dependent on an outside reference group (e.g., certain specialists) or among those with no hope for mobility. Kanter, for example, has noted the tendencies of secretaries to ignore company norms of impersonality and task orientation. "The secretarial function," Kanter (1977) noted "represented a repository of the personal inside the bureaucratic . . . . . . some secretaries were largely defined out of the mobility game, they could afford to carry on the human side of the office." Likewise, Gouldner (1957) has noted the greater deviance of "cosmopolitans" (those with strong external professional affiliations) compared to "locals."

Many other factors may increase the likelihood of deviance, including the amount of dissonance experienced by the role incumbent. Individual deviation is increased by physical separation of the employee from the work group. Similarly, group deviation is increased by the physical isolation of the work group from the rest of the organization (Roethlisberger and Dickson, 1939).

Extreme forms of deviance (e.g., alcoholism) are increasingly recognized as major management problems requiring formal programs, for example, counseling. Research shows that these programs are growing and are effective (Gebhardt and Crump, 1990). More subtle forms of deviance such as rationalization and formation of subgroup norms inconsistent with agency policy are often overlooked but may be even more damaging to the organization. In some cases deviance may be regarded as a tolerable idiosyncrasy of an otherwise "good group citizen" (Hollander, 1958, 1964). Others may be tolerated as negative role examples (Dentler and Erickson, 1959). These are exceptions to the generally strong reaction of organizations against deviance.

MANAGING ORGANIZATIONAL ROLES

Early in this century management theory embraced a "scientific" approach which emphasized industrial engineering (e.g., time and motion studies). It was only with the 1930s that management theory began to emphasize what was called the manager's "responsibility to lead." In other words, new stress was laid on the view that the manager's job, perhaps the primary job, was to manage organizational role expectations and conflicts not simply apply industrial production techniques.

The new viewpoint was associated with such individuals as Elton Mayo and Chester Barnard. Mayo had worked with the Hawthorne experiments (see Roethlisberger and Dickson, 1939). These had suggested the importance of informal group norms in restricting production. This in turn had implied the need for management concern for employee needs. Barnard, a telephone company executive was among the first organization theorists to describe management in non-Weberian terms: an intrinsically cooperative effort resting on a moral purpose inculcated by the manager (see Perrow, 1979; 65;273; Selznik, 1957).

Rensis Likert (1961) has emphasized similar themes in the concept of "supportive management." Supportive management called for the constructive use of conflict, the explicit examination of goals, and a new emphasis on the basic work group (observe that the constructive use of conflict is the antidote for groupthink). Accordingly, organizations may develop to higher levels only by tapping the creative forces represented in conflict management. Conflict management, not blind encouragement of conformity, was (and is) most suited to organizations seeking rapid change in the modern environment.

In the case of explicit examination of goals, Argyris (1957) and others argued that the role demands of most organizations are incompatible with the needs of healthy individuals. Both to integrate personal goals with organizational goals and to reduce role ambiguity (a major generator of stress), goal clarification efforts must be central to the manager's organizational development role. Finally, an emphasis on the basic work group becomes imperative. This emphasis is now central to management because of the recognition of the importance of the basic work group in the socialization of the individual to conformity with or deviance from organization norms. For example, the work group may be enhanced through increasing its social density, a strategy which has been found to reduce role stress and, through greater job feedback, reduce role ambiguity (Szilagyi and Holland, 1980; on measuring role ambiguity see Breaugh, 1980).

An organizing framework for these three emphases is career development. In fact, sometimes role management is used interchangeably with career development. Career development is a vehicle for managing role conflicts. Withdrawal may be channeled into climbing (mobility), aggression into constructive criticism and competition, transformation into anticipatory socialization, and rationalization into personal and management development. A comprehensive career development strategy is far more than training or counseling. It is a basis for organizational control and change which operationalizes organizational assumptions about motivation and leadership discussed in Chapters 3 and 4. When these changes are implemented, public management can be improved, the organization made more effective, and public money saved (Likert, 1981; Likert and Araki, 1986).

It is often assumed that career development is achieved through conformity alone (Mills, 1953; Whyte, 1955). Evidence by Porter and Lawler (1968a, 1968b), however, suggests that upward mobility is most likely to come as the result of differentiating oneself through superior performance, not by being the same as one's coworkers. On the other hand, as Kornhauser has shown in his studies of auto workers (1965), organizations can crush employee motivation by blocking mobility. The alternative to management control through a career development strategy is often the development of powerful, informal social groups within the organization; groups developed by employees to satisfy individual needs not recognized in agency policy.

INFORMAL ORGANIZATION

More than any other single objective, role management is concerned with the agency's response to informal organization. Informal organization is the set of unauthorized behaviors which are routinized parts of the organizational culture of the agency. Informal organization may promote deviant goals, organization goals, or both. It was the promotion of deviant goals which first placed the topic of informal organization high on the agenda of students of administration. In the Hawthorne plant of the Western Electric Company, Roethlisberger and Dickson, working with Elton Mayo, found that the informal organization of workers could countervail management's carefully-designed incentive systems (Roethlisberger and Dickson, 1939). If you recall, in their "Bank Wiring Room" experiment, fourteen workers in a separated work environment were placed on a group piece-work plan under which the more the group produced the more its members received in income. Contrary to engineering theory and the economic man perspective, Roethlisberger and Dickson found that the hypothesized group pressure to increase the paycheck through higher productivity did not materialize. Rather, informal group pressures were mobilized to restrict output. High producers were labeled "rate-busters" while low producers were termed "chiselers." Pressure was put on inspectors to be "one of the guys." The more intelligent and dexterous workers often had the lowest output. Informal group norms centering on such goals as pleasant job conditions and "spreading the work" (job security) proved more powerful than management's incentive pay-centered control system. *The influence of informal groups on the work environment is one of the most important realities of applied management.* The influence of the informal group can be either positive or negative, which depends, in part, on how they are managed. In the past informal groups have been regarded as both threats and opportunities. They are in fact both! Informal groups possesses the potential to be highly functional or dysfunction from the perspective of the organization's goals.

INFORMAL ORGANIZATION AS A THREAT

Early views of informal organization were generally pessimistic. In their classic anthology, *Papers on the Science of Administration* (1937), Luther Gulick and Lyndall Urwick adopted the essentially negative view of informal organization found in the Hawthorne studies (Gulick and Urwick, 1937). Informal organization was seen as the inevitable consequence of bad management. Scientific management, in contrast, would avoid the emergence of harmful employee roles not officially sanctioned. It sought to do this through highly detailed task procedures and time schedules which left virtually no discretion to the rank-and-file employee. Disciples of scientific management sought to break each task into exact sequences of motions which had to be done at prescribed speeds (time-and-motion studies).

Locked into rigidly prescribed patterns, in theory there was no opportunity for the rise of informal, unsanctioned group behavior. In reality, however, discontent over the tight supervision which scientific management entailed led to employee resentment, informal resistance, and even unionism. Gulick and Urwick argued that sound management proceeded from scientific management's assumptions of detailed specification of tasks and schedules according to identifiable principles of administrative science such as clarity of hierarchical lines of authority and adoption of optimal spans of control. When bad management tolerated unclear lines of authority, they argued, workers misunderstood or forgot central organization purposes. Soon workers devoted their energies to their own individual ends and informal work group goals. Likewise, when bad management allowed too large a span of control (as in French bureaucracy), accountability broke down and was replaced by informal organization.

Fear of informal organization was intensified by another principle of administrative science: homogeneity. This principle called for organization of homogenous work groups (e.g., like professionals grouped in staff departments). Since such groups were thought to suffer occupational biases and to be oblivious to the needs of other units, it was particularly important that these groups not be left to develop their own directions. Gulick and Urwick argued forcefully that only clear, hierarchical control administered through a manageable span of control could prevent the dangerous emergence of informal groups which would usurp the powers of management.

Later sociological research popularized the view that informal organization was pervasive and generally negative in association. For example, William Foote Whyte's *Street Corner Society*; (1943) was a notable study demonstrating a high degree of informal organization even in street corner gangs. Whyte's later work, *Money and Motivation* (1955a) showed similar informal organization in work groups. Ways in which workers defeated time-and-motion studies through informal work groups were highlighted in this study. Output restriction was also detailed in numerous other studies which attributed it to such poor management practices as inadequate job security, inadequate reward systems, or unpopular speed-ups (Collins et al., 1946; Roy, 1952; Viteles, 1953; Hickson, 1961).

In the public sector much the same conclusions were reached in Blau's classic study of a New York City employment office (Blau, 1955). Blau found that employment counselors often followed informal group norms rather than agency policies. They would fail to share job listings, neglect job counseling, fail to match the best person to the best job, and show favoritism or discrimination against certain clients. These and other forms of deviance came about through informal group attempts to make work more satisfying and to thwart a quantitative management performance control system.

INFORMAL ORGANIZATION AS AN OPPORTUNITY

Chester Barnard, a founder of modern organization theory, introduced an opposite perspective in the midst of this research supporting a negative management view of informal organization. Barnard, a telephone company executive, argued that informal organization served three highly important and positive functions.

1. *Communication.* Informal communication channels afforded by informal organization allowed more rapid and flexible interactions and responses than would be possible under strict hierarchical organization.
2. *Cohesiveness.* Informal organization was a powerful socializing system regulating members' willingness to serve and contribute to team spirit and mobilization, thereby stabilizing management authority.
3. *Support.* Informal organization provided mutual support for informal group members, enhancing their feelings of self-respect and independence of action.

Barnard thus saw informal organization as a complement to formal organization.

In a two-way influence process, formal organizations created and shaped informal organizations, but they also reflected the organizational culture engendered by them. This concept leads directly to concern for role management as a central function of the administrator.

Much postwar research has reinforced Barnard's positive view of informal organization. In studies of WWII soldiers, for example, Shils (1950) found that informal primary groups contributed to self-confidence and reduced fear. Consequently, soldiers in such groups were less likely to surrender. Similarly, research on Korean War prisoners by Schein (1956) showed the Chinese method of consciously preventing informal group formation (through constant prisoner rotation) led to lower morale, greater sickness, and fewer escapes.

This military research confirmed Mayo's findings that management practices which promoted informal organization (e.g., allowing group rest periods for socialization) led to increased worker satisfaction and productivity (Mayo, 1946). The desirability and inevitability of informal groups was vividly popularized through Roy's (1960) widely-circulated case study of "banana time." Conversely, Trist and Bamforth's (1951) famous study of English coal mining showed how a new technology which disrupted informal organization could lead to plummeting productivity. Current practice in the private sector calls for a shift to a team platform. This movement toward the use of teams will be discussed more fully in Chapter 8. However, we will note at this point that much of logic behind the training of work teams is predicated on managing informal group dynamics so that team efforts can be directed toward organizational productivity (Rees, 1991).

INFORMAL ORGANIZATION: A SUMMARY

It is now recognized that informal organization is critical even in high-control settings like prisons (Social Science Research Council, 1960). In government agencies where authority is less pervasive, even more reliance must be placed on norm-enforcing social pressures of the informal group. On the other hand, limits must be drawn on Barnard's enthusiasm for informal groups. Perrow (1979), for example, has charged that Barnard saw no negative effects in informal organizations because he thought such groups would serve only personal goals which would be overridden by the collective goals of the organization. In reality, informal groups may reinforce collective ends different from those of the agency. Informal work groups represent a powerful force which is not necessarily deviant (as Gulick implied) nor necessarily beneficial (as Barnard suggested). Rather, informal organization is an almost-inevitable facet of organizational life with which the manager must contend. Changing (or reinforcing) informal norms for organizational ends is increasingly recognized as a central management function. It is at the heart of organization development attempts to understand and manage organizational culture and it is central to the role management function of the administrator.

MANAGING ROLE CHANGE

The need for role management is not new. Mary Parker Follett's advocacy of opening up communication and using conflict constructively embodied similar concerns nearly a half century ago (Follett, 1940). Nor is this a need which should be foreign to students of public administration. Theodore Caplow, for example, has shown how role management is relevant even in university settings. Because of discrepancies between university-conferred authority rankings and profession-conferred statuses, Caplow noted, role conflict is common (Caplow and McGee, 1958). Management strategy in universities is often to be passive, allowing power to lie where it might. Caplow charged this laissez-faire attitude is a failure of role management which contributed to a kind of "lawlessness" and heightening of conflict. While some might argue that normative "lawlessness" is in fact the freedom needed for university survival, Caplow's example does strongly suggest the need for an explicit approach to role management. Indeed, the great upsurge in organizational development in the last two decades reflects this. Organizational development (OD), is the planned intervention by groups of specialists employing behavioral science techniques predicated on interaction centered designs (French and Bell, 1995). The purpose of OD is to increase organizational effectiveness. Typically, OD is composed of two phases, organizational diagnosis and organizational intervention. OD starts with a diagnosis of the existing organization culture, norms values, procedures and processes. An evaluation is then made of those features of the organization that facilitate its attainment of its specified goals and those features that inhibit the achievement of those goals. The next phase is the intervention phase in which the organizational development specialists seek to change those dysfunctional features of the organization.

Organizational development has at least six distinguishing features. It emphasizes definite values, such as openness, trust, and collaborate effort. Organizational development seeks to simultaneously meet individuals' needs and the needs of several levels of systems-interpersonal relations, small groups, and large organizations. Organizational development relies on immediate experiences as they occur here and now orientation which often is reflected in "process analysis" of the panoply of personal and institutional forces acting on individuals and groups. Organizational development emphasizes feelings and emotions as well as ideas and concepts and gives preeminence to the individuals' involvement and participation-as subject and object, as generator of data as well as responder to those data in an "action research" sense. Organizational development uses group contexts for choice and change to validate data, to develop and enforce norms, to provide emotional support and identification (Golembiewski et al., 1981, p. 679). Organizational development in the public sector has been employed at various levels of government (Kiel, 1982). Moreover, the range of topics covered has been significant.

> Indeed, public sector OD interventions tend to hunt bigger game. Witness their common emphasis on: racial tension; conflict between individual specialties, individual specialties, and organizational units; community conflict between policy and minorities and basic reorganization; and so on (Golembiewski et al., 1981).

The evidence suggests that OD interventions have largely been successful (Golembieski et al., 1981; French and Bell, 1995). Indeed, organizational development's overall impact in both the public and private sector can be characterized as positive (Golembiewski et al., 1982; French and Bell, 1995). There is some evidence that organizational development is gaining acceptance at an increasing rate (French and Bell, 1995). Moreover, organization development techniques like team-building (see Dyer, 1977; Rees, 1991; West, 1995) have become commonplace in public administration. Organizational development in public and private organizations is surveyed elsewhere (e.g., Golembiewski, 1977; Golembiewski and Eddy, 1978; French and Bell, 1995). We will also discuss organizational development in Chapter 9. We will simply note at this juncture that virtually all of its forms seek formal or informal role change as part of a conscious managerial change effort.

Role management techniques have also become commonplace in individual-centered and intrapersonal interventions. These range from stress reduction

(Frew, 1977) to sensitivity training (Black, 1972) to life/career planning (Storey, 1978) to role negotiation as part of management by objectives (MBO) or other goal-centered control systems (Carroll and Tosi, 1973). There has also been a growing interest in the factors associated with employee "burnout" (Maslach, 1983). In each of these, the focus is on employment of role-changing techniques drawn from social psychology, counseling, and learning theory. In each, management takes an active role in the change process. Informal organization and organizational culture is not taken as a "given," nor is it assumed that role development is a "personal matter" outside the scope of the manager's concerns.

In summary, role conflict, informal organization, and issues of conformity and deviance powerfully affect organizational life. Management must respond through conscious strategies of role management. These strategies are multifaceted and may involve objectives pertaining to motivation, leadership, communication, and virtually any of the other organization behavior topics treated in this volume. Traditional roles and organizational culture are difficult to change. Frequently changed interventions require the catalyzing influence of an outside professional (Bion, 1959; Argyris, 1987). A participatory approach improves role understanding and commitment to role change (Miller, 1980; Burrington, 1987). All approaches involve assessment, goal-setting, and commitment phases and, as such, bear much in common with organizational development techniques. Default on role management responsibilities is associated with the emergence of informal organization and organizational culture commonly deviant from agency norms. Without an appropriate managerial response to the challenge of role management, whether by the traditional "natural leader" or the contemporary "OD specialist," the agency will have a poor basis for organizational communication and decision-making, the topics of subsequent chapters.

MANAGERIAL IMPLICATIONS

Managerial leadership depends critically on the ability of the manager to recognize, understand, utilize, and possibly change the patterns of behavior characteristic of the agency's employees. The behaviors of employees are influenced by both the *formal organization* and the *informal organization*. The *formal organization* is the script for the organization, it establishes a hierarchy of authority and assigns formal roles to individuals within organizations. The informal organization is the parallel organization always present and always exerting influence on roles.

Roles are behaviors expected of people occupying a given position in an organizational setting. Behaviors become routinized over a period of time, allowing them to become anticipated by the manager and other organizational members. Such established behavior patterns are reinforced positively or negatively by sanctions applied by the manager or the informal work group. The management of role behavior is a critical skill.

There are many types of roles. Two broad dimensions divide roles into functional and cultural roles. Functional roles include patterns based on administrative task or function. For example, there are roles associated with the traditional administrative functions of planning, organizing, staffing, directing, coordinating, reporting, and budgeting. Cultural roles, such as those based on nationality, race, or sex. Cross-cultural research suggests that national culture is itself a contingency variable in many management related behaviors. Studies of cultural roles within a given nation have found fewer administrative differences. For example, a variety of studies have found few gender related differences with respect to such dimensions as competitiveness, motivation, decision-making, or analytical skills. Nonetheless, the role of women managers in the workplace requires particular attention by management. Long held role conceptions associate management with stereotypical masculine behaviors and traits. As stated previously, this can place women managers in a double bind if they behave in a stereotypical female role and are judged less effective in their role as managers, or if their management style conforms to male norms, and they are also negatively perceived in terms of social image. It may also explain the "glass ceiling" that many women managers face in certain organizations. Moreover, there may be no differences in the *managerial skills* of men and women however, there may well be differences in *philosophy and managerial style*. These differences may be predicated on female cultural roles.

Roles are a vehicle for insuring conformity. While conformity is often disparaged, organizations could not hold together without it. The inducement of rewards and the force of authority are powerful motivators but no organization can function effectively unless its members share widespread acceptance of and conformity to organizational roles. Managers need to recognize and use this knowledge to their advantage. From an organizational viewpoint, conformity is a method of dealing with actual or potential conflict. Conformity involves the coaptation of existing and potential critics or rivals, strengthening the organization. Conformity at the group level is reflected in group cohesiveness, the degree to which group members desire to stay in the group and abide by its norms. Moreover, by placing individuals under conformity-inducing group pressures, an organizational weakness may be transformed into a strength. Managers must also be equally sensitive to possible negative impacts of organizational conformity, however. There are numerous good reasons for the popular negative reaction to the concept of conformity. Prime among these is the tendency toward suboptimization. That is, the forces of conformity are most effective at the small group level. The norms of the subgroup, however, are often not the norms of the organization in microcosm. The organization may efficiently socialize individuals to subgroup norms while failing to do so for organizational norms. Role conflict arises because individual needs conflict with role demands, because of divergent expectations of a given role by different agency members, or because the same individual may hold two or more conflicting roles simultaneously. Public managers need to be attentive to this fact. In addition, public agencies themselves can have role conflicts.

Informal organization has been seen in the past as the inevitable consequence of bad management. Scientific management, in fact, established a structure that would avoid the emergence of harmful employee roles not officially sanctioned. It sought to do this through highly detailed task procedures and time schedules which left virtually no discretion to the rank-and-file employee. The approached failed! Today the paradigm in the workplace has shifted significantly toward employee empowerment. Employee empowerment is predicated on assumptions of initiative and teamwork, not highly structured tasks and inflexible lines of authority. It is necessary today to work with the informal organization not seek its demise. Sophisticated public managers learn this lesson quickly. It is now recognized that informal organization is inevitable even in high-control settings like prisons. In government agencies where authority is less pervasive, even more reliance must be placed on norm-enforcing social pressures of the informal group. Changing (or reinforcing) informal norms for organizational ends is increasingly recognized as a central management function. It is at the heart of organizational development attempts to understand and manage organizational culture and it is central to the role management function of the administrator.

Finally, role conflict, informal organization, and issues of conformity and deviance powerfully affect organizational life. Managers need to be vigilant to avoid the groupthink and "trips to Abilene." In order to do so, they must respond through conscious strategies of role management. These strategies are multifaceted and may involve objectives pertaining to motivation, leadership, and organizational communication. They may require the manager to seek resources outside their own organization such as an organizational development specialists. Traditional roles and organizational culture are difficult to change, as those seeking to "reinvent government" or establish organizational designs based on total quality management can attest. However, the demands of a global economy and an information age society require that efforts toward change be made.

ENDNOTES

1. Of course, not all studies have found sex independent of behavioral effects relevant to management. Zarmarta et al., (1979) found that males reporting to males resolved conflict more through withdrawal than did males or females reporting to females. Likewise, males reporting to males used less confrontation than females reporting to females. Donnell and Hill (1980), although finding no sex differences on most variables studied, did find women to be more achievement motivated but less open and

candid with colleagues compared to men. Humphreys and Shrode (1978) found more similarities than differences by sex, but did find that women had more difficulty with budgetary and less difficulty with conceptual decisions than did men. There have been differences in dispositional dominance and sex role expectations as they relate to leadership reported as well by Nyquist and Spence (1986). The strength of these relationships is such that they cannot be construed as contradicting the conclusion of Donnell and Hill (1980): that "Women, in general, do not differ from men, in general, in the ways they administer the management process." As stated previously, Helgesen (1990) is among a group of researcher who contend that management style is influenced by the cultural role of women. Specifically, she argues that women express preferences for different organizational designs, the web vs the hierarchy, for example.

2. An excellent training film that vividly brings these points to life is Groupthink Revised Edition, CRM Films, 2215 Faraday Ave, Carlsbad, CA 92008.

REFERENCES AND ADDITIONAL READING

Adams, J. Stacy (1976). "The Structure and Dynamics of Behavior in Organizational Boundary Roles," in M. W. Dunnette, (ed.), *Handbook of Industrial and Organizational Psychology*. Chicago: Rand McNally.

Aldefer, C. P. and C. M. Cord (1970). "Personal and Situational Factors in the Recruitment Interview." *Journal of Applied Psychology*, 54:pp 377–385.

Allen, V. L. (1965). "Situational Factors in Conformity," in L. Berkowitz, (ed.), *Advances in Experimental Social Psychology*, N.Y.: Academic Press, 2:pp 145–146.

Argyle, M. (1957). *The Scientific Study of Social Behavior*. London: Methuen.

Argyris, Chris (1987). "Bridging Economics and Psychology: The Case of the Exonomic Theory of the Firm," *American Psychologist*, 42:No. 5:pp 456–463.

Argyris, Chris (1957). "The Individual and the Organization: Some Problems of Mutual Adjustment," *Administrative Science Quarterly*, 2:No. 1 (June), pp 1–24.

Argyris, Chris (1969). "The Incompleteness of Social Psychological Theory." *American Psychologist*, 24:pp 893–908.

Aries, E. (1976). "Interaction Patterns and Theories of Male, Female, and Mixed Groups." *Small Group Behavior*, 7:No. 1, pp 7–18.

Asch, Solomon E. (1952). *Social Psychology*. Englewood Cliffs, N.J.: Prentice-Hall.

Asch, Solomon E. (1957). "Effects of Group Pressure Upon the Modification and Distortion of Judgments," in H. Guetzkow, (ed.), *Groups, Leadersh and Men*. Pittsburgh: Carnegie Press.

Back, K. W. (1951). "Influence Through Social Communication." *Journal of Abnormal and Social Psychology*, 46:pp 190–207.

Black, K. W. (1972). *Beyond Words; The Story of Sensitivity Training and Encounter Groups*. N.Y.: Russell Sage Foundation.

Barnard, Chester I. (1938). "Informal Organizations and Their Relation to Formal Organizationa," in *Functions of the Executive* (Harvard), reprinted in W. E. Natemeyer, (ed.), *Classics of Organization Behavior*. Oak Park, Ill.: Moore, 1978:pp 239–243.

Bartunek, Jean M. and Christine Reynolds (1983). "Boundary Spanning and Public Accountant Role Stress." *Journal of Social Psychology*, 121(1):pp 65–72.

Bass, Bernard M., C. R. M. Gehee, W. C. Harkins, D. C. Young, A. S. Gebel (1953). "Personality Variables Related to Leaderless Group Discussion." *Journal of Abnormal and Social Psychology*, (January):pp 120–28.

Benne, K. and P. Sheats (1948). "Functional Roles of Group Members." *Journal of Social Issues*, 4:No. 2 (Spring), pp 41–49.

Berkowitz, L. and R. C. Howard (1959). "Reactions to Opinion Deviates as Affected by Affiliation Need (n) and Group Member Interdependence." *Sociometry*, 22:pp 81–91.

Biggart, Woolsey B. and Gary G. Hamilton (1984). "Power of Obedience." *Administrative Science Quarterly*, 29:pp 713–719.

Bion, W. E. (1959). *Experiences in Groups*. N.Y.: Basic Books.

Blau, Peter (1955). *The Dynamics of Bureaucracy*. Chicago: University of Chicago Press.

Breaugh, James A. (1980). "A Comparative Study of Three Measures of Role Ambiguity." *Journal of Applied Psychology*, 65:No. 5 (Oct.), pp 584–589.

Burrington, Debra D. (1987). "Organizational Development in the Utah Department of Public Safety." *Public Personnel Management*, 16:No. 2, pp 115–125.

Camden, Carl T. and Carol W. Kennedy (1986). "Manager Communicative Syle and Nurse Moral." *Human Communication Research*, 12:No. 4, pp 551–563.

Camden, Carl T. (1983). "Manager Communicative Style and Productivity: A Study of Male and Female Managers." *International Journal of Womens Studies*, 6(3):pp 258–269.

Caplan, R. and V. Jones (1975). "Effects of Work Load, Role Ambiguity, and Type A Personality on Anxiety, Depression, and Heart Rate," *Journal of Applied Psychology*, 60:No. 6, (Dec.), pp 713–719.

Caplow, Theodore and R. J. McGee (1958). *The Academic Marketplace*. N.Y.: Basic Books.

Caplow, Theodore (1964). *Principles of Organization*. N.Y.: Harcourt, Brace, and World.

Cardwell, Len (1985). "Managing Women: A Man's View." *Management Education and Development*, 16(2):pp 197–200.

Carroll, S. and W. Tosi, Jr. (1973). *Management by Objectives*. N.Y.: Macmillan.

Collins, O., M. Dalton, and D. Roy (1946). "Restriction of Output and Social Cleavage in Industry." *Applied Anthropology*, 5:No. 3, pp 1–14.

Cooper, C. L. and I. T. Robertson (eds.) (1990). *International Review of Industrial and Organizational Psychology*, Vol. 5. Chichester, England: Wiley.

Dalton, M. (1948). "The Industrial "Rate-Buster': A Characterization." *Applied Anthropology*, 7:pp 5–18.

Dentler, R. A., and K. T. Erickson (1959). "The Functions of Deviance in Groups." *Social Problems*, 7:pp 98–107.

Dollard, John, L. W. Doob, N. E. Miller, O. H. Mowrer, and R. R. Sears (1939). *Frustration and Aggression*. New Haven: Yale.

Donnell, Susan M. and Jay Hill (1980). "Men and Women as Managers: A Significant Case with No Significant Difference." *Organizational Dynamics*, (Spring): 8:No. 4:pp 60–77.

Dunnette, M. D., R. D. Arvey, and P. A. Banas (1973). "Why Do They Leave?" *Personnel* (May–June):pp 25–39.

Dyer, William G. (1977). Team Building. Reading, Mass.: Addison-Wesley.

Emerson, R. M. (1954). "Deviation and Rejection: An Experimental Replication." *American Sociological Review*, 19:pp 688–693.

England, George W. (1967). "Personality Value Systems of American Managers." *Academy of Management Journal* (March):pp 53–68.

Festinger, Leon (1950). "Informal Social Communication." *Psychology Review*, 57:pp 271–282.

Festinger, Leon (1957). *Theory of Cognitive Dissonance*. N.Y.: Harper & Row.

Festinger, Leon (1958). "The Motivation Effect of Cognitive Dissonance," in G. Lindzey, (ed.), *Assessment of Human Motives*. N.Y.: Rinehard and Co.:pp 65–86.

Festinger, Leon, S. Schacter, and K. Bark (1950). *Social Pressures in Informal Groups*. N.Y.: Harper & Row.

Follett, Mary Parker (1940). *Dynamic Administration*. N.Y.: Harper & Row.

French, W. L. and C. H. Bell (1995). *Organizational Development*. Englewood Cliffs, New Jersey: Prentice-Hall.

Frew, D. (1977). *The Management of Stress*. Chicago: Nelson-Hall.

Gebhardt, D. L. and C. E. Crump (1990). "Employee Fitness and Wellness Programs in the Workplace," *American Psychologist*, (February), pp 262–272.

Golembiewski, Robert T., Carl W. Proehl and David Sink (1982). "Estimating the Success of OD Applications." *Training and Development Journal*, 36:No. 4, pp 86–95.

Golembiewski, Robert T., Carl W. Proehl and David Sink (1981). "Success of OD Applications in the Public Sector: Totaling up the Score for a Decade, More or Less." *Public Administration Review*, 41:No. 6, pp 679–682.

Golembiewski, Robert T. (1977). *Public Administration as a Developing Discipline: Part 2, Organization Development*. N.Y.: Marcel Dekker.

Golembiewski, Robert T. and W. B. Eddy, (eds.) (1978). *Organizational Development in Public Administration*. N.Y.: Marcel Dekker.

Golembiewski, Robert T. and R. J. Hilles (1979). *Toward the Responsive Organization: The Theory and Practice of Survey/Feedback*. Salt Lake City: Brighton Publishing Co.

Gouldner, Alvin W. (1957). Cosmopolitans and Locals: Toward an Analysis of Latent Social Roles, *Administrative Science Quarterly*, 2(3)(Dec.):pp 281–292.

Guess, George M. (1985). "Role Conflict in Capital Project Implementation: The Case of Dade County Metrorail." *Public Administration Review*, 45:No. 5, pp 576–585.

Gulick, Luther and Lyndall Urwick, (eds.) (1937). *Papers in the Science of Administration*. N.Y.: Institute of Public Administration.

Guth, William D. and Renato Jagiuri (1965). "Personal Values and Corporate Strategies." *Harvard Business Review*. (Sept.–Oct.):pp 125–126.

Hackman, J. R., (1992). "Group Influences on Individuals in Organizations," in M. D. Dunsette and L. M. Hough (eds.). *Handbook of Industrial Psychology 2ed*. Vol 3. Palo Alto, California: Consulting Psychologists Press, pp 235–250.

Harriman, Ann (1985). *Women, Men, Management*. New York: Praeger.

Harvey, Jerry B. (1974). "The Abilene Paradox: The Management of Agreement." *Organizational Dynamics*, (Summer):pp 128–146.

Harvey, O. J. and C. Consalvi (1960). "Status and Conformity to Pressures in Informal Groups." *Journal of Abnormal and Social Psychology*, 60:pp 182–187.

Helgesen, S. (1990). *The Female Advantage: Women's Ways of Leadership*. Doubleday, New York.

Henderson, Dee W. (1985). "Enlightened Mentoring: A Characteristic of Public Management Professionalism." *Public Administration Review*, 45:No. 6, pp 857–864.

Hickson, D. (1961). "Motives of Workpeople Who Restrict Their Output." *Occupational Psychology*, 35:No. 1 (Jan–Feb):pp 111–112.

Hofstede, Geerte (1980). "Motivating Leadershp and Organization: Do American Theories Apply Abroad?" *Organizational Dynamics*, (Summer), 9:No. 1:pp 42–63.

Hollander, E. P. (1958). "Conformity, Status, and Idiosyncracy Credit." *Psychological Review*, 65:pp 117–127.

Hollander, E. P. (1964). *Leaders, Groups and Influence*. N.Y.: Oxford.

Humphreys, L. W. and W. A. Shrode (1978). "Decision-Making Profiles of Female and Male Managers," *MSU Business Topics* (Grad. School of Business Administration: Michigan State University) 26(4):pp 45–51 (Autumn).

Ilgen, Daniel R., Cynthia D. Fisher, and M. Susan Taylor (1979). "Consequences of Individual Feedback on Behavior in Organizations." *Journal of Applied Psychology*, 64(4) (August):pp 349–371.

Janis, Irving L. (1972). *Victims of Groupthink*. N.Y.: Houghton Mifflin.

Jehn, K. (1994). "Enhancing Effectiveness: An Investigation of Advantages of Value Based Intra Group Conflict," *International Journal Of Conflict Management*, (July), pp 223–238.

Johnson, W. B. and A. E. Packer (1987). *Workforce 2000: Work and Workers for 21st Century*. Indianopolis: Hudson Institute.

Johnson, Mary C. (1980). "Mentors: The Key to Development and Growth." *Training and Development Journal*, 34(7) (July):pp 55–57.

Johnson, T. and J. Stinson (1975). "Role Ambiguity, Role Conflict, and Satisfaction: Moderating Effects of Individual Differences." *Journal of Applied Psychology*, 60(3) (June):pp 329–33.

Kahn, R., E. Wolfe, R. Quinn, and J. Sneck (1964). *Organizational Stress: Studies in Role Conflict and Performance*. N.Y.: Wiley.

Kanter, Roseabeth Moss (1983). *The Change Masters*. New York: Simon and Schuster.

Kanter, Rosabeth Moss (1977). *Men and Women of the Corporation*. N.Y.: Basic.

Keeley, N. (1977). "Subjective Performance Evaluation and Person-Role Conflict Under Conditions of Uncertainty." *Academy of Management Journal* (June):pp 301–314.

Kelley, H. H. and T. W. Lamb (1957). "Uncertainty of Judgment and Resistance to Social Influence." *Journal of Abnormal and Social Psychology*, 55:pp 137–139.

Kiel, David H. (1982). "An OD Strategy for Policy Implementation: The Case of North Carolina State Government." *Public Administration Review*, 42:No. 4, pp 375–383.

Kieler, C. (1969). "Group Pressure and Conformity," in J. Mills, (ed.), *Experimental Social Psychology* (Ch. 11). N.Y.: Macmillan.

Kornhauser, A. (1965). *Mental Health of the Industrial Worker*. N.Y.: Wiley.

Krayer, Karl J. (1986). "Using Training to Reduce Role Conflict and Ambiguity." *Training and Development Journal*, 41(1):pp 49–52.

Lebas, Michael and Jane Weigenstein (1986). "Management Control: The Roles of Rules, Markets and Culture." *Journal of Management Studies*, 23:pp 259–271.

Lefkowitz and Allan W. Fraser (1980). "Assessment of Achievement and Power Motivation of Blacks and Whites." *Journal of Applied Psychology*, (Dec.), 65(6):pp 685–696.

Levinson, H., C. R. Price, H. J. Munden, and C. M. Sulley (1962). *Men, Management and Mental Health.* Cambridge: Harvard.

Lick, Edward J. and Bruce L. Oliver (1974). *Academy of Management Journal*, (Sept.):pp 549–554.

Likert, Jane G., Charles T. Araki (1986). "Managing Without a Boss." *Leadersh and Organizational Development Journal*, 7:pp 17–20.

Likert, Jane G. and Charles Araki (1986). "Managing Without a Boss: System 5." *Leadership and Organizational Development Journal*, 7:No. 3, pp 17–20.

Likert, Rensis (1981). "System 4: A Resource for Improving Public Administration." *Public Administration Review*, 41:No. 6, pp 674–678.

Likert, Rensis (1961). *New Patterns of Management*. N.Y.: McGraw-Hill.

Livingston, J. S. (1969). "Pygmalion in Management." *Harvard Business Review*, 47(4):pp 81–89.

Lott, A. J. and B. E. Lott (1965). "Group Cohesiveness as Interpersonal Attraction: A Review of Relationships with Antecedent and Consequent Variables." *Psychological Bulletin* (Oct.):pp 259–309.

Lyons, T. (1971). "Role Clarity, Need for Clarity, Satisfaction, Tension, and Withdrawal." *Organizational Behavior and Human Performance*, Vol. 6, No. 1 (Jan.):pp 99–110.

Mann, F. C. and J. K. Dent (1954). "The Supervisor: Member of Two Organizational Families." *Harvard Business Review*, Vol. 6 (Nov.–Dec.):pp 103–112.

Maslach, Christina (1983). *Burnout: The Cost of Caring*. Englewood Cliffs, New Jersey.

Mayo, Elton (1946). *The Human Problems of an Industrial Civilization*. Cambridge: Harvard Graduate School of Business Administration.

Miller, Ernest C. (1980). "Hire in Haste-Repent at Leisure: The Team Selection Roles at Graphic Controls." *Organizational Dynamics* (Spring), 8(4):pp 2–26.

Mills, C. Wright (1953). *White Collar: The American Middle Classes*. N.Y.: Oxford.

Mintzberg, H. (1973). *The Nature of Managerial Work*. N.Y.: Harper & Row.

Muldrow, Tressie W. and James A. Bayton (1979). "Men and Women Executives and Processes Related to Decision Accuracy." *Journal of Applied Psychology*, 64(2) (April):pp 99–106.

Mullen B. and C Cooper (1994). "The Relationship Between Group Cohesiveness and Performance: An Integration," *Psychological Bulletin*, 115(2):pp 210–277.

Nadler, David A. (1977). *Feedback and Organization Development*. Reading, Mass.: Addison-Wesley.

Nadler, E. B. (1959). "Yielding, Authoritarianism, and Authoritarian Ideology Regarding Groups." *Journal of Abnormal and Social Psychology*, (May):pp 408–410.

Nalbandian, J. (1990). "Tenets of Contemporary Professionalism in Local Government," *Public Administration Review*. (Nov–Dec), pp 654–661.

Natemeyer, Walter E. and Jay S. Gilberg (1979). *Classics of Organizational Behavior*. Danville, Illinois.

Nelson, Reed E. (1986). "Social Networks and Organizational Interventions: Insights from an Area-Wide Labor Management Committee." *Journal of Applied Behavioral Science*, 22(1):pp 65–76.

Nicholson, Peter J. and C. G. Swee (1983). "The Relationship of Organizational Structure and Interpersonal Attitudes to Role Conflict and Ambiguity in Different Work Environments." *Academy of Management Journal*, 26:1:pp 148–155.

Nyqist, Linda V. and Janet T. Spence (1986). "Effects of Dispositional Dominance and Sex Role Expectations on Leadership Behavior." *Journal of Personality and Social Psychology*, 50:1, pp 87–93.

Pasmore, W. A. (1994). *Creating Strategic Change, Designing the Flexible, High Performing Organization*. New York: John Wiley.

Perrow, Charles (1979). "Complex Organizations: A Critical Essay." 2nd Ed. Glenview, Ill.: Scott Foresman.

Pettigrew, A. (1972). "Managing Under Stress." *Management Today*. (April):pp 99–102.

Pinchot, G. and E. Pinchot (1994). *The End of Bureaucracy and the Rise of Intelligent Organization*. San Francisco: Berrett-Koehler.

Porte, P. C. Andre de la (1974). "Group Norms: Key to Building a Winning Team." *Personnel* (Sep.–Oct.):pp 121–127.

Porter, L. W. and E. E. Lawler (1968a). "What Job Attitudes Tell About Motivation." *Harvard Business Review*, 46(1):pp 118–126.

Porter, L. W. and E. E. Lawler (1968b). Managerial Attitudes and Performance. Homewood, Ill.: Irwin Dorsey.

Posner, John K. and Jody L. Posner (1986). "Stress, Role Ambiguity and Role Conflict," *Psychological Reports*, 55:pp 747–753.

Powell, G. N. (1988). *Women and Men in Management*. Beverly Hills, California: Sage.

Price, James L. (1968). *Organizational Effectiveness: An Inventory of Propositions*. Homewood, Ill.: Irwin Dorsey.

Quirk, Paul (1981). *Industry Influence in Federal Regulatory Agencies*. Princeton: Princeton University Press.

Rabin, Jack (1984). "A Symposium: Professionalism in Public Administration." *State and Local Government Review*, 16:pp 51–68.

Raelin, Joseph A. (1986). "An Analysis of Professional Deviance within Organizations." *Human Relations*, 39:12, pp 1103–1129.

Raia, J. R. and S. H. Osipow (1970). "Creative Thinking Ability and Susceptibility to Persuasion." *Journal of Social Psychology*, 28:pp 181–186.

Rees, F. (1991). *How to Lead Teams*. San Diego, California: Pfeiffer.

Robinson, S. L., M. S. Kraatz, and D. M. Rosseau (1994). "Changing Obligations and the Psychological Contract: A Longitudinal Study," *Academy of Management Journal*, (February), pp 137–152.

Roethlisberger, F. J. and W. Dickson (1939). *Management and the Worker*. Cambridge: Harvard.

Rosenberg, L. A. (1961). "Group Size, Prior Experience, and Conformity." *Journal of Abnormal and Social Psychology*, 63:pp 436–437.

Rosenthal, P. and K. Jacobson (1968). *Pygmalion in the Classroom*. N.Y.: Holt, Rinehart, and Winston.

Roy, Donald F. (1960). "Banana Time: Job Satisfaction and Informal Interaction." *Human Organization*, 18(4).

Roy, E. (1952). "Quota Restriction and Goldbricking in a Machine Shop." *American Journal of Sociology*, 57:pp 427–444.

Sadd, Susan (1979). "Sex Roles and Achievement Conflicts." *Personality and Social Psychology Bulletin*, 5(3) (July):pp 352–355.

Sampson, E. E. and A. C. Brandon (1964). "The Effects of Role and Opinion Deviation on Small Group Behavior." *Sociometry*, 27:pp 261–281.

Schacter, Stanley (1951). "Communication, Deviation, and Rejection." *Journal of Abnormal Social Psychology*, 46:pp 190–207.

Schacter, Stanley (1959). "The Chinese Indoctrination Program for Prisoners of War." *Psychiatry*, 19:pp 149–172.

Schacter, Stanley (1968). "Organizational Socialization and the Profession of Management." *Industrial Management Review*, 9:pp 1–16.

Schacter, Stanley (1971). "The Individual, The Organization, and the Career: A Conceptual Scheme." *Journal of Applied Behavioral Science*, 7:pp 401–426.

Schein, E. H. (1970). *Organizational Psychology*. Englewood Cliffs, N.J.: Prentice-Hall.

Schneier, Craig Eric and Kathryn M. Bartol (1980). "Sex Effects in Emergent Leadership." *Journal of Applied Psychology*, 65(3) (June):pp 341–345.

Schuler, R. (1975). "Role Perceptions, Satisfaction, and Performance: A Partial Reconciliation." *Journal of Applied Psychology*, 60(6) (Dec.):pp 683–687.

Seashore, Stanley E. (1954). *Group Cohesiveness in Industrial Work*. Ann Arbor, Mich.: Institute for Social Research, University of Michigan.

Selznik, Philip (1949). *TVA and the Grass Roots*. Berkeley: University of California.

Selznik, Philip (1957). *Leadersh in Administration*. N.Y.: Harper & Row.

Shapira, Zur and Roger L. M. Dunbar (1980). "Testing Mintzberg's Managerial Role Classification Using an In-Basket Simulation." *Journal of Applied Psychology*, 65(1) (Feb.):pp 87–95.

Shils, E. A. (1950). "Primary Groups in the American Army," in R. K. Merton and P. F. Lazarsfeld, (eds.), *Continuities in Social Research*. N.Y.: Free Press.

Social Science Research Council (1960). *Theoretical Studies in the Social Organization of the Prison*. N.Y.: SSRC.

Smith, R. J. (1986). "Shuttle Inquiry Focuses on Weather, Rubber Seals and Unheeded Advice," *Science* (Feb 28).

Storey, W. (1978). "Which Way: Manager-Directed or Person-Centered Career Pathing." *Training and Development Journal* (Jan.):pp 10–14.

Svara, J. H. (1990). *Official Leadership in the City: Patterns of Conflict and Cooperation*. New York: Oxford University Press.

Szilagyi, A. D. and Winford E. Holland (1980). "Changes in Social Density Relationships with Functional Interaction and Perceptions of Job Characteristics, Role Stress, and Work Satisfaction." *Journal of Applied Psychology*, 65(1) (Feb.):pp 28–33.

Tomkins, P. K. (1993). *Organizational Communication Imperatives: Lessons of the Space Program*. Los Angeles, California: Roxbury Publishing Company.

Trist, E. L. and K. W. Bamforth (1951). "Some Social and Psychological Consequences of the Longwall Method of Goal-Getting." *Human Relations*, 4(1) (Feb.):pp 3–38.

Vasu, Michael L. (1981). "Planning Theory and Planning Practice in the 1980's." *Urban Affairs Quarterly*, 17:1, pp 108–114.

Vasu, Michael L. (1979). *Politics and Planning: A National Study of American Planners.* Chapel Hill, N.C.: The University of North Carolina Press.

Vertz, Laura L. (1985). "Women, Occupational Advancement, and Mentoring." *Public Administration Review*, 45:3, pp 415–422.

Viteles, M. A. (1953). *Motivation and Morale in Industry*, N.Y.: Norton.

Walker, C., R. Guest, and A. Turner (1956). *The Foreman on the Assembly Line.* Cambridge: Harvard.

Wall, J. A. (1974). "Some Variables Affecting a Constituent's Evaluation of a Behavior toward a Boundary Role Occupant." *Organizational Behavior and Human Performance*, 11:pp 390–408.

Webber, R. A. (1974). "Majority and Minority Perceptions: Cross-Cultural Teams." *Human Relations*, 27(9):pp 873–889.

Weaver, Charles N. (1980). "Job Satisfaction in the U.S. in the 1970's." *Journal of Applied Psychology*, 65(3) (June):pp 364–367.

Weiner, M. (1958). "Certainty of Judgment as a Variable in Conformity Behavior." *Journal of Social Psychology*, 48:pp 257–263.

West, J. P. (ed.) (1995). *Quality Management Today.* Washington, D.C.: International City/County Management Association.

Whyte, William Foote (1943). *Street Corner Society.* Chicago: University of Chicago.

Whyte, William Foote (1955). *The Organization Man.* N.Y.: Simon and Schuster.

Whyte, William Foote (1955a). *Money and Motivation.* N.Y.: Harper.

Wilson, P. R. (1968). "Perceptual Distortion of Height as a Function of Ascribed Academic Status." *Journal of Social Psychology*, 74:pp 97–102.

Winther, Dorothy A. and Samuel B. Green (1987). "Another Look at Gender-Related Differences in Leadersh Behavior." *Sex Roles*, 15:1–22, pp 41–56.

Wirth, Clifford and Michael L. Vasu (1987). "Ideology and Decision Making for American City Managers." *Urban Affairs Quarterly*, 22:3, pp 454–474.

Yeager, Samuel J., Jack N. Rabin, and Thomas Vocino (1985). "Feedback and Administrative Behavior in the Public Sector." *Public Administration Review*, 45:5, pp 570–585.

Zarmarta, Raymond F., Manuel London, and K. M. Rowland (1979). "Effects of Sex on Commitment and Conflict Resolution." *Journal of Applied Psychology*, 64(2) (April):pp 227–231.

6
Communication

In any organization, communication is critical to effective management! Communication breakdowns can have draconian effects on public organizations, as in the case of the space shuttle *Challenger* (Graber, 1992, Tompkins, 1993). Conversely, effective communication can enhance organizational productivity. For example, recent research conducted at a number of leading companies has shown that communication is a pivotal element in promoting continuous improvement and organizational learning (Young and Post, 1993). In its most generic sense, communication involves sending and receiving messages over channels. However, communication implies that messages are understood in the sense that the sender intended. Consequently, communication has two essential elements, one is message *transfer*, the other message *comprehension*. As we shall see, both elements are necessary for effective interpersonal and organizational communication (Clampitt, 1991, Hewes, 1994, Tannen, 1994).

Though a critical activity of public sector managers, communication as a phenomenon is not always well understood. Often it is defined in terms of its most limited meaning, the directive(s) a manager issues to a subordinate. Communication, defined in this very limited sense, frequently is focused on the transmission of a message and not necessarily its successful reception. Such a focus has been associated with what has been called an "arrow" manager:

> Arrow managers tend to be straightforward and results oriented. They view communication rather like shooting an arrow at a target. Like the marksman, the speaker seeks to embed an intact message into the receiver so as to achieve the desired results, to hit the bull's eye. Communication is seen as a one way activity based primarily on the skills of the sender. The targets may move, but they never interact with the communicator. Hence, the aim of communication for the Arrow manager is to select the proper words and organize the ideas effectively in order to hit the target. The focus of arrow thinking is on the speaker or sender of the message (Clampitt, 1991, p. 3).

What a great deal of case study and experimental research shows is that just because a message was transmitted does not imply that it was understood in the fashion intended (Jablin et al., 1987; Clampitt, 1991; Tompkins, 1993). Sometimes the consequences of these communication breakdowns are interpersonally and organizationally problematic. At other times, the consequences are tragic. For example, on January 25, 1990, Avianca Flight 52 was heading in for final approach to New York's Kennedy airport when it crashed killing 73 people. Initially, the plane had a comfortable cushion of over two hours of fuel. However, because of a series of delays the plane eventually ran out of fuel and crashed. All during this time the pilots and co-pilot were "communicating" with air traffic controllers. When investigators from the FAA reviewed the cockpit tapes and interviewed the controllers at Kennedy, they discovered that a communication breakdown had caused this crash. The pilots of Flight 52 kept saying they were "running low on fuel." Air traffic controllers told FAA officials that this is a fairly commonly used phrase by airline pilots approaching Kennedy when they are told to assume a holding pattern, prior to getting clearance for landing. Tragically, what the pilots of Flight 52 did not say was that they had an *emergency*. Had they used the word, emergency, they would have been given immediate clearance to land. The cockpit conversations indicated the concern the pilot and co-pilot had about the diminishing fuel reserves. A concern they did not communicate in a fashion that was clear to the air traffic controllers. In effect, a message was *transmitted* but it was not *understood* in the sense that the sender intended.

Clearly, no form of organizational information is effective unless it is both transmitted and understood. In this sense, communication is a two way street requiring a shared commitment between the sender and the receiver of the communication. Management inherently involves the ability to communicate. Mintzberg, in a now classic study on the nature of managerial work, describes the manager as the "nerve center" of the organization's information. The unique access of the manager to all subordinates and special outside contacts confers the power to acquire information:

> In effect, the manager is his organization's generalist with the best store of non-routine information; as monitor the manager continually seeks and receives information from a variety of sources in order to develop a thorough understanding of the organization and its environment; as disseminator the manager sends external information into his organization and internal information from one subordinate to another; as spokesman the manager must transmit information to various external groups; [and] serve outsiders as an expert in the field in which his organization operates (Mintzberg, 1973).

Mintzberg names "sharing information" as a key area of concentration for managers seeking to improve their effectiveness. The only way to share information is to communicate it effectively. Applying Mintzberg's categories to the activities of public sector executives, Lau and Newman (1980) found the communication role to be central to effective management. In an analysis of work diaries they found that a sample of Navy executives spent 22 percent of their time in informational roles: monitoring internal and external information, interpreting, integrating, brainstorming information internally, and transmitting plans, policies, actions, and results to outsiders (Lau and Newman, 1980). Conversely, managerial communication can be a major source of organizational problems. A national study of the role of intra-organizational conflict in the courts found "communication problems" one of the most frequently mentioned sources of conflict encountered in court management (Mays and Taggart, 1986).

In this chapter we will discuss communication from a variety of perspectives. We propose a more comprehensive description of the process of communication. Then we explore both verbal and nonverbal types of communication, the structure of communication, the changing role of information and its impact on management, and the important skill of listening. We conclude with the consideration of a proposed approach to assessing communication effectiveness: the communication audit.

COMMUNICATION AS A PROCESS

The field of organizational communication, lodged in the interstices of the disciplines of organizational behavior and speech communication, by its very nature has an interdisciplinary content (Jablin, et al., 1987; Clampitt, 1991; Hewes, 1994; Tannen, 1994). In addition, the field lacks a prevailing paradigm which would lend unity to its content. Goldhaber, for example, found that in a review of 26 organizational communication textbooks, 39 major topics were explored. But no topic was covered in every book and the majority of topics were covered in less than one-half of the textbooks (Goldhaber, 1979). However, Goldhaber mentions a few concepts which gain general support in this literature review.

1.   Organizational communication occurs within a complex open system which is influenced by and influences its environment:

2.   Organizational communication involves messages and their flow, purpose, direction, and media; and

3.   Organizational communication involves people and their abilities, feelings, relationships, and skills (Goldhaber, 1979).

We adopt the working definition for organizational communication proposed by Tortoriello. Organizational communication, he says, is the study of the flow and impact of messages within a network of interactional relationships (Tortoriello et al., 1978). This definition is enriched by descriptions which portray this communication as a process where messages are created and exchanged within an organizational environment which produces uncertainty for both individuals and groups (Goldhaber, 1979; Clampitt, 1991).

The virtue of these definitions is that they incorporate David Berlo's now classic statement on the "process" character of communication, that is, communication as dynamic, continuous, and ongoing (Berlo, 1960). Communication in this sense is a dynamic phenomenon moving longitudinally in time and space:

Figure 10 is a representation of these definitions which provides the conceptual tools for discussing communication in public sector organizations.

Communication is about creating and exchanging messages between senders and receivers over channels. The source in human communication is the person sending the communication. In order for communication to take place, an objective, expressed as a message to be conveyed by some person is required. This message is encoded in human communication. The channel is the medium through which the message travels, for example, in any public agency there are formal channels and informal channels of communication. In human communication, we are typically interested in conveying a thought to another person; in

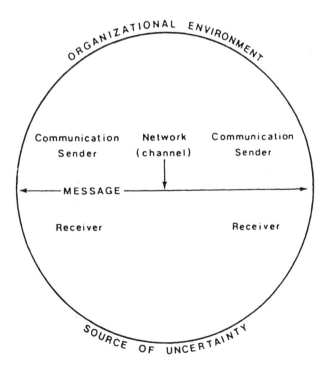

Figure 10   Communication as a process.

other words, this is the purpose of our communication. In order for this to occur, the receiver must decode the message, which typically is expressed using symbols (Hewes, 1994). Human language is a set of symbols used to convey meaning. Mathematics is, also, a symbolic language which conveys meaning to those who are literate in it. However, human language, unlike mathematics, is *inherently ambiguous*. This is to say, that the connotative and denotative meaning of the words that comprise any human language require interpretation. This interpretation provides the potential for distortion in human communication.

> The inherent ambiguity of language can be seen in the words we use, the sentences we utter, and in the countless communication breakdowns we experience. One researcher says that for the 500 most frequently used words in the English language there are over 14,000 definitions. Take, for instance, the word "run." A sprinter can "run" in a race. Politicians "run" races, but not exclusively with their legs. Although a horse "runs" with legs, it uses four of them, which is still a little different than a sprinter. A woman can get a "run" in her hose, which is troublesome, but having a "run" of cards is good. However, having a run on a bank is bad. For a sailor "running" around is not good at all, but a "run" on the wind can be exhilarating. To score a "run" in baseball is different than a run in cricket. Hence one "runs" into the ambiguity of language at every turn even with a simple everyday word like "run" (Clampitt, 1991, p. 26).

The potential for distortion in meaning inherent in language is very evident to public opinion researchers who have engaged in extensive research on question wording, question order and the effects on people's responses (Rea and Parker, 1992). Mueller (1973) found rising levels of support for American foreign intervention to stop subversion if the word "communist" was used in the questions. Indeed, a simple change in wording of a poll can result in a significant change of support for a particular expression of public policy, for example, substituting helping the poor for welfare in a question. Sudman and Bradburn (1982) report research that indicates that words like welfare, socialism, bureaucracy, big business, and federal government have multiple meanings to different people. Consequently, without understanding the precise meaning in a particular context, it is very difficult to interpret survey responses. The substance of the foregoing discussion about the ambiguity of language is best expressed in the joke told by pollsters. Apparently the question "What do you think of Red China?" was asked amid a series of foreign policy questions on a nationwide poll. One answer to this question was "It looks good on a white table cloth." In effect, a message was *transmitted* by the pollster but it was not *understood* in the sense that the sender intended.

Given the inherent ambiguity of language, the sender of a message in the human communication process "hopes" that the message he sent is received in such a way that his other meaning is clear. This qualification is added because the message is encoded by the sender using language and decoded by the receiver during his interpretation of the language used in that message. This decoding by the receiver is conducted through the medium of a filter, a frame of reference, which includes the "the codes of the person's own unique experiences." Some elements of this code include: personal knowledge, attitudes, beliefs, values, sub-cultural or cultural context, gender, capacity for language comprehension, internalized rules for non-verbal behavior, etc. This encoding and decoding process can also be complicated by noise in the channel. Moreover, messages are both verbal (speeches, lectures, conversations) or nonverbal (body language, physical characteristics, vocal cues, personal space) (Goldhaber, 1979; Jablin et al., 1987; Stewart et al., 1996). All of these elements interact to form what we loosely call interpersonal communication.

> Communication takes place beyond general appearance and the spoken word. Posture tells us something about a person's attitude toward others. A slouching, frowning person says something different from the person standing straight and tall. A person continually glancing at a watch may seems to convey a desire to be somewhere else. Real pros at body language can read the precise meaning of the pulling of an earlobe or arms folded across the chest or the gaze out the window, but everyone receives a message of some kind from these gestures. Body language does talk (Arnold et al., 1983, p. 15).

Interestingly, research in human communication has shown that when verbal and nonverbal communication are inconsistent, receivers of communication give greater weight to the nonverbal behaviors in terms of evaluating the senders' feelings (Hayes, 1977; Knapp and Hall, 1992). Given the ambiguity of language, this may be a sound strategy. Research also suggests that people realize that messages received from social actors cannot always be accepted at face value and engage in a cognitive process called "second guessing" which involves providing an alternative interpretation (Hewes et al., 1985; Hewes, 1994).

Whether verbal or nonverbal, the messages that are created and exchanged in an agency travel over channels called communication networks. Communication networks flow from roles and structures that vary from agency to agency. Networks may be formal or informal, and they may channel information vertically or horizontally (Graber, 1992). Messages are communicated through an interaction process. There is constant mutual feedback between sender and receiver so that both parties are communicators, or givers and receivers, at the same time (Tortoriello et al., 1978; Hewes, 1994).

The environment within which communication occurs is a significant part of the communication picture, because of its role in shaping both process and contents of communication. Environmental factors in public sector organizations, including clients, funding bodies, and legislative and executive officials, often shape human communication networks, while changes in political, social and economic environments ensure a ubiquitous uncertainty for public sector managers. Some communication scholars define the principal function of communication as the "reduction of uncertainty" (Farace et al., 1977). Since historically government agencies are established to cope with problems that cannot or will not be resolved by the private sector, and, many of these problems are "wicked problems" in that there is no clearly defined "solution" only "temporary resolutions," the level of uncertainty (the gap between information needed and information held) is heightened for the public manager. Following Berlo's lead, contemporary communication theorists are quick to point out the dangers in describing the communication activity in terms of its discrete components: senders, receivers, messages, channels, and networks. When we examine the components of communication we freeze a process that in the real world is dynamic and constantly changing. Our analytical purpose is served only if we keep in mind the whole as we study its parts.

Communication, as we usually think of it in an organization, is intentional, conscious, directed, and purposeful. For example, the director of the Division for Social Services uses verbal instructions to make his decisions known, he informs his employees about a new case management program, he tells them how it will be implemented, and obtains sufficient information from the case workers to evaluate the new system at each stage of the implementation process. But sometimes managers communicate unconsciously. For example, the same director repeatedly checks his watch while in a conversation initiated by a social worker who is disgruntled about the paperwork generated by the new system. We established earlier that a message is a symbol to which we attach meaning. In the first instance, the social service director is using the symbols of written and verbal communication. In the second example nonverbal symbols were used to communicate meaning.

Watzlawick et al., (1967) capture the significant differences between verbal and nonverbal communication by aligning each type of communication with two distinct systems: the digital and the analog. Digital communication is like an on/off switch; analog communication is like a rheostat. Content messages tend to be transmitted in digital form through verbal communication, which consists of individual sounds, words, and sentences. Nonverbal communication such as voice tone, friendliness, and attentiveness transmits analog messages. Variation occurs by discrete steps in digital communication, by degree in analog communication. The analog, nonverbal communication is more likely to communicate a relationship message, the digital, verbal communication a content message. *All communications have content and relationship dimensions.*

Communication can also be described in terms of information richness dimension; that is, the potential information-carrying capacity of data. Data, as we will use the term in this context, are simply the output of a communication channel. If we array the following forms of communication: face to face communication, telephone conversations, memos, and computer printout, it is clear that interpersonal communication is the highest in information richness and computer printouts the least, in terms of information richness. Why? In face to face interaction the participants have multiple "cues" to employ in reducing uncertainty, verbal messages, body language, facial gestures, tone of voice, dress, physical distance from speaker, etc. (Daft and Lengel, 1984; Knapp and Hall, 1992). Talking with someone on the phone reduces the information richness that we gather from nonverbal cues. This fact may be at the source of the phenomena of meeting someone with whom you have had a series of telephone discussions prior to meeting the person and concluding that they do not "look like" you expected. Now consider reading a memo which suggests multiple interpretations. In such a case, the normal tendency is for a person to seek out the memo's author for clarification or, in other words, to secure more information richness in an endeavor to reduce uncertainty. In other words, to secure other cues that help us read between the lines. Finally, a computer spread sheet, as a communication form, is lowest in information richness. Information richness, or more precisely, the need for it, may explain why the face to face meeting is such an important forum for developing and resolving policy questions in both the public and private sector.

VERBAL COMMUNICATION

In organizations, verbal communication takes place through three distinct types of encounters which will be described subsequently. Each encounter utilizes its own techniques and mediums for communication meaning. For example, in *Communication Encounter 1*, facts, opinions, and ideas are conveyed by management to employees. Techniques typically employed are policy and procedure manuals, employee directives, letters, memos, operational guidelines, and internal agency newsletters; *Communication Encounter 2*, captures various forms of joint consultation in the organization, between management and unions or within work units (teams, quality circles, project members, etc.). Vehicles typically utilized to facilitate this process are structured meetings and problem solving sessions. (Here nonverbal messages may also transmit meaning.) *Communication Encounter 3* refers to the "one on one" dialogue between an individual employee, or applicant, and a manager. This process unfolds through normal day-to-day discussion, occurs as part of periodic performance review or, for the potential employee or promotee, may take place in a formal interview. *Communication Encounter 3* has a very strong nonverbal dimension.

Considering verbal communication in terms of these three sets of organizational encounters helps isolate, and freeze for examination purposes, those places where communication might break down. Typically, barriers to effective organizational communication arise in the effort to translate a specific message through a given medium. Communication breakdown may result from characteristics of the medium or the message. Figure 11 highlights these vulnerable points in the process. With breakdown points identified, the manager can focus on effective remedies.

In the context of *Communication Encounter 1* communication, breakdown may be conditioned by the words chosen or by the medium employed. In some governmental cultures the medium itself impedes effective communication, as in Thailand where the anonymous letter is a "time-honored tradition within the Thai government" (Krannick and Krannick, 1979). In Japan, the Japanese language has different levels of politeness that can greatly effect communication in an administrative setting.

> When a Japanese official speaks to a foreign official, he or she may speak at a very high level of politeness and may, then receive a reply at the same level of politeness. In order to interact and communicate with a Japanese administrator, a foreigner must be familiar with a wide range of politeness. In an organizational relationship, an employee must learn proper manners, which include the use of language and verbal expression. If a person's speech lacks the proper respect, this can easily cause a problem. People react emotionally to the way others speak to them, for the degree of politeness used in speech reflects the degree of respect accorded them by the speaker. A status-conscious Japanese administrator, therefore, tends to be quite sensitive to how he is spoken to. A person inquiring about any sort of service, whether it is information, assistance, or cooperation, is expected to be even more humble and respectful than usual. If a client fails to use a proper expression, a government employee may interpret this as the client's lack of respect. As a result, the employee may be indifferent toward the client and fail to help with the request (Jun and Muto, 1995, p. 130).

In the U.S. the medium of the written word is generally acknowledged as a most useful tool in organizational communication. But in terms of the choice of words, every student of government is familiar with the popular criticism leveled against bureaucratic writing. Examples of *bureaucratic gobblegook* abound in the popular press! One proposal to enhance the clarity of communications offers a tool which rearranges and consolidates content of an administrative memo or

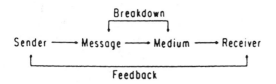

Figure 11   Communication breakdown.

other written document in order of priorities and restricts the uses of verbs to one, written in the active voice and adjacent to the subject" (Silverman, 1980). This "optimum legibility formula" (OLF) stipulates a seven point formula for effective and efficient written communication:

1. Write the complete message as quickly as possible, without premeditated compliance with OLF restrictions.
2. Determine the purpose for the message by listing three or four potential sentence subjects.
3. Decide what to write by answering the six basic journalistic questions: who, what, when, where, why, and how.
4. Rearrange sentences in order of priority, consolidating all sentences with identical or synonymous verbs.
5. Place verbs immediately following their subjects.
6. Eliminate all linking verbs.
7. Use one verb per sentence.

Sometimes *Communication Encounter 1* breaks down because managers think that every detail needs to be communicated. Employees typically don't want to know everything there is to know about their agency. The most important and desired information falls into the following categories:

Job security—facts on the agency's stability, plans for the future growth, intention to expand or reduce the work force, commitment to fair treatment of employees.

Opportunity for advancement—facts on how employees can get ahead, increase their income, improve their working conditions.

Status and recognition—facts on why the employee's job is important; how his "team" rates with the public; how the employee himself has contributed to its success.

What's expected in return—facts on job performance criteria; procedures, policies and rules; standards of conduct; expected level of effort, contribution, and cooperation.

Beyond communicating these items, managers need to be sensitive to information overload. Sometimes, in some agencies, the simple volume of written communication requires the employee to engage in a form of "memo triage" deciding which memos to read and in what priority.

Communication Encounter 2, where joint consultation takes place in a meeting setting, provides management with an opportunity to evaluate employee responses unmatched by any other medium in terms of information richness. Employees may be reluctant to put in writing a criticism that will surface naturally in a group setting. Gestures and facial expressions, between and among the participants, provide helpful clues as to attitudes in a group. Employees may be more likely to raise questions at a meeting than through other channels for upward communication. And, the general verbal as well as nonverbal reaction of the group will help the meeting's convener determine the majority perspective on any individual topic (Jablin, et al., 1987; Hewes, 1994).

Communication in such a meeting often falters because of inattention to the structure of the meeting itself. Improperly planned and structured meetings impede communication by failing to encourage the communication for which the meeting exists, by stressing the wrong message, or by producing a cynicism in employees about the effectiveness of participation. Baker provides some guidelines to ensure meetings are effective mediums for communication (Baker, 1979). Before calling a meeting a manager should:

1. determine alternatives to holding meeting,
2. clearly establish purpose,
3. limit attendance,
4. distribute agenda in advance,
5. circulate background material,
6. choose an appropriate meeting time, and
7. place a limit on the meeting and on each item.

During the meeting the manager must be sure to:

1. start and end on time,
2. place important items at top of agenda,
3. assign time keeping and minutes responsibility,
4. end the meeting with a unifying or positive issue,
5. summarize what has been accomplished, and
6. coordinate time of next meeting.

And after the meeting the manager should take time to:

1. provide timely and complete minutes,
2. follow through on decisions, and
3. conduct a periodic evaluation of the meeting.

Communication Encounter 3 type communication; the messages are transmitted back and forth between an individual manager and a current or potential employee (Tannen, 1994). Effective communication in this one-to-one exchange is highly dependent on the personalities involved. (Strategies encouraging supervisor-subordinate communication will be addressed in our chapter on performance appraisal.) What needs stress here is that an individual's satisfaction (and conversely dissatisfaction) at work has been traced empirically to the quality of communication interaction experience. Communication can both reduce uncertainty (Thayer, 1968) and satisfy needs for affiliation (Timm and Wilkens, 1977; Kalbfleisch, 1993). Some organizations have realized this and embarked on a variety of programs to isolate and correct sources of communication breakdown in the organization. Timm (1968) has argued that supervisor to subordinate communication behavior should be viewed as part of the organizational reward system. Whereas in *Communication Encounter 1* and *Communication Encounter 2* the message is carried largely by words, *Communication Encounter 3* falls into the realm of interpersonal communication where nonverbal messages carry the burden of meaning. The initial employment interview presents one case where the importance of nonverbal transactions in encounter 3 communication has been well documented. Several studies have found the importance of the articulative and nonverbal behavior (eye contact, gesturing, smiling, appropriate tone) in receiving a favorable evaluation in a job interview (Imada and Hakel, 1977; McGovern and Tinsky, 1978; Washburn and Hakel, 1973; Wexley, et al., 1975, Knapp and Hall, 1992). We turn now to an in depth discussion of the nonverbal dimension of communication.

NONVERBAL COMMUNICATION

Nonverbal communication occurs when a message is transmitted by a means other than the spoken or written word. Nonverbal communication includes all the message content in communication interaction except that explicitly encoded through words. Mehrabian argues that three basic dimensions of human emotion and attitudes are expressed nonverbally, immediacy (disliking-liking), status and power relationships (degree of influence of one person over another), and responsiveness (activity versus passivity). Nonverbal communication constitutes the overwhelming majority of any message transmitted during a communication event (Wieman and Harrison, 1984; Mehrabian, 1981). Harris (1970) suggests that 65 percent of social meaning in face-to-face communication is carried by the nonverbal message. According to Mehrabian (1981), 93 percent of general meaning can be attributed to nonverbal messages and only seven percent to verbal. The role of nonverbal communication in interpreting organizational interactions is increasingly recognized as critical. Lewis argues that each of us speaks two languages, one verbal and the other nonverbal (Lewis, in Tortoriello, et al., 1978). The definition of nonverbal communication adopted here is that of the exchange of messages between and among individuals primarily through nonlinguistic means (Jablin et al., 1987; Knapp and Hall, 1992). Some of these nonlinguistic means are kinesics (body language), facial expressions and the use of eye contact, tactile communication, the use of space and territory, paralanguage (vocal but not linguistic communication), and the use of silence and time in communication (Tortoriello et al., 1978; Wieman and Harrison, 1984; Knapp and Hall, 1992).

Using the analogic label to describe nonverbal communication systems as opposed to the digital definition for verbal communication helps to identify and thus to eliminate a major source of communication breakdown. Breakdown occurs when problems arise in translating analogic messages into digital messages. When communicators try to fit the continuous into the discrete, information may be lost or seriously misrepresented. A first step to avoid communication breakdown due to the existence of nonverbal as well as verbal messages is to identify more precisely the modes of nonverbal communication.

Kinesics or Body Language, a well-documented mode of nonverbal communication, has been categorized by Eckman and Friesen (1969) into five types of expressions. *Emblems* are nonverbal behaviors that stand for words: the sign OK, and the peace sign, for example. Often emblems are used to reinforce a verbal message. *Illustrators*; are forms of nonverbal behavior that literally illustrate a message: the parking attendant points to a space while commanding "park here." *Affect displays*; are facial movements which send a message, either intentional as in sticking a tongue out to communicate insult, or unintentional, when a shy employee blushes in response to a compliment from the manager. *Regulators*; such as turning one's eyes away from the speaker to signal loss of interest or nodding one's head to keep communication going regulate all communication. Finally, *adapters* are nonverbal behaviors learned in childhood which meet some need, but which the speaker may not notice. Touching one's head to relieve an itch which in private you might scratch is one example.

Facial Expressions and Eye Contact; are a second category of nonverbal communication. The most visible indicator of emotions and feelings is probably the face (Goldhaber, 1979). But it is eye contact that has been the subject of the most extensive investigation in organizations. Goldhaber summarizes our knowledge about eye contact under the following points:

1. Eye contact seems to occur when people are seeking feedback, when an individual wants to signal open communications, and when an individual is asking for inclusion.
2. Women appear to engage in more eye contact than men.
3. Eye contact increases as communicators increase the distance between themselves.
4. Eye contact may produce anxiety in others.
5. Eye contact does not occur when people want to hide their feelings, when people are physically close, in some competitive situations, when listeners are bored, and when an individual does not want social contact (Goldhaber, 1979).

Tactile Communication; a third nonverbal mode, may be the most primitive form of message sending. Nancy Henley suggests that the message sent is often a message of dominance. In our culture, persons of higher status are permitted to touch others, but it would be a notable break of etiquette for a person of lower status to touch their superiors (Henley, 1977; Wieman and Harrison 1984; Jackson, 1992).

Space and Territory has been studied extensively by ethologists who report that dominant animals in a group have a territory which is distinguished from that of other animals by its greater size. Space and territory emerge in the organizational world as nonverbal communicators of status and power. Mehrabian (1971) notes:

> Higher-status persons of a social group have access to more locations and have more power to increase or restrict immediacy vis-a-vis others than lower status members . . . . . . For instance, among persons of different status within the same institution, such as a school, a business, or a hospital, high-status individuals are assigned larger and more private quarters (p. 34).

Higher status people in organizations are better protected in terms of their territory. For example, it is more difficult to gain access to the governor than to a division head. Higher status people also have more territory to protect. The persons of higher status in American organizations typically seeks corner offices with multiple windows. Persons of higher status will find it easier to "invade" the territory of lower status individuals. Nonverbal behavior communicates a number of messages to those who are observant (Wieman and Harrison, 1984). Moreover, both males and females can employ status and power cues.

> Both males and females can be encouraged to use nonverbal cues that reflect status and power when such cues are appropriate to the communication situation. Instead of using these cues as a reflection of gender stereotypes (men are always dominate and women are always submissive), both sexes can use these cues when the situation calls for them. For example, it may be appropriate for a woman to use status and power cues as the manager of her office just as it may be inappropriate for her male secretary to demonstrate such cues in her office. We should remember that the structure of the situation, not gender stereotypes dictates the use of status and powers cues of interpersonal communication (Stewart et al., 1996, p. 92).

Environment, referring to both the building and rooms in which we work and the arrangements of movable objects like furniture around us, can influence our communication patterns. A desk may serve as a marker to establish personal space. When an office is arranged so that chairs are grouped together, this signals intimacy and informality. When chairs are lined up in front of desk, this is a sign that the desk's occupant has authority and power. At the same time, this formal arrangement may be counterbalanced, in the same office, with a grouping of furniture that is more egalitarian.

Paralanguage, the tone and variation accompanying verbal messages, is a sixth nonverbal mode which may either compliment or contradict a verbal communication. Tortoriello et al. suggest that paralanguage may explain attraction and repulsion between communicators, even when comprehension of a message is unaffected. For example, an employee with a high pitched voice may be denied a job in public relations because a high-pitched voice does not project the image that the organization wants projected (Tortoriello et al., 1978).

The use of *silence and time* shades the meaning of messages between and among people. Silence can indicate support or opposition, create uneasiness, provide a link between messages or sever a relationship (Tortoriello et al., 1978). Time can be an indicator of status, as when a subordinate waits for hours to see a supervisor, or it can be an acknowledgment of mutual respect, when manager and subordinate organize their schedules so as to conserve each other's time (Jackson, 1992; Knapp and Hall, 1992).

Everyone in an organization can become a more effective communicator through increased awareness of nonverbal messages and their impact. Nonverbal messages may serve to repeat, substitute, contradict, complement, or regulate communication (Koehler et al., 1981; Wieman and Harrison, 1984; Leathers, 1992). Finally, nonverbal messages are also gender related and, as we will discuss subsequently, may have an impact on the managerial communication process.

> Gender is reflected in nonverbal cues. In general, women are more adept at encoding (forming) and decoding (translating) nonverbal cues than men, a difference that emerges in childhood and continues into adulthood. In body movement and posture, female and male toddlers and preschool children tend to use different gestures. Girls tend to use more emblems (nonverbal gestures with verbal equivalents) than boys. Throughout childhood development and into adulthood, men use more space than women use to respond freely. As children develop, girls receive more affect displays than boys. As a result, females tend to be better than males at encoding and decoding affect throughout their lives (Stewart et al., 1996, p. 94).

VERTICAL AND HORIZONTAL COMMUNICATION

Thus far we have discussed communication as messages transmitted verbally and nonverbally. We turn now to the channels along which messages flow. What are the patterns of communications in organizations? What effects do the different patterns have on the organizational process? What factors create particular communication patterns?

Within organizations, communication is the foundation of control and coordination. The formal organization dictates the channels for information flow: vertical in direction for formal transactions rooted in the principles of authority and hierarchy and horizontal in direction for transactions emanating from job function (Goldhaber, 1979; Graber, 1992). Vertical communication may be "down-the-line" or "up-the-line" (Conboy, 1976; Graber, 1992). This fact is no less true for the White House than for any other public agency. In an interesting evaluation of the flow of communication in the Reagan White House (Kessel,

1984) devised a communication matrix to isolate those who were receiving the highest number of messages. Using this approach the author was able to characterize the Reagan White House in terms of communication flow. Referring to the previously mentioned matrix the author states:

> The three highest column totals (that is, the number of messages received) were: Ed Meese, 95; Craig Fuller, 90; and Jim Baker, 79. Mike Deaver's total was 55. The other high scores for messages received belong to unit directors. Office of Policy Development Head Ed Harper had a score of 70; chief liaison Ken Duberstein a score of 60; and David Gergen, assistant to the president for communications, 51. The next highest scores belonged to deputy directors. OMB deputy director Joe Wright had a column total of 45, and Roger Porter, deputy director of OPD, 36. The tenth highest score for messages received was counsel Fred Fielding's 30. Of the ten highest scores, eight belonged to assistants to the president and two (the eight and ninth) to deputies. The communication structure of the Reagan White House was centralized and hierarchical (Kessel, 1984, p. 239).

He goes on to compare the Reagan White House and the Carter White House structure by noting that one major difference between the two was "that there simply was more communication in the Reagan White House" (Kessel, 1984, p. 239).

As we noted previously, vertical communication in an organization may be "down-the-line" or "up-the-line." According to Katz and Kahn, down-the-line channels are used to communicate five types of messages:

1. Job instructions; direction on how to do a specific task.
2. Job rationale; information about how one task relates to other tasks in the organization.
3. Procedures and practices; messages indicating the rules of the game in the organization.
4. Feedback; messages telling individuals about their performance on the job.
5. Indoctrination of goals; messages about overall organizational goals and the relationship of the individual goals to organizational goals (Katz and Kahn, 1966).

Logic would suggest that down-the-line communication messages should become more elaborate as they move through levels of the hierarchy, because at each level more specific details might be added to ensure comprehension by subordinates, and because employees want necessary information from their supervisors. But Conboy reports that in fact remarkable attrition occurs as messages move down the hierarchy. One study of 100 industrial managers yielded average information acquisition figures as follows for down-the-line communication.

Board of Directors; 100 percent of communication content
Vice Presidents; 67 percent
General supervisors; 56 percent
Plant managers; 40 percent
Foremen; 30 percent
Workers; 20 percent

Another issue in downward communication concerns how information acquisition is perceived by different people in the organization (Graber, 1992). One study conducted by Likert indicated that supervisors may overestimate the amount of information known by subordinates. Employees often complain that they don't receive enough information about their job performance (Katz and Kahn, 1966). Often the information that is added as the message proceeds down the organizational hierarchy may change the meaning originally intended. But the communication downward may also falter because, as noted earlier, managers may overload employees with messages like bulletins, memos, and announcements, many of which may be of marginal interest to them. Sometimes filtering, or shortening, changing, and lengthening messages as they move down, and power grabbing, or not sharing messages, also frustrate downward communication.

Up-the-line communication occurs when messages flow from subordinate to superior and up the levels of hierarchy. Up-the-line communication is much like the parlor game where one person tells another a story by whispering the story into their ear, and, then that person tells the next person and so on until the story as been told to everyone in the room. At this point, the last person to hear the story and the first person to tell it compare stories, frequently, there is significant divergence in the content of the story. A filtering and weeding-out process has occurred as the story moved form person to person. So it is in organizations! Assuming that the initial message itself is clear, devoid of ambiguity, timely, and contains data relevant to some organizational concern, much distortion occurs as information moves up the hierarchy. Anthony Downs (1967) employing the seminal work of Gordon Tullock, observes that we may postulate a hierarchy of authority containing seven levels with each level reporting to their superiors. And, if we further assume an average span of control of 4 then there are 4,096 officials at the bottom level of this seven level hierarchy. If each official at the bottom level of this organization is gathering 1.0 units of data and transmitting them upward this means that 4,096 units of data are gathered during a given time period. The amount of data that reaches the top level of the hierarchy depends upon the amount filtered out at each screening. If one assumes that half of the information is omitted each time it passes through the next level, the top level will receive 1/64 of all the information, a sum totaling 64 units. Put in other terms, 98.4 percent of the total data gathered will be lost in the upward communication of information through the seven levels of the organization (Downs, 1967, pp. 116–17).

Moreover, it is not just the absolute amount of data that is lost that is of concern, the *quality of the data* that is passed on is also effected. The selection principles employed by those at the bottom of the hierarchy will be different than those at the top, as will their interests, perceptions of reality, allegiance to sub-units of the organization, and the breadth of information they possess. Referring to "A" as the top of the hierarchy Anthony Downs has observed:

> In fact, the selection principles used by officials at each level are likely to be different from those used by other levels for the same reasons. Hence, the information that finally reaches A has passed through six filters of different quality and the facts reported to A will be quite different in content and implication from the "facts" gathered at the lowest level (Downs, 1967, p. 118).

The filtering upward occurs as employees tend to report information that makes them look good and keep silent information that casts them in a poor light. Also, the alienated worker can simply refuse to share information with supervisors because of his or her desire to maintain some control, however meager. Upward filtering has received considerable research attention. It is usually measured directly, by asking respondents to indicate their degree of openness with their superiors, or else indirectly, by measuring the agreement between superiors and subordinates on subordinates' work problems and responsibilities (Monge et al., 1978; Pincus, 1986). Factors found to affect upward filtering include the subordinate's satisfaction (Burke and Wilcox, 1969), the subordinate's trust in the superior (Roberts and O'Reilly, 1974), and the subordinate's own mobility aspirations (Maier et al., 1963; Read, 1962).

Several management theorists have argued that openness of communication between subordinates and superiors is critical to maintaining a successful organizational climate (Likert, 1967; Burke and Wilcox, 1969; Jablin, 1978; Eisenber et al., 1983; Graber, 1992). Some research has found that employees' perceptions of organizational communication are directly related to their levels of job satisfaction and even their performance (Pincus, 1986). Yet, researchers have discovered that subordinates are afraid to tell superiors how they feel (Vogel, 1967), they distort information they give their bosses (Read, 1962; Downs, 1967; Vogel, 1967; Athanassiades, 1973; O'Reilly and Roberts, 1974; Graber, 1992), and they feel that passing negative information to a boss may bring punishment (Blau and Scott, 1962; Argyris, 1966).

Research shows that openness in communication in general will prevail when (1) both superiors and subordinates perceive each other as willing and receptive listeners; and (2) both refrain from responses which might be perceived as neutral-negative or nonaccepting (Jablin, 1978). In a practical vein, Goldhaber concludes from his research on upward communication that sympathetic listening is one of the most efficient ways of increasing the quality of upward communication (Goldhaber, 1979).

So far we have focused on vertical communication, which emphasizes the formal control structure of an organization, its hierarchy, and chain of command. Horizontal communication, in contrast, emanates from functional relationships outlined in the structure of jobs. It refers to the messages exchanged between and among the people and units at the same level in the organizational hierarchy. While the amount of vertical communication may be higher in the typical organization, where estimates of vertical communication run as high as 66 percent (Porter and Roberts, 1976), horizontal communication remains important. Estimates of the amount of horizontal communication hover in the 33 percent range (Porter and Roberts, 1976). However, much communications research suggests the vertical system would be nearly unworkable without considerable flow of information laterally (Burns, 1954; Dubin, 1962; Dubin and Spray, 1964; Guetzkow, 1965; Simpson, 1959).

Typically, horizontal communication is initiated in order to coordinate tasks, solve problems, share information, and/or resolve conflict (Goldhaber, 1979). Though it is a critical part of effective communication in an organization, horizontal communication may falter because of rivalry and specialization of work units without communication avenues linking them, or lack of incentives or rewards for effective communication. As remedies for poor horizontal communication Conboy proposes the following:

Boldly and clearly announce the expectation that horizontal communication will occur.

Put into place mechanisms like routing systems to ensure that horizontal communication takes place.

Design reward systems to reinforce good horizontal communication and discourage hoarding information (Conboy, 1976).

The hierarchical structure of organizations and the functional description of jobs or tasks prescribe certain vertical and horizontal communication patterns in organizations. Also, informal communication networks operate within the work units throughout the organization. Networks specify who talks to whom, how far communicating units are from one another in the network, and ground rules to be followed in communication.

Analysis of typical information flow patterns within most organizations clearly shows that information does not circulate freely to everyone. Some groups are regularly privy to the most important information. Widely know as "old boy" networks, these insiders often develop shared values and expectations. People who do not regularly belong to the insider networks are usually part of other communication networks that share in less politically significant information. Outsiders often differ substantially in the outlook from the in-group. A few of them may be loners who do not communicate regularly with any network. Since messages are interpreted differently as they move from one network to another within the organization or beyond it, they may require explanatory commentary geared to particular needs (Graber, 1992, p. 164).

The location of an individual in a communications network may have significant implications for the organization. Research has found that certain people occupy "key communicator" roles for some topics of concern to the organization; they serve as links between larger groups of people (Taylor et al., 1976; Albrecht, 1978). These "key" people are the ones who most members of the organization can reach through relatively few channels.

Research suggests significant differences in how key communicators and nonkey communicators relate to the organization. Key communicators identify more with their jobs, are more satisfied with downward directed messages, perceive themselves to be closer to management and believe their jobs to be more central in the overall environment (Albrecht, 1979). To the extent that such communication linkages affect assumptions people have about their organization, managers need to keep in mind the communication location of subordinates (Tompkins, 1993).

Poole identifies three aspects of communication networks that determine the shape of communication networks operative in an organization: centrality (the degree to which an individual is at the crossroads of an information flow), connectedness (the degree to which members are inter-linked), and dominance (the degree to which information flow is one-way or two-way) (Poole, 1978). Four network designs that have been studied extensively in experimental situations, the chain, the wheel, and the all channel. Figure 12 depicts these graphically.

Experimental research clearly indicates that the shape of the network influences the process of communication as well as the behavior of individuals in the

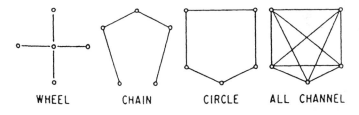

WHEEL   CHAIN   CIRCLE   ALL CHANNEL

Figure 12   Communication network design.

network. Thus these findings hold implications for both job satisfaction and productivity within the organization. The wheel network, where the hub holds the
unique role in collecting, evaluating and dispensing information, seems to work
best where tasks are simple. Obviously the person at the hub is a critical factor,
but this highly centralized communication network achieves high speed and accuracy on simple tasks. On the satisfaction dimension, the person at the hub reports high satisfaction while persons in the spoke positions report low
satisfaction.

The wheel pattern also produces low flexibility to change. The chain network yields the same general results as the wheel, but with a higher level of job
satisfaction than the wheel provides. The circle design, where relationships are
symmetrical, produces high consistency and uniformity in group operation. Job
satisfaction is high, a sense of participation is experienced. On the down side the
circle takes time to operate and accuracy may be low. The all channel, sometimes called the star design, provides high versatility and flexibility. The high involvement provided by everyone to everyone channels yields personal high
satisfaction, but task satisfaction may be lower because of the time-consuming
character of this network.

However, the empirical findings on networks are based mainly on experimental studies where groups perform simple tasks. Some studies indicate that
with more complex problems, the circle network may result in faster and more
accurate performance than the wheel (Shaw, 1954; Mears, 1974). Other studies
show that all groups within the star and chain networks eventually reach the
same levels of performance regardless of structure, whether the focus is on simple or on complex tasks (Carzo, 1963).

Conboy draws three broad conclusions from a review of research on networks that have become part of the research wisdom of the field:

1. The design of a network has a major influence on the outcomes
    processed by that network.
2. There is no universal design. Form and function should be matched
    according to circumstances.
3. Any human communication network should be seen as subject to
    change, modifiable according to the needs of each subsequent task
    (Conboy, 1976).

LISTENING

Communication is a process through which messages are sent and received
along the channels described above. At the interpersonal level the transaction in-

volves at least two communicators and the success of the experience is highly dependent on the listening skills of each (Bolton, 1985). Studies show that we spend nearly one-half of our communication time listening. For public or private sector managers, listening is a critical part of the role: as a source both of new ideas and of understanding employees.

Though the importance of listening is critical to effective management, most of us get low marks in this communication skill. Under normal listening conditions most people, within 24 hours, lose 75 percent of the information gained in a 10-minute presentation. The culprit is poor listening habits (Nichols, 1962; Brown, 1986). Carl Weaver attributes this inattentiveness to the personal risk involved in taking another's ideas seriously (Weaver, 1972). Huseman and Bolton identify typical barriers to listening:

> attending to stimuli that serve to satisfy our own needs
> not attending to stimuli that do not conform to our own models of the world
> filtering based on our own frame of reference; (Huseman, et al., 1976; Bolton, 1985).

Managers need to be sensitive to the purpose of listening in order to sharpen their listening skills. Charles Kelly differentiates between two types of listening guided by distinct purposes. Deliberative listening is listening for information. It includes the ability to hear, analyze, and recall information, and draw conclusions from it (Bolton, 1985). Often empathetic listening is called active listening. Leonard differentiates these types of listening by motivation of the listener:

> The active or empathetic listener strives first to understand the speaker, while the deliberative listener wants first to analyze what the speaker said. In deliberative listening, the listener strives to understand the message for the purpose of using the information contained in the message. Primarily, the listener attempts to evaluate the message. But with active listening, the listener first wants to understand the person, to see and to feel what he or she feels. Deliberative listening is primarily a feeling process (Leonard, 1981, p. 17).

Research suggests that good listening habits can be developed. Regarding deliberative listening or listening for information, 10 guides to good listening proposed by Ralph Nichols have now become part of the conventional wisdom.

1. Find an area of interest in what is being said. Ask yourself: what is the speaker saying that I can use?
2. Judge the content and not the delivery style of the speaker.

3. Withhold evaluation of the speaker's point until you completely comprehend it.
4. Be attentive to central ideas of the speaker, not collection of the facts.
5. Be flexible and adaptable in methods of recording key points of the speaker.
6. Give the speaker your conscious attention; don't fake attention.
7. Resist distractions from the environment.
8. Gain experience through practice in hearing difficult, expository material. Exercise your mind.
9. Identify emotion-laden words that tend to impair your ability to perceive and understand and through reflection and discussion try to diffuse the emotional impact of such words on you. Such words might be redneck, pervert, communist, right-winger, lesbian.
10. Apply the spare time in listening to thinking about what is being said. Most people think about 4 times the rate at which speaking occurs. Use that spare time (Nichols, in Huseman et al., 1970).

While useful, these guidelines for listening principally address deliberative listening, which is focused on information gathering. But as Leonard notes, the good listener listens for all the meanings, those behind the words, not just the obvious meanings. Prerequisites for active listening include:

1. "The listener must want to listen." The desire to listen is highly correlated with the ability to know what to do generally in an interpersonal situation, to be in touch with yourself and what's going on inside of others.
2. "... the listener must be willing to suspend judgment." This point goes beyond merely withholding judgment until the cognitive material is totally comprehended. It invites the listener to genuinely see the issue from the other's point of view.
3. "... the listener must allow and encourage the statement of feelings by the other." Feelings need to be expressed and accepted before dealing with them.
4. "... the listener must be aware of his or her own feelings, and be prepared to integrate them into the interaction where appropriate" (Leonard, 1981).

But beyond these prerequisites for active listening, the messages actually communicated to the speaker by your behavior, shapes the communication encounter (Brown, 1986). Active listening requires that one be sensitive to the nonverbal cues being emitted. Usually labeled "attending behavior" these nonverbal (typically physical) communications tell the speaker, "I'm here, I am interested in you. I want to listen" (Leonard, 1981, p. 16). Bolton includes in attending messages the following:

appropriate body motion
adopting an open posture

leaning toward the other
psychological attention
maintaining good eye contact
positioning yourself at an appropriate distance from the speaker
reflecting attention through facial expressions
attending with vocal cues (Bolton, 1985, p. 33).

Of course many factors external to the communicators influence the quality of interpersonal communication in an organization. Sometimes these factors may be beyond the manager's control. Typical external factors in organizational settings are poor physical conditions such as noise, poor acoustics, a gloomy atmosphere, uncomfortable or inappropriate furniture, and the relative status of the communicators. For the public manager, status is sometimes determined by subtle political relationships relevant in a communication encounter. Awareness of these constraints will focus the listener's attention on taking them into proper account in a communication.

In summary, we note that listening is a skill that can be cultivated. We have pointed to some of the strategies for increasing both deliberative and active listening effectiveness. It is well worth a manager's time and energy to adopt these strategies. A good listener makes better decisions, stimulates better speaking, and is more likely to enjoy the communication experience (Huseman et al., 1970; Bolton, 1985).

THE COMMUNICATION AUDIT

Effective communication is a prime factor in achieving organizational effectiveness (Greenbaum, 1974; Barnard, 1938; Bavelas and Barrett, 1951; Dorsey, 1957; Katz and Kahn, 1966; Bolton, 1985; Graber, 1992). Applied communication research attempts to synthesize our accumulated understanding of the dynamics of communication and develop from it data collection instruments that can ascertain how well the communication system is working (or not working) in an organization. Howard Greenbaum's work on the organizational communication audit advances an outline for managers to follow in assessing communications. At the organizational level the communications audit provide for three stages:

Fact finding; data on the organization's history, objectives, structure, leadership style, organizational character, and communication system is maintained and developed.

Analysis: the extent to which existing practices are achieving objectives of the major communication networks and goals of the organization.

Evaluation and reporting; conclusions based on analysis are drawn about the efficiency and effectiveness of the overall communication system (Greenbaum, 1974).

The International Communication Association has developed a standardized system of five instruments for conducting communications audits in organizations. The five measurement tools are the questionnaire survey, interview, network analysis, communication experiences, and communication diary.

> What could administrators expect to learn from audits? As envisaged, the ICA audit was intended to provide factual and evaluative diagnostic data in all of the major problem areas. It was designed to identify the formal and informal communication networks and the roles played by various individuals in these networks. It could detect underloads and overloads of communication channels. It would provide means to assess the quality of information flowing from various sources and to judge the quality of interpersonal communication relationships. It would describe patterns of actual communication relationships. It would describe patterns of actual communication behavior, identifying sources, channels, topics, and length and quality of interactions. It would provide examples of commonly occurring positive and negative communication experiences. After completing their analysis, the auditors were expected to make recommendations for changes in the communication activities if they were needed to resolve problems or improve the organizations (Graber, 1992, p. 326).

These instruments can be used independently or in combination to yield information on the communication health of an organization. Tables 1 and 2 provide illustrations of these two tools.

The Network Analysis (Table 1) is particularly helpful in providing information on the operational communication network. Respondents report the typical amount of communication with each individual in their unit and with critical personnel outside the unit. Computer analysis identifies all communication links so managers can more readily identify critical actors in communication systems. The communications questionnaire provides for gaining information about the appropriateness of the amount of down-the-line information provided to employees. Respondents indicate both their perception of the amount of information currently received and the amount they would really like to have. Table 2 identifies all of the topics included in this questionnaire.

In effect, agencies' communication systems and individual communication behaviors are sensitive to changes in mission, goal, and environment. The communication audit offers some guidelines for monitoring both communication behavior and climate with the agency. Since communications behavior and climate may enhance or limit an organization's awareness of changed conditions, managers can't afford to ignore this element of organizational life.

Table 1 Communication Audit Network Analysis Instrument

During a typical workday, I usually communicate about work-related matters with the following people through the following channels:

	Identi-fication	Formal organizational structure	Informal (grapevine) organizational structure
Executive			
Stenographer-Secretary	0001	– A B C D E	– A B C D E
Senior Stenographer	0002	– A B C D E	– A B C D E
Executive Secretary	0003	– A B C D E	– A B C D E
Assistant executive director	0004	– A B C D E	– A B C D E
Assistant manager	0005	– A B C D E	– A B C D E
Telephone operator	0006	– A B C D E	– A B C D E
Executive director	0007	– A B C D E	– A B C D E
Administrative and Finance			
Assistant director for administration	0008	– A B C D E	– A B C D E
Typist	0009	– A B C D E	– A B C D E
Accounting clerk	0010	– A B C D E	– A B C D E
Accounting clerk typist	0011	– A B C D E	– A B C D E
Assistant accountant	0012	– A B C D E	– A B C D E
Senior accountant	0013	– A B C D E	– A B C D E
Typist	0014	– A B C D E	– A B C D E
Stenographer	0015	– A B C D E	– A B C D E

Key: A = not at all important; B = somewhat important; C = fairly important; D = very important; E = extremely important.
Source: From Gerald Goldhaber. *Organizational Communication*, Dubuque, Iowa, Wm. C. Brown Pub., 1979, 2nd Ed., pp. 355–357.

Table 2   Questionnaire Survey Topics

Topic	Number of items
1. Amount of information received and needed from others on selected topics.	26
2. Amount of information sent and needed to be sent to others on selected topics.	14
3. Amount of follow-up or action taken and needed on information sent to others.	10
4. Amount of information received and needed from selected sources.	18
5. Timeliness of information received from key sources.	6
6. Amount of information received and needed from selected channels.	16
7. Quality of communication relationships.	19
8. Satisfaction with major organizational outcomes.	13
9. Demographic information.	12
Total	134

Public managers in particular need to be aware of the multiple means for analyzing communication within the organization. This need is heightened because the functional tasks of the public organization often lack goal clarity and because the political environment of many agencies demands frequent reordering of priorities.

MANAGERIAL IMPLICATIONS

Communication is critical to any organization. In its most generic sense communication involves sending and receiving messages over channels. Communication has two essential elements, message transfer and message comprehension. Communication is also a process. It involves both verbal and nonverbal elements. Our verbal communications are filtered through the frame of reference that we bring to the communication encounter. Verbal communication is also made more complex by the ambiguity of language, and the coding and decoding process that is involved in verbal communication. Nonverbal communication occurs whenever a message is transmitted by a mechanism other than the spoken or written word. Research has shown that when verbal and nonverbal contradict each other, people put more faith in the nonverbal information and messages. Nonverbal communication includes the emotional and attitudinal dimensions of communication and constitutes the overwhelming majority of the messages sent and received in a communication encounter.

The environment within which communication occurs is a significant factor for government. For the public sector manager this includes clients, constituents, funding sources and bodies, and the legislative and executive officials. Organizational communication in the public sector is intention, consciousness, direct and purposeful. It can be vertical or horizontal in the organization. In either cases the quantity and quality of organizational communication is effected by organizational design and structure. Managers need to be aware that the quality and quality of information passing up-the-line or down-the-line is subject to distortion. They need to develop strategies that compensate for that distortion. Network research also shows that not all elements of the organization have equal access to information flows. Finally, public managers need to learn how to actively listen during communication encounters. Moreover, they need to be aware that techniques exist to analyze the entire organization in terms of the quality and quantity of communication. The communication audit can detect the formal and informal patterns of communication, the sources of communication, communication roles, as well as overloads and underloads of communication channels.

REFERENCES AND ADDITIONAL READING

Albrecht, T. (1978). "Communication and Perceptions of Organizational Climate: An Empirical Analysis." Unpublished Ph.D. Dissertation, Department of Communcation, Michigan State University. (Cited in Albrecht, 1979.)

Albrecht, T. (1979). "The Role of Communication in Perception of Organizational Climate." *Communication Yearbook 3*, edited by Dan Nimmo, New Brunswick, New Jersey; Transaction Books:pp 343–357.

Angier, M. (1994). "The Debilitating Malady of Boyhood—Should There be a Cure?" *The Beacon Journal*, September 6, 1994:p A8.

Argyris, C. (1966). "Interpersonal Barriers to Decision Making." *Harvard Business Review* (March–April), 44:pp 84–97.

Arnold, David S., Christine S. Becker, and Elizabeth K. Kellar (1983). *Effective Communication: Getting the Message Across*. Washington DC: International City Manager's Association.

Athanassiades, J. C. (1973). "The Distortion of Upward Communication in Hierarchical Organization." *Academy of Management*, 16:pp 207–227.

Baker, Kent H. (1979). "How to Make Meetings Meaningful." *Management Review*, 67:pp 45–47.

Barnard, Chester I. (1938). *Functions of the Executive*. Cambridge, Mass: Harvard University Press.

Bavelas, Alex and D. Barrett (1951). "An Experimental Approach to Organizational Communication." *Personnel*, 27:pp 366–371.

Bell, Daniel (1979). "Communications Technology-For Better or Worse." *Harvard Business Review*, 57:pp 20–45.

Berlo, David K. (1960). *The Process of Communication*. New York: Holt, Rinehart and Winston.

Bolton, Robert (1985). *People Skills*. Englewood Cliffs, New Jersey: Prentice Hall.

Boudewyn, Adri G. (1977). "The Open Meeting-A Confidential Forum for Employees." *Personnel Journal*, 56:pp 192–194.

Blau, P. M. and W. Scott (1962). *Formal Organization*. San Francisco: Chandler.

Brown, J. (1986). *Building Active Listening Skills*. Englewood Cliffs, New Jersey: Prentice-Hall.

Burke, R. J. and D. S. Wilcox (1969). "Effects of Different Patterns and Degrees of Openness in Superior-Subordinate Communication on Subordinate Job Satisfaction." *Academy of Management Journal*, 12:pp 319–326.

Burns, T. (1954). "The Direction of Activity and Communication in a Departmental Executive Group." *Human Relations*, 7:pp 73–97.

Carzo, R. (1963). "Some Effects of Organizational Structure on Group Effectiveness." *Administrative Science Quarterly*, 8:pp 393–424.

Cathcart, R. S. and L. A. Samovar (1974). *Small Group Communication: A Reader*, 2nd edition. Dubuque, Iowa: Wm. C. Brown Company Publishers.

Clampitt, P. G. (1991). *Communicating for Managerial Effectiveness*. Newbury Park, CA: Sage.

Colwill, N. L., and M. Erhart (1985). "Have Women Changed the Workplace?" *Business Quarterly*, Spring 1985:pp 27–31.

Colwill, N. (1993). "Sexist Language Revisited (and revisited and revisited . . .)." *Women in Management*, 3(4):p 4.

Conboy, William A. (1976). *Working Together: Communication in a Healthy Organization*. Columbus, Ohio: Charles E. Merrill.

Cupach, W. R., and B. H. Spitzberg, (eds.) (1994). *The Dark Side of Interpersonal Communication*. Hillsdale, NJ: Erlbaum.

Daft, R. L. and R. H. Lengel (1984). "Information Richness: A New Approach to Managerial Behavior and Organization." in B. W. Straw and L. L. Cummings (eds.) *Research in Organizational Behavior*, 6: Greenwich, Conn: JAI Press.

DiMona, L. and C. Herdon (1994). *Women's Sourcebook: Resources and Information for Everyday Use*. Boston, MA: Houghton Mifflin.

Dorsey, John T., Jr. (1957). "A Communications Model for Administrators." *Administrative Science Quarterly*, 2:pp 307–324.

Downs, A. (1967). *Inside Bureaucracy*. Boston: Little Brown.

Drucker, Peter F. (1988). "The Coming of the New Organization." *Harvard Business Review*, (Jan–Feb, 1988):pp 45–53.

Dubin, R. (1962). "Business Behavior Behaviorally Viewed," in G. B. Strother, (ed.), *Social Science Approaches to Business Behavior*. Homewood, Ill.: Dorsey Press.

Dubin, R. and S. Spray (1964). "Executive Behavior and Interaction." *Industrial Relations*, 4:pp 99–108.

Eckman, P. and W. Friesen (1969). "The Repertoire of Nonverbal Behavior: Categories, Origins, Usage and Coding." *Semiotica*, 1:pp 49–98.

Eisenberg, E. M., P. R. Monge, and K. I. Miller (1983). "Involvement in Communication Networks as a Predictor of Organizational Committment." *Human Communication Research*, 10:pp 179–201.

Farace, R. V., P. R. Monge, and H. M. Russell (1977). *Communicating and Organizing*. Reading, MA: Addison-Wesley.

Ference, T. (1970). "Organizational Communication Systems and the Decision Process." *Management Science*, 17:pp 83–96.

Fernandez, J. P. (1991). *Managing a Diverse Work Force: Regaining the Competitive Edge*. Lexington, MA: Lexington Books.

Galbraith, J. (1973). *Designing Complex Organizations*. Reading, MA: Addison-Wesley.

Garside, S. G. and B. H. Kleiner (1991). "Effective One-to-One Communication Skills." *Industrial and Commercial Training*, 23(7):pp 24–28.

Goldhaber, Gerald M. (1979). *Organizational Communication*. Dubuque, Iowa: Wm. C. Brown Co.

Golen, S. (1990). "A Factors Analysis of Barriers to Effective Listening." *The Journal of Business Communication*, Winter 1990:pp 25–36.

Graber, Doris A. (1992). *Public Sector Communication*. Washington, DC: Congressional Quarterly Press.

Greenbaum, Howard H. (1974). "The Audit of Organizational Communication." *Academy of Management Journal*, 17:pp 739–754.

Guetzkow, H. (1965). "Communication in Organizations." James March, (ed.), *Handbook of Organizations*. Chicago: Rand-McNally.

Hage, J., M. Aiken, and C. Marrett (1971). "Organization Structure and Communication." *American Sociological Review*, 36:pp 860–871.

Hall, R. (1962). "Intra-Organization Structural Variation." *American Sociological Review*, 7:pp 395–408.

Haney, W. V. (1967). *Communications and Organization Behavior-Text and Cases*, 2nd edition, Homewood, Ill.: Irvin.

Harris, D. B. (1970), "Human Intelligence-Its Nature and Assessment." *American Journal of Psychology*, 83(3):pp 455–457.

Hayes, M. A. (1977). "Non-Verbal Communication: Expression Without Words." in *Readings in Interpersonal and Organizational Communication*, 3rd ed. New York: Holdbrook Press.

Henley, Nancy M. (1977). *Body Politics: Power, Sex and Nonverbal Commuication*. Englewood Cliffs, New Jersey: Prentice Hall.

Hewes, Dean, Maudice L. Graham, and Joel Dodger Pavitt (1985). *Human Communication Journal*, 11(3):pp 299–334.

Hewes, D. E., (ed.) (1994). *The Cognitive Bases of Interpersonal Communication*. Hillsdale, NJ: Erlbaum.

Hollandsworth, J. D., R. Kazelskis, Jr., J. Stevens, and M. E. Dressel (1979). "Relative Contributions of Verbal, Articulative, and Nonverbal Communication to Employment Decisions in Job Interview Setting." *Personnel Psychology*, 32:pp 359–367.

Huseman, Richard C., James M. Tahiff, and John Hatfield (1976). Interpersonal Communication in Organizations. Boston: Holbrook Press, Inc.

Huseman, R. C., C. M. Logue, and D. L. Freshley (1970). *Interpersonal and Organizational Communication. Boston: Holbrook Press, Inc.*

Jablin, Frederic M., Linda Putnam, Karlene H. Roberts, and Lyman Porter (1987). Handbook of Organizational Communication: Interdisciplinary Perspective. Beverely Hills, CA: Sage.

Jablin, Frederic M. (1978). "Message Response and 'Openness' in Superior-Subordinate Communication." *Communications Yearbook* 2, Brent D. Rubin (ed.). New Brunswick, New Jersey: Transaction Books.

Jackson, L. A. (1992). *Physical Appearance and Gender: Sociobiological and Sociocultural Perspectives.* Albany: State University Press.

Jun, Jon S. and Hiromi Muto (1995). "The Hidden Dimensions of Japanese Administaration: Culture and Its Impact," *Public Administration Review.* 55(2) (March/April), pp 125–134.

Kaham, Vicki (1986). "Why Assessment Interviews are Worth It." *Training and Development Journal.* May, pp 108–110.

Kalbfleisch, P. J. (ed.) (1993). *Interpersonal Communication.* Hillsdale, NJ: Erlbaum.

Katz, Daniel and Robert Kahn (1966). *The Social Psychology of Organizations.* New York: Wiley and Sons.

Katz, R. and M. Tushman (1979). "Communication Patterns, Project Performance, and Task Characteristics: An Empirical Evaluation and Integration in an R & D Setting." *Organizational Behavior and Human Performance,* 23:pp 139–162.

Kelly, Charles M. (1970). "Actual Listening Behavior of Industrial Supervisors, as Related to Listening Ability, General Mental Ability, Selected Personality Factors and Supervisory Effectiveness." Unpublished Ph.D. Dissertation. Purdue University, 1962. Excerpt first published in Cathcart, Robert S. and Larry A. Samovar, *Small Group Communication: A Reader.* (Dubuque, Iowa: William C. Brown Company Publishers), cited by Leonard (1981).

Kessel, John H. (1984). "The Structure of the Reagan White House." *American Journal of Political Science,* 28(May):pp 231–258.

King, Corwin P. (1978). "Keep Your Communication Climate Healthy." *Personnel Journal,* 57:pp 204–206.

Kirkpatrick, Donald L. (1978). "Communications: Everybody Talks About It, But . . ." *Personal Administrator,* 23:pp 46–50.

Knapp, M. L. and J. A. Hall (1992). *Nonverbal Communication in Human Interaction,* 3rd ed. Fort Worth, TX: Harcourt Brace Jovanovich.

Koehler, J. W., K. W. E. Anatol, and R. L. Applbaum (1981). *Organizational Communication: Behavioral Perspectives.* New York: Holt, Rinehart, and Winston.

Krannick, Ronald L. and Caryl Rae Krannick (1979). "Anonymous Communications and Bureaucratic Politics in Thailand." *Administration and Society,* 2(2):pp 227–248.

Lau, Allan W. and A. R. Newman, (1980). "The Value of Managerial Work in the Public Sector." *Public Administration Review,* 11:pp 513–520.

Lawrence, P. and J. Lorsh (1967). *Organizations and Environment.* Cambridge, MA: Harvard University Press.

Leathers, G. J. (1992). *Successful Nonverbal Communication: Principles and Applications,* 2nd ed. New York: Macmillan.

Leonard, Rebecca (1981). "Acting Listening: Skilled Interpersonal Communication." Unpublished Manuscript, Department of Speech Communication, North Carolina State University.

Lewis, Phillip V. (1975). *Organizational Communications.* Columbus, Ohio: Grid. Cited in Thomas R. Tortoriello. See entry of Tortoriello (1978).

Likert, R. (1967). *The Human Organization.* New York: McGraw Hill.

Likert, R. (1959). "Motivational Approach to Management Development." *Harvard Business Review,* 37:pp 75–82.

Maier, N. R. F., L. R. Hoffman, and W. H. Read (1963). "Superior-Subordinate Communication." *Personnel Psychology,* 16:pp 1–11.

Mays, Larry G. and William A. Taggart (1986). "Court Clerks, Court Administrators, and Judges: Conflict in Managing the Courts." *Journal of Criminal Justice,* 14:pp 1–7.

McGovern, T. V. and H. E. A. Tinsky (1978). "Interviewer Evaluations of Interviewee Nonverbal Behavior." *Journal of Vocational Behavior,* 13(2):pp 163–171.

Mears, P. (1974). "Structuring Communication in a Working Group." *The Journal of Communication,* 24:pp 71–79.

Mehrabian, Albert (1971). *Silent Messages.* Belmont, CA: Wadsworth Publishing Company, Inc.

Mehrabian, A. (1981). *Silent Messages: Implicit Communication of Emotion and Attitudes,* 2nd ed. Belmont, CA: Wadsworth Publishing Company, Inc.

Miller, C., and K. Swift (1988). *The Handbook of Nonsexist Writing,* 2nd ed. New York: Harper & Row.

Mintzberg, Henry (1973). *The Nature of Managerial Work.* New York: Harper & Row.

Monge, Peter R., Richard V. Farace, Eric M. Eisenberg, Katherine I. Miller, and Lynda White (1984). "The Process of Studying Process in Organizational Communication." *Journal of Communication,* Winter, 1984:pp 22–43.

Monge, Peter R., Jane A. Edwards, and Kenneth K. Kirste (1978). "The Determinants of Communication Structure in Large Organizations: A Review of Research." *Communication Yearbook* 2, ed. by Brent D. Rubin. New Brunswick, New Jersey: Transaction Books.

Mueller, J. E. (1973). *War, Presidents and Public Opinion.* New York: Wiley.

Nadler, D. A. (1979). "The Effects of Feedback on Task Group Behavior: A Review of the Experimental Research." *Organizational Behavior and Human Performance,* 23:pp 309–338.

Nichols, R. G. (1962). "Listening is Good Business." *Management of Personnel Quarterly,* 2:p 4.

O'Reilly, C. and K. Roberts (1974). "Information Filtering in Organizations." *Organizational Behavior and Human Performance,* 11:pp 253–265.

Patten, Thomas H., Jr. (1978). "Open Communication Systems and Effective Salary Administration." *Human Resources Management,* 17:pp 5–14.

Planty, Earl and William Machaver (1952). "Upward Communications: A Project in Executive Development." *Personnel,* 28(4):pp 304–318.

Pincus, David J. (1986). "Communication Satisfaction, Job Satisfaction, and Job Performance." *Human Communication Journal,* 12(3), Spring:pp 395–419.

Poole, M. S. (1978). "An Information Task Approach to Organizational Communication." *The Academy of Management Review*, 3:pp 493–504.

Porter, L. W. and K. H. Roberts (1976). "Communication in Organizations." in M. Dunnette, (ed.) *Handbook in Industrial and Organizational Psychology*. Chicago: Rand McNally:pp 1553–1589.

Public Personnel Administration: Policies, Practices, and Procedures. (1973). "Communication with Employees." Englewood Cliffs, New Jersey: Prentice-Hall.

Rawlings, W. K. (1993). "Communication in Cross-Sex Friendships." In L. P. Arliss & D. J. Borisoff (eds.), *Women and Men Communicating: Challenges and Changes* (pp 51–70). Fort Worth, TX: Harcourt Braces Jovanovich.

Rea, Louis M. and Richard A. Parker (1992). *Designing and Conducting Survey Research.* San Francisco, CA: Jossey Bass Publishers.

Read, W. H. (1962). "Upward Communication in Industrial Hierarchies." *Human Relations*, 15:pp 3–15.

Reagan, Priscilla (1986). "Privacy, Government Information, and Technology." *Public Adminstration Review*, 46:pp 629–634.

Reik, T. (1972). *Listening with the Third Ear.* New York: Pyramid.

Richmond-Abbott, M. (1992). *Masculine and Feminine: Gender Roles Over the Life Cycle.* New York: McGraw Hill.

Roberts, K. H. and C. A. O'Reilly (1974). "Failures in Upward Communication in Organizations." *Academy of Management Journal*, 17:pp 205–215.

Romoff, Mark (1978). "Employee Communications in the Federal Government." *The Canadian Business Review*, 4:pp 36–39.

Sadker, M., and D. Sadker (1994). *Failing at Fairness: How Our Schools Cheat Girls.* New York: Simon & Schuster.

Samaras, John T. (1980). "Two-Way Communication Practices for Managers." *Personnel Journal*, 59:pp 645–648.

Shannon, Wayne E. (1978). "One Person Communication." *Training and Development Journal*, 32:pp 20–24.

Shaw, M. E. (1954). "Some Effects of Unequal Distribution of Information Upon Group Performance in Various Communication Networks." *The Journal of Abnormal and Social Psychology*, 50:pp 547–553.

Shuler, R. S. (1979). "A Role Perception Transactional Process Model for Organizational Communication-Outcome Relationships." *Organizational Behavior and Human Performance*, 23:pp 268–291.

Silverman, B. R. S. (1980). "The Optimum Legiblity Formula: A Written Communications Systems." *Personnel Journal*, (July) 59,7:pp 581–583.

Simpson, R. L. (1959). "Vertical and Horizontal Communication in Organizations." *Administrative Science Quarterly*, 4:pp 188–196.

Stewart, Lea P., Pamela J. Cooper, Alan D. Stewart, and Sheryl A. Friedley (1996). *Communication and Gender.* Scottsdale, AZ: Gorsuch Scansbrick Publishers.

Stewart, L. P., and D. Clark-KIundless (1993). "Communication in Corporate Settings." In L. P. Arliss 7 D. J. Borisoff (eds.). *Women and Men Communicating: Challenges and Changes* (pp 142–152). Fort Worth, TX: Harcourt Brace Jovanovich.

Sudman, Seymour and Norman M. Bradburn (1982). *Asking Questions.* San Franciso, CA: Josey Bass Publishers.

Sussman, Barry (1988). *What Americans Really Think*. New York: Random House, Inc.

Summers, Donald B. (1977). "Understanding the Process by Which New Employees Enter Work Groups." *Personnel Journal*, 56:pp 394–397.

Tannen, D. (1990). *You Just Don't Understand: Men and Women in Conversation*. New York: William Morrow.

Tannen, D. (1991). "Teachers' Classroom Strategies Should Recognize That Men and Women Use Language Differently." *The Chronicle of Higher Education*, June 19:pp B1, B3.

Tannen, D. (1994). *Talking from 9 to 5*. New York: William Morrow.

Taylor, J. (1977). "Communication and Organizational Change: A Case Study." Unpublished Ph.D. dissertation, Department of Communications, Michigan State University. Cited in (Albrecht, 1979).

Taylor, J., R. Farace, and P. Monge (1976). "Communication and the Development of Change Among Educational Practitioners." Paper presented to the World Education Conference, Honolulu, Hawaii. Paper cited in (Albrecht, 1978).

Terreberry, S. (1968). "The Evolution of Organizational Environments." *Administrative Science Quarterly*, 12:pp 590–613.

Thayer, L. (1968). *Communication and Communication Systems*. Homewood, Il: Richard D. Irwin.

Timm, P. R. and P. L. Wilkens (1977). *A Model of Perceived Communication Inequity and Job Dissatisfaction*. Paper presented at the National Meetings of the Academy of Management, Kissimmee, FL.

Timm, Paul R. (1968). "Worker Responses to Supervisory Communication Inequity: An Exploratory Study." *Journal of Business Communication*, 16:pp 11–24.

Tompkins, Philip K. (1993). *Organizational Communication Imperatives: Lessons of the Space Program*. Los Angeles, CA: Roxbury Publishing Co.

Tortoriello, Thomas R., Stephen J. Blatt, and Sue Devine (1978). *Communication in the Organization: An Applied Approach*. New York: McGraw Hill.

Truell, George F. (1978). "Communication Styles: The Key to Understanding." *Personnel Administrator*, 23:pp 46–48.

Tucker, J.S., and H.S. Friedman (1993). "Sex Differences in Non-verbal Expressiveness: Emotional Expression, Personality, and Impressions." *Journal of Nonverbal Behavior*, 17:pp 103–117.

Van de Ven, A., A. Delbecq, and R. Koenig (1976). "Determinants of Coordination Modes Within Organizations." American Sociological Review, 41:pp 322–338.

Vogel, A. (1967). "Why Don't Employees Speak Up?" *Personnel Administration*, 30:pp 18–24.

Wallace, William A. and Michael W. Hurley (1986). "Expert Systems as Decision Aids for Public Managers: An Assessment of the Technology and Prototyping as a Decision Strategy." *Public Administration Review*, 46:pp 563–571.

Washburn, P. V. and M. C. Hakel (1973). "Visual Cues and Verbal Content as Influences on Impressions Formed After Simulated Employment Interviews." *Journal of Applied Psychology*, 58(1):pp 137–141.

Watzlawick, P., J. H. Beavin, and D. D. Jackson (1967). *Pragmatics of Human Communication A Study of Interactional Patterns, Pathologies and Paradoxes*. New York: W. W. Norton and Company, Inc.

Weaver, Carl H. (1972). *Human Listening: Processes and Behavior.* New York: Bobbs-Merrill Co., Inc.

Wexley, K. N., S. S. Fugita, and M. P. Malone (1975). "Applicants Nonverbal Behavior and Student-Evaluators' Judgements in a Structured Interview Setting." *Psychological Reports*, 36(2):pp 391–394.

Wieman, J. M. and R. P. Harrison, (eds.) (1984). *Non-Verbal Interaction.* Beverly Hills, CA: Sage.

Wood, J. and C. Inman (1993). "In a Different Mode: Masculine Styles of Communicating Closeness. *Journal of Applied Communication Research*, 21:pp 279–296.

Young, M and J. E. Post, (1993). "Managing to Communicate, Comunicating to Manage: How Leading Companies Communicate with Employees," *Organizational Dynamics* (Summer), pp. 31–43.

7
Decision-Making

The management of the decision-making process is often equated with the study of management. It is thought to be the generalized process to which other considerations of leadership, motivation, role management, and communications are subservient. Herbert Simon, perhaps the most influential of the postwar organization theorists, interpreted complex organizations in terms of a decision-making framework (Simon, 1945). Since that time much research and case study analysis in both public and business administration has been devoted to the study of various dimensions of the decision making process (Forester, 1984; Harmon, 1989; Kaufman, 1990; Simon, 1992; Senge, 1990; Cyert and March, 1992; Zey, 1992; Bazerman, 1994; LaPorte and Keller, 1996).

The decision-making approach is particularly pertinent to public management. Partly, this is because decision-making raises the ethical and political aspects of public administration; that is, public administration as part of the "authoritative allocation of values" function inherent in any political system (Gilman and Lewis, 1996). In the private sector, many decisions on priorities flow almost undiscussed from universal acceptance of the profit motive. A good deal of the decision-making logic of "command and control companies," as Drucker (1988) calls private sector organizations, comes from using profit as the dependent variable against which to compare and contrast other organizational variables. This is not to say, as we stated in a previous chapter, that profit is the only goal that private sector organizations pursue. However, the logic of competition in the marketplace ties the very economic survival of the firm to profit (Milgrom and Roberts, 1992). In other words, profit for a private firm is easily conceived of as the "bottom line." Moreover, *since the major way to realize profit is through efficiency*, that is, using less inputs to produce the same or greater outputs, efficiency becomes the major goal of the rational decision-making process in the private sector (Zey, 1992).

The public sector, by contrast, has a different mission. That mission frequently requires the public sector to choose equity (fairness) at the cost of efficiency, for example, choosing to fund training programs for students with the most severe academic disadvantages. Moreover, public sector organizations are typically forced to perform at a higher level of accountability and to many "publics." This not only brings greater importance to decision-making processes, but makes those decision making processes the objects of public access efforts.

This greater accountability, whether actual or merely potential, leads to more formality and less decision making flexibility in the public sector. In other words, the *context* in which public decision making must take place incorporates many more variables (in addition to efficiency) into the decision-making equation. For example, the general public and elected officials may want to have certain procedures used in making decisions. They may want citizen participation in decision-making regarding service delivery. They may want employee participation in all aspects of civil service decision-making. They may want time consuming procedures to be followed for safeguarding the due process rights of employees (Goodwin and Wilenski, 1984).

Clearly, following any such procedures will render decision-making *less efficient*. Why? Because public participation, employee participation, and employees appeals procedures all introduce delays and utilize other resources. Proponents of efficiency might, therefore, be inclined to oppose such procedures on the grounds that people's preferences can be satisfied better through less costly decision procedures. However, other important values such as impartiality and effectiveness are important aspects of public service, not only in the United States, but across otherwise distinctive cultures (Gilman and Lewis, 1996). In fact, supporters of efficiency must recognize that in the public sector efficiency is only *one value* in the decision-making process. Moreover, because of the political nature of this process, efficiency cannot and should not be the *only* value in the public decision-making process (Etzioni, 1992). Other values such as equity, accountability, due process, etc., have legitimate rights to be included in the calculus of public decision-making.

A considerable body of literature exists on various aspects of decision-making in the public sector (Simon, 1945; Burke, 1986; Harmon, 1989; Cooper, 1990; Zey, 1992; Harmon, 1995). Essentially, two schools of thought emerged in the early literature. One emphasized planning approaches to decision-making that promised greater efficiency, and was predicated on assumptions of organizational rationality. The other focused on incremental decision-making and is based on assumptions about the efficiency of market-like forces in the setting of priorities, substituting the marketplace of influences for the economic marketplace. These two schools were pitted against each other in an important debate between liberals and conservatives after World War II. More recently, concern with the *ethical* dimensions of decision making, from the perspective of the practicing administrator, have emerged (Burke, 1986; Cooper, 1990; and Harmon, 1995). The ethical perspective will be discussed more fully in the ethics chapter. The first two sections of this chapter present by turn the early liberal case for public planning as a preferred decision-making form and the political evolution of thinking about the topic, followed by the post-WW II conservative critique of planning in government. It was in the context of this debate that Herbert Simon advanced his decision-centered approach to public administration in his classic work, *Administrative Behavior* (1945). A third section of the present chapter treats this viewpoint which, for a time, seemed to emerge as a preferable alternative to rational or incremental models of planning and decision-making. Participatory approaches to decision-making are discussed in a fourth section (and discussed at length in the next chapter). The focus in this section is on the empirical studies of individual and group decision-making. The chapter closes with a general discussion of the managerial implications of decision-making theory for the practicing public administrator.

PLANNING AND RATIONAL MODELS OF DECISION-MAKING

When students think of decision-making, they often assume a rational model; that is, a model in which there is a clear relationship between ends and means. This model takes on a number of forms the essential features are: (1) Identify objectives; (2) identify alternative courses of action for achieving those objectives; (3) predict and evaluate the possible consequences of each alternative; and (4) select the alternative that maximizes the attainment of the objectives. This so called "rational decision-making model" always begins with a statement of the goals or objectives to be achieved. Obstacles to the achievement of objectives are inventoried. For each obstacle, alternative solutions are surveyed and the optimal one is selected. Solutions are spelled out into task matrices which relate resources (personnel, materials) to these tasks. Tasks are assembled into a rational, sequential plan through a process, like program evaluation and review techniques (PERT) or other planning processes. Later, costs and benefits are tracked through program budgeting as a database for evaluation and possible revision of the plan selected.

This vision of "rational planning" was at its peak in the United States in the 1930s and 1940s. A symbol of this vision was the National Resources Planning Board, directed by Charles Merriam, a leading political scientist of the 1930s. Political scientists of that era had begun to condemn the "ramshackle character of our national legislative machine," as Edwin Corwin put it in his 1931 presidential address to the American Political Science Association (APSA) (Corwin, 1932). Corwin called on political scientists to put aside questions of power and influence and instead concentrate on issues of management and planning.

This orientation was epitomized the following year when Henry Dennison, an industrialist, was invited to present his view to the APSA on "The Need for the Development of Political Science Engineering" (Dennison, 1932). Related groups such as the Brookings Institution pointed toward the planning models of the French and German advisory economic councils (Lorwin, 1931). By 1934, a vast amount of American literature on social planning was available (see Brooks and Brooks, 1933, 1934), ranging from Chamber of Commerce reports to Harry Laidler's *Socialist Planning and a Socialist Program* (1932). George E. G. Catlin wrote, "The blessed word Mesopotamia of the last decade was 'rationalization'; of this decade, it is planning" (Catlin, 1932).

In a decade, social planning emerged from a concept bordering on sedition to one accepted by nearly all segments of American society. There was a relative consensus in the planning literature on the general vision of using state power to achieve regulation, security, and fairness. Typical was Rexford Tugwell's *Industrial Discipline and the Governmental Arts* (1933). Tugwell, a close advisor of President Roosevelt, argued that the alternative to class conflict in the Depression was a cooperative effort of social planning and regulation of the economy. Social planning themes were predominant in such New Deal innovations as the Blue Eagle (NRA) code authorities and the Tennessee Valley Authority (TVA). Indeed, the vision of national social planning through a country-wide network of TVA-type authorities was promoted by liberal congressmen well into the late 1940s.

Although the vision of national planning fell from grace after World War II, one should not think it disappeared. At the micro-organizational level it prospered with the rise of program planning and budgeting systems (PPBS) in industry in the 1950s and government in the 1960s. At the intergovernmental level, the vision of rational planning was enshrined in the 1971 institution of "A-95 clearinghouses" by the U.S. Office of Management and Budget. Both PPBS and the A-95 clearinghouses illustrated governmental attempts to force disparate agencies and jurisdictions to rationalize and coordinate their efforts. Both also were intended to provide top administrators with rational planning tools for centralized decision-making.

The argument for a rational planning approach to decision-making in the public sector was strong. One of the most sophisticated arguments on its behalf was Karl Mannheim's *Freedom, Power, and Democratic Planning* (1950). Planning was necessary, he argued, because of the collapse of free markets under American capitalism. The rise of large, relatively uncontrolled groups (corporations, unions, interest groups) had eroded the self-regulating marketplace. The collapse of this traditional coordination device, along with the decline of religion as a social control and the failure of the independent regulatory commissions, meant that America needed new forms of social coordination. Since Mannheim rejected totalitarian-type planning, he argued that new, democratic forms of planning had to be found. He believed these would involve; governmental control over the growing monopoly power of the corporations, centralization in most areas of decision-making, strong legislative oversight, social education for democratic citizenship, and governmental initiatives to foster citizen access and group competition.

Although many European democracies moved in directions indicated by Mannheim, America did not. A decade later Gunnar Myrdal (1960) made the same arguments for planning. Although many liberals looked to Sweden, Britain, or West Germany for models of governmental decision-making, direct planning was not a dominant preference even for liberals. Instead, liberals looked to indirect planning through Keynesian economics. Briefly, Keynesianism held that the economy could be controlled by fiscal (e.g., taxes, deficits) and monetary (e.g., interest rates, money supply) policies without recourse to direct means like wage and price controls or nationalization of industry. In fact, postwar liberals believed Keynesian fiscal and economic policies would achieve most of the objectives previously claimed for national social planning. Keynesianism, moreover, was believed to provide a model for doing this on a decentralized basis without resort to odious economic commands, quotas, and controls.

A symbol of this shift in liberal thought was the replacement of Merriam's National Resources Planning Board by the Keynesian-oriented Council of Economic Advisors after World War II. The CEAs indirect controls meant public administration's future did not depend on its capacity to evolve sophisticated rational planning techniques for decision-making. Keynesianism was seen as a means of compensation for the decline of market competition and the consequent erosion of faith in control through Adam Smith's "invisible hand" (the competitive economic market). Interest in planning approaches to decision-making was somewhat restored in the late 1960s and 1970s when Keynesian economics proved incapable of dealing with simultaneous recessionary and inflationary tendencies in the American economy. Civil rights, environmental, consumer, and other social movements of this period also helped the resurgent belief in the need for direct controls and systematic authoritative governmental planning.

The 1980s bore witness to a general retreat from public planning and a diminished confidence in the role government should play in managing our mixed economy. President Reagan ran on a platform in 1980 that pledged to implement the non-Keynesian "supply side" theories of professor Arthur B. Laffer. Laffer's ideas were embodied in the Kemp-Roth Bill and the infamous "Laffer Curve." The philosophical assumption underlying supply side economic theory and legislation holds that when taxation is too high government revenues actually go down because business investment is discouraged. The solution to this dilemma is to reduce taxes sharply for investors and business at a predetermined rate over a specific period of time. A reduction in taxes coupled with a tight monetary policy and curtailment of federal government expenditures, except for national defense, and a reduction in governmental regulation, would presumably allow the unrestrained free market to produce economic prosperity and lower federal government deficits.

The empirical validity underlying supply side economics is currently under dispute among economists and other scholars, although by 1996 the massive federal deficit (and how to reduce it) has become the principal feature on the political and economic landscape. What is not under dispute is that public planning models and those who implement them (civil servants) find themselves on the defensive. They have become, in the minds of many politicians, the "problem" itself rather than the "solution" to the nation's problems. Elmer B. Staats, former Comptroller General of the United States, has observed that both Jimmy Carter and Ronald Reagan essentially ran "against" government and bureaucracy in their presidential campaigns (Staats, 1988). This could also be said of both George Bush and Bill Clinton each of whom promised the end of "big government." Moreover, Wildavsky (1988) argues that both political parties now contain elements opposed to bureaucracy.

The classic debate between the proponents of the "market" versus the "master mind" (free enterprise versus rational public planning and decision-making) has deep roots in American intellectual history. The argument between rational planning models versus market models of decision making will continue to hold a prominent place in the debate about decision-making in the public sector. Because of this fact, we will now turn to an analysis of another major current of this argument, the conservative critique of public planning.

THE CONSERVATIVE CRITIQUE OF PLANNING

Historically, the debate over rational models of decision-making (most planning approaches) emerged from the broader clash of socialism and capitalism. Responding to socialist advocates of governmental planning, depression-era conservatives argued that rational, comprehensive planning models made assumptions that exceeded human capacities for integration and coordination. In practice, the critics charged, such decision-making approaches were misguided and undesirable.

Conservative economists like Friedrich Hayek argued against socialist planning in books like *Collectivist Economic Planning* (1935) and *The Road to Serfdom* (1944). They argued that whenever possible governmental planning should yield to market mechanisms in the making of social decisions. By this they meant that the competition of private producers would, if left to itself, provide the most efficient housing, transportation, recreation and other needs of the nation. In addition to the argument that bureaucrats were invariably noninnovative and government agencies prone to stagnation, it was also held that planning was the antithesis of freedom because, unlike the subtle influence of market forces, planning could only be implemented through coercive directives. Above all, planning was deemed to be inherently inferior because of the absence of a governmental criterion akin to the profit criterion in market decisions based on prices. Unable to set values by a market, governmental planning was seen as inevitably degenerating into elite coercion of the masses "for their own good." Planning was "the road to serfdom."

The conservative, market-oriented perspective on decision-making was popularized in the United States by scholars at the University of Chicago. These included such individuals as Michael Polanyi, Milton Friedman, Edward Banfield, and Charles Lindblom. Writing in *The Logic of Liberty* (1951), Michael Polanyi's arguments illustrated this influential school. Polanyi held that the complex tasks of modern government could be managed only by a market-like system of mutual adjustments which were incremental in nature. That is, Polanyi rejected decision-making by central planners in favor of a give-and-take bargaining process in which a "marketplace" of ideas and influence groups eventually lead to a compromise more appropriate than experts would have made. This incrementalist or bargaining perspective was held to be in contradiction to the planning perspective. Citing Soviet war communism of the 1919–1921 period, Polanyi argued that central planning led to administrative chaos. The choice was between totalitarian central planning or incrementalist decision-making. Middle solutions like "market-socialism" were held to be contradictions in terms, unworkable in practice.

These themes were picked up by Milton Friedman, a Chicago economist who later became famous as an advisor to the Nixon and Reagan administrations. In his *Capitalism and Freedom* (1962), and later in *Free To Choose* (1979), Friedman also took the view that there are only two ways to coordinate governmental decision-making: through central planning or through markets. Planning, however, was intrinsically coercive. Worse, it was unresponsive to democratic preferences. Whereas the market could make billions of decisions reflecting consumer preferences, government responded only through a single yes-no decision every fourth year at presidential election times. The result, Friedman held, was that most governmental programs were unnecessary and undesirable. This analysis led Friedman to a policy of "denationalizing" schools, abolition of professional licensing, termination of social security and public housing, private development of parks and recreation, and other policies substituting private market forces for governmental services. The essential features of the critique of public planning are expressed in his idea that the hierarchy and rigid control required by bureaucracy is the reason for the failure of centralized economies (Senge, 1990).

There are numerous reasons why central planning rarely lives up to expectations. Many were summarized by Charles Lindblom in an enormously influential article in the *Public Administration Review* titled, *"The Science of Muddling Through"* (Lindblom, 1959). Lindblom first lays out, and then calls into question, the assumptions of the rational comprehensive model of planning. In the process he outlines the essential elements of the incremental model of decision-making. A model, he believes, is superior empirically (as a description of reality) and normatively (more consistent with democracy) than the rational comprehensive model. Lindblom outlines the following assumptions of the comprehensive rational planning model. First of all, he notes that the rational model calls for a clarification of values prior to empirical analysis. Next, the rational comprehensive policy formation process proceeds by isolating the specific ends to be achieved and the means to achieve those ends. Additionally, policy under the rational comprehensive model is "tested" by evaluating the extent to which it incorporates the most appropriate means to achieve the desired ends. The next requirement of the rational comprehensive model is that the analysis upon which it is based be comprehensive; that is, the analysis takes into consideration every important factor. Finally, rational comprehensive decision-making relies heavily on theory for the development of policy.

Lindblom systematically calls into question all these assumptions. First of all, he observes that there is no real societal consensus on values and no real measure of majority opinion prior to the public discussion that usually accompanies the development of the policy itself. In other words, values emerge as a part of policy development rather than prior to it. In addition, many policy questions that public administrators face combine a variety of values under one policy; efficiency, service, equity, accountability, and so on. When values conflict, the administrator has no overriding decision criterion akin to the profit motive that would provide him with a ranking of values that the rational comprehensive model calls for:

> Suppose, for example, that an administrator must relocate tenants living in tenements scheduled for destruction. One objective is to empty the buildings fairly promptly, another is to find suitable accommodations for persons displaced, another is to avoid friction with residents in other areas in which a large influx would be unwelcome, How does one state even to himself the relative importance of these partially conflicting values? A simple ranking of them is not enough: one needs ideally to know how much of one value is worth sacrificing for some other values. The answer is that typically the administrator chooses—and must choose—directly among policies in which these values are combined in different ways. He cannot first clarify his values and then choose among policies (Lindblom, 1959, p. 286).

Even where values are clear, the public decision-maker may lack information on the alternative solutions to the problem. Such information can be costly to obtain, if it can be obtained at all. Information costs may be in terms of time, effort, and expense. Incurring such costs may generate an information overload for the agency. Or the information-gathering effort, while comprehensive, may take too much time for the election-oriented political leader. Finally, certain theoretically valid options may be politically unacceptable at a given time, such as using regular military units to patrol the border in an endeavor to stop drug smuggling.

For the above reasons, Lindblom notes that, since administrators cannot formulate relevant values first and then choose among policies, they must, in effect, choose among policies that combine values in different ways. This suggests that in the real world of administration, the means and ends to achieve them are chosen simultaneously because means-ends knowledge is often missing. For example, the means to reduce poverty are not well understood. Many policy alternatives are innovative and social science is too primitive to be able to predict the effects. Diffuse benefits like "social welfare" or environmental quality may be difficult to measure, compounding the problem. Even more fundamentally, decision-makers may not be able to understand what the problem is, let alone comprehensively understand the alternatives. Crime, for instance, is recognized as a problem area, but decision-makers disagree about whether crime is primarily an economic problem (poverty), a psychological problem (criminal personality), a sociological problem (broken families), or whatever. Typically, the nature of the problem will be dependent on situational factors.

Lindblom also notes that the requirement of the rational comprehensive model, to rely on theory is also problematic. Typically, social science will lack an adequate situational theory of the problem. That is, while public administrators and social scientists may understand some general dynamics of a problem, they may not be able to apply this knowledge to differing concrete situations. While theories will abound, the state of the art will not allow the decision-maker to proceed confidently with policy choice and implementation based on a coherent theory. For all the foregoing reasons, Lindblom asserts that it is impossible to test the adequacy of a policy in accordance to the requirements of the rational comprehensive model. To Lindblom, the test of good policy is agreement about the policy itself, rather than the values that underlie it. In some ways, this is a validation of the "politics makes strange bedfellows" observation. For example, in the late 1960s both the Black Panthers and the John Birch Society were vocal opponents of city-county consolidation. It is safe to say their agreement on policy was not predicated on an agreement on underlying values.

The appeal of the incremental model is that it is often seen as the political expression of the market model of economics. In this sense, incrementalists argue that their model is more consistent with the interest group pluralism prevalent in the United States. It is also seen as more consistent with the ideals of democracy since incrementalism calls for policy that results from a competition in the marketplace of ideas. The rational comprehensive-model, correctly or not, is often associated with centralized political and economic systems in which decision-making is reserved to the few. Moreover, incrementalism, according to its proponents, is capable of incorporating the broadest range of values into the policy process. It also as a strategy designed to minimize organizational risk because most changes are incremental, that is, they represent small departures from existing policy.

Much of the debate between the rational-comprehensive and incremental positions center on assumptions about the decision making situation which can and do vary (Forester, 1984; Grandori, 1984; Zey, 1992; Pinchot and Pinchot, 1994). It is argued that decision-making by rational planning can occur only when there is agreement on both goals and means (Nalbandian and Klinger, 1980). Moreover, rational planning appears to work best when the decision has to do with distributive rather than redistributive matters. Distributive policies deal with allocation of resources, whereas redistributive policies—like some land use regulation—deal with reallocating resources from one group to another. Redistributive questions involve far more political intensity and bargaining—something more amenable to incrementalism. Moreover, incrementalism as a decision-making process leans toward consensus, rationalism toward optimization at the expense of consensus (Wimberley and Morrow, 1981).

Because of these limits, empirical studies have frequently shown that national investment in research for rational planning in government is often wasted. Weiss, in *Social Science Research and Decision-Making* (1980), found that not only is research frequently not utilized but governmental decision-makers were so bound by incrementalism and bargaining that they typically disavowed making broad decisions of the type which research was directed. Staats (1980) noted this perception of low decision-making discretion and hence low need for planning studies when, as head of the Government Accounting Office, he looked into the failure to utilize research at the federal level.

There is no clear and immutable answer to the debate between incremental and rational-comprehensive models of decision-making. It may well be that either is appropriate given a particular decision-making situational context. It is clear, however, that much of the recent total quality management and more generic business literature expresses a preference for the greater freedom inherent in "self organizing systems" as opposed to the hierarchy inherent in bureaucracy. Self organizing systems are decision making units based on the inductive features of incrementalism. For example, Pinchot and Pinchot (1994) argue in *The End of Bureaucracy and the Rise of Intelligent Organization* that such self organizing systems based on incrementalism actually lead ultimately to more order not less.

> The free market, as we have seen, is not an isolated case of the superior performance of the self organizing systems over hierarchical controls in human

affairs. Literature, art, science and mathematics are self organizing systems for developing and distributing information. They depend on free choices and free access to stay open for learning and development. In the end, no hierarchy determines what is good art or good science. No vote is taken, no majority rules. Each scientist, each reader, each art critic, each buyer decides for himself or herself (Pinchot and Pinchot, 1994, p. 51).

HERBERT SIMON AND DECISION-MAKING THEORY

If the conservative critique was effective in highlighting the limits of the rational planning model of decision-making, public administration was not won over to the proposed solution of substituting private market goods for governmental services in such areas as recreation and education. Instead, many social scientists sought to erect an alternative decision-making theory which was premised neither on central planning of the radical type nor on abdication to the marketplace as some conservatives advocated. Among the earliest and most influential of these social scientists was Herbert Simon.

From the incrementalist literature on public decision-making it sometimes appeared that governmental decisions were made by thousands of small choices by bureaucrats, with no real control from the top. The image was presented of the political marketplace. Often implied was the notion that it was like the freely competitive economic marketplace, which was not controlled by any consumer or producer. In contrast, research has shown that governmental agencies *are* controlled by decision-makers. Agency outcomes are not the mere result of the market-like effect of thousands of small bureaucratic choices (Etzoni, 1986, LaPorte and Keller, 1996). For example, it has been shown that the higher one's hierarchical rank the more likely one is to participate in decisions (Zeitz, 1980) and change in top public leadership does have a strong and pervasive effect on the substance of decision outcomes (Bunce, 1980; Palmer and Sawhill, 1984; Wood and Waterman, 1994).

Simon was aware of these realities. He also knew, however, that as later research would prove, few managers actually decided things by rational searches for alternative solutions to anticipated problems (Isenberg, 1984; Zey, 1992). The nature of decision-making had to be conceived as a model lying somewhere in between marketing and incrementalism on the one hand and rational comprehensive planning on the other. Simon set forth his compromise model in two famous works, *Administrative Behavior* (1945) and *Models of Man* (1957a), and one co-authored with James G. March, *Organizations* (1960).

Simon's model centered on the concepts of *bounded rationality* and *satisficing*. Bounded rationality meant that decision-makers do reason and plan, but only by searching a few available alternatives, only by seeking to assess a few of the consequences, and only using highly simplified assumptions about cause and effect. Satisficing meant that decision-makers did not really seek the optimal solution, only the first solution that satisfied the minimal criteria they deemed necessary. Simon described his model of decision-making by comparing two kinds of actors in the decision-process; economic man, with his presumed capacities and administrative man more grounded in the real world.

> Economic man deals with the "real world" in all its complexity. Administrative man recognizes the world he perceives is a drastically simplified model of the buzzing, blooming confusion that constitutes the real world. He is content with this gross simplification because he believes that the real world is mostly empty-that most facts of the world have no great relevance to any particular situation he is facing, and that most significant chains of causes and consequences are short and simple . . . Hence, he is content to leave out those aspects of reality—and that means most aspects—that are substantially irrelevant at a given time. He makes his choices using a simple picture of the situation that takes into account just a few of the factors that he regards relevant and crucial (Simon, 1957, p. xxv).

Soon these concepts were widely accepted because they preserved the planning function of the decision-maker but were much more realistic in depicting actual practice. Simon recognized that many decisions did have the appearance of being the uncontrolled results of incremental choices by "the system" or "the marketplace." These he called *programmed decisions.*" Unlike nonprogrammed decisions in which the leadership decision-making role was apparent, programmed decisions were characterized by standard operating routines which left little discretion for those involved. Even routinized decisions were not lacking in control. Actually, a key function of management is the design of those routines and even more important, promulgation and maintenance of the norms and values which make them work. Simon argued for the importance of the managerial role of the socialization of employees to organizational patterns, particularly norms of efficiency and economizing. Like many other functions at top levels of management, this role was not reducible to planning calculations or laws of management science—but neither was it determined by an impersonal, uncontrolled marketplace of incremental choices.

Decision-making under bounded rationality is *not* rationality in the ordinary sense of the word. Also, there is not an expectation that decision-makers are rational in the sense of comprehensive planning. Decisions are seen not as the result of calculations but rather of premises. Moreover, because decisions are the result of premises they may be a function of previous decisions (which the bureaucrat takes as givens and does not reexamine) incorporated into standard operating procedures. Premises provide a system of values and therefore simplify decision-making. This is essential in the real world in which many decisions must be made under time pressure, though it does mean bureaucratic decision-making is only quasi-rational.

Simon recognized that top management must receive feedback on whether management standards are realistic. All levels need to share in a common bank of information about past decisions, organizational objectives, and operating procedures. These communication needs require an abandonment of strictly hierarchical lines of communication but they do not involve an uncontrolled free market. Simon spent a great deal of time seeking to show how his theory translated into practice through the design and formalization of complex communication patterns which reinforce values which are set at the top and specified for the employee in operating routines. The failure to reinforce values that incorporated the free flow of feedback and communication to the top can have profound consequences. For example, the decision-making process that preceded the 1965 escalation of our commitment of ground troops to Vietnam was flawed by the criteria of the free flow of communication and feedback to the top.

In summary, Simon's work represented a critique of the traditional organization theories of men like Weber and Taylor. Simon emphasized the limits of rationality and criticized scientific management principles of hierarchical communication, unitary authority lines, and optimization in decision-making. He also emphasized the importance of managerial control, not through planning instruments, but through influence over organizational values, communication patterns, and operating procedures. Simon's concept of decision-making quickly became accepted by most social scientists as he had developed the best description of organizational behavior to that time. Moreover, Simon's later emphasis on detailed examinations of the decision-making process in case studies also led the way in a new emphasis on case studies in schools of business and public administration. The case approach stood in clear contrast to either scientific management or human relations orientations of Simon's day, both of which centered on seeking certain universal rules or laws of management. Simon's decision-making approach rejected these two viewpoints, saying that they couldn't answer fundamental management questions due to their abstract level of analysis. By examining communications patterns in various decision contexts and drawing conclusions specific to individual case situations, Simon's work was a forerunner of behavioralism and later situational theories of management.

CRITICS AND REVISIONISTS

In the ensuing three decades, Simon's decision-making theory of organizational behavior was itself subjected to as intense criticism as that to which he had put earlier theories. Human relations advocates often saw Simon's model as one in which all values are determined at the top and employees are indoctrinated like automatons into blind allegiance. This seemed to remove all room for self-actualization of the individual (Argyris, 1973a; response by Simon, 1973b). In actuality, however, Simon's model was not inconsistent with self-actualization, as Argyris (1973b) has noted. This is because Simon's concept of rationality was a bounded one which left much room for employee choice and creativity. Though this point was central to Simon's critique of comprehensive rationality, Simon's focus on economizing/efficiency as the dominant organizational value continued to draw the criticism of organizational humanists seeking the fulfillment of other values in agency life (see Guerreiro-Ramos, 1980).

A more fundamental criticism of Simon's model was posed by Charles Perrow (1972). Perrow noted research showing that organizational goals were often largely symbolic. Far from manipulating employees like robots, goals were often of little influence; far less than Simon's theories suggested (see Meyer and Rowan, 1977; Perrow, 1978; Perrow, 1986). Other research, however, suggests that if organizational goals are operationally expressed as "shared meaning," Simon's concepts may have considerable validity (Smirich, 1983).

Other research cited by Perrow indicates that bounded rationality may not be a totally adequate description of reality. Instead, it may often happen that rather than a decision-maker searching for a few alternative solutions to a problem, agency staff with preconceived interest in certain types of solutions will influence the organization to search for problems which are good experimental arenas for those solutions, ignoring perhaps more important problems which aren't (see Cohen et al., 1972; March and Olsen, 1976). This line of thinking is consistent with the view that informal social networks can exert influence that overrides the objectives of the formal hierarchy of the organization (Barnes and Kriger, 1986). Perrow also noted many of these discrepancies between Simon's theories and empirical research (Perrow, 1979). He concluded that while Simon's model was indeed superior to its predecessors, there was a need for a more complex contingency theory of organizational behavior (Harmon, 1989; Harmon, 1995).

Amitai Etzioni, in an important article "Mixed Scanning: A Third Approach to Decision Making," offered another perspective on the topic of decision-making, one very important to public administrators (Etzioni, 1967). In this article he laid out the framework for what he called a third approach to decision-making that combined elements of both the rationalist and incremental approach. He noted that his model of mixed scanning was neither as "utopian" as rationalism, nor as "conservative" as incrementalism. He begins his critique by noting that many of the assumptions of rational/comprehensive planning model presume intellectual and resource capacities that most administrators in the real world don't possess. In this basic sense he agrees with Lindblom, and others, about the unrealistic demands of the rational model for *all* decision situations. He notes, however, that incrementalism itself possesses potential problems as a societal decision-making process. First of all, if all decisions are reached through a process of disjointed incrementalism, not everyone's interests will be equally represented. Etzioni notes that, in fact, those who lack resources in society, the poor and minorities, are very ones least likely to have their values reflected in the "marketplace of ideas" or in the pluralistic intergroup bargaining process that decides which of those ideas become policy. Second, he observes that incrementalism, by its very nature, ignores basic social innovation, since by definition, it looks at marginal changes from existing conditions. He goes on to note that incrementalism can, in fact, be an ideological justification for the status-quo. In other words, administrators can take incrementalism to mean that one should not seek comprehensive and systematic analysis or major policy changes and adopt the position that current practices and policies reflect the best of all possible worlds.

Etzioni also notes that history suggests that most incremental decisions specify or anticipate what he calls "fundamental" decisions. He also goes on to state that the cumulative value of incremental decisions is, in fact, influenced by these fundamental decisions. He provides as an example from the federal budgetary process which appears on the surface to be the classic expression of the incremental approach, but which upon review, reflects the result of a fundamental decision that itself influenced the cold war military build-up, namely, the Korean War:

> The American defense budget jumped at the beginning of the Korean War in 1950 from 5% of the GNP to 10.3% in 1951. The fact that it stayed at about this level, ranging between 9 and 11.3 percent of the GNP after the war ended (1954–1960), did reflect incremental decisions, but these were made within the context of the decision to engage in the Korean War (Etzioni, 1967, p. 388).

He goes on to note other fundamental decisions that America has made such as the space program. He contends that the number of such fundamental decisions that society makes and their influence on subsequent incremental decision-making is greater than the incrementalists admit. He states that what is needed is a model that incorporates the best elements of rationalism and incrementalism. He describes his view of this model of mixed scanning by using the following example worth quoting at length:

> Assume we are about to set up a world-wide weather observation system using weather satellites. The rationalist approach would seek an exhaustive

survey of weather conditions by using cameras capable of detailed observations and by scheduling reviews of the entire sky as often as possible. This
would yield an avalanche of details, costly to analyze and likely to over-
whelm our action capacities (e.g., "seeding" cloud formations that could develop into hurricanes or bring rain into arid areas). Incrementalism would
focus on those areas in which similar patters developed in the recent past
and, perhaps, on few nearby regions; it would thus ignore all formations
which might deserve attention if they arose in unexpected areas. A mixed-
scanning strategy would include elements of both approaches by employing
two cameras: a broad angle camera that would cover all parts of the sky but
not in great detail and a second one which would zero in on those areas revealed by the first camera torequire more in-depth examination. While
mixed-scanning might miss areas in which only a detailed camera could re-
veal trouble, it is less likely than incrementalism to miss obvious trouble
spots in unfamiliar areas (Etzioni, 1967, p. 389).

Mixed-scanning provides an intellectual middle ground between the limited
perspective of incrementalism and the synoptic view of rationalism. It combines the higher order, fundamental decision-making with lower order incremental decision-making into a single model. Mixed-scanning correctly
observes that without the perspective on the "big picture" major variables will
be excluded in any incremental analysis. Moreover, Etzioni (1986) reports a
summary of research that tests the mixed-scanning model and finds many situations in which it is the best description of the policy process. For example, legal
scholars report that the model applies to the evolution of Supreme Court inter-
pretations of the U.S. Constitution with major fundamental decisions (e.g.,
Mapp vs. Ohio, Gideon vs. Wainwright, Brown vs. The Board of Education)
leading the way to incremental decisions that slowly changed basic relationships in society (Etzioni, 1986). Also Springer (1985) reports the results of an
interesting case study of the California Health and Welfare Agency at which he
found a highly sophisticated and quantitatively oriented (big picture) policy
analysis division that influenced the procedures and personnel involved in organizational decision-making. Moreover, the entire agency was itself linked to the
incremental decision-making process of the California State legislature.
Springer correctly observes that this finding is at variance with the conventional
wisdom that policy analysis and decision-makers occupy two different and
alien worlds (Springer, 1985).

It is also important to note that the business literature describes "strategic planning" in terms that have a parallel with mixed scanning. Strategic
planning is defined as those commitments by the firm that are "nonroutine"
and which will have "significant" effects on the long term performance of the
organization, in other words, decisions of a fundamental nature (Frederickson, 1985). A body of literature has developed to elaborated this type of deci-

sion making in business and to explicate the differences between this type of decision-making and routine (incremental) decision-making (Mintzberg, 1978; Gray, 1986).

PLANNING AND PARTICIPATORY APPROACHES TO DECISION-MAKING

Planning in the tradition of scientific management and participation in the tradition of human relations are two of the great themes of public management. Like other great ideas, they are not easily killed. Although the attack on both schools by Simon and others was severe, although it made academics and practitioners alike aware of the limits of facile planning or participatory remedies, the attack did not prevent continuing interest in both types of solutions to organizational decision-making problems.

There were many reasons for the continued salience to and even growth of planning approaches to public administration. First, there were many areas in which calculable solutions did exist, where both ends and means *could* be agreed upon: traffic engineering, the space program, defense procurement, allocation decisions in service delivery. Second, even where ends and means were not consensual, planning tools were often sought out because officials desired the increased coordination they afforded: case management in social services, management by objectives in federal agencies, program budgeting in state and local government. Third, the advent of computer technology, its proliferation to the management level, and the creation of a body of software (e.g., linear programming, spread-sheets, database programs, input-output models, decision support systems, neural networking) enabled decision-makers to handle far more information in a rational manner than officials in Simon's early days dreamed possible.

At a deeper level, the self-interested actions of organizations in a political environment lead to the necessity for planning. This was the theme of another influential work, James Thompson's *Organizations in Action* (1967). His theories were based on the same assumptions about self-interested conflict that the incrementalists had emphasized, but Thompson was led in an almost opposite direction, one which favored planning approaches to decision-making.

Thompson acknowledged that Simon was correct in describing decision-making in terms of bounded rationality, satisficing, and limited searches of alternatives. Thompson, however, criticized Simon's analysis as static, failing to adequately appreciate how searching behavior leads to organizational learning over time. Specifically, Thompson posited four areas which typically characterized this learning process:

1. *Buffering*: Organizations learn to protect themselves from their environments by surrounding their technical cores by input-output structures.
2. *Leveling*: Organizations learn to smooth input-output transactions to reduce fluctuations in activity levels.
3. *Adaptation*: Organizations learn to anticipate changes that cannot be leveled or buffered.
4. *Rationing*: If these three strategies fail to protect the organization's technical core from threat, the organization learns to restrict input or output (e.g., a mental hospital may substitute drug treatment for more time-intensive psychoanalytic treatment). Planning is the inevitable vehicle for pursuit of these four strategies.

Planning, Thompson noted, involves an intrinsic drive for power. Power is needed to control the environment and thereby reduce uncertainty about resources, inputs, markets, clientele, regulations, and the like. Power is manifested in many common organizational strategies. These include vertical integration (the drive to gain jurisdiction over earlier and later phases of production or service, as in TVA's drive toward involvement in all phases of rural development, not just electrification); geographical integration (the drive toward administration through more inclusive jurisdictions, as in the tendency for welfare functions to shift from local to state to federal levels); and input incorporation (the drive to incorporate input-side personnel into agency affairs, as in the tendency of universities to seek to become "total institutions" providing all services needed by students, not just classroom instruction).

The strategies and drives, noted by Thompson, account for the long-term tendency toward organizational complexity and growth. Complexity in turn requires structure. Increase in interdependence is handled through hierarchies and departmentalization and, if that doesn't suffice, through task forces and other more flexible forms. The working of these forms of organization is political. Internal relations in the complex organization are power relations (Pfeffer and Salanak, 1974). The organization becomes governed by power coalitions in a constantly shifting flux of bargaining relationships. This is particularly so in public management, where the task environment is dynamic and means-ends knowledge is rarely perfected. These characteristics increase the range of organizational options for change. This in turn increases both potential opportunities and threats for various coalitions within the complex organization.

In an interesting study of how local governments in the U.S. and Great Britain faced the difficult choice of service reduction necessitated by declining resources, many expressions of Thompson's early concepts can be found. According to Wolman (1983), local governments in both the U.S. and Britain in dealing with fiscal pressures, acted as organizations concerned with maintaining their equilibrium relationship with both their external environment (the citizens) and their internal environment (the organizational staff). Wolman states that the principal goal of local government is the provision of services. It receives the resources to do this from its clients, the citizens. Local governments, when faced with declining resources and the primary mission to provide services, adopted strategies which clearly suggest an organizational planning process that selects from the many logically possible solutions those that do the least violence to the need for support from the organization's internal and external constituencies. The strategies followed by local governments in both the U.S. and Britain were:

> 1) Buying time; drawing on existing resources reserve funds. San Francisco, for example, drew down reserves by 20 million after proposition 13 to avoid reductions in service or staff. Creative bookkeeping; U.S. cities frequently shifted back and forth between accrual and cash accounting, contingent upon circumstances. One time sale of resources; the city of Cleveland, Ohio among others engaged in one time revenue raising device of selling its sewage treatment plant to a regional authority for profit. 2) Seeking more Aid from other levels of government. 3) If spending had to be reduced reducing it through means which do not disturb the external environment, that is, reduction in administrative staff rather than in service delivery people and seeking more efficiency from existing resources. 4) If public employee unions were willing and the institutional structure allowed, local governments could reduce costs through reduction in real service levels rather than cutting personnel. 5) If services had to be cut minimizing their impact by reducing capital expenditures, maintenance, and invisible and marginal activities (e.g., cutting back maintenance schedules for roads, the number of times per week the trees were trimmed; the streets were cleaned; reducing low visibility functions like closing libraries and parks earlier (Wolman, 1983).

In summary, Thompson argued that coping with uncertainty was the essence of administration. It led to a concept of the organization striving for power vis-a-vis the environment, including other organizations. It led to a variety of strategies, all involving increased levels of complexity and planning. Along with this, particularly in organizations of the type often found in the public sector, came the formation of coalitions of power within the organization.

Participatory management theories address the question of how to organize the politics of complex organizations. It is wrong to think of planning and participation as opposites even though their respective roots in the conflicting scientific management and human relations schools might suggest that. Effective planning requires participation (Gray, 1986). If Thompson is correct, the politics of planning, however "scientific" that planning may be, requires human relations skills (Garson and Brenneman, 1981a; Garson, 1981b; Gray, 1986). The general consensus among researchers is that participation in the decision process increases commitment to the decision. Conversely, exclusion heightens alienation from formal channels of decision-making and encourages those excluded to resort to informal organizations (e.g., power coalitions) which may be at odds with organizational goals. For these reasons, interest in participatory management flows directly from Thompson's analysis of organizations in action. Because participation is analyzed at length in the next chapter, little will be said about it here except to note that it is of special importance in public administration compared to business administration. This is a function of the role that public administration has in the authoritative allocation of values. In other words, public administration is a part of the larger political system and involves different normative assumptions about participation than would prevail in the private sector. We shall return to this dimension of organizational participation in the next chapter. At this point we will turn to the applied research that deals with the group decision-making process.

RESEARCH ON GROUP DECISION-MAKING

A concern for participatory methods of decision-making thus led public administration into an area that had formerly been the preserve of social psychologists and behavioral scientists—research on group behavior. Here empirical evidence was found on such questions as "Under what conditions is group consensus most likely?" and "What are the effects of participation on group decision-making?" Evidence was also available on more applied questions like "What is the best size for decision-making groups?" and "How should groups be seated for maximum effectiveness?" In more contemporary terms, this interest in "groups" has been transformed into an interest in "teams" which has been fostered by the growth of Total Quality Movement (TQM) which is based on a team platform approach to work organization. A team is a group with complementary skills who are committed to a common purpose and set of performance goals in the workplace (Katzenback and Smith, 1993). Given the rise of teams in both the public and private sector we will look at more generic literature on groups through the "lens" of teams in the workplace.

Research has found that group decision-making is superior to individual decision-making in certain respects. This finding is at the basis of much of the remarkable growth in the use of teams in the workplace.

> The many revolutions currently going on in organizations, whether through the quality movement, cycle time, reengineering, high performance work systems, or organizational learning initiatives, all have this in common: At their core is a basic shift of day-to-day and feedback systems from the hier-

archy of command to collaboration within and among teams. Project teams, process analysis teams, intrapreneurial new products teams, quality action teams, market forces teams, and so on are used for many purposes and are succeeding where bureaucracy has failed (Pinchot and Pinchot, 1994, p. 67).

In general, research has shown that groups tends to make slower decisions than individuals, but those decisions are of higher quality. There are five reasons for this: (1) groups have a broader fund of knowledge and are in a better position to formulate objectives; (2) groups generate a broader search for alternatives; (3) groups subject alternatives to more critical investigation; (4) groups are more willing to take risks since potential blame is shared; and (5) because groups are inherently participative, group decisions are more likely to be accepted than individual decisions (on advantages of group decision-making see; Natemeyer and Gilberg, 1989, chapters 12–16; Katzenbach and Smith, 1993; Galbraith and Lawler, 1993; Pinchot and Pinchot, 1994 on risk-taking, see Dion et al., 1970; Clark, 1971; Fisher, 1974; Payne et al., 1981; Katzenbach and Smith, 1993).

One major factor in group decision-making that is important for managers to recognize is that groups tend to exhibit a "dynamic" that makes the decisions reached by groups more than the simple additive aggregate of the preferences in the population from which they are drawn (Hirokawa and Poole, 1986; Katzenbach and Smith, 1993; Pinchot and Pinchot, 1994). Also, groups tend to reach consensus on the position initially preferred by the majority of group members more frequently than on the positions held by the minority coalition (Stasser and Davis, 1981). The face to face meeting of groups provides for all types of non-verbal, paralinguistics, and status dimensions that enter the process and which affect the quality of decision-making (Hiltz et al., 1986). Also, in experimental situations where the willingness to take risks was the dependent variable, group evaluations of bets were typically more *extreme* (more risk adverse or risk taking) than the choices of the various individuals who made up the group, although typically in the same direction as individual preferences (Davis et al., 1974).

This is not to say that administrators should invariably opt for or against group or team decision-making. It clearly depends on the nature of the problem. Individual decision-making is not only faster, it may have other advantages in some situations. Individual decision-making, for example, may lead to more ideas generated per individual and to more unique ideas, if the individual would be inhibited in making suggestions before a group (see Taylor et al., 1958; Dunnette et al., 1963). In extreme cases a form of "groupthink" may emerge, whereby group members isolate themselves from negative feedback and, indeed, reality (Janis, 1972). Because of these problems in group decision-making, some managers have preferred methods discussed below such as the nominal group technique, which combines aspects of individual and group decision-making. Clearly, the advantages of group versus individual decision-making depend partly upon *who* the decision-makers are (Katzenback and Smith, 1993). The identity of the decision-makers is the first of several "contingency factors"—situational variables which affect the appropriateness of group decision-making. Participants who are nonsocial, solitary, and independent in personality orientation, for instance, are poor choices for membership in decision-making groups. Individuals with a capacity for abstract thinking (often a function of education and experience), in contrast, are more effective in group decision-making (Hendrick, 1979). Likewise, younger and lower-level organizational members are often more effective in utilizing group processes (Webber, 1974).

Group *composition* is also a contingency factor. Groups that are heterogenous in composition are generally superior in effectiveness compared to homogenous groups (Laughlin et al., 1969; Hoffman and Maier, 1961). Presumably this is because heterogeneity brings a broader range of information, resources, and skills to bear upon the problems discussed. On the other hand, there is some evidence that homogenous groups are more task-oriented and heterogenous groups more social relations-oriented (Reitan and Shaw, 1964). Homogenous groups, therefore, may be superior when group process is unnecessary to identify goals and tasks.

Group *size* is a third contingency factor. In general, the larger the group, the less participation in the decision-making process. Large groups (over fifteen members) tend to generate fewer ideas per member and reach lower quality decisions (Katzenback and Smith, 1993). Moreover, such large groups tend to factionalize into smaller subgroups (see Collins and Guetzkow, 1964; Davis, 1969). Very small groups (under five) are consensual, but also reach lower quality decisions (Hare, 1972). Most analysts recommend medium sized decision-making groups of five to twelve members because groups of this size make higher quality decisions on the basis of more ideas generated per person (Ziller, 1957; Thomas and Fink, 1963; Manners, 1975; Peters and Waterman, 1982; Hirokawa and Poole, 1986). Of this class of more effective-size groups, those in the medium-small end tend to be the most satisfying to participants (Slater, 1958; Hackman and Vidmar, 1970; Katzenbach and Smith, 1993).

Finally, group process is a fourth set of contingency factors. Research suggests, for example, that consensus decision-making is better than methods which reach decisions through leader choice or majority vote (Asch, 1956; Vroom et al., 1969; Katzenback and Smith, 1993). But as we noted in discussing organizational communication, communication network designs can influence behavior of individual group members. For example it seems to be helpful if groups are seated in a democratic manner, as in a circle, rather than in a square, triangle, or other shape placing some individuals in prominence (Hall, 1971). Side-by-side seating leads to less conflict than across-table seating. In general, group process facilitates decision-making when it incorporates participation, openness, equality of status, and security (see Sherif et al., 1955; Natemeyer and Gilberg, 1989, Chapters 12–16; Katzenback and Smith, 1993).

Group decision-making depends not only upon these four contingency domains but also upon other considerations. Groups (teams) function best when the decision task has demonstrable "answers." Teams are more compatible with organizational designs that are customer focused, technology driven, and where speed and simplicity are important elements of comparative advantage (Katzenbach and Smith, 1993; Galbraith and Lawler, 1993; Gross, 1995). Moreover, the use of a "team platform" requires a compensation program designed to reward the team and not merely utilizing some form of variable pay based on individual effort. Compensation schemes based on team incentives and recognition require careful design and implementation (Gross, 1995).

THE DELPHI METHOD, THE NOMINAL GROUP TECHNIQUE, AND COMPUTER MEDIATED COMMUNICATION

The Rand Corporation, a private policy research organization, pioneered the Delphi method of decision-making as a format for achieving group consensus without such problems of group decision-making as the danger of domination by a single aggressive individual, the possible neglect of shyer members, and the tendency for decisions at the end of meetings to be unduly rushed because of time pressure. Moreover, since Delphi groups do not normally meet in a face-to-face context, many of the nonverbal and status effects on the group decision-making process are minimized. The Delphi method was simply a systematic approach to the traditional device of polling experts, whether outside professionals or the organization's own members.

In the Delphi method, decision-making concerns are translated into a written questionnaire which is administered, usually by mail, to a panel of individuals thought to be knowledgeable about a subject. Among the most common uses is to achieve group consensus on anticipated changes for forecasting purposes. Rand, for example, has used Delphi to develop forecasts of trends in population growth, weapons systems development, and automation. It can also be used to project political trends, for organizational goal-setting, or for educational curriculum development. The technique was developed by Rand analysts Norman Dalkey and Olaf Helmer in the 1950s. Delphi, Helmer wrote, "replaces direct debate by a carefully designed program of sequential individual interrogations interspersed with information and opinion feedback derived from a computed consensus from the earlier parts of the program" (Helmer and Rischer, 1959). It normally involves six steps:

1. Identification of a group of experts.
2. Administration of a questionnaire; typically four dimensions are examined:

    a. Direction: e.g., will use of Organization Development (OD) techniques in public administration increase or decrease?

    b. Degree: e.g., how great will be the change in terms of some standard (for example, ratio of OD-related person-hours to total person-hours of all agency functions)?

    c. Time Frame: e.g., when will the event occur (for example, when will 90 percent of all agency employees be involved in at least 20 hours of OD-related functions annually)?

    d. Likelihood: e.g., what degree of confidence does the respondent attach to each of the judgments above?

3. Questionnaire results are statistically aggregated and a second-round questionnaire is administered after the panel of experts receives first-round feedback.

4. The process is repeated until the last round does not increase panel consensus further.

5. Sometimes panelists may be brought together for face-to-face meetings to provide the analysts with further insight.

6. The decision resulting from the Delphi process is reached by the analyst on the basis of group consensus.

Since its development by Rand, the Delphi method has received hundreds of applications in public management, including the prediction of teacher education developments in Canada (Clark and Coutts, 1971), the forecasting of vocational training needs in California (Brooks, 1972), and the projection of developments in public administration as a discipline (Wald, 1973).

Delphi does help avoid group decision-making biases such as the tendency toward group conformity and deference to the views of the highest-status individual. It has not been without its critics, however. Sackman (1975), among others, has noted the following problems of Delphi: bias resulting for the common problem of drop-outs from panels of experts; frequently vague and ambiguous wording of items in Delphi's questionnaires; and the danger that Delphi's very anonymity may encourage panelists to respond in superficial, irresponsible ways. It is also biased toward decision-forcing, encouraging panelist to give *some* prediction even though the real consensus is that prediction on a reliable basis is impossible.

Despite these problems, validation studies of the Delphi technique have shown that it leads to more reliable forecasts than can be obtained through other group-based approaches. Campbell (1966), for example, found that business students could predict the performance of leading economic indicators better using this method than others. Dalkey and Helmer have likewise found experimentally that Delphi is superior to majority vote and leader decision methods of decision-making (Dalkey and Helmer, 1963; Dalkey, 1968). Dalkey (1969) has also found it better than face-to-face consensual methods, as have Breinholt and Webber (1972).

Delphi is clearly a promising decision-making technique. Nonetheless there is some evidence that even higher quality decisions can be attained through such methods as the nominal group technique (NGT), which combine Delphi procedures with the face-to-face aspects of conventional group decision-making. NGT is also a six-step process:

1. A group of 7 to 10 experts or organizational members are selected and meet face-to-face, whereupon they are presented by the analyst with a problem which is to be the focus of decision-making.
2. After individually and silently listing pertinent ideas on paper (e.g., suggestions for solving an organizational problem), each person reveals one of these ideas at a time as the analyst lists them on flip-charts; the analyst continues around the group until all suggestions are listed.
3. After all ideas are listed without comment, the analyst asks for statements of clarification, agreement, or disagreement with each.
4. Using anonymous balloting, group members then tentatively rank the suggestions and the analyst lists by rank order all the suggestions that have received serious consideration.
5. The analyst then leads further clarification as well as elimination of duplicate ideas or ideas which are of low priority.
6. As a final step, group members rate all the remaining ideas anonymously. The idea with the highest average rank becomes the NGT decision outcome.

The NGT approach, Delbecq et al., (1975) has been found by its originators to be superior to Delphi in eliciting the generation of ideas and in securing task involvement. Their colleague, Gustafson (1973), has come to similar conclusions in other research. Burton and Pathak (1978) have found further advantages in the NGT method. These researchers found NGT required only easily-attainable skills, counteracted typical group-problem-solving biases such as dominance by strong personalities, encouraged tolerance for nonconforming ideas and conflicting views, equalized participation to a greater degree than other methods, and promoted a sense of participation and ownership in decisions reached. Burton and Pathak found NGT to be especially valuable for decision-making when agency participants were often inner-directed in personality rather than individuals with strong other-directed social skills. Another contingency of NGT was discovered by White et al., (1980), who found that NGT produced significantly better rates of decision-implementation than decision-making through conventional groups, but only for simple to moderately complex situations. These research efforts suggest that outgoing people making complex decisions may find NGT procedures an unnecessary waste of time. For a wide range of decision-making situations, however, NGT will often lead to more participant satisfaction, higher quality decisions, and more likelihood of decision implementation (on governmental applications, see Mercer and Woolston, 1980). Moreover, NGT procedures are designed to eliminate persuasion or influence on the group. The assumption is that this makes the process more devoid of "politics." However, this assumes that the effect of the politics of persuasion is always negative rather than serving as a means to articulate different values. NGT eliminates some types of group influence, it may increase others, like the enhancing the power of the NGT facilitator and sponsor.

The face-to-face meeting, as we stated in our discussion of the communication process, has the highest information richness, and has long been the method of choice for problem solving among groups within organizations. However, the very information richness provided by the medium allows all forms of nonverbal and paralinguistic factors to effect the quality of the decision-making process. Because of advances in technology and computer networking many organizations are beginning to explore the advantages of electronic mailing lists, electronic forums, discussion groups, Gophers and World Wide Web Services on the Internet (Kling, 1995; Jones, 1995). One specific expression of telecommunication technology is online conferences and electronic forums (Siegal et. al, 1986; Hiltz et al., 1986; Jones, 1995; Sclove, 1995). In an online conference, participants use the keyboard to send and receive messages either at the same time, called synchronous conference, or at different times, called asynchronous conferencing. Increasingly, video is an added feature. An experimental study that compared group problem solving between face-to-face groups with those dealing with the same problem in computer mediated mode found some interesting differences that relate to the process and outcomes of group decision-making (Hiltz et al., 1986). The computer mediated group compared to the face-to-face group exchanged fewer communication units (messages). However, the members of the computer mediated group participated more equally in the decision-making process. Also, the quality of the decisions (they were given a problem to solve "Lost in the Arctic") was no different between the two groups. However, the computer mediated group was less likely than the face-to-face group to reach consensus particularly about issues with a high normative content (Hiltz et al., 1986).

Some researchers suggest that people respond differently in different communication settings of which computer-mediated communication is an example (Siegel et al., 1986). Others contend that the evolution of electronic mail and chat rooms, with more information, in a more timely and convenient manner than previous technologies will enhance the quality of decision-making (Crawford, 1982; Jones, 1995) The growth of the Internet will necessitate an understanding of this technology and its affect on decision-making (Clement, 1994;

Sclove, 1995). In particular the emergence of the virtual organization composed of people distributed in time and space is one of the most important organizational developments of our time (Kling, 1995). And, while the growth of this technology is somewhat more pronounced in the private sector, on-line database searching, computerized conferencing, and electronic forums and workgroups are appearing as features of the public sector workplace (Vasu, 1988; Jones, 1995; Refkin, 1995; Sclove, 1995).

MANAGERIAL IMPLICATIONS

The management of decision-making is in many ways the culmination of the management of organizational behavior in general. Like other behavioral areas in public administration, management of this aspect of agency life is not reducible to simple formulas (Mitchell and Scott, 1987). It is specifically not reducible to either centralized planning and econometric modeling on the one hand nor to blind faith in incrementalism and "muddling through" on the other. Because the management of decision-making is contingent upon so many factors and because a contingency theory of decision-making is still evolving, the discretion of the manager is rather great. Correspondingly, the ability of the textbook-writer to prescribe solutions is rather limited! Nonetheless, a few generalizations can be made for those seeking to apply organizational theories of decision-making to the practical level of the day-to-day management of decisions.

What difference does decision-making theory make for the practicing agency head in the field? Research suggests that not too much investment of time and resources be sunk into the tools of the planners, analysts, and scientific managers. It suggests efforts to design tight, comprehensive, quantitative performance control systems or other centrally planned solutions to complex organizational problems may be misguided. Research and theory also suggests that the manager is wise to invest time and energy into organizational efforts which clarify management's goals, socialize employees to them, and specify them into standard routines. This should not be done in a rigidly planned manner, but it is not a waste for the manager to spend a great deal of time in setting the proper climate in the agency. The agency head should devote time and resources to improving organizational communications. Subordinates must be made aware of values set at higher levels if they are to act upon them.

Louis Gawthrop (1971) is among those who have categorized the management of decisions as falling in three types: the planning mode, the incrementalist mode, and the synergistic mode. These represent alternative styles for organizing decision-making. The planning mode is a prescriptive model under which the manager seeks to generate as many alternatives as possible, assesses the costs and benefits of each, and chooses the optimal solution. Though it allows for consultation, it is typical of what Schein (1969) terms the authority method of decision-making under which power mainly resides in the hands of the manager and his or her expert advisors. The incrementalist mode is characterized by marginal changes in existing budgets and practices. In Schein's terms, it is often the result of the "plop" method (decision-making by default), minority decision-making (presenting the organization with *faits accompli*), or majority decision-making (based on compromise). The synergistic mode, in contrast, is a combination of planning and incrementalist models. It is also a participatory approach. In Schein's terms, it is decision-making by consensus. Sometimes the synergistic mode is taken to be merely decision-making by participation of the human relations type.

The political aspects of the public management of decision-making are manifested in many ways (Denhart, 1984). Kipnis and Schmidt (1980) have shown that for a wide variety of organizations, communications patterns and influence tactics are dependent upon the differential statuses of those involved. Rationality (planning) tactics and approaches increase, for example, as statuses increase in the organization. Decision-making influence tactics also vary simply because some are more effective than others (La Porte and Keller, 1996). Harari et al., (1980) have documented, for example, the greater effectiveness of certain tactics in a public university setting. Specifically, these authors found that the most effective tactic was asking for large changes and settling for moderate ones (as opposed to the foot-in-the-door strategy or the rational-moderate request strategy). Political aspects of decision-making are also inherent in the factionalization apparent in informal organizations and professional networks (Barnes and Krieger, 1986). It is also manifest in differential perceptions of organizational and self-interest, coalition building, and in career-related motivations leading managers to take credit for success and distance themselves from failure (Murnigham, 1985).

Because of the political aspects of administration, successful change cannot be a matter of decision-making by a blueprint imposed from the top. Moreover, much of the literature on decision-making has emanated from business and assumed a private sector context. What can be said with certitude is that managing decisions is a process, not a technique—though techniques like linear programming or the nominal group approach may be useful. In general, the management of decisions starts with the identification of the problem. This sounds obvious but administrators are prone to skip over this step. In the public sector problems are often complex and solutions not obvious. In a health care setting, for example, administrators may leap to the assumption that the problem is lack of resources when the real problem might be conceived of as too much inpatient rather than out-patient care. Indeed, separating the problem statement from the "presumed" but not empirically verified "solution" is an important skill.

The second step is analysis of problem causes in terms of prioritizing problems by three criteria: magnitude of the problem in terms of the value of improvements which could be made; susceptibility of the variables involved to manipulation by the agency; and urgency of the problem in terms of time frame. Brainstorming, prioritizing through paired comparison rankings, nominal group, and a variety of other techniques may be used at this point. In the actual group meetings, at this step, the manager often plays the role of clarifier or summarizer of the progress toward consensus. As in the management of all meetings, certain group process characteristics are desirable. Sometimes an outside change agent can elicit these characteristics better than the perhaps-intimidating presence of the manager (Argyris, 1987). What are these characteristics? They are many: to avoid premature closure, to seek openness and consensus rather than majority vote, to be descriptive rather than evaluative (to reduce defensiveness), to use humor, to be concrete, to focus on the actionable, to avoid stigmatizing "far-out" ideas, to encourage participation of reticent members, to utilize repetition and summaries, to accept conflict, to be generally ego-supportive. As consensus on a decision emerges, typical approaches move toward establishment of task forces or matrix organizations. More broadly, decision implementation should be conceived as a sociotechnical process, not just a technical one (see Davis, 1979). In particular, the role of the informal organization expressed as a network of relationships that forms a parallel organization to the formal lines of authority needs to be considered (Barnes and Craggier, 1986). Moreover, it is important to explicitly assign tasks to people for motivational reasons. Mossholder (1980) has found, for instance, that assigning specific challenging tasks to individuals increases performance levels compared to methods in which the task is assigned without goals. At this stage of the decison process it is important to identify the *stakeholders* in the decision, those who are in a position to influence or be influenced by the decision. It is also important to understand who the *customer* is and what his or her preferences are.

The fourth step of managing decisions is evaluation and feedback. In this phase the manager is charged with developing evaluative measures. These measures will become motivational goals and must be carefully designed and implemented to avoid neglect of performance on unmeasured criteria. Participation in evaluation and feedback increases employee commitment to the change effort, involvement in decision-making, and is one of the most important things a decision-maker can do for his or her organization (Yeager et al., 1985).

The topic of management decision-making eventually leads back to situational factors associated with leadership, motivation, socialization, change, participation, and other organizational behavior topics treated in other chapters. In addition, the private sector recent research suggests that dominance of "rational" approaches to decision-making underplays the role intuition plays in decision-making (Agor, 1984). In fact, in an article "How Senior Managers Think" appearing in the *Harvard Business Review*, Isenberg (1984) contends that whenever the senior managers he studied approached decision-making, rational techniques were always used in conjunction with intuition. Given that decision-making in any type of organization usually takes place in the context of "uncertainty" this finding is hardly surprising. In fact, if decision-making could be reduced to a specific series of steps or techniques then much of the justification for having managers at all would disappear.

The objective of this chapter has been to familiarize the reader with the broad range of orientations toward decision-making as a managerial and organizational activity in the public sector. The three broad traditions of planning, incrementalism, and participation-synergy each come to bear on decision-making in contemporary agencies. The student of organizational behavior can state with confidence that any one approach alone is inadequate. It can also be said that there are some typical techniques which have been found to be particularly effective in managing decisions. Ultimately, however, a contingency theory of decision-making is currently evolving and needs much development before one can expect widespread impact on practitioners in the public sector. Of all the aspects of decision-making contingencies, however, the ones most studied have to do with the contingencies under which a participative approach to decision-making is most effective. This topic is treated in the next chapter.

ENDNOTE

1. The list of activities was adapted form Harold Wolman's list that appears on page 260 of his article. It is not to be implied that all local governments in both nations followed the exact sequence of strategies. For example, the real reduction of wages for public employees was more problematic in the British context. Nonetheless, the author does an excellent job of illustrating the extent to which local governments as organizations can and do have strategies that appear to suggest adaption, buffering, leveling, and rationing.

REFERENCES AND ADDITIONAL READING

Agor, W. H. (1984). *Intuitive Management: Integrating Left and Right Brain Management Skills*. Englewood Cliffs, NJ: Prentice Hall.

Argyris, Chris (1987). "Bridging Economics and Psychology." *American Psychologist, Vol. 42 (5):pp 456–463.*

Argyris, Chris (1973a). *"Some Limits of Rational Man Organizational Theory."* Public Administration Review, Vol. 33, No. 2 (May/June):pp 253–267.

Argyris, Chris (1973b). "Organizational Man: Rational and Self-Actualizing." *Public Administration Review*, Vol. 33, No. 4 (July/August):pp 354–357.

Asch, Solomon (1956). "Studies of Independence and Conformity." *Psychological Monographs*, 1956:pp 68–70.

Barnes, Louis and Mark P. Krieger (1986). "The Hidden Side of Leadership." *Sloan Management Journal*, Fall:pp 15–25.

Bazerman, M. H. (1994). *Judgment in Managerial Decision Making*, Third Edition. New York: Wiley.

Becker, Christine (1979). "Getting Elected is just the Beginning." *Public Management*, July:pp 10–14.

Breinholt, R. and R. A. Webber (1972). "Comparing Dephi Groups, Uninstructed and Instructed Face-to-Face Groups" in D. R. Hampton, C. E. Summer, and R. A. Webber (1978). *Organizational Behavior and the Practice of Management*, Third Edition. Glenview, Illinois: Scott, Foresman:p 257.

Brooks, E. C. (1934). "A Decade of 'Planning' Literature" *Social Forces*, Vol. 12, No. 2 (March):pp 427–459.

Brooks, E. C. and L. M. Brooks (1933). "Five Years of 'Planning' Literature." *Social Forces*, Vol. 11, No. 2 (March):pp 430–465.

Brooks, W. (1972). *North California Research Group Education Study*. Sacramento, California: Office of the Chancellor, California Community Colleges.

Bunce, V. (1980). "Changing Leaders and Changing Policies: The Impact of Elite Successes on Budgetary Practices in Democratic Countries." *American Journal of Political Science*, Vol. 24, No. 3 (August):pp 373–395.

Burke, John P. (1986). *Bureaucratic Responsibility*. Baltimore: The John Hopkins University Press.

Burke, John P. (1984). "Responsibilities of Presidents and Advisors: A Theory and Case Study of Vietnam Decision Making." *Journal of Politics*, Vol 46:pp 830–856 .

Burton, Gene E. and Dev S. Pathak (1978). "Social Character and Group Decision-making." *Advanced Management Journal*, Summer:pp 12–21.

Campbell, R. M. (1966). *A Methodological Study of the Utilization of Experts in Business Forecasting*. Los Angeles: University of California at Los Angeles, doctoral dissertation.

Catlin, George E. G. (1932). Review of C. A. Beard, ed. (1932). *America Faces the Future*, H. Laidler (1932), *The Road Ahead*, and G. Soule (1932), *A Planned Society*, in *American Political Science Review*, Vol. 26, No. 4 (August):pp 730–733.

Clark, R. D., III (1971). "Group-induced Shift Toward Risk." *Psychological Bulletin*, Vol. 76:pp 251–271.

Clark, S. C. and H. T. Coutts (1971). "The Future of Teacher Education." *Journal of Teacher Education*, Vol. 22, No. 4:pp 508–516.

Clement, A. (1994). "Computing at Work: Empowering Action by Low Level Users." *Communications of the ACM*, 37(1):pp 52–63.

Cohen, Michael D., James C. March, and Johan D. Olsen (1972). "A Garbage Can Model of Organizational Choice." *American Sociological Review*, Vol. 17, No. 1 (March):pp 1– 25.

Collins, B. E. and H. Guetzkow (1964). *A Social Psychology of Group Processes for Decision-Making*. New York: Wiley.

Cooper, Terry L. (1990). *The Responsible Administrator: An Approach to Ethics for the Administrative Role*, Third Edition. San Francisco: Josey Bass.

Corwin, Edward (1932). "Social Planning Under the Constitution." *American Political Science Review*, Vol. 26, No. 1 (February):pp 1–27.

Crawford, A. B. (1982). "Corporate Electronic Mail-A Communication-Intensive Applicaton of Information Technology." *Management of Information Science Quarterly*, Vol 6:pp 1–14.

Cyert and March (1992). *A Behavioral Theory of the Firm*, 2nd edition. Cambridge: Blackwell Business.

Dalkey, N. C. (1969). *The Delphi Method*. Santa Monica, California: Rand Corporation Memo RM 5888–PR (June).

Dalkey, N. C. (1968). *Experiments in Group Prediction*. Santa Monica, California: Rand Corporation.

Dalkey, N. C. and Olaf Helmer (1963). "An Experimental Application of the Delphi Method to Use of Experts." *Management Science*, April:pp 458–467.

Davis, J. H., N. L. Kerr, M. Sussman and A. K. Rissman (1974). "Social Decisions Schemes Under Risk." *Journal of Personality and Social Psychology*, Vol. 30:pp 248–271.

Davis, J. H. (1969). *Group Performance*. Reading, Massachusetts: Addison-Wesley.

Davis, Louis E. (1979). "Optimizing Organizational-plant Design: A Complementary Structure for Technical and Social Systems." *Organizational Dynamics*, Vol. 8, No. 2 (Autumn):pp 2–15.

Delbecq, A. L. Van de Ven, A. H. and D. Gustafson. (1975). *Group Techniques for Program Planning*. Glenview, IL: Scott Foresman.

Denhart, Robert B. (1984). *Theories of Public Organizations*. Monterey, California: Brooks Cole Publishing Company.

Dennison, Henry S. (1932). "The Need for Development of Political Science Engineering." *American Political Science Review*, Vol. 26, No. 2 (April):pp 241–255.

Dion, K. L., R. S. Baron and N. Miller (1970). "Group Decision-Making Under Risk of Adverse Consequences." *Journal of Personality and Social Psychology*, Vol. 1:pp 453–460.

Drucker, Peter (1988). "The Coming of the New Organization." *Harvard Business Review*, January–February:pp 45–53.

Dunnette, M. D., J. D. Campbell, and K. Jaastad (1963). "The Effect of Group Participation on Brainstorming Effectiveness for Two Industrial Samples." *Journal of Applied Psychology*, Vol. 47:pp 30–37.

Etzioni, Amitai (1967). "Mixed Scanning: A 'Third' Approach to Decision-Making." *Public Administration Review*, Vol. 27, No. 6 (December):pp 385–392.

Etzioni, Amitai (1986). "Mixed Scanning Revisited." *Public Administration Review*. Vol 46(1):pp 8–13.

Etzioni, Amitai (1992). "Normative-Affective Factors: Toward a New Decision-Making Model," in Mary Zey, (1992). *Decision-Making: Alternatives to Rational Choice Models* Newbury Park, California: Sage

Federickson, James (1985). "Effects of Decision Motive and Organizational Performance Level on Strategic Decision Process." *Academy of Management Journal*, Vol. 28(4):pp 821–843.

Fisher, G. Aubrey (1974). *Small Group Decision-Making: Communication and Group Process*. New York: McGraw-Hill.

Forester, John (1984). "Bounded Rationality and the Politics of Muddling Through." *Public Administration Review*. Vol. 44:pp 23–31.

Friedman, Milton and Rose Friedman (1979). *Free to Choose.* New York: Avon Books.

Friedman, Milton (1962). *Capitalism and Freedom.* Chicago: University of Chicago Press.

Galbraith, J. R., and Edward E. Lawler III, and Associates (1993). *Organizing for the Future.* San Francisco, California: Josey Bass.

Garson, G. David and D. S. Brenneman (1981a). "Resource Rationing in State Agencies: The Management and Political Challenge of Productivity Improvement." *Public Productivity Review*, September:pp 231–248.

Garson, G. David (1981b). "Incentive Systems and Goal Displacement in Personnel Resource Management." *Review of Public Personnel Administration*, Vol. 1, No. 2 (April):pp 1–12.

Gawthrop, Louis (1971). *Administrative Politics and Social Change.* New York: St. Martin's Press.

Gilman, Stuart C., and Carol W. Lewis (1996). "Public Service Ethics: A Global Dialogue." *Public Administration Review*, Vol. 56:pp 517–524.

Goodwin, Robert E. and Peter Wilenski (1984). "Beyond Efficiency: The Logical Underpinnings of Administrative Principles." *Public Administration Review*, Vol 44(6):pp 512–517.

Grandori, Anna (1984). "A Prescriptive Contingency View of Organizational Decision-Making." *Administrative Science Quarterly*, Vol. 29:pp 192–209.

Gray, Dennis (1986). "Uses and Misuses of Strategic Planning." *Harvard Business Review*, January–February:pp 89–97.

Greiner, L. (1967). "Patterns of Organizational Change." *Harvard Business Review*, Vol. 45, No. 3 (May/June):pp 119–130.

Gross, Stephen E. (1995). *Compensation for Teams: How to Design and Implement Team Based Reward Programs.* New York: American Management Association.

Guerreiro-Ramos, Alberto (1980). "A Substantive Approach to Organizations." Ch. 7 in C. J. Bellone, ed., *Organization Theory and the New Public Administration.* Boston: Allyn and Bacon.

Gustafson, D. H. (1973). "A Comparative Study of Differences in Subjective Likelihood Estimates Made by Individuals, Interacting Groups, Delphi Groups and Nominal Groups." *Organizational Behavior and Human Performance*, Vol. 9:pp 280–291.

Hackman, R. and N. Vidmar (1970). "Effects of Size and Task Type on Group Performance and Member Reaction." *Sociometry*, Vol. 33:pp 37–54.

Hall, J. (1971). "Decisions." *Psychology Today*, November:pp 51ff.

Harari, Herbert, Deborah Mohr, and Karen Hosey (1980). "Faculty Helpfulness to Students: A Comparison of Compliance Techniques." *Personality and Social Psychology Bulletin*, Vol. 6, No. 3 (September):pp 573–577.

Hare, A. P. (1972). "Interaction and Consensus in Different Sized Groups." *American Sociological Review*, Vol. 17:pp 261–267.

Harmon, Michael (1995). *Responsibility As Paradox: A Critique of Rational Discourse on Government.* Newbury Park, California: Sage.

Harmon, Michael M. (1989). "'Decision' and 'Action' as Contrasting Perspectives in Organization Theory," *Public Administration Review*, Vol. 49:pp 144–149.

Harmon, Michael M. and Richard T. Mayer (1986). *Organizational Theory for Public Administration*. Boston: Little, Brown and Company.

Hayek, F. A. (1944). *The Road to Serfdom*. Chicago: University of Chicago Press.

Hayek, F. A. (1935). *Collectivist Economic Planning*. London: Routledge.

Helmer, C. and N. Rischer (1959). "On the Epistemology of Inexact Sciences." *Management Science*, Vol. 6:pp 25–52.

Hendrick, Hal W. (1979). "Differences in Group Problem-solving Behavior and Effectiveness as a Function of Abstractness." *Journal of Applied Psychology*, Vol. 61, No. 5 (October):pp 518–525.

Hiltz, Roxanne Starr, Kenneth Johnson and Murray Turoff (1986). "Experiments in Group Decision Making: Communication Process and Outcome in Face to Face versus Computerized Conferences." *Human Communication Research*, 13(2):pp 225–252.

Hirokawa, R. Y., and M. S. Poole, eds. (1986). *Communication and Group Decision Making*. Beverly Hills, California: Sage.

Hoffman, L. R. and M. R. Maier (1961). "Quality and Acceptance of Problem Solutions by Members of Homogenous and Heterogenous Groups." *Journal of Abnormal and Social Psychology*, Vol. 62:pp 401–407.

Isenberg, Daniel, J. (1984). "How Senior Managers Think." *Harvard Business Review*, November–December:pp 81–90.

Janis, Irving L. (1972). *Victims of Groupthink*. Boston: Houghton Mifflin.

Jones, S. G. (1995). *Cyber Society: Computer Mediated Communications and Community*. Thousand Oaks, California: Sage.

Kahneman, J. M. and J. A. Riskind (1979), "Prospect Theory: An Analysis of Decisions Under Risk" *Econometrica*, Vol. 47:pp 262–291.

Katzenbach, Jon R. and Douglas K. Smith (1993). *The Wisdom of Teams: Creating the High Performance Organization*. Boston, Massachusetts: Harvard University Press.

Kaufman, B. E. (1990). "A New Theory of Satisficing." *The Journal of Behavioral Economics*, Spring:pp 35–51.

Kipnis, David and Stuart M. Schmidt (1980). "Intraorganizational Influence Tactics: Exploration in Getting One's Own Way." *Journal of Applied Psychology*, Vol. 65, No. 4 (August):pp 440–452.

Kling, R. (1995). *Computerization and Contraversy: Values, Conflicts, and Social Choices*, 2nd edition. San Diego, California: Academic Press.

Laidler, Harry (1932). *Socialist Planning and a Socialist Program*. New York: Falcon.

LaPorte, Todd R. and Ann Keller (1996). "Assuring institutional Constancy: Requisite for Managing Long-lived Hazards." *Public Administration Review*, Vol. 56:pp 533–545.

Laughlin, P. R., L. G. Branch, and H. H. Johnson (1969). "Individual Versus Triadic Personality on a Unidimensional Completion Task as a Function of Initial Ability Level." *Journal of Personality and Social Psychology*, Vol. 12:pp 144–150.

Lindblom, Chalres E. (1959). "The Science of 'Muddling Through." *Public Administration Review*, Vol. 19 (Spring):pp 79–88.

Lorwin, L. L. (1931). *Advisory Economic Councils*. Washington: Brookings Institution.

Manners, G. E., Jr. (1975). "Another Look at Group Size, Group Problem-solving, and Member Consensus." *Academy of Management Journal*, Vol. 18, No. 4:pp 715–724.

Mannheim, Karl (1950). *Freedom, Power and Democratic Planning*. New York: Oxford University Press.

March, James C. and Johna P. Olsen (1976). *Ambiguity and Choice in Organizations*. Bergen, Norway: Universitetsforlaget.

March, James G. and Herbert A. Simon (1960). *Organizations*. New York: Wiley.

Marini, Frank, ed. (1971). *Toward a New Public Administration: The Minnowbrook Perspective*. Scranton, PA: Chandler.

McCaskey, Michael B. (1979). "The Management of Ambiguity." *Organizational Dynamics*, Vol. 7, No. 4 (Spring):pp 31–35.

Mercer, J. L. and Susan W. Woolston (1980). "Setting Priorities: Three Techniques for Better Decision-making." Management Information Service. *International City Management Association*, Vol. 12, No. 9 (September):pp 1–9.

Meyer, John W. and Brian Rowan (1977). "Institutionalized Organizations: Formal Structure as Myth and Ceremony." *American Journal of Sociology*, Vol. 83, No. 2 (September):pp 340–363.

Milgrom, Paul and John Roberts, (1992). *Economics, Organization, and Management*. Englewood Cliffs, New Jersy: Prentice Hall

Mintzberg, H. (1978). "Patterns in Strategy Formation." *Management Science*, Vol 24:pp 934–949.

Mitchell, Terrence and William C. Scott (1987). "Leadership Failures, The Distrusting Public and Prospects of the Administrative State." *Public Administration Review*, Vol 47(6):pp 445–452.

Mossholder, Kevin W. (1980). "Effects of Externally Mediated Goal Setting on Intrinsic Motivation: A Lab Experiment." *Journal of Applied Psychology*, Vol. 65, No. 2 (April):pp 202–210.

Mumby, D. K., and L. L. Putnam (1992). "The Politics of Emotion. A Feminist Reading of Bounded Rationality," *Academy of Management Review*, July:pp 465–86.

Murnigham, J. K. (1985). "Coalitions in Decision Making Groups: Organizational Analogs." *Organizational Behavior and Human Performanc*, Vol 35:pp 1–26.

Myrdal, Gunnar (1960). *Beyond the Welfare State*. New Haven, CT: Yale University Press.

Nalbandian, John and Donald E. Klinger (1980). "Integrating Context and Decision Strategy: A Contingency Theory Approach to Public Personnel Administration." *Administration and Society*, Vol. 12, No. 2 (August):pp 178–202.

Natemeyer, Walter and Jay S. Gilberg (1989). *Classics of Organizational Behavior*, 2nd edition. Danville, IL: The Interstate Printers and Publishers.

Palmer John L. and Isabel V. Sawhill, eds. (1984). *The Regan Record: An Assessment of America's Changing Priorities*. Cambridge, MA: Ballinger Publishing.

Payne, J. W., D. J. Laughhunn and R. Crum (1981). "Further Tests of Aspiration Level Effects in Risky Choice Behavior." *Management Science*, Vol 30:pp 1350–1361.

Perrow, Charles (1986). *Complex Organizations: A Critical Essay*, 3rd edition. New York: Random House.

Perrow, Charles (1979). *Complex Organizations*, 2nd edition. Glenview, IL: Scott Foresman.

Perrow, Charles (1978). "Demystifying Organizations." In R. Sauri and Y. Hasenfeld, eds., *The Management of Human Services*. New York: Columbia.

Perrow, Charles (1972). *Complex Organizations*. Glenview, IL: Scott, Foresman.

Peters, Thomas J. and Robert H. Waterman (1982). *In Search of Excellence*. New York: Harper and Row.

Peters, Thomas J. (1979). "Leadership: Sad Facts and Silver Linings." *Harvard Business Review*, Vol. 57, No. 6 (November/December):pp 164–172.

Pfeffer, Jeffery and Gerald R. Salanak (1974). "Organizational Decision-Making As A Political Process: The Case of the University." *Administrative Science Quarterly*, Vol 19:pp 135–151.

Pinchot, Clifford and Elyzabeth Pinchot (1994). *The End of Bureaucracy and the Rise of Intelligent Organizations*. San Francisco, California: Berrett-Koehler Publishers.

Polanyi, Michael (1951). *The Logic of Liberty*. Chicago: University of Chicago Press.

Refkin, J. (1995). *The End of Work*. New York: G.P. Putnam.

Reitan, H. I. and M. E. Shaw (1964). "Group Membership, Sex Composition of the Group, and Conformity Behavior." Journal of Social Psychology, Vol. 64:pp 45–51.

Sackman, Harold (1975). *Delphi Critique: Expert Opinion, Forecasting, and Group Process*. Lexington, MA: D. C. Heath and Company.

Saunders, Robert J. (1979). "Improving Policy-making Skills." *Public Management*, July:pp 2–25.

Schein, Edgar (1969). *Process Consultation: Its Role in Organizational Development*. Reading, MA: Addision Wesley Company.

Schull, Fremont, Andre Delbecq, and L. L. Cummings (1970). *Organizational Decision-Making*. New York: McGraw-Hill.

Sclove, R. (1995). *Democracy and Technology*. New York: Gulford.

Senge, Peter (1990). *The Fifth Discipline*. New York: Doubleday.

Sherif, Muzafer, B. J. White and O. J. Harvey (1955). "Status in Experimentally Produced Groups." *American Journal of Sociology*, Vol. 60:pp 370–379.

Siegel, Jane, Vitaly Dubrovsky, Sara Kiesler, and Timothy McGuire (1986). "Group Process in Computer-Mediated Communication." *Organizatonal Behavior and Human Decision Process*, Vol 37:pp 157–187.

Simon, Herbert A. (1957a). *Models of Man*. New York: Wiley.

Simon, Herbert A. (1973b). "Organizational Man: Rational or Self-actualizing?" *Public Administration Review*, Vol. 33, No. 4 (July/August):pp 34–353.

Simon, Herbert A. and Associates (1992) "Decision-Making and Problem Solving," in Mary Zey, (1992). *Decision-Making: Alternatives to Rational Choice Models*. Newbury Park, California: Sage.

Simon, Herbert A., Harold Guetzkow, George Kozmetsky, and Gordon Tyndall (1954). *Centralization vs. Decentralization in Organizing the Controller's Department*. New York: Controllership Foundation, Inc.

Simon, Herbert A. (1945). *Administrative Behavior*. New York: MacMillan

Skok, J. E. (1980). "Budgetary Politics and Decision-Making." *Administration and Society*, Vol. 11, No. 4 (February):pp 445–460.

Slater, P. E. (1958). "Contrasting Correlates of Group Size." *Sociometry*, Vol. 21:pp 129–179.

Smircich, Linda (1983). "Organizations as Shared Meaning," in Louis R. Ponday, Peter J. Frost, Gareth Morgan, and Thomas C. Danbridge *Organizational Symbolism*. pp. 55–65.

Smith, Michael P. and Steven L. Nock (1980). "Social Class and the Quality of Work Life in Public and Private Organizations." *Journal of Social Issues*, Vol. 36, No. 4:pp 59–75.

Staats, Elmer B. (1988). "Public Service and the Public Interest." *Public Administration Review*, Vol. 48(2):pp 601–605.

Staats, E. G. (1980). "Why Isn't Policy Research Used by more Decision-makers" *GAO Review*, Vol. 15, No. 1 (Winter):pp 21–25.

Stasser, G. and J. H. Davis (1981). "Group Decision Making and Social Influence: A Social Interaction Sequence Model." *Psychological Review*, Vol 88:pp 523–556.

Taylor, D., P. C. Berry, and C. H. Block (1958). "Does Group Participation When Using Brainstorming Facilitate or Inhibit Creative Thinking." *Administrative Science Quarterly*, Vol. 23:pp 23–47.

Thayer, Frederick C. (1980). "Organization Theory as Epistemology: Transcending Hierarchy and Objectivity." Ch. 6 in C. J. Bellone, ed., *Organization Theory and the New Public Administration*. Boston: Allyn and Bacon.

Thomas, E. J. and L. F. Fink (1963). "Effects of Group Size." *Psychological Bulletin*, Vol. 60:pp 371–384.

Thompson, James D. (1967). *Organizations in Action*. New York: McGraw-Hill.

Tjosvald, Dean and Deborah K. Deemer (1980). "Effects of Controversy within a Cooperative or Competitive Context on Organizational Decision-making." *Journal of Applied Psychology*, Vol. 65, No. 5 (October):pp 590–595.

Tugwell, Rexford (1933). *Industrial Discipline and the Governmental Arts*. New York: Columbia University Press.

Tushman, Michael (1977). "A Political Approach to Organizations: a Review and Rationale." *Academy of Management Review*, Vol. 2, No. 2 (April):pp 206–216.

Van de Van, A. H. and A. F. Delbecq (1974). "The Effectiveness of Nominal, Delphi, and Interacting Group Decision-making Processes." *Academy of Management Journal*, Vol. 17, No. 4:pp 605–621.

Van Wart, Montgomery (1996). "The Sources of Ethical Decision Making for Individuals in the Public Sector." *Pubic Administration Review*, Vol. 56:pp 525–533.

Vasu, Michael L. (1988). "Information Utilities and Telecommunications Networks for Public Administrators." *Public Productivity Review*, Vol. XI, No. 3:pp 219–227.

Vroom, Victor, Lester Grant, and Timothy Cotten (1969). "The Consequences of Social Interaction in Group Problem-solving." *Organizational Behavior and Human Performance* February:pp 77–95.

Wald, Emanuel (1973). "Toward a Paradigm of Future Public Administration." *Public Administration Review*, Vol. 33, No. 4 (July/August):pp 368–372.

Webber, R. A. (1974). "The Relation of Group Performance to the Age of Members of Homogemous Groups." *Academy of Management Journal*, Vol. 17, No. 3 (September):pp 570–574.

Weiss, Carol H. (1980). *Social Science Research in Decision Making*. New York: Columbia University Press.

White, Sam E., J. E. Dittrich, and J. R. Lang (1980). "The Effects of Group Decision-making Process and Problem-solving Situation Complexity on Implementation Attempts." *Administrative Science Quarterly*, Vol. 25, No. 3 (September):pp 428–440.

Wildavsky, Aaron (1988). "Ubiquitous Anomie: Public Service in an Era of Ideological Dissensus." *Public Adminisration Review*, Vol. 48 (4):pp 753–755.

Wimberley, Terry and Allyn Morrow, (1981). "Mulling Over 'Muddling Through' Again." *International Journal of Public Administration*, Vol. 3:pp 483; b2503.

Wolman, Harold (1983). "Understanding Local Government Responses to Fiscal Pressure: A Cross National Analysis." *Journal of Public Policy*, Vol. 3(3):pp 245–263.

Wood, Dan B. and Richard W. Waterman (1994). *Bureaucratic Dynamics*. Boulder, Colorado: Westview Press.

Yeager, Samual J., Jack Rabin, and Thomas Vocino (1985). "Feedback and Administrative Behavior in the Public Sector." *Public Administration Review*, Vol. 45(5):pp 570–575.

Zeitz, Gerald (1980). "Hierarchical Authority and Decision-making in Professional Organizations." *Administration and Society*, Vol. 12, No. 3 (November):pp 277–300.

Zey, Mary, ed. (1992). *Decision Making: Alternatives to Rational Choice Models*. Newbury Park, CA: Sage.

Ziller, R. C. (1957). "Group Size: A Determinant of the Quality and Stability of Group Decision.' *Sociometry*, Vol. 20:pp 165–173.

8

Worker Participation and Total Quality Management

Increasing worker participation is a common theme in the discussion of organizational behavior in public administration. Today that discussion is typically couched in a broader discussion of total quality management. Participatory management has a long history in the literature of organizations. It was at the heart of the human behavioral attack on classical approaches to organizational behavior, and specifically on Fredrick Taylor's scientific management. Participation also figured prominently in the "new public administration" movement of the 1960s and 1970s which linked aspirations for political democracy with proposals for organizational democracy (Marini, 1971). Today, participatory management, expressed in the form of empowerment, self-directed work teams, and quality circles, is a central tenant of the total quality movement (TQM) in the U.S. and abroad (Crosby, 1984; Imai, 1986; Juran, 1988; Scholtes, 1992; Katzenbach and Smith, 1993; Deming, 1993; Costin, 1994; Imai, 1997). The substance of the human relations and TQM critiques of traditional management is that management control of workers through hierarchical structures reduces workers to the mechanical execution of work programmed by management. This legacy of scientific management must be replaced by worker participation in the decision-making process (Derber and Schwartz, 1983; Walton, 1986; Scholtes et al., 1994; Katzenbach and Smith, 1993; Deming, 1993; Costin, 1994; Lindsay and Petrick, 1997).

Today, participation and TQM are mainstays of current work in the field of organization development and have become major themes in American industry (Lawler, 1992; Cotton, 1993; Jablonski, 1992; Katzenbach and Smith, 1993; Dean and Evans, 1994; Lindsay and Petrick, 1997). Many private sector firms are currently experimenting with various forms of worker participation as a part of a larger quality movement. Private-sector examples cover a full range of models. These models range from, at the low end of the participation scale, profit-sharing plans, in which participation is only nominal, to medium-participation modes, like job enrichment, to high-participation models, like self-directed work teams (Cotton, 1993). The central feature of this participation movement is to reject a central tenant of scientific management, the assumption that ideas, solutions to workplace problems, and organizational policy, *all originate with management*. These worker participation endeavors have a variety of names: "empowerment," "quality circles," "participatory democracy," "participative management," and "self directed work teams." The reasons behind this movement are varied. Research has shown that many employees want to participate (Lawler, 1992; Cotton, 1993; Imai, 1997). Participation is also a critical factor in employee motivation since it is a key to organizational commitment and productivity (Boyle, 1984; Katzenbach and Smith, 1993; Dean and Evans, 1994). Every day more and more private companies worldwide move to the "team platform" as a part of a TQM organizational design. There are many accounts of cost savings, increased productivity, and superior quality related to worker participation programs (Mrockowski, 1984; Lawler, 1992; Katzenbach and Smith, 1993; Dean and Evans, 1994; Poister and Harris, 1997; Lindsay and Petrick, 1997; Imai, 1997).

As stated previously, worker participation today is typically a major element in a larger organizational design shift toward total quality management. Some companies have implemented significant worker participation (empowerment) in the form of self-directed work teams. For example, Ford Motor Company and the United Auto Workers have established joint union-management employee involvement groups in every domestic plant. The Ford Taurus was designed and built using teams. Among the notable companies that have made heavy use of worker participation are IBM, TRW, Honeywell, General Electric, Toyota, Honda, Westinghouse, and Xerox (Mohrman and Ledford, 1985; Katzenbach and Smith, 1993; Imai, 1997). Much of the motivation for the renewed interest in worker participation and teams in the private sector has been pragmatic. Worker participation is recognized as a means to increase organizational productivity and directly affect such factors as employee job satisfaction and absenteeism (Frost, 1986; Marks, et al., 1986; Lawler, 1992).

In effect, much participative management that has been implemented in the private sector have been done so under the assumption that participative management will have a positive net effect on organizational performance and productivity (Mohrman and Novelli, 1985; Lawler, 1992; Katzenbach and Smith, 1993; Lindsay and Petrick, 1997). Participation by workers is also a central theme in the study of decision-making, outlined in the previous chapter, because of its role in broadening the process of choice and selection. Moreover, TQM is now firmly entrenched in the private sector and gaining inroads into the public sector (Harrison and Stupak, 1993; Cox, 1995; Maher, 1995; McGowan, 1995; Swiss, 1995; West, 1995; Poister and Harris, 1997). What is TQM? How adaptable is it to the public sector? Moreover, since worker participation (empowerment) is a central feature of TQM, what are the implications for TQM in public sector organizations? These questions are the focus of the present chapter. We will begin by defining TQM and the role worker participation plays in this new concept of management.

TOTAL QUALITY MANAGEMENT (TQM)

What is TQM? TQM is a new paradigm of management! TQM is both a *philosophy* and *methodology* for managing organizations. TQM includes a set of principles, tools, and procedures that provide guidance in the practical affairs of running an organization (Deming, 1993). Philosophically, TQM has it roots in the human relations approach to management, specifically, it sees organizations as open systems, emphasizes participative management, advocates strategic planning, and has a strong commitment to customer satisfaction (Harrison and Stupak, 1993). Methodologically, TQM is predicated on a strong commitment to the measurement of variance in work processes through statistical process control (SPC), and in comparing organizational work processes through benchmarking (Scholtes, et al., 1988; Amsden et al., 1989; Keehley et al., 1997). TQM is also, fundamentally, a very specific organizational culture, one that seeks to involve and empower all members of the organization in the act of continuously improving how work is done (McNabb and Sepic, 1995; Imai, 1997). The ultimate objective of this continuous process improvement (CPI) is customer satisfaction (Deming, 1993).

In the U.S., TQMs earliest organizational expressions were in the private sector. In government, the Department of Defense and the Department of Agriculture first implemented TQM principles in the 1980s. In 1987, the first National Conference on Federal Quality and Productivity was held, and in 1988 the Federal Quality Institute was established. President Reagan proposed a national quality award modeled on the Deming Prize in Japan in the 1980s. Named after a former secretary of commerce, the Malcolm Baldridge National Quality Award was signed into law in August of 1987. Administered by the Department of Commerce, the Baldridge award is given to organizations that excel on a series of organizational assessment criteria: leadership, information and analysis, strategic planning, human resources, process management, results, and customer focus. These categories are given points, and reflect the core values expressed by TQM. They are the criteria against which organizations under consideration for the award must evaluate themselves. Many private sector organizations employ the Baldridge Award principles as a part of a movement to total quality management and continuous improvement. Increasingly federal, state, and local governments are using the same or similar criteria in their own organizational assessments. In a sense, the Baldridge Award criteria have become the operational definition of quality in organizations. A majority of states, and many local governments, have implemented some form of quality initiative (Cox, 1995; West, 1995). Government agencies that use TQM agree that it is fundamentally different from traditional hierarchical management structures of government (Hyde, 1992; Harrison and Stupak, 1993; Kravchuk and Leighton, 1993; Walters, 1994; Cox, 1995; Maher, 1995; West, 1995; Keehley et al., 1997). Total quality management has many proponents and advocates (Juran, 1988; Crosby, 1984; Deming, 1993; Costin, 1994; Imai, 1997). It has "orthodox" and more reformed expressions (Swiss, 1995). It also has a specific history in the private sector that needs to be examined in order to understand its relevance to government.

TQM is actually a term used to describe the research, managerial philosophy, and thinking of a number of individuals (Shewhart, 1931; Ishikawa, 1982; Crosby, 1984; Imai, 1986; Juran, 1988; Deming, 1993; Imai, 1997). By most accounts, TQM originated when the American Walter A. Shewhart of Bell Laboratories developed a system of measuring variance in production systems. This system is known as statistical process control (SPC).

> Shewhart taught that controlled variation is a consistent pattern of variation over time that is due to *random* or *chance* causes. He saw that there are many chance causes of variation, but the effect of any one of these is relatively small; therefore, which cause or causes are responsible for observed variation is a matter of chance. Shewhart stated that a process that is being affected only by *chance* causes of variation is said to be in a *state of statistical control* (Lindsay and Petrick, 1997, p. 65).

Statistical process control is still the major tool that TQM uses to monitor consistency, as well as to diagnose problems inherent in work processes. One of Shewhart students, W. Edwards Deming, a Yale educated mathematical physicist and U.S. Department of Agriculture and Census Bureau research scientist, was hired to teach SPC and quality control to the U.S. Defense industry during World War II. These methods were considered so important to the war effort that they were classified as military secrets. Ironically, after WW II, most U.S. companies stopped using SPC and TQM-type quality control procedures. However, after WW II, U.S. occupation forces in conjunction with the Japanese Union of Scientists and Engineers (JUSE) invited W. Edwards Deming to lecture throughout Japan on SPC and quality control methodology (Dean and Evans, 1994; Costin, 1994; Lindsay and Petrick, 1997).

Deming always acknowledged his intellectual debt to Shewhart. For example, Deming's Cycle (see Figure 13), an expression of the continuous im-

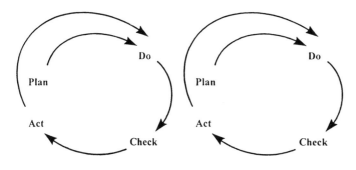

Figure 13   The Deming Cycle.

provement process, was an adaptation of Shewhart's dynamic process of acquiring knowledge which involved steps similar to the classical experiment in science; step 1 form a hypothesis, step 2 conduct an experiment, step 3 test the hypothesis.

Deming's unique contribution was to refine Shewhart's principles into a coherent philosophy expressed in his famous 14 points (Walton, 1986). He also taught the Japanese a series of important lessons that they incorporated into their management practices: (1) that quality is a continuous process of improving work (a journey, not a destination); (2) that customer satisfaction is the ultimate goal of the organization; (3) that the statistical measurement of variance was (is) the best tool available to measure progress toward continuous improvement (Deming, 1993; Dean and Evans, 1994, pp. 37–52; Lindsay and Petrick, 1997). The Japanese were quick to adapt and modify Deming's techniques as well as to add contributions of their own (Ishikawa, 1982, Imai, 1986 and1997). They also recognized Deming's contribution to their own postwar industrial recovery. Deming was credited by the Japanese with being a major force in the "economic miracle" of postwar Japan. To this day, the highest award in Japan for quality is named after W. Edwards Deming. Prior to his death in 1994, one of the highest honors in Japan was to have Deming present at the ceremony. Deming also received the Emperor's medal specifically for his contribution to the economic reconstruction of Japan.

Other Americans, such as Joseph M. Juran, also stressed to the Japanese the importance of involving all departments in the pursuit of quality, and the importance of customer satisfaction, rather than simple adherence to technical specifications. Ishikawa enlarged the ideas of Juran to include as customers "internal customers," those in an organization who depend upon the work output of others. Also, basing his own work in part on the American Behavioral scientists Herbert Maslow (Hierarchy of needs) and Douglas McGregor (Theory Y), he developed the concept of quality circles. TQM today, as practiced in Japan, the U.S. and Europe, is a holistic management philosophy that has evolved over time, and not simply a set of specific techniques like SPC, quality circles, and continuous improvement procedures. In the subsequent section we will more specifically outline the principles and practices of what Professor James E. Swiss calls "orthodox TQM" (Swiss, 1995). We will then evaluate the adaptability of TQM to government.

The Philosophy and Methodology of Orthodox TQM

TQM is Customer, Not Specialist, Driven. Users of products or services define what they want rather than have their needs defined by specialists. In TQM, customer needs and expectations, not agency-established standards, define quality. In fact, quality as concept is defined by the user of the product or service in question. No matter how good your products and services are by some "objective" standard, they cannot be total quality unless they meet your customers needs. A customer is anyone who receives or uses what you produce, or whose service satisfaction depends upon your actions. There are two general types of customers in TQM, internal and external. An internal customer is someone in your organization whose part in the work process comes after yours. An external customer is the ultimate recipient of your product or service. The ultimate purpose of TQM is to exceed the customers expectation, to "delight" them (Deming, 1993; Swiss, 1995; McNabb and Sepic, 1995).

TQM Has an Open Systems View of Organizations Predicated on Mapping Work Processes. One of the major differences between TQM and traditional management theory is in their respective views of individual and organizational performance. Deming (1993) argues for an appreciation of systems thinking. In other words, a police department may be composed of various subsystems: traffic, detectives, internal affairs, and school resources officers. A private company may be composed of subsystems such as purchasing, manufacturing, shipping, and marketing. These subsystems are linked together as internal customers and suppliers working to serve an external customer. Moreover, each subsystem has its own work processes. The management's job, according to Deming, is to *optimize the system.* To Deming it is management that creates work systems, and they are responsible for the success or failure of those systems. While the systems thinking premise is not unique to the advocates of TQM, it has been made famous by Deming's "red bead experiment," which demonstrated the variance explained by the work system versus the individual worker in total results achieved. TQM does not argue that employees are never late, irresponsible, lazy, or inaccurate. TQM does argue that approximately 85% of the problems in organizations are the result of systems (the way management sets up work to be done), and only 15% the result of problems arising from employee mistakes. Therefore, the greatest gains in managerial efficiency are in the area of *improving work systems, not measuring employee performance.* This has led proponents of TQM to argue that managers improve and optimize systems, and to do this they need to understand that an organizational system is composed of a group of linked work processes.

To TQM, work is a series of processes that form systems. These processes can be mapped using various tools and techniques such as flowcharts, histograms, pareto charts, fishbone or Ishikawa charts, scatter diagrams, and control charts. Problems or challenges in a work system usually involve understanding, measuring, and adjusting some element of a work process. For example, the hiring process is a series of linked events that are coupled together to produce an outcome, in this case, hiring someone. Process mapping involves using one of the tools mentioned above to break down the elements of a process so that the manager can understand the steps involved in the process, and therefore, how to improve that process. Again, in TQM a work system is a group of related (linked) work processes. Figure 14 illustrates a payroll process in a southeastern university. It illustrates the components of a process.

First of all, the process has steps. We begin the payroll process with a student being hired by a department chairperson. The process steps follow a sequence that leads to an outcome, the student being paid. At various points in the process, if mistakes are made and not corrected, the checks will not be issued on time. These steps can be mapped which allows us to represent them in a visual fashion. Clearly, the process outcome will depend upon how well the steps are carried out! For example, the second step requires the student to meet with the department administrative assistant and fill out the appropriate paperwork to get the student onto the university computer system. If this step in the process is done incorrectly all the subsequent steps are affected. The logic behind statistical process control is that, by mapping and measuring a work processes, you can both understand and control their output. The assumption is that, if there is a problem in the payroll process, the solution to that problem will be found by improving the steps within the process.

TQM Builds in Quality vs. Quality Control After the Fact. Traditional management in both the product and service arena tolerates errors and waste as long as they do not exceed predetermined standards and specifications set by management experts. The traditional approach to quality control is inspecting things *after* they are produced. Quality assurance in traditional management systems is typically a system of audits and controls imposed after the fact through inspection done by specialists who employ predetermined standards of perfor-

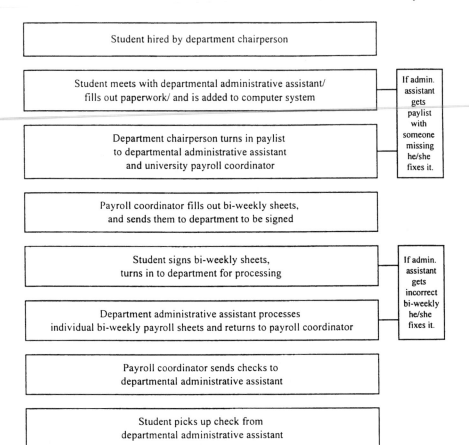

Figure 14   Payroll Flowchart.

mance as their criteria. Traditional organizations expect errors and devote substantial organizational resources to planned rework. TQM, conversely, focuses on improving the work processes (and therefore the system) that create products or services to a point that they are error-free. While error-free may be an ideal, the continuous process improvement cycle attempts to approach this standard as closely as possible. TQM puts quality control and quality assurance back to the line by empowering front line managers and workers. In TQM the quality focus is upstream rather than downstream.

TQM Focuses on Increasing Employee Authority Through Empowerment Rather Than Enhancing Management Authority.   TQM is by no means unique in its commitment to participatory management (Cotton, 1993). However, traditional American management paradigms drew heavily on the work of Frederick Taylor. Taylor believed that work systems needed to be designed so that jobs could be broken down into a series of simple steps that could be accomplished by persons of the most minimal education and talent. Management was paid to think and front line workers to do. TQM believes that workers are assets to be developed rather than a cost to be controlled. TQM advocates management structures that are very different. Typically, TQM advocates "flatter hierarchies." Many staff functions go to workers and first line supervisors. Much emphasis is placed on worker training and retraining. TQM is based on Theory Y conceptions of management. It is team based.

> Once top management has made the long term commitment to quality management, the most important and critical ingredient to achieving a quality commitment throughout an organization is employee involvement, empowerment, training, and teamwork. Work processes can only be improved when all people in the organization, top to bottom and horizontally across functions are involved in making changes. When the intelligence, imagination, and energies of the entire workforce are engaged in the pursuit of the organization's goals, lasting results can be realized. People closest to the problem usually have the best information sources and solutions (Hunt, 1995, p. 15).

TQM Focuses on Continuous Improvement Of Processes Through Data Analysis and Problem Solving Techniques. Traditional management relies inordinately on technological advances such as automation and computers to produce improved quality and productivity. TQM does not ignore these breakthroughs, rather it places more importance on small, incremental, daily gains resulting from attention to enhancing how the work is done. TQM calls this continuous process improvement (Kaizen in Japan). Continuous improvement relies on feedback from customers both internal and external. This feedback is both informal (a stakeholder analysis) and formal (survey research, 1-800 numbers, focus groups, etc.). TQM is data driven! It believes in management by fact, "In God We Trust," everyone else must provide data! Figure 15 illustrates using a TQM tools to achieve a process improvement. The tool is a pareto chart. This chart is similar to one produced by a process mapping team at a southeastern university looking into the reasons why the number of "no checks" had increased so quickly. The process is the same student payroll example we have been using. The pareto chart in Figure 15 lists the causes of no paychecks that were uncovered by a quality team following the process steps outlined in Figure 14. Pareto charts are designed to list causes from most to least and from left to right. A quick inspection of Figure 15 indicates that one step, processing the paperwork, generates the values that are input into the university payroll. This step had a large number of mistakes that resulted in an undesirable outcome of a large number of no checks. It was

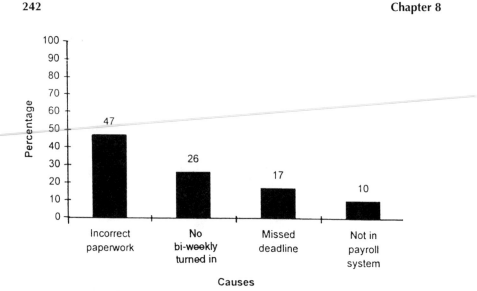

Figure 15   Pareto chart: percentage breakdown of causes of no paycheck for April 1998 (n = 100).

discovered that a new form, reflecting new procedures not adequately understood by the staff, had been implemented in March. A training solution was suggested by the team to deal with the problem.

The Tools Employed by TQM are Designed to Understand and Ultimately Control Sources of Variance in the Production of Product or Services.   TQMs measurement dimension is predicated on the belief that quality is enhanced by reducing the amount of variance in products or services. All work processes produce variance. What is variance? For an illustration of this concept see Figure 16. This is a line chart which is another one of the tools TQM advocates using. This line chart represents what TQM means by variance as a process. The vertical axis includes the number of students in the previously discussed university payroll system, that is, those who did not receive checks in the period outlined January to June (horizontal axis). In TQM terminology, this process expresses variance. In other words, the number of students not getting checks is relatively constant until April when a large spike occurs. However, the process is never perfectly static, there is always some variance.

According to TQM, understanding the source(s) of variance in an organization is management's most important function. Systems speak to managers if they will listen! The system speaks through the variance it produces in outputs over time. The specific tools of TQM, fishbone charts, pareto charts, flowcharts, histograms, bar-charts, process control charts, scatter plots, are collectively, the

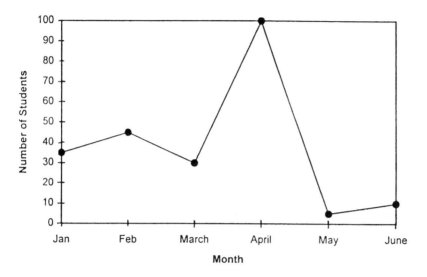

Figure 16   Number of students without paychecks (January–June 1998).

means employed by the organization to determine if a process is within control limits.

> All variation in quality characteristics (dimension, hardness, color) cause loss whether the variation results in defective product or not. Economies in manufacture are natural consequence of reduction in the variation of a quality characteristic. The author divides causes of variation into two sources; (1) the system (common causes), the responsibility of management; (2) special causes, which are under the governance of the individual employee. In the author's experience, losses from the system overshadow losses from special causes. The same principles apply to sales and service (Deming, 1994, p. 94).

Now that we have outlined the central features of TQM let us look at the forces that inhibit the spread of TQM and the participatory management structures which it so adamantly advocates.

FORCES THAT INHIBIT THE SPREAD OF TQM AND PARTICIPATORY MANAGEMENT IN GOVERNMENT

Participatory management and TQM pose unique problems for public administration. On the one hand, a considerable body of evidence based in the human behavioral literature suggests that participatory forms of administration can be more effective in many of the contexts in which government operates (Bryant and Kearns, 1982; Denhart et al., 1987; Cohen and Brand, 1993; West, 1995; Poister and Harris, 1997). Moreover, there is a long tradition of government emulating the managerial developments (like TQM) in the business sector. Also, there are normative (democratic) reasons for advocating participatory management in the public sector. On the other hand, formidable forces unique to the public sector tend to inhibit the spread of orthodox TQM and participatory management. How is public management different? That it is different is now widely recognized (see Curtis, 1980; Fottler, 1981; Whorton and Worthley, 1981; Barrick and Alexander, 1987; Swiss, 1995; West, 1995; Pegnato, 1997). Of the many differences that exist between government and the private sector, some of which we have discussed previously, three major ones impede TQM and participatory management in the public sector.

Accountability

The public sector is more accountable. This is as it should be! Accountability involves the means by which a given public sector agency and its workers deal with the diverse expectations generated by the demands of democratic theory; namely, that public agencies be accountable to the general public through their elected officials (Moe and Gilmour, 1995). Democratic theory holds that government is essentially a series of laws passed by the elected representatives of the people. Bureaucracy is accountable to these elected officials. Accountability is tangibly expressed in the network of rules and procedures (sometimes pejoratively called red tape) that insures accountability. Accountability is a key *control* value in public administration and at the basis of much public law (Moe and Gilmour, 1995; Pegnato, 1997).

The public management implication of accountability is the existence of an authoritative source of control designed to insure accountability The control of public agency actions can emanate from a variety of sources. Control over the agency can come from the system of bureaucracy itself, in which hierarchy forces attention and accountability toward the top. It can emanate from the enabling legislation (laws) that define the function and procedures of the agency and thereby establish formal legal and contractual obligations to which the agency must adhere. Control over the agency also emanates from the professional values of the civil servants themselves whose professional training, e.g., physician, engineer, provides them with standards relative to how they approach their job. Finally, control over the agency can emanate from the political process which creates an environment in which any issue in the public sector can become politicized.

The necessity for control demanded by democratic theory acts as a centralizing force in the organizational design of public agencies. Consequently, it works in opposition to decentralizing features of TQM and participatory management which argues for, among other things, customer satisfaction, flatter hierarchies, and employee empowerment. In addition, business is results-(outcome-) oriented, whereas government is accountable for process as well as outcomes (Denhardt, 1992; Moe and Gilmore, 1995; Pegnato, 1997). What happens to a public manager who is faced with accountability for his or her procedures and results, whose records may be open to public view, and who knows that at any moment public interest groups, investigative journalists, minority representatives, legislative committees, or executive overseers may choose to make almost anything into a political issue? In such a high-accountability setting, the tendency is toward conservative management. The manager is inclined to protect the agency by "going by the book," avoiding risks, and avoiding delegating decision-making powers to those who may be less accountable. The need for tight accountability has a pervasive centralizing effect which often undermines forces for lower-level discretion that participatory approaches require.

Accountability, in fact, is predicated on a core value that mitigates against both empowerment and customer satisfaction. For example, Moe and Gilmour (1995) argue that customer-driven government is incompatible with democratic accountability. The logic here is that bureaucrats trying to meet customer needs might compromise the important democratic value of democratic control to satisfy customer wants. For example, a public agency that "delights" its customers (clients) by providing high levels of service (those not constrained by budget limitations) may do so by leaving the general taxpayer to pick up the tab. Swiss (1995) argues, on more practical grounds, that the real problem is: who is the customer? For example, in the private sector the customer is more easily identified because they "vote with their dollars" when they buy a laptop computer or luxury car. In government, there is typically a disconnection between the provision of services and the payment for those services. Is the customer the public agency's client (e.g., the welfare recipient), or the general public, or both?

> Moreover, government organizations have obligations to more than their immediate clients. Sometimes the agency's important customers- the general public- are not only absent but totally inattentive, and yet the agency must risk offending its immediate customers in order to serve the general public. For example, a government agency that oversees banks and treats banks as customers will greatly damage the public good by keeping banks, in TQM phraseology, delighted. Yet if the agency puts the taxpaying general public first, it will look in vain for their delighted reaction; the general public will remain resolutely uninterested in the agency unless there is a crisis (Swiss, 1995, p. 28).

In terms of empowerment, the demand for accountability clearly acts to constrain movements to empower government employees. An empowered public vs. an empowered private employee are not the same. Employee empowerment is generally predicated on the value of increased *efficiency*. In effect, empowerment leads to greater efficiency in the provision of services, which leads to greater customer satisfaction, which leads to greater market share and profitability. This is a logic which is clearly more at home in the ideology of the private sector. Why? Because, as stated previously, efficiency is only one value in the public policy process and not always the most dominant one. For example, in referring to administrative units in the federal government that are required to both serve and regulate their clients, Joseph A. Pegnato correctly notes that a single-minded commitment to customer service is not in the public interest. What is required is a kind of balancing act between the various values the administrator is expected to optimize.

> The problem of balancing conflicting requirements can be said to apply to the delivery of any governmental service if regulatory compliance overlays delivery of that service, as it often does. Federal officials are routinely challenged by the need to balance conflicting imperatives as accountability, fairness, and due process (Pegnato, 1997, p. 401).

Clearly, any movement for empowerment and customer service must not undermine the principles of accountability that are predicated in democratic theory and public law, and not the entrepreneurial philosophy and values of the private sector (Moe and Gilmour, 1995). In effect, you can only re-invent government so far.

Performance Measurement

The public sector lacks a clear single criterion, like profitability, by which agency performance can be measured. This makes performance measurement (at both the individual and organizational level) in the public sector much more difficult. And, while measures such as "shadow pricing" seek to approximate the information derived from prices and profits, they are just that, approximations. This fact compounds the dilemma outlined above. Large private-sector organizations often attempt to improve efficiency and effectiveness by decentralizing operations to smaller profit centers—units held accountable for profitability, but not required to follow centralized procedures on personnel, production, or other administrative matters. Because means-ends knowledge is imperfect in many areas with which government deals, it is typically more difficult for government to decentralize its operations in a similar fashion. However, the philosophy of TQM and performance management are clearly linked, conceptually and in practice.

> TQM and performance measurement are inexorably linked. TQM assumes the need for integrating productivity measures, strategic plans, evaluations and communication of results: it renews emphasis on defining both the purpose of work activities and the internal and external interrelations and interdependencies of productivity (Nyhan and Marlowe, 1995, p. 333).

Much of what is required from a productivity measurement perspective by TQM is difficult to acquire in many agencies of government. The performance measurement which does exist is typically used to support the budget process or is found in organizations that have a clear production function, for example, highway construction.

By the same token, it is more difficult to adequately measure the performance of many government employees. Many of the success stories of participatory management in the private sector have been justified by the criteria of increased performance in reference to a quantitative standard, for example, "Team Taurus" captured a 12% market share and the car was highly rated by J.D. Powers in terms of quality. Moreover, the illustrations of the success of participatory management that do exist in the public sector tend to be found in agency functions that have a quantitative output, such as claims and restitutions processed, highway maintenance, electronic data processing cost savings, and other operations that have a cost factor associated with them (Denhardt et al., 1987; West, 1995; Poister and Harris, 1997).

Many public employees provide services addressed to problems (e.g., eliminating welfare dependency; rehabilitating criminal offenders) which are little understood. For example, it is difficult to argue that a social worker who handles twice as many welfare cases as another is more effective. Indeed, that social worker may be attaining speed by superficial and arbitrary case treatment which does more harm than good. Also, there is considerable societal disagreement with respect to the function of the prison system. Is it to punish? Is its function to rehabilitate? Because it is hard to measure individual performance without an agreed upon criterion of success, public agencies typically prefer the simpler route of holding employees to certain standard operating procedures established centrally for everyone. While attempts are being made to develop both "objective" and "subjective" measures of such outputs as service delivery, the statistical and measurement problems in the public sector with respect to performance measures are significantly more complex (Swiss, 1995; Wooldridge, 1995; Keehley et al., 1997). Consequently, the argument that "If you'd allow me and my team to decide things autonomously we'd be able to deliver more profit" doesn't apply in the public sector. As we will discuss in the chapter on perfor-

mance measurement in public service, it can be so difficult to document performance that public administrators may have difficulty documenting gains that
might come from a participatory approach. Ironically, compared to business,
public organizations are more accountable but their employees are less accountable! The result is organizations that rely heavily on centralized standard operating procedures (bureaucratic rules) are the antithesis of participatory
management and TQM since these procedures tend to move decision-making up
the hierarchy, inhibit the development of teams, and place more emphasis on individual versus group efforts (Wooldridge, 1995). James Swiss (1995) notes that,
despite the obstacles to performance management in the public sector, a number
of gains have been made in recent years; ironically, the adoption of TQM could
reverse these trends.

> TQM proponents correctly point out that in business, outputs in the form of
> quarterly profit reports represents short term vision and can often lead to goal
> displacement. They fail to recognize that in the very different world of govern-
> ment, it is stressing inputs and processes that represents short term business as
> usual, and therefore focusing in governmental processes is likely to lead to
> goal displacement. In the public sector, a move toward stressing outputs is in
> fact usually a move toward the desired long range vision (Swiss, 1995, p. 30).

Political Legitimacy and Government Culture

The most basic public-private difference that impedes participatory approaches
like TQM is the representative theory of democracy itself and the government
culture that it has produced. Employees are not supposed to participate in decision-making or have autonomy in traditional democratic theory. That theory
holds that the people elect legislatures which make policy and chief executives
who implement policy through appointed officials. These officials' roles are to
carry out day-to-day implementation, not influence policy. The success that recent presidential candidates have had running against the "bureaucracy" underscores the depths of feeling Americans have about this issue. Our political
system thwarts participation in other ways, too. The American political system
has undergone a transition in the last two decades in which the political parties
have declined in their relative influence and special interest groups have increased in their relative influence. Moreover, the mass media now clearly dominates political communication, and significant financial resources are required to
finance campaigns today. This has produced an environment in which ". . . increased reliance by presidents and other partisanly elected chief executives on
transient political appointments for positions formerly filled by long term professional experts" (Newland, 1987, p. 45). Moreover, the turnover of elected officials does not create an environment in which the day-to-day management of
agencies receives high priority from elected officials.

These factors lead to a bifurcated management composition which leads to centralization. On the one hand, the political chiefs, who serve relatively short terms, distrust the long-term civil servants and ordinarily seek to centralize departmental control at the top, not delegate participatory powers to career civil servants, and in effect reduce the policy roles of career civil servants (Rosen, 1986). On the other hand, the civil servants fear the whims of the political chiefs and form powerful employee organizations which support a strong civil service system that protects their jobs. That system, however, is invariably centralized and is a severe obstacle to participatory approaches to management. Thus democratic ideology itself leads to an agency interest group structure which is opposed to organizational democracy! The forces of resistance to participatory approaches to management in the public sector are many. The success of these forces are evidenced in the spread of budgetary and other management control systems at both the federal and state level, and in the centralizing effects of public unionization.

Finally, TQM requires a strong commitment by leadership to culture change since, by almost all accounts, TQM takes years to implement (Imai, 1997). The time frame of many elected officials is the next electoral cycle.

> Successful implementation of a TQM improvement culture in a public agency requires leaders who are cultural change agents, not old style managers who believe in autocratic controls for controlling costs. The new public managers as change agent views TQM as the expectations and behaviors of everyone in the organization as well as those served by it. These expectations are, of course, shaped by the culture, climate, and policies of the organization (McNabb and Sepic, 1995, p. 371).

In many public organizations, the culture and climate mitigates against the implementation of orthodox TQM and participatory management. This is not to say that there are not success stories, we will discuss them in a subsequent section. It is to say, however, if Deming is correct that TQM can only be implemented from the top down as a complete system through committed senior leadership, that this is a problem for many public agencies.

The foregoing discussion might bring into question the relevance of TQM and worker participation to public management, but the obstacles are not the whole story. Below we will outline the forces *favoring* participatory management and "adapted forms" of TQM in public administration.

FORCES FAVORING THE SPREAD OF TQM AND PARTICIPATORY MANAGEMENT IN GOVERNMENT

The argument that TQM and participatory management is on the ascent in American public administration rests on three major assumptions. The first assumption is that the values of our democratic heritage point to organizational democratization as a goal for social development. A second assumption is that the work environment of public administration favors participatory management. Finally, it is contended that participatory management is more efficient and that, as public administration enters an era of austerity, it will be forced by economic necessity to seek out more democratic forms or organization in order to meet the increased demands to run government efficiently. These assumptions are examined below.

American Culture

Functionalist sociologists have long argued that all social systems change through an evolutionary pattern of normative upgrading and specification (Parsons, 1965). Given cultural values which uphold the norms of equality and democracy, this theory predicts that over time organizational life will adapt to better and better specify these norms. Just as upgrading the norms pertaining to the value of equality have gradually led to the inclusion of more groups into full voting and citizenship rights, so one would expect that the social dynamic upgrading the norms pertaining to democracy would gradually lead to fuller and fuller implementation of participatory norms in more and more settings. This should be especially true of *public* administration because of the symbolic role of government in sanctioning cultural values. This line of reasoning suggests that participatory management *should* be implemented for reasons that go beyond its documented effectiveness in increasing some dimension of organizational productivity. In other words, the role of participatory management in the decision-making process can be characterized in terms of the "faith" that some have that it is the right thing to do over and above the "success" that research can demonstrate it has on increasing organizational productivity (Harmon and Mayer, 1986, p. 231; Deming 1993). The same can be said of TQM as a system; its values are very consistent with the norms of equality and democracy.

Moreover, not only is a form of participatory environment relatively widespread in government, the values supporting such an environment are now finding codification in the professional standards of public administrators. This process of value specification and normative upgrading is exactly the type of development predicted by functionalist sociology, cited earlier. *Professional Standards and Ethics*, a workbook issued by the Professional Standards and Ethics Committee of the American Society for Public Administration (ASPA) in 1979, contains many provisions implying a participatory environment, as does the formal Code of Ethics promulgated by ASPA in 1984.

Moreover, the concept of participation in the decision-making process implies responsibility on the part of public administrators which can serve to avoid the "I am just following orders" syndrome. Public administrators implement professional ethics by continually questioning the propriety of standard operating procedures that have arisen through convenience, expediency, pressure, impulse, or inertia. Also, there is no inherent reason to assume that participation is in any way incompatible with the movement for professionalism of the civil service (Hunt, 1995). In fact, there is a strong presumption that the questioning process generated by participatory management procedures will involve all relevant groups, soliciting opposing views, wrestling jointly with moral issues, deciding on some basis involving participatory input if not collective decision-making, and that this can be done within a democratic framework. ASPAs sanctioning of responsibility as a primary professional ethic for public administrators implies affirmatively dealing with moral issues which inherently cannot be resolved through rational analysis of a quantitative problem-solving type. If one acknowledges that expert analysis or benevolent authoritarianism are not appropriate responses to the posited ethic of responsibility, it is almost inevitable that professionalism in public administration comes to be associated with some degree of participatory management.

Type of Work Performed by Public Agencies

In addition to culture, many studies of technology and work organization suggest that the type of work performed by public organizations is conducive to participatory management and by logical extension to TQM.

Public Management as Craft.   Over three decades ago, Blauner found that craft industries were more conducive to participatory consciousness than were assembly-line industries (Blauner, 1964). As George Berkley's well-known text, *The Craft of Public Administration* (1981), suggests, public management more nearly falls in the former category.

Public Management and Interdependence.   Taylor (1971) studied organizational change processes and found highly interdependent contexts to require more intensive interaction and intercommunication of the type afforded by participatory management. Public organizations are more highly interdependent than most business organizations for a number of reasons: political accountability, common revenue base, social nature of the task, and geographic jurisdiction.

Public Management and Innovation. Technological change results in stress, accommodation of which often requires intervention of governmental agencies which mandate new social technologies. Both stress reduction and acceptance of change are goals for which participatory styles of management are highly appropriate. The more processes are innovative and nonroutine, the less feasible are traditional mechanistic, hierarchical management approaches (Perrow, 1967). The socio-technical approach to organization design is based on this principle, using participatory approaches to accommodate the social impact of technological change (Trist and Bamforth, 1951; Emery and Trist, 1959; Davis and Trist, 1972; Cotton 1993).

In general, work technology is a factor in professionalization of the public service. The upgraded competency levels involved in professionalization bring expectations of decision-making roles and participation in the work process. Because public management is a craft devoted to facilitating the social adaptation of an interdependent world to increasingly rapid change, participatory approaches may be of special importance in the government sector.

Efficiency

Participatory management and TQM, it is argued, are on the ascendancy because they are more efficient, not just because they respond to cultural values or are more adaptive to the type of work most agencies do. This assertion needs to be qualified. Some literature on participation has shown participation has no correlation with organizational efficiency, while other studies assert it is a virtual panacea for agency ills Much of the confusion in the literature is based on three methodological problems.

First, there is still limited literature specific to public administration (Poister and Harris, 1997). Given gross differences in public and private administration (e.g., political effects, lack of profit criterion or market controls, civil service constraints, task ambiguity) this deficiency in the literature itself almost prevents generalization about participation and efficiency in government. In addition, a second methodological problem exists in that the dependent variable, efficiency, is notoriously difficult to measure in public administration. Consequently, even if an agency has an experiment in participatory management as a part of a large move to a TQM type organizational design it is unlikely to have in place a means of measuring its effect on productivity. If it does have such a measurement system, the researcher must often question its meaningfulness (e.g., is a manpower program to be rated high because of a high placement rate, even if there is no effect on the unemployment rate? Is a school productive just because its students test well?) The causes of public policy variables are usually only dimly known, complex in nature, and difficult to measure.

A third obstacle in the literature is a corresponding imprecision in the independent variable, participation. Unfortunately, social scientists have frequently made sweeping generalizations about "participation" on the assumption that one type can be equated with another. One author may be discussing full-blown worker self-management, while another may use "participation" merely to refer to the situation in which a traditional hierarchy deigns to ask employees' opinions on some matter. The determinants and effects of different forms of participation may vary and cannot be aggregated meaningfully in some pronouncement that "participation" is efficient (or not efficient) (Lawler, 1986, 1992; Cotton, 1993; Lindsay and Petrick, 1997). TQM in the public sector is still a relatively new phenomenon so its effect on the dependent variable of productivity is not well documented. As stated previously, TQM requires a number of years to produce results in the form of outputs such as productivity (a major measure of efficiency). This was true even in Japanese manufacturing organizations that are now totally committed to TQMs impact on their own productivity. Finally, what is implied by the contention the agency has implemented TQM? Is it the orthodox version outlined by Swiss (1995), or is it a public agency approach labeled TQM that simply incorporates the use of statistical process control and few training seminars on "customer satisfaction," firmly embedded in what is otherwise a traditional command and control bureaucracy?

In a recent and important evaluation of the Pennsylvania Department of Transportation's long standing quality improvement efforts in the area of highway maintenance work quality and labor productivity, Poister and Harris (1997), were able to document (from a cost/benefits perspective) the impact of TQM on highway maintenance. The researchers were able to define and measure a number of critical independent and dependent variables (CPI training, employee attitudes, time spent in TQM team training, labor productivity, and current highway maintenance backlog). They employed a mathematical technique know as path analysis and were able to demonstrate a concrete impact of TQM and its related participatory techniques.

This research was designed to gauge the impact of TQM activities on service delivery in a product-oriented government organization. Most likely, the results should be taken at face value. While based on fairly modest statistical associations, the findings suggest that PennDOT's TQM activities in the highway maintenance area are associated with a 7 percent improvement in overall effectiveness over the long run, with benefits exceeding costs by 35 percent. Thus the results reported here are consistent with the expectation of incremental impacts accumulating over time and provided corroborating evidence that in addition to improvement in organizational culture and processes themselves, TQM activities can impact favorably on the bottom line of service delivery (Poister and Harris, 1997, p. 302).

It should be noted that while this research is an important step in answering vital questions about the impact of TQM and worker participation in the public sector, the public agency in question is unusual in that it had a long term TQM program, highly defined process and output measures, and a production function that distinguishes it from, for example, a social welfare agency. A conclusion about the impact of TQM and full worker participation on public agencies in general must await additional research.

The Political Climate: Public Dissatisfaction and Demands for Change

Proposition 13. The National Debt. Doing more with less! Declining faith in government is becoming the norm. The political climate today is a force for change. Few politicians on either side of the isle disagree, in principle, that we need to reinvent government.

> Public confidence in the federal government has never been lower. Cynicism about American government runs deep. Now more than ever before, our society faces an unprecedented plethora of social ills and political problems. Now more than ever before, we need to turn the powerful currents of change from negative to positive. Before our government can focus on the complex problems facing our country-and the world-today we must earn the trust of the American people. Change is not a Clinton or Gore thing, it not a Democratic or Republican thing. It's a survival thing (Hunt, 1995, p. 397).

Competition in the global economy has resulted in a willingness to experiment with new models of organization in the private sector particularly. Teams, quality circles, flatter hierarchies, empowered workers are being implemented in an effort to increase organizational productivity and product and service quality. As we noted, management practices legitimized in the private sector find followers espousing their applicability to "running government more efficiently " Both the Democratic and Republican parties have embraced major elements of TQM. Much of re-inventing government has, at its root, concepts borrowed from TQM. Moreover, the concept of more efficient and effective government is nonpartisan.

However, when the private sector manager thinks of participation, what comes to mind is employee participation, not customer participation in management. In contrast, the public sector manager quickly thinks of citizen participation but finds the idea of worker participation more problematic for reasons outlined at the start of this chapter. Citizen participation is a long-established aspect of public administration. It is a familiar model rooted in the pioneering work of the TVA and the Agricultural Department in the Depression era (Lilienthal, 1944). Citizen participation was institutionalized in the Administrative Procedures Act of 1946 (e.g., the hearings requirement). During the social turmoil of the 1960s, it became a popular cause (Waldo, 1969). Although the popularity of citizen participation is now mitigated with a greater appreciation of its frustrations and problems (Moynihan, 1969), it is now a well-established part of the repertoire of skills and orientations of modern public managers, particularly in forms allowing for systematic feedback on citizens' reactions to public policies (Stipak, 1980; Fitzgerald and Durant, 1980; Gormley, 1981; Parks, 1984).

The legitimacy of citizen participation can be a bridge to the concept of employee participation in government if efficiency (doing more with less) and better customer service (delighted citizens) are the rationale. If public employees are organized in teams and practicing process improvements that bring about better outcomes at a lower cost, while staying within the framework of democratic accountability, what constituency is there to oppose this movement? In fact, the growing number of governments practicing TQM and participatory management suggests that such a logic is very sound.

MANAGERIAL IMPLICATIONS

Is TQM and participatory management in the cards for public administration because, being more efficient and more in accordance the democratic features of the American culture, it will help governments face the problems of fiscal austerity and declining public confidence in the 1990s and beyond? A qualified "yes" seems in order. However, we essentially agree with Swiss (1995) that what he has called orthodox TQM must be adapted to be implemented in government for the reasons outlined in this chapter. This fact appears to be generally recognized even by proponents of implementing TQM in government. In spite of the obstacles outlined in this chapter, TQM and participatory models of public administration are already evident in American government (Cohen and Brand, 1993; Cox, 1995; West, 1995; Maher, 1995; Poister and Harris, 1997). TQM based organization development, an approach to agency change which typically involves teams, CPI, and a culture of quality are becoming increasingly common. Such TQM efforts usually have as their goals (1) improving labor relations; (2) improving quality of work life; (3) improving productivity through measuring understanding work processes; (4) giving employees some degree of empowerment; (5) focusing on the "citizen as customer;" and (6) promoting team approaches to process problems. Most of these goals are laudable and nonpartisan and are gaining wide support. We believe certain features of TQM are most likely to survive the faddish nature of any new management approach. They are continuous process improvement through increased employee participation (management by fact) and a focus on customer satisfaction.

Traditional American management paradigms drew heavily on the work of Frederick Taylor who believed that work systems needed to be designed so that jobs could be broken down into a series of simple steps that could be accomplished by persons of the most minimal education and talent. The complexity of government and the global economy mitigates against this hierarchical approach, at least across the board. Why? It is simply to expensive and error prone! TQMs belief that workers are assets to be developed rather than a cost to be controlled and that the people closest to the problem need to be involved in fixing it, are more in accordance with the work environment of our time. The emphasis of TQM on worker training and retraining is currently evident at every level of government. TQMs focus on measurement, predicated on the belief that quality is enhanced by continuous process improvement in reducing the variance in products or services, is very likely to endure. It makes good business sense even for government. Also, the success of continuous process improvement and process re-engineering in the private sector are likely to keep these ideas on the agenda of public managers. Recall, much of government work is the result of work processes that frequently cross functional areas. Therefore measuring, mapping, and understanding process are very likely to improve their quality. We also venture to say, on normative grounds, that participatory management *should* be implemented for reasons that go beyond documented effectiveness in increasing some dimension of organizational productivity. In other words, the role of participatory management in the decision-making process can be based on the conviction that it is the right thing to do. Finally, the focus on the citizen as customer is one of the more positive paradigm shifts that TQM has helped to produce. Not withstanding the considerations of the democratic theory of accountability, the belief that the client of public agency deserves the highest quality of service, and that the client should be involved in determining the dimensions of that quality, is in the public interest.

REFERENCES AND ADDITIONAL READING

Adizes, Ichak and E. M. Borgese (eds.) (1975). *Self-Management: New Dimensions to Democracy*. Santa Barbara, CA: ABC-Clio.

Atwater, L. and S. Sanders (1984). "Quality Circles (QC's) in Navy Organizations: An Evaluation" (Technical Report No. FY81–FY83). *San Diego, Navy Personnel Research and Development Center*. (NTIS No. PCA05-MFA01).

Barabba, Vincent P. (1980). "Demographic Change and the Public Work Force," paper, *Second Public Management Research Conference*, Brookings Institution, November, 1980.

Barrick, Murray R. and Ralph A. Alexander (1987). "A Review of Quality Circle Efficiency and the Existence of Positive-Findings Bias." *Personnel Psychology*, 40: pp 579–592.

Bass, Bernard M., V. J. Shackleton, and E. Rosenstein (1979). "Industrial Democracy and Participative Management: What's the Difference?," *International Review of Applied Psychology*, 28(2) (Oct.): pp 81–92.

Bellone, Carl J. (1980). *Organization Theory and the New Public Administration*. Boston, MA: Allyn and Bacon.

Berkley, George (1971). *The Administrative Revolution*. Englewood Cliffs, NJ: Prentice-Hall.

Berkley, George (1981). *The Craft of Public Administration*. 4th ed. Boston, MA: Allyn and Bacon.

Berman, K. (1967). *Worker-Owned Plywood Companies*. (Pullman, WA: Washington State University Press.

Berstein, Paul (1976). *Workplace Democratization: Its Internal Dynamics*. Kent, OH: Kent State University Press.

Blauner, Robert (1964). *Alienation and Freedom*. Chicago, IL: University of Chicago Press.

Bourdon, Roger D. (1980). "A Basic Model for Employee Participation," *Training and Development Journal*, 34(4) (April, 1980): pp 24–29.

Bowman, James A. (1988). "Admission Practices in Master of Public Administration Programs." *Public Administration Review*. 48: p 5.

Boyle, Richard (1984). "Wrestling with Jellyfish." *Harvard Business Review*. January/February, pp 74–83.

Brower, Michael (1976). "Experience with Self-Management and Participation in United States Industry," in Garson and Smith, (eds.) (1967): pp 73–92.

Bryant S. and J. Kearns (1982). "Workers Brains as well as their Bodies: Quality Circles in a Federal Facility." *Public Administration Review*. 42: pp 144; b2150.

Buss, A. (1961). *The Psychology of Aggression*. New York, NY: Wiley.

Campbell, Alan K. (1978). "Revitalizing the Civil Service," *National Civic Review*, 67(2).

Cessaris, Ann C. (1981). "A Soft Approach to Human Relations," *Training*, 18(10) (Oct.): p 64.

Cohen, Steven, and Ronald Brand (1993). *Total Quality Management in Government*. San Francisco, CA: Jossey-Bass Inc.

Conference on Alternative State and Local Public Policies (1977). *New Directions in State and Local Public Policy* (Washington: Conference on Alternative States and Local Public Policies).

Contino, Ronald and Robert M. Lorusso (1982). "The Theory Z Turnaround of a Public Agency." *Public Administration Review* (January/February): pp 66–71.

Costin, Harry (1994). *Readings in Total Quality Management*. New York, NY: Dryden Press.

Costin, Harry (1994) *Total Quality Management*. Orlando, FL: Harcourt Brace and Co.

Cotton, John L. (1993). *Employee Involvement*. Newbury Park, CA: Sage.

Cox, Raymond W. III (1995). "Getting Past the Hype: Issues in Starting a Public Sector TQM Program," *Public Administration Quarterly* (Spring) pp 89–103.

Crosby, Philip B. (1984). *Quality Without Tears: The Art of Hassle-Free Management*. New York, NY: McGraw-Hill.

Curtis, Donald A. (1980). "Management in the Public Sector: It Really Is Harder." *Management Review*, 69(10) (Oct.): pp 70–74.

Davis, L. E. and. E. L. Trist (1972). *Improving the Quality of Work Life: the Sociotechnical Approach*. Philadelphia, PA: University of Pennsylvania Management and Behavioral Science Center.

Davis, T. R. V. (1979). "OD in the Public Sector: Intervening in Ambiguous Performance Environments," *Group and Organization Studies*, 4(3) (Sept.): pp 352–365.

Dean, James W. and James R. Evans (1994). *Total Quality: Management, Organization, and Strategy*. St. Paul, MN: West.

Deming, W. Edwards (1993). *The New Economics for Industry, Government, Education*. Cambridge, MA: MIT Center for Advanced Energy Study.

Deming, W. Edwards (1994) "On Some Statistical Aids Toward Economic Production," in Harry Costin, *Total Quality Management*. Orlando, FL: Harcourt Brace and Co.

Denhardt, Robert B., James Pyle, and Allen C. Bluedorn (1987). "Implementing Quality Circles in State Government." *Public Administration Review*. 47: 4, pp 304–309.

Denhardt, Robert B. (1992). *The Pursuit of Significance*. Belmont, CA: Wadsworth.

Derber, Charles and William Schwartz (1983). "Toward a Theory of Worker Participation." *Sociological Inquiry*, 53(1): pp 61–78.

Dollard, John et al. (1964). *Frustration and Aggression*. New Haven, CT: Yale.

Dorsett, Dennis L., G. P. Latham and T. R. Mitchell (1979). "Effects of Assigned versus Participatively Set Goals, Knowledge of Results, and Individual Differences in Employee Behavior When Goal Difficulty is Held Constant." *Journal of Applied Psychology*, 64(3) (June): pp 291–298.

Driscoll, James W. (1979). "Working Creatively with a Union: Lessons from the Scanlon Plan." *Organizational Dynamics*, 8(1) (Summer): pp 61–80.

Duke, D., B. K. Showers, and M. Imber (1980). "Teachers and Shared Decision-making." *Education Administration Quarterly*, 16(1): pp 93–106. *The Economist* (1976). "The Germans Know How." Sept. 4, p 80.

Emergy, F. and E. L. Trist (1959). "Sociotechnical System Paper," *Institute of Management Sciences*, Annual Meeting, Paris.

Ends, A. Walden and D. J. Mullen (1973). in *Organization Development in a Public School Setting*, J. J. Partin, (ed.), pp 226–247

Evans, M. G. (1970). The Effects of Supervisory Behavior on the Path-Goal Relationship, *Organizational Behavior and Human Performance*, 5 (May): pp 277–298.

Evans, M. G. (1974). Effects of Supervisory Behaviors on Extension of the Path-Goal Theory of Motivation, *Journal of Applied Psychology*, 59 (April): pp 172–178.

Federal Executive Institute Alumni Association (1986). "Questionnaire Results-Special Edition." January No. 67.

Federal Quality Institute (1991). *Introduction to Total Quality Management in the Federal Government*. Washington, D.C.: U.S. Office of Personnel Management.

Feinberg, Lotle E. (1986). "Managing the Freedom of Information Act and Federal Information Policy." *Public Administration Review*, 46(6): pp 615–621.

Fiedler, Fred E. (1967). *A Theory of Leadership Effectiveness*. New York, NY: McGraw-Hill.

Fitzgerald, Michael R. and R. F. Durant (1980). "Citizen Evaluations and Urban Management: Service Delivery in an Era of Protest," *Public Administration Review*, 40(6) (Nov./Dec.): pp 385–394.

Fottler, Myron D. (1981). "Is Management Really Generic," *The Academy of Management Review*, 6(1) (Jan.): pp 1–13.

French, J. R., E. Kay, and H. H. Meyer (1966). "Participation and the Appraisal System," *Human Relations*, 19: pp 3–19.

Frost, T. F. (1986). "The Effects of Quality Circles Upon Job Enrichment Teamwork and Stress." *Quality Circles Journal*, 19: pp 42–45.

Garson, G. David and M. P. Smith, (eds.) (1976). *Organizational Democracy*. Beverly Hills, CA: Sage.

Gold, Kenneth A. (1981). *A Comparative Analysis of Successful Organizations*. Washington, D.C.: U.S. Office of Personnel Management, Workforce Effectiveness and Development Group.

Goldratt, Eliyahu M. and Jeff Cox (1986). *The Goal: A Process of Ongoing Improvements*. New York: North River Press.Gormley, William T. (1981). Statewide Remedies for Public Underrepresentation in Regulatory Proceedings, *Public Administration Review*, 41(4) (July/Aug.): pp 454–462.

Green, Charles N. (1972). The Satisfaction-Performance Controversy, in K. O. Magnuse, (ed.) (1977), *Organizational Development Design and Behavior* Glenview, IL: Scott, Foresman: pp 166–179.

Grouter, Ann C. "Participative Work as an Influence on Human Development." *Journal of Applied Development Psychology*, 5: pp 71–90.

Hamigan, Kathryn R. (1985). "Vertical Integration and Corporate Strategy." *Academy of Management Journal*, pp 397–425.

Harmon, Michael M. and Richard T. Mayer (1986). *Organization Theory for Public Administration*. Boston, MA: Little Brown and Co..

Harrison, Stephen J. and Ronald Stupack (1993). "Total Quality Management: The Organizational Equivalent of Truth in Public Administration Theory and Practice," *Public Administration Quarterly*, 16(4): pp 416–429.

Hellriegel, Don, John Slocum, and Richard W. Woodman (1986). *Organizational Behavior*. New York: West Publishing Co.

Hoover, Larry T. (1996). *Quantifying Quality in Policing*. Washington, D.C.: Police Executive Research Forum.

House, Robert J. and T. R. Mitchell (1974). "Path-Goal Theory of Leadership," *Journal of Contemporary Business* (Autumn): pp 124–138.

Hulin, C. L. and M. R. Blood (1968). Job Enlargement, Individual Differences and Worker Response, *Psychological Bulletin*, Vol. 69.

Hummel, Ralph P. (1987). *The Bureaucratic Experience*, 3rd ed. New York, NY: St. Martin's Press.

Hunnius, Gerry, G. D. Garson, and John Case, (eds.) (1973). *Workers' Control*. New York, NY: Random House.

Hunt, V. Daniel (1995). "A Government Manager's Guide to Quality," in Jonathan P.

West (ed.). *Quality Management Today: What Local Governments Need to Know*. Washington, D.C.: International City/County Management Assoc.

Hyde, Albert C. (1992). "The Proverbs of Total Quality Management: Recharting the Path to Quality Improvement in the Public Sector," *Public Productivity & Management Review*, 16(1): pp 25–37.

Imai, Masaaki (1986). *Kaizen*. New York, NY: McGraw-Hill.

Imai, Masaaki (1997). *Gem Ba Kaizen: A Common Sense, Low-Cost Approach to Management*. New York, NY: McGraw-Hill.

Ishikawa, Karou (1982). *Guide to Quality Control*. White Plains, NY: Asam Productivity Organization.

Jablonski, Joseph R. (1992). *Implementing TQM: Competing in the Nineties Through Total Quality Management*. San Diego, CA: Pfeiffer and Co.

Juran, J. M. (1988). *Juran's Quality Control Handbook*. New York, NY: McGraw-Hill.

Katzenbach, Jon R. and Douglas K. Smith (1993). *The Wisdom of Teams: Creating the High-Performance Organization*. Boston, MA: Harvard Business School.

Keehley, Patricia, Medlin, Steven, MacBride, Sue, and Longmire, Laura. (1997). *Benchmarking for Best Practices in the Public Sector*. San Francisco, CA: Jossey-Bass.

Kravchuk, Robert S. and Robert Leighton (1993). "Implementing Total Quality Management in the United States," *Public Productivity & Management Review*, 17(1), (Fall), pp 71–82.

Latham, Gary P. and E. A. Locke (1979). Goal-Setting: A Motivational Technique That Works. *Organizational Dynamics*, 8(2) (Autumn): pp 68–80.

Lawler, Edward E. (1986). *High Involvement Management*. San Francisco, CA: Josey-Bass Inc.

Lawler, Edward E. (1992). *The Ultimate Advantage*. San Francisco, CA: Jossey-Bass.

Lawler E. E. III and S. A. Mohrman (1985). "Quality Circles After the Fad." *Harvard Business Review*, January–February, pp 64–71.

Lawler, E. E. III, P. A. Renwick, and R. J. Bullock (1981). "Employee Influence on Decisions." *Journal of Occupational Behavior*, 2: pp 115–123.

Levine, Charles (1986). "The Federal Government in the Year 2000: Administrative Legacies of the Reagan Years." *Public Administration Review*, 46(3): pp 195–205.

Lewin, Kurt (1947). Frontiers in Group Dynamics: Concept, Method and Reality in Social Science, *Human Relations*, 1: pp 5–42.

Lewis, Gregory B. and Messung Ha (1988). "Impact of the Baby Boom on Career Success in the Federal Service." *Public Administration Review*, 48(6) pp 951–961.

Lilienthal, David E. (1944). *TVA: Democracy on the March*. New York, NY: Harper and Row.

Lindsay, William M. and Joseph A. Petrick (1997). *Total Quality and Organizational Development*. Delray Reach, FL: St. Luci Press.

Loveridge, Ray (1980). "What is Participation?: A Review of the Literature and Some Methodological Problems," *British Journal of Industrial Relations*, 18(3) (Nov.): pp 297–317.

Magnusen, Karl O. (1977). *Organization Design, Development, and Behavior: A Situational View*. Glenview, IL: Scott, Foresman.

Maher, Julianne G. (1995). "Evolution of a Quality Management Program." *Public Productivity & Management Review*, 18(4) (Summer): pp 387–396.

Marini, Frank, (ed.) (1971). *Toward a New Public Administration: The Minnowbrook Perspective*. Scranton, PA: Chandler.

Marini, Frank "The Minnowbrook Perspective and the Future of Public Administration." in Marini (ed.), *Toward a New Public Administration: The Minnowbrook Perspective*. Scranton, PA: Chandler, pp 345–367.

Marks, M. L., P. H. Mirvis, E. J. Hackett, and J. F. Grady, Jr. (1986). "Employee Participation in a Quality Circle Program: Impact on Quality of Worklife, Productivity and Absenteeism." *Journal of Applied Psychology*, 71: pp 61–69.

McGowan, Robert P. (1995). "Total Quality Management: Lessons from Business and Government." *Public Productivity & Management Review*, 18(4) (Summer): pp 321–331.

McGregor, Douglas (1960). *Human Side of Enterprise*. New York, NY: McGraw-Hill.

McKenna, H. F. (1977). Managing Change in Government. *Civil Service Journal*, 17(4) (April–June): pp 1–29.

McNabb, David E. and F. Thomas Sepic (1995). "Culture, Climate, and Total Quality Management: Measuring Readiness for Change." *Public Productivity & Management Review*, 18(4) (Summer).

Moe, R. C. and R. S. Gilmour (1995). "Rediscovering Principles of Public Administration: The Neglected Foundation of Public Law." *Public Administration Review*, 55(2): pp 135–146.

Mohrman, Susan A. and Gerald E. Ledford (1985). "The Design and Use of Effective Employee Participation Groups: Implications for Human Resource Management." *Human Resource Management*, 24(4): pp 413–428.

Mohrman, S. A. and L. Novelli, Jr. (1985). "Beyond Testimonials: Learning from a Quality Circles Program." *Journal of Occupational Behavior*, 6: pp 93–110.

Moore, Brian E. and T. L. Ross (1978). *The Scanlon Way to Improved Productivity*. New York: NY: Wiley-Interscience.

Mosher, Fredrick C. (1982). *Democracy and the Public Service*, 2nd Ed. New York, NY: Oxford University Press.

Moynihan, Daniel P. (1969). *Maximum Feasible Misunderstanding*. New York, NY: Free Press.

Mrockowski, T. (1984). "Quality Circles, Fine—What Next?" *Personnel Administrator*, June, pp 173–184.

Nadler, David A. and Edward E. Lawler III, (1983). "Quality of Work Life: Perspectives and Directions!" *Organizational Dynamics*, Winter, pp 20–30.

Nalbandian, John and J. Terry Edwards (1983). "The Values of Public Administrators." *Review of Public Personnel Administration*, 4: pp 114–126.

Newland, Chester A. (1987). "Public Executives: Imperium, Sacerdotium, Collegium? Bicentennial Leadership Challenges." *Public Administration Review*, 47(1): pp 45–56.

Nyhan, Ronald C. and Herbert A. Marlowe (1995). "Performance Measurement in the

Public Sector: Challenges and Opportunities," *Public Productivity & Management Review*, 18(4) (Summer).

O'Toole, Laurence, J. (1987). "Doctrines and Developments: Separation of Powers, the Politics-Administration Dichotomy, and the Rise of the Administrative State." *Public Administration Review*, 47(1): pp 17–23.

Parks, Roger B. (1984). "Linking Objective and Subjective Measures of Performance." *Public Adminstration Review*, 44(2): pp 118–127.

Parsons, Talcott (1965). Suggestions for a Sociological Approach to Organizations, *Administrative Science Quarterly*, Vol. 1.

Partin, J. J., (ed.) (1973). *Current Perspectives in Organization Development*. Reading, MA: Addision-Wesley.

Pateman, Carole (1970). *Participation and Democratic Theory* London: Cambridge University Press.

Pegnato, Joseph A. (1997). "Is a Citizen a Customer?" *Public Productivity & Management Review*, 20(4) (June).

Perrow, Charles (1967). "A Framework for Comparative Analysis of Organizations." *American Sociological Review*, 32(2) (April): pp 194–208.

Pfeffner, James A. (1987). "Political Appointees and Career Executives: The Democracy-Bureaucracy Nexus in the Next Century." *Public Administration Review*, 47: pp 57–65.

Poister, Theodore H. and Richard H. Harris (1997). "The Impact of TQM on Highway Maintenance: Benefit/Cost Implications." *Public Administration Review*, 57(4): pp 294–302.

Posner, Barry Z. and Warren H. Schmidt (1986). "Values and Expectations of Federal Service Executives." *Public Administration Review*, 46(5): pp 447–453.

Powell, Reed M. and J. L. Schlacter (1971). Participative Management: A Panacea? *Academy of Management Journal*, June 1971, pp 165–173.

Professional Standards and Ethics Committee (1979). *Professional Standards and Ethics: A Workbook for Public Administrators*. Washington, D.C.: American Society for Public Administration.

Raskin, A. H. (1976). The Workers' Voice in German Company. *World of Work Report*, 1(5) (July).

Rehuss, John A. (1986). "A Representative Bureaucracy? Women and Minority Executives in California Career Service." *Public Administration Review*, 46(5): pp 454–460.

Reuter, Vincent G. (1977). Suggestions Systems: Utilization, Evaluation and Implementation. *California Management Review*, 19 (Spring): pp 78–89.

Rhenman, Eric (1964). *Industrial Democracy and Industrial Management*. London: Tavistock, 1968.

Romzek, Barbara S. and Melvin J. Dubnick (1987). "Accountability in the Public Sector: Lessons from the Challenger Tragedy." *Public Administration Review*, 47(3) pp 227–238.

Rosen, Bernard (1986). "Crises in the U.S. Civil Service." *Public Administration Review*, 46(3): pp 207–214.

Schmidt, Warren H. and Barry Z. Posner (1986). "Values and Expectations of Federal Service Executives." *Public Administration Review*, 46(5) pp 447–453.

Scholtes, Peter R., David L. Bayless, and Gabmel A. Massaro (1994). *The Team: Handbook for Educators*. Madison, WI: Joiner Associates Inc.

Sharkansky, Ira (1984). "Mayor Teddy Kollek and the Jerusalem Foundation: Governing the Holy City." *Public Administration Review*, 44(4): pp 200–304.

Shewart, Walter (1931). *The Economic Control of Manufactured Products*. New York, NY: Van Nostrand Reinhold.

Simmons, John (1980). "Participative Management at the World Bank." *Training and Development Journal*, 34(3) (March): pp 50–54.

Smith, Michael P. and S. L. Nock (1980). "Social Class and the Quality of Work Life in Public and Private Organizations." *Journal of Social Issues*, 36(4): pp 59–75.

Smith, Michael P. (1969). "Self-Fulfillment in a Bureaucratic Society." *Public Administration Review*, 29(1) (Jan./Feb.): 30. *Socialist Thought and Practice* (1981). Third Congress of Self-Managers of Yugoslavia: Symposium Issue, 21, Nos. 6–27 (June-July).

Special Task Force to the Secretary of HEW (1973). *Work in America*. Cambridge, MA: MIT Press.

Steers, R. M. (1975). "Task-Goal Attributes, n-Achievement, and Supervisory Performance." *Organizational Behavior and Human Performance*, 13: pp 392–403.

Stipak, Brian (1980). "Local Governments' Use of Citizen Surveys." *Public Administration Review*, 40(5) (Sept./Oct.): pp 521–525.

Strauss, George (1979). "Workers' Participation: Symposium Introduction." *Industrial Relations*, 18(3) (Fall): pp 247–261.

Swiss, James E. (1995). "Adapting Total Quality Management to Government," in Jonathan P. West, *Quality Management Today: What Local Governments Need to Know*. Washington, D.C.: International City/County Management Assoc.

Thimm, Alfred L. (1980). "The False Promise of Employee Codetermination." *Business and Society Review*, 32 (Winter, 1979–80): pp 36–41.

Trist, L. and K. W. Bamforth (1951). "Some Social and Psychological Consequences of the Longwall Method of Goal-Setting." *Human Relations*, 4: pp 1–38.

Vinzaut, Janet C. and Douglas H. Vinzant (1996). "Strategic Management and Total Quality Management: Challenges and Choices." *Public Administration Quarterly*, 20(2) (Summer): pp 201–217.

Vlaskalic, Tihomir (1981). "A Key Link in the Spreading of Self-Management Practice." *Socialist Thought and Practice*, 21(6,7) (June/July): pp 39–49.

Vroom, Victor and P. W. Yetton (1973). *Leadership and Decision-Making*. Pittsburgh, PA: University of Pittsburgh Press.

Vroom, Victor (1960). *Some Personality Determinants of the Effects of Participation*. Englewood Cliffs, NJ: Prentice-Hall.

Walters, Jonathan (1994). "TQM: Surviving the Cynics." *Governing*, (September) pp 40–45.

Walton, Mary (1986) *The Deming Management Method*. New York, NY: Putnam.

West, J. P. (1995). *Quality Management Today: What Local Governments Need to Know*. Washington, D.C.: International City Managers Assoc.

Whorton, Joseph W. and J. A. Worthley (1981). "A Perspective on the Challenge of Public

Management: Environmental Paradox and Organizational Culture." *The Academy of Management Review*, 6(3) (July): pp 357–362.

Wise, Charles (1985). "Suits Against Federal Employees for Constitutional Violations: A Search for Reasonableness." *Public Administration Review*. 45: p 6.

Wooldridge, Blue (1995). "Overcoming Obstacles to Public-Sector Improvement Efforts." *Quality Management Today: What Local Governments Need to Know.* Washington, D.C.: International City/County Managers Assoc.

Young, Dennis (1972). *How Shall We Collect the Garbage?* Washington: Urban Institute.

Yudin, Yehuda (1975). Industrial Democracy as a Component in Social Change: The Israeli Approach and experience, Ch. 6 in Adizes and Borgese, eds. *Self Management: New Dimensions to Democracy*, (1975).

Zemke, Ron (1981). "What's Good for Japan Might Not Work for You." *Training*, 18(10) (Oct.): pp 62–65.

9
Organizational Change

Organizational change refers to any significant alteration of the behavior pattern of a large number of the individuals who constitute an organization (Gabris, 1983; Heffron, 1989; Pasmore, 1994; Imai, 1997). For example, an organization that seeks to initiate Total Quality Management (TQM) is engaged, fundamentally, in organizational change. In today's global economy, organizational change is frequently discussed within the context of what are called learning organizations, "organizations where people continually expand their capacity to create the results they truly desire, where new and expansive patterns of thinking are nurtured, where collective aspiration is set free, and where people are continually learning how to learn together" (Senge, 1990, p. 3). Learning organizations, in effect, are skilled at organizational change. To understand the nature of organizational change, managers need to look beyond human factors alone (Perrow, 1986; Taylor and Felton, 1993; Imai, 1997). In this chapter, organizational culture and climate, as well as structure, technology and environment will all be represented in models guiding managers who successfully produce organizational change (Senge, 1990; Hofstede, 1991; Kochan and Useem, 1992; Osborne and Gaebler, 1992; Trice and Beyer, 1993; Imai, 1997). This chapter also outlines the critical elements of person-organization interface and proposes strategies which managers can employ to effect change within an organization. We proceed by defining each of the factors relevant to organizational change and then consider the actual change process, the type of organizational learning involved, and the strategies managers may adopt to help organizations change.

ORGANIZATIONAL CULTURE

Organizational culture is a subject of intense interest in both the popular and academic literature. There are a number of books on the topic; Peters and Waterman's, *In Search of Excellence*; Ouchi's, *Theory Z*; Pascale and Athos's, *The Art of Japanese Management*; Schein's, *Organizational Cultures and Leadership*; Hofstede's, *Cultures and Organizations*; Trice and Beyer's, *The Culture of Work Organizations*, and Carroll's, *Big Blues: The Unmaking of IBM*; to name a few. Organizational culture is generally defined in terms of the beliefs and expectations shared by organization members that shape behavior.

> Every organization has culture, that is, a persistent, patterned way of thinking about the central tasks of and human relationships within an organization. Culture is to the organization what personality is to the individual. Like human cultures generally, it is passed on from one generation to the next. It changes slowly, if at all (Wilson, 1989, p. 91).

Organizational culture is reflected in internalized *norms* that *shape perception* and *affect behavior* (Imai, 1986; Hofstede, 1991; Trice and Beyer, 1993). Moreover, research in both the public and private sector underscores the fact that organizational culture concretely influences what happens in organizations (Tompkins, 1993; Carroll, 1993; Pasmore, 1994; Imai, 1997). It does so because the organization's culture filters the ways in which organizational members perceive and emotionally respond to environmental stimuli. In effect, the concept of an organizational culture is another expression of the fact that organizations, themselves, take on features that can be characterized as personality and character:

> . . . cultures are collective phenomena that embody people's responses to the uncertainties and chaos that are inevitable in human experience. These responses fall into two major categories. The first is the substance of a culture-shared, emotionally charged belief systems that we will call ideologies. The second is cultural forms-observable entities, including actions, through which members of a culture express, affirm, and communicate the substance to one another. Clearly, people in organizations develop both cultural substance and cultural forms. Out of these processes, cultures grow. Cultures are a natural outgrowth of the social interactions that make up what we call organizations (Trice and Beyer, 1993, p. 2).

Organizations thus defined have particular ways of thinking, feeling, and acting just as human individuals do, and it is not uncommon to hear explanations of both collective and individual actions in an organizational context stated in terms of deeply ingrained patterns of behavior. For example, the "engineering culture" of the Tennessee Valley Authority (TVA) or the National Aeronautics and Space Administration (NASA) and the "diplomatic culture" of the U.S. Department of State are attempts to capture these ingrained patterns of organizational behavior. It is important to underscore that organizational culture is *not a metaphor*. Organizational cultures are real systems of thought, feeling, and behavior (Trice and Beyer, 1993). They represent what one author calls the software of the mind (Hofstede, 1991). Organizational cultures are tangible and have tangible consequences expressed in such features as organizational design and management systems (Taylor and Felton, 1993).

In *Big Blues: The Unmaking of IBM*, Paul Carroll, a correspondent for the Wall Street Journal, writes that IBM's "culture of optimism," a culture based on enormous past success and characterized by a very hierarchial and bureaucratic culture for a private firm, was to a large measure responsible for IBM's failure to see the growing importance of the microcomputer hardware and software market. A failure in vision that cost them significant market share and resulted in their downsizing. Carroll compares and contrasts IBM's organizational culture with that of Bill Gates and Microsoft, who were working on joint projects in the 1980s. In one expression of the clash of these two cultures, Carroll reports that the Microsoft programmers complained about and criticized IBM programers for their lack of innovation and their inefficiency. In effect, they argued that IBM's bureaucracy did not allow for creativity. For example, the IBM system for measuring productivity in computer programming was defined in terms of *the number of lines of code written*. To programmers from Microsoft, a company with an "entrepreneurial culture" that valued efficiency, this was an absurd approach to developing software.

> One of the biggest fights the IBM and Microsoft developers had came when a Microsoft developer took a piece of IBM code that required 33,000 characters of space and rewrote it in 200 characters, 1/160th of the original space. This was considered rude. Other Microsoft developers then rewrote other parts of IBM's code to make it faster and smaller. That was even ruder. IBM managers then began to complaining that, according to their measurement system, Microsoft hadn't been pulling its weight. Measured in lines of code, they said, Microsoft was actually doing negative work, meaning Microsoft should have been paying IBM for the condensing it was doing.
>
> Microsoft also complained about IBM's unwillingness to change things when problems became apparent. IBMers simply denied that problems existed. Often, the Microsoft programmers said, the IBMers seemed to believe more in the overhead transparencies, or foils, they had prepared to predict the behavior of some software than they did in the tests of the software's actual behavior when it was run on the machine. In fact, the real problem was the IBM culture of optimism which was set by the salesmen who run IBM and those who, as they are groomed for top jobs, run many of the business units within the company. Those salesmen, taught that things always have to be super, eventually discouraged even the typically blunt developers from acknowledging any problems (Carroll, 1993, pp. 101–102).

Organizational culture is manifested in the belief system of the organization and is frequently expressed in language and symbols. Organizational rituals are the behavioral reflections of that belief system (Tierney, 1988). In this sense, behavior takes the form of styles of action which typically reflect responses that have proved successful in the past (Wilkins and Ouchi, 1983). The culture of an organization binds it together and differentiates it from other groups. At the macro level, we can identify the broad outlines of the dominant organizational culture that *public managers share*. The culture of public management is based on a set of values, referred to by Gerald Caiden as our "ideology of public service." The core of these values can be summarized in 7 points.

1. Public administration is a machine for the implementation of the general will, as conceived by the representatives of the people. Government is a public trust to be used in the general interest and not for the benefit of a particular sectional interest.
2. Public officials are servants of the public, not vice versa.
3. Civil officials should be the embodiment of all public virtues they should be hardworking, honest, impartial, wise, sincere, just, and trustworthy. Official conduct should be beyond reproach.
4. Public officials should obey their superior and subordinate their personal interests, unless objection is based on conscientious grounds whereupon they should leave public office before publicly declaring their opposition to governmental policy.
5. Civil servants should perform their duties efficiently and economically.
6. Appointment to public office should be on the basis of merit of person and not on the privilege of class.
7. Public officials should be subjected to the law in the same way as other people (Caiden, 1981).

Other manifestations of organizational culture might take the form of degree of stress given to these general values, or emerge as values represented in some agencies and absent in others. For example, a manager in the state auditor's office may adhere strictly to the rules and regulations for expenditure of public monies; while the managers of a program for severely handicapped children might have a flexible interpretation of expenditure rules because inclusion of children in the program is their first concern. The culture of each organization distinguishes the values of the handicapped services agency from those of the auditor's office. These differences in culture stem from the task or technology of each agency and the environment within which each operates. Organizational culture does not always contribute to agency effectiveness. Elements of some organizational cultures may be dysfunctional in the long run as we can illustrate through our handicapped-services program example. While it may be understandable that program managers adhere to the norm of rule flexibility in determining eligibility, if this value is given free rein program clientele might multiply to the point that the most severely handicapped clients may be neglected because of case overload.

The dominant culture of public sector management is not monolithic. It has evolved through the years and is changing today. Many agencies may have a distinct culture and some subcultures. Cultural change is never easy! One aspect of public management culture undergoing change today is the criteria that governs agency loyalty. Until now the only choices open to the manager who disagrees with the policy actions of supervisors have been to remain silent or to leave the organization. Albert O. Hirschman (1970), in *Exit, Voice and Loyalty*, proposes a third option, "voice," a compromise between silence and resignation. Voice is an attempt to change things in an organization through articulation of member dissatisfaction (Hirschman, 1970). In the 1980s and 1990s this option has been called whistle blowing. In recognition of the need to discourage values which inhibit disagreement within an organization, a Special Counsel's office, linked with the Merit System's Protection Board, has been established in the federal sector. The office handles whistle blowing by receiving and investigating charges of agency or employee misconduct and by providing some protection for anonymous complaints. In addition, many state auditor's offices have established "toll free 800" numbers where citizens (or coworkers) can call in and report abuse of the public trust.

ORGANIZATIONAL CLIMATE

Much of the motivation for organizational change is the changing norms or values outside the organization and is frequently driven by rhetoric and assumptions about the need for increased governmental efficiency and effectiveness (March and Olson, 1983; Osborne and Gaebler, 1992). Sometimes the motivation for change is introduced by changed values of the employees. But again, change does not come easily. Typically it is preceded by a serious problem in the *climate* of the organization.

Organizational climate is a concept closely related to, but distinct from, organizational culture. Like national culture, organizational culture has unique indicators such as myths, symbols, rites, and stories (Trice and Beyer, 1993). Organizational climate is based in attitudes and measures whether people's expectations about what it should be like to work in an agency are met. The concepts of culture and climate can be distinguished from one another by reflecting on our discussions of Douglas McGregor's Theory X, Theory Y. Theory X and Theory Y are expressions of different organizational cultures. Theory X, casting the employees as inherently lazy, leads to attitudes and behavior emphasizing tight control. Theory Y, believing employees to be positively disposed toward work and growth oriented, generates attitudes and behaviors emphasizing employees' autonomy and self direction. Climate; by contrast, relates to the measure of employee acceptance of the prevailing Theory X culture. If many new employees enter the organization with Theory Y values, a "climate problem" will develop. *Why? Because employees do not share the dominant organizational culture value(s).*

An example of a climate problem familiar to many public sector managers centers on criteria for selection in employment. A central element of the public management organizational culture noted above requires that, "appointments to positions should be based on the merit of the person." But the real world of politics often dictates selection on the basis of political affiliation and participation. While most managers acknowledge someplace for patronage appointments, debate centers on how many appointments should be political and how politics should weigh against other factors. A state executive who objected to political appointments as an unacceptable transgression of the "political" aspects of government into the "administrative aspects" would experience a climate problem in dealing with his or her agency. In governmental organizations climate problems can emerge when employees perceive substantial deviation from the merit norm produced by patronage pressure.

Often organizational culture and climate are imperceptible to managers in the thicket of agency decision-making. Yet both climate and culture can either foster or impede change efforts. Sometimes managers turn to organizational development specialists to diagnose these subtle dimensions of an organization's readiness for change. Typically, such consults look for incongruence either between organizational culture and actual practices (a problem of climate), or between organizational culture and new agency goals. A lack of fit gives the organizational development consultant a starting point for developing a change plan. But culture and climate are not the only factors that shape change efforts. Organizational structure, technology, and environment also come into play.

STRUCTURE, TECHNOLOGY, AND ENVIRONMENT

Literature which focuses on the interaction of structure and technology to explain organizational behavior is usually labeled structural analysis. Some structural analyses also incorporate the concept of organizational environment. Structure, technology, environment, and their interaction may influence the direction and limits of organizational change. Here we simply describe those concepts as they appear in the organizational literature.

Organizational structure refers to the coordinating system in an organization, including job descriptions, the policies and procedures for coordinating jobs, and the management roles charged with securing coordination. Technology refers to the network of tasks tied to the organizational goal. Those activities that have to be accomplished together with the equipment and people necessary to accomplish them constitute the technology of the organization (Lincoln et al.,

1986; Taylor and Felton, 1993). Public agencies are founded because of the need to serve some public purpose. This policy objective calls forth specific technology and structures fitting the agency mandate. Since public sector managers don't start with people and shape structure and technology to fit, rather vice versa, some elements of structure and technology need to be treated as control variables in any discussion of organizational change. However, managers should be cautious about treating structure and technology as absolutes. Organization theory literature helps put these factors in perspective.

The structural approach to organizational analysis makes the assumption that organizational roles characterize the types of people who should occupy them. Thus people in those roles exhibit the expected traits and behaviors. Kanter (1977) characterizes the implications of structural arrangement in this way: "Positions carry a particular structure of rewards. The structures of rewards, in turn, channel behavior, setting people on a course which ties them further into their roles, makes them even more a product of their situations." Five basic assumptions underlie the structural analysis model:

1. The nature of the total organizational system is important in shaping the relationship of any employee to work.
2. Employees' choices about how to behave in a particular organization is rational and adaptive. It reflects strategic decisions directed toward managing a situation.
3. The structure of an organization does not so much control as it limits in the sense of restricting the range of options and confronting the individual with a characteristic set of problems to solve.
4. The content of a job as reflected in the formal job description and its location in the organizational hierarchy has much to do with how people actually behave.
5. Formal task and formal location of position have much to do with an incumbent's ability to demonstrate competence in an organization (Kanter, 1977).

Structural analysis is often accompanied by a further analysis which sometimes sees technology as the determinant of structure and thus of behavior. One working definition of technology in this context is:

> For our purposes, technology is comprised of the tools, the work rules, the information (such as technical drawings and job specifications), machines and equipment, and other artifacts that are used to convert the system's input into its product. For these technological objects, the emphasis is on what they will "do" to the input when it is made available. (Taylor and Felton, 1993, p. 54).

Blair and his associates have shown, for example, how technology is associated with hierarchy, specialization, increase in supervisory ratios, and increase in worker responsibility and skill levels (Blair et al., 1976). The thesis that organizations differ in their tasks and therefore in the way they are run (Perrow, 1986) garnered some support in the empirical studies of Joan Woodward in the early 1950s. Her research on British manufacturing firms found an empirical relationship between technology or the nature of production systems, patterns or organization, and business success (Woodward, 1972).

An organization's environment is another element often considered when assessing the impact of structure and technology on efforts toward change. Organizations, whether public or private, are open systems which interact with the environment. Political, economic, legal technological, and social dimensions of the environment shape the interaction by providing resources necessary to achieve organizational objectives. While some degree of firmness of organizational boundaries is necessary to maintain organizational identity, all organizations are vulnerable to environmental influences. Lawrence and Lorsch (1967) point to the accessibility of critical information in the manager's environment as the major factor in shaping how organizations are structured. Uncertainty in the environment reflects the gap between the information a manager needs to achieve organizational objectives and the information she holds at a particular point in time. From the managerial viewpoint, the seriousness of the problem posed by environmental uncertainty depends on the rate at which information changes, the time span of feedback, and the certainty of information gained at any particular point in time. All organizations do not face the same type of environment. In a classic article, Emery and Trist (1965) use movement to differentiate environments. They describe environments as either political and random, placid and clustered, disturbed and reactive, or turbulent.

In the public sector, there are many instances of managers attempting to manage their environments. When program directors develop and cultivate outside constituents, when public relations officers nurture good relationships with the press, and when managers succumb to pressures to promote a loyal party worker over a more worthy civil servant, we see examples of public servants engaged in exchange with critical forces in their environment. Some literature in organizational analysis treats structure, technology, and environment as virtual determinants of organizational action, with debate centering principally on how these variables interact and what causes what. The most deterministic of this literature sees technology as the prime cause of most effects we observe in organizational life. But our review of this literature concludes that while there may be some independent effects of technology on an organizational structure, (Aldrich, 1972; Child, 1972; Child and Mansfield, 1972) and in turn on behavior, this impact does not justify the technological determinist view (Kochan and Useem, 1992; Taylor and Felton, 1993; Imai, 1997). Studies of Mohr (1971) and Melman (1971) for example support the conclusions that in relation to the employees' participation dimension of organizational structure, technology is not a significant determinant. Mohan's review of the general impact of various context factors concludes that none of the casual connections we have been discussing are sufficient determinants in and of themselves. Rather in organizational change efforts, normatively committed organizational leadership is the key variable (Mohan, 1972; Senge, 1990; Kochan and Useem, 1992; Osborne and Gabler, 1992; Galbraith and Lawler, 1993). We turn now to considering how managers deal with these dimensions of organizational life to effect change.

ORGANIZATIONAL LEARNING AND ORGANIZATIONAL CHANGE

Chris Argyris (1980) offers the most useful conceptualization of organizational change in the literature today. He adopts a learning metaphor to describe the alternative change models. Organizational learning occurs whenever a mismatch is detected and corrected by an organization. The Argyris learning model is based upon a mental construct which sees an organization as a system. The basic assumptions of system theory are central to this analysis.

Systems theory sees an organization as a system which can be identified by some sort of boundary which differentiates the organization from its environment. Systems are process based in nature and can be conceptualized in terms of a basic model which stresses input, throughput, output, and feedback. Overall the systems operation can be explained in terms of striving to fulfill systems needs geared toward survival. Units within an organization can be viewed as subsystems with their own systemic characteristics. Some agreement exists that distinctions must be made between individual and organizational learning. Though individual learning is important to organizations, organizational learning is not simply the sum of each member's learning. Organizations, unlike individuals, develop and maintain learning systems that not only influence their immediate members, but are then transmitted to others by way of organization history and norms. (Fiol and Lyles, 1985, p. 804; Senge, 1990; Kochan and Useem, 1992; Tompkins, 1993; Galbraith and Lawler, 1993).

Moreover, the operation of the entire system is empirically visible in the behavior of its constituent elements. Boundary transactions internally between subsystems and externally via the environment are critical features of organizational life (Burrell and Morgan, 1979; Taylor and Felton, 1993). From the vantage point of organizational learning the critical concept is feedback. In systems theory, feedback describes the process whereby information concerning the outputs or the process of the system is fed back as input into the system, perhaps leading to change in the throughput process and/or future outputs. The feedback loop is the path feedback follows from output to subsequent feedback and new input.

Adopting a systems framework, Argyris outlines two types of learning occurring in organizations: single loop learning and double loop learning. *Single loop learning is like a thermostat that senses it is too hot or too cold and adjusts the heat accordingly* (Argyris and Schon, 1978; also see Fiol and Lyles, 1985; Taylor and Felton, 1993). Single loop learning occurs when a match between intentions and results is produced or a mismatch is corrected without having to question the organizational assumptions and policies (Hedberg, 1981). For example, a new procedure for mailing social security benefit checks or for correcting errors in the way welfare payments are distributed illustrates single loop learning. The distinction here is between learning and adaptation. The former involves the understanding of reasons beyond the immediate event, the latter simply means defensive adjustment. This implies that simple adaptation (with no understanding of causal relationships) may be a part of learning, but that learning can involve a great deal more (Fiol and Lyles, 1985, p. 805; Tompkins, 1993; Imai, 1997).

Using the thermostat analogy, double loop learning would occur if one asked if the thermostat concept itself was appropriate. In the social security check example, double loop learning would occur if the organization considered reformulating the entire social security program. *Double loop learning is typically associated with the kind of inquiry which resolves incompatible organizational norms by setting new priorities and weighing of norms or by restructuring norms themselves* (Argyris and Schon, 1978; Fiol and Lyles, 1985). Single loop learning problems are the ones most typically encountered by public sector managers. Think about the manager of a unit charged with processing certification forms for participation in a supplemental income program for hearing disabled citizens. The manager observes that nearly a third of the employees are falling below the performance standard for the number of certification requests processed per month. This performance standard, of 20 applicant reviews per month, was established after a study preceding the initial implementation of the entire disabled benefits program and was based upon the projected workload for each employee with certification responsibilities. When the manager of the unit responds to this feedback by counseling the employees that their performance level must be raised in order to meet the standard, without questioning the performance standards themselves or the quality of performance accomplished, we have a case of single loop learning. This case illustrates the strengths and weaknesses of the single loop model. The minimum criterion of 20 forms per month served as a good performance measure in the past and was perhaps a fitting measure for most units involved in the program. Clearly, some numerical measure is necessary in order to aggregate performance ratings across units for purposes of comparing relative productivity. In other words, important organizational purposes are served by maintaining this numerical indicator of performance. It is an important management information tool. But this very tool may inhibit double loop learning essential to effectiveness of the overall benefits program. Perhaps the applicant certification review process requires more time for the hearing disabled applicant who is the subject of this unit's program than does the review process for certification of other types of disabilities which are handled by other units in the department. Alternatively, it may be that the norm of 20 certification reviews per month is simply too high given the number of hearing impaired applicants or potential applicants in the population. In either case, simply counseling the employees to certify more applicants inhibits learning about the real source of the problem. In other words, the real source of the problem may require a thorough statistical process analysis of the work not simply counseling employees.

However, there are significant potential disincentives for a manager of a unit engaging in double loop learning. If the truth is that the number of hearing impaired who were certifiable initially was overestimated and that the high early numbers were simply a function of backlog which has now been taken care of, finding out the truth would not serve the personal interest of the manager in charge of the hearing impaired program. It might mean reduction in staff and therefore reduction in organizational status. Another example in the affirmative action area illustrates the same point. A deputy secretary in a state agency is placed in charge of implementing a new women in management program. After hearing from the governor's council on the status of women of the need to place more women in management, the deputy sends out a memo and asks 5 division heads to submit the names of five women who might be eligible for advanced management training. Next, with the list of 25 names in hand, the deputy invites all of these women to attend a state-sponsored executive development program. Much to his surprise he finds only two women willing to accept this offer of advancement.

Following a single loop model the deputy concludes: "women do not want to advance in this organization. The need for affirmative action doesn't exist." The short term disincentives for engaging in double loop learning for this manager are clear. If the fault for lack of interest in advancement does not lie in the women, it might lie in the organization; a conclusion with personally and organizationally threatening consequences. Chris Argyris captures the essentials of this organizational change paradox illustrated in both examples above. "The difficulty is that in real life, truth is a good idea when it is not threatening. If truth is threatening, the appropriate tactics and games will be displayed to reduce the threat while covertly distorting the truth" (Argyris, 1980).

This discussion of organizational learning illuminates the problem of organizational change. While change by accommodation and adjustment can occur within a single loop learning model, conditions of modern public organizations call for a deeper capacity to change, or for double loop learning. For example, an agency that attempt to implement Total Quality Management that requires a change in the organization's philosophical and measurements systems must go well beyond accommodation and adjustment. While we are concerned with both types of learning we invite managers to focus particularly on ways that double loop learning might be enhanced by the following managerial change strategies.

MANAGERIAL CHANGE STRATEGIES

One thing that we know about the change phenomenon is that it has two parts corresponding to the concern for production and the concern for relationship dimension. There is a technical part, the goal redefinition and/or reorganization that needs to be implemented and a social part, the feelings, values and attitudes of people involved in its implementation and impact. The strategies managers adopt should be sensitive to both parts of the change experience. Kotter and Schlesinger (1979) outline four managerial approaches to change sensitive to both dimensions.

Education and Communication

Change is effected through the force of information. This strategy assumes a fairly solid latent consensus which will easily emerge once information is provided and misinformation dispelled. Dissemination of studies and model regulations is an example of this type of strategy.

Participation and Involvement

Change is effected on the basis of the commitment which results from participation in decision-making. This approach assumes that a large number of actors can reach a mutually acceptable compromise if they are allowed to interact on a face-to-face basis. Conferences with a working agenda are an example as are many organization development strategies.

Negotiations

This is similar to participation, but only a few actors are involved. The approach assumes there are distinct points of view about the change in question and that powerful interests must be directly represented and reconciled. Retreats of top management may illustrate this strategy.

Authoritative Determination

Change is effected by directives from the top. This strategy assumes that consensus is so obvious or, at the other extreme, so impossible, that participation and negotiation are inappropriate. This strategy suggests a plan involving efforts directed toward the top management levels, not toward the much larger numbers of users and affected parties. Quite possibly managers would involve elements from each of these approaches developing a change strategy fitting to a particular case.

BASIC POINTS ABOUT MANAGING CHANGE

In thinking about a strategy for a broad change effort involving many factors, in many jurisdictions or subsystems, managers should consider the literature on organizational development (OD). OD is the applied expression of organizational change theory which holds that change efforts involve distinct stages or phases (see French, 1969; Gabris, 1983; French and Bell, 1984; Kochan and Useem, 1992).

On the basis of a review of eighteen diverse change efforts, Greiner (1967) has usefully summarized six phrases typical of such an OD effort:

1. Pressure and arousal: awareness of the problem at top levels of management; placing the problem as a priority agenda item; legitimation of lower levels treating the problem as a priority.
2. Intervention and reorientation: call for reexamination and change, legitimated by top management but often facilitated by an outside newcomer as a catalyst (a consultant, a manager from another line division, a staff support professional, or a new agency head).
3. Diagnosis and recognition: a shared process of inventorying problems.
4. Invention and commitment: search for alternatives on a collaborative basis.
5. Experimentation and search: provisional decision-making and trial implementation.
6. Reinforcement and acceptance: publicity for performance improvement, reward for improvement, integration of change with training and support systems.

The classic formulation of change through organizational development reduces the process to three stages. Kurt Lewin (1947, 1951) identifies these stages as: (1) unfreezing, by the introduction of new information or experiences which change old value priorities; (2) changing, by actual decision-making which sanctions new processes; and (3) refreezing, by reliance on training, rewards, and other means to perpetuate the new system. The thought is that managers must avoid the temptation to just do stage 2, ignoring the need for laying the preliminary groundwork for later follow-up on decisions about change.

The first stage has certain typical features. As one researcher has shown (Huse, 1975), the first stage usually requires certain concrete efforts to "unfreeze" the situation by decreasing resistance to change. Examples of considerations here are the following: (1) have you communicated effectively evidence showing the change is helpful to those who must decide on change?; (2) have you considered how the change will threaten to diminish the prestige and authority of relevant actors?; (3) have you afforded relevant actors an opportunity to be part of the change process from the start?; (4) have you sought to legitimize the change by securing the support of the highest levels of management from the beginning?; (5) have you provided a means whereby actors can share their perceptions, thereby establishing peer reinforcement of new change-oriented attitudes? These may seem to be common sense rules, but many managers planning change efforts either forget them or assume they can safely ignore one or more of them. In most cases all five considerations are really necessary.

Change action begins with diagnosis, but managing change is a snowballing process. A vision of change starts at the center, others are involved and the vision is refined, then a wider group is brought in and this changes goals further, until eventually all the actors are brought into the network and goals are crystallized in a decision. This is very different from "marketing," in which a preset product is sold without change to an audience. In managing change, the audience is progressively brought into the "production process." In introducing an affirmative action program, for example, the audience of potential users, higher level managers, etc., is brought progressively into the change effort. Ordinarily representatives of each type of actor are brought in at the outset, the more prestigious the representatives the better. What these representatives usually do at the outset is engage in diagnosis. Where are women and minority group members now in the respective units? What have been the retention/advancement patterns regarding them in the past? What are the special problem areas?

There is extensive literature on organizational diagnosis (Levinson, 1972; French and Bell, 1984; Kochan and Useem, 1992; Pasmore, 1994). However, the core of diagnosis is simply engaging in some effort to find out: (1) what the current situation is; (2) what people think the situation to be; and (3) what people perceive as the obstacles. An impressive array of techniques can be used in diagnosis ranging from brainstorming to survey research to Lewin's "force field analysis." Whatever the form taken, action begun in diagnosis provides feedback which is then the focus of the middle stage, the changing process.

Depending on the strategy adopted, the changing process will involve a large or small number of people. A three-day working conference on equal employment opportunity involving a couple of hundred participants would be a participatory approach to an affirmative action program. The authoritative approach to the same program might be a retreat or planning session involving only a few key decision-makers. Regardless of the strategy, however, the middle stage, the changing process, has a few typical features.

First, the middle stage involves face-to-face decision-making meetings, whether small meetings or large conferences, they demand substantial skill. Our communications chapter highlights the art of meeting management and points out aspects of nonverbal communication to which managers must be sensitive. It is worth noting that such decision-making meetings have a typical sequence whether they are stretched out over many meetings or condensed in one. The recommended typical sequence is as follows: (1) legitimation of the change objective by the highest-ranking officials possible; (2) presentation of diagnostic findings by a representative planning team, documenting the need to change and widespread readiness to change; (3) introductory activities involving those attending in sharing perceptions on the subject; (4) brainstorming of what's good, what's wrong, what changes would help, and what obstacles remain (often done in small groups which report back to the whole); (5) participative establishment of goals; (6) formation of task groups addressed to action steps and obstacles. Generally speaking, these steps are helpful whether the decision-makers are a large conference or a small set of key officials. The less the consensus and commitment of the decision-makers, the more each step is necessary.

The third stage of the change process is more or less important, depending on whether you are instituting a new procedure or eliminating a former problem. The follow-up or "refreezing" stage in managing change is less critical in an effort like deregulation, where the outcome is to be elimination rather than institution of activities. To the extent new activities are required by a change, as in the example of instituting a new AA program, it is necessary that they be reinforced by being built into reward systems, into performance appraisals, MBO reporting, and incorporated into professional association activities. In the case of deregulation, such as discontinuing an ongoing effort, most of this sort of unusual change consideration is irrelevant. Nonetheless, follow-up should also provide for some system of evaluation of the change, with provisions for the decision-making group to review and refine the change at a later point.

MANAGERIAL IMPLICATIONS

Organizational change refers to any significant alteration of the behavior pattern of a large number of the individuals who constitute an organization. Organizational change in a global economy is increasingly necessary to survival. Edward Deming and the Total Quality Management movement, for example, requires organizations to change both their philosophy and managerial methodologies in order to implement (TQM). In order for managers to change organizations they must understand important features of the organizations in which they work.

All organizations have a culture. Organizational culture is generally defined in terms of the beliefs and expectations shared by organization members that shape behavior Organizational culture is reflected in internalized *norms* that *shape perception* and *affect behavior*. Research in both the public and private sector underscores the fact that organizational culture concretely influences what happens in organizations. It does so, because organization culture filters the ways in which organizational members perceive and emotionally respond to environmental stimuli. In effect, the concept of an organizational culture is another expression of the fact that organizations, themselves, take on features that can be characterized as personality and character. Managers need to be aware of their organizational culture.

Organizational climate is a concept closely related to, but distinct from, organizational culture. Like national culture, organizational culture has unique indicators such as myths, symbols, rites, and stories. Organizational climate is based in attitudes and measures whether people's expectations about what it should be like to work in an agency are met. Climate is attitudinal and is based on acceptance of the prevailing culture. If many new employees enter the organization with values different from the dominate organizational culture, a "climate problem" will develop. Why? Because employees do not share the dominant organizational culture value(s). Organizational climate problems can at times reach problematic proportions. Managers may need to consider organizational development or change interventions.

Managers need to understand that organization can learn (and forget). Organizations, in fact, change through the learning process. We identified two types of learning occurring in organizations: single loop learning and double loop learning. Single loop learning is like a thermostat that senses it is too hot or too cold and adjusts the heat accordingly Single loop learning occurs when a match between intentions and results is produced or a mismatch is corrected without having to question the organizational assumptions and policies Using the thermostat analogy, double loop learning would occur if one asked if the thermostat concept itself was appropriate. Double loop learning is typically associated with the kind of inquiry which resolves incompatible organizational norms by setting new priorities and weighing of norms or by restructuring norms themselves.

The classic formulation of change through the intervention of organizational development reduces the organizational change process to three stages. Kurt Lewin (1947, 1951) identifies these stages as: (1) unfreezing, by the introduction of new information or experiences which change old value priorities; (2) changing, by actual decision-making which sanctions new processes; and (3) refreezing, by reliance on training, rewards, and other means to perpetuate the new system. Organizational change action begins with diagnosis, but managing change is a snowballing process. A vision of change starts at the center, others are involved and the vision is refined, then a wider group is brought in and this changes goals further, until eventually all the actors are brought into the network and goals are crystallized in a decision. This is very different from "marketing," in which a preset product is sold without change to an audience. In managing change, the audience is progressively brought into the "production process." Managers have a number of change strategies available to them; education and communication, participation and involvement, negotiation, and authoritative determination. Which change strategy is appropriate to which agency depends upon the agency's technology, structure, and environment, as well as climate and culture.

REFERENCES AND ADDITIONAL READING

Aldrich, H. E. (1972). "Technology and Organizational Structure: A Re-examination of the Findings of the Aston Group." *Administrative Science Quarterly*, Vol. 17 (March):pp 26–43.

Argyris, C. (1980). "Making the Undiscussable and its Undiscussability Discussable." *Public Administration Review*, 5(6):pp 205–211.

Argyris, C. and D. A. Schon (1978). *Organizational Learning: A Theory of Action Perspective*. Reading, MA: Addison-Wesley.

Blair, P. M., C. M. Falbe, W. McKinley, and P. R. Tracy (1976). "Technology and Organization in Manufacturing." *Admininstrative Science Quarterly*, Vol. 21 (March):pp 20–40.

Blasi, A. (1980). "Bridging Moral Cognition and Moral Actions: A Critical Review of the Literature." *Psychological Bulletin*, 88(1):pp 1–45.

Brookfield, S. D. (1987). *Developing Critical Thinkers: Challenging Adults to Explore Alternative Ways of Thinking and Acting*. San Francisco, CA: Jossey-Vass Publishers.

Brown, P. G. (1986). "Ethics and Education for the Public Service in a Liberal State." *Journal of Policy Analysis and Management*, 6(1):pp 56–68.

Burns, T. and G. M. Stalker (1961). *The Management of Innovation*. London: Tavistock Institute.

Burrell, G. and G. Morgan (1979). *Sociological Paradigms and Organizational Analysis*. London: Heinemann.

Caiden, G. E. (1981). "Ethics in the Public Service." *Public Personnel Management*, 10:pp 146–152.

Carroll, P. (1993). *Big Blues: The Unmaking of IBM*. New York: Crown Publishers.

Child, J. (1972). "Organization Structure and Strategies of Control: A Replication of the Aston Study." *Administrative Science Quarterly*, 17 (June):pp 163–177.

Child, J. and R. Mansfield (1972). "Technology, Size and Organization Structure." *Sociology*, 6 (September):pp 369–393.

Cooper, T. L. (1984). "Citizenship and Professionalism in Public Administration." *Public Administration Review*, 44 (Special Issue, March):pp 143–156.

Cooper, T. L. (1987). "Hierarchy, Virtue, and the Practice of Public Administration: A

Perspective for Normative Ethics." *Public Administration Review*, 47 (July/August):pp 320–328.

Cranton, P. (1994). *Understanding and Promoting Transformative Learning: A Guide for Educators of Adults.* San Francisco, CA: Jossey-Bass.

Daft, R. (1983). *Organizational Theory and Design.* St. Paul: West Publishing Company.

Dalton, G. W. (1978). "Influence and Organizational Change." *Organizational Development in Public Administration*, (R. T. Golembiewski and W. B. Eddy eds.). New York: Marcel Dekker, Inc.

Doig, J. W. (1983). "Placing the Burden Where it Belongs." Paper prepared for panel on "Anti-corruption Strategies in Public Agencies," National Conference of the American Society for Public Administration, New York, April 16–19.

Edmondson, A. C. (1996). "Three faces of Eden: The Persistence of Competing Theories and Multiple Diagnoses in Organizational Intervention Research." *Human Relation*, 49(5):pp 571–594.

Fiol, M. C. and M. A. Lyles (1985). "Organizational Learning." *Academy of Management Review*, 10(4):pp 803–813.

Fincher, C. (1986). "What is Organizational Culture?" *Research in Higher Education.* 24(3):pp 325–328.

Fleishman, J. L. and B. L. Payne (1980). *The Teaching of Ethics VIII: Ethical Dilemmas and Education of Policy Makers.* New York: Institute of Society, Ethics and the Life Sciences, The Hastings Center.

French, W. L. and C. H. Bell (1984). *Organizational Development.* 3rd ed. Englewood Cliffs, NJ: Prentice Hall.

French, W. (1969). "Organizational Development: Objectives, Assumptions and Strategies," reprinted in *Classics of Organizational Behavior*, (W. E. Natemeyer, ed.) Oak Park, Ill.: More Publishing Company.

Gabris, G. (1983). "Organizational Change." in *Organization Theory and Management* (T. Lynch, ed.), New York: Marcel Decker.

Galbraith, J. R. and E. E. Lawler (1993). *Organizing for the Future: The New Logic for Managing Complex Organizations.* San Francisco, CA: Jossey-Bass Publishers.

Garvin, D. A. (1993). "Building a Learning Organization." *Harvard Business Review*, 71 (July–August):pp 78–92.

Greiner, L. (1967). "Patterns of Organizational Change." *Harvard Business Review*, 45(3) (May/June):pp 119–130.

Hedberg, B. (1981). "How Organizations Learn and Unlearn." In *Handbook of Organizational Design* (D. C. Nystrom and W. H. Starbuck eds.), London: Oxford University Press.

Heffron, F. (1989). *Organization Theory and Public Organizations.* Englewood Cliffs, NJ: Prentice-Hall, Inc.

Hellriegel, D., J. W. Slocum, and R. W. Woodman (1986). *Organization Behavior.* St. Paul, MN: West Publishing Co.

Hirschman, A. O. (1970). *Exit, Voice and Loyalty.* Cambridge MA: Harvard University Press.

Hofstede, G. H. (1991). *Cultures and Organizations: Software of the Mind.* New York: McGraw Hill Book Company.

Hunt, D. E. (1974). *Matching Models In Education.* Toronto, Canada: The Ontario Institute for Studies in Education.

Huse, E. F. (1975). *Organization Development and Change.* New York: West Publishing Company.

Imai, M. (1997). *Gemba Kaizen: A Commonsense, Low-Cost Approach to Management.* New York: McGraw Hill.

Imai, M. (1986). *Kaizen: The Key to Japan's Competitive Success.* New York: McGarw Hill.

Isaacs, W. N. (1993). "Taking flight: Dialogue, Collective Thinking, and Organizational Learning." *Organizational Dynamics,* 22 (Autumn):pp 24–40.

Kanter, R. M. (1977). *Men and Women of the Corporation.* New York: Basic Books.

Kastelic, F. (1974). "Innovation, Involvement, and Contemporary Service Organizations." *Journal of Sociology and Social Welfare,* 1 (Summer):pp 233–243.

Kaufman, H. (1985). *Time, Chance and Organizations.* Chatham, New Jersey: Chatham House Publications Inc.

Kaufman, H. (1976). *Are Government Organizations Immortal?* Brookings Institution.

Kochan, T. and M. Useem (eds.) (1992). *Transforming Organizations.* New York: Oxford University Press.

Kotter, J. P. and L. A. Schlesinger (1979). "Choosing Strategies for Change." *Harvard Business Review,* (March/April):pp 106–114.

Lawrence, P. R. and J. W. Lorsch (1967). "Differentiation and Integration in Complex Organizations." *Administrative Science Quarterly,* 12:pp 1–47.

Levinson, H. (1972). *Organizational Diagnosis.* Cambridge, MA: Harvard University Press.

Levitt, B. and J. G. March (1988). "Organizational learning." *Annual Review of Sociology,* 14:pp 319–340.

Lewin, K. (1947). "Frontiers in Group Dynamics." *Human Relations,* 1 (June):pp 5–41.

Lewin, K. (1951). *Field Theory in Social Science.* New York: Harper Brothers.

Lilla, M. (1981). "Ethics' and the Public Service." *The Public Interest,* 63 (Winter):pp 3–17.

Lincoln, J. R., M. Hanada, and K. McBride (1986). "Organizational Structures in Japanese and U.S. Manufacturing." *Administrative Science Quarterly,* 31:pp 338–364.

Little, J. C., Jr. and N. J. Cayer (1996). "Experiences of a learning organization in the public sector." *International Journal of Public Administration,* 19,(5):pp 711–730.

Loevinger, J. (1977). *Ego Development.* San Francisco, CA: Jossey-Bass.

Melman, S. (1971). "Managerial versus Cooperative Decision Making in Israel." *Studies in Comparative International Development,* 6:pp 47–58.

Mertins, H. and Brannigan, P. J. (eds.) (1982). *Professional Standards and Ethics: A Workbook for Public Administration.* Washington: American Society for Public Administration.

Mintzberg, H. (1983). *The Sructuring of Organizations*. Englewood Cliffs, NJ: Prentice Hall.

Mohan, R. P. (1972). "A Preliminary Model of Organizational Renewal." *Indian Journal of Social Research*, 13 (December):pp 179–153.

Mohr, L. (1971). "Organizational Technology and Organizational Structure." *Administrative Science Quarterly*, 16 (December):pp 444–459.

Nozick, R. (1974). *Anarchy, State, and Utopia*. New York: Basic Books, p 130.

Osborne, D.and T. Gaebler (1992). *Revinventing Government: How the Entrepreneurial Spirit is Transforming the Public Sector*. New York: Addison-Wesley Publishing Company, Inc.

O'Toole, J. J. (1979). "Corporate and Managerial Cultures." *Behavioral Problems in Organizations*, (Cary L. Cooper ed.). Englewood Cliffs, NJ: Prentice-Hall.

Ouchi, W. G. and A. L. Wilkins (1985). "Organizational Culture." *Annual Review of Sociology*, 11:pp 457–482.

Ouchi, W. (1981). *Theory Z*. Readings, MA: Addison-Wesley.

Pasmore, W. A. (1994). *Creating Strategic Change*. New York: John Wiley & Sons.

Pascale, R. and A. Athos. *The Art of Japanese Management*. New York: Warner Books.

Perrow, C. (1986). *Complex Organizations: A Critical Essay*. 3rd ed. New York: Random House.

Perrow, C. B. (1970). *Organizational Analysis: A Sociological View*. Belmont, CA: Wadsworth Publishing Company.

Peters, T. and R. Waterman (1982). *In Search of Excellence*. New York: Harper and Row.

Ruitt, D. G. (1971). "Choice Shift in Group Discussion: An Introductory Review." *Journal of Personality and Social Psychology*, 20:pp339–360.

Rawls, J. (1971). *A Theory of Justice*. Cambridge, MA: Belknap.

Rest, J. (1987). *Moral Development: Advances in Research and Theory*. New York: Praeger.

Rohr, J. A. (1978). *Ethics for Bureaucrats*. New York: Marcel Dekker, Inc.

Roosevelt, T. (1976). "Managing the Psychological Contract." in *Organizational Behavior and Administration*. 3rd ed. (P. Laurence, L. Barnes, and J. Horsch eds.). Homewood, Ill: Richard D. Irvin.

Rubin, I. (1982). "Managing the End: Death and Dying in Public Organizations." *Public Management*. (March).

Sayles, L. R. (1958). *Behavior in Industrial Work Groups: Prediction and Control*. New York: John Wiley.

Schein, E. (1985). *Organizational Culture and Leadership*. San Francisco, CA: Jossey-Bass.

Schein, E. (1993). "On dialogue, Culture, and Organizational Learning." *Organizational Dynamics*, 22 (Autumn):pp 40–51.

Schwartz, H. and S. M. Davis (1981). "Matching Corporate Culture and Business Strategy." *Organizational Dynamics*, (Summer):pp 30–48.

Senge, P. (1990). *The Fifth Discipline*. New York: Doubleday.

Singh, J., R. J. and D. J. Tucker (1986). "Organizational Change and Organizational Mortality." *Administrative Science Quarterly*, 31:pp 587–611.

Sprinthall, N. and R. Sprinthall (1988). "Value and Moral Development." *Ethics: Easier Said Than Done*, 1(1):pp 16–21.

Stein, B. A. and R. M. Kanter (1980). "Building the Parallel Organization: Creating Mechanisms for Permanent Quality of Work Life." *Journal of Applied Behavioral Science*, 16:pp 371–388.

Swieringa, J. and A. Wierdsma (1992). *Becoming a Learning Organization.* Workingham, England: Addison-Wesley Publishing Company.

Szanton, P. (1981). "So You Want to Reorganize the Government." in *Federal Reorganization: What Have We Learned?* (Szanton, ed.) Chatham, NJ: Chatham House Publishers, Inc.

Taylor, J. C. and D. F. Felton (1993). *Performance by Design: Socio Technical Systems in North America.* Englewood Cliffs, NJ.

Thompson, D. (1985). "The Possibility of Administrative Ethics." *Public Administration Review*, 45(5) (September/October):pp 555–561.

Tierney, W. G. (1988). "Organizational Culture in Higher Education." *Journal of Higher Education*, 9(1) (January/February):pp 2–20.

Toffler, A. (1970). *Future Shock.* New York: Bantam Books.

Tompkins, P. K. (1993). *Organizational Communication Imperatives: Lessons of the Space Program.* Los Angeles, CA: Roxbury Press.

Trist, E. L. and K. W. Bamforth (1951). "Some Social and Psychological Consequences of the Longwald Method of Goal Setting." *Human Relations*, 4(1):pp 3–38.

Trice, H. M. and J. M Beyer (1993). *The Cultures of Work Organizations.* Englewood Cliffs, NJ: Prentice Hall.

Ulrich, D., M. A. Von Glinow, and T. Jick (1993). "High-Impact Learning: Building and Diffusing Learning Capability." *Organizational Dynamics*, 22:pp 52–67.

Walker, J. and R. H. Guest (1952). *The Man on the Assembly Line.* Cambridge, MA: Harvard University Press.

Wilkins, A. L. and W. G. Ouchi (1983). "Efficient Cultures: Exploring the Relationship Between Culture and Organizational Performance." *Administrative Science Quarterly*, 28:pp 468–481.

Wilson, J. Q. (1989). *Bureaucracy:What Government Agencies Do and Why They Do It.* New York: Basic Books.

Woodward, J. (1972). *Industrial Organization: Theory and Practice.* London: Oxford University Press.

Woodward, J. (1958). *Management and Technology.* London: HMSO.

10
Management Systems

Management systems are *tools* for directing large complex organizations toward specific ends. Management, itself, is the coordination of human and capital resources to achieve specific organizational outcomes or goals. In a systems sense, organizational inputs are transformed into organizational outputs through *management* which is the mechanism employed to effect this transformation (Bartlett and Goshal, 1994; Pasmore, 1994). Management systems are the tools used to link the organization's strategic planning process to its operational units and processes (Swiss, 1991). In other words, strategic planning sets the organization's overall policy goals, that is, what the organization wants to accomplish and how it plans to accomplish its goals (Gray, 1986; Nutt and Backoff, 1992; Mintzberg, 1994b; Bryson, 1995). The strategic planning process defines who the agencies' clients are. It also defines the mission and vision of the agency as well as the overall policy objectives (Bryson, 1995). Strategic planning also determines in what specific ways these clients are to be served, as well as what service and resource priorities will dominate. Operations, on the other hand, refers to the day to day tasks of the organization; teaching the students, patrolling the streets, approving the subdivision plans, etc. Management systems are the *link between strategic planning and operations* in the organization (Swiss, 1991; Ammons, 1995).

Strategic planning, itself, is an ongoing process. It is a disciplined effort designed to create fundamental organizational decisions and actions (Bryson, 1995, pp. 4–5). Strategic planning is a set of *procedures and concepts* that allows managers to think and act strategically. The strategic planning process involves a series of steps:

1. Initiating and Agreeing on a Strategic Planning Process.
2. Identifying Organizational Mandates.
3. Clarifying Organizational Mission and Values.

4. Assessing the Organization's External and Internal Environments.
5. Identifying the Strategic Issues Facing the Organization.
6. Formulating Strategies and Plans to Manage the Issues.
7. Reviewing and Adopting the Strategies and Plan.
8. Establishing an Effective Organizational Vision.
9. Developing an Effective Implementation Process.
10. Reassessing Strategies and the Strategic Planning Process (Bryson, 1995, pp. 23–37).

Management systems are the techniques or tools that the manager employs in order to gain adequate feedback with respect to the linkage between what the organization is doing (operations) and what it should be doing (policy objectives or goals). In this sense, any management system is a feedback system with specific criteria that include:

1. Setting initial standards. Using the policy directives from above as guidelines, the manager sets organizational goals for the period covered, whether it is a week, a month, a quarter, or a year. For example, to process 5,000 patients this quarter.
2. Collecting information on progress. During the period covered, the manager collects information on how the organization is performing. For example, have 5,000 patients been processed?
3. Taking remedial action. This third step isn't always necessary. But if the previous step reveals that organizational goals are not being attained, the manager will take remedial action to correct the shortfall (Swiss, 1991, p. 3).

Management systems involve setting standards first and then taking action. They are output oriented (Swiss, 1991; Ammons, 1995; Ammons, 1996). The information generated by management systems can be used to increase decision-making efficiency and/or to influence behavior by manipulating incentives. Management systems provide a form of control over the organization and enhance the efficiency of the management endeavor.

There are a variety of management systems. Management systems is a broad umbrella term that subsumes specific techniques that have, as one common feature, a focus on some type of output measure (Swiss, 1991; Swiss, 1995). Another common feature of management systems is that they provide information on how the organization is operating while providing standards against which to compare this information. The organization is then able to judge (evaluate) how well it is operating (Ammons, 1995; Ammons, 1996). In the private sector, management systems are typically referred to as "management control systems." Management control systems emphasize the "control" that management can gain over the organization by having adequate information on which to predicate decision-making. In addition, management systems provide the control, implicit in using the information generated by the management system, in directing employee behavior toward specific organizational goals. This is achieved by linking incentives to specific outputs, for example, tracking market share and linking merit pay to increases in market share. Management information systems (MIS) and information resource management (IRM) have become synonymous with types of management systems which employ computer hardware and databases to assist managers (at all levels) in collecting and tracking organizational information. Both of these terms have come to mean much more than the narrower rubric of data processing. Given the importance of information management to the future of organizations, we have devoted a separate chapter to information, computers, and organizational theory. For the purposes of this chapter, both MIS and IRM will be considered particular expressions of management systems in that they provide information that can be used to evaluate organizational outputs as well as provide the information necessary to create incentives to conform to organizational goals.

In the public sector one useful clarification is provided by Swiss (1991,1995), who divides management systems on the basis of the goals or outputs that they track. Some management systems set goals personally in face-to-face meetings; management by objectives (MBO), a topic we discuss in the chapter on performance evaluation, is an illustration of this type of management system. Other management systems set goals and measure outputs by a more impersonal system, such as using some set criteria such as engineered standards (standard times). Standard times are the time it should take to complete a particular task based on recording the performance of experienced workers; for example the average amount of garbage collected by a team of four, expressed in tons, on a route of specific size and configuration. This type of management system is termed production monitoring system (Swiss, 1995). Production monitoring systems typically track organizational outputs, whereas techniques like MBO and its hybrids tend to track individual outputs (Poister, 1995).

Most management systems have their origin in the private sector. In the private sector management systems are designed to increase effectiveness and efficiency. Effectiveness is the ability to produce the desired outcome. Thus a fire department that puts out fires is effective. Efficiency, on the other hand, is measured by how well organizational resources were used in achieving that outcome. A fire department that uses less manpower and trucks to put out fires of the same size is more efficient. In other words, effectiveness is focused on the *final outcome*, did you get the job done? Efficiency emphasizes the process from the perspective of inputs employed per unit of output produced (Rosen, 1995).

When applied to the public sector, management systems generate political effects and frequently engender political resistance. This is in many ways a function of the differences between public and private organizations (Bower, 1983; Ring and Perry, 1985; Swiss, 1991; Swiss, 1995; Tracy and Jean, 1995) For example, Bower (1983) observed that private sector organizations strive to make the most efficient and effective possible use of all the resources at their disposal. Moreover, they are measured in terms of their results. Many management systems are tools toward this end. However, Bower contends that "political" organizations seek to insure that the system treats people fairly (the equity dimension). Accordingly, we measure public managers primarily by the legitimacy of their internal processes and by accountability standards. This is not to say that efficiency and effectiveness are not important to public organizations. However, they do not (and cannot) have the predominance that they must have in market organizations. A recognition of the factors inherent in management systems and in the public sector environment is an important precondition in the success of management systems in government (Osborne and Gaebler, 1995). It is also a major focus of this chapter, *which will not deal with management system techniques per se as much as the socio-technical considerations inherent in their implementation.*

Many of the problems in any attempt to implement management systems in government have to do with the unique characteristics of the public sector. For example, the lack of profit as a goal. The fact that public organizations have far more legal constraints on their internal and external actions than do private organizations. The fact that the goals of public sector organizations must include equity, as well as efficiency and effectiveness. The fact that public sector goals in general are more ambiguous and consequently more difficult to quantify. Finally, democratic accountability frequently requires procedural rules that compromise efficiency. These realities of public sector life make the direct adoption (without modification and planning) of management systems by the public sector impossible.

> Those who speak glibly of "bringing business techniques to government" in order to make it more businesslike are missing these differences. It is futile to attempt to transfer techniques, approaches and systems from the private sector to the public sector without adaptation. They simply will not work (Swiss, 1991, p. 9).

Because management systems are becoming more and more a part of the fabric of public organizations it is important to focus on the history of their implementation in the public sector. This history suggests that political and human behavioral dimensions of organizational life must be considered when attempting to introduce a management system into a public agency. It is also important to keep in mind the problems inherent in measuring outputs, as well as the context and constraints that public organizations present to the implementation of management systems.

PUBLIC SECTOR APPLICATIONS OF MANAGEMENT SYSTEMS

In the last three decades there has been a shift in public administration toward greater application of organizational behavior concepts to management. At the same time there has been a proliferation of management systems designed to assist management decision-making such as program planning and budgeting systems (PPBS), zero-base budgeting (ZBB), and management by objectives (MBO), to name a few. All these systems involve the systematic relating of organizational goals to personnel and budgetary data. As systematic, often quantitative techniques, the systems approaches are often seen as "hard" task-centered tools which contrast with the "soft" person-centered methods drawn from the study of human behavior. In spite of apparent tensions it is a thesis of this chapter that management systems and human behavioral approaches function best when they are seen as complementary. All human organizations are *socio-technical*. In other words, the technical dimensions of the organization are influenced by the human behavior within the organization. The reciprocal is true as well, the technical system influence aspects of human behavior.

The application of management systems to human resource questions goes back some way in American public administration, antedating John F. Kennedy's installation of program budgeting (PPBS) in the Department of Defense. Planning, programming, and budgeting systems (PPBS) was a system which required that budgets correspond to program categories (that is, to objectives). By grouping expenses by program category it was possible to employ PPBS in making judgments about the costs and benefits of one program compared to another. Zero-base budgeting (ZBB), popularized under President Carter, required agencies to submit three budgets rather than one; a cutback budget, a stand-pat budget, and an expansion budget. This, too, was intended to increase the decision-making powers of top management. Management by objectives (MBO), was emphasized during the Nixon administration and focused on the coordination of individual work plans with organization goals, and these with the budget. All three systems, like most others, increased information available to top decision-makers, enabling top management to make more effective decisions.

The literature suggests an increasing proliferation of management systems techniques designed to measure individual and organizational outcomes in governmental units (Poister 1984; Poister, 1995; Alter, 1995; Griesemer, 1995; Ammons, 1996). In fact, the capacity of many governmental units; that is, the ability to achieve its objectives in the context of voter expectations, resources and the problems it faces, is increasingly being measured in terms of its administrative techniques. For example, MBO is being employed to evaluate the upper-levels of urban managers (Ammons, 1995).

Gremillion et al., (1980) reported on the benefits of PPBS in the U.S. Forest Service. Amid economic cutbacks, PPBS-type analyses may find increased applicability. Even at the federal level after the departure of the ZBB advocates of the Carter era, substantial elements of ZBB have been left in place (Draper and Pitsvada, 1981). For its part, MBO has been reinforced by its potential linkage with the rapid growth of management information systems (MIS), as in hospital administration (see Spano et al., 1977; Granvold, 1978; McConkie, 1979; Moore and Staton, 1981; Swiss 1991; Swiss, 1995).

In view of the proliferation of management systems techniques it is important to remember the need to integrate the implementation of these management systems with behavioral concerns and techniques of the sort discussed in this book. Our premise is that both must be integrated for effective realization of the objectives of either. We begin with a discussion of human behavioral concerns in the design of management systems. The following section treats the question of evaluation and research design in implementation of management systems. A concluding section presents common managerial problems in applying (or not applying!) behavioral concepts to systems applications.

DESIGN CONCERNS IN MANAGEMENT CONTROL SYSTEMS

The introduction of a management system is commonly perceived as a relatively technical matter by most agency employees. It is seen as emphasizing forms, budgetary data, and analytic constructs somehow tied to "management planning" and perhaps (fear and trembling!) to job evaluation and merit pay (Swiss, 1991; Swiss, 1995). Thus the management system appears on the scene as something of an unknown and, like most unknowns, it elicits a certain automatic resistance to the changes it brings. Ironically, such management systems are usually created to improve communication, coordination, and feedback. In the absence of careful attention to human behavioral design concerns, however, implementation of these systems can easily backfire.

There are three major design issues in implementing a management system which demonstrate various ways management system implementation can fail in public agencies. These issues are *influence differentiation, suboptimization, and goal displacement*. Influence differentiation; refers to problems associated with participation and control, or lack thereof, in management systems. Suboptimization; refers to design failures in process integration in systems implementation. Finally, goal displacement; refers to the potential behavior-distorting effects of the information/tracking system established in conjunction with a management system. Each of these design issues is briefly outlined below.

Many management systems involve issues of power, influence, and control in an explicit way. Since a major purpose of a management system is to facilitate the flow of information to top management for analysis and review, management systems appear, in effect, to be centralizing. Just as the introduction of human behavioral interventions like autonomous work groups may threaten the established influence structure from the point of view of management, the introduction of management systems may seem to employees to be merely a further tightening of oversight and control. While the tightening of control by management can be productive for the agency, there are many circumstances (the opposite of the contingencies favoring participatory management) in which it can be harmful.

Problems arising from the failure to join human behavioral interventions with management system implementation are discussed in the "Central City" case later in this chapter. The point here, however, is simply to establish the concept that management system design must recognize the political (power) dimension of agency change (Swiss, 1991; Bryson, 1995). This is done through systems design which emphasize influence integration rather than influence differentiation.

Influence differentiation is the normal mode by which agency members perceive power in the organization. That is, influence is perceived to be differentiated by function and level. Higher organizational levels exert greater influence over more functions. Low-level employees exert less influence over fewer functions. The influence differentiation mode, however "natural," carries with it an internal tension. On the one hand, power in the agency tends to be viewed as zero-sum in nature: *the more influence the employees have, the less management has and vice versa.* On the other hand, the purpose of management systems is to motivate the employee to contribute more to broader functions of the agency normally reserved for higher levels. That is, the management system is an appeal to the employee to identify with such broader organizational concerns as productivity and achievement of agency goals. The influence differentiation mode, however, does little to legitimize such an appeal. On the contrary, it fosters an ambiguous push-pull mentality in which the employee is expected to be subordinate in influence level and functional domain but also expected to be integrated in the functional concerns of higher levels.

Influence differentiation is not an abstract theoretical construct for systems implementation. In fact, it is probably the single most common cause of widespread cynicism toward management systems, accounting for their often transitory or faddish nature in public administration. Influence differentiation is not an inevitable orientation toward the agency's power structure. As Tannenbaum has noted of organizations taking an influence integration approach, by involving both systemic and human behavioral innovations, both managers and employees can come to understand that influence is neither one-way nor zero-sum. It can be true, as Tannenbaum found of the organization member, that "while he controls more, he is not controlled less" (Tannenbaum, 1962 in Natemeyer, 1978). In planning management systems like ZBB, PPBS, or MBO, participative approaches do more than overcome resistance to change and increase employee satisfaction. They encourage a team perspective oriented toward exchange of ideas and feedback rather than an hierarchical perspective rooted in command and acquiescence. By providing concrete experiences with two-way influence and illustrations of nonzero-sum decision-making, a participatory approach fosters the influence integration mode of perceiving management systems, a prerequisite for successful systems implementation.

> Regardless of the ultimate outcome of particular experiments, the principle has been established beyond doubt in innumerable instances: Workers will be far more efficient if they have a hand in designing own work than if work design is performed by management and handed down for compliance (Pinchot and Pinchot, 1994, p. 6).

Suboptimization is the second of the major design concerns in systems implementation. When large agencies are divided into divisions or units which have the design responsibility for implementing a management system, there is a possibility if not likelihood that suboptimization will occur. Suboptimization is the design of a management system to meet unit goals not coordinated with agency goals. For example, PPBS may operate effectively within a purchasing division of a state department, achieving all its goals of efficiency, documentation of costs and benefits, and so on; yet it may be impeding larger organizational goals like responsiveness (PPBS may slow other units down) or decentralization (PPBS may be based on specialized skills provided centrally).

Suboptimization is really part of the broader design problem of goal displacement. The most pernicious form of goal displacement is when the process itself becomes the goal. Goal displacement is the opposite of goal congruence; the close alignment of the personal goals of the organization's members with the goals of the organization as a whole.

> As the name suggests, goal displacement occurs when an organization or its members begin to pursue goals other than the "proper" organizational ones. The problem of goal displacement is not confined to management system in fact it afflicts organizations without such systems in a far worse form. For example, a small town's public library may be open only during the day because its employees prefer these hours, despite the fact that this schedule makes it far more difficult for the public to use the library. This is a clear example of goal displacement; the organization is being run as if the goal were the comfort of the employees rather than the benefit of the public (Swiss, 1991, p. 90).

All management systems select certain information for performance monitoring and decision-making purposes. There is an old aphorism "what is measured counts" and this pretty well sums up the problem of goal displacement. Goal displacement occurs when employees in an organization seek to deliver output that is measured and ignore outputs that are not measured. For example, if a state employment security commission's stated goal is job placement and success is measured in quantitative terms by the number of applicants interviewed, there will be an incentive to interview the applicant quickly with little follow up. If the management system measures success by the number of applicants successfully placed, the incentive will be to "cream" that is, concentrate on the applicants with the most experience and education, those easiest to place. In both the above cases goal displacement has occurred (Swiss, 1991; Osborne and Gaebler, 1995).

The data gathered in a management control system are critical because they carry fundamental assumptions about the purpose of the system. If information and purpose are mismatched, several breakdowns occur:

1. Desired purposes cannot be served rationally.
2. Time and resources spent in data collection are wasted.
3. Employees will displace behaviors in favor of measured performances.

It is not true that "some data are better than none" in the case of management systems. It is entirely possible to sabotage an otherwise satisfactory organizational process through imposition of an inappropriately designed management control system.

The fundamental problem of management systems is that without proper consideration of the human dynamics, employees will distort behavior to display improvement on measured indicators. This is, indeed, one of the key *intended* effects of management systems—but it assumes that the agency or individual performance measures required by the management system *accurately* reflect the full range of intended performances. A measure which taps produced units per person-days is fine for a management system if efficiency in production is the only performance desired. Such an indicator would not measure quality, effectiveness, or other values. Either the management system must be designed to measure all significant performance areas or the management system must be supplemented by other broader behavior-assessing approaches (e.g., performance appraisals, program reviews) which are presumed to do so. Otherwise employees will devote their energies toward showing achievement solely on that which is measured by top management, in this case efficiency (Osborne and Gaebler, 1995; Rosen, 1995).

Some general rules for avoiding the worst aspects of goal-displacement in management systems do exist (Swiss, 1991). The first is employing multiple measures. Because using only one measure (e.g., the number of tickets issued by a patrolman on a specific shift) will lead employees to neglect unmeasured attributes, it is always prudent to measure multiple attributes. The second rule is to employ nonsystematic measures. In other words, you should avoid using the management system as the only source of information and the only criteria for evaluation. This is particularly important in light of the fact that management systems are important factors in budget, promotion and personnel evaluations. Consequently, there is a real incentive for employees to manifest the behaviors that the system measures. Much of the logic of using sources over and above the management system emanates from the "reasonable man" approach in law. The reasonable man approach holds that not all contingencies can be addressed in a contract and that parties to a contract have the obligation to act reasonably. Therefore, if a clerical person significantly increased their measured output while at the same increasing the error rate significantly and by being impolite with clients, a "reasonable man" approach would dictate that the increased error rate and impolite behavior to clients should be considered in any evaluation of the employee (Swiss, 1991). The third rule is for managers to establish intermediate measures for management systems. All public programs have multiple effects; some immediate and produced directly and others delayed and produced by the ripple effect (Swiss, 1991; Swiss, 1995). Outputs can be arrayed in a "chain of outputs" that separate these types of outcomes. For example, the immediate outcome measure for an educator may well be increased reading and math comprehension scores. However, these outcomes may well be designed to facilitate more intermediate goals down the chain such as providing students with job skills, making them better citizens, etc. By distinguishing between immediate and intermediate goals and by placing these outcomes in a "chain of outcomes" the manager can avoid "not seeing the forest for the trees."

The basic choice inherent in the design of many management systems is the tradeoff between simplicity and complexity. Simple management systems are easier to administer and are less costly. Complex management systems may involve less goal displacement but administrative burdens may become prohibitive. A simple management system in the Postal Service, for example, might focus on number of mail items delivered per postal worker-day. It might be, however, that this rate has been changing due to changes in transportation, population density, technology, and other factors. A more complex measure might be percent increase in number of items delivered per postal worker-day compared to the trend line. This productivity measure alone could encourage neglect of quality, however, so a more complex system might also track a measure of client satisfaction or of accuracy of delivery. Other potential measures might include damage control, employees' health and safety, or a range of philatelic services. By tracking all possible measures, the Postal Service's management system might easily wind up with two or three dozen unit and individual performance measures. Even then the possibility would still exist that some important dimensions might be neglected.

Neglected areas typically are those at the periphery of the agency's role. In public agencies these might include issues such as whether the management systems should track environmental impact concerns, whether it should track indirect social impacts of policies, or whether the system should seek to measure data on political ramifications of policies. Typically, management systems avoid such areas. Forcing such concerns into the rigid formats of management systems would only make matters more controversial. But if environmental, social, or political impacts are not part of the management system, the agency cannot afford to ignore such considerations. The inevitable conclusion is that the management system must be designed not to replace but only to augment a broader, less explicit decision-making process which does consider wider issues.

All measurements on which management systems are based are subject to controversy. Even long-standing, routinized measures like the consumer price index or the unemployment rate, by way of comparison, are subject to intense intra bureaucratic debate and conflict. The same sort of intra organizational conflict is inevitably part of the formal or informal processes of any agency which seeks to implement a management system. Designing a management control system is a complex process involving important value choices. Because value choices are involved, top management must participate in the establishment of a management system (Bryson, 1995). Management must be intimately associated with the system and must stand behind the development process. Agencies opting for the easier, less expensive, simple management control systems must either have unusually simple configurations of outputs or must be prepared for strong dysfunctional goal displacement effects. On the other hand, agencies which opt for more complex measures must be capable of long-range planning. That is, the evolution of such measures involves trial and error to find an appropriate balance between over measurement leading to excessive burden on the one hand or under measurement leading to excessive goal displacement on the other.

This trial and error process cannot be accomplished in one or two years. Establishment of a management control system makes sense only if the agency can reasonably anticipate future stability. Aside from external considerations (e.g., change in political administrations), such stability is typically based on agencies which has, through organization development or some indigenous approach to human resources, undergone a process of goal clarification, consensus-seeking, and commitment-making. Without the process requiring the application of human behavioral skills, the management system will soon collapse due to poor design associated with the problems of influence differentiation, suboptimization, and goal displacement.

THE RELEVANCE OF RESEARCH DESIGN
TO CONTROL SYSTEMS

Administration under a management control system is different from routine management and consequently data collected under a management system are rarely the same as information collected prior to system installation. In considering the redesign of information collection for a new management system, decisions are made which will determine its success. Two common mistakes occur at this point:

1. Because of the heavy actual and psychological investment in the old data system there is strong pressure to make do with the old forms and procedures. Because new forms of data collection are expensive in time and energy there is also pressure to collect only the most readily available data, which is not necessarily what the management system may require.
2. For data which is available, there is a tendency to assume that the more, the better.

In contrast, the appropriate approach is to gather all the information actually required by the assumptions of the management system, and no more.

Knowing what data will fill the needs of a given management system is an issue dependent on the particular system and the particular agency. In general, however, the procedure is to develop a list of indicators through a trial-and-error process which seeks to minimize goal displacement and other problems discussed above. The indicators developed will ordinarily include elements in each of the major agency functions: personnel, budgeting, scheduling, service delivery, and so on. These indicators are then translated into reporting forms used in a research design.

You may be thinking, "Research designs are for academic study. I thought we were dealing with management control systems! Why do we need a research design at all?" Let's back up. What is it we are trying to get at in a management control system? In general we are trying to measure the relationship between the inputs we control and the outputs we want. Inputs include time, personnel, technology, and resources. Outputs include changes in clients, delivery of services, impacts on environments, and accomplishment of tasks. As we stated previously, the relationships are socio-technical. That is, they depend not only on a given means-ends technology (e.g., a structured job training program) but also on the social relationships among staff and clients.

It is true that research design is not needed in simple organizational environments in which the means-ends technology is both fully known and is fully determinant. By definition, in such simple systems we already know the input-output relationships that management control systems are intended to explicate. For that matter, in such simple contexts there is no need for a management control system at all, only routine reporting of input and output levels. In simple settings, management control systems only serve to quantify and justify agency operations, but management decision-making is not improved by having such systems and their cost in effort and resources is not justified.

At the other extreme, there is no need for research designs or management control systems in hyper complex administrative environments in which inputs and outputs are constantly changing, variables cannot be measured, or objectives are diffuse in nature. For example, the attempt to implement PPBS in the U.S. State Department was largely a failure. In extremely complex environments management control systems again become costly and unnecessary burdens. At best they may assist decision-making in some smaller, less complex subsystem of the agency.

Management control systems and the research designs that go with them are appropriate for organizations in a middle range of complexity. Such middle-range organizations are too complex for mere common sense to be adequate on the one hand, but not so complex on the other hand that they are beyond the state of the art of management control systems. While control systems advocates and consulting firms often sell such systems as universal in applicability, they are not. The attempt to apply them in inappropriate context leads to organizational problems of the first magnitude.

HOW RESEARCH DESIGN FITS IN

A management control system tracks data on inputs and relates them to outputs. Note the two parts: tracking and relating. Tracking data on inputs and outputs is the most obvious part, typically embedded in PPBS budget forms, MBO objective reports, performance evaluation systems and so on. This is the traditional management part. While the reporting may be more systematic and well-designed, the tracking function is not different in kind from pre-control system information management in most agencies. What makes control systems different is the analytic part which identifies presumed relationships of inputs to outputs. This relating process requires a research design because tracking and relating are two different processes.

In installing a management control system like ZBB, managers tend to fixate on the tracking part. After all, this is the data on which they make decisions. The control system's monthly reports of input levels (e.g., person-hours, expenditures) and program outputs (e.g., cases processed, social impacts, downtime, and externalities) seems at first glance all the manager needs. It is perfectly possible to design a management system with tracking as the only function.

A management control system, in contrast, requires the addition of a relating or analytic function. *How* are inputs related to outputs? *How* are costs related to benefits? In organizations of medium complexity the answers to these questions are often not obvious. We may know that 100 person-hours will result in an average of 1,000 papers being processed, but we are unlikely to know how many client effects will result. We are even less likely to know why sometimes many effects result and at other times there are few effects. Likewise it would be nice to know why units in some geographic areas are more effective than other units within the agency, or why the cost-benefit ratio is changing over time for the agency. These are control questions which require system changes beyond simple tracking. A management control system provides systematic means-ends analysis of this data using control variables. That is, cause-effect relationships are presented not on the basis of mere correlations which stand out from the tracked data (e.g., the units with more personnel have more output) but also take into account other variables (control variables) which may be at work (e.g., controlling for education, larger units may have less output since the output of educated staff is proportionately higher but educated staff are concentrated in the larger units, making them seem to have more output merely because they are larger).

Management systems such as MBO, PPBS, or ZBB may be used with solely a tracking function, or they may be operated in a more complex and sophisticated manner as management control systems. The latter require reliance on a research design. These range from the inexpensive but error-prone to the expensive but scientific. The most expensive and sophisticated are experimental designs as in the New Jersey Maintenance Experiment on guaranteed minimum wages and their social effects. Experimental designs require both randomly-selected treatment (receiving the income maintenance payments) and control (not receiving) groups, as well as time series data both before and after the treatment. Quasi-experimental designs are far more common, relying on such methods as time series analysis, replication, or other forms of multivariate analysis. Nonexperimental designs include before-after studies and comparisons of the given program with national norms.

Management systems and human behavioral approaches not only can but must be joined in attempts to establish management systems. The reasons for this have to do with the contributions that the organizational theory and organizational behavior literature have to make to processes which (1) start with questions about value clarification, as management systems do; and (2) require in their implementation a lengthy period of commitment-making and process refinement, as management systems also do. In this section on research design, we have sought to add the additional point that the most important management control questions require a systems approach which incorporates research into causal relationships. While this could be done in an autocratic manner by an elite group of experts, it is probably best done by thinking of the organization as a self-evaluating agency (see Wildavsky, 1972). That in turn requires a reliance on human behavioral concerns to prevent the management system's implementation fall into one of the numerous pitfalls discussed in the next section.

THE IMPLEMENTATION OF MANAGEMENT SYSTEMS

Although usually thought of as a "hard" intervention technique, implementation of a management system requires a full measure of attention to the so-called "soft" details of human behavioral considerations. Increasingly, systems analysts, industrial engineers, and others oriented toward "hard" approaches are involved in human behavioral intervention techniques as well. Without them, implementation of management systems often becomes unproductive. In this concluding section we present a real-world public-sector case study of just such an unsuccessful attempt to implement a management system. The pitfalls of implementation divorced from human behavioral approaches are outlined, followed by a summary of other managerial considerations in applying human behavioral concepts to management systems.

The Case of Performance Enhancement Monitoring Systems in Central City

The performance monitoring system (PEMS) was installed on a pilot basis in Central City's Department of Administration. Amid considerable fanfare, Mayor J. R. Givens, a lawyer who had campaigned "to put the city back on business management principles," announced that PEMS symbolized his administration's dedication to administrative reform. The system, he said, would soon spread throughout city government and lead to savings of hundreds of thousands of dollars. Secretary Susan Kiley, head of the Department of Administration and a close associate of the mayor, was equally committed to PEMS and saw it as an opportunity to demonstrate her professionalism in carrying out the mandates of the major.

Secretary Kiley had learned of PEMS from the mayor of a neighboring city and had brought it to the attention of Mayor Givens. Both saw PEMS as a general management system which could be implemented quickly for immediate demonstrable payoffs. Its purpose was to raise employee productivity through improvement of performance standards, task processes, and limitation on the number of personnel assigned to tasks. Tasks would be measured and performance standards set, after which a routine performance tracking system would document employee performances, whether above or below standard. To minimize implementation problems, there was to be no attempt to interface PEMS with existing performance appraisal personnel, or budgeting systems all of which continued as usual. To save money and time, PEMS omitted any organization development component.

While PEMS meant some extra work for the various department heads, Givens and Kiley felt that the demonstration effect of the benefits in the Department of Administration would soon overcome resistance to change. In addition, there was the political fact that this was a key symbol in Givens's program and Givens, as a strong mayor, could command the allegiance of his department heads.

Kiley slated the start-up of PEMS for fall 1998, with the first phase to be completed in the three major agencies of the Department of Administration by June 30, 1999. The following time schedule was adopted:

1. September 1 to October 15 training of PEMS analysts by consultants.
2. October 15 to November 1 orientation of agency employees to PEMS in general orientation sessions.
3. November 1 to January 15 time and motion studies measuring task accomplishment for employees in lower organizational levels; measurement at higher levels accomplished through analogous but more flexible techniques.
4. January 15 to April 15 (matching of standard times calculated on the basis of task measurement) with estimated manpower needs; calculation of projected agency workloads.
5. November 1 to April 15 simultaneously conducting process consultation to make recommendations regarding more efficient procedures, needed equipment investments, or changes in scheduling and assignments of personnel.
6. April 15 to May 15 formulation of recommended position changes (cuts to be made through attrition) and process changes, with opportunity for agency heads to respond.
7. May 15 to June 1 final report to the mayor; recommendation of reversion of net savings to the city council; preliminary negotiation of PEMS expansion plans.

On September 1, 1998, the mayor and some sixteen individuals gathered at the temporary PEMS office within the Department of Administration. Delegated by their agencies to receive PEMS training were a broad range of personnel, including civil engineers, personnel analysts, and administrative assistants, even secretaries. Some had training in PPBS or other management systems, but others had not. Of those who had such exposure, the experiences were sometimes with failed systems. As a group they were younger personnel, energetic and eager for an opportunity to expand their career horizons through new professional experiences. Although their training was only six weeks in duration, it was intense and left the PEMS analysts highly motivated.

Although few questions were raised by employees at the general orientation sessions, when actual PEMS analysis began in November the analysts found
considerable employee resistance to measurement. In some agencies resistance
was greater than in others. When position cut recommendations were made in
April, these problems came to a crisis point.

When that point was reached the mayor, preoccupied with other problems, was presented with a difficult decision. The proposed cuts were opposed
by his agency heads, who felt the PEMS system was not taking all important
considerations into account. When these agency heads appealed to the mayor to
restore their cut personnel, the mayor ruled in their favor, preferring to go with
known and trusted political allies rather than an uncertain new management
system. The PEMS office found itself unable to argue with the mayor or, for
that matter, with the city Personnel Office and Budget Office, both of which
supported the agency heads argument that their original position justifications
had been properly documented and approved demonstrating need, PEMS
notwithstanding.

Though PEMS was completed in the Department of Administration and
considerable savings identified, other departments failed to adopt it. Identified
savings reverted to the City Council which, while pleased, was preoccupied with
other matters. The PEMS analysts were eventually returned to the same positions
from which they had been borrowed. Their home-agency superiors showed little
interest in the PEMS project. In the end, some process changes were made and a
number of low-level clerical and service positions were eliminated. The distribution of these cuts was not very different from that brought about by position
freezes previous mayors had imposed. Nonetheless, when a new productivity
system was installed two years later, some of the PEMS lessons were incorporated and the PEMS implementation attempt was, at a minimum, a useful, if not
always appreciated learning experience for city government.

Lessons of the Central City Case

What are the lessons of a case like PEMS in Central City, from a human behavioral point of view? There are many. For our purposes, however, ten can be identified for brief discussion.

1. Rational Systems Versus Human Systems

There is a common but mistaken belief that if a system works it will spread
by the force of its own example. This argument equates the demonstration effect
in the public sector with the effect of competitive advantage in the private marketplace. Unlike the business marketplace in the public sector there is no force
equivalent to the profit motive as tied to consumer choice. The mere demonstration that a particular innovation is worthy is rarely in itself a strong motivator for

change when installation of a new management system has high costs in terms of personnel, resources, and opportunities. While it might be rational to expect change on the basis of demonstration that a management system is cost-effective, the reality is that human systems respond in a more complex manner requiring other motivators be built into the project design.

2.   The Limits of Command

In Central City it was assumed that the mayor's political authority would suffice to effect whatever changes were not motivated by the demonstration effect. While this might be true in some circumstances, the PEMS planners did not realistically assess the limits of political authority. If political command is to be the central motivator in a management system implementation, it must be more than a mere initial blessing; it must be a strong, continuing direct involvement by the chief executive. Chief executives, however, can rarely devote adequate time to management system implementation. Policy matters seem more important, the management system seems technical and mystifying, and there is an assumption that administrative matters should be something subordinates take care of. Beyond publicizing systems like PEMS as symbols ("Yes, we have one!") the chief executive will rarely find political advantage in associating with the details of management systems design and implementation. In fact, to the extent the system envisions personnel and program cuts, the chief executive may want to maintain considerable distance from these details so as to preserve his options.

3.   Equity For Major Actors

Every successful system implementation rests on a self-reinforcing incentive structure. In Central City, all system benefits reverted to the city council (albeit with political status benefits accruing to the Mayor and Secretary of Administration). This has a certain rationale in public administration since the legislative branch is supposed to make allocation decisions. In reality, however, not much can be said in favor of a system which fails to distribute benefits among those whose support is necessary for system success. For example, it would have been a better design to revert part of savings back to agency heads for funding of new, approved projects using savings derived from productivity-related cuts brought about by PEMS. A willingness to design a system with incentives for all major actors requires a relatively high degree of managerial sophistication, sacrificing short-run gains for the top actor (e.g., the city council) in favor of greater long-run gains through greater system effectiveness based on an equitable incentive system.

4.   Equity For Minor Actors

Most management systems impact lowest-level employees more adversely than managerial employees. Ironically, it is these employees who have the least to say about their tasks. To the extent they are performing tasks inefficiently or unnecessarily, it is often their superiors who are to blame. On the other hand, since personnel costs are a high percentage of total costs in public administration, and since lower-level personnel are the bulk of all personnel costs, it is inevitable that savings engendered by a management system will come heavily through position cuts at lower levels. These in turn bring demoralization and opposition (particularly in unionized jurisdictions). Although a policy of layoffs through attrition is a major remedy, it should be recognized that the implementation of management systems has major externalities in the form of social costs. Part of the system benefits should be dedicated to these costs as, for example, through establishment of relocation and retraining funds.

5. Process Needs

It is tempting to treat human behavioral approaches as an unnecessary frill. Why not take the direct approach to implementing a system like PEMS? The direct approach, it is reasoned, would save considerable time and money. Human behavioral corollaries to management system implementation are necessary for three reasons, however: (1) because general orientation meetings are an inadequate way to overcome almost-inevitable employee resistance to change; (2) because participation in the system design process is necessary to invest managers and employees with a sense of ownership in the system; and (3) because the organization must be acculturated to better understanding of each actor's role and needs in the new system to be implemented. Goal-setting, team-building, and other thrusts of organization development and like human behavioral approaches are fundamental to achieving a design responsive to these three needs.

6. Time Frame

Organizational change is a process which requires a longer time frame than does a technical change requiring only a solution. If a chief executive forges ahead with management system installation in a short period, and one year is too short, adequate organization development programs, adequate training programs, and adequate negotiation of coordination of the new system with old arrangements cannot be undertaken in time. Without these, failure follows.

7. Staffing Needs

Central City staffing was inadequate because junior personnel were selected to become PEMS analysts. This role called for them to come into agencies as outsiders, evaluate management practices, and recommend budget cuts for senior agency heads. This sort of "whiz kid" strategy occasionally works, as when under President Kennedy, Secretary of Defense Robert McNamara installed

PPBS using a junior staff. But in that case junior status was counterbalanced by prestigious professional credentials and a triumphant success record in private industry. Lacking both position and professional status, the Central City PEMS analysts lacked the credibility to effectively defend their recommendations. Affected managers rightly claimed equal or greater professionalism in their opposition to PEMS recommendations, arguing that a six-week training program could not produce analysts of high caliber. And in fact, the short training program was inadequate to establish analyst self-confidence, let alone credibility with skeptical superiors.

8. Career Development Needs

The Central City PEMS system lacked a career development program for its analysts (just as it was isolated from all other Personnel Office functions). Although seemingly small, this was a critical omission. A key incentive for participation as a PEMS analyst was the prospect of career development. In practice, returning analysts found that back in their home agencies their PEMS experience was ignored. Instead, they found they were now out of touch with agency plans and programs and had to catch up to reestablish themselves. Needless to say, this was demoralizing to the analyst staff and was a significant factor in the discrediting of the PEMS program.

9. Program Coordination Needs

Management control systems are often marked by a self-defeating faddishness. PPBS, ZBB, and other systems come and go in rapid succession. When a new system like PEMS is to be tried, it faces an expectation that it too will soon pass. Officials prepared to "hunker down" for a year while it blows over. The passing of each system makes implementation of the next more difficult. This is so not only because of the skepticism faddishness breeds but also because each successive system leaves lingering residues which compete with the new system. Although requiring a much longer time frame, ideally the new system would be thoroughly coordinated with existing procedures in personnel, budgeting, and other "overhead" functions.

10. Setting Expectations

Most management systems are oversold initially, setting the stage for later disillusionment and abolition. By presenting the PEMS system as appropriate for all aspects of tasks at any level, in any department, a commitment was made to implement PEMS even in complex settings where it was inappropriate. Task measurement for lower-level employees, for example, was universalized into performance measurement for all employees. Unfortunately, the failure of performance measurement for nonroutine higher-level jobs then becomes generalized as a judgment that all task measurement is invalid. Once this expectation is set, strong pressure exists to shift away from the rejected function toward other functions. In the case of PEMS at Central City the shift was toward process consulting (providing particularlistic advice about agency-specific tasks), a function which varied greatly from agency to agency. In essence, as PEMS failed to meet unduly high expectations regarding its core technology (task measurement) it shifted toward peripheral functions The setting of over-high expectations leads routinely toward goal displacement, often followed by fragmentation of the management system.

MANAGEMENT IMPLICATIONS

At almost every point the management of systems implementation involves human behavioral considerations treated in the literature on administration (see Garson and Brenneman, 1981a, 1981b; Bryson and Roering, 1988; Swiss, 1991; Swiss, 1995). For example, Britan (1981) studied a major productivity program in the U.S. Department of Commerce and found that the relative failure of the program to achieve substantial results was understandable only through an emphasis on examination of personal understandings and relationships of the sort studied by students of organizational behavior. Wallach (1979) likewise emphasizes the importance of training in system changes. With regard to human behavioral approaches of the participatory type, the need for these is highlighted in Draper and Pitsvada's study (1981) of ZBB, emphasizing investment in the system through participation. Likewise, participatory methods are viewed as critical in Gregg and Diegelman's (1979) study of productivity systems in the Law Enforcement Assistance Administration and by Simon (1978) in his study of management information system development and the need for team approaches.

To the student of human behavior in organizations, many of the considerations outlined in this chapter will seem like common sense. Unfortunately, they are not! In the real world of public administration it is more common than not to find even the most elementary human behavioral approaches ignored in favor of "hard," "direct," and "rational" implementation of management systems. Often, when such methods later fail, the organization's members are faulted as being too uncooperative or too ignorant to implement the system. We hypothesize that in the vast majority of such instances the system in question displayed poor incentive system design, failure to utilize organization development approaches, omission of human resource planning (e.g., career development), and other failures to apply human behavioral approaches. What is needed is a recognition of the sociotechnical nature of public organizations. The concept of the public manager as the controller of technical systems must be abandoned in favor of the concept of the public manager as designer of social as well as technical systems for the agency.

REFERENCES AND ADDITIONAL READING

Ackermann, R. (1992). "Strategic Direction Through Burning Issues: Using SODA as a Strategic Decision Support System." *OR Insight*, 5(3):pp 24–28.

Agranoff, R. (1989). "Managing Intergovernmental Processes." In J. L. Perry (ed.), *Handbook of Public Administration*. San Francisco: Jossey-Bass.

Ammons, David N. (1996). *Municipal Benchmarks: Assessing Local Performance and Establishing Community Standards*. Thousand Oaks, California: Sage Publications.

Ammons, David N. (1995). *Accountability for Performance:Measuring and Monitoring in Local Government*. Washington D.C.: International City\County Management Assocation.

Alter, Allan E. (1995). "Silicon Valley Civics." in David N. Ammons, *Accountability for Performance: Measurement and Monitoring in Local Government*. Washington D.C.: International City\County Management Assocation.

Bachrach, P. and M. S. Baratz (1963). "Decisions and Non-Decisions: An Analytical Framework." *American Political Science Review*, Vol. 57:pp 632–642.

Bartlett, C. A., and S. Ghoshal (1994). "Changing the Role of Top Management: Beyond Strategy to Purpose." *Harvard Business Review*, Nov./Dec., pp 79–88.

Berry, F. S. and B. Wechsler (1995). "State Agencies Experience with Strategic Planning: Findings from a National Survey" *Public Administration Review*, 55(2):pp 159–168.

Bower, Joseph L. (1983). "Managing For Equity." *Harvard Business Review*, July/August.

Britan, G. M. (1981). *Bureaucracy and Innovation: An Ethnography of Change*. Beverly Hills, California: Sage Publishing Company.

Bryson, J. M. and William D. Roeing (1988). "Initation of Strategic Planning by Governments." *Public Administration Review*, 48(6):p 995–1003.

Bryson, J. M. (1990). "Know Thy Stakeholders." Government Executive, 22(4):pp 46.

Bryson, J. M., and F. K. Alston (1995). *Creating and Implementing Your Stratigic Plan: A Workbook for Public and Nonprofit Organizations*. San Francisco: Jossey-Bass.

Bryson, J. M. and C. B. Finn (1995). "Development and Use of Strategy Maps to Enhance Organizational Performance." In A. Halachmi and G. Bouckaert (eds.), *The Challenge of Management in a Changing World*. San Francisco: Jossey-Bass.

Bryson, J. M. (1995). *Strategic Planning For Public and Nonprofit Organizations*. San Franscisco: Jossey-Bass

Churchill, Neil C. (1984). "Budget Choice: Planning vs. Control." *Harvard Business Review*, July/August:pp 150–163.

Crow, Micheal and Barry Bozeman (1983). "Strategic Public Management." in John M. Bryson and Robert C. Einsweiler, (eds.), *Strategic Planning Threats and Opportunities For Planners*. Washington, D.C.: Planners Press.

Daley, Dennis (1992). *Performance Appraisal in the Public Sector*. Westport, CT: Quorum.

Draper, Frank U. and B. T. Pitsvada (1981). "ZBB-Looking Back After Ten Years." *Public Administration Review*, 41(1):pp 73–75.

Eadie, Douglas C. (1983). "Putting a Powerful Tool to Practical Use: The Application of Strategic Planning in the Public Sector." *Public Administration Review*:pp 447–452.

Ford, Charles H. (1980). "Manage by Decisions, Not by Objectives." *Business Horizons*, 23(1):pp 7–18.

Garson, G. David (1981). "From Policy Science to Policy Analysis: A QuarterCentury of Progress?" *Policy Studies Journal*, 9(4) (Special Issue L2):pp 535–543.

Garson, G. David and D. S. Brenneman (1981a). "Limits of the Rational Model of Resource Rationing." *Southern Review of Public Administration*, 5(1):pp 5–21.

Garson, G. David and D. S. Brenneman (1981b). "Incentive Systems and Goal Displacement in Personnel Resource Management." *Review of Public Administration*, Spring:pp 1–12.

Gawthrop, Louis C. (1984). *Public Sector Management, Systems, and Ethics*. Bloomington, Indiana: Indiana University Press, p.173.

Granvold, D. K. (1978). "Supervision by Objectives." *Administration in Social Work*, 2(2):pp 199–209.

Griesemer, James R. (1995). "The Power of Performance Measurement: A Computer Performance Model." in David N. Ammons, *Accountability for Performance: Measurement and Monitoring in Local Government*. Washington D.C.: International City\County Management Assocation.

Gray, Danial H. (1986). "Use and Misuses of Strategic Planning." *Harvard Business Review*, Jan./Feb.:pp 89–97.

Gregg, James M. and R. F. Diegelman (1979). "Red Tape on Trial: Elements of a Successful Effort to Cut Burdensome Federal Reporting Requirements." *Public Administration Review*, 39(2):pp 171–175.

Gremillion, Lee L., J. L. McKenney, and P. J. Pyburn (1980). "Program Planning in the National Forest Service." *Public Administration Review*, 2(3):pp 226–230.

Grizzle, Glona (1984). "Devloping Standards for Interpreting Agency Performance: An Exploration of Three Models." *Public Administration Review*, 44(2):pp 128–129.

Halachmi, A. and Boydston, R. (1991). "Strategic Management with Annual and Multi-Year Operating Budgets." *Public Budgeting and Financial Management*, 3(2):pp 293–316.

Hayes, Robert H. (1985) "Strategic Planning-Forward in Reverse." *Harvard Business Review*, Nov./Dec.:pp 111–119.

Herman, R. D., and Associates (1994). *The Jossey-Bass Handbook of Nonprofit Leadership and Management*. San Francisco: Jossey-Bass.

Hirsh, Richard F. (1986). "How Success Short-Circuits the Future." *Harvard Business Review*, March/April:pp 72–76.

Honadle, Beth W. (1981). "A Capacity-Building Framework: A Search for Concepts and Purpose." *Public Administration Review*, 41(5):pp 575–580.

Huse, Edgar A. (1980). *Organization Development and Change*, 2nd Edition. St. Paul, Minn.: West.

Kemp, R. I. (1993). *Strategic Planning of Local Government*. Jefferson, N.C.: McFarland.

Landau, Martin and Russell Stou Jr. (1979). "To Manage is Not to Control: or the Folly of Type II Errors." *Public Administration Review*, 39(2):pp 148–156.

McConkie, Mark L. (1979). "Classifying and Reviewing Empirical Work on MBO: Some Implications." *Group and Organization Studies*, 4(4):pp 461–475.

McGreggor, Eugene B. Jr. (1988). "The Public Human Resource Puzzle: Strategic Management of a Strategic Resource." *Public Administration Review*, 48(6):pp 941–950.

McTighe, John T. (1979). "Management Strategies to Deal with Shrinking Resources." *Public Administration Review*, 39(1):pp 86–90.

Mintzberg, H. (1994a). "The Fall and Rise of Strategic Planning." *Harvard Business Review*, Jan./Feb., pp 107–114.

Mintzberg, H. (1994b). *The Rise and Fall of Strategic Planning*. New York: Free Press.

Mitroff, I. T. and C. M. Pearson (1993). *Crisis Management: A Diagnostic Guide for Improving Your Organization's Crisis-Preparedness*. San Francisco: Jossey-Bass.

Moore, Perry (1980). "Zero-Base Budgeting in American Cities." *Public Administration Review*, 40(3):pp 253–258.

Moore, Perry D. and Ted Staton (1981). "Management by Objectives in American Cities." *Public Personnel Management Journal*, 10(2):pp 223–232.

Nanus, B. (1992). *Visionary Leadership: Creating a Compelling Sense of Direction for Your Organization*. San Francisco: Jossey-Bass.

Natemeyer, Walter E., ed. (1978). *Classics of Organizational Behavior*. Oak Park, IL: Moor Publishing Company.

Nutt, P. C. (1984a). "A Strategic Planning Network for Non-Profit Organizations." *Strategic Management Journal*, Vol. 5:pp 57–75.

Nutt, P. C. (1984b). "Types of Organizational Decision Processes." *Administrative Science Quarterly*, Vol. 29:pp 414–450.

Nutt, P. C. and R. Backoff (1992). *trategic Management for Public and Third Sector Organizations: A Handbook for Leaders*. San Francisco: Jossey-Bass.

Nutt, P. C., and R. Backoff (1995). "Strategy for Public and Third Sector Organizations," *Journal of Public Administration Research and Theory*, 5(2):pp 189–211.

Osborne, David, and Ted Gaebler (1995). "The Art of Performance Measurement." in David N. Ammons, *Accountability for Performance: Measurement and Monitoring in Local Government*. Washington D.C.: International City County Management Assocation.

Pasmore, William A. (1994). Creating Strategic Change. New York: John Wiley and Sons.

Peters, Thomas J. (1980). "Management Systems: The Language of Organizational Character and Competence." *Organizational Dynamics*, Volume 9, Summer:pp 2–26.

Pinchot, Clifford and Elizabeth Pinchot (1994). *The End of Bureacracy and the Rise of Intelligent Organizations*. San Francisco: Berett-Koehler Publishers.

Poister, Theodore H. (1984). "The Use Management Tools in Municipal Government: A National Survey." *Public Administration Review*, 44(3):pp 215–223.

Poister, Theodore H. (1995). "Productivity Monitoring: Systems, Indicators, and Analysis." in David N. Ammons, *Accountability for Performance: Measurement and*

Monitoring in Local Government. Washington D.C.: International City\County Management Assocation.

Ring, Peter S. and James L. Perry (1985). "Strategic Planning in Public and Private Organazations: Implication of Distinctive Contexts and Constraints." *Academy of Management Review*, Vol.10:pp 276–286.

Rosen, Ellen Doree. (1995). "Measuring Productivity." in David N. Ammons, *Accountability for Performance: Measurement and Monitoring in Local Government.* Washington D.C.: International City\County Management Assocation.

Sauser, William I. Jr. (1980). "Evaluating Employee Performance: Needs, Problems, Possible Solutions." *Public Personnel Management*, 9(1):pp 11–18.

Simon, Sidney H. (1978). "Personnel's Role in Developing an Information System." *Personnel Journal*, 57(11):pp 622–625.

Spano, R. M., T. J. Kiresuk, and S. H. Lund (1977). "An Operational Model to Achieve Accountability in Social Work in Health Care." *Social Work in Health Care*, 3(2):pp 123–141.

Swiss, James E. (1995). "Performance Monitoring Systems." in David N. Ammons, *Accountability for Performance: Measurement and Monitoring in Local Government*. Washington D.C.: International City\County Management Assocation.

Swiss, James E. (1991). *Public Management Systems: Monitoring and Managing Government Performance*. Englewood Cliffs: New Jersey Prentice Hall.

Tannenbaum, Arnold S. (1962). "Control in Organizations: Individual Adjustment and Organizational Performance." *Public Administration Review*, 7(2):pp 236–257.

Tracy, Richard C. and Ellen P. Jean (1995). "Experimenting with SEA Reporting in Poland." in David N. Ammons, *Accountability for Performance: Measurement and Monitoring in Local Government*. Washington D.C.: International City\County Management Assocation.

Wallach, Arthur E. (1979). "System Changes Begin in the Training Department." *Personnel Journal*, 58(12):pp 464–484.

Wildavsky, Aaron (1972). "The Self-Evaluating Organization." *Public Administration Review*, 32(5):pp 509–520.

Zedlewski, Edwin W. (1979). "Performance Measurement in Public Agencies: The Law Enforcement Evolution." *Public Administration Review*, 39(5):pp 488–492.

11
Information, Computers, and Organization Theory in Public Management

The study of computer information systems is multi-disciplinary, fragmented among hundreds of disparate concerns often of a narrow, applied nature (Studer, 1972). Attending a national meeting such as that of the Association for Computing Machinery immediately reveals that this is a field which brings together odd bedfellows, ranging from sociologists broadly concerned with technology and social change to programmers concerned only with developments regarding a particular computer language. Although theories *for* information systems management, such as TQM, have been applied to computer environments (CAUSE, 1994; Collins, 1994), and although the value of information systems in implementing theories like TQM is recognized (Hendrick, 1994), theories *of* information systems have received less attention. However, in spite of its generally theoretic nature (Cooper, 1988 p. 92), organization theory applies to information systems as it has to traditional public administration areas (Garson, 1989a).

Labels used to designate the field of information systems illustrate a gradual evolution toward broader themes of greater theoretical significance. Early on the term "data processing" was a synonym for information systems, denoting the processing of large transaction databases (e.g., accounts receivable) by mainframe computers. Later management information systems (MIS) became a more common term, indicating that information systems were not just transaction processing but also included systems for human resource management, financial analysis, project planning, and the full range of management functions. Even more recently, information resource management (IRM) has taken center stage, differentiating a concern for higher-management decision-making needs in contrast to middle management MIS needs (Jackowski, 1988). These semantic differences are, of course, not accepted by all writers. Authors like Cooper (1988, p. 76) use "MIS" to describe "IRM" concerns for research on strategy, public policy, effectiveness issues, and information requirements analysis, while others

311

may use "IRM" to refer to routine transaction processing. Regardless of semantics, the central point is that information systems as a field has become more differentiated and more theory-oriented over time.

POLICY STUDIES VERSUS ORGANIZATION THEORY

Sharon Caudle's widely circulated 1987 essay indicated one direction in which organization theory for MIS/IRM needs to develop. This essay, and the National Academy of Public Administration study which followed, faulted public administration educators for emphasizing computer technology at the expense of information resource management and strategic information planning (Caudle, 1987). Caudle's essay drew on Paul Strassman's *The Information Payoff* (1985), a book which urged refocusing MIS on information for productivity enhancement, productivity measurement, questions of employee attitudes and motivation, on organization design/structure questions, and on issues of privacy and security.

Caudle urged public administration educators to focus on basic questions. What is information for? Does it support the agency mission? Who uses information and for what decisions? What types of reports are wanted? Who are the external users. Where does information come from? How is reliability assured? How is security assured? How is speed and timeliness assured? Who is responsible? Who pays? What strategies exist for preventing information systems from assuming a life of its own? Who is allowed to read and write data? What is the impact or penetration of MIS within the agency and its environment? How is information disseminated? What property rights exist regarding information created? What competition with the private sector is allowed? What provision is made for data archiving? For data elimination? To maintain data integrity? How are data linked for retrieval? What are the organization inputs to MIS design? How is MIS evaluated?

These and other questions make up the study of information systems from a policy studies perspective. They quickly lead to study of policy formation, implementation, government decision-making, communications, budgetary analysis, and other public administration fields.[1]

> The use of modern computers in scientific and engineering research over the last three decades has led to the inescapable conclusion that a third branch of scientific methodology has been created. It is now widely acknowledged that, along with the traditional experimental and theoretical methodologies, advanced work in all areas of science and technology has come to rely critically on the computational approach. Accordingly, for the advancement of the scientific and technological base of our nation, it is essential to maintain the U.S. leadership advantage in scientific computing (Rheinboldt, 1985, p. 5).

Policy studies tend to focus on supporting management decision-making and operational productivity. However, the quotation above reminds us that there is an epistemological dimension to information systems as well. Epistemology refers to information technology impacts on issues of data use, research methods, and theory development (Morell, 1989). That is, while the push for information resource management has come from those concerned with applied policy knowledge (sometimes at a high level), there is an equally if not more critical pure research dimension as well.

This pure research dimension is, of course, organization theory of information systems. Ultimately the well-founded conception of information systems, built on sound organization theory, may be as important to the nation's information infrastructure as are applied policies for creating IRM coordinators or instituting information needs assessments in major agencies. Pure research on information technology, the study of organization theory, plays a singularly significant role because it seeks to provide the context of meaning from which all else proceeds—or so its developers wish.

TYPOLOGICAL FRAMEWORKS AS ORGANIZATION THEORY

Though not organization theory in the view of this author, many would accept as theory various typological frameworks set forth to provide a set of intellectual boxes by which to organize information about the complex and rapidly-changing world of computing and MIS. Most of these frameworks draw from systems theory vocabulary, itself based on computer imagery. There are almost as many typological frameworks of MIS/IRM as there are professors of it, and many of them quite useful (see Anderson, 1985).

One of the best known typologies is that by Ives et al., (1980), whose framework synthesized several earlier efforts and was used by them to classify some 300 doctoral dissertation on MIS subjects. This framework depicts the information system (IS) as embedded in the organization environment, which in turn is embedded in an external environment. The IS itself is divided into three environments: those associated with primary users and their applications, with development, and with operations. Using this set of categories various authors have successfully organized vast MIS research literatures (e.g., Lyytinen, 1987a; Cooper, 1988). discussing, for instance the interface of the IS with the external environment or with the organization, and identifying IS problems associated with use, development, or operations.

The most interesting typologies are those which are empirically grounded. That is, they emerge not from abstract reasoning but from real-world needs, sometimes involving the joint activity of many scholars and practitioners (Glaser and Strauss, 1967). For instance, Wellar's (1988) typology was used by the Urban and Regional Information Systems Association (URISA) to organized its research agenda conference sessions. Loosely following the systems theory concepts of input-throughput-output, Wellar organized MIS research issues into a tripartite division:

1. Database Development (access, archiving, assembly, documentation, formats, integrity, quality, sources, structures, standards, transfer, relating, and sampling of data);
2. Technical and Technological Initiatives and Implications (benchmark testing, systems integration, complex database systems, geographic information systems, expert systems, and artificial intelligence);
3. Institutional Impacts, Adjustments, Structures, Functions, and Relationships (managerial impacts, public impacts, productivity effects, evaluation, decision support and strategic planning, user education, conflict resolution, and futurism).

Another grounded typology is implicit in the structure of special interest groups which have emerged over the 40-year history of the Association for Computing Machinery (ACM). The ACM now has formal groups of scholars and practitioners who have chosen to band together in 31 areas of concern[2], constituting a form of typology (Cochran, 1987, p. 869).

Typologies use generalized categories the way a file cabinet uses drawers to organize information. They may serve as convenient checklists of considerations in certain circumstances. But typological frameworks lack a propositional basis and thus are of relatively little use in the way a guidebook is useful. Organization theory is looking for guidebooks, not file cabinets. Typologies, however grounded in successful actual use, are not theory in the sense of others to be discussed below. They are simply meant to be a set of boxes to organize knowledge. Typologies may be called frameworks or even theoretical frameworks, but by their nature, they do not (and are not meant) to predict patterns of growth, to explore effects of economic or other determinants, or to understand the cause and effect of impacts of information technology. In short, they are not organization theory in the definition used in this chapter.

STAGES-OF-GROWTH THEORIES OF MIS

The leading early attempts at organization theory for information systems focused on developing a stage theory of its evolution. Prior to the "microcomputer revolution" and MIS decentralization in the 1980s, information systems seemed to evolve according to a predictable pattern which made an organic, stages-of-growth theory seem natural.[3]

Classic Stage Theory: Maturation of the Center

Early stages-of-growth concepts were explored by Robert Anthony (1965), who developed a theory of organization development based on the transition from operations to control to planning issues, with each stage marked by the dominance of a different level of business structure. But it was a later writer, Richard Nolan (1973, 1977, 1979; see also Gibson and Nolan, 1974), who set forth what became the most widely accepted stage theory. Nolan first envisioned four and later six evolutionary stages leading MIS from infancy to maturation of the central management information system unit within the organization. Nolan believed that unless forces external to the MIS process intervened (e.g., a major turnover of top management), organizations would progress through these stages, rarely skipping any one of them:

1. INITIATION: functional departments utilize computers to reduce costs; end-users are largely oblivious to the changes; top management is not much involved. Computing starts in the payroll, benefits, accounting and billing units. Most departments and most users are quite isolated from the ADP unit, which is organized into two small subdivisions: (1) the analyst and programmers, and (2) the computer operators. Top management exercises little control. Inexperience leads to various fiascos and blunders. Equipment vendors, notably IBM, provide assistance to larger accounts to protect their market reputation.

2. CONTAGION: cost-reducing applications proliferate; users display growing enthusiasm; some end-users become programmers; top management control remains lax. In the second stage the earlier success of the accounting department leads other units to attempt computerization. User enthusiasm increases and applications proliferate. The ADP unit becomes overextended and backlogs develop or outright delivery failures occur. The initial responses of the ADP unit are to request more staff and to place them under their best ex-programmers and extechnical staff people. These are individuals who are promoted into ADP management in spite of the fact they lack the training, experience, and perhaps even the ability for management, instead having credentials in technical areas. Top management sees the need for greater professional managerial control and coordination.

3. CONTROL: rising costs force management to hold some users more accountable; there is a growing concern for documentation of MIS applications; a "DP" function is formalized at the middle management level. In this stage, management creates a formal, professional organization structure for MIS. Often outside professionals are hired. Stage two informality is displaced by stage three formal procedure. User charges for computing are systematized. The ADP unit develops its

own professional elite culture, creating further distance between itself
and end users. Top management recognizes the MIS administrator on
a collegial basis, if not actually incorporating this role into the top
management inner circle. The ADP unit is now seen as an MIS unit,
and it struggles to serve the increased needs for base functions (e.g.,
accounting) and also top management decision support reports. Middle and lower managers' needs are often neglected.

4.   INTEGRATION: The central "DP" (data processing) office becomes
     fully established; applications are retrofitted to a standard database
     technology; end-users must justify new applications as cost-effective
     and must get clearance; the overall theme is catching up with the
     needs resulting from pent-up user demands from stage three.
5.   DATA ADMINISTRATION: The organization focuses on creating an
     integrated applications system with emphasis on shared data and com-
     mon systems.
6.   MATURITY: Planning and control become a central focus of manage-
     ment; applications are well integrated with information flow within
     the organization; shared data and common systems are regarded as a
     strategic resource.

The problem with Nolan's stage theory was that it tended to place the "end
of history" somewhere in the late 1970s insofar as MIS development was concerned. In an S-curve of development, slow initial growth gave way to fast succession of middle stages, then leveled off at a plateau (maturity). The
"microcomputer revolution" of the 1980s was not predicted by Nolan's "maturity" stage. The decentralization it brought seemed to threaten two decades of
evolution toward centralized integration, undoing so much that had been
achieved over a long period of time (Nolan, 1979).

Although Nolan's stage theory was found to fit a number of cases and to be
useful for analytic purposes (e.g., Herzlinger, 1977; Guimaraes, 1981; McFarlan,
1981; Saarinen, 1987), it did not fare well among the critics. A review of the literature by Benbasit et al., (1984) found its testable propositions not to be supported. Likewise, King and Kraemer (1984) found in Nolan's stage theory
conceptual problems which accounted for the failure to validate it. Other studies
found the stage theory to be plausible in some respects but to be contradicted by
evidence in others (Lucas and Sutton, 1977; Goldstein and McCririck, 1981;
Drury, 1983).

Many of the criticisms had to do with Nolan's description of the later
stages of growth and incompatibilities with actual developments of the 1970s
and 1980s. Some scholars tried to adapt its basic theory of maturation to fit
the world of the 1980s. Some preferred a simplified four-stage model, with
the fourth being "maturity" (McFarlan and McKinney, 1983, p. 183; Murray,

1988, p. 230). Enslin (1984) advocated a five-stage pattern: (1) introduction of ADP for cost-reduction purposes, usually in the financial area; (2) ADP spreads to other functional areas throughout the organization; (3) management realizes that the huge promised cost savings of ADP are illusory and there is a moratorium on computer investment; (4) attention comes to center on MIS as an approach to greater organizational effectiveness, not necessarily cost minimization; and (5) the organization moves toward creation of an MIS oriented toward management decision-making using an organization-wide database.

Yet other authors such as Lockhart (1981), extended Nolan's basic schema to six stages, the last of which pointed toward information resource management as the culmination of a mature data processing organization. An ethnographic study by Mathew (1994), though not explicitly testing Nolan's theories, provided support for it in viewing the evolution of information systems management as one guided by the production ethos of "Fordism," a drive for managerial control over all organizational processes, using TQM and other strategies to reconcile classic assembly-line production principles with contemporary organizations' need for flexibility.

A Second Stage Theory: Functional Information Integration

Where Nolan's stage theory focused on the maturation of the center, a second stage theory version focused on the integration of information processes. Where Nolan's theory was structural in emphasis, this second stage theory was functional in nature. That is, in this second set of stage theories, "information integration" was not equated with structural centralization as Nolan had believed. Rather functional integration could be achieved with decentralized structure according to the second stage theory. This made the second stage theory more consistent with the rise of distributed client-server processing in the 1985–1995 period (see Wong, 1988).

A recent contribution to stage theory of the functional information integration genre, reflecting intellectual movement away from the first set of stage theories to the second, is that of Huff et al., (1988), who apply Nolan's maturation concept to end user computing—a phenomena central to criticisms of Nolan's early work. These authors see five stages to end user computing:

1. Isolation. Experimentation without major use of job-relevant data.
2. Stand-Alone. Job-relevant data is entered manually and is not exchanged among applications.
3. Manual Integration. Data are exchanged by physical transfer of disks or by manual local area network transactions.
4. Automated Integration. Data are transferred routinely and automati-

cally among personal workstations and mainframes using automated processes built into applications software.

5. Distributed Integration. Applications are part of a network which transparently accesses data, the location of which does not matter to the end user.

This theory clearly assumes an organization-wide evolution toward distributed information integration, the hallmark of this second set of stage theories and its point of differentiation from the other two.

Looking back over the short history of management information systems and projecting into the future, authors such as Marchand and Kresslein (1988) discerned four stages of MIS growth. These four stages relate to intrinsic tendencies within management information systems toward the ever greater integration of information, culminating in information resource management (IRM):

1. *Physical Control, 1900–1960*: Based on typewriters, telephones, filing cabinets, adding machines, and microfilm, management practices centered on issues having to do with organizing records, correspondence, reports, directives, and other paperwork in terms of physical office design and layout.

2. *Automation, 1960–1975*: Based on early data processing, word processing, duplication, and telecommunications, management practices centered on issues of technical efficiency, often leading to functionally separate word processing centers, duplication centers, data processing centers, and telecommunications units.

3. *IRM, 1975–1985*: Based on distributed data processing, integrated voice/data communications, multi-function workstations, and microcomputers, management practices focus on issues of linking IRM to agency-wide planning processes and horizontal integration of information across the agency.

4. *Knowledge Management, 1985–?*: Based on expert systems and decision support software, management issues are integration of information and policy planning throughout the agency with high interdependence of information technology and decision-making at all levels.[4]

As agencies matured through these stages, Marchand and Kresslein believed, the status of IRM administrators would tend to increase. "Recognition of an organization's dependence on effective knowledge management," they stated, "will become an essential management attribute and influence the basic operating philosophy of senior managers in government and business" (p. 411).

In broader terms, Marchand and Kresslein saw information resource management evolving from fragmentation, reaction, and project orientation toward integration, proactive policies, and agency-orientation. Information itself tends to evolve from being a "free good" of an unstandardized nature with limited user access to being standardized and available on networks at a fee. Users evolve from low literacy, limited involvement, and low awareness to high skill, high expectations, and broad participation in the IRM arena. Staff evolve from centralized, technical orientations to orientations toward distributed processing, user-orientation, and emphasis on broad management skills. Finally, the agency office itself evolves from having a few stations and only pilot electronic mail with limited connectivity toward integrated networks of many personal computers, teleconferencing, and integrated voice, data, and even video communications (Marchand and Kresslein, 1988, pp. 446–7, Table 10).

Functional stage theory of information systems generally corresponds to the history of computer hardware. The *mainframe* model was the traditional mode. All data processing was handled by MIS staff using centralized mainframe computing facilities. The *mainframe network* model expanded access through decentralized workstations wired into the mainframe. A third model was *distributed processing*, in which minicomputers, workstations, and microcomputers in various functional and geographic divisions of the organization are used to process data and feed it to the central mainframe with which they are networked. The thrust is to use electronic networks and information centers to retain and enhance the linkage of the end-user manager to the entire data management system and to maintain the integrity and comprehensiveness of the departmental mainframe database system (Danziger and Kraemer, 1986). From a functional theoretic viewpoint, thus similar functions (e.g., control) may be performed by a variety of mixes of structural alternatives.

POLITICAL PROCESS MODELS

As Sullivan (1988, p. 8) has noted, early strategic planning in MIS was drawn to the "organization development notion that all companies will—and should—move along a similar trajectory in their adoption of technology, resulting in a predictable series of problems and characteristic solutions." Where the dynamic of stage theories is the supposed inner telos of information systems to unfold according to predictable stages, the dynamic of political process models is the hypothesis that information systems will unfold according to predictable political conflicts. Political process models fall into three subtypes: sociotechnical process, planning process, and political process.

Socio-Technical Models

One of the grand-daddies of all stages-of-growth models is Lewin's famous model of unfreeze—move—refreeze, which has become the basis of much of organization development theory (Lewin, 1952). Of special relevance to information technology is that this stage theory of organizational change was central to socio-technical systems (STS) analysis, developed as a managerial tool by the Tavistock Institute under Emery (1959) and Trist (Trist et al., 1963; Trist, 1981).

Lewin notwithstanding, sociotechnical authors focus not on stages but on social and political dynamics. The central concept is not "stages" but "stakeholders," their "interests," and ensuing forms of conflict and cooperation. Socio-technical analysis emphasizes "human assets" in the form of employee information and knowledge, capacities, and skills, centering organization change and management development through a participatory, group-centered method (Susman, 1976; see also Mumford, 1984). Socio-technical approaches, in turn, have been applied to information systems by a number of researchers (Mumford, 1983; see also Ginzberg, 1978; DeMaio, 1980; and Alter, 1980).

STS is a theory which views the organization as a self-regulating system which adapts to change through learning. It assumes that there should be simultaneous and balanced development of social and technical systems through each stage of information technology development. As organization theory, STS tends to emphasize human relations and organization dynamics, overcoming conflict through participation and recognition of stake-holding in the change to be effected. Normatively, STS is a consensus model of organizations, not a conflict model. Interest conflict is seen as resolvable through improved communication and organization development (OD). This leads STS practitioners to an applied focus on specific OD interventions.

Planning Process Models

Sullivan (1988) is illustrative of authors who seek to put the organization theory of information systems in the service of the planning needs of MIS management and staff. Designing decision support systems is an important subsidiary focus in the planning model. MIS units and professionals are seen as destined to play a greater role in analyzing data for the organization, involving them in performance and productivity issues, in identification of critical success factors, and in general organizational planning processes. The planning process model sees an evolution from planning *for MIS organization design* toward strategic planning *for the entire organization* by the MIS unit.

A conceptually similar variant on the planning model was provided by Caudle (1988, p. 796), who suggested a "needs hierarchy" model. Caudle identified three needs levels: (1) first the "IRM governance base" must be established, uniting top management support and resources with organizational planning and evaluation processes involving IRM and other resource management functions in an end-user-oriented capacity; (2) then computer. telecommunications, and other information systems in the "information technology base" must be moved from the existing level of technology management to the higher level of information management; and (3) an "information management base" utilizing this technology must be constructed which starts with information needs assessment and uses data management for decision support. Caudle argued that satisfaction of needs at one level opened up a focus on the needs issues of the next stage.

Where socio-technical models of political process are based on human relations/human dynamics consensus models arising from social psychology, the planning model is based on management science, particularly the field of decision science. Where socio-technical models when applied lead to organization development interventions, planning models when applied lead to re-engineering of the flow of information through organizations and the creating of information-tracking and executive decision support systems.

The planning model has the potential to be very controversial. From one viewpoint, it places the information resource manager at the pinnacle of planning for the organization. It could be construed as a call to displace others from critical staff planning functions. Needless to say, this imperialistic understanding of the stages-of-planning vision of MIS evolution did not go uncontested. "Obviously," Venner (1988, p. 17) wrote, "it is not the responsibility of the MIS department to provide strategic direction for the enterprise." Venner urged limiting MIS's role to informing management of what technology can do and supporting information needs as end users define them. He would not create a new integrated information resources management structure for organizational planning, as apparently envisioned by Sullivan or Caudle. In fact, the trend of computer science professionalization is not toward challenge to the CEO but rather toward alignment with the corporatist movement (Frechet, 1993).

Political Process Models

Both socio-technical and planning models are usually presented as consensus rather than conflict theories of political process, particularly by American authors. In countries with stronger union traditions, these same models may be presented in ways which emphasize interest differences and conflict. In Norway, for example, where by law labor-management agreements are required to establish major computer information systems, planning processes are viewed as including a much larger component of bargaining and conflict than one finds discussed by Sullivan, Caudle, or most American writers on planning. In Scandinavia, the theory of information systems planning centers on "systems development by negotiations" (Kubicek, 1983; Ciborra and Bracchi, 1983; Nygaard, 1983).

Negotiation is acknowledged as important by American writers, of course. For instance, Markus and Robey (1983) define "organizational validity" as MIS design conforming to user psychology and organizational power structure, arguing that it is brought about by negotiation among different interests to achieve integration of differences. The concept of "constructive resolution" (Franz and Robey, 1984) centers on negotiation. Lanzara's imagery of information systems development processes as games also makes negotiation central (Lanzara, 1983), as does exchange theory and its cousin, contract theory (Ouchi, 1979, and applied to information technology by Ciborra, 1981, 1984).

Still, while negotiation is acknowledged in models discussed above, one may differentiate "political process models" which see interest conflict as something that will never be "resolved" or "integrated," much less "overcome." These conflict models assert that political processes drive all organizational systems, including the information subsystem (on political process models of information technology, see Keen, 1981; Markus, 1983; Markus and Pfeffer, 1983; Markus and Robey, 1983; Hirschheim et al., 1984; Robey, 1984; Kling and Iacono, 1984b).

Political process models push to center stage a focus on bargaining among interest groups. Viewing IRM as political management of a planning process involving bargaining addresses criticisms of much existing planning process theory, namely, that it seeks to rationalize and suppress conflict through institutionalizing more powerful planning processes. Specifically, the political process conception of planning brings together Venner's concerns for interests of functional units and existing or potential IRM interests Caudle emphasizes. It should be emphasized that IRM as political management of a planning process also implies that IRM is best conceived as a *role* played by chief executives and others, not simply as a *position* like that of "IRM Manager."

Integrating interest group theory (Garson, 1978) with planning process models would make frameworks such as Caudle's more realistic as organization theory even in the American context (see the case study of interest groups in MIS by Overman and Simanton, 1986). Moreover, some specific IRM reforms advocated by Caudle in her model, such as information needs audits, have been criticized for their individualistic rational-man premises and failure to place needs as perceived by managers in the context of the broader organizational environment (Huber, 1981, 1983). Excessively cybernetic models of organizations lurk close to the surface of some planning process models, presuming an organization theory based on lack of conflict in planning—a long-noted major failing of many such models and their associated techniques (Mason and Mitroff, 1973; Keen, 1981; Ciborra, 1984).

Conflict theory is asserted most forcefully by phenomenologists studying computing and human behavior, contrasting, for example, the feelings of empowerment of managerial computer users compared to perceptions by "involuntary users" of computing (social workers are cited as an example) that such technology is not neutral, but instead is an omnipresent force monitoring and controlling work (Karger and Kreuger, 1988, p. 115).

The Phenomenological Perspective. Phenomenologists emphasize the intersubjective nature of computing—that is, computing not only appears different in nature to different people (the subjective element), it also appears different in nature according to how it is embedded in social networks (the intersubjective element). Based on this, phenomenologists are led to emphasize the paradoxical nature of computing, inconsistent with any "stage" theory, "consensus" theory, or other unified theory of information systems.

On the optimistic side, some studies which could be construed as belonging to this viewpoint, such as that by Sherry Turkle (1984), have brought attention to the evocative capacities of computers and their potential role in the mastery process by which the development of the creative spirit unfolds for children and for us all. *Cybersociety* (Jones, 1995) sets forth theories about theorizing an electronic reconstruction of community through electronic networks.

On the other hand, the phenomenological school can be quite pessimistic. Lyman (1984, 1988), for example, associates computers, particularly the computerization of writing, with the decline of "narrative culture" in favor of "technical culture." This is seen as a process in which the role of the writer/author is diffused and then devalued. Lyman thus sees a shift in emphasis from interpretive craftsmanship to mere techniques of information retrieval, diminishing the status and authority of the writer. Lyman generalizes this pessimistic perspective by arguing that social science reason is a cloak for professional-technical hegemony (Lyman, 1982). The technical rationality of computerized social science is seen as an "angry" mode of discourse that effects social control by imposing shame on those not partaking of its methods. People are transformed into things by devaluing experience and discourse in favor of computer data and technical rationality. Lyman is supported by Blank (1988), citing Ragin (1987). Blank sees social science shifting from the richness of case-oriented research to the confines of variable-oriented research—a function of the rise of computers in research organizations. Extending this argument, Berg (1994) traces computational culture from eighteenth-century origins, contending it effects a social acceleration which threatens the fabric of society.

Rens (1984) carried views similar to Lyman's even further, superseding Marxist emphasis on control of the means of production with a new world view of dialectic determinism based on control over the means of communication, of which computerized information is emerging as the leading form. However, Marxist scholars like Siegel (1986) see no such hegemonic struggle, arguing that computer tools are just that—tools which may enhance decision-making in certain respects but which will not change the moral basis of decision-making.

Phenomenological themes are cast in a theory of organizations by W. F. G. Mastenbroek (1988), in his essay on "Information Systems, Organization Design, and Organization Theory." Mastenbroek argues that computing is best understood as a system of feedback to and from subjective users who must be motivated to participate through "action learning." He develops a network theory of organizations which emphasizes paradoxes, polarities, and dilemmas as tension-balances among units which become both more autonomous *and* more interdependent as the organization becomes more differentiated and more integrated as a result of computer technology. Mastenbroek's synthesis of organization theory brings out the links between phenomenological themes of paradoxes and intersubjective networks on the one hand, and the view of organizations as networks of politics, power, competition, conflict, and communication as emphasized by the communications and control perspective discussed at the end of this chapter.

ECONOMIC THEORIES OF MIS

Phenomenological Marxism is not the predominant type. Siegel (1986), writing in the *Monthly Review*, has come as close as anyone to expressing the Marxist point of view. It is at once a stages-of-growth theory and class conflict political process theory. The stages are:

1. development of digital computing by teams sponsored by American, British, and German military and intelligence agencies;
2. privatization of public investment in computing after the war, resulting in near-monopolistic market hegemony by IBM;
3. technological innovation in integrated circuits and microprocessors leading temporarily to a more competitive situation marked by superficial radicalism (e.g., future founder of Apple Computer, Steve Wozniak building and selling electronic devices to bypass the AT&T billing system, according to Siegel, or future IBM microcomputer head Bill Gates simultaneously "crashing" all CDC computers in the Cybernet network; a "hacker" ethic of breaking copy protection and sharing software);
4. eventual IBM reassertion of market hegemony, even in microcomputers, and the maturing of Apple Computer into conventional corporate giants.

In the Marxist view, computing and microcomputing are tools, like typing. Although the ruling class has larger and more sophisticated tools, whether computers or printing presses, those who oppose them also use the same tools to put out newsletters, generate mailing lists, edit radical magazines, assist the Marxist government of Nicaragua with data processing, and otherwise oppose the powers-that-be.

In sum, the Marxist theory of information technology is that there is no unique impact of computing because computing is just another tool and the computer industry is like the rest of capitalism. Insofar as Marxist theory of information technology has practical implications, it is in holding that the decisions of MIS planners are not neutral but are part of a political process model as discussed above, albeit one seen in terms of class rather than group interests (Ehn and Sandberg, 1979). This leads back to treating information technology issues as a particular case of other struggles over workplace democracy (see Hunnius et al., 1973; Garson, 1974, 1977; Kubicek, 1983; Sandberg, 1985).

At almost the other end of the political spectrum, another economic model of MIS also leads back to the political process model. In *Datawars*, Kraemer et al., (1987) used the framework of supply and demand to analyze federal use of computer modeling. "Supply" factors included such variables as availability of sound theory, good computer simulations, high quality data, talented experts, and organizational readiness to design, produce, and implement computer models (e.g., national econometric models for the Congressional Budget Office). "Demand" factors included political priority of the subject matter of the model and political needs of the decision-makers. "A supply of good models and their promotion by modeler organizations might enhance model implementation and use," the authors found (p. 31), "but they will not generate use in the first instance. What generates model use is policy need and political saliency." That is, like the Marxists, the authors found computing to be the a tool of higher decision-makers, not an independent force from below or even a technical-rational matter as so much of the MIS literature wrongly implies.

Thus there is seeming agreement across highly divergent political perspectives that economic theories of MIS point only to the relative unimportance of the economics of MIS as the locus of independent variables in social analysis and organization theory, that it is a tool in nature, and that other dimensions, such as the political, and other paradigms, such as control models, may be more salient.

Nonetheless, in considering theoretical models for explanation and prescription in public management information systems (PMIS), Bozeman and Bretschneider (1986) have proposed a theoretical framework which emphasizes another type of economic distinction: public sector vs. private sector differences. Whereas most research on MIS and PMIS largely ignores extra-organizational factors, these authors asserted that the economic context (public or private) was the most important variable in constructing prescriptive theory in this field.

Bozeman and Bretschneider noted that four broad categories of differences existed between the public and private sectors. Among the economic differences distinguishing the public sector were relative absence of competition, inability to transfer ownership of equipment, and the greater value attached to public service features. In the political dimension, differences included greater interdependency, the need for representativeness, and different public expectations. In the workplace dimension, the budget time frame was shorter, media attention greater, and accountability greater. Finally, in the personnel dimension the public sector, with its civil service system, was more rigid and prone to "red tape". Bozeman and Bretschneider asserted that such public-private differences led to ten different prescriptions for PMIS as compared to private-sector MIS.[5]

While acknowledging that there "may be at least as many similarities as differences" between PMIS and MIS, Bozeman and Bretschneider argued that the factors they had outlined meant that "the trend of divergence between PMIS and business practice will likely accelerate" (Bozeman and Bretschneider, 1986, p. 485). It is possible to demonstrate a number of statistical differences between public- and private-sector computing, such as the greater pervasiveness of PCS in government due to a more information-intensive work environment (Bretschneider and Wittmer, 1993). However, without repeating the arguments here, an empirical study by the author suggests that at nearly every point there is reason to think the alleged public-private differences are nonexistent or of marginal importance (Garson, 1987b). This is in line with the finding of others that economic distinctions are relatively less important to organization theory for MIS. On the other hand, the numerous political factors cited by Bozeman and Bretschneider constitute important insights but ones which could be better cast in the context of a political process than an economic model.

PUBLIC GOODS THEORY OF INFORMATION SYSTEMS

Public goods theory is an alternative economic approach to information systems. Public goods theory assumes free markets are best for management and distribution of any commodity or service, except in certain areas where markets have difficulty. Difficulties arise when achieving excludability is difficult (situations in which consumption cannot be limited to those meeting the vendor's terms, as in the classic case of lighthouses). Difficulties also have difficulty when subtractibility is low (situations where one individual's consumption of the good nonetheless leaves the good intact for the next consumer, as in the case of weather forecasts).

In public goods theory, private goods tend to be consumed subtractibly on an excludable basis (e.g., automobiles) while public goods are consumed jointly on a nonexcludable basis (e.g., efforts to control organized crime) (Ostrom and Ostrom, 1977). Public goods theory carries the normative suggestion that political influence should be greatest and market influence least to the extent that goods are public rather than private. Other examples of public goods are earthquake forecasts, pollution control, and mosquito abatement.

Information systems have clear collective aspects. For instance, there is the benefit to democratic values of assurance that the transactions of business and governmental organizations can be held to public scrutiny. The fundamental collective and therefore public aspect of information access is the essential role it plays not only in citizenship but also in lifelong education, whether occupational, avocational, social, or intrinsic. The telecommunications aspects of IS are associated with collective consumption of basic freedoms of expression and thus bear the same publicness as public utilities such as telephone systems. And, of course, publicness is also affected by the negative public goods aspect of information systems in their capacity to pose a threat to privacy rights.

Pure public goods cannot be divided into marketable portions because consumption is almost entirely collective. Pure public goods therefore have a 'free rider' effect: if purchased privately, the rational median voter would not choose to expend funds on the public good because the benefit will be conferred anyway. To take a private sector example, collective bargaining representation confers collective benefits on entire work groups. Rational workers have no incentive to pay union dues since they will be represented anyway. The publicness of collective bargaining justifies political influence such as regulations forcing employees to pay dues in order to avoid free riders.

However, most goods are not purely public or purely private. Classic public goods theory usually spoke in terms of such a dichotomy, but the "publicness" of most goods is dimensional, not dichotomous. That is, many goods, including major information systems, are mixed goods with both public goods and private goods aspects. For instance, in the case of information systems, for instance, impacts of IS on privacy rights are an important public goods aspect. At the same time, information is routinely marketed as a private goods commodity, much like soap or automobiles.

Mixed goods like information systems raise special questions. For instance, consider another mixed good, education, as provided by one hypothetical economy in which that service is distributed solely on a market basis, and a second hypothetical economy in which all education is publicly provided. Public goods theory centers on the question of how the education service levels provided in the two hypothetical economies would differ, which ordinarily they will. Mixed goods are characterized by a gap (the "publicness surplus" between service levels when distributed by market economics and service levels when distributed by public means. In the case of education, for instance, a pure market approach might yield lower overall levels of educational service, adversely affect equity by increasing choices for the affluent while restricting choices for the poor. Likewise privatization might displace generalist curricula with occupational curricula more closely tied to immediate payoffs. In the recreational area it is similarly commonly assumed that state parks and the like have benefits to the commonweal which transcend uses of fee-payers alone. In other areas, such as public libraries, a pure market approach might find the level of demand inadequate to support a purely fee-based service altogether, as has been found by numerous public transportation companies which have experimented with a self-supporting fee basis.

In the area of information access, the surplus is the amount that would have to be provided in the form of income redistribution to enable all information consumers to be as informed as they would be under an economy in which information access were provided publicly. A privatized information access culture has appropriated the publicness surplus to private organizations, the profitability of which may be contingent on perpetuating distributive injustice.

Those goods and services which achieve their optimal distribution solely through market forces should be and usually are private. Those with a strong element of publicness, however, require subsidy, taxation, or regulation to achieve their optimal allocation.

With public goods theory as background, how does the concept of "publicness" relate specifically to information systems? Information access is a mixed good. It is neither a purely public nor a wholly private good. Access can be linked to the consumption of particular users who may be charged fees like other private goods. However, information access is also a public good in the sense that public libraries are.

Although particular units of information can be consumed individually and thus can be private goods, information usually is not subtractible (one person's use leaves information intact for the next user) and information access infrastructure taken as a whole is consumed collectively. For instance, credit bureaus may sell consumer information as a private good on a record by record basis but if the credit bureau has instituted privacy safeguard procedures normally these protect privacy regardless of payment or nonpayment of fees. Lack of subtractability and presence of collective consumption aspects bring information systems closer to public goods status. The larger and more information-inclusive the information system, the more it has an element of "publicness." The policy implications sanction the need for regulation of credit bureau information systems.

The courts have held that "Public interest means something in which the public, the community at large, has some pecuniary interest, or some interest by which their legal rights or liabilities are affected" (*State v. Crochett*, 206 Pac 816, 817). That pecuniary interest is the publicness surplus. More broadly, the Supreme Court has held "Property does become clothed with a public interest when used in a manner to make it of public consequence, and affect the community at large . . . When . . . one devotes his property to a use in which the public has an interest, he . . . must submit to be controlled by the public for the common good" (*Munn v. Illinois*, 94 U.S. 113, 126). In this light, large-scale information access systems would seem to be developments of strong public consequence and community effect, opening the door to public control as, for example, through resource redistribution linked to public goods, whether rendered by a government agency or by a corporation.

In summary, the ownership of information, never a well-defined area, has become far more controversial in recent years as a result of the rapid expansion of computing and related telecommunications in the last decade. These issues have emerged largely in systems owned by corporate entities during a politically conservative era in which property rights are being vigorously reasserted and the concept of the public interest is on the defensive. When ownership rights are ascendant over opposing public interests, corporate entities assume policy-making powers which substitute for public processes.

Public goods theory shows information systems and the services they provide may be seen as mixed goods, often imbued with several aspects of publicness. The analysis of such public goods suggests that professions associated with them follow relatively predictable patterns which may be summarized by the concept of private government. In carrying out regulation of the publicness of information systems as a mixed good and doing so under private aegis, a form of private government develops which is prone to a number of dysfunctional tendencies among which are the development of vested professional property rights and ordered markets.

The productive base of the American economy is changing. Over a quarter century ago, Machlup (1962) calculated that the production of information formed about a third of the American gross national product. By 1978 the proportion was estimated to be half (Porat, 1978). In the aftermath of the "microcomputer revolution" of the 1979–1985 period, the U.S. Office of Technology Assessment (1988) estimated that two dollars out of every five spent on new plant and equipment in the United States was going into computing and telecommunications. These changes give credence to those who state that America has shifted from a manufacturing economy to being an "information society." Just as the advent of the manufacturing economy brought Progressive legislative controls over the means of production, so public goods theory predicts that the coming of the information society will be associated with parallel struggles for legislative oversight of the means of information.

SOCIAL IMPACT RESEARCH AS ORGANIZATION THEORY

Perhaps the best-known body of research on computing in the public sector in this regard is that associated with the Urban Information Systems (URBIS) group at the University of California, Irvine. In a convenient summary, Kraemer and King (1986) have summarized these findings under six headings:

1. Organization Structure: Computers can facilitate either centralization or decentralization. Since managers like centralization and since there is a tendency for organizations to centralize over time, it appears that computerization at one date leads to greater organizational centralization later on, but this is not cause and effect. While man-

agers are increasingly dependent on computer-generated information and while information systems create the possibility of increasing the span of control (at the expense of middle management—see Wigand, 1988), in fact managers who are most satisfied with MIS use support staff to mediate between themselves and the computer environment, so the predicted flattening of the organization need not occur (Kraemer, Danziger, Dunkle, and King, 1993). Computing is a tool which can be used for centralization or decentralization (Kraemer et al., 1987).

2. Employment: In spite of widespread early fears that automation would lead to widespread unemployment, there is little evidence to contradict the contention that, overall, in the long run, computing creates as many jobs as it displaces. The causes of employment are so complex, however, that firm research and conclusions are impossible.

3. Decision-Making: Although expert systems may have a dramatic impact in the future, at present computing (a) facilitates organization of data for decision-makers (e.g., identifying exceptional transactions from among many, for selection for possible management action); and (b) forcing discipline on decision-makers (computer decision support models require decisions by managers about what is important to measure, how to measure it, and what the issues are).

4. Quality of Work Life: A study of 2,400 government workers by Danziger and Kraemer (1986) showed that for three-quarters, computing increased their sense of accomplishment, contradicting predictions that computing would be "de-skilling" and would lead to alienating jobs. Likewise, outside data handling professionals, computing seemed to be associated with decreases in time pressure and therefore with a better working environment.

5. Management: There is no universal set of rules for effective management of computing resources. Instead, the data processing manager is in a supply and demand marketplace, trying to maximize the data processing unit's position by justifying itself in terms of service to clients, trying to socialize each new wave of managers to data processing ideology, and in general seeking to mobilize internal and external supports for data processing development and maintenance;

6. Politics: Computing is not a power base for technocrats, as some have predicted, but instead is a powerful tool for the status quo as organizational elites control who benefits from computing and use computing power to control information and the power associated with it.

Although each of these points summarizing major thrusts of impact research is plausible, there is room for disagreement. For example, studies of impacts of telecommunications on organizational structure (e.g., Turoff et al., 1989) generally show a decentralizing and democratic effect.

Hierarchical rigidity is eroded by increased communications, and telecommunications can override traditional pyramidal management structures. However, this difference may be accounted for by the fact that Kraemer and King focus on departmental MIS units, not on organizations as a whole. This focus is more consistent with findings of tendencies toward centralization: the staff MIS function may become centralized even as the organization as a whole becomes more heterogenous, dispersed, and decentralized in its various operations. Moreover, the telecommunications research is more suggestive of future impacts rather than substantial past trends, upon which the URBIS group has concentrated.

In spite of various critiques, the URBIS approach, summarized by Kraemer and King, seems relatively sound in most respects. At the time the Kraemer and King (1986) article appeared, Garson was conducting a survey of officials identified by their respective state personnel directors as being the most knowledgeable about MIS in human resource functions (Garson, 1987). Although not a general sample, it asked officials about aspects of social impact theory as summarized by Kraemer and King:

1. Organization Structure: consistent with Kraemer and King, the respondents were about equally divided on whether computerization had or had not had a centralizing effect in state personnel, and this equal division was what would be predicted given a like division of response over whether there was a general tendency in personnel toward centralization.

2. Employment: also consistent with Kraemer and King, few respondents saw a significant effect on employment levels.6

3. Decision-Making: Only about a third reported use of computer models, noted by Kraemer and King (1986, p. 491) as the most notable application in decision-making, but this is expected since personnel is not in the forefront of computer application.

4. Quality of Working Life: Only about 10% of the respondents perceived computing to have a de-skilling effect, again supporting Kraemer and King.

5. Management: supporting Kraemer and King, some 4/5 reported establishment of information centers, reflecting client orientation, although only 40% reported that computing in personnel was enhanced by a widely used system of training, which should be a key element in the information manager's efforts to socialized employees and upper management.

6. Politics: contrary to Kraemer and King, however, very few respondents would agree that computerization has reinforced the status quo,

giving more power to those already powerful in the organization; most felt that computerization had made some units or individuals more powerful than they would have been otherwise (although one quarter did agree with this).

Thus, Kraemer and King's summary of important dimensions of impact research was upheld by Garson's survey in all respects except one. Even here, inclination of respondents heavily involved in MIS to see new political forces emerging rather than reinforcement of the status quo could easily be challenged as merely subjective, reflecting human tendencies to enhance one's own status. On the other hand, whereas one might have expected denial of anything but scientific neutrality, the willingness of the respondents to see computing as increasing the power of some who would not otherwise have it does suggest that issues of control are close to the surface.

THE COMMUNICATION AND CONTROL PERSPECTIVE

Kling, one of several scholars associated with this line of research, has emphasized institutional control as a key issue (Kling and Iacono, 1984a, 1984b). In such an institutional control model, each member of an organization system exerts control on each other member. In part computing amplifies the vertical controls from management to worker but the increase in interdependence associated with computing also brings, at least in the inventory management system studied, increased lateral influences among workers as peers, intensifying employee work involvement along with it. However, as Kling (1980) pointed out in an earlier study, a segmented institutional model often provides the context for such processes. That is, organizations are segmented among many different interest groups which conflict as technological change proceeds, altering power bases as this occurs.

Interestingly, the focus on control and its amplification has become popular in social psychological studies of computing. This view is articulated by Caporael and Thorngate (1984, p. 11) and Jackson (1987), who argue that computers function to amplify whatever social forces and problems exist within an organization. These authors hold the amplification principle to be true particularly of organizational control of behavior, thus forming a potential bridge to Perrolle's concern with the communications and control paradigm, to be discussed below.

Amplification as a theory is supported by such studies as that by Robey (1981), who found that computing can facilitate a variety of organizational structures, depending on the situation; Olson and Primps (1984), who found telecommuting increased the sense of control for professional workers, already traditionally high by this dimension, and decreased control for clerical workers; and Marx and Sherizen (1986), who found computerized monitoring of employee performance increased employee reactance levels, amplifying prior tendencies. This is similar to Kraemer and King's observation (1986) that computerization can amplify preexisting organizational tendencies toward either centralization or decentralization, or Jackson's note (1987, p. 236) that computers can be used either to enrich jobs from a design viewpoint or to better follow autocratic practices of job segmentation and performance surveillance.

The most comprehensive effort to link organization theory to the control themes which run throughout social impact research is found in the work of Perrolle (1986, 1987a, 1988), who has sought to unite the diverse findings from social impact research into an explicit theory she labels the 'communication and control paradigm.' This paradigm is in a direct line of thought which is central to her discipline, sociology, and for which some mileposts are (1) Tonnies' concept of the emergence of society from community (gemeinschaft vs. gesellschaft); (2) Durkheim's themes of social differentiation and integration; (3) Weber's description of the process of institutionalization and bureaucratization; (4) Parsons and the functionalists' emphasis on communications and culture as a social control system; and (5) March and Simon (1958; see also Simon, 1969) and systems theorists' casting of cybernetics as a model of social self-equilibration, and Simon's emphasis on decision premises as reflected in the communications structure of organizations (see Galbraith, 1977, on organizations as information-processing entities, and systems theorists who emphasize control systems, such as Landry and Le Moigne, 1977).

Communications and control also are themes in various critical social research schools such as (1) Marxist discussion of the role of intellectuals and of cultural hegemony; (2) Habermas's (1979, 1984) theory of communicative action; (3) other phenomenological viewpoints emphasizing intersubjectivity in the communication of knowledge (Boland, 1985; Karger and Kreuger, 1988); and (4) one might even cite popular culture theories of the "media is the message" genre (McLuhan, 1964). For instance, Janson et al., (1993) test Habermas's "communicative action" theory in MIS case studies, showing how MIS success or failure is accounted for by use or misuse of communicative action in responding to design uncertainty and user resistance.

Perrolle (1988) views the communications and control paradigm as one which is an extension of mainstream sociological work, interpreting computing as an extension of social understanding of the Industrial Revolution, yet broad enough to be accepted by conservative and critical theorists alike. Perrolle examines communications and control in the context of four MIS-related research literatures. With regard to human/technology interface research, the communications and control paradigm shifts the focus from ergonomics as a neutral extension of scientific management onto a focus on the extent to which computer systems designs do or do not serve control functions (e.g., worker surveillance). In the area of information production the paradigm focuses attention on control issues surrounding changing views on the ownership of information. In research on the computerization of work, the communications and control paradigm focuses on equity issues (does computing differentially affect women or minorities?) and other policy issues (e.g., the political uses of computer models such as the 'Limits to Growth' or more recent 'Nuclear Winter' models). In artificial intelligence research, the communications and control paradigm leads Perrolle (1988) to focus on the struggle of some intellectual workers to define as "routine expertise" the work of other, possibly less creative intellectual workers, over the vehement objections of the latter.

By defining the communications and control paradigm very broadly, Perrolle runs the risk of merely noting that the topics of communications and control are common themes in almost all theories, a true but not very interesting or helpful fact. What the paradigm does do, however, is shift the focus from computers to social structures and processes such as effects of computerization on the family, school, and other institutions (Perrolle, 1987a, pp. 102–127). In summary, the communications and control paradigm is not so much predictive social theory as it is a predisposition which assumes that the communications aspects of computing are the most important, and that the issues of control and power which arise from this are the most interesting.

CONCLUSION

As an ideal type, theories are constellations of hypotheses which form a system that allows accurate prediction. Organization theory should lead to predictions about organizations, and organization theory for information technology should lead to the ability to make predictions based on hypotheses which link that technology to variables which arise in an organizational context. Using organization theory of information technology, for instance, we would be able to make accurate predictions regarding growth patterns in MIS, success factors (or failure factors) in implementation of information technology, effective decision support mechanisms for management, and we would be able to forecast the effects of changes in one or another class of factors, such as economic forces.

Organization theory in the foregoing sense is a goal of some. The reality is that validated hypotheses in MIS and IRM are not plentiful, much less linked to encompassing predictive theories. Obstacles to theory development abound, including lack of standard terminology, unavailability or low quality of data, and rapid change in the subject of study, made more challenging by its interdisciplinary nature. In this discouragingly complex real world, the objectives set for an organization theory of information technology may be lower than the ideal. Reasonable objectives would be for such a theory to point us toward the important issues, organizing research around a map of major concepts, and suggesting interesting hypotheses relating to them.[7]

A theory with these limited but very worthwhile objectives is emerging. The presentation of such a theory, its conceptual map, and associated hypotheses is beyond the scope of this paper and what follows is *not* that, although it is the basis for a later work of this type. Instead this chapter concludes by synthesizing the foregoing streams of thought about organization theory for information technology into what comes closest to the emerging consensus. Not wanting to succumb to the "Columbus complex" endemic to academic theoreticians, one may follow Perrolle's lead in calling this the "communications and control paradigm", but the description of the model which follows hopefully clarifies and expands that paradigm. Hopefully also, the model appears to be common sense, but that the discerning reader will note that it incorporates crucial theoretical elements omitted by one or another research tradition considered in isolation from the others.

MANAGEMENT IMPLICATIONS

People play various roles as employees of organizations, which in turn exist within a set of successively more comprehensive environments which the manager must understand and work with. While the objectives of organizations vary, all organizations share in common a primary need to acquire the control necessary to discharge their functions. In fact, the drive for control over environmental factors is at the core or the manager's responsibility for strategic planning. Strategic planning tools associated with communication have become progressively more important until today they are the most significant category from the point of view of control.

Information technologies are part of socio-technical systems which amplify the effects of various communications tools, affecting their control characteristics. Information technologies do so in any or all of three processes: by identifying information needs in relation to objectives, by organizing and analyzing information, and by enabling linkages among actors, linkages which in the case of computer technology are of a largely instantaneous and often automatic nature. Information resource management is a fundamental, perhaps *the* fundamental managerial responsibility. Yet all too often managers take information systems for granted and inappropriately (and irresponsibly) delegate powers over it to lower-level staff.

The drive to acquire environmental control needed to fulfill organizational objectives applies not only to organizations, but also to sub-organizational units, even to employees as individuals, as well as to other groups, interests, and classes in the organization's environment, and to national and global entities. All these entities use information communication tools. These entities interact with, exchange among, bargain with, conflict with, and even play games with and symbolically manipulate one another in many domains, the most important of which is the use of information communication tools for purposes of control. Good information systems support strategic planning by the manager to play these games well.

Information resources management is a formal or informal role of one or more members of the organization, whether or not computers are used. Ideally, responsibility for this role is placed at the highest level of the organization. The primary function of this role is to manage the political processes which surround planning and implementation of such systems. This political process reflects both conflict over objectives and differences over functional alternatives for agreed objectives among the various entities enumerated above. Different societal, reference market, and organizational cultures affect the nature of the political process, giving varying emphases on imposed structural controls, negotiated solutions, market outcomes, and group consensus.

The management of information technology is highly heterogenous, but its most important divisions concern (1) impacts associated with the interfaces between the organizational, reference market, social, and global environments; (2) planning for the processes of information needs identification, information organizing and analyzing, and information linking; (3) managing associated political processes; and (4) invention, development, and implementation of hardware and software applications mandated by the prevailing forces. This heterogeneity is best encountered by a manager with extensive social and political skills and experiences in addition to technological expertise.

ENDNOTES

1. See Aines (1988). Aines has been a technical consultant to three presidential science advisers and has been active in seeking a new national information policy under a new administration.
2. The areas are these:
    1. Automata and Computability Theory
    2. ADA Programming Language
    3. APL Programming Language
    4. Computer Architecture
    5. Artificial Intelligence
    6. Business Data Processing and Management
    7. Biomedical Computing
    8. Computers and the Physically Handicapped
    9. Computers and Society
    10. Computer and Human Interaction

11. Data Communication
12. Computer Personnel Research
13. Computer Science Education
14. Computer Uses in Education
15. Design Automation
16. Documentation
17. Computer Graphics
18. Information Retrieval
19. Measurement and Evaluation
20. Microprogramming
21. Management of Data
22. Numerical Mathematics
23. Office Information Systems
24. Operating Systems
25. Programming Languages
26. Security, Audit, and Control
27. Symbolic and Algebraic Manipulation
28. Simulation
29. Small and Personal Computing Systems and Applications
30. Software Engineering
31. University and College Computing Services

3. In the sections which follow, various theories of information technology are categorized according to their major conceptual emphases. It should be noted, however, that specific authors frequently acknowledge central points made by colleagues grouped in another category. Likewise, various authors' statements have implications in the context of other authors' models, perhaps of an unconsidered or unintended nature. No claim to comprehensiveness is made regarding summaries of each author's perspective. However, the assumptions associated with each category and with the authors treated within each do form the bases for alternative organization theories regarding information technology. The failure of most authors to distinguish explicitly among these conceptual bases has been a significant obstacle to theory development.

4. Marchand and Kresslein's discussion of planning leads into the third variant of stage theory (planning), discussed following. Their central emphasis on integration, however, has led to discussion of their theory together with others in the second variant (information integration). Dates for the four stages are approximate and overlapping, of course.

5. The ten differences were these:

    1. PMIS projects cannot be evaluated primarily on efficiency as are MIS projects; for example, problems with computer matching of welfare and bank account information in Massachusetts AFDC administration led to suits against the state and a realization that due process needed higher priority than efficiency.

    2. Because civil service prevents spot bonuses and most forms of monetary recognition for good work, "side-payments" are common in the private sector; thus, Bozeman and Bretschneider assert, for example, computing equipment is distributed as a substitute reward in the public sector, interfering with PMIS planning and integration.

3. Political uncertainties in the budget process in government require PMIS to be more incremental, whereas private MIS administrators can plan more comprehensively.

4. There is greater fragmentation and interdependency in PMIS, Bozeman and Bretschneider assert, as in computer sharing of information among various levels of law enforcement, motor vehicles, courts, and other agencies.

5. Because the heads of public agencies tend to be political appointees, the PMIS head is better kept relatively insulated from the top whereas private-sector MIS literature usually urges the MIS chief report directly to the chief executive.

6. Leasing and time-sharing of computer equipment is more important in the public sector because government agencies cannot sell their older equipment, nor do they get tax depreciation benefits as do their private sector counterparts.

7. PMIS systems require a longer testing period than do private MIS projects of a similar nature. This is because of the different and often higher public expectations of government and the need for greater accountability, more checks, and the public outrage which occurs when, for instance, computer error allows a dangerous criminal to be released from prison as happened in a case in Georgia.

8. PMIS managers find less use of computer systems for control purposes than do their private counterparts because of greater employee resistance and because managers trade control for accountability.

9. PMIS has fewer labor-saving benefits than MIS, in part because of a rigid civil service system and because public jobs sometimes serve double-duty as a social "safety net" guaranteeing employment.

10. Finally, staffing is much more difficult in PMIS because government pay scales are not competitive, resulting in difficulty of recruitment, high turnover, and generally lower skill levels. PMIS systems design must take account of this.

6. Employment impacts are discussed in a symposium on the subject, in the Spring, 1989, issue of the *Social Science Computer Review*, Vol. 7, No. 1. Articles in the symposium do not contradict the position taken by Kraemer and King.

7. These are the three steps of theory building as set forth in Schendel and Hofer, eds., 1986: 386).

REFERENCES AND ADDITIONAL READING

Ahituv, N. and S. Neumann (1984). "A Flexible Approach To Information System Development", *MIS Quarterly*, V. 8, N. 2: 69–78.

Aines, Andrew A. (1988). "U.S. Recognizes Information Age, But Is It Too Late?", *Government Computer News*, July 22: 103.

Alter, S. (1980) *Decision Support Systems: Current Practice and Continuing Challenge* (Reading, MA: Addison-Wesley).

Anderson, Ronald (1985). "A Classification Of The Literature On Computers and Social Sciences," *Computers and the Social Sciences*, V. 1, N. 2: 67–76.

Anthony, Robert N. (1965). *Planning And Control Systems: A Framework For Analysis*

(Boston: Division of Research, Harvard Graduate School of Business Administration).

Attewell, Paul and James Rule (1984). "Computing and organizations: What we know and what we don't know,", *Communications Of The ACM*, V. 27, N. 12 (Dec.): 1184–1192.

Bemelmans, M. A., (ed.) (1984). *Beyond Productivity: Information Systems Development For Organizational Effectiveness* (Amsterdam: North-Holland).

Benbasit, I., A. S. Dexter, D. H. Drury, and R. C. Goldstein (1984). "A Critique Of The Stage Hypothesis: Theory And Empirical Evidence", *Communications Of The ACM*, V. 27, N. 5 (May): 476–485.

Berg, R. Dreyer (1994). "Our Computational Culture: From Descartes to the Computer," *A Review of General Semantics*, V. 51, N. 2 (Summer): 123–144.

Blank, Grant (1988). "New Technology and the Nature Of Sociological Work", *The American Sociologist*, V. 19, No. 1 (Spring): 3–15.

Boland, R. J., Jr. (1978). "The Process and Product of System Design", *Management Science*, V. 24, N. 9: 887–898.

Boland, R. J., Jr. (1985). "Phenomenology: A Preferred Approach To Research On Information Systems," in Mumford, Hirschheim, Fitzgerald, and Wood-Harper et al., (eds.) (1985): 193–202.

Boland, R. J., Jr. and W. Day (1981). "The Process of System Design: A phenomenological Approach," in Ginzberg and Ross, (eds.) (1982): 31–45.

Bozeman, Barry and Stuart Bretschneider (1986). "Public Management Information Systems: Theory and Prescription", *Public Administration Review*, Special Issue, November 1986: 475–487.

Bretschneider, Stuart and Dennis Wittmer (1993). "Organizational Adoption Of Microcomputer Technology: The Role Of Sector," *Information Systems Research*, V. 4, N. 1 (March): 88–108.

Briefs, U., C. Ciborra, and L. Schneider, (eds.) (1983). *Systems Design For, With, And By The Users* (Amsterdam: North Holland).

Bryce, M. (1987). "The IRM Idea," *Datamation*, V. 33, N. 8: 89–92.

Caporael, L. (1984). Computers, Prophecy, and Experience: A Historical Perspective," *Journal of Social Issues*, V. 40, N. 3: 15–29.

Caporael, L. and W. Thorngate (1984). "Introduction: Towards The Social Psychology Of Computing," *Journal of Social Issues*, V. 40, N. 3: 1–13.

Caudle, Sharon L. (1987) "High Tech to Better Effect," *The Bureaucrat*, Spring 1987: 47–51.

Caudle, Sharon L. (1988). "Federal Information Resources Management After the Paperwork Reduction Act," *Public Administration Review*, V. 48, N. 4 (July/August): 790–799.

CAUSE (1994) "Managing Information Technology as a Catalyst Of Change." Track III: The Impact of Quality. Boulder, CO: CAUSE. In *Managing Information Technology as a Catalyst Of Change; Proceedings of The CAUSE Annual Conference* (San Diego, CA, December 7–10, 1993).

Ciborra, C. U. (1981). "Information Systems and Transactions Architecture," *Journal of Policy Analysis and Information Systems*, V. 5, N. 4: 305–324.

Ciborra, C. U. (1984). "Information Systems and Organizational Exchange: A New Design Approach," in Bemelmans, (ed.) (1984): 135–145.

Ciborra, C. U. and G. Bracchi (1983). "Systems Development and Auditing in Turbulent Contexts: Towards a New Participative Approach," in Wysong and de Lotto, (eds.) (1983): 41–52.

Cochran, Anita (1987). "ACM: The Past 15 Years, 1972–1979," *Communications of the ACM*, V. 30, N. 10 (October): 866–872.

Collins, L. W. (1994). "TQM Information-Systems—An Elusive Goal," in *Joint Commission Journal on Quality Improvement*, V. 20, N. 11 (Nov.): 607–613.

Cooper, Randolph B. (1988). "Review Of Management Information Systems Research: A Management Support Emphasis," *Information Processing and Management*, V. 24, N. 1: 73–102.

Danziger, James N. and Kenneth L. Kraemer (1986). *People and Computers: The Impact Of Computing On End Users in Organizations* (NY: Columbia University Press).

DeMaio, A. (1980). "Sociotechnical Methods for Information Systems Design", in Lucas, Land, Lincoln, and Supper, (eds.) (1980): 105–122.

Dertouzas, Michael and Joel Moses, eds. (1980). *The Computer Age: A Twenty-Year View* (Cambridge, MA: MIT Press).

Drury, D. H. (1983). "An Empirical Assessment of the Stages of Data Processing Growth", *MIS Quarterly*, V. 7, N. 2 (June): 59–70.

Ehn, P. and A. Sandberg (1979). "Systems Development: Critique Of Ideology and The Division of Labor in the Computer Field", in Sandberg, (ed.) (1979): 34–46.

Emery, F. E. (1959). *Characteristics Of Socio-Technical Systems* (London: Tavistock Institute of Human Relations).

Enslin, W. L. (1984). "Information Systems Management," pp. 75–93 in J. Rabin, S. Humes, and B. S. Morgan, (eds.), *Managing Administration* (NY: Marcel Dekker, 1984).

Fick, G. and R. H. Sprague, (eds.) (1981). *Decision Support Systems: Issues and Challenges* (Amsterdam: North Holland).

Franz, C. and D. Robey (1984). "An Investigation of User Led System Design: Rational and Political Perspective," *Communications of the ACM*, V. 27, N. 9 (Sept.): 1202–1209.

Frechet, Guy (1993). "Professional and Corporatist Temptations Among Computer Scientists," *Recherches Sociographiques*, V. 34, N. 1 (Jan.–April): 89–110.

Galbraith, J. (1977). *Organization Design* (Reading, MA: Addison-Wesley).

Garson, G. David (1974). *On Democratic Administration and Socialist Self-Management: A Comparative Survey* (Beverly Hills, CA: Sage Publications).

Garson, G. David (1977). *Worker Self-Management in Industry: The West European Experience* (NY: Praeger).

Garson, G. David (1978). *Group Theories of Politics* (Beverly Hills, CA: Sage Publications).

Garson, G. David (1987a). *Computers In Public Employee Relations* (Alexandria, VA: International Personnel Management Association).

Garson, G. David (1987b). "Human Resource Management, Computers, and Organization Theory," American Political Science Association, 1987 Annual Meeting, Chicago.

Garson, G. David (1989a). "Computer-Related Research and Instruction for MPA Programs in the 1990s," *New directions in Public Administration Research*, V. 2, N. 1 (April): 1–13.

Garson, G. David (1989b). "Review of Datawars," *Social Science Computer Review*, V. 7, N. 1 (Spring).

Gibson, Cyrus F. and Richard L. Nolan (1974). "Managing The Four Stages Of EDP Growth," Harvard Business Review, V. 52, N. 1 (Jan./Feb.): 76–88.

Gilchrist, B., Ed. (1977). *Information Processing 77* (Amsterdam: North-Holland).

Ginzberg, M. J. (1978). "Steps Towards More Effective Implementation of MS And MIS," Interfaces, V. 8, N. 3: 295–300.

Ginzberg, M. J. and G. Ariav (1986). "Methodologies For DSS Analysis and Design: A Contingency Approach to Their Application," *Proceedings of the Seventh International Conference for Information Systems* (1986).

Ginzberg, M. J. and C. Ross, (eds.) (1982). *Proceedings Of The Third International Conference On Information Systems*, Ann Arbor, MI, Dec. 13–15. The Institute of Management Sciences.

Glaser, B. G. and A. Strauss (1967). *The Discovery Of Grounded Theory: Strategies for Qualitative Research* (Hawthorne, NY: Aldine Publishers).

Goldstein, R. C. and I. McCririck (1981). "The Stage Hypothesis and Data Administration: Some Contradictory Evidence," *Proceedings of the Second International Conference on Information Systems*, December, Boston, MA: 309–324.

Guimaraes, Tor (1981). "Understanding Implementation Failure," *Journal of Systems Management* (March): 12–17.

Habermas, Jurgen (1979). *Communications and The Evolution Of Society* (Boston: Beacon Press).

Habermas, Jurgen (1984). *The Theory Of Communicative Action* (Boston: Beacon Press).

Hendrick, Rebecca (1994). "An Information Infrastructure for Innovative Management of Government," *Public Administration Review*, V. 54, N. 6 (Nov.–Dec.): 543–550.

Herzlinger, Regina (1977). "Why Data Systems in Non-Profit Organizations Fail," *Harvard Business Review* (Jan.–Feb.): 81–86.

Hirschheim, R. A., F. Land, and S. Smithson (1984). "Implementing Computer-Based Information Systems in Organizations—Issues and Strategies," pp. 356–369 in *Proceedings Of The Interact-84* (Amsterdam: North Holland).

Huber, G. P. (1981). "Organizational Science Contributions to the Design of Decision Support Systems," in Fick and Sprague, (eds.) (1981): 45–55.

Huber, G. P. (1983). "Cognitive Style as a Basis for MIS and DSS Designs: Much Ado About Nothing?," *Management Science*, V. 29, N. 5: 567–577.

Huff, Sid L., Malcolm C. Munro, and Barbara H. Martin (1988). "Growth Stages Of End User Computing," *Communications of the ACM*, V. 31, N. 5 (May): 542–550.

Hunnius, Gerry, G. David Garson, and John Case, (eds.) (1973). Workers' Control (NY: Random House).

IBM (1981). *Business Systems Planning—Information Systems Planning Quide. Application Manual*, Third Edition (IBM Pub. GE20–0527–3).

Ives, B., S. Hamilton, and G. Davis (1980). "A framework for Research in Computer-Based Management Information Systems," *Management Science*, V. 26, N. 9: 910–934.

Jackowski, Edward M. (1988). "Developing an Information Resource Management Plan," *Public Productivity Review*, V. 11, N. 3 (Spring): 3–12.

Jackson, Lee A., Jr. (1987). "Computers and the Social Psychology Of Work," *Computers and Human Behavior*, V. 3, N. 3/4: 251–262.

Janson, M. A., C. C. Woo, and L. D. Smith (1993). "Information Systems Development And Communication Action Theory," *Information and Management*, V. 25, N. 2 (Aug.): 59–72.

Jones, Steven G. (1995). *Cybersociety: Computer-Mediated Communications and Community* (Thousand Oaks, CA: Sage Publications).

Karger, Howard Jacob and Larry W. Kreuger (1988). "Technology and the 'Not Always So Human' Services," *Computers in Human Services*, V. 3, Nos. $^1/_2$: 111–126.

Keen, Peter G. W. (1981). "Information Systems and Organizational Change," *Communications of the ACM*, V. 24, N. 1 (Jan.): 24–33.

Kersten, G. E. (1985). "NEGO—Group Decision Support System," *Information and Management*, V. 8: 237–246.

King, John Leslie and Kenneth L. Kraemer (1984). "Evolution and Organizational Information Systems: an Assessment of Nolan's Stage Model," *Communications of the ACM*, V. 27, N. 5 (May): 466–475.

Kling, Rob (1980). "Social Analyses of Computing: Theoretical Perspectives in Recent Empirical Research," *Computing Surveys*, V. 12, N. 1: 61–110.

Kling, Rob and Suzanne Iacono (1984a). "Computing as an Occasion for Social Control," *Journal of Social Issues*, V. 40, N. 3: 77–96.

Kling, Rob, and Suzanne Iacono (1984b). "The Control of Information Systems Development After Implementation," *Communications of the ACM*, V. 27, N. 12 (Dec.): 1218–1226.

Kraemer, Kenneth L., J. N. Danziger, D. E. Dunkle, and J. L. King (1993). "The Usefulness of Computer-Based Information to Public Managers," *Management Information Systems Quarterly*, V. 17, N. 2 (June): 129–148.

Kraemer, Kenneth L., Siegfried Dickhoven, Susan Fallows Tierney, and John Leslie King (1987). *Datawars: The Politics of Federal Policy Making* (NY: Columbia University Press).

Kraemer, Kenneth L. and John Leslie King (1986). "Computing and Public Organizations," in *Public Administration Review*, V. 46, Special Issue (Nov. 1986).

Kubicek, H. (1983). "User Participation In System Design: Some Questions About the Structure and Content Arising from Recent Research from a Trade Union Perspective," in Briefs, Ciborra, and Schneider, (eds.) (1983): 3–18.

Landry, M. and J.-L. Le Moigne (1977). "Towards a Theory of Organizational Information System—a General System Perspective," in Gilchrist, (ed.) (1977): 801–805.

Lanzara, G. F. (1983). "The Design Process: Frames, Metaphors, and Games," in Briefs, Ciborra, and Schneider, (eds.) (1983): 29–40.

Lewin, Kurt (1952). "Group Decision and Social Change," in Newcomb and Hartley, (eds.) (1952): 330–344.

Lockhart, G. (1981). "Information Processing By Stages," *Management Today* (September): 120–140.

Lucas, H. C., F. Land, T. Lincoln, and K. Supper, (eds.) (1980). *The Information Systems Environment* (Amsterdam: North Holland).

Lucas, H. C., Jr. and J. A. Sutton (1977). "The Stage Hypothesis and the S-Curve: Some Contradictory Evidence," *Communications of the ACM*, V. 20, N. 4 (April): 254–259.

Lyman, Peter (1982). "Being Reasonable: On Anger and Order in Middle Class Culture," *Society for the Study of Social Problems*, 1982 Annual Meeting.

Lyman, Peter (1984). "Reading, Writing and Word Processing: Toward a Phenomenology of the Computer Age," *Qualitative Sociology*, V. 7, Nos. 1/2 (Spring/Summer): 75–89.

Lyman, Peter (1988). "Sociological Literature in an Age of Computerized Texts," *The American Sociologist*, V. 19, N. 1 (Spring): 16–31.

Lyytinen, Kalle (1987a). "Different Perspectives on Information Systems: Problems and Solutions," *ACM Computing Surveys*, V. 19, N. 1 (March): 5–46.

Lyytinen, Kalle (1987b). "Information System Failure: A Survey and Classification of Empirical Literature," *Oxford Survey of Information Technology*, V. 4.

Machlup, Fritz (1962). *The Production and Distribution of Knowledge in the United States* (Princeton, NJ: Princeton University Press).

Maggi, L., J. L. King, and K. L. Kraemer, (eds.) (1984). *Proceedings of the Fifth International Conference on Information Systems* (NY: Society for Management Information Systems).

March, J. G. and Herbert A. Simon (1958). Organizations (NY: Wiley).

Marchand, Donald A. and John C. Kresslein (1988). "Information Resources Management and the Public Sector Administrator," in Rabin and Jackowski, (eds.), 1988: Ch. 15.

Markus, M. Lynne (1983). "Power, Politics, and MIS Implementation," *Communications of the ACM*, V. 26, N. 6 (June): 430–444.

Markus, M. Lynne and J. Pfeffer (1983). "Power and the Design and Implementation of Accounting and Control Systems," *Human Relations*, V. 36: 203–226.

Markus, M. Lynne and Daniel Robey (1983). "The Organizational Validity of Management Information Systems," *Human Relations*, V. 36, N. 3 (March): 203–226.

Martin, James (1983). *Managing the Data-Base Environment* (Englewood Cliffs, NJ: Prentice Hall).

Marx, G. and S. Sherizen (1986). "Monitoring on the Job: How To Protect Privacy As Well As Property," *Technology Review*, V. 89, N. 8: 62–72.

Mason, R. O. and I. I. Mitroff (1973). "A Program for Research on Management Information Systems," *Management Science*, V. 19, N. 5: 475–487.

Mastenbroek, W. F. G. (1988). "Informational Systems, Organizational Design, and Organizational Theory," *M & O* (Netherlands), V. 42, N. 6 (Nov.–Dec.): 430–442.

Mathew, Biju (1994). " Structure and Power in Information Technology Environments: A Genealogy of Organizational Systems." Doctoral dissertation, University of Pittsburgh, Pittsburgh, PA.

McFarlan, Warren (1981). "Portfolio Approach to Information Systems," *Harvard Business Review* (Sept.–Oct.): 142–150.

McFarlan, Warren and James L. McKinney (1983). *Corporate Information Systems Management: The Issues Facing Senior Executives* (Homewood, IL: Irwin, 1983).

McLuhan, Marshall (1964). *Understanding the Media* (NY: McGraw-Hill).

Morell, Jonathon A. (1989). "The Impact of Information Technology on Research: An Agenda for Social Science Investigation," Ch. 14 in Nagel and Garson, (eds.) (1989).

Mumford, E. (1983). *Designing Human Systems—The ETHICS Method* (Cheshire, England: Manchester Business School).

Mumford, E. (1984). "Participation: From Aristotle To Today," in Bemelmans, (ed.) (1984): 95–104.

Mumford, E., R. A. Hirschheim, G. Fitzgerald, and A. T. Wood-Harper, (eds.) (1985). *Research Methods in Information Systems* (Amsterdam: North Holland).

Murray, J. Michael (1988). "Information Systems and Data Processing Organizations: Functions, Evolution, Structure, and Issues," in Rabin and Jackowski, (eds.), 1988: Ch. 7.

Nagel, Stuart and G. David Garson, (eds.) (1989). *Research Annual on Advances in Social Sciences and Computers*, Vol. 2 (Greenwich, CT: JAI Press).

Newcomb, T. M. and E. L. Hartley, (eds.) (1952). *Readings in Social Psychology* (NY: Holt).

Nolan, Richard L. (1973). "Managing the Computer Resource: A Stage Hypothesis," *Communications of the ACM*, V. 16, N. 7 (July): 399–405.

Nolan, Richard L. (1977). *Management Accounting and Control of Data Processing* (NY: National Association of Accountants).

Nolan, Richard L. (1979). "Managing the Crisis in Data Processing," *Harvard Business Review*, March–April: pp. 115–126.

Nygaard, K. (1983). "Participation in Systems Development—The Tasks Ahead," in Briefs, Ciborra, and Schneider, (eds.) (1983): 15–25.

Olson, Margrethe H. and S. Primps (1984). "Working At Home with Computers: Work and Nonwork Issues," *Journal of Social Issues*, V. 40, N. 3: 97–112.

Ostrom, Vincent and Elinor Ostrom (1977). "Public Goods and Public Choice." in E. S. Savas, (ed.), *Alternatives for Delivering Public Services: Toward Improved Performance* (Boulder, CO: Westview Press,) p. 7–49.

Ouchi, W. G. (1979). A Conceptual Framework for the Design of Organizational Control Mechanisms," *Management Science*, V. 25, N. 9: 833–848.

Overman, E. Sam and Don F. Simanton (1986). "Iron Triangles and Issue Networks of Information Policy," pp. 584–589 in *Public Administration Review*, Vol. 46 (Nov. 1986).

Perrolle, Judith A. (1986). "Intellectual Assembly Lines: The Rationalization of Managerial, Professional, and Technical Work," *Computers and the Social Sciences*, V. 2, N. 3: 111–121.

Perrolle, Judith A. (1987a). *Computers and Social Change: Information, Property, and Power* (Belmont, CA: Wadsworth).

Perrolle, Judith A. (1987b). "Conversations and Trust in Computer Interfaces," *Eastern Sociological Society*, Boston.

Perrolle, Judith A. (1988). "The Social Impact of Computing: Ideological Themes and Research Issues," *Social Science Computer Review*, V. 6, N. 4.

Porat, Marc U. (1978). "Communication Policy in an Information Society." in Robinson, (ed.) (1978).

Rabin, Jack and Edward M. Jackowski, (eds.) (1988). *Handbook of Information Resource Management* (NY: Dekker).

Ragin, Charles (1987). *The Comparative Method: Moving Beyond Qualitative and Quantitative Strategies* (Berkeley: University of California Press).

Rens, Jean-Guy (1984). "Revolutions in Communications: From Writing to Telematics/Revolutions Dans La Communication: De L'Ecriture A La Telematique," *Sociologie et Sociétés*, V. 16, N. 1 (April):13–22.

Rheinboldt, W. C. (1985). "Future Directions in Computational Mathematics, Algorithms, and Scientific Software," *Society for Industrial and Applied Mathematics*, Annual Meeting, Philadelphia, PA.

Robey, D. (1981). "Computer Information Systems and Organization Structure," *Communications of the ACM*, V. 24: 679–687.

Robey, D. (1984). "Conflict Models for Implementation Research," in Schultz, (ed.) (1984).

Saarinen, Allan O. (1987). "Improving Information Systems Development Success Under Different Organizational Conditions," in URISA, 1987, Vol. II: 1—12.

Sandberg, A., (ed.) (1979). *Computers Dividing Man and Work* (Malmo, Sweden: Arbetslivscentrum).

Sandberg, A. (1985). "Sociotechnical Design, Trade Union Strategies and Action Research," in Mumford, Hirschheim, Fitzgerald, and Wood-Harper, (eds.) (1985): 79–92.

Schendel, D. E. and W. Hofer, (eds.) (1979). *Strategic Management* (Boston: Little, Brown).

Schultz, R. L., (ed.) (1984). *Management Science Implementation* (NY: Elsevier).

Siegel, Lenny (1986). "Microcomputers: From Movement To Industry," *Monthly Review*, V. 38, N. 3 (July–August): 110–117.

Simon, Herbert (1969). *The Sciences of the Artificial* (Cambridge, MA: MIT Press).

Strassman, Paul A. (1985). *Information Payoff: Transformation of Work in the Electronic Age* (NY: Free Press, 1985).

Studer, Paul A. (1972). "From Multidisciplinary to Interdisciplinary Research: Effects of Information Systems on Formal Organizations," *Journal of the American Society for Information Science*, V. 23, N. 6 (Nov.–Dec.): 343–352.

Sullivan, Cornelius H. (1985). "Systems Planning in the Information Age," *Sloan Management Review*, V. 27, N. 1 (Winter): 3–11.

Sullivan, Cornelius H. (1988). "The Changing Approach to Systems Planning," *Journal of Information Systems Management*, V. 5, N. 3 (Summer): 8–13.

Susman, Gerald I. (1976). *Autonomy at Work: A Sociotechnical Analysis of Participative Management* (NY: Praeger).

Swanson, B. E. (1984). "Organizational Designs for Software Maintenance," in Maggi, King, and Kraemer, (eds.) (1984): 73–82.

Trist, E. L. (1981). "The Sociotechnical Perspective," in van de Ven and Joyce, (eds.) (1981): 19–75.

Trist, E. L., G. W. Higgins, H. Murray, and A. B. Pollack (1963). *Organizational Choice* (London: Tavistock Publications).

Turkle, Sherry (1984). *The Second Self: Computers and the Human Spirit* (New York: Simon and Schuster).

Turner, Judith (1982). "Observations on the Use of Behavioral Models in Information Systems Research and Practice," *Information Management*, V. 5, N. 3: 207–213.

Turoff, Murray, Roxanne Starr Hiltz, and Miriam Mills (1989). "Telecomputing: Organizational Impacts," Ch. 9 in *Research Annual on Social Sciences and Computers*, Vol. 2 (Greenwich, CT: JAI Press).

U.S. office of Technology Assessment (1988). *Technology and the American Economic Transition*. Washington, DC: Superintendent of Documents.

Van de Ven, A. H., and W. F. Joyce, (eds.) (1981). *Perspectives on Organization Design and Behavior* (NY: Wiley).

Venner, Gary S. (1988). "Managing Applications as a Software Portfolio," *Journal of Information Systems Management*, V. 5., N. 3 (Summer): 14–18.

Wellar, Barry S. (1988). "Research Agenda Sessions, URISA '88," *URISA News*, No. 98 (July): 3.

Wigand, Rolf T. (1988). "Integrated Telecommunications Networking and Distributed Data Processing," in J. Rabin and E. Jackowski, (eds.), *Handbook of Information Resource Management* (NY: Dekker. Ch. 9).

Wong, Peter J. (1988). "Expert Systems Emerge from Academia," *Computer Technology Review* (January): 10.

Wysong, E. M. and I. de Lotto, (eds.) (1983). *Information Systems Auditing* (Amsterdam: North Holland).

12

Performance Appraisal

In a summary of literature on organizational design and systems analysis published in 1965, Haberstroh drew two broad conclusions from his review of performance measurement research: "First, performance reporting is omnipresent and necessarily so. Second, almost every individual instance of performance reporting has something wrong with it" (Haberstroh, 1965). Performance appraisal remains both omnipresent and problematic today (Daley 1992; Zalesny and Highhouse, 1992; Gross, 1995).

Performance appraisal is a pivotal *management technique* with a number of purposes and dimensions. It involves a systematic evaluation of the employee by his or her supervisor or some other qualified person(s) who is familiar with the employee's performance on the job. The purposes for which performance appraisal can be employed are twofold: *judgmental* and *developmental* (Daley, 1992). Performance appraisal in its judgmental expression directly impacts a number of workforce decisions such as promotion, demotion, pay, transfer, and retention. From a judgmental perspective, performance appraisal is explicitly linked to extrinsic rewards and punishments and is an expression of the command and control model of authority (Daley, 1992, p. 16). From a developmental perspective, performance appraisal seeks to "add value" to the employee by developing intrinsic motivation and providing opportunities for training and professional growth (Daley, 1992).

Performance appraisal is fundamentally a form of *measurement* and, therefore, involves questions of validity (are we measuring what we think we are?) and reliability (is that measurement stable over time?). Performance appraisal takes many forms. It may be conducted by means of a standardized instrument that is adapted to the needs of a particular organization. It may involve peer assessment. Performance appraisal may also be designed to measure team rather than individual performance (Nord, 1979, Nalbandian, 1981; Ammons and Rodriguez, 1986; Dulewicz, 1991; Zalesny and Highhouse, 1992; Gross, 1995).

Performance appraisal, as a form of measurement, attempts to evaluate employee work output. Moreover, since performance appraisal is typically an important factor in salary and promotion decisions, performance appraisal is one mechanism by which organizational rewards and sanctions are invoked. As such, performance appraisal is inherently controversial and can affect employee motivation and organizational commitment (Pearce and Porter, 1986; Zalesny and Highouse, 1992; Daley, 1992). Many performance appraisal systems are predicated on assumptions similar to those of expectancy theory; that is, for a performance system to work most job holders must expect that their performance will lead to positive rewards before they will expend the effort that leads to productive performance (Perry et al., 1989). If the performance appraisal system is perceived as unrelated to those rewards, for whatever reason, then its ability to motivate people toward increased productivity and other goals is compromised (Schneier et al., 1986; Daley, 1992)

Today, employee and public demands for better performance appraisal systems is greater than ever before. This demand is a function of budgetary constraints and the anti-bureaucratic climate that has been prevalent since the Carter administration. These factors have led to increased calls for more "efficiency" in government. In 1978 Congress passed the U.S. Civil Service Reform Act (CSRA). In 1984, largely to deal with shortcomings of the CSRA, it created the performance management and recognition system (PMRS). Both of these endeavors attempted to relate a performance appraisal system to an increase in job performance. The "pay for performance" movement, along with calls for increased "productivity," have spread to the state level, resulting in an ever increasing demand to measure and direct public sector employee performance at all levels of management (Ammons and Rodriguez, 1986; Pearce et al., 1985; Halachmi and Holzer, 1987; Ammons and Condrey, 1991; Daley, 1992).

Moreover, performance appraisal has important implications for affirmative action programs and equal opportunity. Since the passage of the Civil Rights Act of 1964, American courts have sought to mandate objective personnel practices.

> While the employment of objective performance appraisal techniques and processes should be an ordinary occurrence. It has, unfortunately, all too often taken legal intervention with its implied threat of negative sanctions to introduce their practice. American management practices, especially when applied to the public sector, are notorious in their seeking out shortcuts and short circuits. Unfortunately, little effort is often expended on validating many of these easier alternatives. The extension of the *Griggs v Duke Power Company* (1971) decision to clearly include performance appraisal systems (Connecticut v Teal, 1982) changed all this (Daley, 1992, p. 5).

Performance appraisal implicitly raises questions of perceived equity versus merit in the workplace These are the types of questions that involve conflicting values and are not likely to be resolved in the short run (Rabin, 1984; Perry, 1986; Daley 1992). In short, performance appraisal is an important topic on the agenda of most public sector managers throughout the 1990s and beyond. In this chapter we will review the performance appraisal process by first defining terms and concepts related to measurement and addressing the needs of the organization regarding performance appraisal and the context within which those needs unfold. Then we explore alternative approaches for achieving performance assessment objectives and specify criteria to be considered in a model system. Finally, we discuss the very specific managerial skills required in the assessment interview as well as discuss the managerial implications of the performance appraisal literature.

ORGANIZATIONAL NEEDS: EVALUATING PERFORMANCE

Performance appraisal is an exercise in measurement. It is an effort at "formally, rationally, and objectively organizing our assessments of others" (Daley, 1992, p. 14). All measurement is the attempt to define and quantify some aspect of reality (Nunnally, 1967). Measurement involves questions of reliability, validity, operational definitions, and constructs. Since many performance appraisals are conducted with standardized protocols that seek to objectively assess the performance of others, a brief discussion of the terms and concepts that underlie the psychometrics of performance measurement is necessary.

Measurement typically involves providing an operational definition of a construct. For example, if an organizational researcher is attempting to study the work attitudes of "southerners" in the U.S. he or she must be in a position to define the "south" and "southerner." Is the "south" the states that formed the Confederacy? If it is then Texas and Florida are in the "south." Accordingly, residents of south Florida, residents of the Virginia cities that rim Washington D.C., and the Research Triangle Park area of North Carolina are southerners. However, many scholars and native southerners would argue that the areas just mentioned are characterized by a high migration of people from outside the region who now equal or outnumber the indigenous population and that these areas and their residents do not represent the "south" or true "southerners." They might go on to contend that Texas is not in the "south" but rather in the "west." In so doing, they have rejected a historical/geographical definition of the south. In its place they may choose to define the south as that section of the U.S. where English is spoken with a "southern accent" imposing instead a linguist definition of the south. In the process, they would in all likelihood extend the definition of the "south" beyond the eleven states of the Confederacy, as well as eliminate some sections of those states once a part of the Confederacy, for example, the southern part of Florida. Others might argue that to be a "southerner" you would have to be born and raised in the south imposing a sociological definition on the region and its inhabitants. Still others would argue preferences for food and music define a true member of the region insisting on a cultural definition of both the "south" and a "southerner."

What is the answer to this dilemma? Is the "south" a historical/geographical, a linguistic, a cultural, or a sociological region of the United States? It is in fact *all of them* since the "south" is a construct with no fixed or immutable *real* definition. For a particular purpose, however, such as research about work attitudes, each of these operational definitions of the south would be appropriate, although each independently could lead to different people being defined as southerners. In effect, there is no real definition of the south only operational definitions. Similarly, there is no real definition of a southerner, only an operational one. Operational definitions of constructs are necessary because language is inherently ambiguous. Without an operational definition we could never be sure which of a wide variety of dimensions of a construct (e.g., the linguistic or geographical) is being employed in a particular context. However, once we are presented with an operational definition we may or may not agree that it captures all the dimensions of the construct. Nonetheless, we at least know how it was measured, for example, the south for this study of work attitudes included people residing in the eleven states of the Confederacy and we can evaluate any conclusions resulting from the research accordingly.

The relationship of performance appraisal to the previous discussion is that in a performance appraisal system we seek to measure constructs that have a variety of dimensions. Simply stated, if you are measuring performance in the workplace, one of the first steps is to define the dimensions of performance you seek to measure. Let's take a look at one performance measurement process using as an example the management excellence inventory (MEI). MEI is a tool developed by the U.S. Office of Personnel Management (OPM) for use by federal agencies and is predicated on a competencies-based model of effective management. The model contains characteristics common in varying degrees to management at all levels of government and in different organizational settings (Flanders and Utterback, 1985; Daley, 1992). *Effective management*, like the south, has no "real" definition only operational definitions. Effective management is a construct with a variety of dimensions and therefore potentially different operational definitions. What is important is that these dimensions be job related. The MEI attempts to establish the "what" or content dimension of effective management. It also attempts to define the "how" or behavioral dimension of effective management. The content dimension in the MEI is broken down into categories that include the following: external awareness, interpretation, representation, coordination, work unit planning, work unit guidance, budgeting, material resources administration, personnel management, supervision, work unit monitoring, and program evaluation. The behavioral dimension includes: broad perspective, strategic view, environmental sensitivity, leadership, flexibility, action orientation, results focus, communication, interpersonal sensitivity, and technical competence (Flanders and Utterback, 1985). Each of these terms attempts to capture some element of the construct effective management and are job related. Each of the terms listed above has an operational definition. For example, the MEI provides the following definition for supervision by specifying the following behavioral indicators.

Make daily work assignments to subordinates.

Help subordinates identify their development needs and means for meeting them.

Explain task expectations so that each subordinate clearly understands his or her role.

All performance appraisal systems attempt to measure how well (or badly) employees are doing relative to some standard. Moreover, the goal of performance appraisal is to increase organizational effectiveness. The chosen performance measures must be reliable or stable over time. They must also be practical in that they are accessible to the organization's managers and are regarded as appropriate by those being measured. Finally, they must represent behavior or results over which the employee has actual control (Zalesny and Highhouse, 1992; Daley, 1992). However, not all performance appraisal systems meet these criteria equally well. In fact, some performance appraisal systems measure performance quite inadequately. As stated previously, job-relatedness has emerged as the chief standard used to evaluate a performance appraisal instrument. This is both a requirement of good measurement and a requirement of the courts who have consistently reaffirmed and explained requirements for job relatedness (*Brito v Zia Company; Ramirez v Hofheinz,1980; Zell v United States*). The case law in this area makes it incumbent on public managers and their organizations to develop performance appraisal systems that discriminated between employee solely in terms of their job performance. Moreover, the burden is on the organization to be able to prove the existence of a relationship between the performance appraisal system and job performance.

There has been a movement away from performance appraisal systems which measure traits to those that focus on behaviors. This movement has occurred to make performance measures more valid and reliable because behaviors (He or she makes daily work assignments to subordinates) are less subjective than traits (He or she shows judgment). While the topic of validity and reliability are mathematically quite complex, a basic understating of these topics is important to the practicing manager. When is a measure valid? Broadly speaking, validity is the degree to which a measure (test or performance appraisal instrument) measures what it is supposed to measure. Reliability, on the other hand, is the degree of internal consistency or stability of the measuring device over time. For example, an anatomy test administered in Russian to a group of top notch American medical students might be very reliable. They would do consistently poorly over time. However, such a test would *not* be a valid measure of the students knowledge of anatomy, since low scores on the test would reflect a lack of understanding of Russian and not anatomy. Since all performance appraisal systems attempt to measure and rank individuals on some performance dimension, we need to be certain that performance appraisal instruments are valid, that they measure what they are supposed to, for example, performance on the job, and reliable, that the measurement is stable over time (Borg and Gall, 1983; Heller, 1986).

There are many obvious reasons that performance appraisal needs to be valid and reliable. Human resources represents the largest and most valuable factor of production in the public sector. As such, the organizational capacity for "clear thinking" on performance appraisal has always been important. Now, however, three new factors in the environment of human resource management place more stringent demands on performance appraisal systems. First, the reluctance of the public to pay higher taxes, the continuing demand for public services, and the spiraling costs of producing and delivering existing goods and services, have placed extraordinary productivity demands on government. Well-constructed and implemented performance appraisal is often relied on as a panacea for meeting this challenge. While effective performance can't reduce these conflicting environmental pressures, it may provide the basis for a more rational managerial response to the legislative alert to bureaucratic waste. Performance appraisal can also be an important tool in defining the work that the organization and its members have been designated to perform and help to evaluate the contribution of organizational members toward that end (Huettner, 1988).

Second, increased demand for equitable treatment of employees has challenged performance appraisal systems. Valid and reliable performance appraisal instruments can demonstrate equity to groups protected under various equal employment opportunity (EEO) laws and regulations. Because performance appraisals are used in making a variety of selection decisions including promotion, merit raise, compensation, training, and transfer, they must meet the standards promulgated by the various EEO guidelines. In other words, performance appraisal is a selection procedure and as such may be grounds for a charge of discrimination (Heller, 1986). In this context, performance appraisal measurement that attempts to delineate the job and task competencies of various types of positions will have a direct impact on the comparable worth controversy. In the case AFSCME v State of Washington (1983), decided under Title VII of the Civil Rights Act of 1964, the federal court found that the state of Washington had intentionally underpaid women in female dominated state jobs. They used as a standard of comparison male dominated jobs. This case set into motion a stream of litigation in the U.S. Courts, and has generated proposed legislation in Congress. Comparable worth may well be the employment issue of the 1990s and beyond (Sullivan, 1985). The history of the comparable worth controversy has been outlined by George Sape in an important article "Coping with Comparable Worth" appearing in the *Harvard Business Review*:

> Wage comparability surfaced as a discrete issue within the broader framework of EEO concerns when women's activists groups realized that "equal pay for equal work," the traditional standard for determining pay discrimination, left some important sources of pay disparity unaddressed. This standard is set forth in the 1963 Equal Pay Act, which predates Title VII, and addresses wage disparity not as a civil rights matter but merely as one of a series of pay administration questions embodied in the Fair Labor Standards Act. Moreover, in adopting the Equal Pay Act, Congress specifically rejected the comparison of men's salaries when the job could not be shown to be equal or substantially equivalent.
>
> As women's understanding of workplace discrimination evolved, their attention shifted from problems of equal pay to the issue of comparable pay. This shift was premised on the realization that even though the Equal Pay Act was correcting pay rates in substantially equivalent jobs held by both men and women, such jobs represented only a portion of those jobs women held. Most women-dominated jobs, in fact, had no equivalent male comparisons and were thus outside the scope of the Equal Pay Act (Sape, 1985, p. 146).

Advocates of comparable worth want to have employers evaluate the job components and make a decision on those aspects of job content that the employer believes should determine the overall worth of the job. This would require an extensive investment in performance appraisal and evaluation systems. After evaluating all of the jobs based on their job components and required competencies, proponents want employers to set rates of pay based on these job evaluations independent of external or market data (Sullivan, 1985). Advocates of comparable worth are characterized as seeking "internal equity." Opponents of comparable worth argue that the competitive market not "fair pay" levels, should determine the wage structure and that job evaluation systems for all of the nation's employers would be a logistical nightmare, too costly, and too bureaucratic (Sullivan, 1985). Opponents of comparable worth are characterized as seeking "external equity" that is, letting the marketplace set the wage rate for jobs. While it is too soon to determine the outcome of this controversy, it is clear that comparable worth, affirmative action, and all performance appraisal systems involved in selection and promotion of people in the workplace will remain under scrutiny given the increasing diversity of the workforce.

In a more general context than comparable worth, Dena Schneier reports that the courts have found the use of performance ratings to be discriminatory when:

They are based on subjective and ill-defined criteria.

They might be affected by sexual and/or racial bias.

They are not collected and scored under standardized conditions, thus affecting their reliability and validity.

The content of the rating instrument is not based on a careful job analysis.

They are not shown to be job related through proper validation studies (Schneier, 1978, Heller, 1986; Craigh et al., 1986; Daley, 1992).

The last reason that more attention must be paid to performance appraisal is the ascent of public sector unions. Performance appraisal systems have been targeted as an important subject in public sector arbitration. In the federal workforce this trend has been accelerated by the required consultation with labor organizations in federal agency design of performance appraisal programs (Federal Personnel Manual, Chapter 430). William Holley's analysis of arbitration decisions focusing on the performance appraisal component of collective bargaining agreements provides guidance to public sector managers (Holley, 1978). Typical examples of actions where arbitrators rule in favor of the grievant include:

1. When the employee has been denied the right to review performance appraisal records.
2. When performance appraisal systems are altered without consultation with union officials.
3. When appraisals are administered at improper times.
4. When a performance appraisal form doesn't meet the requirements and specifications of the collective agreement.
5. When employees are not made aware of performance standards that will be used in appraisals.

In taking adverse action against employees, there is one point managers shouldn't ignore. When an employee is discharged on the basis of negative performance appraisal, the burden of proof rests on the employer to justify the discharge. Arbitrators have also required employers to demonstrate that performance standards are in fact attainable. As a strategy for preventing endless challenges to management decisions, public sector managers are advised to anticipate increasing union interest in performance appraisal and design performance appraisal programs that are sensitive to the thinking of union representatives.

OBJECTIVES OF PERFORMANCE APPRAISAL SYSTEMS

Typically, performance appraisal systems are adopted in order to serve one or more of the following objectives:

1. Management development—to provide a framework for developing employees by identifying and preparing individuals for enlarged responsibilities.
2. Performance measurement—evaluating individual employee accomplishments and measuring the relative value of an employee's contribution to the overall task of the organization.
3. Performance improvement—identifying areas of individual weakness and devising strategies for strengthening employees accordingly.
4. Compensation—determining salary and merit pay based upon performance.
5. Identifying potential—targeting candidates for promotion or transfer within the organization.
6. Feedback—discussing actual performance level against the organization's performance standards for an employee.
7. Manpower planning—evaluating the present supply of human resources for replacement planning.
8. Communications—providing a setting for open exchange between supervisors and subordinates (Lazer and Wikstrom, 1977; Craigh et al., 1986; Daley 1992).

Most performance appraisal systems cannot meet all these objectives simultaneously. One survey which asked 25 private sector human resource managers to list problems encountered with performance appraisal found the first item listed to be the conflicting and multiple uses of performance appraisal. Though the practical advantage of a multipurpose appraisal system is clear, its pitfalls should be acknowledged. We can illustrate this point by analyzing four broad kinds of performance appraisal: development planning, work review, compensation review, and human resource allocation planning.

In *development planning*; which exists to improve the individual's skills and motivate individuals to take initiative for their own professional development, the manager is the consultant. As such he or she helps, supports, and evaluates the employee. The employee is the initiator, risk taker, creator, and definer of the situation. By contrast, in the *work review*, which is supposed to improve short-range productivity, the manager assumes the role of boss, director, controller, and evaluator. In this context the employee is a subordinate, responding to direction, although perhaps suggesting ideas. In the *compensation* review; where the purpose is to motivate effort and to improve productivity, the manager is clearly an appraiser who evaluates the employee and judges his or her comparative value. Here the employee becomes his or her own advocate, evaluating and negotiating with the manager. Finally, in the *human resource planning* situation; where performance appraisal is used to assure long range productivity and organizational effectiveness, the manager evaluates and recommends. In the human resource planning context, the employee is basically a salesperson promoting him or herself in light of the organization's long-range plans. Clearly, each of these appraisal situations gives rise not only to different, even incompatible roles, but also calls for different managerial skills, occasions different processes, and stimulates different problems (Lazer and Wikstrom, 1977; Malinauskas and Clement, 1987; McGregor, 1988; Daley, 1992).

Critical to effective performance appraisal is the manager's firm grasp of the purpose of each review. To the extent that purposes may be in conflict, effective management of the system demands awareness of the tension points. Organizations and managers must clearly define what they want performance appraisal to do for them. With criteria established and roughly ranked, organizations and managers can be prepared to explore alternative forms of performance appraisal technique. Before turning to specific appraisal techniques, however, general characteristics of an effective performance appraisal system should be addressed.

In promulgating its performance appraisal system for a federal employee, the U.S. Office of Personnel Management suggests the following list of characteristics as providing a frame of reference for effective performance appraisal systems:

1. Performance is measured against established comprehensive standards which are written in a clear and explicit style and communicated to the employee at entry on the job and at the beginning of the appraisal period.

2. Performance appraisal information is used for specific purposes, e.g., to determine developmental needs, awards, and retention and not for vague abstract reasons, such as appraisal for promotion potential unrelated to a particular type of job.

3. Appraisal criteria and techniques are appropriate to the specific purposes for which the appraisal is being done.

4. The information produced is useful for work-related decisions.

5. Data are as objective, reliable, and valid as possible.

6. Instruments for performance review and appraisal are easy for the participants to understand and use.

7. Supervisors are appraised in terms of how competently they perform their supervisory duties.

8. Employees are kept informed about methods and purposes of appraisals.

9. A process exists which allows for impartial resolution of complaints and review.

10. Employees are promptly notified in writing and preferably orally, too, of the results of their performance appraisal. To prevent misun-

derstanding about whether the appraisal was given or what the appraisal contained each employee is asked to indicate by signature and date, the receipt of the appraisal, not agreement with it.

11. Employees' performance appraisals are kept current.
12. There is no attempt to satisfy all the management purposes of the appraisal at a single annual discussion of performance. Systems provide additional opportunity for supervisors and employees to discuss, improve, and plan for job performance.
13. Employees are informed about the steps the agency will follow in using appraisal information to make decisions to reward, promote, reassign, train, retain in RIF, or demote employees (Levinson, 1980; Perry et al., 1989; Daley, 1992).

CONTEXT FACTORS AFFECTING PERFORMANCE APPRAISAL

Both task characteristics and organizational arrangement need to be taken into account in designing a performance appraisal system (Dornbusch and Scott, 1975; Schneier et al., 1986; Daley, 1992). Task, complexity, goal clarity, and predictability all bear on the appraisal process.

If a task is highly complex, such as provision of human services by public agencies, evaluation criteria need to be established for all parts of the process and costs in time and effort need to be weighed in order to learn the level of measurement for subtask achievement. Also, when goals are highly diffuse, as in the public sector, they do not allow for clear specification of performance properties. Efforts to impose specificity may result in goal transformation or goal displacement (Dornbusch and Scott, 1975; Schneier and Beatty, 1979; Pearce and Porter, 1986; Zalesny and Highhouse, 1992). Haberstroh warns that "performance measures should reflect real goals, for they surely will become operational goals in the day-to-day work patterns of affected personnel" (Haberstroh, 1965). Finally, if a task outcome is predictable, assessment of performance on the basis of results may yield inaccurate information. Outcomes may be unpredictable when factors other than the skill of the employee control performance. Potential controlling factors could include budget contingencies, client cooperativeness, and inept policy-making (Dearden, 1987).

Organizational arrangements such as visibility of task performance also affect performance appraisal options. Many types of performance are difficult to observe because of the nature of the job, because of resistance of employees to observation, or because of prohibitive costs. Also, many employers may be conducting evaluations within a complex authority system, thus producing increased opportunity for miscommunication. For example, studies indicate that appraisals might be skewed by an appraiser's awareness, while evaluating subordinates, that he or she is also being evaluated by a superior (McGuire, 1980). Next, task interdependence is a feature of organizational life with important implications for performance appraisal. Often, particularly in public sector organizations, single outcomes cannot be traced to the contributions of individual employees. Typically, it takes a contribution from a number of functional sources to produce a desired result. When operating within the context of high task interdependence the organization might try to segment the units in which the service is produced so links can be made between individual performance and outcomes (Gross, 1995).

The distribution of power in the organization will also be reflected in the evaluation process and is a principal factor in shaping the design of performance appraisal systems. Disagreement between evaluator and employee in terms of what and how to evaluate is resolved in both the public and private sector according to the distribution of power. This explains both the pressure on the part of the appraisee, who is often represented by a union, to gain influence on the appraisal process, and the capacity of the management to escape appraisal in many organizations. When appraisers either have little input into setting the criteria for appraisal, or when they are powerless in their own positions, evaluation will suffer, no matter the design (Dornbusch and Scott, 1975).

Rosabeth Moss Kanter suggests that the reliability of formal performance measures tends to be greatest when the following conditions prevail in an organization.

1. The purpose of the appraisal is clear.
2. Tasks are simple.
3. Goals for the task are clear.
4. Outcomes are predictable.
5. Tasks are relatively independent.
6. Task performance is observable.
7. Criteria for performance are set by those later assessing performance.
8. Appraisers feel secure in their own jobs and have no personal stake in hurting the performer.

However when complexity, interdependence, power concerns, and multiple appraisal purposes increase, then so must flexibility of the appraisal system and sensitivity to its limitations (Brinkerhoff and Kanter, 1980).

PERFORMANCE APPRAISAL TECHNIQUES: A SURVEY

In this section we will survey eight performance appraisal techniques and explore two promising appraisal methods in depth.

Essay Appraisal

This technique asks appraisers to write a short narrative statement covering a particular employee's strengths, weaknesses, areas for improvement, potential, and so on. The method is often used in the selection of employees when written recommendations are solicited from former employers, supervisors, or teachers. Supervisors are free to rate performance without being constrained to rate specific attributes or responsibilities. The major disadvantage with essay appraisal is its variability in standards applied. This free form method invites supervisors to comment on different aspects of an employee's performance. While useful as part of an employee development and promotability assessment, essay appraisals are difficult to combine and compare and thus provide little assistance in salary or merit pay administration. This inability to systematically compare employees to one another across any dimension of performance, of course, limits its utility in ranking employees. Finally, a good or bad appraisal may be more of a function of the evaluator's writing ability than the level of performance of the employee.

Graphic Rating Scale

A typical graphic rating scale assesses a person on quality and quantity of his or her work and on a variety of other factors that vary with specific jobs. Often included are personal traits such as flexibility, cooperation, level of motivation, and organizational ability. Employee performance on these items is then rated using a set of adjectives listed in some form of ordinal scale (poor, fair, acceptable, good, excellent). Sometimes, quality and quantity of work, job knowledge, and planning ability are also rated. The predetermined scale allows the supervisor to assess employees on an underlying ordinal scale that can be converted into a numerical analysis (poor = 0, fair = 1, acceptable = 2, good = 3, excellent = 4). Graphic rating scales typically allow supervisors wide latitude in interpreting terms. This, in conjunction with heavy personal trait focus, produces varying standards of comparison used across raters. However, the graphic scale does produce more consistent quantifiable data than the essay appraisal, and thus lends itself more to compensation decision-making. Some combination of essay and graphic rating scale remains a common form of performance appraisal (Lacho et al., 1991; Daley, 1992).

Field Review

This type of appraisal is used as a check on reliability of the standards used among raters. A member of the personnel or central administrative staff meets with a small group of raters from each supervisory unit to go over ratings for each employee and to identify areas of dispute and to arrive at a usable standard. This group judgment technique tends to be more fair and valid than individual ratings. Though it is considerably more time consuming, when the principal individual assessment method is an essay, or graphic rating scale, the field review provides critical information on rater variation. This is especially necessary if performance appraisal is to be used in salary administration, since inter-rater reliability can effect measurement outcomes.

Forced-Choice Rating

There are many variations of this method, but the most common version asks raters to choose from among groups of statements those which best fit the person being evaluated, and those which least fit. The statements are then weighted and scored in much the same way psychological tests are scored. The theory behind this type of appraisal is that since the rater does not know what the scoring weight for each statement is, he or she cannot play favorites. A member of the personnel staff applies the scoring weight to determine the rating. Though this approach does aim for fairness, it rankles managers who feel they don't need to be "tricked" into making honest appraisals. Obviously the usefulness of this appraisal is highest for making salary determinations and is lowest as a counseling or planning instrument in the appraisal review.

Critical Incident Appraisal

Supervisors are asked to keep a record on each employee and to record actual incidents of positive and negative behavior. The evaluator's focus is on those behaviors that make a difference in executing a job effectively. This method is beneficial in that it deals with actual behavior rather than abstractions and thus provides factual incidents to discuss with an employee. But on the negative side, it is time consuming for the supervisor and it shares the free-form problem with essay appraisals. It is susceptible to varying standards of comparison and thus has limited use in salary administration.

Management By Objectives (MBO)

In this approach employees are asked to set, or help set, their own performance goals. Objectives are usually described in terms of performance standards or results, but employee development objectives are often included. Periodically employees and supervisors monitor progress against objectives and at the end of an appraisal period employees and supervisors assess performance against each objective. MBO has considerable merit in its involvement of the individual in setting standards by which he or she will be judged and its emphasis on results rather than on abstract personality characteristics.

The disadvantage of MBO is in it's susceptibility to the use of varying standards to establish performance objectives. Proper administration of MBO requires considerable time and skill. It is most appropriate for positions that require individual goal setting. Moving down the organization it is important to recognize the manipulative potential of MBO in which pseudo-participation substitutes for genuine employee involvement. If management intends to impose work standards and objectives on lower level employees it should be done openly and explicitly.

Performance Standards

This approach provides for the organization to explicitly lay down work standards instead of asking employees to set goals and objectives. The work standards technique establishes work and staffing targets aimed at increasing productivity. Under work standards the organization develops or alters position descriptions for each position to reflect all the major responsibilities and standards of performance. When realistically used and when standards are fair and visible it can be an effective type of performance appraisal. The most serious problem is that of comparability. With different standards for different people, it is difficult to make comparisons for purposes of promotion.

Assessment Centers

Assessment centers are gaining popularity for the prediction and assessment of future potential (Dulewicz, 1991). Typically, individuals from different areas are brought together to spend two or three days working on individual and group assignments. Lets take a selection example, a group of candidates may be brought together and given an "in basket" assignment and a number of scenarios about focused on approaches to a particular budget or policy problem. A group of evaluators from the department and external to it serve as evaluators. The pooled judgment of the observers is used to produce an ordered merit ranking of participants for the job. The technique is not limited to selection. The greatest drawback of this system is its time and cost. But its substantial advantage is its potential impact on equal employment opportunity. Since assessment centers are based on simulating managerial activities, they may give people currently invisible and imbedded deep in the organization a chance to demonstrate their potential to higher management in an organization (Oberg, 1972).

Given these basic performance appraisal techniques, what is the pattern of use in the public sector? At the federal level a new performance appraisal system, characterized as the "cornerstone" of the Civil Service Reform Act of 1978, is now in place. It represents a combination of several methods above and includes identifying critical elements of an employee's position, developing objectives, job related performance standards for those elements, periodic progress reviews, and a direct relationship between appraisal of performance and pay (Brown, 1982; Perry et al., 1989). Various types of performance appraisal systems are found in state and local government and survey data reporting current practices across these units of government suggest substantial variation in practices within jurisdictions. An Urban Institute study of fifty states, twenty-five counties, and twenty-five cities, conducted in the late 1970s, reported the following. Fifty of the hundred governments used systems that involved supervisor ratings of individual employees; either essay appraisals or rating instruments with nonspecific performance factors. Sixteen jurisdictions used systems in which employees were appraised on the basis of their achievement of performance targets. In the remaining governments, individual departments determined their own appraisal systems (Greiner et al., 1981). More recently, Poister and McGowan (1984), report that over 59% of the municipalities they surveyed employed MBO and that over 67% employed some type of performance monitoring. A survey by Daley, (1991) of 303 smaller cities and towns indicates a preference for objective systems. MBO is the technique of choice for the evaluation of upper management in city government (Ammons and Rodriguez, 1986). The two performance appraisal methods receiving most attention in the literature, management by objectives (MBO) and behaviorally-anchored rating scales (BARS) systems offer attractive alternatives to public managers. Both avoid the subjective nature of the previously discussed techniques and are considered objective performance appraisal systems in that they emphasize detailed job analysis (Daley, 1992, p. 80).

MANAGEMENT BY OBJECTIVES

MBO is a basic management and control system that can be used directly in individual performance appraisal (Ammons and Rodriguez, 1986; Swiss, 1991, Daley, 1992). As a management system, objectives or goals are established for the organization, each unit, each manager within each unit, and each employee within a work area (Moore and Scott, 1983). The focus in this goal setting phase is not on the behavior of the employee but on the effectiveness of the employee's contribution to organizational goals. Introduced by Peter Drucker in 1954, management by objectives is based upon a theory of motivation that assumes employees will be more productive if they participate in setting their work objectives. MBO originated as a means for senior managers to translate strategic plans into plans that could be implemented. While there are many variants of MBO, three steps are common to most.

Mutual Goal Setting

Supervisors and subordinate meet to establish results employees will achieve. Objectives established should meet the following criteria:

1. They should be linked to the important objectives of the supervisor.
2. They should represent the employee's most significant responsibilities.
3. They should be achievable with reasonable effort and within existing resource limitations.
4. They should include for supervisors managing aspects such as planning and staff development.
5. They should be stated precisely enough so that there is little chance of misinterpretation or disagreement over meaning (Allen and Rosenberg, 1968; Daley, 1992).

Coaching: Working Toward Goals

After objectives are set, employees typically enjoy substantial freedom in achieving them. But in some adaptations of MBO, coaching on the part of supervisors is strongly encouraged both to guide and to lend support to employees. The supervisor may intervene to take stock of where the work stands relative to expected results, to exchange any new relevant information, or to jointly take a look at anticipated problems. Coaching skills help the manager capitalize on the needs of employees. Participation is an important concept in MBO appraisal systems. Goals and objects are designed to be worked out in a collegial manner. Goal setting is an effective process, in and of itself, because it helps to focus and direct the efforts of individuals in the agency. It also provides a target(s) in what can be a very diffuse environment. The process of goal setting also allocates resources needed to achieve these goals (Moore and Scott, 1983; Ammons and Rodriguez, 1986; Swiss, 1991).

Reviewing Performance

In this third step within MBO, performance is appraised in terms of goal attainment. The performance review is carried out in the form of a formal discussion between the supervisor and the subordinate at the end of a work period. The purpose is to reach agreement on what was done well and what improvements are needed. In performance review it is important to keep in mind extraneous factors that may have influenced the objective levels of accomplishment such as recent legislation, budgetary uncertainty, and the whole network of other factors we have discussed.

The potential pitfalls of MBO have been catalogued in the literature (Beatty and Schneier, 1977) and focus primarily on the goal setting step. In mutual goal setting MBO may falter because of:

1. Overemphasis on objectives to the neglect of means.
2. Tendency to focus on short term results.
3. Temptation to include results already achieved.
4. Tendency to name results easily attainable.
5. Objectives established are not in the control of the employee.
6. Significant conditions under which objectives to be achieved are ignored such as decreasing cost by 15 percent without decreasing services.
7. Too many objectives may be stated, not distinguishing important objectives from unimportant objectives.

While goal setting is an especially delicate part of the MBO process, this appraisal system may falter because of a manager's neglect at the "working toward goals" or "performance review" stages. Failure of MBO may be attributed to a lack of coaching skill and willingness to apply it, or to inattention to performance review. Even with the most finely-focused goals statement MBO, as a performance appraisal device, will prove inadequate to the task when the second and third steps of the process are neglected.

BEHAVIORALLY ANCHORED RATING SCALES

While MBO focuses on employee effectiveness, behaviorally anchored rating scales (BARS) focuses on employee behavior. BARS is most effective with groups of individuals whose job descriptions can be standardized, as compared to MBO which can be tailored to individual job descriptions. BARS handles behavioral processes where outputs are more measurable than outcomes (Daley, 1992, p. 79). Also concerned with getting results, BARS identifies with the critical areas of a job and describes more or less effective job behaviors in getting results. Combining two of the approaches to performance appraisal discussed above, performance standards and critical incident, BARS appraisal instruments are based on characteristics of a job or job family. BARS appraisal instruments are constructed through the following steps:

1. Jobs to be appraised are identified.
2. Job incumbents, their managers, or both identify dimensions of the job critical to results, and write several statements describing behavior that is especially effective and especially ineffective in gaining results. Then several statements are written describing neither especially effective or ineffective behavior.
3. Statements are grouped into performance dimensions by scale designers, discarding statements that are not job specific, not observable or do not fall within one of the job dimensions. Statements assigned to a job category by at least 75 percent of the job incumbents or managers are retained.
4. Each statement is evaluated by each scale designer. Statements are assigned a scale value from 1 (very ineffective performance) to 7 or 9 (very effective performance). Within the performance dimension the mean and standard deviations are calculated for all statements. The mean rating provides the scaled level of effectiveness for each statement. The degree of agreement among raters on the scale values is indicated by the standard deviation, with a statement typically retained if its standard deviation is less the 1.5 (Goodale, 1977; Edwards, 1983, Swiss, 1991; Daley, 1992).

Specific measures which attempt to define performance dimensions and scale values in behavioral terms have been recommended by numerous researchers (Campbell et al., 1973).

BARS is a particularly useful technique if the manager gives high priority to feedback. BARS reflects a passive form of participatory management by involving the employee as a stakeholder in the performance appraisal process. By removing the ambiguity of performance appraisal, it helps reduce employee anxiety and provides the employer with very specific direction in advising the employee on performance improvement. In terms of a critical performance appraisal consideration, BARS may point the way toward less subjective and ultimately more valid performance appraisal. Additionally, because BARS is a quantitative technique, appraisal scores can be tied to salary structure and ranges of scores on BARS can be tied to different level of merit raises (Beatty and Schneier, 1977). BARS requires extensive advance work by the organization in designing their instruments and as a consequence is expensive (Daley, 1992).

We have described MBO as a broad management and control system that could have individual appraisal applications. BARS, by contrast, is an individual appraisal device with potential to catalyze an entire organization. The spinoff effects of BARS may touch the whole human resource management area. BARS may identify behavioral criteria on which to make decisions and design selection tests; it may identify specific behavioral training objectives; and it may highlight areas of poor performance in the organization where special reward structures may be installed (Beatty and Schneier, 1977; Edwards, 1983).

In terms of performance appraisal alone, managers turn to BARS because it addresses several major problems in performance appraisal feedback. Kearney (1978), identifies four compelling advantages to the BARS system:

1. Clarification of differences between behavior, performance and results.
2. Emphasis of appraisal based on observed and measurable job specific behaviors.
3. Improved observation and evaluation skills of managers through their participation in scale construction.
4. Participation of job incumbents in identifying performance dimensions and identifying and scaling job behavior thus reducing disagreement over what constitutes satisfactory performance.

Disadvantages of BARS, however, are also evident:

1. The jobs of those to be appraised must be relatively stable in content and the BARS emphasis is on inputs rather than outputs and results.
2. There must be several people performing a job to spread the cost of scale development.
3. Managers must be able to observe subordinates on a systematic basis.
4. Since pooled judgments are used, enough managers and job incumbents must be available to construct the scale.
5. BARS systems need constant attention and must have a training component.
6. BARS systems can be costly (Kearney, 1978; Daley, 1992).

Both MBO and BARS appraisal systems rest on the assumption that quality appraisal is a dynamic process, not a yearly event. Both techniques trade on a high level of participation by persons ultimately using the appraisal system. MBO, with its effectiveness emphasis, fits best where managers and employees make direct and measurable contributions to the task. In contrast, BARS may be more appropriate where individual contributions to overall effectiveness may be hard to trace. Schneier and Beatty propose that organizations consider integrating MBO and BARS systems by asking employees:

1. What (i.e., results) are you to contribute to this organization in measurable terms?

Table 3 An Integrated MBO/BARS Performance Appraisal

Job Title: Unit Supervisor of Personnel Action Processing Section
Job Objective: Ensure prompt accurate processing of all personnel action forms
Method of Measurement: Quantity

Processed Forms in Unit	Present	Date	Target	Date	Actual
% errors causing return					
% forms processed by day following receipt					

INSTRUCTIONS: Please indicate what you believe to be the typical behavior of this unit supervisor based on your observation of his/her performance.

CHECK ONE

_____ Excellent: Supervises total clerical processing of all personnel action forms. Maintains up to date knowledge of procedures and rules related to processing. Assists employees in proper processing methods and trains new employees. Attends all staff meetings involving procedures for processing forms to offer technical assistance on processing. Offers suggestions to forms development supervisor on form improvement.

_____ Very Good: Stresses the importance of immediate form processing. Has good knowledge of processes and procedures. Communicates knowledge to employees. Trains new employees. Communicates knowledge to employees. Trains new employees and offers technical assistance to staff when requested to do so. Asks employees to be timely in form processing.

_____ Good: Is able to answer questions from subordinates and staff on form processes and procedures. Once a year holds update session on new developments in form processes and procedures.

_____ Average: Gives information to subordinates on form processes and procedures but fails to stress the importance of timeliness in form processing.

_____ Below Average: Answers questions of subordinates on procedures but responses are not always accurate.

_____ Poor: Gives wrong information on response queries about proper processing of personnel action forms.

_____ Unfavorable: Fails to plan form processing work. Doesn't get forms processed in time to facilitate line manager's needs.

How could this manager improve his/her performance in the area of percent of correct personnel forms processed that is not included in the above description?

2.   How (i.e., behaviorally) do you expect to make this contribution or ac-
     complish this objective? (Schneier and Beatty, 1979).

Traditional MBO would be used to answer the first question and BARS
would be used to deal with the second (Beatty and Schneier, 1977). Table 3 provides a sample form illustrating the use of this MBO/BARS integration.
       In this illustration the Unit Supervisor of the Personnel Action Processing
Section is able to set performance expectations which are measured against qual-
ifiable measures of effectiveness, such as percent errors causing returned forms.
Additionally, an employee can point out to his manager the desired behavior
which he exhibited, even though it may not have contributed directly to the nu-
merically stated goal. Raters can also identify deficiencies which help in counseling and training decisions for employees.

Appraisal Interview

The appraisal interview, part of whatever appraisal system is in use, may be the
most difficult aspect of the process for most managers. Behavioral science research on the characteristics of the effective employee performance and development interviewing exists (Maier, 1958; Meyer et al., 1965; French et al., 1976;
Kay et al., 1965). Increasingly, evidence suggests that knowledge of interviewing skills and practicing their use strengthens the effectiveness of the session
(Burke, 1970; Malinaukas and Clement, 1987; Ferns and Rowland, 1990; Zalesny and Highhouse, 1992). Maier has argued that there are both skills and
methods requiring attention in performance appraisal. "This differentiation between skill and method is important because the goal of the interview determines
which method should be used to achieve it; and once we have clarified the
goals . . . the problem of developing the necessary skill is greatly simplified"
(Maier, 1958). Maier distinguishes between three methods of interviewing: The
"tell and sell" interview, which aims to let the employee know how he or she is
doing and to encourage compliance with an improvement plan; the "tell and listen" interview, which aims to communicate evaluation and provide for the re-
lease of defensive feelings; and the "problem solving" interview, when the
principal aim is to stimulate growth and development in the employee.
       The "tell and sell" method calls for salesmanship and patience on the part
of the appraiser. The employee is assumed to respond to positive or negative incentives extrinsic to the job itself and the appraising task is to make those connections clear. Patience is called for in managing conflicts that will develop. The
flow of communication is top down and thus such appraisal interviews tend to
perpetuate existing values. The "tell and listen" method calls for skill in listening
and reflecting feelings as well as summarizing the responses of the appraisee.
The appraiser plays the role of counselor, and motivation lies largely in breaking

down resistance to change. Also, the supportive counseling climate in itself is a motivating factor. In addition to these extrinsic motivations, if the interview results in solving a problem in the nature of the job itself intrinsic motivation is encouraged. Some upward communication is possible here as the employee responds to the employer's comments. In a third interviewing method, "problem solving," the interviewer should be skilled not only in listening to and reflecting on the employee's feelings but also in posing exploratory questions that will yield new ideas about the job and the organization. Sensitively reflecting these new thoughts back to the employee individually and in the context of summarizing is a critical appraisal skill in this method.

While some extrinsic motivations are always present, an intrinsic motivation is assumed in inviting the employee to discuss his/her job, how it might be restructured for greater productivity, and how the manager can contribute to the improved productivity effort. Motivation in this model flows from increased employee freedom and responsibility. Two-way communication, with the stress on bottom up flow, aims at mutual learning, free growth, and nurturing conditions for change. Here the active listening skills discussed in the communications chapter are particularly helpful.

Communications theory recognizes that two messages are communicated in any interpersonal exchange, a content message and a relationship message. The content has to do with what the manager and employee say, while the relationship message concerns the feelings involved in the exchange. Cohen has argued for special attention to process in performance discussions (Cohen, 1979). In the "tell and sell" method of appraising, the manager dominates the discussion and may be satisfied if she or he communicates main points. The subordinate listens passively, may feign acceptance of supervisor's assessment, but may privately harbor anger toward the critic and resentment at the exclusion of discussion. Because of traditional role expectations, this may happen even if the communications climate between the two individuals is relatively good. Cohen proposes using "process," or stopping the conversation wherever either party feels the need to make an observation that would strengthen the relationship, as a mechanism for improving performance discussion. Special conditions calling for the use of a process comment include the following:

1. When the purposes of the meeting seem not to be clear enough.
2. When there is inadequate opportunity to express ideas or share information.
3. When there is a feeling that one is not influencing the meeting as much as one wants to.
4. When the meeting tends to be dominated by one person.
5. When there appears to be not enough trust.
6. When individual needs and purposes start not being met.

7. When the discussion starts to get off target and becomes less concrete.
8. When differences in viewpoint tend to be handled, not in an adult manner through discussion and rational problem solving, but by either avoidance or imposition (Cohen, 1979).

The appraiser then has two issues to attend to: first, what method of conducting an appraisal interview is appropriate in a particular situation, and second, what attending skills are needed. Research on the content and process of appraisal interviews provides some general guidance in making this choice (Malinauskas and Clement, 1987; Zalesny and Highhouse, 1992 ; Daley, 1992).

There are conflicting views on the impact of providing performance feedback in the appraisal interview. Meyer et al., (1965) report that negative feedback, or the discussion of performance weaknesses, depresses goal achievement while positive feedback has little effect. In contrast, Cummings (1973) reports that feedback results in a more positive view of appraisal and Beveridge (1974) qualifies this point by specifying that criticism needs to be directed towards performance, not the individual employee. There is substantial evidence to suggest that on balance stressing strengths and weaknesses is the most supportive strategy for future performance (Fletcher and Williams, 1976; Stone, 1973; Fletcher, 1973). A participative approach in appraisal interview has been found most successful (Bassett and Meyer, 1968; Fletcher, 1973; Beveridge, 1974). Moreover, feedback, in general, has been identified as having a positive overall impact on the attitudes and job perceptions of public employees. Conversely the absence of feedback has been associated with negative job related attitudes in the public sector (Yeager et al., 1985).

MANAGERIAL IMPLICATIONS

Performance appraisal is a management control tool historically used to measure individual performance. Today managers should regard performance appraisal as a pivotal management technique designed to measure both individual and team performance. Additionally, managers need to conceptualize performance appraisal in both its judgmental and developmental expressions. In its judgmental expression, performance appraisal is a major element of a command and control organization impacting promotion, demotion, pay, transfer, and retention. In this sense, it is explicitly linked to extrinsic rewards and punishments. From a developmental perspective, performance appraisal seeks to develop intrinsic motivation by providing opportunities for training and professional growth. With a trend toward increased employee participation in organizational decision making and the heightened awareness of employees as a valuable resource, performance appraisal is now asked to measure employee potential and to create the context for heightened employee involvement in the overall planning process.

Performance appraisal is fundamentally a form of measurement and, therefore, involves questions of validity (are we measuring what we think we are?) and reliability (is that measurement stable over time?). Performance appraisal as a form of measurement attempts to evaluate employee work output. Moreover, since performance appraisal is typically an important factor in salary and promotion decisions, performance appraisal is one mechanism by which organizational rewards and sanctions are invoked. As such, performance appraisal is inherently controversial. Many performance appraisal systems are predicated on assumptions similar to those of expectancy theory; that is, for a performance system to work most job holders must expect that their performance will lead to positive rewards before they will expend the effort that leads to productive performance. If the performance appraisal system is perceived as unrelated to those rewards, for whatever reason, then its ability to motivate people toward increased productivity and other goals is compromised.

Today, employee and public demands for better performance appraisal systems is greater than ever before. The demands are a function of; budgetary constraints, the anti-bureaucratic climate, and the court's role, which all contribute toward moving performance appraisal toward objective measures of performance predicated on standards of job related measures. Performance appraisal clearly has important implications for affirmative action programs and equal opportunity. Performance appraisal implicitly raises questions of perceived equity versus merit in the workplace. These are the types of questions that involve conflicting values and are not likely to be resolved in an era where the workforce has become more diverse.

Managers need to be aware of two current problems: (1) confusion over what performance appraisal is supposed to do and (2) placing expectations on a single performance appraisal system that may be conflicting or contradictory. It may be that managers ask too much of performance appraisal, asking more of it than it can accomplish well. Effective public sector managers should know what they want from a performance appraisal, and opt for systems capable of producing that end while remaining aware of the contextual features limiting the capacity of any system and the interpersonal skills necessary to deliver the chosen system.

REFERENCES AND ADDITIONAL READING

Allen, Peter and Stephen Rosenberg (1968). "Formulating Usable Objectives for Manager Performance Appraisal." *Personal Journal*, (November):pp 626–629, 640.

Ammons, David N. (1987) "Executive Satisfaction with Managerial Performance Appraisal in City Government." *Review of Public Personnel Administration*, 8(1):pp 33–48.

Ammons, David N. and Stephen E. Condrey (1991). "Performance Appraisal in Local Government: Warranty Conditions." *Public Productivity and Management Review*, 14(3):pp 253–266.

Ammons, David N. and Phillip A. Nietzielski-Eichner (1985). "Evaluating Supervisory Training in Local Government: Moving Beyond Concept to a Practical Framework." *Public Personnel Management*, 14(3):pp 211–230.

Ammons, David N. and Arnold Rodriguez (1986). "Performance Appraisal Practices for Upper Management in City Governments." *Public Administration Review*, 46(5):pp 460–467.

Ashford, Susan J. and Anne S. Tsui (1991). "Self-Regulation for Managerial Effectiveness: The Role of Active Feedback Seeking." *Academy of Management Journal*, 34(2):pp 251–280.

Basset, G. A. and H. H. Meyer (1968). "Performance Appraisal Based on Self Review." *Personal Psychology*, 21:pp 421–430.

Beacham, S. T. (1970). "Managing Compensation and Performance Appraisal Under the Age Act." *Management Review*, (10):pp 51–57.

Beatty, Richard W. and Craig E. Schneier (1977). *Personnel Administration*. Reading, MA: Addison-Wesley Publishing Co.

Beveridge, W. E. (1974). "Attitudes in Three Work Organizations." *Management Education Review*, 5(2):pp 68–74.

Borg, Walter R. and Meredith D. Gall (1983). *Educational Research*, Third Edition. New York: Longman, p 936.

Brinkerhoff, Derick W. and Rosabeth Moss Kanter (1980). "Appraising the Performance of Performance Appraisal." *Sloan Management Review*, Spring:pp 3–14.

Brown, Robert W. (1982). "Performance Appraisal: A Policy Implementation Analysis." *Review of Public Personnel Administration*, (2), (Spring):pp 69–85.

Burke, Ronald J. (1970). "Characteristics of Effective Performance Appraisal Interviews." *Training and Development Journal*, March:pp 9–12.

Calhoun, Richard and Thomas H. Jerdee (1976). *Coaching In Supervision*. Chapel Hill, NC: Institute of Government.

Campbell, James E. and Gregory B. Lewis (1986). "Public Support for Comparable Worth in Georgia." *Public Administration Review*, 46(5):pp 432–437.

Campbell, J. P., M. D. Dunnette, R. D. Arvery and L. V. Hellervik (1973). "The Development and Evaluation of Behaviorally Based Rating Scales." *Journal of Applied Psychology*, (10):pp 15–22.

Cederblom, Douglas (1991). "Promotability Ratings: An Underused Promotion Method for Public Safety Organizations." *Public Personnel Management*, 20(1):pp 27–34.

Cohen, Arthur M. (1979). "Using Process in Performance Discussion." *Supervisory Management*, March:pp 33–36.

Craigh E., Richard Schneier, and Richard W. Beatty (1986). "How to Construct a Successful Performance Appraisal System." *Training and Development Journal*. 40(4):pp 38–42.

Cummings, L. L. (1973). "A Field Experimental Study of the Effects of Two Performance Appraisal Systems." *Personnel Psychology*, 26:pp 409–502.

Daley, Dennis (1984). "Gender-related Differences Among Iowa Public Employees." *Public Personnel Management*, 3(3):pp 345–354.

Daley, Dennis M. (1990b). "Great Expectations or a Tale of Two System Employee Attitudes Toward Graphic Rating and MBO-Based Performance Appraisal." *Public Administration Quarterly*, 15(2):pp 188–209.

Daley, Dennis M. (1991c). "Performance Appraisal as an Aid in Personnel Decisions: Linkages Between Techniques and Purposes in North Carolina Municipalities." Paper presented at the Annual Meeting of the American Political Science Association.

Daley, Dennis M. (1992). *Performance Appraisal in the Public Sector: Techniques and Applications*. Westport, CT: Quorum Books.

Dearden, John (1987). "Measuring Profit Center Managers." *Harvard Business Review*, Sep/Oct:pp 84–93.

Dornbusch, Sanford M., and W. Richard Scott (1975). *Evaluation and the Exercise of Authority*. San Fransisco: Jossey-Bass, p 145.

Dulewicz, V. (1991). "Improving Assessment Centers." *Personnel Management*, June:pp 50–55.

Edwards, Mark R. (1983). "Product Improvement Through Innovations in Performance Appraisal." *Public Personnel Management*, 12(1):pp 13–26.

Ferns, G. R. and K. M. Rowland, (eds.) (1990). *Performance Evaluation, Goal Setting, and Feedback*. Greenwich, CT: JAI Press.

Flanders, Loretta R. and Dennis Utterback (1985). "The Management Excellence Inventory: A Tool for Management Development." *Public Adminstration Review*, 45(3):pp 403–410.

Fletcher, Clive (1973). "Interview Style and the Effectiveness of Appraisal." *Occupational Psychology*, 47:pp 225–230.

Fletcher, Clive and Richard Williams (1966). "The Influence of Performance in Appraisal Interviews." *Journal of Occupational Psychology*, June:pp 75–85.

French, J. R. P., E. Kay and H. H. Meyer (1976). "Participation and the Appraisal System." *Human Relations*, 19:pp 3–20.

Goodale, James G. (1977). "Behaviorally-Based Rating Scales:Toward an Integrated Approach to Performance Appraisal," in W. Clay Hammer and Fred L. Schmidt (eds.) *Contemporary Problems in Personnel*. Chicago: St. Clair Press.

Greiner, John M., Harry P. Hatry, Margo P. Kass, Annie P. Millar and Jane P. Woodward (1981). *Productivity and Motivation*. Washington D.C.: The Urban Institute Press.

Gross, Steven E. (1995). *Compensation for Teams: How to Design and Implement Team Based Reward Programs*. New York: American Management Association.

Haberstroh, C. J. (1965). "Organizational Design and Systems Analysis," in J. G. March (ed.) *Handbook of Organizations*. Chicago: Rand McNally.

Halachmi, Arie and Marc Holzer. (1987). "Merit Pay, Performance Targeting and Productivity." *Review of Public Personnel Administration*, 7(2):pp 80–91.

Heller, Philip S. (1986). "EEOC Standards: What Makes for a Good Test?" *Personnel Journal*, July:pp 102–105.

Holley, William H. Jr. (1978). "Performance Appraisal in Public Sector Arbitration." *Public Personnel Management*, 7(January–February):pp 1–5.

Huettner, Charles H. (1988). "Job Task Systems Management of Government Organizations." *Public Administration Review*, 48(4):pp 783–789.

Kay, E., H. H. Mayer, J. R. French (1965). "Effects of Threat in a Performance Appraisal Interview." *Journal of Applied Psychology*, 49:pp 311–317.

Kearney, William J. (1978). "Improving Work Performance Through Appraisal." *Human Resource Management*, Summer:pp 15–23.

Lacho, Kenneth J., G. Kent Sterns, Maurice F. Villere (1979). "A Study of Employee Appraisal Systems of Major Cities in the United States." *Public Personnel Management*, March/April:pp 111–125.

Lacho, Kenneth J., G. Kent Stearns and Robert Whelan. (1991). "Performance Appraisal in Local Government: A Current Update." *Public Productivity and Management Review*, 14(3):pp 281–296.

Lawler, Edward E., III. (1990). *Strategic Pay: Aligning Organizational Strategies and Pay Systems.* San Francisco: Jossey-Bass.

Lazer, Robert and Walter Wikstrom (1977). *Appraising Managerial Performance.* New York: The Conference Board.

Levinson, Priscilla (1980). *A Guide for Improving Performance Appraisal.* U.S. Office of Personnel Management: Government Printing Office.

Lovrich, Nicholas. (1989). "Managing Poor Performers." In James L. Perry (ed.), *Handbook of Public Administration.* San Francisco: Jossey-Bass, pp. 412–425.

Maier, W. R. F. (1958). *The Appraisal Interview: Objectives Methods and Skills.* New York: John Wiley.

Malinauskas, Barbara K. and Ronald W. Clement (1987). "Performance Appraisal Interviewing for Tangible Results." *Training and Development Journal*, February:pp 74; b279.

McGregor, Eugene B. (1988). "The Public Sector Human Resource Puzzle: Strategic Management of a Strategic Resource." *Public Administration Review*, 48(6):pp 941–950.

McGuire, Peter J. (1980). "Why Performance Appraisals Fail." *Personnel Journal*, September:pp 744–746, 762.

Meyer, H. H., E. Kay, J. R. P. French, Jr. (1965). "Spilt Roles in Performance Appraisal." *Harvard Business Review*, 43 (January–February):pp 123–129.

Moore, Michael L. and Dow Scott (1983). "Installing Management by Objectives In a Public Agency: A Comparison of Black and White Managers, Supervisors, and Professionals." *Public Administration Review*, 43(2):pp 121–126.

Morrison, Elizabeth Wolfe and Robert J. Bies (1991). "Impression Management in the Feedback-Seeking Process: A Literature Review and Research Agenda." *Academy of Management Review*, 16(3):pp 522–541.

Nalbandian, John (1981). "Performance Appraisal: If Only People Were Not Involved." *Public Administration Review*, 41(3):pp 392–396.

Nord, Lloyd G. (1979). *Participative Performance Appraisal: A State-Wide Application.* Washington, D.C.: U.S. Office of Personnel Management, pp. 45–52.

Nunnally, Jum C. (1967). *Psychometric Theory.* New York: McGraw Hill.

Oberg, Winston (1972). "Make Performance Appraisal Relevant." *Harvard Business Review*, January–February:pp 61–67.

Pearce, Jone L. and Hyman W. Porter (1986). "Employee Responses to Formal Performance Appraisal Feedback." *Journal of Applied Psychology*, 71:pp 211–218.

Pearce, Jone L., W. Stevenson and James L. Perry (1985). "Managerial Compensation Based on Organizational Performance: A Time Series Analysis of the Impact of Merit Pay." *Academy of Management Journal*, 28(June):pp 261–278.

Perry, James L. (1986). "Merit Pay in the Public Sector: The Case for a Failure of Theory." *Review of Public Personnel Administration*, 7(1):pp 57–69.

Perry, James L. (1988–1989). "Making Policy by Trial and Error: Merit Pay in the Federal Service." *Policy Studies Journal*, 17(2):pp 389–405.

Perry, James L., Canala Hanzlik and Jone L. Pearce (1982). "Effectiveness of Merit-Pay-Pool Management." *Review of Public Personnel Administration*, 2(3):pp 5–12.

Perry, James L. and Theodore K. Miller (1991). "The Senior Executive Service: Is It Improving Managerial Performance." *Public Administration Review*, 51(6):pp 554–563.

Perry, James L., Beth A. Petrakis, and Theodore K. Miller (1989). "Federal Merit Pay, Round II: An Analysis of the Performance Analysis and Recognition System." *Public Administration Review*, 49(1):pp 29–38.

Poister, Theodore. H. and Robert T. McGowan (1984). "The Use of Management Tools in Municipal Government: A National Study." *Public Administration Review*, 44(3):pp 215–223.

Sape, George P. (1985). "Coping with Comparable Worth." *Harvard Business Review*, May–June:pp 145–152.

Schneier, Craig E., Richard W. Beatty, and Lloyd S. Baird (1986). "How to Constuct a Success Performance Appraisal System." *Training and Development Journal*, 40(4):pp 38–42.

Schneier, Craig E. and Richard W. Beatty (1979). "Combining BARS and MBO: Using an Appraisal System to Diagnose Performance Problems." *The Personnel Administrator*, September:pp 51–60.

Schneier, Dena B. (1978). "The Impact of EEO Legislation on Performance Appraisals." *Personnel*, July–August:pp 24–35.

Slack, James D. (1990). "Information, Training, and Assistance Needs of Municipal Governments." *Public Administration Rewiew*, 50(4):pp 450–457.

Stone, T. H. (1973). "An Examination of Six Prevelant Assumptions Concerning Performance Appraisal." *Public Personnel Management*, November–December:pp 408–414.

Sullivan, John F. (1985). "Comparable Worth and The Statistical Audit of Pay Programs for Illegal Systemic Discrimination." *Personnel Administrator*, March:pp 102–111.

Swiss, James E. (1991). *Public Management Systems: Monitoring and Managing Government Performance*. Englewood Cliffs, NJ: Prentice-Hall.

Thompson, Paul H. and Gene W. Dalton (1970). "Performance Appraisal: Managers Beware." *Harvard Business Review*, February:pp 60–68.

U.S. Merit Systems Protection Board (1990a). *Why Are Employees Leaving the Federal Government? Results of an Exit Survey*. Washington, D.C.: Government Printing Office (May).

U.S. Merit Systems Protection Board (1990b). *Working for America: A Federal Employee Survey*. Washington, D.C.: Government Printing Office (June).

U.S. Merit Systems Protection Board (1992). *Federal First Line Supervisors: How Good Are They?* Washington, D.C.: Government Printing Office.

Yeager, Samuel T., Jack Rabin, and Thomas Vocino (1985). "Feedback and Administrative Behavior in the Public Sector." *Public Administration Review*, 45(5):pp 570–575.

Zalesny M. D. and S. Highhouse (1992). "Accuracy in Performance Evaluation." *Organizational Behavior and Human Decision Processes*, February:pp 22–50.

Zigon, J. (1994). "Making Performance Appraisal Work for Teams." *Training*, (••):pp 58–63.

13
Management Ethics

The application of management ethics is one of the most challenging facets of good management. It requires action based on a firm grasp of organizational concepts and theory. Unlike decision-making in the areas of performance appraisal, management systems, and information technology—where research has provided a smorgasbord of well-described and tested techniques and strategies—applying management ethics to everyday situations presses the innovative capabilities of the public manager. Public managers must create the ethical understanding which will guide them.

At a fundamental level this ethical core was recognized by our intellectual forefathers. The literature surrounding the Pendleton Act of 1883, which enacted the basic framework for modernization of the public sector, is replete with ethical overtones. But in the 1920s, as scientific management brought a businesslike orientation to government and an engineering mentality to administration, ethical reflection became passé. New thinking focused on workflow and physical-layout analyses as private-sector management contributions worthy of adoption by public managers (Dvorin and Simmons, 1972).

Through much of the twentieth century, students of organizational behavior in the public sector have been playing catch-up with their private-sector counterparts, striving to describe public-sector organization by making adjustments to theories and concepts generated for analysis of private-sector organizations. This approach to defining research questions and seeking usable theories has had significant implications for the range of subjects considered. Models of organizational behavior in the private sector are founded on the assumption of one overriding principle which precludes most ethical debate: the principle of maximization of profit. This means that organizational behaviors are judged as "good" or "bad" depending on how they contribute to making a profit.

Though the public-sector setting always encouraged ethical discourse, public organizations relied on managers who emulated the private sector, discouraging ethical considerations. But the events of the 1970s changed all that. Briefly, two factors triggered renewed concern with public-management ethics: the dramatic drop in public confidence in social institutions, and the Watergate affair. The first the public ascribed to the failure of leaders to act ethically (Bowman, 1981). The second confirmed their feelings by revealing corruption and betrayal of public trust at the pinnacle of democratic government.

The 1980s saw little to assuage the public alarm. Through the 1980s we witnessed a series of Washington events that contributed to the clamor for a higher ethical standard in the operation of our government. The Iran-gate affair, former Attorney General Edwin Meese's involvement with the Wed-Tech imbroglio, scandals in defense-contract procurement in the Pentagon, and the demise of the all-powerful Speaker of the House, Jim Wright, suggested that corrupt or at least ethically questionable practices unfold not only at the pinnacle of democratic government, but also at the middle and lower levels of management.

Regarding the Iran-gate controversy, it is clear that there was some kind of "deal" entered into by high-level governmental officials, and that those incumbent officials chose not to enlighten the public about the nature of that "deal." In itself, of course, there is no wrong in government officials sheltering information as a requirement of national security. But the public debate around Iran-gate focused public attention on a potentially more serious problem. As one journalist put it in the summer of 1987, "A great deal of shelter has been taken over the months in . . . technicalities to disguise what actually happened . . . caught saying no when the truth was yes, public officials have said that in some metaphysical sense only they seemed to grasp, they were telling the truth . . . I think the issue is that the injunction against lying is being repealed by our leaders" (Greenfield, 1987).

The case of Edwin Meese and his business dealings with his law-school classmate, E. Robert Wallach, points up the public's requirement that the country's chief law official both abide by and appear to abide by the law. An independent council report issued in July 1985 provided the following fragments of a story. Mr. Wallach, a close friend of Mr. Meese, was representing Bruce Rappaport, who was a principal player in a major Iraqi oil-pipeline project. During that time period, Mr. Meese was confronted with the possibility of a large bill for Mr. Wallach's services related to Mr. Meese's confirmation hearing that year. Mr. Wallach had also arranged for a $40,000-per-year job for Mr. Meese's wife. While under these obligations to Mr. Wallach, Mr. Meese took several steps, dubbed "unusual activities" by the independent council's report, to promote the Iraqi pipeline. The final report concluded that the evidence did not support that Mr. Meese knowingly traded official actions on the pipeline for personal favors. However, as special investigator James C. McKay suggested, Mr. Meese had the equivalent of a "tin ear" for the harmonies of the government's ethics law.

Also in the late 1980s, the four-year investigation of the Dingle Committee in Congress revealed the extent to which blatantly unethical and illegal practices infect some of the procurement activities in the defense establishment. The prototypical case was that of William Parkin, covered extensively in the press. Mr. Parkin had served as one of the Navy's most powerful contracting officers in the Pentagon from 1966 until he retired in 1983. Starting in late 1986, Mr. Parkin, working as a defense consultant, paid more than $15,000 to obtain "inside information" on a pending Navy contract, and passed the information on to his client, Hazeltine Corporation. The FBI's taped conversations suggested Mr. Parkin "served as a middleman who paid government employees for inside information and sold it to contractors," according to a *Wall Street Journal* report (*Wall Street Journal* September 2, 1988).

Finally, in June 1988, Congressman Newt Gingrich filed a complaint that eventually led the House Ethics Committee to charge Speaker Jim Wright with 69 violations of House rules. The most serious charge accused Wright of benefiting from a corporation set up to covertly funnel illegal gifts to him and of avoiding House limits on speaking fees by selling his book in bulk to unions and other groups. In May of 1989, Jim Wright announced his resignation as Speaker.

Ironically, less than a decade later, we have witnessed the narrow survival of another Speaker of the House. The House Ethics Committee excused Speaker Newt Gingrich with a reprimand and fine after he admitted that he had failed to seek proper legal guidance before using the proceedings of his tax-exempt foundation to finance a college lecture course, broadcasted nationwide by satellite. The Speaker acknowledged that the class was aimed at the partisan goal of electing a Republican Congress, and that he had turned in false information to ethics committee investigators. As in earlier decades, ethical concerns in the 1990s have been bipartisan, with alarm being expressed in the press and the public about the campaign financing practices of both political parties. The use of presidential invitations to the White House as a fund-raising tool may have gained the lion's share of headlines in 1997, prompting a public outcry for strict scrutiny of political fund-raising across the board. The perceived problems abound: the use of "soft money" by unregistered organizations without disclosure to influence elections, the misuse of government offices and staff for political purposes, abuses of power in coercing campaign contributions, and promises of special access to government and elected officials are among the most prominent as this book goes to press. Suzanne Garment captured the unfortunate spirit of the 1990s in the title of her book *Scandal: The Culture of Mistrust in American Politics* (1991).

However, there are signs of hope. One of the most striking features of the ethics crises of the mid-1990s was their focus on elected rather than appointed officials. Progress has been made, particularly in the organization of a structure for teaching and monitoring ethics in appointed positions, especially at the federal-government level. Still, one common response to the citation of news clips on unethical actions among officials, elected or appointed, is to decry the deterioration of a formerly intact moral code; others demur, arguing that things are really no worse than they ever were and that the "ethical crisis" is a product of the media (Josephson, 1988, p. 3). But as one analyst points out, this comparative approach misses the point. "It doesn't much matter whether our ethics are better or worse . . . Times are different and there is a problem. We must face up to the fact that the cumulative effect of several major incidents puts a spotlight on ethics" (Josephson, 1988, p. 3).

So, in the waning years of the 20th century, as in the waning years of the 19th century, students and officials of public-sector organizations are again discussing the ethical dimension of organizational behavior. But where the ethically sensitive "reformer" of a century ago found a fairly straightforward remedy to the "morality" problem in government organizations, today's observer confronts complexity and ambiguity. In most areas of management, we try to provide managers with answers. Treatment of ethics requires a different approach, stimulating managers to ask the right questions.

But, like other areas of management, our discussion of ethics assumes that the practice of ethics can be improved by learning. True, ethics is not taught in the way management systems is taught, and a person's sense of ethics develops over time. Still, one overcomes obstacles to ethical behavior by developing ethical consciousness, competency, and commitment. Education addresses ethical consciousness and competency (Sprinthall and Sprinthall, 1990). Commitment, as in all aspects of good management practice, depends on the practitioner.

Ethical consciousness and ethical competency imply an awareness of current thinking on the nature of the ethics issue and a capacity to utilize current knowledge to follow ethical strategies of action. First, we compare today's disparate definitions of public management ethics to the apparent consensus on "the ethical question" a century ago. Next, we describe three major avenues managers may take in thinking about ethics. Finally, we advance a matrix capturing the major dimensions of variation and fit a strategy to each intersection.

ETHICS DEFINED

When governmental reformers argued for passage of the Civil Service Reform Act of 1883 (the Pendleton Act), their argument was moral. A striking unity of perspective prevailed on the character of the moral challenge occasioned by the spoils system. The reformers were persons deeply concerned with liberty who saw "spoils" as enslaving the body politic (Van Riper, 1958). Civil service reform was held forth as the instrument for elevating the moral tone of political life (Van Riper, 1958). Quite simply, civil service reformers of the Guilded Age defined ethics in government as synonymous with civil service reform (Cooper, 1994, p. 4). But today the consensus of our ethically-confident Victorian forefathers is gone.

Even a casual reading of contemporary public-management ethics literature reveals competing definitions. Often ethics is defined for the practicing manager as a "set of standards by which human actions are determined to be right or wrong" (Bowman, 1981). This vision is followed up by studies of practitioners' use of and response to the American Society for Public Administrators Code of Ethics (Bowman, 1990, 1997). A related but distinct perspective views the task as inculcating administrators with values of law and legal tradition (regime values) (Rohr, 1989). Some definitions stress the subjective nature of managerial ethics: "An ethical problem is one where at least some of the actors actually perceive a dilemma of competing ethical criteria (or ethical criteria competing with pragmatic considerations) being raised by some action" (Godfrey and Zashin, 1981). Others take the vantage point further and suggest revising the objectivist approach to ethics so as to shift attention away from the "facts of the matter" and the rules involved. This interpretive perspective would emphasize the personal-development agenda of the people involved (McSwain and White, 1987). Still other definitions shift the focus of ethics to impact: "[Ethics] is concerned primarily with the impact of decisions on people within and without organizations, individually and collectively. Any action which has a present or potential impact on human beings involves ethics" (Evans, 1981). One author turns to the concept of administrative discretion and sees the exercise of individual power at the root of ethics for the public manager (Worthley, 1981). And however ethics is defined, increasingly scholars agree with John Rohr that expertise in the ethics domain is central to the administrator's claim of competence (Rohr, 1996).

To a great extent these different perspectives represent numerous role or value-sets which are the sources for the decisions that administrators must make (Van Wart, 1996). The common thread which runs through most definitions of ethics is some notion of obligation (Waldo, 1980).[1] Taking the concept of obligation as a common theme, it is possible to identify three distinct approaches to analyzing public-management ethics today. Each approach yields a dichotomous variable. The first approach focuses on the agent bearing the obligation, the individual or the organization. The second approach considers the negative or affirmative nature of the obligation incurred. The third approach analyzes loci of response to the obligation, or whether the source of the regulation is internal or external. While this way of partitioning the ethics field does not deny obvious interdependencies across approaches, it is a mechanism for sorting through current analyses.

APPROACHES TO ETHICAL ANALYSIS[2]

The Moral Agent: Individual or Organization

In the early 1970s Harlan Cleveland observed that "The first line of defense against anti-public actions by Public Executives is to develop their own moral sensitivities" (Loucks, 1981). Lodging responsibility for ethical judgment with individual administrators underpins the popular press' admonitions to public officials. Fitting with this perspective, the postmortem on the Watergate experience in the mid-1970s diagnosed the affair as a problem of character failure, and in the decade of the 1990s presidential debates focus intensely on questions of character. However, after decades of revelations about the ethically questionable practices managers often abide, we conclude the "flawed character" diagnosis may be simplistic.

Managers on the front line rarely encounter issues that present themselves as involving a choice between "doing the right thing" or "doing the wrong thing." On the contrary, managers typically report that the first question confronting them when they believe they are facing a moral dilemma is whether or not they have any right to self-consciously treat their decision as an ethical one. Before even getting to "what is good" or "what is moral," most managers ask: "What right do I personally have to exercise moral judgment in this case?" (Powers and Toffler, 1980; Toffler, 1986). Does this dilemma call for responsible action from me or from the organization? Public administration literature points to the complexity of this question (Harmon, 1995) and to the competing perspectives on answers (Burke, 1996; Cooper, 1996).

But, from the practitioner's perspective, one may ask: Is this distinction between individual and organizational ethics a valuable one? A positive response requires rejecting two popular concepts of ethics that excuse or shield individual culpability. Dennis Thompson urges the rejection of both the "ethics of neutrality" and "the ethics of structure" to excuse individuals for personal responsibility for their actions. The neutrality ethic asserts that administrators should not follow their own moral principles, but neutrally follow the policies and decisions of the organization. The ethics of structure holds that not administrators, but the organization should be held responsible for decisions (Thompson, 1985). Thompson rejects both as a substitute for individual responsibility. Quoting Robert Nozick, he concludes, "Responsibility is not a bucket in which less remains when some is apportioned out" (Nozick, 1974, p. 130).

Personal ethics determines right or wrong individual behavior in interaction with others in the organization. Organizational ethics serves to set the parameters and specify the obligations for the organization itself, and defines the context within which personal ethical decisions are forged. Probing the natures of personal ethics and organizational ethics in a public-agency setting provides a firm basis for considering critical areas of interaction.

On the personal or individual level, available evidence suggests that

". . . managers are interested in ethical issues and can identify them as being associated with rules and standards, morals, right and wrong, and values of honesty" (Bowman, 1981). Empirical studies available indicate that most administrators reject the claim that concern with ethics is a passing fad in government (Bowman, 1990, 1997). The source of the ethical dimension for the individual public manager is his/her authority to take action affecting persons inside and outside the organization (Worthley, 1981). Given that authority, Stephen Bailey describes the mindset needed for ethical behavior in the public service as a blend of moral qualities and mental attitudes. The requisite mental attitudes include awareness of moral ambiguity inherent in the public service, appreciation of contextual forces that play in decision situations, and sensitivity to the "paradoxes of procedures" which might lead to rules frustrating responsible action. Qualities supporting ethical attitudes are optimism, courage, and charity, or a willingness to lose oneself in public service (Bailey, 1965). While such a mindset may well equip a public manager for ethical decision-making, the real world of practicing administration often challenges these qualities to their limits. The public employee is expected to behave competently, efficiently, honestly, loyally, responsively, fairly, and accountably with no clear directions on priorities. Worthley describes in rich detail the competing claims placed on the individual moral actor in the public agency today:

> At the micro level, the level of the individual employee, this is no smooth environment in which to work. The tax auditor reviewing a tax return is faced with supporting efficiency (reviewing the most returns possible), fairness (taking time to inform me of what he is doing and giving me an appeal), accountability (responding to his appointed superior who says to take it easy on middle income returns), and the rule of law (doing precisely what the regulations stipulate). The caseworker faces the rule of law (which specifies eligibility), responsiveness (listening to all applicants), honesty (reporting the exact income figures), expertise (judging whether an applicant is truly in need), and efficiency (processing the most cases possible). And the supervisor is expected to be responsive (understanding and sympathetic to subordinates), fair (treating all subordinates with the same standard), legal (enforcing the rules and conforming to civil service regulations), and expert (handling each subordinate with managerially sound methods). What does one do? (Worthley, 1981).

It is in this context that the organization emerges as the institution capable of either guiding individual members through this series of ethical tugs-of-war or compounding and rigidifying ethical dilemmas. Bowman reports that, when faced with ethical dilemma, people turn first to the immediate organization itself for help (Bowman, 1981). But with the growth of organizations in both size and complexity has come a diffusion of responsibility and accountability, so that there are no specific persons charged with setting standards (Bowman, 1981). When individual judgment reflects group norms, the organization becomes the moral community, the referent for determining right from wrong (Bowman, 1981). With the organization as the moral community, the supervisory role incorporates some elements of the moral advisor; public managers become norm-setters (Rizzo and Patka, 1981).

Here the empirical data are alarming. Bowman reports in his national studies of public administrators that in 1989 and 1996 many supervisors were under pressure from top levels of their organizations to compromise standards (50% in 1989 and 46% in 1996) and that a majority doubt that ethical standards of elected and appointed officials are as high as those of career civil servants (60% and 55% respectively) (Bowman, 1990, 1997).

It is in the interaction between individual and organizational ethics that some of the most difficult issues and greatest opportunities arise. From the vantage point of the organization, the atmosphere cultivated can foster either integrity or baseness among employees. An organization which presses individuals to achieve results while disregarding means fosters unethical behavior (Bowman, 1981). The individual who challenges the agency must weigh his or her own assessment of right against that of the organization. In cases of unresolvable conflict it may be necessary for the individual to leave the organization. But typically, conflicts between individual and organizational judgment of "good" center on a competing claims issue. For example, one public manager reported the following dilemma to us:

> Recently I encountered a problem involving my interpretation of the law as opposed to the division director's interpretation of the law. Based on my experience in another program, I am certain that case law in this area supports my interpretation. While it was my desire to request an "opinion" from the office of the state attorney general in an attempt to receive the favorable ruling for a client, the director vetoed this and ruled the case closed. My dilemma was this: Should I have informed the client to request an opinion from the AG's office, thereby going over the head of the director, or should I honor the order of the director and close the case?

Viewed from the perspective of the organization as a whole, broad program interests might be served by the director's decision to close the case. Perhaps the division director wanted to delay a premature ruling in the hopes that a ruling at a later point would benefit a larger proportion of the program clientele. The competing claims at stake in this case would be those of the individual client versus those of the entire program clientele. After weighing the interests involved, the administrator recounting this dilemma must still consider his or her own ethical burden: What powers does the individual administrator have? What obligations go with these powers? What are the limits of one's authority and responsibility?

George Graham advises the administrator to be guided by the following rules when such dilemmas arise:

> Recognize that the rules of the game permit him to contest a decision made by his own organization, but not yet final, by going to other organizations within the government . . . only when he can honestly ensure himself 1) that a mistake is being made on an issue of major public importance; 2) that his judgment is unbiased by personal or partisan, as opposed to public interest, considerations 3) that the risk he runs of being forced out of government is justified by the importance of the issue; and 4) that what will be lost by the decision outweighs the value of his probable future usefulness to the government if he continues in government . . .
>
> [Finally] resign if he cannot accept valid interpretations of the law by higher administrative authorities which would control his action . . . (Graham, 1974).

The literature focusing on the nature of the moral agent touts a prescriptive theme. It sees the organization as capable of encouraging or discouraging ethically appropriate behavior. The manager is held accountable for setting the atmosphere for the unit or agency. Managers determined to cultivate an ethically sensitive climate in an agency could provide mechanisms for making ethical concerns a matter of normal consideration, such as introducing ethics into training programs. These managers would promote or reward those employees who welcome an open and ethically sensitive atmosphere (Godfrey and Zashin, 1981).

However, we conclude this section by acknowledging that much remains to be done on this front. Bowman's national survey of practitioners finds that an affirmative organizational strategy that encourages ethical behavior and actively deters problems describes the experience of less than 7% of respondents in 1989 and only 11% in 1996 (Bowman, 1990, 1997).

NATURE OF OBLIGATION: NEGATIVE OR AFFIRMATIVE

A second question designed to sharpen the ethical skills of public managers asks: what is the nature of the obligation of administrators to act? When does the situation give rise to negative responsibilities? When are affirmative responsibilities engaged? The guideline presented here suggests that negative responsibilities are more stringent than affirmative responsibilities, or that the responsibility to avoid harm to others is a more stringent obligation than the responsibility to help others. In an essay on corporate ethics, Mike Rion uses a personal example to illustrate this point:

> Suppose you encounter a beggar soliciting donations as you walked down the street of a large city. Should you make a contribution? Should you aid

her to find shelter or even take a continuing interest in her welfare? The answers are not obvious, for they depend upon your understanding of why persons must beg, your charitable commitments and priorities, and your financial means. Judging affirmative responsibilities to do good to others can easily lead to disagreements about values and appropriate roles but if asked whether you should intentionally push the beggar off her chair into the rain puddle, surely all moral agents would say that you should not. Morally, we agree that we should not harm others (Rion, 1980).

Traditionally, ethics in public administration has meant the negative obligation to do no harm, to avoid injury. The admonition to avoid waste, public deception, and other abuses of power is directed toward abstaining from doing injury to one's managerial role. No one disputes that the administrator bears a negative obligation to avoid injuring others in the execution of public service. But the nature of injury requires careful analysis. Rion offers, as a core definition of harm, the following:

1. physical injury, including direct assault, impairment of health, deprivation of food, clothing, and shelter;
2. deprivation of freedom, including political rights and personal choices;
3. violation of certain moral principles such as promise keeping, truth telling, and justice (Rion, 1980).

The manager's challenge is to understand the nature of harm involved in a particular action and then to balance that action against another potential harm inflicted by nonaction or by an alternative action. Elsewhere, Mark Pastin has referred to this ethical tool as "end-point ethics" (Pastin, 1986). Take the following case related to us by one administrator:

Client discharge from a teenage drug abuse rehabilitation program is a primary treatment goal of my agency. Discharge is considered only when a client's treatment team reaches consensus about the client's readiness. Recently a treatment team's decision to discharge a young woman from the program was strongly objected to by her parents. Adamant about continuing program treatment for the girl, the parents used influence with a legislator on the appropriations committee to put pressure on the agency head. I am the intermediary between the agency head and the treatment teams. The agency head asked me to intervene and halt discharge plans. He believes there may be some chance the treatment team was wrong in its discharge decision. He also suggests that the level of funding for the entire program and therefore the capacity to meet clients' needs in general may be jeopardized by this discharge decision.

Clearly, this case presents potential for injury on a number of fronts. In order to analyze the nature and extent of injury, the manager first asks who the principal "stakeholders" are in this dilemma. Stakeholders are the parties affected by a decision. They might include individuals, groups, and organizations. Next, managers ask what rights or interests does each party have. Finally, the manager considers the nature of all the conflicting values among the stakeholders and rates the relative importance of each value. Doing harm to the interest of some stakeholders might derive from avoiding injury to other stakeholders. In the ethical dilemma reported above, the stakeholders would include at least the following:

the teenage girl;
the parents;
the treatment team;
the legislator;
the agency head;
the other clients of the program;
the administrator reporting the dilemma.

Each of these parties has a potential to be injured by the administrator's response. Avoiding injury to all parties is not possible in this case. Often this kind of ambiguity dominates decision-making in the public sector. But the task of the administrator is to sort out these potential injuries and, within his or her authority, to select the least injurious decision from the value rankings derived from thoughtful analysis. Viewed from this perspective, though the most stringent obligation of the administrator is to avoid doing harm, defining this obligation in particular context is difficult.

This negative notion of avoiding injury is reflected in the public ethics literature in John Rohr's discussion of the "low road" approach to management ethics. The "low road" emphasizes adherence to formal rules and regulations, the thrust of which are to keep government managers "out of trouble" (Rohr, 1978). It finds empirical expression in ethics codes, financial disclosure regulations, and broader conflict-of-interest statutes. While often the first response of an agency newly sensitized to the ethical dimension of organizational life, this negative stress can lead to channeling all ethical reflection into "avoiding infractions." Ultimately, some argue, it can trivialize ethics in management.

THE KEW GARDENS PRINCIPLE: BETWEEN AVOIDING INJURY AND DOING GOOD

Conventionally an ethical distinction is made between the obligation to avoid doing harm to others (negative responsibilities), sometimes called the "low road," and doing good (affirmative responsibilities), referred to by Rohr (1978) as the "high road." But before turning to a discussion of this high road, we need to consider those instances falling in between, where a manager may have an opportunity to correct harm caused by others. Some ethicists have argued that managers have an obligation not only to avoid inflicting injury but also to correct injury caused by others. Referred to as the "Kew Gardens Principle" a label borrowed from the widely publicized murder in the Kew Gardens section of New York City, witnessed by 30 silent bystanders, the principle tries to highlight conditions triggering obligatory actions. The analysis from the Kew Gardens perspective suggests action is obligatory to the extent that the following conditions prevail:

1. Need—There is a clear need for aid.
2. Proximity—The agent is "close" to the situation, not necessarily in space but certainly in terms of notice.
3. Capability—The agent has some means by which to aid the one in need without undue risk to the agent.
4. Last Resort—No one else is likely to help (Rion, 1980).

The Kew Gardens Principle is offered as a tool to guide managerial decision-making. As Rion suggests: "When claims are pressed on managers by various stakeholders, the four considerations outlined may be useful in sorting through whether the managers are obliged to act" (Rion, 1980). Take as an example the following dilemma reported to us by a state-government executive.

> A major part of my responsibility requires making decisions affecting private property. I have to make these decisions as fairly and uniformly as possible. Recently, a property owner used his influence with my superiors in the organization to gain a reversal on a property decision I had made. I can accept this reversal of my decision as "how things are." The problem is such actions make it difficult to justify denying reconsideration to other property owners. This week I received a call from a reporter who had caught wind of an allegation of unequal treatment and favoritism in the handling of private property decisions by our office. He wants to know why some property owners receive favorable consideration and others are refused. He indicates knowledge of the recent reversal of my decision. I can easily avoid lying by a no comment. Only my superior and I have the true information about what happened.

The question is: does this manager have a more stringent obligation to respond than that imposed by the affirmative obligation to do good? The Kew Gardens Principle suggests that a more stringent negative obligation might exist. The public has been injured by favoritism toward a single property owner (need). The manager in this case is close enough to the situation to have the vital information (proximity). Whether or not he/she could act without jeopardizing his or her job or future effectiveness in the organization is uncertain (capability). It does appear that the manager in this case may be the only one who can come to the aid of citizens at large (last resort).

To summarize this discussion of the nature of moral obligation for the manager up to this point, the basic moral principle admonishes managers to avoid doing injury to others. Careful ethical reflection is required to actually define an injury in terms of all stakeholders involved and to weigh injuries caused by others, according to the Kew Gardens Principle. This principle identifies an area where there is a less stringent obligation than in the requirement to avoid injury, but a more stringent obligation than in the affirmative obligation to do good. In the world of public administration this principle might be the thrust behind institutionalizing protection for whistle-blowers in organizations.

AFFIRMATIVE OBLIGATION: DOING GOOD

The negative responsibilities are discussed above as the most stringent because "they are minimal; without adherence to these obligations, our generous deeds would be to no avail . . . In contrast, affirmative responsibilities extend to all human needs and open up a range of actions beyond the resources and capacities of the individual agent" (Rion, 1980). The range of affirmative responsibilities is set by the resources and distinctive roles managers and agencies represent. Since the "good to be done" in the world is boundless, efficiency and effectiveness regarding primary tasks require parameters on administrative action in this sphere. Evans reports that in the last decade, the traditional notion of government ethics has notably expanded to suggest that administrators actively undertake socially just acts (Evans, 1981). And "social equity" has taken its place along these other principles as one of the central values of the field of administrative ethics (Cooper, 1994, p. 13). It requires public managers to actively work for social equity, for only then can a public agency be ethical and just (Evans, 1981). The proactive drive for social equity can be channeled outside the organization by public-policy making and within the organization through personnel practices. Its adherents criticize the older negative tradition for merely proscribing unethical acts. Clarke and McInturff indict the negative approach because it constructs a value system which does not encourage positive behavior (Clarke and McInturff, 1981). Those who advocate the affirmative notion of ethics call for the development of the moral administrators of the future. They campaign for ethics training for managers that stresses the achievement of social equity.

While this affirmative obligation concept has received considerable treatment in the literature (Dvorin and Simmons, 1972; Fredrickson, 1974), many observers question whether practicing administrators typically subscribe to such an expansive obligation. Research on this question is limited, but one study by Evans of 790 public administrators in California does suggest that age is a significant variable shaping adherence to the affirmative-obligation stance. Both older and younger administrators support a negative obligation concept; they feel people should not be manipulated and that administration behavior should be honest, efficient, and nonabusive (Evans, 1981). But significant age differences emerge on the issue of affirmative responsibilities: "Younger respondents believe that an organization should proactively advocate social equity and allocate its resources accordingly." Older respondents, by contrast, believe government should refrain from this proactive stance (Evans, 1981).

One author has described this affirmative obligation as analogous to the exercise of creativity. "Creativity [at work] is literally doing something outside of the domain of the laws by which the world predictably works" (Pastin, 1986, p. 103). He sees this expression of creative energy as part of the total "responsibility" package for the manager, though he acknowledges that "to be responsible, you must act independently of where the payoffs are" (Pastin, 1986, p. 103).

But for all public administrators the affirmative impulse stems from a recognition that "public administration is not neutral, nor 'objective,' nor anonymous" (Miller, 1993), and a belief that the polity is best served through a public administration involved in public discourse about goals to be achieved (Miller, 1993).

SOURCE OF REGULATION: INTERNAL OR EXTERNAL

The distinction between internal and external regulation composes a third facet of management ethics. Our analysis asks whether the effort to shape ethical decision-making comes from within or without the moral agent, which can be either a person or an organization. If agents are controlled externally, this means their behaviors are chosen by whether they are rewarded or not (Foster, 1981). If agents are controlled internally, theoretically, ethics in government will not rely on implementation of often sporadic external controls that can be circumvented.

In a now-classic exchange on this issue published in the 1940s, Carl Friedrich and Herbert Finer staked out polar positions. Friedrich (1940) took the position that a public lacking professional and technical expertise could not effectively oversee administration action. He argued that trust should be placed in professional managers' internal values as a guarantee against abuse of administrative discretion. In contrast, Finer (1941) argued for strengthening political institutions to curb bureaucratic power. In current literature, this tension is reflected in Fox's analysis of multilateral accountability versus unilateral accountability in public service. Fox asks the questions: "Where's the proper locus of ethical agency? Where's the authority to interpret the public interest and to act to advance it?" The unilateral (Finer) view sees public administrators as accountable through their political bosses who must stand for elections. Hence external control, exercised through investigating commissions, auditing agencies, and oversight committees, is the proper instrument for ethical monitoring. The multilateral view argues that all public servants, elected and nonelected, are accountable to the public (Fox, 1981). Logically, widely spread ethical responsibility will result in more ethical action (Fox, 1981). In agreement with Friedrich, Fox also sees professional norms and standards as a meaningful source of ethical behavior.

The empirical world of public management reflects both perspectives on ethical agency. Herbert Simon's discussion of professionalism and neutrality among public servants explains internal regulation in its classic form. Simon argues against an ethically neutral public service in favor of one highly committed to goals dictated by professional standards and values. He sees corruption as more likely to occur in a neutral value-free professional corps than in a heavily value-laden one. Accordingly, professional codes rooted in positive, goal-oriented values are the best regulating mechanisms for ethical action in public organizations (Simon, 1967). But, as Gunn points out, the public at large is no longer willing to trust professional norms: "confused by conflicting evidence over the risks of exposure to a range of hazardous substances, shocked by revelations of such occurrences as the Tuskegee Syphilis experiments, and overwhelmed by disclosures of payoffs, bribery, immoral conduct, etc., of public officials, the public has demonstrated its desire for more control over the decision-making process" (Gunn, 1981).

This building realization of the need to forcefully articulate those values by which public administrators work led to the promulgation of the ASPA Code of Ethics in 1988, the revision and reaffirmation of the ICMA Code in 1987, and the revision and reaffirmation of the ASPA code in 1995. The codes themselves illustrate both internal and external controls.

Advocates of financial disclosure laws and regulations anchor the "external" end of the continuum. Aimed at detecting and determining conflicts of interest, financial disclosure laws are at the substantive core of most state ethics codes (Hays and Gleissner, 1981). Though financial disclosure regulations vary regarding who and what they cover and how they are enforced, their more expansive versions have come under attack in recent years. One line of criticism is rooted in fears that: (1) excessive severity of financial disclosure laws will weaken the capacity to recruit public servants (2) the cavalier treatment of privacy inherent in financial disclosure laws might make public servants insensitive to the privacy of citizens they serve, and (3) financial disclosure laws may treat public officials unjustly by confusing a condition of a "conflict of interest" with actually committing an offense (Rohr, 1981).

On the other hand, financial disclosure requirements serve many jurisdictions as the sole mechanism for warding off conflict of interest. Public-opinion polls confirm a dramatic drop in the public's confidence in social institutions during the 1970s (Bowman, 1981). The allegations and investigations continuing through the 1980s reinforced public skepticism about government (Garment, 1991). The argument for financial disclosure regulation is that public confidence can only be bolstered and sustained by an external mechanism clearly in place. It provides a real and symbolic obstacle to private exploitation of public goods.

The passage of the Ethics in Government Act of 1978 signaled that a political consensus had been achieved on these points. This legislation expressed the Congressional will to preserve and promote public confidence in the integrity of federal officials through financial disclosure, past-governmental employment restrictions and independent investigations of alleged wrongdoing by government officials (Public Law 95). This legislation provided for the first public financial-disclosure requirement for high-ranking officials and employees of the federal legislative, executive, and judicial branches. However, in 1985 Congress amended the act to give the President authority to require any officer or employee in the executive branch to submit a confidential financial disclosure report. This amendment resolved some ambiguity in the 1978 Act that may have exempted some executive-branch personnel from any form of disclosure. To implement these provisions, the Act established the Office of Government Ethics and authorized the appointment of an independent counsel to investigate charges of criminal activity by high-ranking executive branch officials (U. S. Office of Government Ethics, 1996).

The Office of Government Ethics holds responsibility in six broad areas:

1. *Regulation*: To develop rules and regulations pertaining to the substantive areas covered by the statute as well as the entire field of conflict of interest and ethics in the executive branch.
2. *Review of financial disclosure reports*: To review, in conjunction with ethics officials at the agency levels, disclosure reports for nominees under review for Senate confirmation.
3. *Prevention*: To train and educate agency ethics officers and employees regarding standards of conduct and conflict of interest laws.
4. *Interpretive advice and guidance*: To assist individuals in identifying and avoiding ethical violations, and encourage uniform interpretation of ethics laws and regulations.
5. *Enforcement*: To monitor agency ethics programs by comprehensive, periodic reviews.
6. *Evaluation*: To evaluate the effectiveness of ethics laws and regulations and recommend appropriate legislative action (Ethics Newsgram, 1986).

The federal Office of Government Ethics and its counterpart agencies in state and local governments may appear to be the quintessential example of "external" regulation of ethical behavior. However, it is important to highlight that even here the "training" function is critical, and training can be directed toward Friedrich's concern with bolstering a manager's "internal" values as a guarantee against deviance.

MATRIX SUMMARIZING DIMENSIONS OF VARIATION AND THEIR INTERACTION

The preceding discussion poses ethical questions designed to stimulate manager-ial thinking on the ethical dimension of life in the public sector organization. The matrix presented in Table 4 uses each of three perspectives on ethical decision-making. This summary does not claim to be comprehensive, but rather highlights areas for ethical reflection.

MANAGERIAL IMPLICATIONS

Few managers are highly skilled in articulating ethical issues. Still, behavior in organizations is determined largely by someone's consideration of appropriate or "right" action. Today public managers need to acquire skills in ethical reasoning in order to understand behavior within the organization, and to find their own way through the moral ambiguity pervading many administrative decisions. The start-ing point for both understanding and steering one's own course is asking the right questions (Bradley and Wilkie, 1974). Personal moral competence (Brousseau, 1995) is central to ethical action in public administration.

The model adopted here is one which urges managers to ask the right ques-

Table 4 Strategies for Ethics Intervention in a Contemporary Ethical Analysis Matrix

	Individual		Organization	
	Internal regulation	External regulation	Internal regulation	External regulation
Affirmative obligation	Establish as performance measures proactive behaviors/part of performance appraisals	Establish rewards for excellence external to the organization, e.g., bonuses as in the Senior Executive Service	Modify organizational culture to affirm the proactive roles	Appoint and empower Advocacy Boards for government programs
Negative obligation	Select and promote employees exhibiting traditional virtues, e.g., honesty, promise keeping	Enact financial disclosure laws, conflict of interest statutes, governmental codes of ethics	Institutionalize protections for whistle-blowers	Appoint and empower legislative over-sight committees

tions. To advocate managers asking questions at all is to reject the view that public-administrative behavior can be described as either "administrative Darwinism" (where managers pursue self-interests) or Weberian idealism (where dutiful civil servants move in obedience to bureaucratic superiors). Rather we stand with those who see administrative discretion as both legitimate and unavoidable (Warwick, 1981). On that basis we conclude that administrative "choice" must inform and be informed by organizational behavior theory and concepts. We end our text on "management ethics" to stress this point. Ethical decision-making involves evaluating the impacts of managerial actions on affected parties and justifying those impacts in terms of ethical principles. Ethical problems typically imply a mixture of benefits and help for some, and damage and harm for others (Hosmer, 1987). But deciding the "right" thing to do is often just the start of the administrative process (Hosmer, 1987). As we focus on issues of motivation, leadership, and roles, or on the group dynamics accompanying communication, decision-making, and participation, or on facilitating organizational change, we engage in a process fraught with choices. Applying organizational behavior knowledge to management ethics means using theory and concepts to enlighten those choices and ease their implementation.

We began this book by defining management as simply the organization and direction of resources to achieve a desired result. We conclude by noting that, in the public sector in particular, managers are obliged to manage with self-conscious reflection on the public interest involved. We see public managers of the future as moving beyond the naive morality of the founders of the American Civil Service System (Stewart, 1982) to become ethically mature administrators, sensitive to the responsibility incurred in managing public organizations and willing to ask questions about right and wrong.

ENDNOTES

1. This chapter adapts Waldo's distinction between "moral" and "ethical." Moral signifies right behavior in an immediate and customary sense; ethical signifies right behavior as examined and reflected upon (Waldo, 1980).
2. This discussion of "Approaches to Ethical Analysis" is drawn in part from Debra W. Stewart, "From Expunging Evil to Moral Judgment: The Pendleton Concept of Ethics in a Contemporary Ethics Matrix," in *Centenary Issues of the Pendleton Act of 1883*, David H. Rosenbloom, (ed.). New York: Marcel Dekker, 1982.

REFERENCES AND ADDITIONAL READING

Bailey, Stephen K. (1965). "Ethics and the Public Service." In *Public Administration and Democracy*, Roscoe C. Martin, (ed.). Syracuse: Syracuse University Press.
Bowman, James S. (1981). "The Management of Ethics: Codes of Conduct in Organizations." *Public Personnel Management* 10:pp 59–66.

Bowman, James S. (1997). "Ethics in Government: From a Winter of Despair to a Spring of Hope." Forthcoming in *Public Administration Review*.

Bowman, James S. (1990). "Ethics in Government: A National Survey of Public Administrators." *Public Administration Review* 50:pp 345–353.

Bradley, David and Roy Wilkie. (1974). *The Concept of Organization*. Glasgow: Blackie.

Brousseau, Patricia L. (1995). "Ethical Dilemmas: Right vs. Right." *Spectrum* 68, no. 1 (Winter):pp 16–24.

Burke, John P. (1996). "Responsibility, Politics and Community." *Public Administration Review* 56 (Nov/Dec):pp 596–599.

Clarke, Michael and Patrick McInturff (1981). "Public Personnel in an Age of Scientificism." *Public Personnel Management* 10:pp 83–86.

Cooper, Terry L. (1996). The Paradox of Responsibility: An Engima. *Public Administration Review* 56 (Nov/Dec):pp 599–604.

Cooper, Terry L. (1994). "The Emergence of Administrative Ethics as a Field of Study in the United States," In *Handbook of Administrative Ethics*. New York: Marcel Dekker, pp 3–30.

Dvorin, Eugene P. and Robert H. Simmons (1972). *From Amoral to Humane Bureaucracy*. San Francisco: Canfield Press.

Dvorin, Eugen P. and Robert H. Simmons (1977). *Public Administration*. Port Washington, NY: Alfred.

Evans, James W. (1981). "A New Administrative Ethic?: Attitudes of Public Managers and Students." *Public Personnel Management* 10:pp 132–139.

Finer, Herman (1941). "Administrative Responsibility in Democratic Government." *Public Administrative Review* 1 (Summer):pp 335–350.

Foster, Gregory D. (1981). "Legalism, Moralism and the Bureaucratic Mentality." *Public Personnel Management*. 10:pp 93–97.

Fox, Charles J. (1981). "Civil Service Reform and Ethical Accountability." *Public Personnel Management* 10:pp 98–102.

Fredrickson, H. George (ed.) (1974). "Symposium on Social Equity and Public Administration." *Public Administration Review* 1 (January/February):pp 1–51.

Friedrich, Carl J. (1940). "Public Policy and the Nature of Administrative Responsibility." *Public Policy* 1:pp 3–24.

Garment, Suzanne (1991). *Scandal: The Culture of Mistrust in American Politics*. New York: Time Books.

Godfrey, E. Drexel and Elliot Zashin (1981). "Integrity in Work and Interpersonal Relations." *Public Personnel Management* 10:pp 110–118.

Graham, George A. (1974). "Ethical Guidelines for Public Administrators." *Public Administration Review* 1 (January/February):pp 90–92.

Greenfield, Meg (1987). "Giving Truth a Bad Name." *Newsweek*. 27 July:p. 64.

Gunn, Elizabeth M. (1981). "Ethics and the Public Service: An Annotated Bibliography and Overview Essay." *Public Personnel Management* 10:pp 172–178.

Harmon, Michael M. (1995). *Responsibility as a Paradox: A Critic of Rational Discourse on Government*. Newbury Park, CA: Sage.

Hays, Steven W. and Richard R. Gleissner (1981). "Codes of Ethics in State Government: A Nationwide Survey." *Public Personnel Management* 10:pp 48–58.

Hosmer, La Rue T. (1987). "The Institutionalization of Unethical Behavior." *Journal of Business Ethics* 6, no. 16 (August):pp 447–449.

Loucks, Edward A. (1981). "Bureaucratic Ethics from Washington to Carter." *Public Personnel Management* 10:pp 77–82.

McSwain, C. J., and O. F. White (1987). "The case for lying, cheating, and stealing: Development as ethical guidance for managers." *Administration and Society* 18, no. 4:pp 411–432.

Miller, Hugh T. (1993). "Everyday Politics in Public Administration." *American Review of Public Administration* 23, no. 2 (June):pp 99–116.

Nozick, R. (1974). *Anarchy, State and Utopia*. New York: Basic Books.

Pastin, M. (1986). *The Hard Problems of Management: Gaining the Ethics Edge*. San Francisco: Jossey-Bass.

Powers, Charles and Barbara Toffler (1980). "Overview of Reading Materials for the 1980 Institute of Ethics in Management." Catalina, CA: Institute on Ethics in Management.

Rion, Michael (1980). *Ethical Principles*. Columbus, Indiana (mimeographed).

Rizzo, Ann-Marie and Thomas J. Patka (1981). "The Organizational Imperative and Supervisory Control." *Public Personnel Management* 10:pp 103–109.

Rohr, John A. (1996). "Professional Ethics and Public Administration." (Speech delivered at the National Conference on Public Service Ethics and the Public Trust, St. Louis, MO, February 29–March 2.)

Rohr, John A. (1989). *Ethics for Bureaucrats: An Essay on Law and Values*, 2nd ed. New York: Marcel Dekker.

Rohr, John A. (1978). *Ethics for Bureaucrats*. New York: Marcel Dekker.

Rohr, John A. (1981). "Financial Disclosure: Power in Search of Policy." *Public Personnel Management* 10:pp 29–40.

Simon, Herbert (1967). "The Changing Theory and Changing Practice of Public Administration." In *Contemporary Political Science*. Ithiel de Sola Pool, (ed.). New York: McGraw-Hill.

Sprinthall, Norman A. and Richad C. Sprinthall (1990). *Educational Psychology: A Developmental Approach*. New York: McGraw-Hill.

Stewart, Debra W. (1982). "From Expunging Evil to Moral Judgment." In *Centenary Issues of the Pendleton Act of 1883*. David H. Rosenbloom, (ed.). New York: Marcel Dekker.

Thompson, Dennis F. (1985). "The Possibility of Administrative Ethics." *Public Administration Review*. Rpt. in *Ethical Insight, Ethical Action*, Elizabeth K. Keller, (ed.). Washington, DC: International City Managers Association, 1988:pp 29–41.

Toffler, Barbara Ley (1986). *Tough Choices: Managers Talk Ethics*. New York: Wiley.

United States. Office of Government Ethics (1996). *Fourth Biennial Report to Congress*. (March):p. 7.

Van Riper, Paul P. (1958). *History of the United States Civil Service*. Evanston, IL: Row, Peterson and Company.

Van Wart, Montgomery (1996). "The Sources of Ethical Decision Making for Individuals in the Public Sector." *Public Administration Review* 56, no. 6 (November/December):pp 525–533.

Waldo, Dwight (1980). *The Enterprise of Public Administration.* Novato, CA: Chandler and Sharp.

Warwick, Donald P. (1981). "The Ethics of Administrative Discretion." In *Public Duties: The Moral Obligation of Government Officials.* Joel Fleishman, et. al., (eds.). Cambridge, MA: *Harvard University Press*:pp 93–127.

Worthley, John A. (1981). "Ethics and Public Management: Education and Training." *Public Personnel Management* 10:pp 41–47.

Index

Abilene paradox, 136
Accountability, 19, 244–246, 289
Administrative discretion, 394
Ambiguity of language (*see also*
    Communication), 164,
    165
American Society for Public
    Administration Code of
    Ethics, 250, 391

Behavioral approaches to leadership
    (*see* Leadership)
    Fiedler contingency theory,
        106–108
    Hersey and Blanchard, 108, 109
    Michigan studies, 98–100
    Ohio State studies, 101, 102,
        125
    participation, 98–100
    path goal, 104–105
    social/task leadership behavior,
        100–103
Behaviorally anchored rating scales
    (BARS) (*see also*
    Performance appraisal)
    advantages, 364–366
    defined 365, 366
    disadvantages, 366
    integrated MBO\BARS appraisal
        systems, 367

Change (*see* Organizational change)
Climate (*see* Organizational climate)
Communication
    as a process, 161–167
    audit, 183–186
    communication audit network
        analysis instrument, 185
    listening, 180–183
    non-verbal communication,
        171–175
    network designs, 179, 180
    verbal communication, 167–171
    vertical and horizontal
        communication, 174–180
Computers
    communication and control
        perspective, 332–334
    economic theories of MIS,
        324–326
    functional information
        integration, 317-319
    information resources
        management vs.
        management information
        systems, 311–313
    phenomenological perspective,
        324
    policy vs. process models, 319
    political process models,
        321–323

[Computers]
  planning process models, 320,
    321
  public goods theory of
    information systems,
    326–329
  social impact theory, 329
  stages of growth theory of MIS,
    314–317
  typological frameworks as
    organization theory, 313,
    314
Civil Service Reform Act of 1978,
    80
Civil Service Reform Act of 1883
    (Pendelton Act), 377, 380
Culture (*see* Organizational culture)

Decision-making
  adaptation, 212
  buffering, 212
  computer mediated, 220, 221
  conservative critiques of
    planning, 200–205
  critics and revisionists, 208–211
  efficiency vs. other values in the
    policy process, 195–197
  group decision-making, 214-217
  Herbert Simon's critique and
    decision-making, 205–208
  leveling, 212
  mixed scanning, 209, 210
  participatory approaches to
    decision-making, 213
  planning and rational models
    of decision-making,
    197–200
  programmed decisions, 206
  rationing, 212
  satisficing, 41
Delphi technique (*see also* Decision-
    making), 217–219

Deming Cycle (*see also* Total
    Quality Management),
    237
Deviance, 141, 142 (*see* Roles)
Drive or tension reduction theory,
    61–63

Empowerment (*see* Total Quality
    Management)
Ethics
  competing claims, 384
  financial disclosure, 387, 391,
    392
  Iran-gate, 378
  Kew Gardens, 387–390
  obligation, 381, 384–393
  regulation, 381, 390–392
  responsibility, 382, 384, 387
Ethics in Government Act of 1978,
    392

Formal organization, 123–126
Freudian psychoanalytical theory,
    62

Garbage can model of decision
    making, 42, 43
Gender and communication,
    172–175
Gender roles, 126, 127
Goal displacement (*see also*
    Management systems),
    291–295
Group composition (*see also*
    Decision-making), 216
Group decision-making, 134–137
Group-maintaining role, 125
Group size (*see also* Decision-
    making), 216
Groupthink, 134, 135

Hawthorne effect, 36

Hawthorne studies, 36–38
Hygiene factors (*see also*
    Motivation), 71

Informal group (*see* Hawthorne
    studies)
Informal organization, 123–125
Informal organization as a threat,
    144, 145
Informal organization as an
    opportunity, 146, 147

Kinesics or body language (*see also*
    Communication), 173

Leadership
    behavioral approaches to
        leadership, 97–103
    contingency theories, 110
    defined, 89–91
    leadership vs. management, 92,
        93
    path-goal theories, 106
    situational leadership, 108–110
    trait approach, 93–96
    traits and organizational
        effectiveness, 96, 97
    transactional leadership,
        110–113
    transformational leadership,
        110–113
Listening, 180–183

Management systems
    central city case study, 300–306
    defined, 286
    design concerns, 291–297
    goal displacement, 293–295
    influence differentiation, 291–292
    management by objectives
        (MBO) 290, 291, 360,
        362–364

[Management systems]
    planning, programming and
        budgeting (PPBS), 290
    public sector applications, 290
    public sector vs. private sector,
        289
    research design, 298–300
    suboptimization, 293
    zero-based budgeting (ZBB),
        290, 291
Management by objectives (MBO)
        (*see* Performance appraisal
        and Management systems)
Maslow's hierarchy of needs (*see
        also* Motivation), 65
Messages in communication (*see
        also* Communication,
        160–162)
Motivation
    acognitive approach, 68
    basic motivation theory, 59, 60
    cognitive approach, 60–64
    context, 56–59
    expectancy, 74–77
    extrinsic motivation, 78–81
    human growth and development
        theory, 64–67
    intrinsic motivation, 78–81
    two factor theory, 70–74
Motivation strategies for managers
    establish goals, 82
    link rewards to performance,
        82
    manage equity issues, 82
    provide for job enrichment, 83

Nominal group (*see also* Decision-
        making), 219–221

Operant conditioning (*see also*
        Motivation), 67, 68
Organizational behavior, 2–4

Organizational change
  basic points, 277
  defined, 277
  double loop learning, 274, 275
  environment, 272, 273
  managerial strategies, 276
  organizational climate, 269, 270
  organizational culture, 265–269
  organizational development,
    277–279
  organizational learning, 273, 276
  single loop learning, 274, 275
  stages 277–279
  structure, 270, 271
Organizational culture
  defined, 265, 268
  ideology of public services, 268
  norms, 266
Organizational development
  management of roles (see also
    Organizational change),
    147–149
Organizational learning: (see
    Organizational change)
Organization theory
  approaches to, 26, 27
  bureaucratic politics approach,
    47–52
  classical approach, 30–35
  decision-making approach, 38–43
  defined, 4-6
  expectancy value theories, 63,
    64
  human relations approach, 36–38
  neo-human relations approach,
    43–45
  systems approach, 45–47

Paralanguage (see also
    Communication), 173, 174
Participation (see Worker
    participation)

People vs. task skills (see also
    Leadership), 101–103
Performance appraisal (see
    Behaviorally anchored
    rating scales [BARS])
  appraisal interview, 368
  assessment centers, 361
  case law, 351–353
  comparable worth, 353
  context factors, 357–358
  critical incident appraisal, 360
  defined, 347, 349
  developmental, 347
  developmental planning, 355,
    356
  EEO, 352
  forced choice rating, 360
  field review, 359
  graphical rating scale, 359
  judgmental function, 347
  management by objectives
    (MBO) 362–364
  measurement dimensions,
    349–354
  performance standards, 361
  reliability, 351–354
  techniques, 358–362
  validity, 351–354
Public organizations
  differences in problems faced,
    20, 21
  economic differences, 16–18
  political differences, 18–20
Public vs. private organizations (see
    also Public organizations),
    6–9, 243–249, 289
Role of government
  controlling externalities, 11–13
  insuring equity, 13–15
  providing a framework for law
    and order and economic
    stability, 15, 16

[Role of government]
   providing public goods, 13
Roles
   dynamics of conformity and
      exclusion, 130-133
   managing role change through
      organizational develop-
      ment, 147–149
   negative functions of conformity,
      137
   positive functions of conformity,
      133
   psychological dimensions of role
      conflict, 141
   role conflict, 137–140
   role conformity, 126–130

Satisficing, 41
Stakeholders, 223, 387
Stimulus response model (*see also*
      Motivation), 59

Tactile communication (*see also*
      Communication), 172
Theory X (*see also* Motivation),
      68–70
Theory Y (*see also* Motivation),
      68–70
Total Quality Management (TQM)
   accountability in the public
      sector, 244–246
   continuous process improvement,
      241
   decision-making in teams, 214,
      215
   defined, 235
   Deming cycle, 237
   effectiveness, 253
   efficiency, 252, 253
   empowerment, 240, 245
   forces favoring adoption,
      249–255

[Total Quality Management (TQM)]
   forces opposing adoption,
      243–249
   group and team decision-making,
      214–217
   open systems, 238
   orthodox TQM, 238–243
   performance management,
      246–248
   political legitimacy, 248, 249
   process mapping, 238–243
   quality control, 240
   reinventing government, 254
   statistical process control (SPC),
      236, 242, 243
   taylorism, 255
   type of work done by public
      agencies, 251
   tools, 241–243
   variation, 242, 243
Task roles, 125
Teams (*see* Group decision-
      making)

U.S. Office of Government Ethics,
      392

Verbal communication, 171–175
      (*see also* Communication)
Vertical and horizontal comm-
      unication in organizations
      (*see* Communication),
      174–179

Watergate, 378, 382
Wicked problems, 21
Worker participation (*see* TQM)
   efficiency, 252, 253
   participatory management,
      233–234
   TQM and participatory
      management, 235